Jew, Christian, Muslim

Jew, Christian, Muslim

Faithful unification or fateful trifurcation?
Word, way, worship and war in the Abrahamic faiths.

Kenneth L. Vaux

Wipf & Stock
PUBLISHERS
Eugene, Oregon

Wipf and Stock Publishers
199 West 8th Avenue, Suite 3
Eugene, Oregon 97401

Jew, Christian, Muslim: Faithful Unification or Fateful Trifurcation?
Word, Way, Worship and War in the Abrahamic Faiths
By Vaux, Kenneth L.
Copyright©2003 by Vaux, Kenneth L.
ISBN: 1-59244-363-X
Publication date 9/29/2003

Contents

Acknowledgement

The author is grateful for the insights and help offered by
Bill Chu, John Duff, Lorenzo Fincher, David Jones, Joey Lenti,
Peter Mageto, Kevin Olson, Stan Schade, Bert Vaux
and the First Presbyterian Church – Evanston.

Part I. Word: Akedah, Theology and Messiah

Introduction

There is silence all around. The Baptist appears, and cries: "Repent, for the Kingdom of Heaven is at hand." Soon after that comes Jesus, and in the knowledge that He is the coming Son of Man lays hold of the wheel of the world to set it moving on that last revolution which is to bring all ordinary history to a close. It refuses to turn, and He throws Himself upon it. Then it does turn; and crushes Him. The wheel rolls onward, and the mangled body of the one immeasurably great Man, who was strong enough to think of Himself as the spiritual ruler of mankind and to bend history to His purpose, is hanging upon it still. That is His victory and His reign.[1]

Prelude

The Alsatian polymath deciphers and configures the world akedically. For him the early Christian symbol of the lamb cradling the shepherd's crook was the clue to all wisdom, power and reality.

> Worthy is the lamb that was slain and hath redeemed us to God by His blood to receive power, riches, wisdom, strength, honor, glory and blessing...[2]

We expect such vision from one who comfortably consorts with Bach's "Sheep may safely graze", or Mark's little apocalypse in chapter 13, or with patients suffering with malaria in Lambarene, or "Le mystère du pauvre et de la riche (Calvin)". The riddle of suffering and resurrection is well known to the sublimely original and critical Strasbourg Calvinist.

Alongside this profound and enigmatic text of Schweitzer, striking in its paradoxical power, positioning life and authority in One bounden unto death, like the immolated lamb of the Apocalypse reigning over the cosmos in the book of Revelation, I offer another scene, this one from a contemporary film, one which paints the picture I wish you to view and contemplate in this study. In Robert Duvall's film, *The Apostle*, Sonny, played by Duvall, is confronted by a racist mob intent on bulldozing the wooden, country church that the preacher has racially integrated. Though a broken and flawed figure, Duvall has made the Apostle a wounded healer, a crazed prophet, one who vicariously embodies a justice and sacrificing empathy for his poor parishioners. As the bigot begins to bulldoze the shanty-sanctuary, with redneck Billy Bob Thornton at the controls, Sonny kneels on the ground with his bible in front of the dozer, reminiscent of the reverend Jim Reeb who in 1964 was run over and crushed on that vicious deathwheel in the red mud of Mississippi. Here, in this tense scene, in pure Abraham-Isaac redemptive rescue, the dozer stops and, like Isaac, the offering is spared. Now God and good have prevailed. In a Faustian fury of soul with the full warfare of good and evil, God and hell, a decision of grace has won. As in Tienanmen Square, the great tractor grinds to a halt. The bigot persecutor Saul

---

[1] Albert Schweitzer, *The Quest of the Historical Jesus*, (New York: Macmillan, 1906), p. 370.
[2] G.F. Handel, "The Messiah," after Revelation 5:12.

becomes Paul, the purveyor of grace. Old Deuteronomy restores a world-worn Jellico cat and a new day has begun.

Do not lay your hand on the child...(Genesis 22)

One more picture. Here Vermeer-like dark shadows obscure nearly all shafts and shadows of light. Martin Gilbert, the Oxford historian, reports on the Nazi genocidal *Wehrmacht* as it rolled into Poland in 1939:

> "In the first ten days of the German advance onslaughts against unarmed, defenseless civilians were carried out in more than a hundred towns and villages. In the city of Czestochowa, home of thirty thousand Jews, 180 Jews were shot on September 4, 'Bloody Monday'. At the village of Widawa, home of one hundred Jewish families, the Germans ordered the rabbi, Abraham Mordechai Morocco, to burn the Holy books. He refused, whereupon they burned him, with the Scrolls of the Law in his hands."[3]

As in Fourth Maccabees (c. 18-55 CE), where the seven sons and their mother recall Isaac's faithfulness to endure their own torture and death rather than abandon Torah, in Judaism, martyrdom is to suffer and die painfully for the sake of the "Way"—"to sanctify and unify...THE NAME." In Jesus' words, it is to "keep my commandments" (John 14:15 ff.)

> "Hear O Israel—The Lord our God is One...You shall have no other gods...You shall love the Lord...with your Life...You shall not defame... THE NAME..."

Jesus and his observant Jewish companions may have carried on their robes the *Tephilim* capsules containing SHEMA and DECALOGUE, expressions of the obedient piety of Second Temple Judaism. They knew the "Way" and the requisite witness. So also do the three pictures of Schweitzer, Duvall and Gilbert. They show a hostile world, driving its relentless way, seeking to crush the good. The Creator/Commander confronts the Destroyer/Tempter in the human travail of faith, flesh and obedience. The pictures show vicars of the good and exemplars of faith evoking then submitting to that pent-up violence of the sinful world (*Peccata Mundi*). They succumb to it, holding the tablets of the Way of God in hand, transforming violence into victory, even in death. Yet in Kierkegaardian paradox, their defeat is victory. The scenes concern Holocaust —the burning of innocents in a furious attempt to quench the truth. They depict the paschal mystery of the Book of Revelation, which is also the mystery of the enigmatic suffering of humanity: the Immolated Lamb holding the books of God (*biblion*, Revelation, ch. 5), reigning over the universe.

---

[3] Martin Gilbert, *The Holocaust* (New York: Holt, Rinehart and Winston, 1985), p. 87.

Purpose

My opening words are apocalyptic and provocative. This is as it should be. Real life and revelation about its meaning are cataclysmic:

With righteousness he shall judge the poor

> He will smite the earth with the rod of his mouth . . . the wolf shall dwell with the lamb. . .
> (Isaiah 11)

This Isaianic text presents an eschatological vision. It depicts a justice-grounded condemnation of the "world as it has become" in favor of a "promised world to be"- a "world as it was meant to be." Like apocalyptic insight, eschatology is the human perception of what is really real. This means that in a world where there is a God there is also a history behind history, a reality beyond reality. Embedded in a realm behind the provocative events of this day are the meanings drawn in the Isaiah text. Victor Hugo has it right in *Les Misérables*. As Napoleon, or we ourselves, go our merry way, pretending that we control events—another purpose is at work, a redemptive purpose, guiding the flow of history, bearing significance beyond the tacit and visible events.

The overarching thesis of this work is that a filial affinity is to be found among the three Abraham faiths, an affinity which, when nurtured, invigorates the member religions and sustains faith, justice and peace in the world. When severed and antagonized, the particular faiths are distorted and the world is threatened and terrorized.

Introduction: Thesis and Caution

This book has been in the making for twenty years. My career-long search to recover the Jewish roots of Christianity has amplified, in these recent years, marked by 9/11/01, to comprehend Islam and thus complete the Abrahamic triptych. That this tableau has been torn asunder, I believe, is the clue to much of the evil of modern times. In recovering that common heritage lies the hope for justice and peace in the world. To touch and gauge the pulse of that implicit purpose I propose to show the connection between Torah and Akedah. The way of God with this world and the way that we relate to God in faith are captured in these great symbols. These motifs are the interpretive instruments of theodicy. They point us to the meaning of good and evil, engagement and estrangement, in a God-derived and destined cosmos. The Abraham-Isaac episode in Hebrew tradition is a powerful source for the formation of the primitive Christian Gospel. Islam arises in the mystery of history to correct the distorted piety and restore the impeded *prolepsis* of those sister faiths. The ethical story and the eucharistic sequel, Torah and GOSPEL, contribute the Hebraic/Christic essence that the Apostle Paul calls "The Gospel of God" (Romans 1:1). These two symbols are the key to deciphering the hidden redemptive process in natural, historical and human reality. Like the Throg's Neck and George Washington bridges joining the three land masses of Manhattan, Bronx and Long Island, Torah and Akedah bridge the ethical homeland tradition of Judaism with that of the more massive islands of her two irascible sons, the exuberant Christian and the Ebionitic Islamic traditions. These three Abrahamic peoples—three billion—or nearly one half of the world's population—is home-gathered, reconciled and reanimated in their respective and synergistic global missions and destiny by these poignant symbols, of Torah and Akedah.

The thesis which I offer will affirm that Akedah, the central common interpretive story of faith and ethics of Abrahamic religion *Jew,* (Judaism, Christianity and Islam), rightly interprets the human problem and prospect and in its synthetic comprehension of God and world, of salvation and social justice, offers reconciliation to our broken world—redemption and resurrection.

> ...And we beheld His glory, a glory as of an only born son [*MONOGENOS*]...
> (John 1:14)

I contend that the Torah/Akedah axis helps us to decipher the nature and history of God, fathom the riddle of the human condition and restore the ethical/salvational dimension to human existence. These realities are incomprehensible and unattainable without the normative signal of Torah and the interpretive symbol of Akedah, all evolving within the process of temptation. Ever since my first studies of Nazi medicine and Holocaust in the 1960s, my work has sought to reconcile the awkward estrangement of Judaism and Christianity. Rejecting on theological grounds the thesis that there are two concurrent and severable faiths and bibles (the God of Israel is One...), I have sought *rapprochement* as being necessary for the wholeness and authenticity of each faith. When Hebrews follow *Elohim,* when Jesus in Aramaic addresses God his Father as *El'lah* and when Muslims submit to *Allah,* this One God is acknowledged. When the Dean of my Medical School (University of Illinois), Andrew Ivy, sought the "Laws of Humanity" to convict Hitler's willing physician-executioners at Nuremberg, he reached for this universal substance. When America and Israel condemn world law and world court, they resist this efficacy.

Among the three Abrahamic faiths, Judaism, Christianity and Islam, Torah is the most salient ethical theme of this universal tradition, and Akedah the most salient common theological theme. Ultimately a theology which seeks universality and truth interprets four phenomena. Indeed, these are the quadrilateral parameters of theology:

> The story (activity) and reality (being) of God
> The human condition
> The enigma of history and
> The travail of nature

6

Theology responds to Kant's salient questions:

What can I know, believe and hope ?

Phrased religiously these might read—

Where do I find home? How can I be saved? Where am I going?

Ethics respond to Kant's question of practical reason—"What must I do?"

Philosophy and theology as normative disciplines seek to interpret human phenomena and divine noumena within a cohesive natural/preternatural whole that is rationally coherent and ethically convincing. Elucidating these two salient pathways of insight—one metaphysical the other meta-ethical—holds the promise of fashioning a credible and convicting world-view and of affirming anew the possibility of justice and peace in the world.

The reader already finds here a contemporary *PESHER* or *MIDRASH* on Akedah. Just as the genetic code can be deciphered to unravel the biological mysteries of life, so also the biblical text can be displayed to decipher "what God is doing in the world." (Paul Lehmann) From the beginning of biblical religion this parable has been used to fathom and interpret the meaning of God and of human existence. Akedah is the paradigmatic text of man's love for and duty to God. It is the deciphering codex of the "Way" of God in the world, of faith and works. It is the text, par excellence, of the nature and purpose of divinity and humanity.

Akedah is invoked to decipher in and find deliverance through the experiences of people—Israel in their Canaan consolidation, in exile in Babylonia, in suffering under the Greek and Roman colonialists, in the agony of the crusades, in the twentieth century holocaust. It is the pervasive symbol interpreting reality in the Christian worldview explaining the life, suffering, death and resurrection of Jesus, the martyrdom of early Christian witnesses at the hands of the Romans, and more generally of the vicissitudes of history and of human experience "under the cross." Akedah also reads the historic agony of Islam.

In the two millennia of human history shaped by the biblical tradition, a christological view of nature, history and human destiny have developed in the akedic spirit. Islamic theology, philosophy and cultural world-view follow suit. This work is offered as an appreciative midrash in the constructive spirit of Jon Levenson and Shalom Spiegel rather than in the deconstructive appraisal of Carol Delaney.

I believe that the most fundamental reality is the reality of God and the divine *ORDO SALUS*: suffering, death and transfiguration. Akedah portrays that

7

synthetic vision. It best deciphers all codes: genetic, generational, world-historical, cabbalistic.

In this systematic theology I attempt to lay out a comprehensive treatise containing an ethical, eucharistic and evangelical Faith, for which I adopt the classical catechetical format or structure of belief. Now, in this prolegomenon, I offer an elucidation of the *leitmotif* of that more expansive work. Indeed in all of my writing in ethics and theology I have unconsciously drawn on the akedic metaphor as I have tried to weave the normative thread of an understanding of redemptive suffering, yielding resurrection. As in my study I turned more and more to Jewish literature reading works like Shalom Spiegel's THE LAST TRIAL and Jon Levenson's THE DEATH AND RESURRECTION OF THE BELOVED SON I came to find in Akedah a clue to fathoming meanings that I had learned empirically across the years in work in the medical and religious world. Now I wish to spell out that assumed and undeveloped theme in some detail so that those who have honored me as readers will see that unspoken premise more fully unfolded. In this work I also wish to struggle with this central idea in my own faith system, which is also the center of my philosophy of life and history. Reaching the age of sixty and having had the privilege of teaching Bioethics, then Just-War and Economic ethics, all the while pondering fundamental themes of theology, has afforded me a theoretical atmosphere and a practical laboratory to probe this highly profound and problematic theme. Add to that the personal challenge: At threescore years one begins to feel disintegrations of body and mind even amid that gracious integration of mind called contingency as the illusion of self-sufficiency fades. Torah-laced Akedah affirmed for me the mystery that even in disintegration and dissolution was wholeness, death was life. I now wish to test that paradoxical thesis with considerate and critical readers.

Akedah

The best biblical metaphor for this organizing and interpretive motif in my work is the Akedah, subsuming, as it does, the essence of Torah. Akedah weaves together a tapestry of meta-ethical and metaphysical threads: creation, command, temptation, evil, sacrifice, reconciliation, new life. In sum, Akedah is the symbol of the perennial human obedience, offering and obeisance—the work (worthship) of existence. It is the receptor in the human soul, personal and collective, which responds to Torah which is the received and perceived Word, Way and Will of God for the world. Akedah is loss into life, since the God of Torah delivers eternal life through the suffering and death of the Righteous One. In more secular and humanistic terms Akedah ponders three great queries:

What is right and good in the world?
What has gone wrong?
How is righteousness (SHALOM) reconstituted?

From the beginning of human history and especially from the inception of communal existence, where James Breasted locates what he calls the DAWN OF CONSCIENCE, a perception of opprobrium has accompanied human actions. By this I mean that wherever human beings appear, we find a sense of commendation or condemnation, a belief, in philosophical language, that our deeds are praiseworthy or blameworthy, both before our family and fellows and before the mysterious divine power in the world.

All literary and cultural artifacts point to humans as *homo religiosis*. Persons always and everywhere have a sense of ought grounded in ultimacy. This inherent and inculcated moral sense finds in both human and divine presence and judgment the bivalence of command and rescue. Our lives are called into question and released by the other to grace as possibility. Command or deontological requirement is preemptive moral direction—prophylactic and preventive in nature. The mandate "Do Not Kill," for example, conveys a duality of blessing and curse, promising reward as we honor life in concrete action and conversely conveying dire consequence as we violate another's life and good.

These proddings and pangs of conscience experienced both before and after our deeds find expression in personal and communal rituals of expiation and propitiation. It is here, at this nexus of divine-human association in the dynamics of spirit and conscience that Akedah/Torah arises. Akedah splits and unites. Torah guides. It is responsibility (German *Verantwortung*)—answerability to the moral call—that leads Abraham, Sarah and Isaac to resolve to mount Moriah (*Yahweh yireh*, God will provide), there to recognize the ultimate obligation of "no other gods" and obedience to *vox dei*. That same filial obedience leads Jesus, that other "only beloved son," to offer in Gethsemane, at the platform of Mount Golgotha, "Your will be done."(Matthew 26:42)

Akedah is the parable of all of life, as Philo teaches in his work *On Abraham*. The story has a universality as it finds analogy in all of human experience. In this symbol the physical and spiritual worlds find resonance. In conjoining ultimate reality to the tragedy and thrill of this time/space world, we see its perennial currency. Its ultimacy as a symbol is not only grounded in Hellenistic philosophy, as in Philo, or in some Jungian eternality of forms as in René Girard's *Violence and the Sacred* or his reflections on Job. It is found concretely in the documentary and textual history of the Akedah. This paradigmatic story arises before Israel begins her parochial history and it verges into universal history as Israel's political existence wanes in the late Roman Empire. Jacob, who will become Israel, is yet to come, indeed that resultant particular history..."your descendents shall be as the sands of the sea, as the stars of the sky..." is the resurrection gift of Akedah. The parochial history of Christendom and *Dar al Islam* also phase, in turn, into the universal history of the modern world—the ultimate gift of the Akedah.

The textual tradition, though rooted in the archaic mists of patriarchal times, is finally redacted late, during the Exile. In that long season of captivity (boundedness) and homelessness (perhaps the history of Jesus' own family before they return to Galilee), the sensitivities of the Hebrew people are turned to a vision of pathos, suffering and deliverance that shapes their expectancy and their ethos. Original and universal sin and salvation now convict the conscience. Their pathos is now joined to the lament and Hallelujah of all humanity.

> Comfort, my people...your warfare is accomplished.
> (Isaiah 40:1-2)

Summary

Before we trace that textual heritage, let us summarize our argument, which seeks to establish the thesis that Akedah joined to Torah restores an ethical dimension to theology and fashions a more explanatory and adequate worldview.

If Akedah captures the theological essence of Abrahamic faith (Judaism, Christianity, and Islam), and if Torah is their common ethical substance, then conjoining these two symbols may present the occasion for *rapprochement* and renewal among these faith movements now so violently separated and alienated. The enduring strife for survival in Israel, the demonization of Arabic Islam in the West and the accusation, in the Islamic world, that Anglo-American culture is the "great Satan," all show that the tragic Abrahamic history of Holocaust, Crusade and Jihad still goes on. The babes still wrestle in the womb of the matriarch of humanity. If we can show that the unfolding history of Akedah and Akedah interpreted by Torah has normative power and that the histories of God, humanity, nature and society corroborate this value, then the contours of a new theology and ethic will begin to emerge.

Caution

In Nicholas Ray's film *Bigger than Life*, the overweening father, played by James Mason, after years of pathological indulgence, actually comes to the point of wishing to sacrifice his son. The news this week carries the frightful story of a father infecting his baby with HIV, believing that this would enable him to afford health care for the infant. The sad saga of misguided parental love/hate relationships with their children, a general contempt for children in the culture and other sociological insights will lead us to great caution in the use of Akedah in our family life and in our theology. We must not superimpose our violent human propensities onto our theological world-view.

Feminist theology, along with other liberationist strands of thought, critiques the theme of suffering and sacrifice as perpetuating a patriarchal and masochistic tendency in religion, one which denigrates human freedom, opportunity and wholeness. Akedah can become an instrument of violence, especially against women and children. Carol Delaney's *Abraham on Trial* masterfully explores

10

this critique. Theories of vicarious atonement and sacrifice have fallen under corrective critique in recent theology. We must not superimpose a cultural chauvinism and a destructive hegemony over women, children, the old, the poor, the weak and those ethnically different onto our theology.

A final caution is offered in a striking observation made by one of the preeminent scholars in the field of our inquiry. Roland de Vaux, in his *Studies in Old Testament Sacrifice*, has found that in ancient civilizations (e.g. Greece, Carthage, Phoenicia) it is the wealthy and impious who tend to engage in child sacrifice:

> Human sacrifice is attested most clearly in some societies which are relatively evolved and prosperous materially while morally decadent.[4]

Similar studies in India seem to show that those of means seek to assuage guilt and appease fate by this kind of offering. We must not superimpose on a theological view our unease over exploitation and expropriation of the goods of life from others. As much as is possible, theology must transcend the cultural residue. Forgiveness, liberation, justice and peace, not persistent bad conscience, is the call of humanity. Despite the validity of these profound critiques of Akedah, the imperatives of true piety and just ethics encourage us to continue searching this motif, especially as it is chastened by Torah. We now begin our argument, laying a foundation for a positive theology of Akedah-Torah.

A. Biblical Overview

The Bible is replete with reference and allusion to Akedah. From Genesis 22 to Revelation 5, some thirty references witness to the formative influence of the story. Events such as Passover and Temple, New Year and Exodus, crucifixion and resurrection, are grounded in the symbol.

Akedah arises into human experience out of the vast prehistory of the human race through the legendary memory of those who share the Abraham—Isaac – Jacob complex. Abraham is, in one way, the first historical human at the dawn of concrete Mesopotamian history concurrent with the Egyptian Amenhotep and the Babylonian, Hammurabi. Salvation history is profiled in this fragile family. Abraham, Sarah and the first-born Ishmael and the late-born son Isaac, are introduced as the pioneers of faith-born humanity.

Akedah finds concrete articulation as constitutive events ground the religious and ethical history of Israel in the Passover Exodus, half a millennium later. The historical moment of Moses begins and ends with Akedic infanticide. Moses is rescued into Pharaoh's family from the Egyptian genocidal attempt to depopulate the rapid and threatening fecundity of this servile Habiru population. This saving and constitutive epic ends with a Passover rescue of the Hebrew

---

[4] Roland de Vaux, Studies in Old Testament Sacrifice, p. 53. Part I. Word: Akedah, Theology and Messiah.

children, whose blood-smeared doors (recalling the blood of Isaac) turn away the plague-breathing God of Israel who kills the progeny of the demoralized Egyptians who persistently refuse to "let my people go." The saga of fathers and sons, which began with Adam and Cain and Abel, Abraham and Isaac, then Jacob, Joseph and brothers, will stretch to David and Solomon, Elijah and Elisha and finally to Joseph and Jesus. This only begotten, beloved child is one born in akedic rescue amid Herod's cruel infanticide. Another born out of season, Paul, will refer to Jesus' people as the "firstborn" of the resurrection (I Corinthians). Akedah permeates both testaments.

The following texts include the established body of Akedah reference in the Jewish and Christian tradition. Here is my own selection of salient passages - allusions to Akedah - which are replete in scripture and extra-biblical literature. Passages are drawn from the Jerusalem Bible.

The biblical texts of Akedah are as follows:

> Genesis 22:1-18, 37:3-12, 42:29-36
> Exodus 4:19-23, 22:28,29, 34:19,20
> Judges 11:29-40
> II Kings 3:26,27
> II Chronicles 3:1
> Psalms 40:1-3,6-8
> Isaiah 30:33
> Jeremiah 19:5-6
> Isaiah 53:3-12
> Jeremiah 20:25,26
> Zechariah 12:10
> Jeremiah 19:5,6
> Ezekiel 20: 25,26
> Micah 6:6-8
> Sirach 44:19-23
> Judith 8:25-27
> I Maccabees 2:52
> Jubilees 1717:15-18:19
> Wisdom 10:5
> Mathew 2:13-18
> Matthew 3:16-17, 17:4,5
> John 1:14 1:29, 3:16, and 10:17-18
> Romans 8:31-37
> Hebrews 2:9-18, 11:17-19,12:1,2
> James 2:20-23
> Titus 2:14,15
> Revelation 5:6,11,12

Extrabiblical texts that can be added to this corpus include these:

4Q 180 (Qumran), 4 Maccabees 13:2ff, Song of Deborah 32:1-4, 40:2, Pseudo Philo Biblical Antiquities 18:5, 2 Syriac Verse Homilies.

Genesis 22

1 After these things God tested Abraham, and said to him, "Abraham!" And he said, "Here am I."

2 He said, "Take your son, your only son Isaac, whom you love, and go to the land of Mori'ah, and offer him there as a burnt offering upon one of the mountains of which I shall tell you."

3 So Abraham rose early in the morning, saddled his ass, and took two of his young men with him, and his son Isaac; and he cut the wood for the burnt offering, and arose and went to the place of which God had told him.

4 On the third day Abraham lifted up his eyes and saw the place afar off.

5 Then Abraham said to his young men, "Stay here with the ass; I and the lad will go yonder and worship, and come again to you."

6 And Abraham took the wood of the burnt offering, and laid it on Isaac his son; and he took in his hand the fire and the knife. So they went both of them together.

7 And Isaac said to his father Abraham, "My father!" And he said, "Here am I, my son." He said, "Behold, the fire and the wood; but where is the lamb for a burnt offering?"

8 Abraham said, "God will provide himself the lamb for a burnt offering, my son." So they went both of them together.

9 When they came to the place of which God had told him, Abraham built an altar there, and laid the wood in order, and bound Isaac his son, and laid him on the altar, upon the wood.

10 Then Abraham put forth his hand, and took the knife to slay his son.

11 But the angel of the LORD called to him from heaven, and said, "Abraham, Abraham!" And he said, "Here am I."

12 He said, "Do not lay your hand on the lad or do anything to him; for now I know that you fear God, seeing you have not withheld your son, your only son, from me."

13 And Abraham lifted up his eyes and looked, and behold, behind him was a ram, caught in a thicket by his horns; and Abraham went and took the ram, and offered it up as a burnt offering instead of his son.

14 So Abraham called the name of that place The LORD will provide; as it is said to this day, "On the mount of the LORD it shall be provided."

15 And the angel of the LORD called to Abraham a second time from heaven,

16 and said, "By myself I have sworn, says the LORD, because you have done this, and have not withheld your son, your only son,

17 I will indeed bless you, and I will multiply your descendants as the stars of heaven and as the sand which is on the seashore. And your descendants shall possess the gate of their enemies,

18 and by your descendants shall all the nations of the earth bless themselves, because you have obeyed my voice."

Comment:

From the dawn of the age of human sacrifice, which Roland de Vaux argues arises perniciously at the dawn of human civilization (Breasted) in times of human prosperity and concomitant guilt, it was believed that blood must be shed for life to go on. Perpetuation of progeny and prosperity required propitiation for sin. Abraham's saga both perpetuates and repudiates this ancient ritual, especially child sacrifice. We find two distinct literary strands woven into this text. The first (vs. 1-10) uses *Elohim* as the name of God. This is the God of power and justice. The second portion employs the name *Yahweh* (the Lord), the God of rescue, mercy and surprise.

Genesis 37

3 Now Israel loved Joseph more than any other of his children, because he was the son of his old age; and he made him a long robe with sleeves.

4 But when his brothers saw that their father loved him more than all his brothers, they hated him, and could not speak
peaceably to him.

5 Now Joseph had a dream, and when he told it to his brothers they only hated him the more.

6 He said to them, "Hear this dream which I have dreamed:

7 behold, we were binding sheaves in the field, and lo, my sheaf arose and stood upright; and behold, your sheaves gathered round it, and bowed down to my sheaf."

8 His brothers said to him, "Are you indeed to reign over us? Or are you indeed to have dominion over us?" So they hated him yet more for his dreams and for his words.

9 Then he dreamed another dream, and told it to his brothers, and said, "Behold, I have dreamed another dream; and behold, the sun, the moon, and eleven stars were bowing down to me."

10 But when he told it to his father and to his brothers, his father rebuked him, and said to him, "What is this dream that you have dreamed? Shall I and your mother and your brothers indeed come to bow ourselves to the ground before you?"

11 And his brothers were jealous of him, but his father kept the saying in mind.

Comment:

The saga of fathers and beloved sons permeates the Genesis document. The coincidence and contradiction of divine command and human love throughout exemplifies the complexity of the divine character and the ambiguity of the human condition. Judah (Judas) betrays Joseph (Jesus) then for 20 pieces of silver (inflation even then).

Genesis 42

29 When they came to Jacob their father in the land of Canaan, they told him all that had befallen them, saying,

30 "The man, the lord of the land, spoke roughly to us, and took us to be spies of the land."

31 But we said to him, 'We are honest men, we are not spies;

32 we are twelve brothers, sons of our father; one is no more, and the youngest is this day with our father in the land of Canaan.'

33 Then the man, the lord of the land, said to us, 'By this I shall know that you are honest men: leave one of your brothers with me, and take grain for the famine of your households, and go your way.

34 Bring your youngest brother to me; then I shall know that you are not spies but honest men, and I will deliver to you your brother, and you shall trade in the land.'"

35 As they emptied their sacks, behold, every man's bundle of money was in his sack; and when they and their father saw their bundles of money, they were dismayed.

36 And Jacob their father said to them, "You have bereaved me of my children: Joseph is no more, and Simeon is no more, and now you would take Benjamin; all this has come upon me."

Comment:

Abraham Isaac, Jacob, Joseph—fathers and sons. The saga of duplicity, evil and death characterizes life bracketed by command and moral temptation. The reward of faithful (obedient) living is righteousness and life (Perpetuation). Kidnapping, slavery and oppression are concentric ripples of the violation of Decalogue at rung #7 ("Do not steal"). We are all active and complicit in this patricide and parricide act as we precipitate and participate in the betrayal of the beloved son. The redemptive drama ensues, as the life-giving potency of that evil becomes clear. The word adorns each offering of the God-beloved child… "You meant it for evil – God uses it for good."

Exodus 4

19 And the LORD said to Moses in Mid'ian, "Go back to Egypt; for all the men who were seeking your life are dead."

20 So Moses took his wife and his sons and set them on an ass, and went back to the land of Egypt; and in his hand Moses took the rod of God.

21 And the LORD said to Moses, "When you go back to Egypt, see that you do before Pharaoh all the miracles which I have put in your power; but I will harden his heart, so that he will not let the people go.

22 And you shall say to Pharaoh, 'Thus says the LORD, Israel is my
first-born son,
23 and I say to you, "Let my son go that he may serve me"; if you
refuse to let him go, behold, I will slay your first-born
son.'"

Comment:

In the drama of the suffering, death and revival of the first-born child, we
find a spiritual/moral oscillation between the poles of condemnation and rescue:

Moses in the bull-rushes.
The plague against Egypt's first-born,
Passover Herod's Infanticide
Another Holy family's sojourn in Egypt
The spared son now sacrificed in Golgotha
The apostolic construal of Jesus' cross as *Pascha*
(Passover)

Exodus 22

29 "You shall not delay to offer from the fullness of your harvest and
from the outflow of your presses. "The first-born of your sons you shall
give to me.

Comment:

The command for unswerving loyalty

...Have a God
...No other gods (Luther)

sets in motion the dynamic of temptation. The demand for first fruits and first
born is the ultimate test, woven, as it is, paradoxically in the legal structure of
Torah, which condemns killing. From the recesses of early culture, some
semblance of a structure of righteousness (the evil eye) intuits the realities of
unrighteous offense and redemptive offering. Here is focused the mystery of
existence, torn between time and eternity.

Exodus 34

19 All that opens the womb is mine, all your male cattle, the firstlings
of cow and sheep.
20 The firstling of an ass you shall redeem with a lamb, or if you will
not redeem it you shall break its neck. All the first-born of your sons
you shall redeem. And none shall appear before me empty.

Comment:
The mystery of the gift of life entails thanksgiving and reciprocal justice
(because loved ...we love). This proffered gift requires loyalty, all-surpassing

trust, even willingness to forsake the filial bond. The primacy of faith entails fear and trembling.

Judges 11

29 Then the Spirit of the LORD came upon Jephthah, and he passed through Gilead and Manas'seh, and passed on to Mizpah of Gilead, and from Mizpah of Gilead he passed on to the Ammonites.

30 And Jephthah made a vow to the LORD, and said, "If thou wilt give the Ammonites into my hand,

31 then whoever comes forth from the doors of my house to meet me, when I return victorious from the Ammonites, shall be the LORD's, and I will offer him up for a burnt offering."

32 So Jephthah crossed over to the Ammonites to fight against them; and the LORD gave them into his hand.

33 And he smote them from Aro'er to the neighborhood of Minnith, twenty cities, and as far as Abel-keramim, with a very great slaughter. So the Ammonites were subdued before the people of Israel.

34 Then Jephthah came to his home at Mizpah; and behold, his daughter came out to meet him with timbrels and with dances; she was his only child; beside her he had neither son nor daughter.

35 And when he saw her, he rent his clothes, and said, "Alas, my daughter! You have brought me very low, and you have become the cause of great trouble to me; for I have opened my mouth to the LORD, and I cannot take back my vow."

36 And she said to him, "My father, if you have opened your mouth to the LORD, do to me according to what has gone forth from your mouth, now that the LORD has avenged you on your enemies, on the Ammonites."

37 And she said to her father, "Let this thing be done for me; let me alone two months, that I may go and wander on the mountains, and bewail my virginity, I and my companions."

38 And he said, "Go." And he sent her away for two months; and she departed, she and her companions, and bewailed her virginity upon the mountains.

39 And at the end of two months, she returned to her father, who did with her according to his vow which he had made. She had never known a man. And it became a custom in Israel

40 that the daughters of Israel went year by year to lament the daughter of Jephthah the Gileadite four days in the year.

Comment:

The tough implication of Akedah – The Hebraic-Christic rendering of primal love entailing sacrifice is that without it Abraham, Sarah, Isaac, and the world would be lost. The gruesome Cross of Christ is necessary that the world might be saved. In the great Pauline ascension/coronation text, the precondition of "sitting at the right hand," of "the joy set before him" was "enduring the cross,""despising his shame."

(Hebrews 12:2) Commenting on the Jephthah's Daughter text and obliquely to the analogous Iphigeneia in Aulis (Euripides), where sacrificial loyalty is pledged for military victory (averting greater sacrifice), Jon Levenson writes:

> Abraham will have his multitudes of descendents only because he was willing to sacrifice the son who is destined to beget them[5].

> God proves faithful to the hoary imperative to slay one's firstborn son, yet Jesus lives. As in the first Akedah and in the story of Joseph, the son can be enjoyed and the promise sustained only if he is exposed to death itself.[6]

2 Kings 3

26 When the king of Moab saw that the battle was going against him, he took with him seven hundred swordsmen to break through, opposite the king of Edom; but they could not.

27 Then he took his eldest son who was to reign in his stead, and offered him for a burnt offering upon the wall. And there came great wrath upon Israel; and they withdrew from him and returned to their own land.

Comment:

A "pagan" instance of idolatrous child sacrifice? Don't be too sure. Mesha is king of Moab. He fights against Israel and the sacrifice of his first-born son succeeds. Again Levenson conjectures that the provocative act strikes terror and awe into the Israelite army. They know the currency of the Moabite national deity—*Chemosh*. The act of son-sacrifice insures that subsequent defeat is not only at the hands of *Chemosh*, but also of Yahweh, the Lord of history. Finally, they perceive the enduring claim of the ultimate loyalty stipulates of Decalogue (c.1-3), even to the point of laying down that which is most beloved.

2 Chronicles 3

1 Then Solomon began to build the house of the LORD in Jerusalem on Mount Mori'ah, where the LORD had appeared to David his father, at the place that David had appointed, on the threshing floor of Ornan the Jeb'usite.

Comment:

The perpetuity of piety and people, of religion and nation are founded, established and anchored on Akedah–the primal and paradigmatic act of faithful

---

[5] Jon Levenson, *Death and Resurrection*, p. 13.
[6] Ibid., p. 223

obedience. Here Torah was transfigured into faith. Here salvation was irrevocably positioned in THE WAY. The foundation of continuation and culmination of worldly and otherworldly reality rests on this archaic glacial rock, this Jebusite fortress, this Solomon's pedestal, this Golgotha, this Muslim Dome of the Rock, this summit to which all nations shall stream as they "beat their swords into plowshares" and resolve to "study war no more."

Psalm 40

1 I waited patiently for the LORD; he inclined to me and heard my cry.

2 He drew me up from the desolate pit, out of the miry bog, and set my feet upon a rock, making my steps secure.

3 He put a new song in my mouth, a song of praise to our God. Many will see and fear, and put their trust in the LORD.

4 Blessed is the man who makes the LORD his trust, who does not turn to the proud, to those who go astray after false gods!

5 Thou hast multiplied, O LORD my God, thy wondrous deeds and thy thoughts toward us; none can compare with thee! Were to proclaim and tell of them, they would be more than can be numbered.

6 Sacrifice and offering thou dost not desire; but thou hast given me an open ear. Burnt offering and sin offering thou has not required.

Psalm 102

1 A prayer of one afflicted, when he is faint and pours out his complaint before the LORD. Hear my prayer, O LORD; let my cry come to thee!

2 Do not hide thy face from me in the day of my distress! Incline thy ear to me; answer me speedily in the day when I call!

3 For my days pass away like smoke, and my bones burn like a furnace.

4 My heart is smitten like grass, and withered; I forget to eat my bread.

5 Because of my loud groaning my bones cleave to my flesh.

6 I am like a vulture of the wilderness, like an owl of the waste places;

7 I lie awake, I am like a lonely bird on the housetop.

8 All the day my enemies taunt me, those who deride me use my name for a curse.

9 For I eat ashes like bread, and mingle tears with my drink,

10 because of thy indignation and anger; for thou hast taken me up and thrown me away.

11 My days are like an evening shadow; I wither away like grass.

12 But thou, O LORD, art enthroned for ever; thy name endures to all generations.

13 Thou wilt arise and have pity on Zion; it is the time to favor her; the appointed time has come.

14 For thy servants hold her stones dear, and have pity on her dust.

15 The nations will fear the name of the LORD, and all the kings of the earth thy glory.

16 For the LORD will build up Zion, he will appear in his glory;

17 he will regard the prayer of the destitute, and will not despise their supplication.

18 Let this be recorded for a generation to come, so that a people yet unborn may praise the LORD:

19 that he looked down from his holy height, from heaven the LORD looked at the earth,

20 to hear the groans of the prisoners, to set free those who were doomed to die;

21 that men may declare in Zion the name of the LORD, and in Jerusalem his praise,

22 when peoples gather together, and kingdoms, to worship the LORD.

23 He has broken my strength in mid-course; he has shortened my days.

24 "O my God," I say, "take me not hence in the midst of my days, thou whose years endure throughout all generations!"

25 Of old thou didst lay the foundation of the earth, and the heavens are the work of thy hands.

26 They will perish, but thou dost endure; they will all wear out like a garment. Thou changest them like raiment, and they pass away;

27 but thou art the same, and thy years have no end.

28 The children of thy servants shall dwell secure; their posterity shall be established before thee.

Comment:

Worship throughout Judeo-Christian history alludes to Akedah. What began as corn and horse sacrifice cruelly yet sublimely transmutes into offering of beloved children. The propitiary offering even of the king modulates into vicarious slaying/roasting of the substitutionary lamb, eventually culminating in the offering of prayer. The transaction of wonder and felt obligation, then thanksgiving at received grace, is ultimately transformed into communal adoration and alymosary service

…. Present your bodies…a living sacrifice (Romans 12:1) This is reasonable service….

Isaiah 30

33 For a burning place has long been prepared; yea, for the king it is made ready, its pyre made deep and wide, with fire and wood in abundance; the breath of the LORD, like a stream of brimstone, kindles it.

Jeremiah 19

5 and have built the high places of Ba'al to burn their sons in the fire as burnt offerings to Ba'al, which I did not command or decree, nor did it come into my mind;

6 therefore, behold, days are coming, says the LORD, when this place shall no more be called Topheth, or the valley the son of Hinnom, but the valley of Slaughter.

7 And in this place I will make void the plans of Judah and Jerusalem, and will cause their people to fall by the sword before their enemies, and by the hand of those who seek their life. I will give their dead bodies for food to the birds of the air and to the beasts of the earth.

Comment:

Just south of the wall of Jerusalem is an old garbage pit, the ruins of the horrors of the Moloch, the fire-eating god. Here is Gehenna, the hell-like blast-ovens of child sacrifice. This site of blasphemy, idolatry, filial abuse and murder always looms in the background as Israel articulates and communally affirms its law. When the Decalogue is antiphonally recited at Jerusalem at the *Pascha* assembly or when the blessings and curses are chanted from the mountainsides at Shechem or Hebron, this WAY of sacrifice, salvation and social justice is being enacted. The flames and fumes of Topheth acridly cloud the air. Israel's WAY is profound antipathy to pagan ritual in the name of life and serene *YAWEH* devotion. Yet at the heartbeat of this piety and justice rests that solemnity kept on Holy nights, the wonder of self-giving Agape.

God so loved the cosmos (that lost, derelict, beloved world)
(John 3:16)

Isaiah 53

3 He was despised and rejected by men; a man of sorrows, and acquainted with grief; and as one from whom men hide their faces he was despised, and we esteemed him not.

4 Surely he has borne our griefs and carried our sorrows; yet we esteemed him stricken, smitten by God, and afflicted.

5 But he was wounded for our transgressions, he was bruised for our iniquities; upon him was the chastisement that made us whole, and with his stripes we are healed.

6 All we like sheep have gone astray; we have turned every one to his own way; and the LORD has laid on him the iniquity of us all.

7 He was oppressed, and he was afflicted, yet he opened not his mouth; like a lamb that is led to the slaughter, and like a sheep that before its shearers is dumb, so he opened not his mouth.

8 By oppression and judgment he was taken away; and as for his generation, who considered that he was cut off out of the land of the living, stricken for the transgression of my people?

9 And they made his grave with the wicked and with a rich man in his death, although he had done no violence, and there was no deceit in his mouth.

10 Yet it was the will of the LORD to bruise him; he has put him to grief; when he makes himself an offering for sin, he shall see his

21

offspring, he shall prolong his days; the will of the LORD shall prosper in his hand;

11 he shall see the fruit of the travail of his soul and be satisfied; by his knowledge shall the righteous one, my servant, make many to be accounted righteous; and he shall bear their iniquities.

12 Therefore I will divide him a portion with the great, and he shall divide the spoil with the strong; because he poured out his soul to death, and was numbered with the transgressors; yet he bore the sin of many, and made intercession for the transgressors.

Comment:

The conjunction of "beloved son" (*agapetos* in Septuagint), *Yahid* ("Favored one" in Hebrew texts) and "servant of Yahweh" (Isaiah 53) is complicated but crucial. The melding of images of Akedah and suffering servant is decisive in the formulation of early Christian Kerugma, which constitutes the Pentecost witness. Paul Van Buren has shown in *According to the Scriptures* that the first apostles to whom it fell to formulate the Gospel (*Evangelion*) of the meaning of Jesus' life, suffering, death, resurrection, ascension, and spirit return, reached for the great traditions of Akedah and suffering servant. In this convergence the mystery of ignominious suffering, grotesque death and restoration of the beloved son made sense. These elements, in many ways offensive to the logic and reason of both Hebrew and Hellene (I Corinthians 1:17ff) molded a conviction which found in One humiliated, scourged, wounded and despised a king, savior, messiah and Lord the creator and inheritor of all creation (Revelation 5). Akedah joined to suffering servant provided the rationale for such wisdom.

Jeremiah 31

9 With weeping they shall come, and with consolations I will lead them back, I will make them walk by brooks of water, in a straight path in which they shall not stumble; for I am a father to Israel, and Ephraim is my first-born.

15 Thus says the LORD: "A voice is heard in Ramah, lamentation and bitter weeping. Rachel is weeping for her children; she refuses to be comforted for her children, because they are not."

Zechariah 12

10 "And I will pour out on the house of David and the inhabitants of Jerusalem a spirit of compassion and supplication, so that, when they look on him whom they have pierced, they shall mourn for him, as one mourns for an only child, and weep bitterly over him, as one weeps over a firstborn.

Comment:

Two strains of mourning run through Hebrew history. They both resonate in Akedah. Tears decry the agonies of injustice; tears greet the pangs of

22

redemption. The Sermon on the Mount crowns as blessed those poor, those who mourn, those who are persecuted for the sake of righteousness (Matthew 5). This is the akedic mystery.Rachel weeps for her lost children in Sara, Rebecca, Mary and all the mothers they represent. Sons (and daughters) are lost before the Hasmonean governors, outside the walls of Jerusalem, at the sword of the crusaders in Mainz, or on the ramparts of Paris, Normandy, Nelson Mandela's Robben Island or Jenin, Palestine. The weeping and wailing is the *Lachrimosa* of the Requiem Mass.

Jeremiah 19

5 and have built the high places of Ba'al to burn their sons in the fire as burnt offerings to Ba'al, which I did not command or decree, nor did it come into my mind;

6 therefore, behold, days are coming, says the LORD, when this place shall no more be called Topheth, or the valley of the son of Hinnom, but the valley of Slaughter.

Ezekiel 20

25 Moreover I gave them statutes that were not good and ordinances by which they could not have life;

26 and I defiled them through their very gifts in making them offer by fire all their first-born, that I might horrify them; I did it that they might know that I am the LORD.

Comment:

"The lady doth protest too much, methinks."[7] The rise of Christianity with its akedic rendition and interpretation of the Cross of Christ heightens a critical tension in the mother-faith of Judaism from which it springs. Was Isaac actually sacrificed as some Midrash contends? Did the father-God actually command the sacrifice – then the counter-command? Jesus is enigma. Here father Abraham actually follows through and offers the son to death. The prophets keenly feel this equivocation:

- The moral imperative to love God above all loves even to the point of yielding one's deepest love.
- The moral imperative not to harm or kill.
- The vociferous disavowal
- "I didn't command it"
- "I didn't do it"
- "The thought never crossed my mind"

---

[7] William Shakespeare, *Hamlet*, III, ii, 242.

it betrays the difficulty even of the biblical writers and editors to fathom the ethical quandary of Akedah – "kill…don't kill." The profound theological crisis of human life can only be explained in this paradox. If humans are to live, they must die. To live to God necessitates "dying to sin," Akedah interprets the truth about God, the human condition, nature and history as it discloses the meaning of those dimensions of reality. This book seeks to elucidate that claim.

Micah 6:6-8

What shall I bring before the Lord
and bow before the High God
Shall I come with burnt offers
Or the yearling calf?
Will the Lord be pleased with a thousand rams,
Or ten thousand rivers of oil?
Shall I give my firstborn for my transgression,
The first of my body for the sin of my soul?
Man, he has showed you what is good;
What does the Lord require of you
But to do justice, love mercy, and to walk humbly with your God?

Comment:

The biblical and prophetic struggle continues with the 8th century prophets. The drama of sacrifice must continue but not with the automatic and customary gifts. The essence of sacrifice (service) is affirmed as the ministry of justice and kindness and following in the Lord's way, which is saving relationships, and serving obedience. A direction begins which will eventuate in the sublime contradiction of Akedah, "Present your bodies… a living sacrifice" (Romans 12:1).

Sirach 44:19-23

Abraham, 'the father of a multitude of nations,'
Tarnished not his glory;
Who kept the commandment of the Most High and entered into a covenant with Him:
In his flesh He engraved him an ordinance, and in trial he was found faithful.
Therefore with an oath He promised him 'To bless the nations in his seed,'
To multiply him as the dust of the earth and to exalt his seed 'as the stars;'
To cause them to inherit 'from sea to sea, and from the river to the ends of the earth.'
And as to Isaac also He promised it likewise, for his father Abraham's sake;
And the blessing of all predecessors rested upon the head of Israel;

"And He titled him with the dignity of firstborn," and gave him his inheritance;
And He set him in tribes, so as to be divided into twelve.

Judith 8

All this being so, let us rather give thanks to the Lord our God who, as he tested our ancestors, is now testing us. Remember how he treated Abraham, all the ordeals of Isaac, all that happened to Jacob in Syrian Mesopotamia while he kept the sheep of Laban, his mother's brother. For as these ordeals were intended by him to search their hearts, so now this is not vengeance that God is exacting on us but a warning inflicted by the Lord on those who are near his heart.

Book of Jubilees 17:15-18:19

15 his name Nebaioth; for she said, 'The Lord was nigh to me when I called upon him.' And it came to pass in the seventh week, in the first year thereof, [2003 A.M.] in the first month in this jubilee, on the twelfth of this month, there were voices in heaven regarding Abraham, that he was faithful in all that He
16 told him, and that he loved the Lord, and that in every affliction he was faithful. And the prince Mastema came and said before God, 'Behold, Abraham loves Isaac his son, and he delights in him above all things else; bid him offer him as a burnt-offering on the altar, and Thou wilt see if he will do this command, and Thou wilt know if he is faithful in everything wherein Thou dost try him.
17 And the Lord knew that Abraham was faithful in all his afflictions; for He had tried him through his country and with famine, and had tried him with the wealth of kings, and hadtried him again through his wife, when she was torn (from him), and with circumcision; and had tried him through
18 Ishmael and Hagar, his maidservant, when he sent them away. And in everything wherein He had tried him, he was found faithful, and his soul was not impatient, and he was not slow to act; for he was faithful and a lover of the Lord
[Chapter 18]

1,2 And God said to him, 'Abraham, Abraham'; and he said, Behold, (here) am I.' And he said, Take thy beloved son whom thou lovest, (even) Isaac, and go unto the high country, and offer him
3 on one of the mountains which I will point out unto thee.' And he rose early in the morning and saddled his ass, and took his two young men with him, and Isaac his son, and clave the wood of the
4 burnt offering, and he went to the place on the third day, and he saw the place afar off. And he came to a well of water, and he said to his young men, 'Abide ye here with the ass, and I and the

5 lad shall go (yonder), and when we have worshipped we shall come again to you.' And he took the wood of the burnt-offering and laid it on Isaac his son, and he took in his hand the fire and the

6 knife, and they went both of them together to that place. And Isaac said to his father, 'Father;' and he said, 'Here am I, my son.' And he said unto him, 'Behold the fire, and the knife, and the

7 wood; but where is the sheep for the burnt-offering, father?' And he said, 'God will provide for himself a sheep for a burntoffering, my son.' And he drew near to the place of the mount of

8 God. And he built an altar, and he placed the wood on the altar, and bound Isaac his son, and placed him on the wood which was upon the altar, and stretched forth his hand to take the knife

9 to slay Isaac his son. And I stood before him, and before the prince Mastema, and the Lord said, 'Bid him not to lay his hand on the lad, nor to do anything to him, for I have shown that he fears

10 the Lord.' And I called to him from heaven, and said unto him: 'Abraham, Abraham;' and he

11 was terrified and said: 'Behold, (here) am I.' And I said unto him: 'Lay not thy hand upon the lad, neither do thou anything to him; for now I have shown that thou fearest the Lord, and hast

12 not withheld thy son, thy first-born son, from me.' And the prince Mastema was put to shame; and Abraham lifted up his eyes and looked, and beheld a ram caught...by his horns, and Abraham

13 went and took the ram and offered it for a burnt-offering in the stead of his son. And Abraham called that place 'The Lord hath seen', so that it is said the Lord hath seen: that is

14 Mount Sion. And the Lord called Abraham by his name a second time from heaven, as he caused

15 us to appear to speak to him in the name of the Lord. And he said: 'By Myself have I sworn, saith the Lord. Because thou hast done this thing, And hast not withheld thy son, thy beloved son, from Me, that in blessing I will bless thee, And in ultiplying I will multiply thy seed. As the stars of heaven, and as the sand which is on the seashore. And thy seed shall inherit the cities of its enemies,

16 And in thy seed shall all nations of the earth be blessed; Because thou hast obeyed My voice, And I have shown to all that thou art faithful unto Me in all that I have said unto thee: Go in peace.'

17 And Abraham went to his young men, and they arose and went together to Beersheba, and Abraham [2010 A.M.]

18 dwelt by the Well of the Oath. And he celebrated this festival every year, seven days with joy, and he called it the festival of the Lord according to the seven days during which he went and

19 returned in peace. And accordingly has it been ordained and written on the heavenly tablets regarding Israel and its seed that they should observe this festival seven days with the joy of festival.

Comment:

Hebraic akedic midrash seeks to fathom the mystery of God as explicating human meaning and reciprocally illuminating the riddle of the human condition, nature and history. Sirach finds Abraham the first faithful human and therefore the progenitor of true humanity. For Judith the purpose of Akedah is not cruel vindictiveness or vengeance – some cosmic punishment – but an ordeal to make right the heart of those near and dear to Him. As Christian midrash will come to elaborate, the gift of faith is to create righteous humanity. Jubilee ties the fulfillment of humanity on Earth to this primal act of obedience in faith, the essence of Torah/Akedah. When because of him the earth was drowned, it was wisdom again who saved it... (Wisdom)

Matthew 2

13 Now when they had departed, behold, an angel of the Lord appeared to Joseph in a dream and said, "Rise, take the child and his mother, and flee to Egypt, and remain there till I tell you; for Herod is about to search for the child, to destroy him."

14 And he rose and took the child and his mother by night, and departed to Egypt,

15 and remained there until the death of Herod. This was to fulfill what the Lord had spoken by the prophet, "Out of Egypt have I called my son."

16 Then Herod, when he saw that he had been tricked by the wise men, was in a furious rage, and he sent and killed all the male children in Bethlehem and in all that region who were two years old or under, according to the time which he had ascertained from the wise men.

17 Then was fulfilled what was spoken by the prophet Jeremiah:

18 "A voice was heard in Ramah, wailing and loud lamentation, Rachel weeping for her children; she refused to be consoled, because they were no more."

Matthew 3

16 And when Jesus was baptized, he went up immediately from the water, and behold, the heavens were opened and he saw the Spirit of God descending like a dove, and alighting on him;

17 and lo, a voice from heaven, saying, "This is my beloved Son, with whom I am well pleased."

Matthew 17

4 And Peter said to Jesus, "Lord, it is well that we are here; if you wish, I will make three booths here, one for you and one for Moses and one for Eli'jah."

5 He was still speaking, when lo, a bright cloud overshadowed them, and a voice from the cloud said, "This is my beloved Son, with whom I am well pleased; listen to him."

John 1

14 And the Word became flesh and dwelt among us, full of grace and truth; we have beheld his glory, glory as of the only Son from the Father.

John 1

29 The next day he saw Jesus coming toward him, and said, "Behold, the Lamb of God, who takes away the sin of the world!

John 3

16 For God so loved the world that he gave his only Son, that whoever believes in him should not perish but have eternal life.

John 10

17 For this reason the Father loves me, because I lay down my life, that I may take it again.
18 No one takes it from me, but I lay it down of my own accord. I have power to lay it down, and I have power to take it again; this charge I have received from my Father."

Comment:

Gospel texts betray their akedic character by the way in which they portray the historical setting (e.g. Herod's slaughter of the innocents); construe and interpret the Christ-event (e.g. the crisis at Caesarea Philippi); employ Abraham/Isaac meanings to phrase the theological content of the proclamation and use simple linguistic hints employing images such as "only begotten son", "beloved son", "lamb of God", "voice from heaven". These cryptic texts signal Akedah.

The synoptics and John tell a story with a very clear point. They do not chronicle the sequence of life events. They drive to the point:

...that you may believe (Luke 1:1-4)
and have life in His name (John 20:31)

Agapetos

A crucial appropriation of Akedah into the Christian Kerugma is found in the instances where the Greek word AGAPETOS is used inconjunction with *o huios mou*.

The key passages are: Matthew 3:17, Mark 1:11, Luke 3:22, Matthew 17:5, Mark 9:7, II Peter 1:17, Matthew 12:18, and Mark 12:6 (parallel: Luke 20:13).

Comment:

These verses identify Jesus with Isaac and the martyr church with the akedic Christ. The parable of the servants, the son and the vineyard fully explicates the akedic message. Servant after servant is sent to collect the owner's portion of the yield of the vineyard. Each emissary is either beaten or killed. Finally the Lord's own "beloved son"—the heir himself—becomes the final envoy. "Surely they will heed my own son." But, the tenants violently and greedily kill and cast to the wolves, even this precious one. "What will the Lord of the vineyard do now?"

Acknowledging the akedic reference saves this passage from the insinuation of anti-semitism and from vindictive interpretation. Out of love, God willingly commissions the beloved son to be exposed to the violence of human sin. The father, Abraham, Godself, did not hold back the only-begotten (*monogenos*) and dearly beloved (*agapetos*) son. The text can best be read in this way. God willingly and knowingly turned the beloved son over to danger (the risk of sin) and death (the cost of sin). Faithfulness, even unto death, is pioneered for humanity by both Abraham and Isaac. God as father can and will raise the beloved son from the wound of violence and from the ashes of death. The son has the power to lay down and raise up his own life. (John 10:18, cf. Matthew 28:18) God is able from the stones of human destruction and desolation to raise up "children of Abraham." (Matthew 3:9)

Luke 16:19-31
19 There was a rich man who was dressed in purple and fine linen and lived in luxury every day.

20 At his gate was laid a beggar named Lazarus, covered with sores

21 and longing to eat what fell from the rich man's table. Even the dogs came and licked his sores.

22 The time came when the beggar died and the angels carried him to Abraham's side. The rich man also died and was buried.

23 In hell, where he was in torment, he looked up and saw Abraham far away, with Lazarus by his side.

24 So he called to him, "Father Abraham, have pity on me and send Lazarus to dip the tip of his finger in water and cool my tongue, because I am in agony in this fire."

25 But Abraham replied, "Son, remember that in your lifetime you received your good things, while Lazarus received bad things, but now he is comforted here and you are in agony.

26 And besides all this, between us and you a great chasm has been fixed, so that those who want to go from here to you cannot, nor can anyone cross over from there to us."

27 He answered, "Then I beg you, father, send Lazarus to my father's house,

28 for I have five brothers. Let him warn them, so that they will not also come to this place of torment."

29 Abraham replied, "They have Moses and the Prophets; let them listen to them."

30 "No, father Abraham," he said, "but if someone from the dead goes to them, they will repent."
31 He said to him, "If they do not listen to Moses and the Prophets, they will not be convinced even if someone rises from the dead."

Hebrew and Christian scriptures redound with references to Abraham. They therefore obliquely refer to Akedah, that crucial event in Abraham's biography which confirmed the virtue of his piety and insured his global and eternal progeny. Abraham and his beloved son, Isaac, are the progenitors of righteous—true and good—humanity. The story of the rich man and Lazarus annunciates the theological-ethical matrix that is the substance of Akedah. The matrix unfolds in this way:

- Injustice prevails in a thoughtless, God-demeaning, humanly disdainful world
- Through this provocation divine righteousness turns to wrath
- Prevailing grace offers the required sacrifice for redemption and reconciliation.

The Lukan story of the justice crisis of wealth and poverty (a manifestation of the sin of the world) speaks of moral apathy, of warning and of final justice. The pericope concludes with the frightening yet liberating truth that messianic shalom will remain suspended while the great gulf of injustice and inequity endures. Just as the historic specificity of Akedah is the repudiation of childsacrifice, the metaphysical meaning of this parable is the prophetic condemnation of human injustice—rich to poor, well to sick—hardheartedness which is damnation.

Romans 8

31 What then shall we say to this? If God is for us, who is against us?
32 He who did not spare his own Son but gave him up for us all, will he not also give us all things with him?
33 Who shall bring any charge against God's elect? It is God who justifies;
34 who is to condemn? Is it Christ Jesus, who died, yes, who was raised from the dead, who is at the right hand of God, who indeed intercedes for us?
35 Who shall separate us from the love of Christ? Shall tribulation, or distress, or persecution, or famine, or nakedness, or peril, or sword?
36 As it is written, "For thy sake we are being killed all the day long; we are regarded as sheep to be slaughtered."
37 No, in all these things we are more than conquerors through him who loved us.

Comment:

Paul's experience of Christ crucified, now alive, shapes the theology of the Gospels, it gives contour to the construal of Hebrew faith which will be the foundation for Christian proclamation and theology (teaching of the Apostles). Akedah, joined to the liberating vision of the Servant of Yahweh, now the glorified Son of God attested in Hebrew Torah and prophets, proclaimed by the martyr Stephen, mediated by the Pentecost Spirit, formed the heartland of this theology. Paul learned it in Damascus and Syria. It was refined through great tension with Jesus' family and the Jerusalem Christians headed by Jesus' brother, James. It finds expression in the birth and nascent growth of the early Jesus congregations in Asia Minor, Aegea and Rome. Paul's akedic theology is epitomized in chapter 8 of his Epistle to the Romans.

Written to solicit (1) An ethical witness in the form of a gift of compassion to be sent back to the famished Jerusalem community and authorized by that beneficence for (2) an evangelical mission to Spain, Paul places his akedic christology at this crux of the letter.

The features of the theology are:

- The gift of the "beloved son" portends a flow of subsequent blessing (8:32 –35ff)

- These provisions sustain through persecution and apparent calamity

- This new entourage of Isaac, like the risen lamb, are "more than conquerors" (37)

- All this is grounded in the loving father and son who "laid down" life for us.

- In this inspiration we ought not withhold (*Pheidomai*—Romans 8:32, Genesis 22:12,16) but lay down sustenance and evangelical endeavor which is our reasonable sacrifice(12:1).

Hebrews 2

9 But we see Jesus, who for a little while was made lower than the angels, crowned with glory and honor because of the suffering of death, so that by the grace of God he might taste death for every one.

10 For it was fitting that he, for whom and by whom all things exist, in bringing many sons to glory, should make the pioneer of their salvation perfect through suffering.

11 For he who sanctifies and those who are sanctified have all one origin. That is why he is not ashamed to call them brethren,

12 saying, "I will proclaim thy name to my brethren, in the midst of the congregation I will praise thee."

13 And again, "I will put my trust in him." And again, "Here am I, and the children God has given me."

14 Since therefore the children share in flesh and blood, he himself likewise partook of the same nature, that through death he might destroy him who has the power of death, that is, the devil,

15 and deliver all those who through fear of death were subject to lifelong bondage.

16 For surely it is not with angels that he is concerned but with the descendants of Abraham.

17 Therefore he had to be made like his brethren in everyrespect, so that he might become a merciful and faithful high priest in the service of God, to make expiation for the sins of the people.

18 For because he himself has suffered and been tempted, he is able to help those who are tempted.

Hebrews 11

17 By faith Abraham, when he was tested, offered up Isaac, and he who had received the promises was ready to offer up his only son,

18 of whom it was said, "Through Isaac shall your descendants be named."

19 He considered that God was able to raise men even from the dead; hence, figuratively speaking, he did receive him back.

Hebrews 12

1 Therefore, since we are surrounded by so great a cloud of witnesses, let us also lay aside every weight, and sin which lings so closely, and let us run with perseverance the race that is set before us,

2 looking to Jesus the pioneer and perfecter of our faith, who for the joy that was set before him endured the cross, despising the shame, and is seated at the right hand of the throne of God.

Comment:

This is a thoroughly akedic text. The sacrifice of a God against sin for the life of the world is epitomized in the man of faith who suffers with and for humanity, becoming in his service the "great high priest." The parade of the faithful shows us THE WAY on which we too must go.

James 2

20 Do you want to be shown, you shallow man, that faith apart from works is barren?

21 Was not Abraham our father justified by works, when he offered his son Isaac upon the altar?

22 You see that faith was active along with his works, and faith was completed by works,

23 and the scripture was fulfilled which says, "Abraham believed God, and it was reckoned to him as righteousness"; and he was called the friend of God.

Titus 2

14 who gave himself for us to redeem us from all iniquity and to purify for himself a people of his own who are zealous for good deeds.
15 Declare these things; exhort and reprove with all authority. Let no one disregard you.

Comment:

The hidden, albeit profound pervasive presence of Akedah in Christian scripture, must be attributed to the adversarial relationship that arose between Paul and James, Gentile and Jewish Christians. A thoroughly biblical and Hebraic metaphor, Akedah was regrettably submerged especially in the Paul, Augustine and Luther pathway of faith. To my mind, Paul was distorted by the Gentile, antinomian, even anti-Semitic impulses of what would become the Constantinian, Latin and Protestant theological heritage. Yet despite Luther's attempt to decanonize James, he made it. Today the thrilling recovery of Jewish literature in the dawning age of Christianity illumines again the akedic thrust of our biblical faith. Faith and works are reciprocal codependent qualities of the religious life. The divine nemesis, the *imago dei* and *imitatio dei* for this age as all ages is the *doulos theou* - the servant of God (therefore of the world) - patterned on the One who in obedience to his father "loved us and gave himself for us."

Revelation 5

6 And between the throne and the four living creatures and among the elders, I saw a Lamb standing, as though it had been slain, with seven horns and with seven eyes, which are the seven spirits of God sent out into all the earth;
11 Then I looked, and I heard around the throne and the living creatures and the elders the voice of many angels, numbering myriads of myriads and thousands of thousands,
12 saying with a loud voice, "Worthy is the Lamb who was slain, to receive power and wealth and wisdom and might and honor and glory and blessing!"
13 And I heard every creature in heaven and on earth and under the earth and in the sea, and all therein, saying, "To him who sits upon the throne and to the Lamb be blessing and honor and glory and might for ever and ever!"

Comment:

Crown him with many Crowns,
The Lamb upon his throne;
Hark! how the heavenly anthem drowns

All music but its own.
Awake, my soul, and sing
Of him who died for thee,
And hail him as thy matchless King
Through all eternity.
Matthew Bridges, 1851

B. Toward a Biblical Theology of Akedah

Time now to interpret this array of texts. Numerous technical questions and controversies swirl around this motif and midrash of Akedah "Binding," "splitting,"— the Hebrew word can refer to the tying down of Isaac on the pyre, to the splitting of the logs for the fire, to the parting of the sea of reeds. We must ask whether the ubiquitous practice of child-sacrifice in the ancient world was practiced or proscribed in Israel. Strange that a practice so vehemently repudiated (Jeremiah 19:5,6) should supply the *Leitmotiv* for Israel's messianic message to the world. What was the nature of the abandonment, then moral abhorrence of the practice of human sacrifice? What shift in religious and moral consciousness brought about the cultural – liturgical movement from material to human to animal to representational sacrifice (prayer, eucharist, justice)? The thesis of this author is that Akedah is at the normative center of biblical theology.

To probe these questions, we need to posit a new theology of Akedah, one which will think through all of the ambiguities and contradictions prompted by the biblical material. It will identify the guiding ideas, then the operational values, which arise from these admittedly perplexing materials.

The underlying theological understanding in Akedah is the pain in the heart of the God who goes out in love to his wayward and lost son in the creation. The doctrine of divine regretting [Genesis 6:6-7], repenting or pining contends that God literally inflicts pain on Himself by willing creation, allowing freedom, abiding rebellion and then going out in forgiving, reconciling love. In the very being of God we do not find passive and abstract nature but what Robert Bresson calls "The holy agony."

To lay out this biblical theology let us first offer biblical-theological reflection on some of the textual material just overviewed. We will then weave these threads of biblical theology into a normative garment for which we can then in the subsequent chapters seek empirical corroboration and application from actual patterns and processes of secular life. First, some biblical ruminations about

- Temptation and Trust in Job
- Faith and Works in Paul
- Command and Lamb in John

34

- Fear and Rest in Hebrews

1. Temptation and Trust in Job

The Akedah saga in scripture is set in the genre of temptation. The book of Genesis explores this genre. It is the "book of temptations." In their freedom, Adam and Eve confront the choice to obey or disobey, to doubt or believe, to act out that intrigue or remain true. As proto-humans they try to do well but usually fall. Cain and Abel and their offspring both pioneer creative energy and succumb to violence. A strange twist about sacrifice occurs in these scenarios of temptation as the offering of the firstborn lamb of Abel proves more savory (unjustly we feel) than the sprouts of Cain. Then with Noah—his uncanny truth and trust only to unravel again in the unruly son—Shem, Ham, Japheth—and the unruly and audacious mob. Then Abraham emerges from the mists of mythic story—the first historical person. His life is a saga of temptation—of command—choice—consequences—rescue:

- Leave Haran or stay stuck in Pleasantville (The same temptation that would test those incarcerated in luxuriant Egypt.)
- The trial of childless Sara, Ishmael, Isaac
- The crisis with Lot, at Sodom
- The covenant carved in the flesh (circumcision) and
- Akedah

Job's temptation is paradigmatic of this and every story. Temptation is the lot of every human being. Living as we do on the plane bisecting time and eternity, earth and heaven, our lives oscillate in the tension between "is" and "ought." We all experience Paul's quandary "the good I know, I can't do" and "the evil I abhor is the very thing that I do." (Romans 7:15 ff.)

Job's experience posits this temptation in the moral-theological structure of the universe. His story is a parable of life. The prologue posits a heavenly adversary, associated with adversity, plague, even death, contending with a somewhat passive deity, one quite prepared to expose (give over, lay down) his child, in freedom, to be afflicted in order to see if faith holds.

Job introduces us to the tempter as "avenger" (wrongly translated "redeemer" in Job 19:25) and as "destroyer." This evil adversary seems to have been given license to harass, torture, even kill. In Jewish lore God delivers the first-born of Israel from the "destroyer" by the blood of the paschal (Passover) lambs. This deliverance recalls Isaac's deliverance from that other "angel of death." Alan Segal notes that Jesus contemplates his death in Gethsemane Garden, at the foot of the Mount of Olives, a space in Jewish lore, sacred to the "destroyer." In a sermon appended I wonder whether on his last night prayer in that garden Jesus looked across the Kidron valley up at Mount Zion, and whether he remembered the Akedah of Isaac, believed in his day to have occurred there on that pinnacle, and contemplated his own offering.

Trust and temptation are interwoven antinomies in the divine/demonic/human intercourse. The crux of the matter is the question of whether Job's blamelessness and faithfulness is conditioned by his prosperity. If all this were to be torn away – health, wealth, even family –would his true colors show through?

Now the Lord is tempted by the tempter: "Lay your hand upon all that he has and he will certainly curse you to your face." (1:11)

This is the structure lying behind Akedah. Well-being and life itself are threatened. Children are taken but restored. Job lived to see four generations of sons and grandsons (Job 1:18-19, 42:13-16). It is an ethical parable. Torah and Decalogue with their vertical and horizontal challenge are pronounced. What is your ultimate loyalty
and trust? What commitment do you have to others?

Two elements are here in the structure of temptation and trust: We see that life is a process of being "given over" (*paradokein*) (Isaiah 53, Romans 8) in order to be "taken up". An allusion to the "cursed one who hangs on the tree" (Deuteronomy 21:22, 23). John's Jesus claims "If I be lifted up I will draw all people to myself." (John 12:32) The paradox of the ordeal of temptation, be it Israel in the Sinai wilderness or Jesus in the Judean wilderness, is that the ordeal purifies, clarifies and fortifies for the impending mission.

Universally interpreted, the human predicament of adversity or persecution clarifies the soul since it comes from and leads to God. It is an adventure into sin, yes. Exertion of equivocal freedom, yes. But ultimately we are truly free because we are divine creation. Damnation or salvation really ensue both immediately and ultimately. This is inevitable in the Trinitarian ontic construal of reality where divinic, anthropic and demonic dimensions interplay. The freedom with which the creator imbued the world process
allowed agony yet insured victory.

The human project of culture – technology, science, the arts, in some sense even religion itself – is the search for protection from the terror of this insult. It is a projection of a vicarious victim to bear the insult. The vicar – be it a scapegoat, a victimized sub-population, animals or nature itself – absorbs the punishment – the price for the exploitation and injustice of life. Yet even what we intend for evil, God works for good.

2. Faith and Works in Paul

This understanding of the human project as a muting of sin and deflection of judgement leads to a deeper discussion of the phenomenon of human work. Paul lifts this AKEDIC crisis to yet another level.

He writes to the Corinthians:

> ...Our paschal lamb, Christ, has been sacrificed.
> Therefore let us keep the feast not with
> The old leaven of malice and evil but with
> The new leaven of sincerity and truth.
> (I Corinthians 5:8)

Paul views the outward projection of the moral crisis of humanity on to some scapegoat, even on to some code on to which adherence can be imputed as righteousness, as destructive of freedom and faith.

Paul views Jesus/Messiah as a total substitutionary sacrifice, standing in as vicar or lamb for humans who are totally without virtue and salvific efficacy. This view of the incapacity of repentance and righteousness in humans is totally inconsistent with the view of human nature in Hebrew religion and scripture. While Paul's view heightens the concentration of salvific efficacy in the Akedah, it diminishes the prelude and postlude of human responsibility. Paul leads into and out of Akedah by emphasizing the personal infusion of Spirit. Existence, *en Christou*, as the new righteousness.

In the provocative section of the second letter to Corinth, Paul says that the Christic transformation of the human community toward its original authenticity and its eschatic new being is not based on "stone tablets" (Decalogue) or Letters (the Antioch dispatch?) but on the "fleshly tablets of the heart." (2Corinthians 3:3) Paul's view is that the human moral crisis has been once for all transacted in the AKEDIC Christ. Now the law has been transcended and new life, conceived existentially, is conveyed by the indwelling Holy Spirit. Yet as Scott Hafeman[8] has shown, this new covenant of Jeremiah 31 is the vivification of the old covenant. In Paul we meet Moses revivified, not repudiation or supercessionism.

This view is articulated in the letter to the Galatians. A most fascinating conjunction and juxtaposition, law and lamb, Torah and Akedah, is found in Paul's letter to the Galatians. We may assume that in Paul's time that this Asia Minor faith community was strongly shaped by Judaism through the Passover liturgy and Torah ethics. The epistle raises the concerns about judaizing the

---

[8] Scott Hafeman, *Paul, Moses and the History of Israel*. Munich: Mohr, 1995.

gentile believers, especially on the issues of circumcision, kosher foods and works-grounded faith. The salient Midrash on Akedah is chapter 3.

> ...You began your walk of faith in the spirit. Will you now complete it in the flesh? Growth in God comes by listening in faith, not living by works.... Abraham heard God ("go out from Chaldea, give your beloved son") and believed and he was righteous (progeny) ... The just shall live therefore by faith. Those who seek to live the law are cursed. It is written that those who live by the law (written in the books) fail and are cursed. Christ redeemed us from the law's curse. He was made curse for us, for it is written, "cursed is every one who hangs on the tree."
> (Galatians 3:3-13, my translation.)

Paul—the Pharisee–theologian–evangelist–is offering a very subtle and searching rendition of Akedah. He seeks to go to the heart of God's giving of the beloved son and the meaning of that restatement of righteousness for humanity. In my view Paul is giving a particular twist to several Judaic themes–law, Akedah, servant, curse, righteousness–in order to restore Israel's universal mission of "light to the Gentiles" and "God-fearing righteousness" and to object to the trivialization of scribal and pharisaic ethics and the "threatened" tyranny of law in the Jerusalem priesthood. I cannot believe that Paul rejects Torah or Decalogue. Just as Jesus said that not one jot or tittle would pass from the law and just as Paul affirmed "the law of Christ," this antinomianism is surely a reaction against the virulence of the Jerusalem establishment priests, under threat both externally from Roman paganism and internally from Jamesian, Nazaritic, Hasidic, and Zealotic radicals call for reform. I cannot imagine Paul repudiating the law. The new company of Paul and Judaism scholars such as E.P. Saunders, Geza Vermes and others move in this direction.

- You shall love the Lord your God with all your being
- You shall have no other gods
- You shall not kill

Paul's agenda is rather to renew the life and way of God (piety and ethics) within the soul of the human being. The living Christ, accessible in the Holy Spirit of God into the heart and soul of believers is the end- all of Paul's mission. This new relationship conveyed in the eternal yet earth–seeking Christ embraced, for Paul, all that there was of truth, sacrifice and law into the new being. The Holy Spirit, we must recall, is the gift of *Shavout* festival, the celebration of the law. Paul's fascinating juxtaposition of the curse of the tree elaborates this doctrine. Though Paul wrongly chafes under James' and Jerusalem church authority he rightly joins in the Jamesian spirit, the *pietas* and ethos of God's giving love, which is our "living sacrifice." (Romans 12)

In this sense, Paul anticipates the Johannine synthesis of the lamb with the books (law) within the Akedah symbol. He restores prophetic and psalmic piety:

"I desire righteousness, not sacrifice" (Hosea 6:6)
"I waited for the Lord–He heard my cry
He lifted me from the pit (Joseph) and set me on the rock
Sacrifice and offering you do not desire
…In the volume of the book it is written
I delight to do your will, O my God.
Your law is engraved on my heart."
(Psalm 40:1-8)

We summarize Paul's akedic theology.

We might ask at this point that all-searching question which holds the redemptive secret:

- Why did God command Abraham to sacrifice Isaac?
- Why did God give over Jesus to die for the world?
- Why do we age and waste away if God is the Lord of life, redemption, of the future?
- Why is goodness and justice under assault in world history and in the history of nature?

Scholars of nascent Christianity rightly attribute the Apostle Paul for imbedding akedic belief and behavior into the faith. Wayne Meeks, for example, shows how Paul's theological ethic of the cross of Christ becomes the paradigm for christic existence.

> Paul's hortatory rhetoric is an expandable set of analogies,…between the story of Jesus' crucifixion and resurrection and the desired dispositions and behavior of believers. This transformation of what ….was for Paul the basic message of Christian faith into a malleable polysemic trope was perhaps the profoundest and most enduring contribution that Paul made to Christian speech and thought.[9]

Quoting Paul's rebuke of the smugness of the Galatian congregation

> …forbid that I should boast—save in the Cross of Christ through which the world is crucified to me and I to the world (6:14)

Meeks summarizes:

> …for Paul to speak of the crucifixion is always to imply the resurrection. Therefore, a Kierkegaardian "repetition", in which faith simultaneously gives

---

[9] Wayne Meeks, *The Origins of Christian Morality* (New Haven, Connecticut: Yale University Press, 1993).

up and gets back-transformed-the desired object, catches better the double movement of Paul's concern. [10]

The biblical answer, I believe, is the baptism of Jesus to the demur of John the Baptist: " How can I baptize you?"... "that all righteousness must be fulfilled." (Matthew 3:15)

What might this mean?

Several premises build up an understanding of the biblical rendition of righteousness:

- The law becomes ethicized as the way of life in God for the world.
- God posits law to bind himself with his creature in relationship.
- Divine and human conduct is therefore regulated by this law.
- God's Way (command) is right because God is righteous.
- While the world condemns to death, God saves to life the one who obeys' the Way'.
- The Way of God therefore, not jogging, proper diet, kindly disposition, etc., is the way of life.
- The ultimate command is to give one's life to God (witness).
- The end of law (Torah) is *Tikkun Olam*—the healing of the world.

Abraham's question at Sodom and Gomorrah is the *Leitmotiv* of his existence:

"Shall not the judge of all the earth do right?" (Genesis 18:25)

The mystery of Akedah and the crucifixion is found in the restitution of this way of healing (restitution) for the world.

3. Command and Lamb in John

A more Hebraic rendition of the akedic heritage comes from the Johannine circle–John the Baptist through John the Apostle, those who compose and redact the Gospel of that name, to the Elder of the Epistles of John, culminating in the visionary of Patmos and then the Asia Minor Churches–one deeply steeped in the song of Akedah. Here Logos is defined by Law and Lamb, as these symbols are woven into the Paschal mysteries and ultimately into the mission of the immortal, now regnant, lamb of God. The Gospel begins with an Akedah song:

- He came to his own...and gave them power to become sons of God (1:12)

---

[10] Ibid., p. 64.

- We beheld his glory...as of the only son (*monogenos*) (1:14)
- John saw Jesus and said..."behold the lamb of God who takes away the sin of the world." (1:29)

The *Leitmotiv* of the genre is the conjunction of Lamb and Law

If you love me you will keep my commandments (14:21)
Keep my commandments—continue in my love—I keep the Father's commandments and continue in his love
That my joy might remain in you and your joy be full (15:9-11)

This is Akedah: Willing obedience to God's command agape–self-sacrificial love–yielding joy in heaven and on earth.

... There is joy in heaven as one sinner repents (Luke 15:7,10)
... For the joy set before him–he endured the cross (Hebrews 12:2)

Our research shows that the moral structure of the Johannine corpus, especially John's apocalypse, is Torah, especially the ethical charter of Decalogue. From the Nash Papyrus we know that second temple Judaism, in the second century before Christ, oriented its religion and legal life around the Shema and Decalogue. This fact is corroborated by the fact that the book of revelation, like 4 Ezras, is fashioned in *"dekalogische Struktur"*.

My analysis of the contribution of *Bet Johannan* to akedic conviction centers on 3:16 of the Gospel and the first letter of one bearing the name of that school.

...As Moses lifted up the serpent in the wilderness, so must the Son of man be lifted up so that all who believe receive eternal life. For God so loved the world that he gave his only son (*monogenos*) so that all who believe shall not perish, but receive eternal life. (3:15,16)

Being "lifted up" (Greek *huphōthō*, Hebrew *nasah*) seems to be used by Jesus as a mingling of the themes of akedic hanging on the tree (crucifixion) and ascension. The lifting up therefore is deemed necessary to cancel sin and to release the spirit. The first letter similarly juxtaposes death and life, murder and release, which is the akedic essence of the Johannine theology.

We know that we have passed from death to life because we love the brethren.
He who does not love his brother abides on death.
Whoever hates his brother is a murderer.
We know that no murderer has life abiding in him.
Herein we perceive the love of God because He laid down his life for us.
We therefore ought to love the brethren.
I John 3:14-16

41

Lying behind this theology, Jewish (Jon Levenson) and Christian (Raymond Brown) scholars agree is the Isaianic servant. In Isaiah 53 the grotesque, leprous servant will "teach the way" because "he poured out his soul to death." Obedient unto death, this lad (Isaac, servant) atones vicariously for the very violent ones who killed him. Here again we see the intricate relation between law and obedience, transgression, violent death, vicarious sacrifice, rescue and renewal.

The genius of Akedah is expressed in the Hymn which the agnostic son of the Down Ampney Vicarage—Ralph Vaughan Williams—set to the words of Bianco da Siena (d.1434). One feels here the deepest spiritual meaning of Mount Moriah.

> Come down, O Love divine, Seek out this soul of mine,
> And visit it with thine own ardor glowing;
> O Comforter, draw near, Within my heart appear,
> And kindle it, thy holy flame bestowing.
> O let it freely burn, Till earthly passions turn
> To dust and ashes in the heat consuming;
> And let thy glorious light Shine ever on my sight,
> And clothe me round, the while my path illuming.

4. Fear and Rest in Hebrews

The most fully akedic book in the bible is the letter to Hebrews. Two biblical texts preface our comments:

> "Do not touch the child – I now know that you fear God"
> "You have not withheld your only beloved son"
> Genesis 22

> " He sent his beloved son into the vineyard saying they will fear
> my son–but they killed him and threw him out of the vineyard"
> (Mark 12:6 ff. – Isaiah 5:1)

Hebrews throughout echoes Akedah

> … You are my son–I have begotten you …
> (Hebrews 1:5)

> He took on him the seed of Abraham (2:16)
> He himself has suffered and was tempted (2:18)

> There remains therefore a rest for the people of God
> Therefore fear, lest any come short of it. (4:9ff)

> By faith Abraham when tried offered up Isaac…Trusting that God

was able to raise him up …even from the dead.
(11:17 ff).

As Isaac's merit brings rescue, so the merit of Jesus' cross grounds his resurrection. Akedic or priestly logic agrees with Jon Levenson who writes:

"… as in the first aqedah and in the story of Joseph (with Jesus) the son can be enjoyed and the promise sustained only if he is exposed to death itself."[11]

While the mother of seven martyred sons in IV Maccabees can boldly belittle father Abraham for offering only one son and not finishing it off at that, God, Jesus' father, stays true to his promise. He goes through with it. This is the thrust of the poignant clause " he did not withhold."

A crucial issue clarified in the akedic cosmology of Hebrews is the role of the adversary/destroyer in the ordeal of temptation. As Levenson shows the heavenly adversary of Jubilees 17:15-16 is the mysterious destroyer, let loose in the Passover in Exodus 12:21-23—that force in death and life which will "get through " when divine immunity or protection is withdrawn.

"When he withdraws his breath they collapse back to dust." The "ashes" or bloodstain of Isaac is to God the memory that bars the door from ferocious mortal affliction. In Hebrews we recall this destroying force:

… Just as the children are flesh and blood, he took on the same that through death he might destroy him that had the power of death.
Hebrews 2:14

The Sabbath or rest envisioned in Hebrews is the resurrection victory over the tempter in his adversarial/destroyer function. The fear of death (Hebrews 2:15) is the antithesis of rest. The dynamics of Akedah accomplish rest for the people of God.

Id al-Adha, also called the "major festival" or "sacrificial feast," is the commemoration or reenactment of the Abraham-Isaac (Ishmael) offering throughout the Islamic world. On this day the ancient universal ritual of the sacrificial lamb, the Hebrew ritual of Passover and temple sacrifice and the Christian liturgy of Eucharist are celebrated. Capturing the salvific and ethical essence of the sacrifice (resurrection victory over temptation, sin and death) by its rendition of this primal atoning act, Muslims worldwide purchase or secure from their own flock the kid without blemish or imperfection, cook it and cut it for one's own restoration, then distribute the major portion to the poor. While the Druses here celebrate the Cain/Abel sacrifice, for most Muslims the constitutive memory and hope is the Abrahamic Akedah.

---

[11] Jon Levenson, *Death and Resurrection of the Beloved Son*, Yale, 1994, p. 223.

These reflections from what might be called "Biblical Theology" can now be woven into a more coherent and systematic theory. There is a philosophical, ethical and esthetical dimension to the theology or *Weltanschauung*, which proceeds from the metaphor of Akedah.

Philosophy and Akedah

> "Venerable Abraham ... you knew first that higher passion, the holy, pure and humble expression of the divine madness."[12]

Terence Malick, the celebrated filmmaker of *Badlands* and *Days of Heaven* resigned to study philosophy for two decades before producing his prize-winning *The Thin Red Line* in 1998. He studied great thinkers, including Søren Kierkegaard, whose study of Abraham/Isaac, *Fear and Trembling*, has influenced the film. The film (see appendix sermon "The Gift of the Beloved Son") probes the philosophy of Akedah.

Kierkegaard, one of the stalwarts of modern philosophy, seeks that balance of critique and conviction which is the genius of philosophy. Kierkegaard condemns worldly philosophy such as that of Hegel, who attempts a grand synthesis of meaning from science, culture, history and religion. He fashions a radical conviction based on sheer freedom and decision grounded in the irreducible truth of human existence. As with his *Nachfolger*, Martin Buber, "I-thou" is the crux of reality for Kierkegaard.

Kierkegaard is critical of human apotheosis and deification and facile identification of culture with truth and good. Humans are radically contingent beings respective to deity and responsible to others. He focuses on existence and pioneers the philosophy of existentialism. He then highlights the phenomenon of suffering and hope, decision and practice. Akedah adapts well to this philosophy.

Akedah penetrates the very heart of philosophy in its critical and convictional dimensions. As theory and praxis, Akedah portrays a story to interpret and animate life and death. Like the exacting scalpel of that akedic epistle to the Hebrews, the word of truth (or love of wisdom: philosophy) pierces to the membrane dividing bone and marrow (matter and thought), soul and spirit (Hebrews 4: 12). Modern linguistic philosophy, as derivative of thinking such as Wittgenstein and A. J. Ayer, as of the German/French school of Hegel, Husserl, Heidegger, Saussure, Girard, Levinas, Derrida and Ricoeur seek to cut through the imprecise use of language. In Akedah research, the work of Shalom Spiegel (*THE LAST TRIAL*), and Jack Miles (*GOD: A BIOGRAPHY*) note the cleavage in usage of the Hebrew in Genesis 22 between the designations "God" and " The LORD (Yahweh)".

---

[12] Søren Kierkegaard, *Fear and Trembling*, p. 12.

"God" is the creator and destroyer. This is the God who reigns from the thrones of mercy and justice (Psalm 89). Here is One transcendent and arbitrary– benevolent and malevolent, just and merciful, aloof and companioning. "The LORD" is slow to anger and plenteous in mercy (Psalm 103:8), a characterization that seems incompatible with the first command of Akedah. While this duality in the linguistics about God are unnerving, this may be a liberating value of critical thought which depicts the true complexity of the divine being. Just as the necessity of matter and anti-matter is necessary to fathom physical reality, there may be a paradoxical complementarity of the being and action of God. Just as a parent's love for a child requires discipline, not *laissez-faire*, the back-to-back thrones of justice and mercy may conceal the fact that justice is mercy and mercy, justice.

Akedah is a depiction of reality. The ultimate reality is God. Philosophy is the science of reality. Akedah is the paradigmatic symbol of the God who gives and takes, takes and gives. As a potent risk of temptation and paradox, God releases then reclaims the creation. In Israel's history, God liberates in freedom then binds in command. This mystery is rationalized by Augustine, Luther and Kierkegaard who affirm that in God and with our fellow humans—servitude is perfect freedom. God commands "Be fruitful," then imposes circumcision. God gives us over (*paradokein*) to our willful disobedience, then wins us back to a free willing obedience. The heart of it all is that God, through self-giving and the offering of his son, guides us to the way of life.

This setting forth of a divine pattern and pathway we find offensive. We want to go our own way. This primary process of denial leads to the fashioning of other ultimacies and efficacies. As humans we will usually follow what works. We assert various idolatries and immoralities to fill the void. Here philosophy is a salutary instrument, critiquing beliefs and values. It guides a discipline of iconoclasm and worthy belief, discerning false loyalties and destructive behaviors.

We either honor and follow high religion - Abrahamic faith which transcends our petty beliefs and values - or we succumb to natural, cultural religion. This latter expression caters to our own needs and fears. Primitive sacrifice insures a way of life, to appease a vengeful or capricious deity, to guarantee fertility or fecundity of fields and families. AKEDIC sacrifice, subsuming Torah, weaving faith into human justice, tempers an authentic commitment. The prehistory of Akedah in naturalistic, human sacrifice is such a concession to popular deities. From the dawn of history, sacrifice is homage to the "powers that be." In this sense it exhibits a primal and commendable piety.

> ... That which could be known of God Deity (Godhead) and power were evident in the creation
> (Romans 1:19:20).

Yet, though graceful in potential, when unchastened by transcendence, this natural religious and moral impulse, uninspired by the Holy Spirit and unguided by the will of God, leads to idolatry and immorality – false and insidious constructions. Far from being innocent, these constructions are insidious. They constitute the universal evil called the fall. They wreak havoc in the earth as all violence is rooted in that rudimentary lie and misdirection:

> Claiming to be wise they became fools…
> Changed the truth of God into a lie…
> They worshipped the creature more than the creator
> …Being filled with all unrighteousness
> (Romans 1:22-32)

Jack Miles suggests that

> "The Lord (Yahweh) acts because of his own feelings, his regrets; God (Elohist) because a cleaning destruction is what the world needs"[13]
> (Genesis 6:5-8)

This duality in the perceived being and action of God presents crisis (judgment) to human existence. This anxiety provokes either faithful lure or faithless evasion out of the nexus of freedom in the human heart and mind. Here, as Luther claimed, arises faith or idolatry (C-1, *Larger Catechism*). [14]

It is at this point that we either cling to the theology of grace in the cross of Christ, or we enact the crucial violence of sacrifice. Rejecting the child of Bethlehem leads us to Herodian infanticide. We are either crucified with Christ (Galatians 6:14) or we perpetuate the crucifixion.

The mountain of the gods is the primitive version of the Athens Agora or the Gladiators' arena. It is the scene of the ultimate clash of visions and values. Here the drama of justice transpires with reasoning and bargaining. The drama concerns life and death. The mountain confirmation engages disease and health, feast or famine, fate and death. These great impulses drive the Incas or Siberians up those sacred mountains with goat or horse or child. This is Sinai, the summit of reasoning together and of the command of righteousness. Here we present body and mind, conviction and conscience, as living sacrifice.

On these holy mountains–Moriah, Olympus, Sinai, Carmel, Transfiguration, Golgotha–earth-shaking crises occur. Here we find the rendezvous at dawn of dueling deities. Contenders and presenters are put to the test. On Akedah

---

[13] Jack Miles, *God: A Biography*, New York: Knopf, 1995, p. 34.

[14] I will refer to the Commandments according to the Reformed list, with the abbreviations C-1 - C-10.

mountain we have theophany–True God appears. The medium of Akedah—sacrifice, blood, fire, wind—the elements of SHAVOUT/Pentecost—test the worthiness of offerings, the worship of God. The Gods themselves on Olympus or Sinai find themselves in contention with humans. The Greek gods can be cajoled or bribed. Even Yahweh is tempted by the hardheartedness of the people (Hebrews 3:16ff).

Philosophy—the human enterprise which seeks to expose, exegete and extol truth—takes on new forms in our postmodern age. Today secular philosophy has displaced religious philosophy. While deconstructive critique is intense and salutary, affirmation of truth and reality is intellectually suspect. At last, in the early years of this new millennium, we begin to weary of relativism as ultimate truth. Yes, human perception and articulation is always conditioned, partial and situational—even religion. Yet this awareness is itself evidence for the quest for objective and universal reality. Akedah sensitively responds to human relativity and divine ultimacy.

Philosophy also seeks the *summum bonum*, ultimate good. As we construct a new theology of Akedah, moral philosophy plays a critical role.

If the character of God is the primary reading, and if the vindication of God's goodness as the purpose of God's justice wins out as the outcome of Akedah, then a close secondary import is human character and the akedic rendition of the structure of good and evil. A philosophy underlies a manner of life. In Israel's biblical history, Mount Moriah becomes the setting for the temple mount (II Corinthians 3:1) connecting the sacrifice of Isaac with the ministrations of the Torah life charter and its sacrificial/sacerdotal cult in Jerusalem.

This connection of law and lamb is reaffirmed when the book of Jubilees associates Isaac's sacrifice with Passover (17:15-18:19). The importance of our thesis is seen today as you mount the upper levels of the great Jerusalem mosque, the Dome of the Rock and find there at the apex the crude plateau believed to be the place in Moriah where Abraham took Isaac for Sacrifice. This Holy site, also the ascension site of the prophet Mohamed, is surrounded by the old city of Jerusalem. Israeli soldiers patrolling the street are close to the Via Dolorosa and Calvary; here also are The Holy Sepulcher and the other Holy sites of Christendom. The three Abrahamic or akedic faiths seem to hold the destiny of the world in their hands. Indeed, as the Prophets foreknew ... The nations shall stream to Zion and there 'beat their swords into plowshares" (Isaiah 2:4, Micah 4:3) or the eschatological reversal (Joel 3:10).

The import of this association for world history is that the moral structure of life in a God - sustained world is the essence of the meaning of Akedah. What is the progression of points of argument linking the theological assumptions of Akedah with the nature of human ethics? Here is the compendium as I see it:

- The turning out (evolving) in freedom of humans as divine icons (*Imago dei*) precipitated self suffering and autonomy (becoming a law to one's self)

- The sin of the world created new conditions for alienation and reconciliation (law incites sin and grace)

- The outgoing of God in law and love (servant and son) sought to repair the breach and recover "THE WAY" for creation.

- Living the law provokes the violence of the sin-entangled world. In Jewish perspective the martyr, the ultimate righteousness, potential even in Gentiles, is one who suffers for the sake of the commandments ("The Name").

- The people's vindication and perpetuation would require the expiatory act of righteousness and grace – animated recommitment to the way (faith, willingness to offer one's dearest to God and one's living as "wholly acceptable" sacrifice: (Romans 12) "It was Yahweh's good pleasure to crush him with pain; if he gives his life as a sin offering, he will be offspring and prolong his life, and through him Yahweh's good pleasure will be done (Isaiah 53:10)." The seed of Abraham is inseminated and disseminated.

Our argument now unfolds into the following thesis: Human wrong is to visit suffering on the heart of God and into the flesh of our fellow humans and in wounding the organism of the earth. It is to perpetuate violent Akedah into the earth as we deny the release of new life through violence and death.

The "good" in moral philosophy is that highest excellence which the human mind and conscience can conceive.

Great philosophers from Philo to Kierkegaard have found in Akedah the foundational paradigm of the moral human condition and the reality of reality. How does this simple, one might say crude, metaphor, assume such profound meaning? The symbol is complex: a rescue ram is caught in the mountain briars as Abraham unsheathed a knife. It is the Passover lamb slain as a rescue–a warning to all sword-wielding infant-killers–sparing Moses in the bulrushes, sparing Hebrew children in the Passover plague, sparing the Holy family from Herod's infanticide. It is the lamb–Son of God—tied to the Roman's crucifixion tree— which will forbid future killing as deterrence. It is the envisioned immolated Lamb reigning on the throne of John's Apocalypse to which all earth's rulers ultimately bow. This is the biblical panorama of Akedah.

The Aesthetics of Akedah

Akedah, as we have seen, speaks of God and of the moral character of God relating to the world in judgment and mercy. These are the two sides of the divine nature or the two thrones of God's dealing with humanity (Psalm 89). Akedah is also the prime symbol for the pathos of humanity. The enigma of suffering is the heart of that pathos. In Platonic tradition this is the dark side of light, the *nihil* underlying cosmos. Developing this human aesthetic implication of Akedah will help us fathom the universality and efficacy of the symbol. A good way into this subject is to ponder the biblical metaphor of Rachel "weeping for her children…who are gone."

Although this deep lament that echoes (Jeremiah 31:15, Matthew 2:18) through the ages, from Egypt's first infanticide from which Moses drifted to life, to the Passover deliverance at the Red Sea, down to Herod's order at the time of Jesus' birth, Rachel's children are actually Joseph and Benjamin (Genesis 46:19) "Who are gone." When Reuben returns to the pit where the brothers had abandoned Joseph he cries, "he is gone." Psalm 40, a great akedic text, picks up on the theme:

He inclined to me and heard my cry
He lifted me from the horrible pit
and set my feet upon a rock (40:2).

When the brothers, without Benjamin, appear before the Egyptian Prime Minister to request food, again they tremble, "the youngest is with our father and one is no more." (42:13) Like Moses, Joseph has become a vizier of the overlord. Joseph and Benjamin are *yedid*—beloved of the Lord. Like Abraham and Sarah, these boys are the miraculous children of Judah's and Rachel's old age, and the lament is all the more bitter.

Much of the moving rabbinic literature on Akedah finds the mother weeping over the lost son. In several texts Sarah has long deep distress resisting the commission of Abraham. A Syriac voice homily of the sixth century is representative:

I begin to lay before the / the story of holy people. Abraham, father of nations, / for one hundred years as though a single day. Stood at God's gate / asking, amid groans and with supplication and prayer, that he should have a son by Sarah. This is granted. Then God called out to Abraham: "Offer up to me your son as a whole offering / on one of the mountains I shall tell you of."

So Abraham begins to sharpen a knife. Sarah sees this, and her heart groans. She asks Abraham to reveal what he is hiding from her to which he replies that, "this secret, women cannot be aware of." Sarah reminds him that they were as one in entertaining guests who turned out to be angels and begs that she now be allowed to share with Abraham, whom she calls "drunk with the love of God," in the sacrifice of her only son. Then to Isaac she says:

"When you go with your father, / listen and do all he tells you …Stretch your neck like a lamb. /… Lest his mind be upset and there be a blemish in his offering." Listen … to the words of your mother / and let your reputation go forth unto generations to come." Sarah lets them depart; they reach their

49

destination and make ready to ascend the mount. As Isaac prepares to carry the wood,

A Voice says: " I shall put in him strength... "And in this shall I too carry / my cross on the street of Sion, "When I go down to Golgotha / I will effect the salvation of Adam."

So father and son begin to gather stones and build the pyre They became workers for God, / the old man and his son, equally.

The Threefold One blessed them / for they became (workers) for his Being.

Isaac tells Abraham that he knows that he is about to be sacrificed and requests that he be bound tightly, lest he spoil the offering. Abraham is much relieved to hear that Isaac is not praying to be spared what God has commanded. Abraham proceeds with the offering, but is stopped by a Voice from on high that tells him:

"Your offering is accepted... You have become [father] to thousands without number." "And without mention of your name, Abraham, / an offering shall not be accepted."

Abraham turns and finds a lamb "hanging on the tree," which

He offers in place of Isaac. Upon their return home, Abraham tells Isaac to wait while he sees how Sarah will receive him. She welcomes Abraham, bringing water to wash his feet, and says:

"Welcome, blessed old man, / husband who has loved God. Welcome, O happy one, / who has sacrificed my only child on the pyre;

Welcome, O slaughterer, / who did not spare the body of my only child."

Sarah asks for a full report of how Isaac died and whether he wept, and Abraham assures her that Isaac did not. Sarah says:

"May the soul of my only child be accepted, / for he hearkened to the words of his mother."

Sarah grieves that she was not present and has not even seen the place where her only child, her beloved, was sacrificed.

Suddenly, Isaac comes in. Sarah rejoices, saying:

"Welcome, O dead one come to life."

She asks Isaac, "What did your father do to you?" Upon hearing his report, she says:

"Henceforth, my son, it will not be 'Sarah's son' / that people will call you,

"But 'child of the pyre' / and 'offering which died and was resurrected.'

And to you be the glory, O God, / for all passes away, but You endure."
[15]

Summary: Sacrifice for Sin—the Heart of Akedah
Martyrs in the Jewish tradition suffer pain, dying for the sake of the law—especially sanctifying and unifying the divine name (Shemah – C1, 2,3.). In IV Maccabees, an expansive Akedah text, the martyrs of Israel's faith to the increasingly belligerent Roman Empire are conceived in terms of "self-offering … as atonement for the sins of Israel."

Two centuries hence when the Christian martyrs' witness against an idolatrous Empire is conceived in the book of Revelation, it is as the sacrificial lamb is offered for the "sins of the world" (Revelation 5, Isaiah 53).

The lingering heritage of Abraham and Isaac in the Hebrew heritage is that of a loving and faithful father offering an obedient and submissive son. One good, innocent and just offers himself and is offered for the sake of sinners; Isaiah 53:7,10. [16]

In delivering his soul to death … He took away the sins of many.
(Isaiah 53:12)

Being bound or chained to bear the punishment of the sin of the world, being handcuffed and leg-bound in the dungeon, is the qualification of the "Servant of God." Just as one is captive or sold into slavery (servanthood), so here one willingly submits to the cords and lashes of a criminal justice apparatus to gain (ransom) release for those similarly incarcerated. Charles Wesley (1739) captures the theme:

My imprisoned spirit lay, fast bound in sin and nature's night; Thine eye diffused a quickening ray; … I woke the dungeon flamed with light.

My chains fell off, my heart was free, I rose went forth and followed thee.

"The ashes of Isaac" becomes the heart of Israel's offertory even as the temple is transmitted to synagogue worship. The SHOFAR, or the pulverized ash of the ram's horn, signifies the sacrifice of Isaac. The blowing of the SHOFAR at new

---

[15] Quoted in Paul Van Buren, *According to the Scriptures* (Grand Rapids, Michigan: Eerdmans Press, 1997), p. 44.

[16] See Geza Vermes, *Scripture and Tradition in Judaism* (Leiden: Brill, 1961), p. 117ff.

year signifies the victory of redeeming love over besetting sin. God's way prevails as resurrection strives and thrives against the force of the demonic. Christian liturgy is born in this Akedic Passover festival. Akedah is prayer that the divine healing love will override human destructive violence. From the third century in Genesis *RAB* to the 12th Century sephardic liturgy of Fez, Akedah becomes the celebration and petition for divine forgiveness. "Remember thy favor sworn on Mt. Moriah." In the third portion of this study we will explore Jewish-Christian *rapprochement* embedded in such piety and prayer.

C. Corroborations of Akedah: History

Listen to the lambs...all a cryin'
He shall feed His flock like a shepherd
And carry the young lambs in his bosom.

History itself bears out this akedic thesis. Just north, down the Rhine from Schweitzer's university town of Strasbourg, is the ancient Roman city of Mainz. Here in the turbulent months following Pope Urban II's sermon at Clermont in November of 1095, which launched the first Crusade, events occurred which gave rise to one of the most poignant Akedah texts ever penned, this in human blood. In his masterful way Shalom Spiegel chronicles the story:

> *In the Synagogue on the eve of Rosh-ha-Shanah one still reads a penitential prayer, its language reminiscent of the Chronicle of 1096, about the martyrs of Magenza (Mainz), maggen we-zinah, "Shield and Buckler of every congregation." At first the Jews of that city tried to take refuge behind the fortified courtyard of the archbishop and to defend themselves. "Young and old donned armor and with weapons girded themselves, and with R. Kalonymous the Parnas in the lead...they made their way to the gate to battle against the vagabonds and the townspeople... But oh, Because of our sins the enemy prevailed and captured the gateway." And then the Jews discovered that the mobsters had broken through the castle courtyard and there was no way out except through apostasy, they resolved to delay no further: "Their voice rang out because all hearts were at one: 'Hear, O Israel, THE Lord... is One.' Ours is not to question ways of the Holy One, blessed be He and Blessed be His Name, for it is He who gave us His Torah, He who commanded that we die and be slain for the unification of his Holy Name...Oh our good fortune if we do His will! Oh, the good fortune of everyone slain and butchered and killed for the unification of His name. There is none better to sacrifice our lives to than our God. Let everyone who has a knife inspect it lest it be flawed. Let him come forth and cut our throats for the sanctification of Him who Alone lives Eternally and finally leteach man cut his own throat. Whereupon all of them, men and women, rose and slew each other. The tender of heart put on courage and themselves cut the throats of their wives and*

children, yea, babes. The tenderest and daintiest of women cut the throat of her darling child...Women bared their necks to one another in order to be offered up for the Unification of the Name. So a man treated his own son and his own brother; so a brother his own sister; so a woman her own son and daughter; so a man his own neighbor and comrade, bridegroom his bride, lover his beloved—here is one sacrificing and then himself being sacrificed, and there another sacrificing and himself being acrificed—until there was no flood of blood, the blood of husbands running together with that of their wives, the blood of their fathers with that of their children, the blood of their brothers with that of their sisters, the blood of masters with that of their disciples, the blood of bridegrooms with that of their brides, the blood of those who chant the liturgy with that of those who compose the sacred songs, the blood of babes and sucklings with that of their mothers; and so they were slain and sacrificed for the Unification of the Glorious and Awesome Name... Ask ye now and see, was there ever such a holocaust as this since the days of Adam? When were there ever a thousand and a hundred sacrifices in one day, each and every one of them like the Akedah of Isaac son of Abraham? Once at the Akedah of one on Mount Moriah, the Lord shook the world to its base!...Oh heavens, why did you not go black, O stars, why did you not withdraw your light, O sun and moon, why did you not darken in your sky?" When in one day one thousand and one hundred pure souls were slain and slaughtered! Oh the spotless babes and sucklings. Innocent of all sin, oh the innocent lives! Wilt Thou hold Thy peace in the face of these things, O Lord?" [17]

(Spiegel comments)

Questions like these, raging laments from hearts in a whirlpool of torment, recur in the synagogue poetry of that generation, ringing every note on the scale of grief and shock:

O Lord, mighty One, dwelling on high! Once,
over one Akedah, Ariels cried out before Thee.
But now how many are butchered and burned!
Why over the blood of children did they not raise a cry?
Before that patriarch could in his haste sacrifice his only one,
It was heard from heaven: Do not put forth your hand to destroy
But how many sons and daughters of Judah are slain.
While yet He makes no haste to save those butchered, nor those cast on the flames.
On the merit of the Akedah at Moriah once we could lean,
Safeguarded for the salvation of age after age.
Now one Akedah follows another, they cannot be counted. [18]

---

[17] Shalom Spiegel, *The Last Trial* (New York: Judah Goldin [Shocken Books], 1950).
[18] Ibid., p. 72.

No, the memory of Mount Moriah had not faded; it continued to instruct every one who followed the course of sanctification of the name. But for the victims of the Crusades it was impossible not to feel that their sufferings and sacrifices exceeded by far everything endured by the original Akedah father and son. So the synagogue poets, *payyetanim*, go on singing the praises of their contemporary fathers and sons, who enacted to the last line everything reported in rabbinic sources of Abraham and Isaac, and surpassed that:

> *How the outcry of the children rises!*
> *Trembling, they see their brothers slain.*
> *The mother binds her son lest he be blemished as he startles,*
> *The father makes a blessing before slaughtering the sacrifice.*
> *To their mothers in grief the tender children say,*
> *Offer us up as a whole burnt offering! We are wanted on high!...*
> *With their fathers the sturdy young men plead,*
> *Quick! Hurry to do our Creator's will...*
> *His father tied him, who was offered on Mount Moriah,*
> *Who prayed he should not kick and disqualify the slaughter.*
> *But we without being tied are slain for His love...*[19]

This moving text, now woven into the fabric of the Jewish liturgy, draws the connection in meaning between historical events and the trans-historical, between the physical realm and the metaphysical. The rich tradition of Akedah affects this same sacrament, which is the normative yield of secular, biblical faith, into world history.

How complex and convoluted a religious act—the bishop of Mainz seeks to protect, the religiously inflamed crusaders seek to kill. The crusaders themselves are profoundly conflicted. Consider the mixture of worthy and unworthy motives:

- To sanctify the divine name and secure a place for that presence in the world
- To wrest the Holy Land from infidels
- To cleanse the Holy Roman Empire of Jews and Muslims.

Indeed the entire sequence of religio-military conquests is morally suspect:

- The coercive Christianization of the Byzantine Empire
- The military conquest of Islam through to the OttomanEmpire
- The Crusades

---

[19] Ibid., p.75.

In this chapter of corroborative evidence we will trace the development of the doctrine of Akedah using a discerning tool to distinguish authentic from aberrant expressions within that vast literature, history and experience about sacrifice and suffering. In the case that we are exploring, we will argue that Akedah finds authenticity when it is rooted in the Torah drama of rescue and deliverance from sin and bondage through forgiveness, drawing on the divine qualities of justice and mercy.

Sheer infanticidal, fratricidal or homicidal violence is anti-Akedah. In no way does it participate in redemptive mercy. That any group would feign divine command in some act of cruel violence confounds conscience. Butchering an African Tutsi or Hutu in a Rwandan cathedral; disemboweling the Armenian Bishop in a New York City church; slaying Mexican peasants as they huddle for sanctuary in a Chiapas church; rocketing down a Palestinian child as he huddles against the wall, is not Akedah but brutal and blasphemous murder. To make our moral and theological case we must therefore discern among instances of sacrifice. Some involve violent usurpation of divine prerogative and denigration of divine command. Other cruciform acts convey the redemptive mystery of God. What is the difference?

The executions of Amerindians by Puritans or by Conquistadores, however rationalized as righteous deeds, were not. The martyrial acts at Masada, the Roman coliseum or Mainz prove our case linking a moral structure with the sacrificial act. Serving God, shunning idols and sanctifying the Name are imperatives of Torah. Killing, raping, desolating someone's home, lying or expropriating another's livelihood are prohibitions of that same Torah.

Akedah affirms that righteousness and therefore resurrection ultimately prevails even though suffering has penultimate power and sway. This is why, in the image of Revelation, ethics (the scroll of Torah) is handled by the lamb. For life to receive the blessing of rescue and resurrection it must pass the tribunal of righteousness, which threatens judgment, suffering and death. The condemnation of the death sentence (Romans 1:28) is relieved only in the vicarious rescue of the innocent lamb. Now from the ashes of the ram's horn resounds the Shofar's summons to new life.

> Though the cause of evil prosper,
> Yet the truth alone is strong;
> Though her portion be the scaffold,
> And upon the throne be wrong,
> Yet that scaffold sways the future,
> And, behind the dim unknown,
> Standeth God within the shadow,
> Keeping watch above his own.
> James Russell Lowell, 1845

To first rehearse the theological purpose of my work, it is my conviction that in the history of God and salvation, Jesus united the religion of justice with the religion of sacrifice. Justice and mercy kiss (Psalm 89) in the ongoing being and action of God. Soteriology and axiology blend. Judaism is the tradition, par excellence, of obligation, and Christianity, of acceptance. At one level my project seeks to restore Jewish ethics to Christian belief. We may hope to thus remedy that historical amorality of Christendom, which tragically marches from crusades to colonialism to Auschwitz. At the root of this crisis I find the Pauline-Lutheran distinction between faith and works to be mischievous and artificial, and the reciprocal excommunication of Israel and the Church a great tragedy of world history.

The Paul-James deal to attenuate the ethical rigors of Judaism for Gentile converts (Acts 15) and the "*Shamoneh Esreh*" addition to the Eighteen Benedictions ('MAY THE NOSRIM AND MINIM {Nazareth Gentiles and Antinomians} COME TO RUIN') seal this animosity for millennia until the European Holocaust. Now, at least in major Christian communions, the door has been reopened to our parental faith. In rejoining Akedah and Torah and re-synthesizing faith and works we may find again the missing "Heart piece" of these long alienated religious traditions and restore the biblical integrity of DECALOGUE, 1 John and James to Judeo-Christianity. Perhaps then can we seek rapprochement with Islam and fathom and ameliorate the agonies of Palestinian intifada, Israeli fear, Iraqi infanticide via sanctions and Taliban atrocities. But then came the "ATTACK ON AMERICA." (9/11)

That great servant of Jewish-Christian theology, Paul Van Buren, builds on the binding Abrahamic doctrine that Torah is Yahweh's instrument to heal the world. This shows how the story of Israel and the Church is to offer emancipatory redemption into the world. Yet amid crisis we find confidence.

> Israel's great story unfolded in the Torah. Appealed to in the Prophets, celebrated and rehearsed in the Psalms, [philosophized and moralized in Wisdom]... is the choosing of this people as his special possession and his instrument for dealing with all the nations. The story contained the truth about God and the truth about the world; it was the key to all mysteries. [20]

Akedah is the story of demand, death and deliverance. In the more apocalyptic tenor of Exile and Hasmonean Judaism and in primitive Christianity, it becomes the story of retribution, redemption and resurrection.

I see five permutations of Akedah in the history of Divine/Human truth:

- In pre-biblical and parallel traditions we find sacrifice functioning to appease or please the deity in order to avert calamity, to win wars, to

---

[20] Paul Van Buren, Op. Cit., pp. 26-27.

secure harvests, to assure fertility or more generally, find the forgiveness of sins.

- In Hebrew and Christian faith sacrifice is transformed into the response of faith and love to the command and excellence of God.

- Throughout biblical and subsequent time Akedah entails refusing blasphemy and idolatry by living and dying for the sanctity and unity of "The Name" (C-3).

- In Christian faith Akedah involves living in the crucifixion/resurrection as Jesus redeems the fallen world.

- Serving one's God, one's nation, one's family and friends by laying down one's life for the other sustains the akedic heritage.

With this premise before us let us now see that theology is human reflection of God—worldward and world-Godward. It is revelation and reason. Cohen, the priest, draws God down and lifts people up. In the theological heart of this book we now show how Akedah discerns divine-Human mystery in 1) the History of God, 2) the Human Condition, 3) the Travail of Nature and 4) the Saga of History. Each of these natural phenomena is an intimation of eternity.

1. The History of God

The history of God is the Akedah of God. Akedah deciphers the code of what God is doing in the world. Karen Armstrong's moving *HISTORY OF GOD* (1993) and *THE BATTLE FOR GOD* (2000) take you into a realm and catch you up in a saga where humans seek to respond to the God who is met in the Abrahamic faith traditions. She then helps you formulate understandings of that engagement (logos) and live out with intensity the mandates that flow from those faith formulations. The story Armstrong tells is captured in the great missionary hymn:

O Zion, haste, thy mission high fulfilling…
Publish glad tiding, tidings of peace;
Tidings of Jesus, redemption and release.
…Tell how he stooped to save his lost creation,
And died on earth that man might live above.
Mary Ann Thomson, 1868

The long and turbulent annals of human history can be read as Armstrong's *HISTORY OF GOD* and *BATTLE FOR GOD* or Jack Miles' *BIOGRAPHY OF GOD*. World history unfolding is the travail, terror and triumph of those meetings, clashes, campaigns, and conversions—with that sublime presence. "The struggle of life," as one Chinese student told me, "is to know and make known the life of God."

The religions of time and history—the Abrahamic faiths that receive and envision a God who leads—seem to lay particular emphasis on the dynamic qualities of deity and on the construal of life as struggle or test. What is the akedic understanding of the history of God in Judaism, Christianity and Islam?

Judaism

Judaism's Akedah is formative for all subsequent Abrahamic faith and for human history. Cutting through archaic and primordial religion where abstract cosmic force and substance perdures in infinite stasis and superstition, Abraham and his offspring Israel, meet, then introduce to history, a God who speaks and acts. This God goes out, cares, yearns, seeks, gives and hopes. This God is by definition disturbing and disruptive. Despite the Genesis cosmology—crafted in the crisis of Exile—which claims that divine word and will, stills a restless disorder, drawing cosmos from chaos, in truth the creature is now put on edge, on guard. Humans now find themselves under observation and expectation. The God of creation, of the garden, is one who pries and intrudes, one who won't leave us alone.

Yahweh God, who presents himself as "I am" or "I will be," becomes known as demand and draw, requirement and acceptance, setting the world in directional purpose and enlisting faithful community in that endeavor. "*Tikkun Olam*," as the rabbis taught (the healing of the world), or the "Kingdom of God," is the sustaining goal for the world.

Abraham is *al Kahalil*, yes, the friend of God. Like Jesus at the Emmaus rest stop, God sat down to meal with Abraham. Yet Armstrong reminds: "He inspires terror and insists upon distance."[21] Singular devotion is demanded even in that age when the plurality of deity was self-evident. "No other gods" makes sense only when there is an experienced pantheon. The attempt to make Yahweh the only God might seem plausible if times were good and the deuteronomic blessings and relief of adversities ensued. But this God was no "font from whom all blessings flow." This one puts folk to the test, takes them toward the unknown, sets in motion a spiritual journey that can best be called "an ordeal." Here the akedic character of the nature of history and the history of God comes into focus. God has gone out to the world in loving risk. In freedom, humanity is invested with responsibility and destiny. Divine venture and human plight meet to precipitate crisis, well depicted by the electric fingertouch on the creation fresco of the Sistine ceiling. Akedah is inevitable within this potent crossfire. Emmanuel, God with us, requires holiness and compatibility. Estrangement demands price. Finding out who we are provokes us to examine where we have gone wrong, what we have become and where we need to go.

The heart of the crisis, which requires costly reconciliation, is moral. God wills the fulfillment of life and the just ordering of interhuman associations and relationships with the world. Humans strive for self-aggrandizement and exploitation of others and the world. God wills that the creation be sustained and

---

[21] Armstrong, Karen, *A History of God* (New York: Ballantine, 1993), p. 21.

flourish. Man seeks to tear it apart and use it up in self-indulgence. A *dénouement* or *Götterdämmerung* is provoked. The options remain: God must be banished (Nietzsche), humanity destroyed or costly rapport purchased. Akedah propounds this salvation story. Judaism effects this with rigorous covenant, chastening martyrial history, culminating in Holocaust, and exacting Diaspora. Apocalyptic Judaism and Christianity resolve the crisis in suffering messiology, Islam in Ishmael's travail, a perpetual sacrifice in the face of the world's violence—all Akedah.

In the liturgical and calendric history of Israel we find a clue to the Hebraic theology of Akedah. The Abraham/Isaac tradition is celebrated not on Yom Kippur, the Day of Atonement, but on Rosh Hashanah, the new year. According to the Rosh Hashanah liturgy this is "... a day of remembrance, a day for blowing the shofar (ram's horn, Isaac's vicar), a holy convocation, a memorial for the departure from Egypt." This dating signifies that in the history and character of God, Akedah is not primarily a matter of sacrifice and expiation, but a matter of victory, resurrection and new life.

For Judaism, Akedah is a historical legacy. The history or destiny of God's redemptive Way in the World is woven into Akedah. Akedah is a proto-martyrial and paradigmatic moment—a precedent of faith by which sacrifice all subsequent generations will live. In the Talmud of Genesis Rabah, MIDRASH on Akedah from fourth or fifth century C.E., the event is spoken of as a "living memorial," something like the dynamic perpetuity of the "cross of Christ." It is not only an ancient example of faith, but an expression of faith with ongoing efficacy. The history of God, in other words, is a redemptive history. The constitutive events of Israel's history, Exodus, Sinai and Exile, for example, not only signal the constant and ongoing character of God, but carry on a liberating chastening spirit among the faithful community. In Rosh Hashanah, the ram's horn of Isaac celebrates Sinai and the overture of law into the world. As Carol De Laney summarizes, the horn "...created on the sixth day of creation...is a clarion call of God's ongoing rule over creation and will sound again in the last days."[22] Weaving together etiology and eschatology in the history of God with the world further corroborates our thesis of reconciling salvation and social justice. Akedah signifies Passover and temple sacrifice as well as Exodus, exile and all aspects of historical deliverance. It parables the faith and work of God in the world.

Another aspect of the history of God in Hebrew history arises from this complementarity of salvation/sacrifice and liberation/justice. These themes focus on the controversial issue of messianic history and the question: "Who is the messiah?" Isaiah 53, one of the great "servant" texts of the exilic author Isaiah introduces the paradoxical vision of the servant as leper:

---

[22] De Laney, Carol, *Abraham on Trial* (Princeton, New Jersey: Princeton University Press, 1998), p. 119.

"As one from whom we turned our faces…"
"…One despised and rejected"
"Bruised for our iniquity…" (Isaiah 53)

How does *yahid*, "the favored one," the servant, the beloved son (*agapetos*), become the "despised one"? Assuming that this is both a personal, proleptic text and a public text (referring to an individual yes, but primarily to the corporate community—to the social history of the people), the history of God is a process which seeks to shape an individual and communal Akedah—a way of life.

The sheep that "before its shearer is silent" (Isaiah 53:7) is one who bears the iniquity of all persons who like "sheep have gone astray" (v. 6). Resonating with this the calendric book of Jubilees, Judaism times Akedah at the moment when the Passover lambs are sacrificed in the temple. History, as *Heilsgeschichte* (holy history), is the story of God. For Hebrew writers, biblical and extra-biblical, that story involves risky out-going, a covenant, a bearing of the burden caused by breach of that covenant and misspent freedom. The way of God follows through in justice and love, concluding in a gift of life and an ensuing redemption. In this saga Judaism is the "light to the world."

The enigmatic history of the Jewish people raises troubling implications of the history of the God of Israel. In deuteronomic biblical theology God leads the faithful people to prosperity (Promised Land) and leads a faithless and unjust people into punishment and exile. The history of persecution, martyrdom, ghettoization and Holocaust bring conflict and anguish in light of this heritage. "Why did the skies not blacken?" asks Arno Mayer, Princeton's historian of the European Holocaust, echoing the akedic suicide at Mainz. The silence, disengagement, even justice of God, becomes deeply problematic. To the mind of this privileged Christian observer of God's chosen people, one who agonizes over this persecutorial history and the church's complicity and causality in it, I ask whether the akedic history of God may in some way interpret that horror. Ironically, God's people Israel, along with the poor and despised of the world, may bear the messianic cross out through time.

> To sum up this cursory overview of the history of God in Hebrew religion, God is a god of word, will, wisdom and way. Primordial, Parmidean religion resists the notion of divine expression and historical activity, especially when that manifestation is concrete. Buddhism, for example, resists even the notion of the existence of God (which may also be a biblical belief). Abraham and the patriarchs, prophets and priests dare to follow and meet Yahweh in concrete, disturbing and communicative presence. Divine disclosure is concrete, direct command received by Abraham, Jacob, Moses or the prophets.

Word is a prime quality of the history of the God of Israel. Without this, Akedah is hallucination. That God is good will and not the peeved and petulant deity of the Greek gods or the tribal deities of forest and swamp and that this purposive God is One whose works are animated by clear intention and goals is the insight of Abraham and Israel.

...That the earth be filled with the knowledge of God (Colossians 1:9)
...That righteousness surround the earth

Tikkun Olam

...For the sustenance and healing of the world.

These characteristics of an historically active God are borrowed from long precedents in the ancient Near and Far East. Temptation rises within this modality of divine action. Wisdom is that quality of perspicacity, of suspension of passion and immediacy, of muting a rash judgment. Wisdom literature is about the conjunction of DECALOGUE ("way"), sacrifice and instruction. Through the *Imago dei* Israel views the self and situation *sub specie aeternitatis*. Wisdom is the counsel of reality. It concerns parental love and consideration. It prompts filial piety and obedience. It suffuses Akedah.

Finally, and most critically, the history of Yahweh is a story of the Way. That this God gives a "Way" for the world through its people is the ground of Akedah. "Way," being "on the way," or "being wayward" is the meaning of Akedah. The word Torah, the title given to the foundational law of the Hebrew tradition can better be translated as "Way" or "instruction." That "Way" finds precedents in perennial wisdom and in universal law, e.g. the Noachic covenant in Genesis 9 designed for the entire human race. It then focuses in more particular codes such as the DECALOGUE, Mosaic and Levitical code. It finds *sequellae* in the Christian Sermon on the Mount or in "the Antioch dispatch" (Acts 15) or "law of Christ" (Galatians 6:2).

If the God of history is a God of "the Way," then not only is there a pattern of meaning within history, but history itself is a "way." The radical theologians of providence—Augustine, Calvin, and the Puritans—accent this. Rather than a random and meaningless sequence of events, history is proceeding with direction toward intended purpose. *Chronos* has been imprinted with *Kairos*. History is sacred history.

Akedah involves annunciation of that "Way". It involves progression and transgression of that 'way'. It involves the tension set in motion by adherence (martyrdom) and by disobedience. It involves cutting through in judgment and restitution. It involves culmination and fulfillment of the 'way'. The drama of

Akedah, personified in the Abraham/Isaac instance, reenacted in Joseph and the Sons of Jacob, is culminated in Jesus, carpenter's son–Son of man–Son of God.

Christianity

Christianity is founded in this Akedic/Yahedic (beloved son-servant tradition). Jesus sustains the heritage of Isaac. Ironically the most ahistorical sect of Judaism—Christianity creates the most palpable and problematic history. A decidedly apolitical itinerant Galilean rabbi-teacher becomes the occasion for the political transformation of movements called Jewish-, then Gentile-Christianity. These, in turn, transform the Western world and in recent centuries, global society. The Akedah for this movement becomes the way of suffering transformation or of triumphing catastrophe. In the spirit of Torah and DECALOGUE, the early Christian movement was called "The Way." "See how they love each other" was an early designation. It was an irenic, pacifist movement that eventually, created an empire. Initially, the resistance to Roman power was less exaggerated in either establishment Judaism or even the apocalyptic Judaism that gave it birth. With its foundational constituency gathered from secularized workers, people of the land and Jesus' own family circle of Davidite Galileans, the movement focused on simple Torah righteousness ("love of God and neighbor") and ethical piety. As it proceeded into Paul's Gentile mission and the apostolic conversion of the Roman Empire, the Christian community became a mystically-derived ("Christ in me"), Spirit-driven, evangelical movement. God had come near to his long exiled people, "those who walk in darkness have seen a great light." This intense experience and vision of new existence (*"en Christou"*) categorically displaced the more eclectic piety of the Hellenistic world where one could be both Jew and Christian. It became a forceful worldly commitment that eventuated in the Constantinian Christian Empire. This phenomenon of the fourth and fifth centuries precedes the rise of Islam by a handful of generations. Islam may in fact be caused by the neglect of Arabia in both Judaism and Christianity. In any case, radical and existential piety became state religion. All this would contribute to the akedic history of the Christian God. Now in the frightful anti-Semitic then and anti- Islamic debacle from Constantine to the Crusades to Holocaust, Abraham's call to kill the "beloved son" overcame the call to save and sustain. The forwarding groundwork of Akedah is given in discernment of the God of Israel who has become "The God and Father of our Lord Jesus Christ." In the primitive Christian community, the God story has undergone a subtle but earth-changing transformation. In Fitzmyer's *Romans,* for example, he argues that those caught up in the Jesus movement, especially the nascent gentile Christian side of the movement, interpret the Messianic event-life, obedience, suffering, death, resurrection of Jesus in akedic terms, i.e. in terms of vicarious sacrifice for the people of Israel and the world. No similar usage is found in first century Hebrew texts:

"…That Isaac was to be sacrificed on behalf of Israel, or on behalf of anyone else, is never mentioned."[23],[24]

In my thesis, the early Christian apostles and the apologists of the first three centuries learned Akedah from Israel through the mediation of Hebrew Christians like James the brother and Mary the mother of Jesus and from the Jerusalem congregation.

They in turn gave theological history an akedic twist as Pauline, Petrine, Lukan, Markan, even Johannine schools, slowly accent existential consciousness. "Christ in you" mysticism, spirited enthusiasm, along with a decided turn against performance of the "The Way" ensues. Experience, not performance, became central to salvation. The sacrifice quality of Akedah often takes hold without the ethical component. To me this is the danger as salvational Christianity stripped of Jewish ethics leads to the cultural accommodation of the Christianized/Roman Empire. Before long Holy War, then crusade, is being waged against not only Islam but against Diaspora Israel.

Two fundamental concepts derived from Judaism, but distinctively different, shape the Christian God-story. The first is the concept, inimical to Judaism, at least in its triumphalist caste, that Jesus is the crucified messiah and that indeed God is *THE CRUCIFIED GOD* (Jurgen Moltmann). This rendition of the story of God is drawn from Jewish messianic literature about the son, the servant, the savior (messiah) in texts such as Psalm 2, 22, 89, 110, Isaiah 42 and 53. But these texts are measured and interpreted by the experience of the life and teaching, but more the suffering, death and resurrection of Jesus. This lens into the Christ-event shapes both the Jewish and the Christian God-story. It is not far from the mark to say, from what we know today of faith and ethics from the first century B.C.E. through to the Christian era, that Judaism forms Christianity and Christianity forms Judaism. This reciprocity and mutual formation with all gifts of its grandeur and danger focuses in Akedah.

The second concept involves the logic and necessity in this very concept of the crucified messiah. I just state it now for later development. In the tale of the will of God for the world Jesus must live, suffer, die and be raised for the efficacy of his destiny and for the "Way" of God to be accomplished. There is no resurrection without the death and no death without the resurrection. Pain and deliverance is reality concomitant with creation and freedom. This paradoxical confounding of Jewish messianic logic is buttressed by a plethora of New Testament texts which seek to fathom the Jesus experience both pre- and post-resurrection and to refute heretical tendencies to disjoin cross and crown.

---

[23] Fitzmyer, J., *Romans: Anchor Bible.* (New York: Doubleday, 1993), p. 531.
[24] Ibid.,p.532 ff.

From this theology arises the more normative akedic history of God in Christianity as the "Lamb of God" heritage which leads Quakers and Mennonites, for example, to call the war of God in history the "war of the lamb." In John Howard Yoder's classic description (*THE POLITICS OF JESUS*) the "war of the lamb" is the powerful witness of martyrdom. Here Christians, like Dietrich Bonhoeffer, take up the cross and follow the Lord, living out the Gospel of God in keeping the commandments, enacting social justice in the love of God and care for the poor. This provokes the vengeful ire of the world inciting "persecution for righteousness sake" (Matthew 5). The war of the lamb is thus "filling up the sufferings of Christ" (I Peter 1:1ff) as Akedah is reenacted as the ongoing merciful sacrifice of the Son of God for the sin of the world. In this tradition, paschal mystery perpetually reenacts the grace of Akedah, Passover, the temple of slaughter of the lambs, the crucifixion, the white robes of the martyrs. The composite offering of body and blood, life and death, eucharistically enlivens the church and world. The blood of God mingles in the tragedy of the world, even in the gnarled ruins of the World Trade Center.

The summary of the Christian story of God is to show us One who so suffered, one compassionate...

...For God is love.

Islam

I know so little about Islam. It has taken me 60 years to esteem her as a sister faith. I am still not well impressed with Quran as scripture and I decry the antics of fundamentalist militants as much as I do the acts of Jewish religious belligerents or Christian crusaders. But I find myself looking more carefully these days at Islam for two reasons: First, in the aftermath of the events of September 11, 2001, the whole world is prompted to better understand Islam. Second, in recent history, Muslims act more faithfully for the poor. In Africa, and throughout the Middle East, Muslims are the champions of the oppressed. All too often Jews and Christians defend the privileged. That to me is an akedic sign. The third attraction has come as I ponder Akedah. This later-day sister Abrahamic faith seems to fathom most completely and acutely the Abraham/Isaac sacrifice. At the ending of *Haj*, or the feast of the sacrifice (*Id al adhai*), Muslims the world over bend the neck in prayer, recalling Isaac's contrite obedience. At this season Muslim families sacrifice the lamb, analogously in faith, submit the carcass to the flame, then share the roast with the poor. What is the history of God (Allah) in Islam, which supplies Akedah? Carol Delaney observes:

> "...Because Islam is conceptualized as a return or recall to the one, true original religion given in the beginning to Abraham, his story may be

more actively present in Islam than in either Judaism or Christianity."
[25]

Abraham was a *Bar mitzvah*, a son of the "Way" of God, who was prophesied to be an idol buster (iconoclast) so much so that King Nimrod of Babylon had all the first-born sons slaughtered. In that recurrent imagery Abraham survived because his mother hid him in a cave. (Those who visit the rock cave in Bethlehem purporting to be the "stable" of Jesus birth recall the force of this image).

The connection between command, obedience, and transgression in Akedah is profound in Islam. The iconoclast strictly adheres to the structure of C 1-3 where "no other gods," "no false idols" and no defamation of "the Name" are strictly enjoined. In my view this connection between command, prevalent idolatry and blasphemy, injustice and evoked sacrifice, is the essence of Akedah. Abraham is called to sacrifice Isaac (or Ishmael) as adherence to "first fruits law" (Exodus 22:28, 29) It is also to test Abraham's loyalty ("no other gods") and his subordination of all other values, even his prized *agapetos*, the long belated, only beloved son. Isaac is also a penitential and vicarious sacrifice. He is offered on behalf of the sin of the people and for the perpetuation of the people (seed of Abraham). The rich tapestry of the act is expression of Torah faithfulness.

Muhammad rebuilds the *Ka'ba*, the temple of God, with the black stone (the staying hand of God?) as a recounting of Akedah. Henceforth the *Haj*, the journey of the faithful, will reenact the journey (and trial) of Abraham. This pilgrimage now becomes the paradigm for the meaning of God and our life.

The essence of the Muslim history of God is that of restoration. In human disobedience the world has gone wrong and despoiled creation. Only an expression of human righteousness can recover the primeval harmony of God with his creature. In Judaism, Torah restores this concourse and congress.

"...make straight in the desert a highway for our God." (Isaiah 40)

Jesus, the Son of God effects the atonement and incarnates that way for christendom. In Islam, in the spirit of law and Gospel (*Injil* and *Taurut*), Abraham becomes the prototype and representative of faithful and righteous humanity having accomplished rapprochement.

Let us now turn from the history of God to the history of man for further corroboration of Akedah.

---

[25] DeLaney, p. 184.

2. The Human Condition

> Sometimes I feel I'm almost gone...
> A long way from home...

The tribulation of bodily existence is also corroboration of Akedah. The old spiritual captured the feeling of my dad as I wrote these words. At 86 years, the crisis of an infection, septic shock, intensive antibiotic therapy, an operation for a tumor in the colon, a weak heart and chronically low platelets left him exhausted, unable to stand or walk and afraid that he would be confined to bed or a wheel chair for the remainder of his days. He saw his life slipping away and he was scared.

Six weeks earlier he was well and strong, traversing the country, visiting his family, working in the shop, tending the yard, "getting on" despite the grief for loss of his dear companion of 50 years—my mom. To this oldest son watching and un-watching sympathetically from the side, it raised another Akedah question: Why must the culmination of one's days be accompanied by pain and suffering, loss and bereavement? Is there some secret providence in life that renders these tragedies triumphs? Does this altar of sacrifice end in rescue and new life? Or is the destiny of persons demeaning atrophy, loss of mind and muscle, then slow disgrace, helplessness, utter dependence, death and extinction? Dad's bony frame, swimming, we fear deliriously *inter feces et urinam*, still bore the little smile. I believe he knew the akedic, Christic secret.

In Abrahamic terms, is the end of the faith journey an altar of sacrifice, or do we find there provisions and rescue—renewal of life and blessed progeneration out into history? And what of the intricate equations of why and wherefore? Why in the subtle intricacy of command and temptation is the sacrifice necessary? Does our biological existence in some mysterious way symptomize Paul's "sting" of the fall? Are the agonies of existence vicarious both in terms of cumulative consequences and proleptic possibilities? Do we pay the price for what we have done and what we will receive?

There is a solemn and sublime story to life and death of the human body and mind. In a *Chicago Tribune* update of Kinsey's "In America" sex studies, we see that as we age, sex becomes more pleasurable and less frequent. Finally we reach that ultimate point of ultimate non-existent delight. Vitality in the organism wanes as self breaks down and burns out until its culmination—its fulfillment! Crazy-madness-paradox.

We are all brought low, brought down, pulverized, atomized akedic ashes to ashes, dust to dust. Eva becomes Adama, life, dirt, humus-humorous. But still the akedic Shofar blasts in the exultant shout of the creed: "...in the clear and certain hope of the resurrection."

Why does approaching demise, why does the culmination or conclusion of one's life (a theological appraisal) entail so much pain, frustration, suffering, fear and frequent indignity? The years are 70 or 80, today 80 or 90...

Yet is their length sorrow and dismay as we are consumed...under thy wrath.
(Psalm 90)

Could it be that in the grand scheme of things, aging into death is training ground, or a punishment? Is disintegration and dissolution the natural reparation for the good days of youth? Is it perhaps an unfortunate weight of morbidity and mortality, built up by decades of neglect, perhaps avoidable with bean sprouts, exercise, eugenics, stem cell miracles, or ozone therapy and cryogenics?

The disrepair and disintegration of our bodies is ultimately an issue of the redemption of bodies, i.e., the ultimate destroying of these poor vessels, within the purview of the creator/consummator of existence. A close exegesis of Romans chapter 8 and glancing attention to cognate (often contradictory) biblical tests will be necessary to lay the foundation for this dimension of Akedah.

Infection is the principal lethal force among living beings in the universe. It is the antithesis of replication, reproduction and development, "dust to dust." Yet even here we ponder the mystery of seed that "we must die to live." Most persons and perhaps animals throughout the course of evolution have succumbed to microbial demise, often secondary to some other cause in the organism like malignancy, organ failure or depressed immune response.

A range of the theological questions arises when we seek corroboration for Akedah from the human story, especially from the condition of morbidity and mortality. Life's course may be sheer, meaningless accident (incidental, as in medieval philosophy), and life itself may be "an accidental (happenstance) collection of atoms destined to extinction in the vast death of the solar system."[26] We invoke Akedah and suggest meaning rather than absurdity.

Secondly, there is the ethical question: Is good and evil somehow involved in the history and current epidemiology of disease? Put curtly, does human injustice and impiety contribute to the causation and intensification of illness? In some sense do we harm ourselves and each other by projecting evil onto a cosmic plane? Is there, in the sense of Job's temptation, some "destroyer" who, with divine allowance, robs us of happiness and health, prosperity, even threatening life itself? Is this challenge in the very axis of our being somehow

---

[26] Bertrand Russell, *A Free Man's Worship* (London: Unwin, 1976, p. 73).

caught up in the history of God? Is this the burden of the allowance and the risk of human freedom?

The History of Disease
The fact that we perceive human history to be progressive in the sense of overcoming vectors of morbidity—bubonic plague, smallpox; then achieving impulses of vitality such as non-toxic childbirth, anti-microbial therapy, etc.—invites reflection into the history of disease. Is medical history genuine progress or a trade-off with ambiguous consequences? Obviously the pattern of disease has changed across human history. The progress of science, technology, hygiene and public services has shifted. The burden of disease, at least in some advanced sectors of the world has changed from acute, treatable infectious diseases where children and young adults die en masse, to the diseases of aging, chronic diseases, and chronic disability.

Global epidemiology of those forces which injure and kill people shows a frightful disparity between the rich and the poor world. In Africa, India, Bangladesh, parts of Asia and the Middle East, Latin and South America, we have rampant morbidity in malnutrition (e.g. infant mortality) and infectious diseases (e.g. River blindness, AIDS, malaria, tuberculosis). The International AIDS meeting in 2000 in Durban, South Africa depicts a severe crisis. 70% of the near 40 million cases in the world are found in Africa. Life expectancy will soon begin crashing towards 30, which it has not been since the medieval times of the Bubonic plague. South Africa, Uganda and other countries have such dramatic increase in disease incidence that up to 50% of children in those societies may face death by AIDS. Mid-summer 2000 also saw AIDS cases dramatically increasing even in United States cities: San Francisco, Chicago, Newark, Washington D.C. An author in the journal *SCIENCE* some years ago may have accurately forecast that the two dominant diseases in the world early in this new century will be AIDS and Alzheimer's. Infant mortality has doubled and life expectancy is halved in this section of the world when compared with the affluent North. In the well-to-do world, the blessings of health and longevity bring another burden. As the spectrum of morbidity is pressured toward the right two things happen: incidence of mental illness intensifies, and throwbacks to earlier pathologies in the evolution of disease such as viral and fungal infection also intensify.

| Infections | Heart & Vessel Disease | Cancer | Mental Illness |

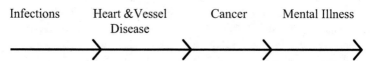

Historical pressure (prevention, antibiotics) pushes intensity toward the right and left side of chart. The incidence of neuromental pathologies, e.g. depression, Alzheimer's and throwbacks to AIDS, tuberculosis, to viral and fungal infections on the left, mount in these times.

In the United States, for example, death rates from influenza, pneumonia and tuberculosis have decreased and approached zero, while death from cardiovascular disease and cancer, has remained high. [27]

In important cognate studies, Christine Cassell and others have shown that we have selected the diseases that will become more prominent among us (epidemiology) by virtue of the fact that the diseases we have deselected by either successful treatment or prevention now are chronic and debilitating. Eliminating the infections that killed men in early life and women in childbirth necessarily increase the incidence of prostate disease (benign and malignant) in men and breast cancer and Alzheimer's in women. It is simply a process of filling in the vacuum left in a world where morbidity and mortality are constant. Cassell goes on to decry the fact that while we have selected by deselecting from the panorama of diseases for, say osteoporosis and arthritis, we have failed to take measures in medical research, pharmacological care and health care provision to remedy and care for the sicknesses in people which we have made inevitable.

Health, disease and mortality statistics show that we live in two worlds: one rich, one poor. This gives rise to the charge that injustice (mal-distribution of wealth) is a cause of disease. Mortality statistics in the developing world are double those of the developed world. Even in the US, the poverty sub-culture, what has been called a third world within the first, experiences roughly twice the morbidity and premature mortality as the affluent middle class population, this includes:

- Tooth decay
- Back Pain
- Diabetes
- Cancer
- Hypertension and most other disease categories. A black man living in Lawndale, an inner city census tract in west Chicago, can expect to live twelve fewer years than a white male in Evanston.

Epidemiologically speaking, the spectrum of disease that arises epidemically among the people also has an akedic color, i.e., sacrifice on behalf of and at the hands of the sinful world. In 1997 the ten leading causes of death (and percentage of total deaths) in the US were:

- Heart disease 31.4%
- Cancer 23.2%
- Stroke 6.9%

---

[27] Vital Statistics: *World Almanac 1999*, p. 873.

- Accidents 5.8%
- Lung diseases 4.8%
- Pneumonia/Influenza 3.8%
- Diabetes 2.7%
- Suicide 1.3%
- Kidney diseases 1.1%
- Liver diseases 1.1%

Scanning this list and these data raises obvious remarks on an earlier question: is social injustice and individual irresponsibility a cause in human disease? Is disease a sign of something gone wrong in the creation? If so, the phenomenon of human experience may corroborate the Akedah thesis. But these observations and interpretations are only a facile way of recognizing a deeper fracture within human flesh and within the body of humanity. This wound cries out against the powers of evil toward the power of God for the grace of deliverance. The human oblation is felt on earth from the dawn of creation.

> The whole creation groans in the travail...
> We groan within our selves as we
> Wait for the redemption of our body...
> We are killed all the day long...regarded
> As sheep for the slaughter...
> (Romans 8)

Human disease, even death therefore, is a specter that we seek to do something about. The stigmata of the Fall or the Four Horses of the Apocalypse: war, disease, famine, death (Revelation 6) become not so much enigmas to which we submit, but entities to be construed as enemies, resisted in the arduous and apocalyptic contention of good and evil. Famine, writes Nobel Laureate Amartya Sen, is caused by poverty.

Conclusion

Three conclusions can be offered to verify the corroboration, which the human condition displays toward and receives from Akedah. They concern: A) The preeminence of life over death, B) The positive rendition of suffering and death and C) The affirmation of sacrificial justice and caring love as the enduring essence of redemption.

A.   A fundamental premise of Akedah is that life has the final word over death. The final word at Moriah is not sacrifice and death, but rescue and resurrection. Life is a preeminent value in the Semitic theistic anthropology that emerges with the shadowy Haj of Abraham from Haran. The wandering faithful band— bound in hope which we call the *Habiru*, give to the world the assertion that the prime interpretive value in this God-loved world is *l'hayim*—LIFE. A global health and well-being therefore is not a desirable dream or a worthy ambition, but an imperative, fundamental human right, a required condition which makes anything less, blasphemous.

As I write, fifty-eight persons from the Hunan province of China are found dead in the sealed capsule of a Belgian lorry at Port Dover, England. Modern slaves, they had sold themselves to the ruthless criminal traffickers who sell the bodies of workers, women and children to the more affluent and opportune sectors of the world. Mexican hopefuls perish by the hundreds in the Southwestern U.S. deserts. The injustice of the global economic disequilibrium has fashioned the breach of C-8 through C-10 ("no stealing" and "envy") as disparate affluence amid poverty and hard-heartedness prevail. The affluent and acquisitive nature of the North Shore community in which I live assures (by the very nature of justice) that Chicago will be a culture of theft.

Health, a derivative and correlate of life, must not be reduced to a commodity—a matter of purchase and selling. The U.S., which spends four thousand dollars per person annually for health care—far in excess of any other nation, ranked 37th in a recent UN study in health standards among nations of the world. This is a global disgrace in its co-modification of health and life. Akedah, our common Abrahamic ethics, should prompt us to show the world that life and dignity, not death and servility, are preeminent values.

B.   Part of the materialistic and acquisitive ethos that has been fashioned in this land, which ought to be animated by Judeo, Christian and Islamic values, is the biblical association of anxiety, acquisitiveness and fear of death. The rich farmer of Jesus' story harvested the fields, filled his silos, then settled in for the night in his secure armchair of negligence, only to be shocked by the angel of death. This is parable to our nation and world (Luke 12:16 ff., cf. also Matthew 16:24-26).

Breach of the commands of justice and forsaking sharing the proffered generosity (Ezekiel 18:7) prompts us to hold on and cling desperately to what we have—our possessions. We come to live by another delight, rather than by the righteousness of God (Matthew 6:33). Letting go and giving away are akedic virtues grounded in that sublime DECALOGUE MIDRASH of the Sermon on the Mount.

The "life" value can be exaggerated and serve wrong when we witness a furious mania to prolong life and deny death. Lest we see contradiction between point one, "choose life," and this point, recall the words of Pierre Teilhard de Chardin:

> "...We must resist death with all our force
> for that is our fundamental human destiny.
> But when, in the course of life we face
> death, we must experience that paroxysm of
> faith in life and receive death as falling into
> a greater life." [28]

Accepting mortality is a correlate of the love of life. Abrahamic trust in the reliable promise of God ("your seed...") and Christic trust in that father who is "able far beyond our imagination," fathoms that strength is hidden in weakness, that in death we are in life. When this consciousness animates persons and peoples, justice rather than physical immortality becomes the central passion. We in America now live in the idolatry of lifeprolongation, within which we pay perhaps 20% of the annual health care expenditure (over $1 trillion a year) in the final months, weeks and days of our lives. This, while hundreds of millions of lives around the world languish with treatable afflictions: AIDS, malaria, river blindness, intestinal infections, and the like.

C. Sacrificial justice, rather than futile personal justification, is the akedic purpose of life. Abraham gave over his only beloved son as did the God and father of Jesus-Messiah for the remedy of sin and the healing of the world (*TIKKUN OLAM*). This self-abnegating justice in concern for others is the ultimate corroboration of Akedah.

In an important sociological history, Rodney Stark attributes the dramatic rise of Christianity in the Roman Empire to akedic impulses of giving and caring. The prevalent ethic of power, despair, infanticide and abandonment yielded to a new outlook finding meaning and suffering under the cross. This prompted the hope for eternal life beyond death and the staying ministry of nursing for the sick and dying. In the akedic mystery of death into life, justice and care displaces violence and disdain. Abraham's promise has been fulfilled.

A Final Word
Let us think carefully of how the existential and epidemiological portrait of health and disease that we have sketched relates to Akedah. Akedah is a parable of human life under God. A parable addresses an ultimate truth in an earthly story: seeds are sown on three soils with different yields—an analogical truth of divine seminal activity and human receptivity (Matthew 13). Akedah is an historical parable of the same order of the other Abrahamic and patriarchal narratives, grounded in history, all elaborate in meaningstories: Lot's wife,

---

[28] Teilhard, Pierre, *Le Phenomène Humain*. (New York: Harper and Row, 1955), p. 311.

Sodom and Gomorrah, Jacob's dream, Joseph's coat all are parables of divine/human meaning.

The story of Abraham and Isaac has emerged in biblical history as the dominant parable for the way that God deals with people and the way that human experience is interpreted within the divine purview. The experiences of life and death, health and suffering, are analogies or parables between the story of God and the human story. Akedah mediates each reality to the other.

Akedah is a normative parable. It speaks to questions such as:

- What is going on in human life?
- Ought it to be this way?
- What has gone wrong?
- Why has it become this way?
- What is needed to make it right?

This range of normative questions probe a sphere of human experience, in this case health and disease, lifting it into the normative realm— The realm of ought. A glimpse of another reality redefines this reality. Akedah is the interpretive icon of life's meaning.

One powerful way that the akedic reality of frightful journey, terrifying judgment, suffering and final rescue all undergirded by assuring, trustworthy promise, is expressed is to superimpose a faith picture from transcending reality upon this wretched scene. Even for a modern New York City couple, a quaint Victorian vision overruled harsh reality. My mother left me the following poem in the family bible which she passed on after her own difficult life's end/beginning experience. (Mom died after being mute for several years with end-stage Alzheimer's).

Safely Home

> I am home in Heaven, dear ones;
> Oh, so happy and so bright!
> There is perfect joy and beauty
> In this everlasting light.
> All the pain and grief is over,
> Every restless tossing passed;
> I am now at peace forever,
> Safely home in Heaven at last.
> Did you wonder I so calmly
> Trod the valley of the shade?
> Oh! But Jesus' love illumined
> Every dark and fearful glade.
> And he came himself to meet me

In that way so hard to tread;
And with Jesus' arm to lean on,
Could I have one doubt or dread?
Then you must not grieve so sorely,
For I love you dearly still;
Try to look beyond earth's shadows,
Pray to trust our Father's will.
There is work still waiting for you,
So you must not idly stand;
Do it now, while life remaineth–
You shall rest in Jesus' land.
When that work is all completed,
He will gently call you Home;
Oh, the rapture of that meeting,
Oh, the joy to see you come.

The Travail of Nature

I take my cue here, not from Loren Eiseley's apocalyptic visage of nature "a vast whirlpool of destruction" opening up with man's appearance on earth, but with Teilhard's benign, even sublime view of the same appearance.

In an appendix to *Le phenomène humain* (The Human Phenomenon), Pierre Teilhard writes from Rome on October 28, 1948, "Some remarks on the place of break through & breakdown, of good and evil in world in evolution."[29] He acknowledges "The negative of the picture" and "The abysses between the peaks." He proceeds to address:

- The evil of disorder and failure
- The evil of decomposition
- The evil of solitude and anxiety and
- The evil of Growth

He concludes that:

...in one manner or the other, it still remains true that, even in the view of the mere biologist, the human epic resembles nothing so much as a way of the cross. [30]

Following hard on the heels of corroborative evidence for Akedah from the history of God and from the human condition, we now reflect on the travail of nature. If Akedah is the most illuminating metaphor, not only of divinity, but of humanity, then it should find increasing explanatory power here. In the last section I employed another grand Romans text on the agony of nature struggling with the birth pangs of bodily redemption (Romans 8).Now this passage of the

---

[29] Ibid., p. 311.
[30] Ibid., p. 312.

great scientist-philosopher acknowledges a similar perspective on the "hope" to which nature has been subjected. Chardin's nature-mysticism sees in the processes of genetics, biological evolution, cosmology and anthropology, a memento of divinity in a world subjected to freedom and hope. He finds colossal grandeur, order, purpose, wonder, splendor, and complex beauty. He also sees distortion and limitation, risk and seemingly inevitable calamity, a shadow, a fierce El Greco-like stormy skyline over a sunny, sublime view of Toledo. With Teilhard, one is not sure whether this dark-side, this negative, is a necessary valence of the complete picture, or not. His profoundly optimistic and confident rationalism, reminiscent of Albertus Magnus, does not embrace an akedic candor until this postscript.

To show that nature's actual portrait is akedic, I will first explore the implication of Teilhard's confession, that "even in the view of the mere biologist the human epic resembles nothing so much as a way of the cross." I will specifically refer to the human genome project. This window into not only scientific knowledge but also therapeutic technology, shows the travail of nature as a corroboration of Akedah. I will next offer a larger vision of that travail with reference to the powerful insights of the eminent anthropologist, Loren Eisely. Before I offer this analysis, a word about the association I am suggesting between idea (Akedah) and matter (nature).

Penultimate or "natural" reality is a reflection of ultimate reality because "nature," what we explain with knowledge and tame with technology, is, in part, a product of human imagination. Nature is not only an objective, external reality, it is defined by what Kant called both pure (*reine*) and practical (*praktische*) reason (*Vernunft*). In this latter realm we impose certain "oughts" and "hopes" onto nature or intuit them as emergent. We thus allow an ethical phenomenon like Akedah to penetrate the thing in itself (*Dinge an Sich*). As Kierkegaard in his great akedic MIDRASH wrote:

"The ethical is the universal and as such it is the divine." [31]

Teilhard has been criticized for not adequately dealing with genetics. Even though his monumental work was done in the nineteen forties and early fifties, writers like Julian Huxley argue that he should have dealt with that albeit nascent science and with the admittedly brutal phenomenon of natural selection.[32] Eiseley has argued that man is always positivist and progressivist, detailer and dreamer. "He has a belief in seen and unseen nature ... both pragmatist and mystic."[33] Teilhard strikes this delicate balance, perhaps allowing the mystic more range.

---

[31] Kierkegaard, *Fear and Trembling*, p. 64.

[32] Teilhard, *Phenomenon of Man*, p. 21.

[33] Eiseley, Loren, *The Firmament of Time* (New York: Atheneum, 1974), p. 4.

On June 26, 2000, President Clinton announced that the Human Genome Project had been completed. In an exaggeration, he called it the greatest scientific event in history. The 50,000 genes have been characterized by NIH and Celaro Genetics Corp.

President Clinton and Prime Minister Tony Blair celebrated the completion of Government and private efforts to map the entire human genome.

Mr. Clinton:

- "We are learning the language by which God created life."
- "We are fathoming the secret of God's good creation."
- "We have learned from the Genome Project what we had learned from the ancient faiths, 'all are created equal'."
- "The most important fact of life is our common humanity."

My reflections were less exuberant:

- Today we celebrate the revelation of the first draft of the book of life.
- Humans now begin to read the book that up to now only God could read... Tailor-made medicine for disease will follow. "Pharmaco-genomics," the derivative technology, will require discriminating use as we develop and administer drugs.
- Fears seek to create perfect human, superman—Genetic purity.
- Government will use information to discriminate—will insurers discriminate?
- The poor in other countries will not have access to these developments

Nicholas Wade wrote in the following Sunday *New York Times*:

...Over the next few years, we should read [the] behavioral instructions whatever they are—instincts to slaughter or show mercy, the contexts for love and hatred, the taste for obedience or rebellion—the determination of human nature [and character].

Wade continues:

The Genesis account (following Frances Collins' remarks),... tells us there were two trees in the Garden of Eden, The Tree of Knowledge (of good and evil) and the Tree of Life. God evicted Adam and Eve because he feared that, having tasted the Tree of Knowledge, his problem tenants would eat next of the tree of life and live-forever. The genome, to borrow the Genesis writer's metaphor, is surely represented by both trees, entangled around each other like two strands of the double helix. Have we not now broken back into the garden

76

for a second bite? From the Tree of Knowledge we will learn to read the programming instructions that shape human nature and determine the implicit survival rules of human societies. From the Tree of Life we will learn to fix the programming errors that limit longevity and, should we choose, to change the program so as to extend life span many decades.[34]

As one begins to address the subject of genetics and the human genome project, one becomes aware of a primal tension inherent in human endeavors, noted by Eiseley, that of "taming and terror." Eiseley suggests that man believes in the destruction of worlds and the voice out of the whirlwind, precisely because he now possesses power at the heart of the atom.[35] In human genetics we delve into the most fundamental structure and substance of human life itself. The mingled response of attractive awe and foreboding fear, the primal spiritual/ethical response noted by Rudolf Otto in the *IDEA OF THE HOLY*, and in Malinowski's studies of magic and science, is even more pronounced here in genetics than in interventions in the physical universe.

I remember in the 1960's when Dr. Le June, the French physician-scientist who first described Trisomy 21-Down Syndrome, pleaded that the world not use his genetic knowledge to search for and destroy the "down" fetus—to no avail! Knowledge irresistibly led to technology, and the values of people—aesthetic, material, ethical, and the rest—values edifying and destructive—came into play. It still remains a frightening fact that every destructive human idea ever developed from nuclear explosion to biological warfare has always eventually been used. The argument today is that if you prohibit it in Chicago, we'll do it in the Bahamas.

The connection of the Human Genome project with the Akedah symbol which we employ to philosophically fathom, theologically discern, then ethically direct the scientific/technical enterprise, is obvious. We use the phrase "amniotic" probe. "The lamb" we open up, split and expose fetal cells and tissue. The lamb (*amnio, agnus*) is offered to the court of confrontation between the just and unjust impulses of humanity and the justice and mercy of the Holy One. The power is over life and death. The question of "who shall live and who shall die?" goes to the very essence of Abrahamic temptation.

Human motivations are also always ambivalent. Kierkegaard has dissected the intentions and emotions of Abraham as he journeyed toward Mount Moriah. In the genetics quest, do parents seek to cure diseases (e.g. severe combined immune deficiency), to learn to live with an anomaly (Down syndrome), or to enhance physical attributes (human growth hormone for achondroplasia)?

---

[34] Wade, Nicholas, "The Four Letter Alphabet That Spells Life."*New York Times*, 2 July, 2000, p. 4.

[35] Eiseley, p. 3.

The NIH and Celero Genomics Corporation have finished the initial probe and description of the some 50,000 human genes in the Genome. Will the knowledge be placed on the Internet and be made available free to all? Will it be shared privately for commercial utilization? The Abraham/Sarah/Isaac crisis is personal and familial, but more importantly, it is generic, social and cosmic. The command and act draw all humanity to the altar. The decision is representative for all. The structures of humanity's memory and future are at stake. Francis Collins, the physician-scientist (pioneer in cystic fibrosis) who leads the NIH Human Genome Project, frames the project in a profound spiritual/ethical/scientific context. In an article reflecting on these deeper dimensions he writes:

- If Jesus Christ, in his short time on earth, spent so much time on healing…those who follow him should consider this especially important.

- The Human Genome Project is a natural extension of our commitment "to heal the sick."

- Understanding the [genetic basis] of complex diseases like diabetes will "facilitate new treatments."

- "The work of discovering [speaking of CF project] is a form of worship."

- Breast cancer is a very powerful paradigm for what is happening in molecular medicine. A gene for breast cancer called BRCAI was unmapped in 1990 and identified precisely in 1994. A woman with a misspelled copy of BRCAI from family with a high incidence of breast cancer has a 50% risk of getting breast cancer by the age of fifty, with a life-long risk of about 85%. In the general population, about one in 200 women have a hereditary susceptibility to early-onset breast cancer. In the Jewish population, it is one in 40.

- We are all walking around with 4 or 5 genes that are really spoiled and another 10 or 20 that are moderately altered in a way that is not good for us.

In a poignant comment as the completion of the Genome Project was announced, Collins mourned the death, that preceding day, of his sister-in-law from breast cancer:

> I have to tell you…this morning is a bittersweet experience… She died much too soon, of breast cancer. The hope and promise…of the genome and the tools…came too late for her.[36]

---

[36] *New York Times*, 27 June, 2000, D. 8.

It reminded me of the moving, though somewhat naïve, remark of my dean in Houston, Dr. Michael Debakey, at the death of our chief of neurology:

> We regret the untimely death of our colleague. It teaches us how much we have yet to learn in medicine.

The akedic mystery offers that in the purview of God no one ever dies too early or too late. The God of Abraham and Job is the "giver" and "taker" of life. Collins concludes:

> My prayer for all of us is that we find wisdom. James 1:5 reads: "All who lack wisdom, let them ask of God, who gives to all freely and without reproach and it will be given to them." [37]

My purpose (and prayer) in this section of the essay is to show a correspondence between the parable of Abraham and the history of nature as instanced by genetics. Francis Collins' exuberant and ecstatic, yet realistic, appraisal of The Human Genome Project resonates with Akedah. A breach has opened up within creation. This break ("spoiled genes") [despoiled creation] elicits divine command and human quest (task)—the Abrahamic/Isaac ventures of faith. The act assuages the anguish of creation and the story of perpetual seed life goes on in renewed grace. The theological mystery follows this cycle:

- The Way of God leads to life.
- Digression from that Way necessitates sacrifice, salvation, and rescue, which reestablishes life in The Way.

Abraham, writes Kierkegaard, might have heroically killed himself in Isaac's stead (as any loving father would).

> "...He would have been admired in the world, and his name would not have been forgotten; but it is one thing to be admired, and another to be the guiding star, which saves the Anguished." [38]

"...To save the anguished" may be the deepest meaning of Akedah and the purpose of the Human Genome Project. Following his sojourn in Berlin, Kierkegaard knew that his beloved Regina was engaged to another man and that while his philosophical legacy might endure, his physical legacy would not. From this background he may have asked of the relative worth of intellectual and the generational legacy in the broad destiny of "saving the anguished."

---

[37] Collins, Francis S., "The Human Genome Project," in *Genetic Ethics*, ed. John Kilner, et al. (Grand Rapids, MI: Eerdmans Publishing Co., 1997), p. 95-102.
[38] Kierkegaard, p. 35.

Dan Kevles, the eminent social historian of science, positions the "Scientific search for the 'Holy Grail' of biology" to the monk Gregor Mendel's discovery of the laws of inheritance in the year 1900. The ensuing century has been one of sinister violence and sublime victory. The "Way of God," which is the "Way of Life" in the face of death, has been served in myriad ways, culminating in the salutary yield promised in the Human Genome Project (Francis Collins' "Heal the Sick" graces that quest). Nazi and Stalinist genetics and the broader cultural manias have disgraced the human race and offered perpetual decalogic warning to morally guide the project. Today's hacks hawking embryos or creating embryos for sale and research, follow this train of disgrace.

The moral imperatives to heal the sick, save and enrich life (C-6: Sustain Persons/do not kill) and seek justice (C-8: Help the needy/do not steal) are enormously enlarged in the divine gift of the Genome project. The destructive and unjust potentials are also evident. The project is morally equivocal thus resounding the akedic structure of good and evil. It also portends the akedic dimensions of organization and destination. Robert Sinsheimer, in many ways the pioneer of the project, wrote:

> "For the first time in all time, a living creature understands its origin and can undertake to design its future. "[39]

The akedic act remits the past and portends the future. The "seed" of humanity (Adam's seed) provokes the crisis and extends the promise. Sinsheimer's evaluation of the Genome Project lifts it into the redemptive realm. The promise to Abraham was born in the gift.

Isaac and the God of the Beloved Son (John 3:16) graces the realm of matter and nature. Conversely, the Genome project, efficacious in the realm of biological nature, is fraught with ethical and spiritual significance.

Theoretical and practical innovations will fall along the good/evil axis as the Genome project unfolds (see chart). Some acts will assert human sinfulness, pride, violence and injustice. They will contradict/veil the way of Torah and redemptive Akedah. Others will affirm trust, faith collaboration, and human fulfillment within that redemptive way. The axis might look as follows:

---

[39] Quoted in D. Kevles, "Out of Eugenics: The Historical Politics of The Human Genome" in Kevles, D. and L. Hood, *The Code of Codes* (Cambridge: Harvard University Press, 1992), p. 18.

Torah

↓

- Disease-free existence?
- Genetic therapy to mute violent, antisocial, and self-destructive behavior?
- Genetic Tech issues, e.g. screening, diagnosis, therapy to cure diseases that decimate the poor?
- Food research & development (e.g. grain, fish) to feed the hungry?
- Commercial exploitation that will further accentuate the gap between rich and poor?
- Enhancement of normal qualities (size, intelligence) constructing superman, ultimate deicide?

ANTI-Torah

The deep paradox of Abrahamic and biblical religion is the way in which the spiritual and material are interwoven. Not only does nature fold into history, both in etiology and eschatology, but ultimate reality converges with this world of time and space. Creation and incarnation, space and time, as Alfred North Whitehead has shown, proceed from Judaism and Greek philosophy, to create the worldview of modern science. The Human Genome Project, as the latter-day manifestation at the end of the century of genetics and at the culmination of millennia of human eugenic/dysgenic ambition, is a fully akedic ritual.

Loren Eiseley proposes a full human science and a comprehensive unified theory, which accords with and corroborates Akedah. He begins such an appraisal by noting the imposition of human mind on matter to form a view of nature in *THE FIRMAMENT OF TIME*. This imposition renders nature akedic because the human dynamics of reason and the irrational, good and evil, are woven into the fabric of nature as human perception and intervention. The struggle to assure justice and avert evil therefore is a dynamic of Akedah and of nature itself.

Dealing with disorder, disease, dissolution and death within nature is nature's first akedic distinction. Eiseley first points out that from the beginning of human history life was assumed, death was considered "unnatural." "It shouldn't be," was the way that this contradiction planted itself in human consciousness and conscience. Yet the contradiction goes deeper. Death, it appears, is a salutary condition for life. The processes of development and evolution ensure that organisms must die and yield to new genetic variants. In more human language, one generation succeeds another transmitting knowledge, wisdom and skill which capacities are progressively honed by the successors. On deeper thought, death is a grace concealed as an offense. As my teacher Paul Ramsey would say, the genetic mania (of cloning and Genome project) that all persons to come after be like us or somehow "be us," is the aberration. It is the cry against God to perpetuate not the living God who makes all things new, but to sustain myself in perpetuity. The demand for immortality shares some of the same life-negating irony.

In akedic terms, the ashes of Isaac or the fossils of the earth are the life source of the phoenix. In the mystery of God, death is the portal of life. This salutary process goes on when God is the killer, not man. "The Lord gives, The Lord takes ...blessed is the name...." Man's killing is the violent contradiction of God's way:

> "...biocide, pesticide, homicide, fratricide, infanticide, suicide, genocide, deicide, become the mania of humans gone wrong."
> (See Kenneth Vaux, DEATH ETHICS)

The phenomenon of survival and extinction of species is one fraught with moral and spiritual ambiguity. On the one hand, natural selection and "survival of the fittest" allow the procession of life forms to continue in the face of changing environmental challenges. That the dinosaurs disappeared from earth may be neither value nor disvalue in the history of God and the history of nature. On the other hand, extinction of species, especially the rapid cascade of loss since the industrial age, manifests human thoughtlessness, greed and violence—breaches of "The Way."

The static continuity of species was a theological axiom in bygone centuries because humans could not conceive the dispensability of their own kind. This esteem for human beings is commendable and very much in keeping with Abrahamic religion. On the other hand, this tradition, especially in its apocalyptic and eschatological tendency, denies ultimate divinity to this world, even humanity, and dares to affirm that the kingdom of God can only emerge with the emerging calamity, even the dissolution of this world.

Darwin, writes Ernst Mayer in *Scientific American* (July 2000), creates the philosophy of Biology by establishing four principles:

- The non-constancy of species (evolution itself)
- Branching evolution (common ancestor)
- Gradual evolution (non catastrophe)
- Natural Selection

Imbedded in this philosophy is what Mayer calls an "Ethics of survival and reproductive success which, though seemingly selfish, really shows that altruism and harmonious cooperation are forwarded by evolution." [40]Yes, there is violence, loss, death in natural process, but it is conducive to new life—Akedah. I find this philosophy and ethic harmonious with the biblical worldview and ethic that I have described as akedic. In both systems the elements of faith, hope, and love override the negatives of harm, injustice and despair.

Darwin, contends Eiseley, made death benign or natural. Ignoring this fundamental premise of the biblical tradition, which questioned whether the human project was the prime value of creation, Darwin and his followers domesticated death. Hitler's ultimate social Darwinists sought to bring death and life within human control in the euthanasia and eugenics programs. Constructing his data on the empirical realm in which death is observed and construed in terms of natural causality, the broader phenomenon of death as ethical and spiritual in causality and in perception was neglected. Here the Pauline notion of death as "The wages of sin," as the consequence of wrongful life, comes into play as a factor in the etiology of morality.

Death is a stigma within creation. By stigma I mean a sign that points to a larger context of meaning. In akedic purview, death signals to us the discord in creation. The wrong that has been let loose, the crisis and judgment that human life falls under results in a human dialectic of sacrifice and redemption as we seek, through science, technology and medicine to right flaws, ameliorate pains and optimize goods. Eiseley identifies this moral dimension of the history of nature in his famous passage on the "whirlpool":

> It is with the coming of man that a vast hole seems to open in nature, a vast black whirlpool spinning faster and faster, consuming flesh, stones, soil, minerals, sucking down the lightning, wrenching power from the atom, until the ancient sounds of nature are drowned in the cacophony of some thing which is no longer nature, something muted which is now loose and knocking at the world's heart, something demonic and no longer planned—escaped it may be—spewed out of nature, contending in a final giant's game against it master.[41]

Still, a serenity and hope is the final word as Eiseley signatures his book with the words of Shelley:

> The splendors of the firmament of time
> May be eclipsed, but are extinguished not...
> ...Death is a low mist which cannot blot
> The brightness it may veil.

Human life in thought and act is free. It either evokes or provokes the goodness of creation. Torah, "The Way," ultimately orders Creation. Eiseley observes a long-range crisis/calamity in nature associated with the appearance of humans. It

---

[40] Mayer, Ernst, "Darwin's Genius," *Scientific American*, July 2000, p.17.
[41] Eiseley, pp. 123-124.

is what ancient religious texts called the fall and what historical empires saw as the subjugation and exploitation of nature. In the history of nature human aggression against life forms and other humans infects the creation. Meanwhile, human justice and care liberates the world.

This bivalent enterprise crescendos into modern history. The age of science, technology, industry and globalization brings the beneficence/maleficence quotient of human creativity into an acute phase. Now it accelerates abruptly and apocalyptically into a crisis that is at once chronic and contained.

Humans enter what might be the climactic age of their time on earth. Global warming is the thoughtless yield of human greed. Many signs point to a convergence of destructive energies that cannot go on much longer. Scientists of humans on the earth, like Richard Leakey, place the odds at less than 50% that humans can endure on the earth through one more neglectful and violent century. What began in the nineteenth century as presumed deicide may turn out to be ecocide, specicide, and eventually global suicide. Unless, we awaken again, obey akedic command and find life.

The Saga of Human History
    Finally, history, like Nature, is a human interpretive construct molded from a basis of facts, events and data. What history had to do with Akedah struck my mind as I read accounts of the persecution of Christians at the hands of the Roman Empire and of Jews along the Rhine at the hands of the Crusaders. These historical crises were interpreted in terms of the Abrahamic/Isaac story. All other historic calamity from earthquake, to famine, to war, to September 2001's infamous "Attack on America" yield to the same interpretive matrix.

Akedah became a paradigm for those who would die for faith or for Torah, 'for righteousness' sake' (Matthew 5). For God, loyalty expressed unto death–Abraham, Isaac, Job, Jesus–was a verification of faith, which was then vindicated by bestowal of the grace of life restored. Life is grace in biblical tradition. It is not natural, not necessary, not a human right. It is gift. By right and necessity life should not be. In the cosmos stillness and non-being is the norm. In akedic terms even when life erupts from the bed of non-existence, sacrifice and death, not life and renewal, is the natural necessity. Yet…

Resurrection is verified where strife against the demonic thrives.
William Stringfellow

The history of humans on earth is punctuated by crises of death against life, of justice against injustice. These akedic temptations are often exacted in the guise of economic, territorial, military and political confrontations. History is always the conflict between egoism and nationalism against reciprocity and cooperation. When viewed as persecution, prosecution or tribulation, these same episodes called wars can be seen as transactions of justice and are therefore corroborations of Akedah. Paralleling what we have called the history of God is a history of conflict that I propose is not only an analogy too, but an expression of Akedah. The final portion of this book on creed and crusade will elaborate this section.

While the border disputes, clan and tribe rivalries and national battles of all peoples share such justice features of exploitation, victimization, persecution and eventual appeasement and settlement, and while other regional ethnic-religious encounters through the ages (e.g., Japan-Korea, India-Pakistan) always have deep elements of sacrifice and injustice, I have been struck by what might be called the akedic episodes of history which would include:

- Israel's struggle to establish the presence of Yahweh in world history.
- Jewish and Christian martyrdom at the hands of the Roman Empire.
- The crisis of Constantinian then crusading Christendom against Judaism and Islam.
- Amerindian genocide at the hands of European conquistadors and settlers.
- The final calamity of historic Christendom: The Nazi Holocaust.
- The dislocation of Palestinians at the hands of the state of Israel.
- Continuing ecocide/genocide in Africa and the poor world at the hands of the global economy.
- The outlash of vehemence and violence of terrorists, focused in the Middle East and in Western Asia, against Israel and America. The World Trade Center, the Pentagon and the global economy are seen as instruments of injustice.

Before sketching this corroborative historical line we need to reflect on the nature of war as sacrifice in the cause of justice and relate that to Akedah.

Each Memorial Day, I watch with care the celebration on the Washington Mall for the fallen heroes of American wars. On this day in all nations people honor those who gave their lives to defend their country, their freedom, and their democracy against tyranny. The military history of our young nation looks with gratitude on the war for independence against England; ignores the wars to remove and concentrate Indians, anguishes over the fratricide of civil war, while extolling Abraham Lincoln and condemning slavery; slips over the wars of land expansion against Mexico; glories in the wars of defeating the evil of fascism and communism; flags in zeal in reflecting on Vietnam and Grenada; renews transient glory in the Gulf War and is totally confused about Somalia, Bosnia, Kosovo, Afghanistan and Iraq and the less noted struggles against genocide and for human rights. Now we ponder the highly ambiguous *avant-garde* of war-terrorism.

On the Washington Mall, the litany of sacrifice of sons and daughters on the battlefield and of hard-working "Rosie-The- Riveters" at home takes on subtle changes each year. Was Vietnam the "Good War" that we deem World War II to have been? Who were the real patriots and heroes in Vietnam, Nicaragua and South Africa? The final song of the commemoration "Let there be peace on earth…" commendably laments the loss of persons (especially innocents, women, the old, children) on all sides. It now defies Prime Minister Margaret Thatcher and, with Archbishop Runcie, it prays for Argentinian and British fallen at Falklands. It yearns for that eschaton where "…swords will be beaten into plowshares and we will study war no more." It may be proleptic that the first heroes of the first war on global terrorism are firefighters and NGOs (e.g., the Red Cross).

War expresses the two modes of trial and temptation. Human malice or mistake is one explanation of temptation (see James 1:13- 15). The view of the etiology of war asserts an evil force or fatality. John Sossinger in his classic *Why Nations Go to War* holds the former view:

> … Mortal men make the (decision about war). They make them
> in fear and trembling … In most cases they were not evil men
> bent upon destruction but frightened men entrapped in self-delusion.[42]

On the eve of the "Attack on America," the world has come to realize that there are countless individuals in the world who are willing to die to confront and punish what they feel are America's "Evil Ways." Osama Bin Laden orchestrates one such network. The Taliban party, until recently ruling in Afghanistan, may be possessed by a similar martyr impulse. For many in the Arabic and Islamic world America's evil is its support and funding of Israel's occupation and violence toward the Palestinian people. This mode of aggression against the world is symbolized by the Pentagon.

Others focus their lethal rage on the exploitative side of the global economy orchestrated from the "now in rubble" World Trade Center. What is that litany of evils that would animate such life and death sacrifice? As Americans,

- we have contributed to and in some ways are behind the massacre and disinheritance of the Palestinians;

- we throw our weight around the world—from Korea to Vietnam to Grenada to the Gulf War;

---

[42] Sossinger, John, *Why Nations Go to War* (New York: St. Martin's Press, 1974), p. 2.

- we have grown ostentatiously rich at the expense of the rest of the world, acting as if the world owes us a living;

- we indulge in this luxuriant, apathetic, drug-riddled, MTV, indulgent manner of life at the expense of a poor and suffering community both within our nation and without;

- our military and intelligence patrols and surveys every inch of the globe, but God forbid that another nation try to do the same.

The indictment is in part valid. The Palestinian extermination and expulsion (Israel had 30% Palestinian Christians 20 years ago— now it has 3%) has been supplied 'cash and copters' by the American government. We cannot and should not dismiss the profound moral revulsion in much of the world over this official American sponsorship of violence against the inhabitants of Palestine. The Arab world and the entire morally sensitive world feels solidarity with the Palestinians.

But America and Israel are seen as enemies today because of our rightful response to the most grotesque inhumanity of all history—the holocaust of European Jews. The numbing guilt of not having intervened until it was too late, indeed of acting in complicity by rejecting European Jews and not speaking out, causes us to be silent now. The harsh clouds beneath the crumbling World Trade Center Towers are the direct legacy of the ashes of the Auschwitz ovens. A century of evil has precipitated the akedic offering of some 4,000 persons in lower Manhattan. Their ashes waft across the seas from Manhattan and rest at Auschwitz on the ash of 6 million others together to yearn for a Phoenix to arise from the dust and for a newer world set right.

Vicar-Victim...

Ancient and modern construals of war are similar. In either case we see an akedic interpretation of war. Sons are taken out to terrifying unknown places full of terror. They go in trust, out of loyalty to patria and to patrie and mother land ...*Dulce et Decorum est*. While rescue may ensue (North Sea rescues in World War II, MASH units in Vietnam), victory usually entails victims. "Danny Boy" is the plaintive war song of all nations. War also often involves righteousness or justice. Just war theory elaborates the causes (*Jus ad bellum*) and conditions (*Jus in bello*) which justify war. If Isaac is offered for the sin of the people and for their perpetuation, the soldier is often a holy offering, redeeming and regenerating a people. The main parallel with Akedah, to my mind, is the fact of innocent redemptive sacrifice. Jews interpret suffering at the hands of Assyria, in the Roman wars, at the hands of crusaders along the Rhine, or the demonic Nazi State, as saving akedic martyrdom. Early Christian persecution, which is the historical backdrop of much of the New Testament, or missionary martyrs in Ecuador or China, is received as Isaacic or Christic sacrifice. If war is construed akedically or theodically, it must reflect the righteousness, or as Abraham Lincoln reflected, that the judgments of God are "true and right altogether."

The hegemonic theory of war's etiology and execution holds that power vacuum invites invasion. *Terra Nullus* invites occupation, and weakness and vulnerability invites attack. Pure Darwinian war theory finds that the weak create imbalances and disequilibria of power which the strong must exploit, or be themselves, in turn, taken over. While these biological, evolutionary, territorial and class theories of the origin of conflict have fallen out of vogue in our age which is fascinated to watch the weak under attack ("The Survivors" TV series), even using pity to protect the vulnerable (e.g. Kosovo, Albanians), the theory retains some currency. I relate and appropriate this theory as corroboration of Akedah by adding a moral dimension. To me, power, wealth and the desire for expansion are often inversely related to righteousness. Justice respects the several habitats of nations because of a more generous and reciprocal view of personal and societal relations. The impulse to make war is to wound and kill the innocents, a child immolation proscribed in Akedah, not the worthy sacrifice proffered by it.

Thucydides' hegemonid theory of war held that when natural divisions and balances (hierarchies) of power eroded, trouble inevitably ensued. When Hellas concentrated power and joined it to aggressive hunger and the need to humiliate, war ensued. To appropriate this natural law and hierarchical theory to akedic theory, we may say that war comes as injustice and erodes the structural *shalom* of nations. The Second World War, in this case might be caused in part by the economic dislocation imposed in the settlement of the First World War. The Gulf War might be caused, in part, as much by the dislocation of Arab peasants by the land appropriations of Israel and by unjust international economic policies (oil) as by Saddam Hussein's fantasies of power. In my view, the panorama of modern wars—Serbia in Bosnia and Kosovo, Russia in Afghanistan, France, then the U.S., in Vietnam—are wars of inverted Akedah. The vulnerable party may be overwhelmed in the vehemence of battle but is vindicated by a deeper historical righteousness. The quip "winning the battle but losing the war" refers to this akedic phenomenon.

I believe that the outcomes of conflict are often confounded in the inscrutable mystery of God. Losers may be winners. The Indians of Chiapas may prevail over the right-wing conquistadors. In Africa the conquered and colonized peoples may ultimately succeed. This mystery is captured in the Lawrence Housman/Geoffrey Shaw Hymn:

> Father eternal, Ruler of creation, / Spirit of life, which moved ere form was made,
> Through the thick darkness covering every nation, / Light to man's blindness, o be thou our aid:

Races and peoples, lo we stand divided, / And sharing not our own griefs, no
joy
can share;
By wars and tumults, love is mocked, derided, / His conquering cross no
kingdom wills to bear
Thy Kingdom come, O Lord thy will be done

Analysts of history in general, and conflict and war in particular, refrain from moralizing appraisal. This contrasts with theological appraisals of history where interpretations of events, of the rise and fall of nations, are replete with notions of good and evil. When scientific historians imbue history with meanings, e.g. Toynbee and Spengler, or when theologians ponder the pattern of events and the sequence and consequences of actions, they often appeal to motifs such as pride/humility, justice/injustice or complex metaphors of meaning such as Akedah/CROSS. I pose here a *Heilgeschichtliche* mode of reflection, which discerns divine patterns of judgment and rescue within the historical process. Let me offer a review of the preceding historical moments showing akedic significance. I begin with recent events and work backwards precisely because in our "positivistic" post-modern, post-Marxist, post-Christian age, explicit akedic texts are not as available as in earlier texts.

A.   I mention at the end of a historical continuum a first example: the crisis of genocide and ecocide at the hands of a global economy, especially in Africa. Case in point: the International Conference on AIDS concluded (July 15, 2000) in Durban, South Africa. Thirty percent of young persons in this newly emancipated nation may be infected with the virus. Part of the crisis is the dislocation entailed in the global economy where young men must go far away, even abroad, to find employment in the mines, diamond pits and other industry. This fracturing of families contributes to the rampant pandemic. Beyond that brought about by diseases, Ebola, malaria and the like, homicide is also caused by the flaring and fearful tribal and fratricidal wars—Congo, Rwanda, Kenya, Uganda, Sierra Leone, Liberia, Sudan, Ethiopia and Eritrea. Although causation is complex in these conflicts, the destructive effects of the hegemony and the wrongful and harmful paternity of colonialism contribute. This is the dark side of akedic warning "do not lay a hand…"

B.   The penultimate crisis I lift up is ironic verging on the tragic. We see this in the contemporary world as we learn again as President Clinton or Bush meets with Barak or Sharon of Israel and Yassir Arafat of Palestine. The pilgrim akedic people in world history, the Jews, have become the oppressors of the Palestinians. The persecuted become persecutors. A mass of people have been cast out of their homes, concentrated in Gaza, exiled as refugees in camps in Lebanon and Jordan, discouraged and exiled to Michigan and incarcerated by disconnected apartheid sectors in their own land.

Neither side has a monopoly on violence or on terrorism. A passenger jet slices into the 60th floor of the World Trade Center. Hamas explodes a bus bomb in West Jerusalem. Dr. Goldstein, a Brooklyn transplant, mows down worshippers in a Hebron mosque. A Palestinian child is shelled to death as he huddles with his dad against a Jerusalem wall. An Israel reservist is stomped to death, burned and dropped from the window of a Ramallah police station. Ever new sacrifices will be called for before resurrection, *Shalom*, can arise. Peace (*shalom*) can only be fashioned upon justice. Martin Buber and Karen Armstrong envision a shared community where all three Abrahamic/akedic peoples—Jews, Christians and Muslims—will together inherit the land and cause the desert to flower. Here might arise on Zion, the citadel of peace where all the nations of the world will come up in reconciliation.

The complexities of political and military history often have to do with strong exploiting weak, privileged scapegoating the vulnerable. In some sense, this is the irony of the last half-century of tragic history in Palestine, only with an inversion. A people that "Christian Europe" sought to eliminate, i.e. scapegoat elsewhere if they could not be eliminated, ends up in a land of severe poverty and vulnerability—a wounded sheep assaulting that black goat.

The Palestinian/Israeli moment of akedic history refers us back to the last confrontation when akedic imagery was used to interpret what was happening—these are the World Wars fought against fascism in Europe and Asia. In addition to Jewish MIDRASH crying out to the God of Abraham on behalf of the sacrificial son, even Christian Europeans offered the same plaintive groan.

C.   Contemporary Jewish thinkers hesitate to imbue the Holocaust with any meaning, any death and resurrection interpretation. Arno Mayer asked, "why did the sky not darken?"[43] Elie Wiesel gazes with horror into an endless NIGHT. Many agree with Nietzsche who said that Holocaust offers final proof that we have killed God and all meaning with our iniquity. Yet while full of furious sadness and guilt, some writers, like Wilfred Owen, dare to invoke the image of Akedah.

Michael Brown in a salient essay reviews a variety of modern Jewish writers who respond to the Holocaust in terms of the Akedah.[44]

---

[43] Mayer, Arno, *Why did the Skies not Darken?* (Princeton: Princeton University Press, 1981), p. 72.

[44] Brown, Michael, "Biblical Myth and Contemporary Experience: The Akedah in modern Jewish Literature." *Judaism* 31 (1): 99-111, 1982.

The twentieth century, the double millennium, is the century of genocide. We have witnessed the near complete termination of the Eastern Armenians, the Jews of Europe, Stalin's forced starvation in Ukraine, Cambodia, Rwanda, ethnic cleansing in Bosnia and Kosovo. Within this cascade of horror, the European *SHOAH* is definitive. The cultural crisis of Germanic Europe in this century completes the dejudaization of Christianity and in the process, severs the spiritual and ethical cord of vitality from Western civilization. *SHOAH* completes the supercessionism of corpus Christianum. In this, the most violent century the world has ever known, hundreds of millions have been killed. With our enhanced tools of destruction, can the human race continue? We are back to Loren Eiseley's "Whirling cesspool" or Teilhard's *MASS UPON THE EARTH*. The sacrifice of the children of the earth—especially mothers and innocents, threatening the perpetuation of the human race—is an akedic prolepsis. The Abrahamic, even Noachic, covenant is breached and all life is threatened. "The way" of God life for the world has been rejected for the human way of violation.

D.   An earlier anticipation of this same war, this same akedic crisis, comes with the colonial violation committed by European *Corpus Christianum* in the spawning centuries of the modern era—the fifteenth through the seventeenth centuries. The eruption from congested and war-weary European lands, the commercial exploitation, the military assault, the missionaries with too much baggage, disposed to denigrate the indigenous cultures, filled the boats with merchants, militia and missionaries. Durban 2001 rightly condemns racism and slavery (and Israel expropriation) as unjust violence. The English, Dutch, Portuguese and French in Africa, the British in India, the Dutch and French in Asia, the Spanish and English, the Dutch and French in the Americas. These, among other colonial misadventures, culminate in the dispossession, concentration and genocide of the indigenous peoples, in our case the Amerindians. This crisis presages and predetermines the European genocide of Jewry. It has now become clear that the roots of Nazi Eugenics and Euthanasia are found in America. (See D. Kelves).

I have been suggesting a history of crisis, which sees continuum where one injustice and trauma leads on to the next. The celebration of justice is a long arm overarching history. All conflict is embraced within the context of human violence and sin, retribution and reconciliation. The history of social upheaval and war, in other words, is the history of Akedah. This prime metaphor to fathom sin and suffering, death and resurrection, therefore relates the historic phenomenon of the plight of the weak and poor, the exploitation by the powerful and rich to a deeper trans-historic pattern of meaning. In this sense the injustice done to the American Indians is not only a symptom of an underlying malaise in the dominant and privileged Western culture, but it is caught up in the same akedic judgment, sacrifice and restoration for:

> God is working His purpose out as year proceeds to year. God is working His purpose out and the time is drawing near. Nearer and nearer draws the time, the time that shall surely be, when the earth shall be full glory of God as the Waters cover the sea.

In Dee Brown's classic *BURY MY HEART AT WOUNDED KNEE* we have an akedic rendition, not only of that particular crisis of the Great Plains tribes but also of the greater crisis of the white man's intrusion into the aboriginal world. Injustice, sacrifice and the death are not transacted without a witness. In akedic terms God sees (*Yahweh Yireh*) and remembers. Justice works its righteousness slowly and in circuitous fashion, but it is conclusive.

E. The Masterpiece of akedic MIDRASH is Shalom Spiegel's, *THE LAST TRIAL*. At the center of this text is his translation and exegesis of the poetic lament of Rabbi Ephrahim Bar Jacob of Bonn. This text ends with the signature of Ephrahim or Jacob, BE-MIGHTY in-Torah and in-*MITSVOT*. The text fulfills the commitments of its author, a twelfth-century German Rabbi, to Torah and into commandment. The text has now taken its place as identical with Akedah itself.

As we have shown in the earlier section on the genocidal pogrom of the first crusade along the Rhine, the historical background of the poem is the futile attempt of the church and bishop to protect the Jews from the marauding crusaders. Like the father Abraham who in some MIDRASH goes through with the sacrifice against the divine voice, or like Wilfred Owen's, "But he would not, and slew half the seed of Europe, one by one..."—anti-command becomes gleeful vengeance.

The Crusaders were inflamed not only to reclaim the Holy places and lands, but to cleanse the lands of the offensive presence of Muslims and Jews. To sanctify and unify the name through self-sacrifice was the impulse on all sides. Abrahamic fratricidal conflict is doubly heinous from the ancient animosity between the Isaac and Ishmael tribes, through perennial clashes of Jews and Christians, even Jewish Christians like Jesus and James, his brother, which provoked animosity from Gentile Christians. The Pope is not welcome today by Ukraine Orthodox. From the dawn of Messianic times, through the crusades, medieval ghettos and pogroms, from Nazareth down to Palestine today, fratricidal animosity wretches the world-Akedah.

Not only do faith families draw each other's blood mercilessly, but they also do so lustily as if fulfilling some *MITSVOT*. Violation of DECALOGUE: metaphysical presumption, manipulation of persons, mischievous *porneia*, military power, material possessions. A text of the lethal assault of the crusades on the archbishop's courtyard in Mainz is telling:

> ...because of our sins, the enemy prevailed.

Not only did the defenders' strength fail, but also YAHWEHGodself-shield and buckler preeminent (*Rosh ha-Shavah* Service) yielded to the blood thirst. As the crusaders wielded the bloody sword, they probably sang, "Lift High the Cross" and chanted the mischievous Gospel words "His blood be on us and our children...." Thus the lineaments of Deuteronomic Theology were shattered where God gives victory to the righteous and defeat to the sinners.

For four millennia, the establishment of God's name and kingdom in the world has been accompanied by violence and bloodshed. If we resort to the Apostle John's memory of Jesus' searching High Priestly words, this sibling animosity condemns the world to unbelief.

> That they...
> > ...May be one...
> > > ...so that the world may believe...
> (John 17:23).

Most of the warfare history, which we have reviewed, reveals the delusion of one or even both sides that God or righteousness was on "their side." The self-sacrifice was therefore warranted, indeed mandated. Jewish, Christian and Muslim soldiers believe more or less the same creed, that death in battle is death in the Lord and instant translation into God's kingdom. That question came as the Jews defended at Mainz, confronted the same conviction in the Crusader, or as the Palestinian Arab confronted today's Israeli soldier.

Gratefully, for the peace of the world, Judaism and Christianity, especially post-Constantine and Crusade Christianity, removes the category of killer as martyr so that killing the infidel is not a God-sanctioned act. It may be high patriotism or sublime altruistic sacrifice, but it is not a saving oblation. Akedah call II has perhaps at long last succeeded call I.

F.   So we are drawn to the paradigmatic battle, 'the mother of all battles" as our JIHADIC brethren might say, the contention for the survival of the presence and name of the God of Israel and martyrdom of both

Jews and Christians at the hands of the Roman Empire. Akedah recall, writes Spiegel, begins with events during the Hasmonean travail (2nd century BCE) as these are projected forward into the Hadrianic travail (2nd century CE) by Jewish faithful who will not bend the knee to "other gods," even unto death. The period between the Maccabean revolt c.160 BCE and the Bar Kochba revolt c.160 CE is the crucial age when mother Judaism gives birth to two sons—Christianity and Rabbinic Judaism. If we allow that diaspora Jewish Christianity, often called "Ebionism" (God's poor), forms the exile preconditions for what will become Islam, then all three children of Abraham find their nativity in a world history formed in this fateful span of three centuries.

To my reading, the history of religion of this period, not the eighth-century BCE, is the axis-time of human history. Here, law and salvation meet. It is *KAIROS* (fullness of time) for Akedah. Ancient spiritual traditions; Israel's eighth century prophets embodying Torah in the social structure, Buddha, Zoroaster, Greek and Egyptian high religion; the noble ethical systems of China, all yield their heritage of justice and righteousness as these now mingle with the salvation cults of Mithra and Dionysus. Out of this convergence emerge the sublime salvation and faith of Jesus Christ, the way of James toward Jewish Christianity and the way of Paul, the Hellenistic Jew. Social justice now joins hands with saving faith to form an akedic vision of redemption. The Pauline view joins the soaring reaches of Greek Philosophy and Roman Stoicism, transforming the west while the Jamesian view stressing Torah and Paschal moves East. Both versions of the singular vision disturb and perturb the established deities and pieties of the age. Three centuries of Jewish and Christian martyrdom ensue, punctuated by the Roman-Jewish wars, the destruction and dismantling of Jerusalem, the mass suicide of MASADA and the rapid evangelization of the Roman Empire. We now begin to see the irony unfold. At the very time that the final Bar Kochba is suppressed and Judaism ceases forever to be a worldly power, Polycarp and Ireneaus preside on ecclesiastical thrones at Smyrna and Lyons.

During these decades, thousands of Jews and Christians go silently or militantly to their martyr deaths. Whether they knew, as Edward Gibbon would sketch in the eighteenth century, that the martyr-blood would be the seed of the church (or of the sublime genius of Talmudic Judaism) we do not know. We do know that human history turned in a decisively akedic direction. With the convergence of Torah and Gospel, temptation, death and transfiguration have fashioned a new spirituality and ethos and injected world history with an intensified yet violent trauma and redemptive drama. We now turn to characterize that new manner of life, as *pax Romana* becomes *regnum Christi*.

We have surveyed four parameters of secular life that corroborate the secular/sacred notion of Akedah. The history of God, the Human condition, the enigma of Human history and the travail of nature all resonate with an akedic understanding of reality. Having offered this *apologia* for the *Leitmotiv,* let us now elaborate and commend the akedic lifestyle as a pattern for goodness and justice in God's world.

D. An Akedic Lifestyle

Faith in order to works – Works in order to faith.

Princeton's Walter Lowrie, the great translator and analyst of Kierkegaard, summarizes the existential philosophy grounded in faith, which is the essence of the great Dane's proposal for humanity. I take this teaching as a contemporary apostolic and akedic *Didache* and *Didascalia*—a charter for how we should be, believe and behave. It provides a charter for an akedic lifestyle. Kierkegaard summarizes his philosophy of life as a paradox (think of Hegel's dialectic) where the inevitable antithesis of God and man, of eternity and temporality, frames a creative tension where "God's understanding of what man ought to be and man's" confront his being. This yields an ethical maturity where self-realization "involves decisiveness of spirit," a radical relationship where a person's "strength consists in weakness, his victory in defeat."[45]

The lifestyle he commends is one of faith, active in love and hope. Lowrie sees *Fear and Trembling* as the architectonics of this manner of life, which we have held as one where good works (Torah) are absorbed into salvation. The elements of this decisional faith are:

- Particularity of relationship with GOD (no intermediary)
- Infinitive resignation (vis a vis finite goods)
- Double movement of spirit as resignation becomes relation (to God to others)
- Fearful teleological suspension of the Ethical (e.g. Abraham)[46]

The akedic manner of life is unfolded in *Fear and Trembling.* Here a radical revolution of consciousness is affected where universal ethical consciousness is transmuted into the Christian consciousness of sin and forgiveness and into a more general normative perception of good and evil. Before explicating and elaborating this manner of life let us add the depiction of dying into life via faith-loyalty as the "Way of God." This is the modus vivendi of the martyrial

---

[45] Kierkegaard, *Fear and Trembling.* (New York: Doubleday, 1954), p. 16.
[46] Ibid., p. 16.

existence of First Century (CE) Jews, God-fearers and Christians. It comes in Daniel Boyarin's masterful study.[47]

The faith/piety of this formative age finds clear expression, claims Boyarin, in the Prayer of Polycarp and the Prayer of Eleasar in IV Maccabees 6:27-29, both texts grounded in Isaac's Akedah. Boyarin sees a mingling of images which converge in a picture of a "Way of life," which is perfectly depicted in Jesus in the Sermon on the Mount:

> … Roman generals devotion, with its Greek analogues, chaste Greek and Roman wives (and virgins) threatened with rape, Maccabees, gladiators, Socrates, Jesus on the Cross, even Carthaginian child sacrifice.[48]

This *exemplum* captures the genius of Jewish-Christian ethics, of the biblical manner of life. Pauline antinomianism and moral freedom has not yet severed grace from law. Stoic, Egyptian and Babylonian elements still influence Hellenistic Judaism. It is an ethic of working-faith or faithful work.

In this chapter we will first trace the contours and characteristics of the akedic life pattern following Kierkegaard and other *midrashim*. We will conclude by sketching the proscriptions and prescriptions (abstentions and actions, Barth) of a contemporary akedic lifestyle. Though Kierkegaard develops his ethical theology in *EITHER/OR* and *REPETITION*, the focus of his suasion on the moral life is found in what he considered to be his greatest work, *FEAR AND TREMBLING*. Early in this work he makes clear his disdain for systematization and speculation in ethics. He seeks the universal imperative that is rooted in concrete active existence and for this reason turns to the proto-human and ultima-human Abraham. The treatise consists of a prelude, panegyric and a problemata in three parts.

A checklist of ethical axioms can be extracted showing an akedic pattern of life.

- The command to obey in faith sends shudder through the soul.
- Breaking commands sends one on a journey into the unknown.
- The innocent mother's child is carried along unknowingly into that crisis.
- The "Hero" or "Poet" rescues the wanderer from moral oblivion.
- The hero is moral guide—the subject and object of one's love.
- Through the "Hero" (Abraham) we know of eternal consciousness constituting the sacred human bond.

---

[47] Boyarin, Daniel, *Dying for God: Martyrdom and the Making of Christianity and Judaism*. (Stanford: Stanford University Press, 1999), p. 117.
[48] Ibid., p. 117.

- Human heroism is measured by the greatness of one's love.
- "Divine madness" is highest human passion (the Paroxysm of faith).
- "This world is in bondage to law of indifference while in world of spirit ...only he that works gets the bread, he who was in anguish finds repose, he who descends the underworld rescues the beloved, only he who draws the knife gets Isaac" (p. 38).
- The life of responsibility is one of "labor, heavy laden...fear & dread."
- Moral authenticity is being condemned a "would be killer" before the God who commands the mandatory sacrifice as "first-fruits offering."
- Authentic humanness must confront "divine madness."
- The "sword of God slays and saves."
- God tempts (allows adversary to tempt), yet God is love.
- God must be loved with "all one's soul," i.e. even unto death.
- Loving God in faith reflects glory on God (*summum bonum*).
- Infinite resignation leads to "suspending the ethical."
- "Though he slay me, yet will I love him" (Job 13:15).
- "He resigned everything infinitely, and then grasped everything again by virtue of the absurd" (p. 51).
- Knight finds right in self, not in external law (Luther's).
- Self is receptor of spirit – will of God.
- In the finite world the only thing that can save one is the absurd grasped through faith. The encasement and enslavement of finitude finds release in God known in contradiction to the world.
- The pathway to this release of life is command obedience through faith.
- Resignation (renunciation) is the eternal consciousness [love of God in Faith (obedience)].
- Irony and humor (the absurd) inhere in faith.
- Temptation (*ANFECHTUNG, FRISTELSE*) is assertion of particularity against universal.
- Yet in faith particulars (individuals) transcends the universal & touch the absolute.
- Abraham's act is absurd (*skandalon*) like the cross of Christ.
- It is beyond reason, logic, goodness, even justice.
- Human duty to God is absolute; therefore ethics is relative (C-1,2,3).

- The relational call of God (word, will, command) is the ultimate good.
- The will of God is a solitary path.
- Distress and dread is the paradox of faith.

We have reviewed the masterpiece of modern akedic MIDRASH—Kierkegaard's *FEAR AND TREMBLING*. All who seek to fathom the agony of the two recent centuries—the collapse of optimism, war, genocide, poverty, yet hope—adjourn to this text. It has become the template for the meaning of existence in our world. Its struggle with theodicy and its spoken honesty are echoed in Elie Wiesel's *NIGHT*, Terence Malick's *THIN RED LINE* and Jacques Derrida's *DONNER LA MORTE*.

Theodicy, temptation, Torah, "THE WAY"—the basic constituents and characteristics of human life, under God, in the world—are trials where our ultimate devotion, our *raison d'être* is called into question. When humanity is granted freedom in the divine creation, the duel of faith (righteousness) with denial (disobedience) is set in motion. It is John Donne's death duel—*ANFECHTUNG*—yielding victory.

In the history of thought, Kierkegaard has been associated with Luther, locating the preeminence of faith over works in the religious life. On closer look, Kierkegaard's fascination with temptation and Akedah shows that he is not proposing a facile "suspension of the ethical" but a rigorous integration of faith and works as synergetically constitutive of the good life. The conjunction of the salvific and the ethical is secured in his doctrine of love. In the spirit of the Psalms, Jesus, Paul, Augustine and Luther, Kierkegaard shows that the highest passion—the *SUMMUM BONUM* of life is the love of God, known in outgoing care, epitomized in the greater love of laying down one's life for one's friends" (John 15:13). Love, for John—always agapic and akedic, infinite and finite, whole and broken—is inseparably divine and human.

On this impulse Alice Walker (*THE COLOR PURPLE*) notes that the first black woman in South Africa who publicly declared that she had AIDS was stoned to death by her community (prompted, no doubt, by vindictive, self-righteous, infectious males). In her new book of stories, *THE WAY FORWARD IS WITH A BROKEN HEART*,[49] she writes of the agony that accompanies human growth. The first story deals with the anguish of living in the segregated South with her biracial daughter and husband Melvyn Leventhal. Yet in a faith deeper than suffering, even death, she envisions "a love more radical than violence," where friendship and amity extend, even to enemies.[50]

---

[49] Walker, Alice, *The Way Forward is with a Broken Heart*. (New York: Random House, 2000).

[50] See Gusson, Mel, "An Explorer of Human Terrain," *New York Times*, 26 December, 2001, p. B1, 10.

Touching on suffering love and the Johannine School again puts us in touch with Paschal traditions of Jewish Christianity. Further biblical ground for an akedic lifestyle is found in another Hebraic- Gospel text which dwells on command and sacrifice, temptation, faith and works—THE LETTER OF JAMES.

The key to understand what we have called a Paschal or akedic ethic which we contend is endemic to Judaism and therefore Christianity, is the blending of piety and performance, faith and works, all anchored in what we believe is the constitutive paradigm of biblical faith—what Jon Levenson calls THE DEATH AND RESURRECTION OF THE BELOVED SON. This ethic, rooted in the Abraham/Sarah/Isaac complex and in the Jesus as Christ event and history, is that which is lived out and articulated by the brother of Jesus.

James, the brother of Jesus, perhaps the one referred to as the 'Righteous Teacher' or 'Teacher of Righteousness,' in the Dead Sea Scrolls, was said to have knees worn bare like the Camel's from his constant intercession for the people. His own teaching and leadership of the Jerusalem Church and his martyr death in 62 CE, exhibits an akedic pattern. He was the recognized authority in the Mother Church in Jerusalem to whom Peter, and even reluctantly, Paul, come to honor.

In a pivotal text in the Gospel of Thomas the disciples ask Jesus,

"After you have gone who will be great over us?"

Jesus answers

"In the place where you are to go, go to James the Just for whose sake heaven and earth came into existence."
(G. Thomas, 12)

James, called *ZADDICK* or 'Just One,' is identified with the eternal, pre-existent 'Righteous One' of the Jewish mystical tradition (*KABBALAH*).

Sustenance and recovery of this tradition of faith and life is difficult for several reasons. Three ecclesiastical developments in
early Christianity, especially in the time around Constantine, suppress and minimize the importance of James and of Jewish Christianity. Especially obscured is the 'moral exemplar' tradition.

1. In stressing the "virgin mother" tradition not only is the biblical 'Davidic,' 'Nazorite,' genealogical heritage compromised but fantastic gesticulations are set in motion conjecturing on the origins of Jesus' family, including James.

2. Catholic orthodoxy also develops the tradition of Peter's apostolic primacy which obscures the fact that James was the First Bishop—in Jerusalem.

3. Under the influence of Paul, Jewish ethics, Torah, and especially the fine points of Rabbinic casuistry, were deemphasized in favor of the primacy of faith for salvation.

These distortions harm the biblical concept of the interpenetration, interdependence and reciprocal integrity of faith and works. In Matthean DIDACHE, Syrian DIDASCALIA, Sardis PASCALIA as well as in other Semitic-Christian ethical instruction we sense the residue of a primitive Jewish-Gospel ethic which after the Roman-Jewish wars (66 CE) would disappear with the Diaspora into Pella, Syria, Iraq, even Arabia. It is this religio-moral LIFEWAY which historians believe surfaces a few centuries later in the base communities of Islam. What are the characteristics of that WAY, that manner of life, that lifestyle?

In the first place we find a total synthesis of what Christian tradition has tended to polarize—faith and works. *HESED* and *ZEDEK*, piety and justice. Devotion toward God and righteousness toward one's neighbors are of one piece. These dimensions are totally inseparable in Jewish and Jewish-Christian religion. In this cache of literature and tradition, which we can now identify as firmly normative and orthodox, the teaching of James, Qumran and the John the Baptist corpus holds true. As the body is baptized in the water of the river Jordan, the soul is being purified with the baptism of behavioral righteousness. A body/soul transformation is being effected. Repentance, judgment, baptism of water and spirit—in activity exquisitely spiritual and physical—the Covenant (circumcision) is enacted in soul and heart (the very being) personal and communal. Jesus submits to this baptism and the Baptist defers to Jesus' Spirit bestowal. The GOOD LIFE (all righteousness) is thus fulfilled (Matt.3: 15).

James' exposition of the WAY OF LIFE is given in three main pericopes:

> James, a servant of God and of the Lord Jesus Christ, To the Twelve tribes in the Dispersion: Greeting. Count it all joy, my brethren, when you meet various trials, for you know that the testing of your faith produces steadfastness. And let steadfastness have its…full effect, that you may be perfect and complete, lacking in nothing. If any of you lacks wisdom, let him ask generously and without reproaching, and it will be given him. But let him ask in faith, with no doubting, for he who doubts is like a wave of the sea that is driven and tossed by the wind. For that person must not suppose that a doubleminded man, unstable in all his ways, will receive anything from the Lord.
> (James 1:2-8)

The opening passage announces an akedic theology of history as the author links the recipients of the letter (the twelve scattered tribes of Israel) to the history of those persecuted for the divine WAY and NAME:

> Count it all joy ...when you undergo various trials (1:2) for this gentle (exemplary) endurance strengthens faith in patience.

Faith is thus connected to persecution and therefore to commandment obedience as this is the source of the fury of the persecution.

> Blessed are those who are persecuted for righteousness sake...
> (Matthew 5:10)

Faith, in Jewish Christianity, is never disjoined from good works. The dynamics of salvation are repentance for misdirection—*METANOIA*—the change of mind, heart and direction, then righteous action to verify resurrection and new direction.

The 'Formula of Joy' affirms that the deepest contentment (*XAPAN*) comes when faith tested, triumphs. The direct allusion to Abraham/Isaac is clear. The persecution being experienced is the direct result of hearing command and keeping faith. When Abraham or Job was tested, God's faith prevailed as righteousness. Israel in the wilderness fails in faith. To stay with and continue on in God involves not only not denying, forsaking, defaming or negating God but in living out THE WAY. Faith entails persevering in believing and doing THE WAY. That Confession and life-manner will always stir up rage and rejection from the unbeliever and the unethical-from authorities and antagonists. In a sequence of active nounsreminiscent of the Beatitudes in the Sermon on the Mount—characteristics of the "good life" are sketched:

TESTING>>>>>PATIENT

ENDURANCE>>>>>PERFECTION (v. 4)

The person who is perfect (*TELEION*) has been brought to completion of life's potential by the indwelling action of God yielding good works. "Wisdom," in its biblical meaning, is the free and joyous living of the law. Virtue, therefore, is the gift received when temptation (trial) is successfully confronted.

> The law of the Lord is perfect, reviving the soul:
> The testimony of the Lord is sure, making wise the simple.
> The commandment of the Lord is pure, enlightening the eyes.
> The fear of the Lord is clean, enduring forever:
> The judgements of the Lord are true and righteous altogether.
> (Psalm 19)

101

The connection of persecution, perfection and performance of law is vital to James.

> My brethren, show no partiality as you hold the faith of our Lord Jesus Christ, the Lord of glory. For if a man with gold rings and fine clothing comes into your assembly, and a poor man in shabby clothing ….also comes in, and you pay attention to the one who wears the fine clothing and say, "have a seat here, please," while you say to the poor man, "Stand there," or, "sit at my feet," have you not made distinctions among yourselves, and become judges with evil thoughts? Listen, my beloved brethren…. Has not God chosen those who are poor in the world to be rich in faith and heirs of the kingdom which he has promised to those who love him? But you have dishonored the poor man. Is it not the rich who oppress you, is it not they who blaspheme the honorable name which was invoked over you? If you really fulfill the royal law, according to the scripture, "you shall love your neighbor as yourself," you … do well. But if you show partiality, you commit sin, and are convicted by the law as transgressors. For whoever keeps the whole law but fails in one point has become guilty of all of it. For he who said, "Do …. not commit adultery," said also, "Do not kill." If you do not commit adultery but do kill, you have become a transgressor of the law. So speak and so act as those who are to be judged under the law of liberty. For judgment is without mercy to one who ha shown no mercy; yet mercy triumphs over judgment.
> (James 2:1-13)

The logic and movement of the moral life continues:

- Wisdom contours the moral life toward equity (1-4).
- God has chosen the poor of the world to be rich in faith (5).
- The rich persecute the world (6).
- This injustice is blasphemy and breach of the "ROYAL LAW" (8).
- In divine demand for perfection a single breach violates the entire law (9 ff).

This last cabbalistic notion verifies the biblical/Pauline thread which affirms that… "all have sinned and come short" (Romans) and that "none is righteous" (Psalm 14). James contends that justice and mercy toward the poor is a measure of compliance with the entire law. Here is where 'hearing' and 'doing' the law usually part company. The law of love (Royal Law, Law of Freedom) superinscribes both the Godward imperatives (no disbelief, idolatry, defamation) and the Humanward imperatives (no killing, immorality, lying, stealing, coveting). All are gathered together into one indissoluble structure in the mythical-wisdom text,

> …who offends in one point of the law, violates all (10).

How is this pericope instructive of an akedic lifestyle? As we have shown at the outset, salvation and social justice are inextricably interwoven. In sacrifice,

Isaac is called on to bear the weight of death-consequence required by humanity's breach of the Royal Law. But not only death but life is embedded in the sacrificial act. Isaac also carries on his tree—humanity's proleptic redemption, the seed of the future—the seal of the protopromise to Abraham. In this concentration of the vicarious act that is victory for humanity, victim becomes victor. In an akedic hermeneutic Jesus bears *peccata mundi*. The Cross in this sense is the ultimate fulfillment of the Law. Obedience unto death of the Beloved Son is requisite unto humanity's resurrection and life. Only thus is righteousness fulfilled, the law renewed and new resurrection life made possible. Our rightful response to this 'wondrous love' is to love and serve the poor.

Two elements of this pericope have particular akedic bearing: God's bias toward the poor and condemnation of the violence of the rich. Abraham abandons all estate, prosperity and progeny—all future and heritage—to offer Isaac. He accepts the ultimate poverty of giving over his only long-awaited, only begotten, dearly beloved Son. God favors and rewards this relinquishment. As a human act, it offers an ultimate *mimesis* of the God whose very nature is to give and give-over. Secondly, as de Vaux has shown, child-sacrifice is an indulgence of the affluent in the ancient world, where the rich sought to deflect the divine wrath from the guilt of their acquisitiveness and its attendant violence. As with the primal sacrificial act of Cain and Abel (Genesis 4) God condemns the guilt sacrifice and honors the simple sacrifice of the pure heart. The two akedic commands therefore commend the poor and condemn the rich:

> Take your only son,
> Do not lay a hand on the boy,
> (Genesis 22)

The paradoxical yield of akedic ethics is therefore a summons to relinquish wealth with its commensurate demands for power and control in order to become truly rich and free. We are called to release the oppressed (break their chains) by chaining ourselves in service to the poor. To paraphrase Luther, it calls us to be "perfectly free Lords" and "perfectly dutiful servants of all." This is the twofold impulse of Akedah.

> Who is wise and understanding among you? By his good life let him show his works in the meekness of wisdom. But if you have bitter jealousy and selfish ambition in your hearts, do not boast and be false to the truth. This wisdom is not such as comes down from above, but is earthly, unspiritual, devilish. For where jealousy and selfish ambition exist, there will be disorder and every vile practice. But the wisdom from above is first pure, then peaceable, gentle, open to reason, full of mercy and good fruits, without uncertainty of insincerity. And the harvest of righteousness is sown in peace by those who make peace.
> (James 3:13-18)

The posture of being bent down in sacrificial worship is the essence of wisdom. *COHEN*, the Hebrew word for Priest, is one who bends down in identification with the poor and needy (*ANAWIM*) in order to lift up the people. The God of wisdom is the prophetic God who in justice "casts down the mighty and elevates the lowly" (I Samuel 2:7-8, Luke 1:48 ff.).

Abraham's offering of Isaac affirms the decalogic offering of one's life to God and to the neighbor. The wisdom ethics of James is similar to that imbedded in the Qumran community. Three snares must be avoided: riches, impurity, and idolatry. Three modes of life are commended: simplicity, integrity, and faith through justice. This is the extracted essence of the DECALOGUE. This is akedic lifestyle.

Akedah in Contemporary Philosophy

We must now draw this part of our discussion to a close by relating its content to contemporary issues. As I complete this study while on study leave in Paris, I ponder a nineteenth century fresco by H. Flandrin, circa 1840, a diptych on the central nave-arch of the 11th century Romanesque Paris church, St. Germain-de-Près. This was the congregation of Le Fevre d'Etaples, the great forerunner of Jean Calvin. The couplet theme is quite common in European art from the Middle Ages on. Here, as on the fresco on which Luther meditated at *Schlosskirche,* Wittenberg, the Akedah and the CROSS OF CHRIST are juxtaposed side by side. The great medieval monastery of St.Germain was considerably diminished in the Revolution, although the violation was not as complete as in Notre Dame de Paris where the "mountain of reason" was built over the altar. I use this diptych against the background of violent revolution that created modernity to review a sequence of great modern French thinkers who variously construe the meaning of Akedah for our time. Camus and Girard, Derrida and Levinas, represent those who have addressed the spiritual/moral/intellectual crisis of modernity as we struggle with human freedom and responsibility and seek to hear the ever-obscure divine voice.

Camus

Albert Camus searches for the "hero" amid existential anguish, the tribulation of freedom, moral tragedy and the absurd. Like Kierkegaard, he elevates existence to the ultimate category of reality, while unlike the Dane, he suspends the question of God. Until just this year with the publication of ALBERT CAMUS AND THE MINISTER by Howard Mumma at the American Church, Paris, we have known little of Camus' spiritual pilgrimage. The essay by Rene Girard, "Camus' Stranger Retried"[51] focuses even more on Camus akedic reflection seeking to decipher the Hero, sacrifice, violence and the search for resolution of the moral life.

L'Étranger is not an evil man, merely numb and unaffected. He doesn't cry at his mother's funeral but rather views it with detachment as he does a film the

---

[51] Harold Bloom, ed., *Albert Camus. Modern Critical Views.* (New York: Chelsea House, 1989).

next day. His heroism is neither courage or faith but victimization before a cruel legal system. The command of righteousness and necessity embodied in the law crushes him in the same way that Javert hounds Jean Val Jean in LES MISÉRABLES. The tragedy of Meursault, a boring *petit bourgeois*, is an accidental murder that, as with so many, he stumbles into! Like Abraham he didn't deserve this, he didn't will the violence. In Girard's view a more ubiquitous and perennial violence, one which supercedes human will, even thought, victimizes man. A kind of *Fatum* presides over our human lives bringing not only our heroism but our non-engagement to a tangled calamity. Camus' treatment of "Hero" in THE STRANGER as in Dr. Rieux in THE PLAGUE deals with the two possible notions of temptation. The Greek tragic view sees the vice of circumstance crushing the proud, yes, but also the supposedly innocent—the bystander. Temptation in a Hebraic perspective (evocative of culpability) is found in the provocative discussion in the book of Jesus' brother James.

> ...do not say I am tempted by God (or fate, or the system)
> ...God cannot be tempted by evil and He tempts no one
> ...temptation comes when we are drawn away in lust, in enticement
> (James 1:13, 14)

Even Camus acknowledges duty and complicity. In the famous shooting scene Meursault confesses, "all I had to do was turn, walk away...but I fired four shots more into the inert body...and each was another loud, fateful rap on the door of my undoing" (p.3).

Camus' free and just man (e.g. Dr. Rieux in *La Peste*) is in accord with the Akedic vision. He ventures into the unknown. He takes the risk of decision and responsibility. He bears vicariously both the violence and the thoughtlessness of the system (the fallen world), he hears the voice of command and consciousness. He follows or flees. As he offered in his creed at the Nobel Prize acceptance speech, "freedom (love) is not to withdraw but to engage the other."

Girard

René Girard, like Camus, lifts the archetype of Abraham/Isaac up to the light of anthropological scrutiny. Drawing on Freud and Levi-Strauss, he deals with the crisis addressed by Delaney where intrafamilial violence erupts in parricide or infanticide as part of the malevolence of desire. Girard launches his classic *VIOLENCE AND THE SACRED*[52] with a discussion of Akedah. He notes how in primitive sacrifice the complicated *equivoce* is enacted where the sacred one must be killed, and that one is sacred because he is to be killed. He then posits a sacred source to the very impulse to sacrifice, like Meursault in Camus' *THE STRANGER*, the sacrifice is given a kind of excuse, an indifference. In

---

[52] Girard, René, *Violence and the Sacred*. (Baltimore: Johns Hopkins University Press, 1972).

offering the victim one extends in this suspension of the ethical (Kierkegaard) the right to substitute a surrogate victim.

In the even more primitive Akedah in Genesis 4, Cain's plant sacrifice is rejected in favor of Abel's succulent ram. Girard conjectures that the tale speaks of the necessity and tragedy of the vehicle of the vicar, of substitutionary sacrifice. He notes that in the Islamic story of Akedah, the ram delivered to rescue Isaac is the very one sacrificed by Abel, for his offering. Girard sees these archetypal stories as illustrative of a social situation where violence is generally muted and sublimated by subtle forms of sacrifice (e.g. scapegoating, class denigration) so as to sustain social functions, such as survival. The Darwinist distortion of the survival instinct animates the human belief/action that life is a process "of eat or be eaten" thus setting in motion the perpetual sacrifice of some (e.g. foreign workers procuring starvation-wages) so that our life here flourishes.

The evil of "unworthy sacrifice" must be redeemed by "worthy sacrifice." The sacred for Girard is not the commanding, justice-demanding, evil disrupting force that Abraham hears as first among humans and Jesus (and Socrates) obey as they resolutely go to the altar of public and religious iniquity. His "sacred" is the enforcement of stability and status quo. The sacred is that oppressive force identified by Freud, Marx and Nietzsche as the very antithesis of human freedom and good. Girard wrongly identifies the sacred with social prejudices and conformity systems. These are not THE SACRED. The sacred is persistently opposed to, persistently overturning, these idolatrous and immoral structures.

The *SACER* in Roman culture is not the privileged "destroyer" of persons. He is the "accursed," the one who must be done in or "run out" so that popular indulgence and immorality can go its merry way. The expulsion or execution of SACER is necessary to obliterate the presence of the sacred from human society so that she may live unperturbed in injustice.

Commenting on Girard's insight that ancient sacrifice "feeds" the destructive violence of people into the gods so that stability and fecundity are purchased, Richard Mouw resorts to "the free sacrifice that occurred at Calvary" where the problem of human violence can only be solved by having our violence taken up" into the life of the triune God, to be transformed there into something good that is then given back to us as a gift."

Akedah, as Girard would rightly conclude in his Jansenist philosophy, is the intrusion of the good will and demand of God into the resistant human community. It first signals what the prophet Micah eventually intuits in his Akedah, that the Divine abhors our sacrifices and demands justice.

...with what offering shall I come before the Lord

106

...with ten thousand rivers of oil
...with my first-born for my transgressions
...He has shown you what is good...he requires you to
...do justice, love mercy and walk humbly with your God.
(Micah 6:6-8)

Derrida

In his essay "La Pharmacie de Platon,"[53] Jacques Derrida alludes to the practice in Plato's Athens where a scapegoat (*PHARMAKOS*), a surrogate victim, kept on hand for calamities such as plague (Camus), famine, foreign invasion, or internal dissension, was led through the streets of Athens before his execution. Referring to Plato's ascription of the Sophists as (*PHARMAKON*—poison) and Socrates as (*PHARMAKON*—remedy) Derrida affirms the classic cleansing and healing role of philosophy in expelling error and injustice not only in the violent confrontation of clear thought and precise language (Socrates to Nietzsche), but in the concrete life witness of a "good person."

Derrida and the classic philosophical heritage deliteralizes the historical events of Abraham/Isaac and Jesus/Golgotha in favor of a presentation of the death and transfiguration accessible to persons as error and violence yield sway to truth and justice in one's thought and action and speech.

Derrida on Death

The postmodernist, deconstructionist agenda is a kind of Akedah. The lurid physicality of human arrogance and violence preserved in ancient myths and conserved in classical systems of reality doctrine (including religion) must be sacrificed at the altar of reason, critical language and unflinching demythologized honesty. Only thus are humans freed from the oppression of untrue systems of thought and violent manners of behavior. Freud, Marx and Nietzsche are invoked as martyrs to the manias of modernity with its authenticity-obliterating ideas and its complicity with oppression.

Derrida's most masterful Akedah essay is chapter 3 of THE GIFT OF DEATH.[54] The chapter is inspired by Kierkegaard's *FEAR AND TREMBLING*. Derrida proclaims the most fundamental human experience to be that of the *MYSTERIUM TREMENDUM* where the overwhelming "gift of infinite love" touches the finite being of the person causing him to tremble. Exegeting Paul's letter to Phillipians 2:12,13 he relates this response of being to *Mysterium Tremendum* in terms of 1) "working out" the ethical life in the presence of numbing silence and temptation that takes one to the verge of hell and 2) in the prospect of "giving over one to death," an analogue of the "gift of death" of Akedah.

---

[53] Derrida, Jacques, *La Dessemination*. (Paris, 1972), pp. 71-197.
[54] Derrida, Jacques, *Donner la Mort*. (Chicago: University of Chicago Press, 1995), part of the larger *L'Ethique du Don*.

Like Levinas, Derrida stresses the intertwining of command, temptation, absence and presence under the symbol of Akedah where the "totally other" (*"tout autre"*) commands the ultimately cruel deed ("offer the life of your beloved") to put his faith to work, to give over to death. Derrida is more favorably taken by Kierkegaard than is Levinas. The phenomenon of faith is an equivalent good to ethics. He acknowledges the power of image where in all of life "I sacrifice to the other... everyone being sacrificed to everyone else in this land of Moriah that is our habitat every second of every day." [55]

Derrida concludes this chapter with the moving passage toward the end of Kierkegaard's *FEAR AND TREMBLING*:

> ...there was no one who could understand Abraham. And yet what did he achieve? He remained true to his love. But anyone who loves God needs no tears, no admiration; he forgets the suffering in the love. Indeed, so completely has he forgotten it that there would not be the slightest trace of his suffering left if God himself did not remember it, for he sees in secret and recognizes distress and counts the tears and forgets nothing. Thus either there is a paradox that the single individual stands in an absolute relation to the absolute, or Abraham is lost. [56]

Levinas

Of the circle of important French intellectuals of the modern era the one most amenable to our thesis is Emmanuel Levinas. In introducing a philosophy of transcendence, he gives room in recent critical thought to the great line of philosophical thought stretching to Plato but accenting thinkers influenced by Akedah such as Halevy, Pascal and Kierkegaard.

Levinas offers a human philosophy with kinship to biblical and akedic thought by agreeing with Plato that the essence of transcendence is the "Good," the "Ethical." Taking this theme into Kierkegaard and twentieth century existentialists like Camus, he finds the prompting of the "good" (which now is also the true) in the demand or the command that the other (*AUTRUI*) makes upon me. This is the genius of responsibility that is the essence of humanity. Levinas also picks up early on the Abrahamic theme of violence as it is developed in thinkers like Girard and Derrida.[57] Violence has several akedic meanings. It first signals the perturbation of conscience or consciousness as the divine command (presence) erupts in the mind and soul. It also causes the awareness of "the other" to displace self-protection and self-interest. Finally it allows the demand of transcendence (the God of Abraham, Isaac and Jacob: Pascal) to intrude love into the will, sublimating the dangerous expressions of desire.

---

[55] Ibid., p. 69.

[56] Kierkegaard, *Fear and Trembling*, p. 81.

[57] Levinas, Emmanuel, "Violence and Metaphysics" in *Writing and Difference*. (Chicago: University of Chicago Press, 1978).

In two sections of a salient essay, "God and Philosophy,"[58] he directly alludes to Akedah. He first contends that at the very heart of consciousness is emotion or anxiety which "upsets imperturbability and starts 'fear and trembling' before the sacred."[59] Transcendence enters immanence, rupturing subjective lock in terms of presence or command, (see *LIBERTE ET COMMANDEMENT*). The INFINITE changes our consciousness because of its two meanings: 1) "non"—it is the contradiction of everything finite cf. [C-1— "no other gods"] and, 2) "within"—it becomes reality, not just concept or projection.

The idea of the infinite is then "taken up as love."[60] This recalls Geza Vermes' notion that the heart of the struggle as Akedah seeks to decipher divine and human meaning is to affirm that God is love and that love is the peculiar essence of human destiny. In a moving passage Levinas seems to offer direct allusion to Akedah. Speaking of the "trauma of awakening" when transcendent presence comes within us as the demand of "The Other," he writes of its unprecedented wonder and terror:

> This putting in (the finite presence into Being) without a corresponding recollecting devastates its site like a devouring fire, catastrophing its site (Micah 1:3-4)...It is a dazzling where the eye takes in more than it can hold, an igniting of the skin which touches and does not touch (*touche pas*) what is beyond the graspable and burns[61]

The passage recalls for Levinas the torching theophany of Abraham (Genesis 18:27, interceding for Sodom) and Moses' self-dissolution (Exodus 16:7). We conclude again with the Ralph Vaughn Williams akedic hymn:

> Come down o love divine, seek show this soul of mine
> and visit it thy Holy flame bestowing...
> O let it freely burn, till earthly passions turn to dust and
> ashes in its heat consuming.[62]

We have set the stage for a detailed explication of the Jewish substance of Christian, then Muslim, Theology and Ethics. To this we now proceed with a review of Way, Worship and War. We have shown the inextricability of ethics and salvation (faith) in the Abrahamic heritage. We now need a fine-grained analysis of the moral life to verify and amplify that vital connection.

---

[58] Levinas, Emmanuel, *Basic Philosophical Writings*. (Bloomington, IN, 1996).
[59] Ibid., p. 173.
[60] Ibid., p. 175.
[61] Ibid., p. 139.
[62] DOWN AMPNEY, 1906, words by Bianco da Siena, d. 1434.

Part II. Way: The Decalogue and Ethics

Introduction

> "Your law is perfect,
>   enlivening the soul."
>   Psalm 19

I invite you to explore with me an ethical system structured on the Ten Commandments. When the tribes of Israel converged on SHECHEM for covenant renewal, when Jesus preached on the Mount or conversed with the rich young man about eternal life or when the Qumran teachers wore their phylacteries inscribed with the ten words and when Iranian Muslims kneel at Mosque for Moral Instruction, inculcation and inspiration, we are introduced to various attempts to comprehend and promulgate the broad ethical structure of life. This moral structure would be summarized by that Teacher, by John his anticipator and Paul his annunciator as the synthetic love commandment. All three died for this righteousness. Though the world cannot abide its radiance, the light of its right will never go out. When we today search for meaning and wholesomeness in our sexuality, when we seek to be responsible parents of children and children of parents, when we make life or death, business or vocational decisions, when nations decide for war or peace, or adjudicate war crimes or peace treaties, we probe for that same fundamental structure. Theology begins with this search for an authentically and fully human responsibility in the world. If not death awareness, then moral awareness may be the spring of religion. An ethical reality is found at the historic roots of Godconsciousness among all the world's peoples. Some discrepancy between life as it has become and what life is meant to be is at the source of doctrines like creation and fall, redemption and sanctification. Ethics, in this sense, anticipates theology. I begin this part of our reclamation of Judaism into a Christian framework by relating this wisdom to a still semi-nomadic—now modern—Islam, and by laying a structure of ethical theology in scripture, tradition, and the contemporary world. I suggest that the Ten Commandments provide a sound and comprehensive picture of morality adequate to guide contemporary morality and to ground law, moral philosophy, and public policy. To establish that case, I will review recent scholarship on the Decalogue that shows its ethical authenticity and applicability. I will first reason this case by reviewing the 1) nature, 2) history, and 3) ethical implication of the Decalogue.

My work here is influenced by the searching study of Paul Lehmann, *Decalogue and a Human Future*,[63] the completion of his theological ethics. His book, grounded in Luther's Larger Catechism, applied those insights to contemporary morality. My point of entry into the history of ethics will be the Renaissance-Reformation in France. That ethos, along with the German Reformed (Heidelberg Catechism of 1562), Scottish (Scots Confession of 1560), and English Puritan (Westminster Confession of 1649) constitutes my own ecclesial-

---

[63] Paul Lehmann, *Decalogue and a Human Future* (Grand Rapids: Eerdmans, 1995).

ethical heritage and one that has dynamically shaped not only western history but also non-western history (e.g., South Africa, South Korea). I am especially intrigued by the juncture of personal and political theology and ethics in the crucial period when Bucer and Calvin collaborated in Strasbourg (*1538-1541*). In all I seek to consult Jewish and Muslim sources to effect the rapprochement of our broader project. Where filaments of Judaism survive in Christendom, as at Basel, Switzerland, with its exemplary resistance to anti-Semitism in both parochial and public life, examples of our envisioned partnership are evident.

The ethical substance of the Decalogue is meditated to modern experience through traditions of moral initiation and instruction such as Hebrew school and bar and bat mitzvah, Catholic, Orthodox and Protestant catechesis and Muslim learning. The Decalogue's ethical wisdom is also embedded in the laws of nations, charters of human rights, and international law. It is embodied in humanistic philosophy in thinkers as diverse as Kant and Mill, Habermas and Derrida. I have come to believe, as I have learned from my colleague, Michael Perry at Northwestern University, now Wake Forest, that all public ethics are finally grounded in religious and moral ultimacies and values and that secular philosophy or syncretistic morality is not adequate to undergird a believable and workable public ethic. So I will try in this work to refresh these biblical springs, clear away the debris, and watch if the flow can again nourish our moral wasteland.

As I have written this book I have visited in some depth three societies: Greece, Turkey, and Israel. These nations along with Italy and Syria are the geographical settings of the bible. In this study I seek to seriously revisit biblical ethics. These three peoples also struggle today to express a religiously grounded public ethic.

Together with Armenia, Greece is a fascinating example of a nationstate seeking to live out a Byzantine-Orthodox public ethic. Turkey is seeking to create an Islamic state, albeit European and secular at the same time. Israel, in the throes of agonizing conflict, seeks the same kind of rapprochement between Judaic-Orthodoxy, secularpluralism, and concord with Palestinian Muslims and Christians.

This biblical and contemporaneous probe of three lands and my citizenship in America colors this inquiry. Following some introductory reflections, the Decalogue will be explored in its nature, history, and implication. We will finally explore, *ad seriatum*, the Ten Commandments in their biblical, historical, and contemporary relevance.

The Nature of the Decalogue
In the first ten days of the German advance into Poland, onslaughts against unarmed, defenseless civilians were carried out in more than a hundred towns and villages. In the city of Czestochowa, home of thirty thousand Jews, 180 Jews were shot on September 4, "Bloody Monday." At the village of Widawa,

home of one hundred Jewish families, the Germans ordered the rabbi, Abraham Mordechai Morocco, to burn the Holy books. He refused, whereupon they burned him, with the Scrolls of the Law in his hands.[64]

> And behold, one came up to him saying, 'Teacher, what good deed must I do, to have eternal life?' And he said to him, 'Why do you ask me about what is good? One there is who is good. If you would enter life, keep the Commandments.' He said to him, 'Which?' And Jesus said, 'You shall not kill, You shall not commit adultery, You shall not steal, You shall not bear false witness, Honor your father and mother, and, You shall love your neighbor as yourself.' The young man said to him, 'All these things I have observed; what do I still lack?' Jesus said to him, 'If you would be perfect, go, sell what you possess and give to the poor, and you will have treasure in heaven; and come, follow me.' When the young man heard this he went away sorrowful; for he had great possessions
> (Matthew 19: 16-22).[65]

> Six hundred and thirteen commandments were given to Moses...David came and reduced them to eleven. For it is written: *A Psalm of David. O Lord, who shall sojourn in thy tent? Who shall dwell on thy holy hill? (1) He who walks blamelessly, (2) and does what is right, (3) and speaks truth from his heart; (4) who does not slander with his tongue, (5) and does no evil to his friend, (6) nor takes up a reproach against his neighbor; (7) in whose eyes a reprobate is despised, (8) but who honors those who fear the Lord; (9) who swears to his own hurt and does not change; (10) who does not lend his money at interest, (11) and does not take bribe against the innocent. He who does these things shall never be moved (Ps. 15.1-5)...*Isaiah came and reduced them to six, for it is written: *(1) He who walks righteously (2) and speaks uprightly; (3) he who despises the gain of oppressions, (4) who shakes his hands, lest they hold a bribe, (5) who stops his ears from hearing of bloodshed, (6) and shuts his eyes from looking upon evil (Isa. 33.15)* . . Micah came and reduced them to three,for it is written: *He has shown you, O man, what is good; and what the Lord require of you but (1) to do justice, (2) and to love kindness, (3) and to walk humbly with your God (Micah 6.8)...*Isaiah came again and reduced them to two, for it is written: *Thus says the Lord: (1) Keep justice (2) and do righteousness (Isa. 56.1). Amos came and reduced them to one, for it is written: For thus says the Lord to the house of Israel: (1) Seek me and live*
> *(Amos 5:4).*[66]

> 'As the father has loved me so have I loved you; abide in my love. If you keep my Commandments, you will abide in my love...'
> (John 15: 9-10).

---

[64] Martin Gilbert, *The Holocaust*. New York: Holt, Rinehart and Winston, 1985, p. 87.

[65] All quotations from the Scriptures are from the Revised Standard Version (RSV: ed. Herbert G. May and Bruce M. Metzger, NY: Oxford University Press, 1962, 1973), unless indicated otherwise.

[66] R. Simlai, *bMakkot,* in Geza Vermes, *The Religion of Jesus the Jew (Minneapolis: Fortress, 1993) 44.*

Therefore one must be subject, not only to avoid God's wrath but also for the sake of conscience. For the same reason you must also pay taxes, for the authorities are representatives of God, attending to this very thing. Pay all of them their dues, taxes to whom taxes are due, revenue to whom revenue is due, respect to whom respect is due, honor to whom honor is due (Romans 13: 1-7). Owe no one anything, except to love one another; for he who loves his neighbor has fulfilled the law. The Commandments, 'You shall not commit adultery, You shall not kill, You shall not steal, You shall not covet,' and any other Commandment, are summed up in this sentence, 'You shall love your neighbor as yourself.' Love does no wrong to a neighbor; therefore love is the fulfilling of the law (Romans 13: 8-10). Besides this you know what hour it is how it is full time for you to wake from sleep. For salvation is nearer to us now than when we first believed; the night is far-gone, the day is at hand. Let us then cast off the works of darkness and put on the armor of light; let us conduct ourselves becomingly as in the day, not in reveling and drunkenness, not in debauchery and licentiousness, not in quarreling and jealousy. But put on the Lord Jesus Christ, and make no provisions for the flesh, to gratify its desires (Romans 13: 11-14).

Legacy

The Ten Commandments sum up or focus God's history with Israel and the world, the purpose of which is to instill God's way with the nations (Psalm 105:45). The Hebrew bible is a literary construction exemplifying the way in which Decalogue violation leads to the calamity of Israel's history and by portent, with the universal history of humankind.

When Ezra and/or the fifth century priests and scribes assemble the Hebrew bible, each of the first books (after Genesis) shows the result of a violation of a particular commandment which, after the sequence of breaks of all commandments, will bring down the house of cards, the failure of the Davidic project and the demise of the national existence of Israel. David Noel Freedman summarizes:

> "The purpose of the author/editor (of the Hebrew bible) was to show how God created Israel to be his people and then formally sealed the relationship through a covenant that was concluded between them at Sinai/Horeb, mediated by Moses, and summarized or epitomized in the Decalogue. Israel's subsequent history could be told in terms of successive violations of the commandments— one by one, book by book, until Israel ran out of options and possibilities and was destroyed as a nation, and its people taken away into captivity."[67]

With Freedman I take a radically serious view of the DECALOGUE. For me it encapsulates our duty to God and to our fellows, the essence of belief and practice, and the conjunction of salvation and social justice. It is a radical doctrine in the etiological and eschatological sense conveying the will of God

---

[67] David Noel Freedman, *The Unity of the Hebrew Bible*, Ann Arbor: University of Michigan Press, 1999, p.39. See especially *The Nine Commandments*, Harper and Row, 2000.

about how our life was meant to be and how it ought to be. Like Kabbalic Judaism and Kieslowski's visual rendition, each command points to all others as each comprehends all and all comprehends each. I believe that Jesus was nurtured in the Second Temple matrix of faith and life and would have daily recited the Shemah and Decalogue. The influence of the Ten Commandments has been lasting and pervasive. Law-keeping and law-breaking has measured human history. Tenacious adherence—even death-grasp all the way to flippant discard—have marked their reception throughout the ages. Yet reminiscence haunts us. Who can forget Rembrandt's illumined brow of Moses in Berlin's Stadtmuseum (looking all like the furious Solzhenitzyn), smashing the tablet; or the cortege of angels surrounding Moses on Ghiberti's great bronze doors on the baptistery of Florence; or William Blake's florid and flowing depiction of the finger etching God in the Scottish National Gallery in Edinburgh? Or Krzysztof Kieslowski's series of films, "The Decalogue"? Or Charlton Heston in Cecil B. DeMille's film? Or the raucous film, "The History of the World," with Mel Brooks as his mosaic self stumbling down the smoke-shrouded mountain, jostling three stone tablets: "I have here 15—" (whoops—smash—one crashes to the ground)—"I have here Ten Commandments." God only knows what we may have missed!

Ten Commandments: *asereth haddebarim, verba decem, eusebian pietas, dexa logion*—ten little words — a perfect ten. For millennia they have grounded duty on their solid direction. Children for ages have established here their bar and bat mitzvahs and confirmations. From earliest teachers, Christian civilization has anchored catechesis, instruction in faith, what Luther in his 1528 sermons saw as our inculcation into humanness, in these salient ten words. From Clement in his second century pedagogy, through Augustine in *De Dekalogue*, to Robert Grosstesta in *De Deum Mandatis,* from Oxford scholars in 1209 to Aquinas in the *Summas*, to Luther and Calvin in their sixteenth-century catechisms, throughout all Christian tradition—the full-orbed theology and ethic for Christians has been anchored in the Ten Commandments and its companion authorities the Lord's Prayer and the Creed. In the Old English Prayer Book, godparents in baptism pledge that "they will chiefly provide that s/he (the child) may learn the Creed, the Lord's Prayer and the Ten Commandments in the vulgar tongue and all the other things which a Christian ought to know and believe to his soul's heart. Until very recently every Anglican Church had engraved on the east wall this three-fold foundation of the Christian faith and life.

With its inimitable word-building construction, the German language reduces the rich tablets literally to ten not-so-succinct words:

> Word one—no other gods—*Fremdgotterverbot*
>
> Word two—no graven images—*Bilderverbot*
>
> Word three—name of the Lord—*Blasphemieverbot*

Word four—Sabbath day—*Sabbatgebot*

Word five—honor mom and dad—*Elterngebot*

Word six—do not kill—*Totungsverbot*

Word seven—do not commit adultery—*Ehebruchsverbot*

Word eight—do not steal—*Diebstahlverbot*

Word nine—do not bear false witness—*Falschzeugnisseverbot*

Word ten—do not covet—*Begehelichkeitsverbot*

DeMille's ten single words are engraved in the Canaanite language, since Hebrew did not yet exist. Stone slabs of Sinai red granite. Today synagogue doors often have the simple ten Hebrew letters.

No documents yet discovered have the blue-robed, bejeweled Moses of a thousand nineteenth century colored church windows with two great slabs bearing the Roman numerals 1-10. Indeed, when the Hexateuch in Numbers 10 speaks of the ark as the Ark of the Covenant, or when Exodus 38 calls the sacred tent "the tabernacle of witness," it is by virtue of those concisely etched plates residing within the vehicle.

Indeed, it is not until our lawless twentieth century that we have dropped this classic architecture of religious instruction. Even a great theologian like Emil Brunner could say that the Ten Commandments offered no concrete ethical instruction to us today. Imagine that, and they're etched in stone! How trenchant and troubling our autonomy had become. Without the binding power of Decalogue, the "pious" redneck can lynch a black man or rape his wife and the baptized Nazi officer can torch the rabbi even with the scroll in hand. And who can forget Judge Moore and his block of granite in the Alabama Courthouse.

The Decalogue has become the moral charter of world civilization. This is especially true as human rights-oriented democracies now flourish in the world, the irresistible cause of and sequel to freedom and economic enterprise. All international agencies of law and human rights, The Hague, The World Parliament, and the global associations in Geneva and Strasbourg cherish this heritage. In particular, the Decalogue is the centerpiece of the ethical theology of Judeo-Christian culture.

The headline texts in this chapter from Christian Gospel and Epistle lift up certain preliminary considerations as we formulate the structure of an ethical theology for our world where the Semitic traditions, Judaism and Islam, are enriched by the Christian movement, which in modern times has circumnavigated the globe. In a subtle, but important point, Crüsemann argues that modern ethics, indebted to the Christian heritage, has distorted the prophetic justice that Torah brings to worldly law by accenting love of neighbor while ignoring love of stranger. The Christian meaning of Decalogue must be examined.[68]

The striving and pious, rich young man approaches Rabbi Jesus just after a series of lessons about the innocent righteousness of children (Matthew 19). "What must I do to achieve eternal life?" he asks. "Follow the Commandments," says the teacher, citing in particular **C-6, -7, -8,- 9**, and **-5**.[69] Then he adds the altruistic particle from the great Levitical summary: "You shall love your neighbor as yourself."(Leviticus 19: 18).

What meaning can we extract from this Gospel moment? First, the Commandments in this compact form are extant and authoritative in Jesus' time and in his messianic consciousness. There is no hint of suspension or replacement. Recent New Testament scholars, E.P. Sanders and Geza Vermes in particular, have recovered this long neglected aspect of Jesus' life and teachings. The Ten Commandments were part of the daily prayers during the second temple period. Both Josephus and Philo report that they were the only "words" proclaimed by God.[70] Word, will and way of God center here. Throughout the apocrypha, pseudepigrapha and Philo the title Son of God is attributed to the righteous one, one who keeps the Decalogue.[71] This law is written indelibly into the moral structure of reality. It proceeds from the very Word of God. Secondly, the commands are sufficiently captured in the law of love that embraces God, neighbor, and self. Finally, and this is a radical elaboration of the ethics of Judaism, code obedience must be anchored in a life of self-abnegation and volitional commitment. "I have followed these from my childhood." "One thing you lack—sell all that you have, give it to the poor, then come and follow me." As we will see in the most vital times of Christian witness, as with Judaism in its noblest moments, faithfulness to the Commandments involves not only nominal strictness to these good rules but also a disposition toward God's way as one is freed from lesser loyalties. The heart given to God is the foundation of ethics.

In the spirit of Beatitudes 1 and 3, James writes: "...God has chosen the poor of this world to be rich in faith...heirs of the kingdom promised to those who love him. In despising the poor...you blaspheme the name in whom you have been called. If you fulfilled the royal law of scripture...you will love your neighbor as yourself...and do well (James 2: 5, 7, 8). The spiritual essence of meeting the thundering God of Sinai on the mountain of Sinai or of the Beatitudes is to meet One moved with concern and compassion toward the poor, One who considers

---

[68] Frank Crüsemann, *The Torah* (Minneapolis: Fortress Press, 1996) 5.

[69] I will refer to the Commandments according to the Reformed list, with the abbreviations C-1 - C-10.

[70] E.P. Sanders, *Jesus The Jesus and Judaism,* 1985; *Jerusalem from Jesus to Mishna,* 1990; Paul, 1991. G. Vermes, *Jesus the Jew,* 1973; *The Gospel of Jesus the Jew,* 1981; *The Religion of Jesus the Jew,* 1992.

[71] G. Vermes, *The Religion of Jesus the Jew,* (Philadelphia: Fortress, 1993) 38.

hatred, hurt and apathy toward the poor itself blasphemy, One who reigns in a kingdom of justice where love is the royal law.

A Jewish legend ties this ethical principle to the Exodus experience. It is said that, once the people had come successfully across the sea of reeds through the miraculous tunnel of escape, the angels looked down and were singing as the Egyptians were swept away and drowned. The Lord, Yahweh, stilled their delight. The dying Egyptians were his children, too, the work of his hands.[72]

Actually, Jesus' conflation of the two imperatives from Hebrew scripture, though novel in text, is traditional in spirit.

> Love the Lord your God with all your heart and soul and mind and
> strength....Love your neighbor as yourself
> (Mark 12:30-31).

When the rabbi sits with his disciples on the mountain of the Beatitudes, his repetitive provisos, "But I say to you" in no sense offer repudiations of or even intensifications of Torah, they were simply warnings against mechanical performance of the moral life and calls to heartfelt and willful adherence to the Way.

What is the nature of this ethical charter that has so mastered the human heart, mind, and will? Here we ask about its character, not about its derivation and influence, which we will examine in the sections to follow. What manner of proclamation, writing, orally recited and silently-memorized word, could so claim and change the world? What sort of message could charter human rights, ground the laws of nations, guide personal behavior and be attributed to the very voice and etching of God? The fundamental nature of the text is *dabar*, divine speech. Natural phenomena—thunder, clouds, smoke—shroud and attend the annunciation. The principles are announced as eternal, as if they had always been valid. They are not creations of Moses' mind, nor are they mere cultural accretions. To relativize or temporalize them is to violate their essential nature. The Kabbalist and mystical traditions of Judaism exert this indelible character by claiming Decalogue or Torah to be coexistent with God before the creation of the world. That created angels would go astray; that the world and humans would be created to counter the fall; that humans in turn would yield to temptation; that they in turn would be redeemed—all this is present...In the beginning...Decalogue words are twice blessed. They assert their claim upon humanity despite our repudiation of them. Incensed by the Golden Calf violation of what even then was presupposed as being understood and binding, Moses pleads for a rewrite. The finger of God accedes in mercy. Now the tablets are given holy home in the Ark of the Covenant, the tent sanctuary at the Shiloh tabernacle and finally, the Jerusalem Temple. By finger or voice, there is the

---

[72] Louis Ginsberg, *Legends of the Jews,* 7 vols., Philadelphia, 1946, 1947.

articulation of divine will in the very midst of God's ineffable yet evocative presence. It seems to say this is word enough, law enough, knowledge enough, presence enough.

Moses is the prime priest—*Cohen*—he pleads humanity up God-ward. He also bends God down human-ward. Priest—*Cohen*— lifts up and draws down. With the power of Michelangelo's "Creation of Humanity" on the Sistine ceiling, the divine finger is proffered to the human reach. God, whose thoughts and ways are not ours, is humanly coerced into forthcoming and communication. Humans, who seemingly prefer to be left alone, are confronted and addressed. A cosmic dialogue across time and eternity, world and God, has been enacted. It will forever be touch and go, often eclipsed, and sometimes radiating the divine reflection.

The biblical believer who would anchor her ethical theology in Decalogue must trace the tradition through a fascinating array of passages. The allusion and counter-allusion, reference and crossreference, runs throughout Scripture. Traces of the Decalogue are found in Torah and Prophets, wisdom and writings, Gospels and Epistles. After the primary "ethical" Decalogue in Deuteronomy 5: 6-18, there is the second primary text, the "primal" Decalogue in Exodus 20: 2-14. The "cultic" Decalogue Exodus 34: 10-26 elaborates and extends the now-embodied tradition toward liturgy, holiness and celebrative purposes. Leviticus 18:6-17 and 18:20 expand the sacral, familial, and sexual bearings of the tradition. Psalm 15 describes the festal setting and Ezekiel 18:5-9 is one of many prophetic utterances that further elucidate the commitment. The reader will want at this point to trace the scriptural legacy that continues into the New Testament with passages such as Matthew 19, John 15, Romans 13. Throughout this book I will rehearse and recall the various appropriations of the Decalogue throughout scripture.

The nature of the Decalogue has been seen as *vox dei*, as an eternal consort to the deity, as natural law, as apodictic (unmediated) utterance, as a societal formulation based on trial-and-error experience. It has stood the test of time and although it has often hardened into harsh legalism violating its intrinsic spirit, it has never been repudiated. My thesis in this study is that it still serves humanity well as an ethical standard for life. It is the light of our life, lamp to our path. It is fully consonant with the grace of Jesus' Gospel. Its nature is evocative. When put to the test, it works. It illumines, guides and inspires. It safeguards, trusts and sustains commitments. It inclines our living toward God, toward neighbor, toward stranger, even enemy, and in sacred stewardship toward the natural world. It is the manner of life that naturally flows when God is your friend.

In the delicate nature of mandate or command, the Commandments reach beyond our natural propensities, challenge us with a transcending possibility, strongly condemn our perversion and injustice, and envision for us optimal individuality and community. Following Paul Lehmann's analysis of Decalogue after Luther's *Grosser Catechismus*, it is a morally descriptive document rather than a condemnatory or juridical one. It sets forth a charter for fulfilled humanity.

History of the Decalogue

The nature and character of this deontological charter for humanity is further clarified as we trace the history, particularly the religious history, of the Decalogue. A good entry point into the story is through the writing of the deuteronomic historians. Well into Hebrew history, centuries after Exodus and conquest, after the monarchy of Saul, David, and Solomon, well into the twilight of the early prophets and the mounting assault of neighboring powers, a renaissance of the law enlivens the common life of Israel. Dates are debated, but it is certainly later than the eighth century prophets and after the fall of the northern kingdoms as Sargon II (721 BCE) conquers Samaria. King Josiah of Judah has invigorated the Hebrew community by his reforms of church and state (II Kings 22 ff.). He was Bar Mitzvah, a son of the covenant, "who did what was good, veering neither to the left or the right" (vs 2). The priest Hilkiah discovers the book of the law in the temple and as it is read to the King, he tears his clothes as he realizes how far wrong he and his people have gone. An intriguing picture! What had been lost or forgotten? Was it like the billing records of Arkansas legal transactions that suddenly appeared in the residential rooms of the Clinton White House? Was it like the Nixon tapes? Whatever happened, it jarred and renewed conscience. Something that had been lost was now remembered. As when Ezra reads the law to those returned from the exile at the gates of the old city in Nehemiah 8, Life was recalled to its rightful loyalty. It was a shattering experience; the foundations shake. The people are redrawn to the rudiments and reestablished on the fundaments of divine reality.

Frank Crüsemann has ventured to trace in Israel's history the pathway of the Decalogue's development within the broader structure of law. Theologically speaking, he contends that we find an inseparable conjunction of command and promise, covenant and obligation, law and gospel in the biblical tradition. Rejecting the misconstrual of the Paul-Luther tradition, Crüsemann affirms with Karl Barth that Torah (Decalogue) is integral to faith and that "law is the form of the Gospel." Only as this rich ethical tradition is recovered can we hope to address moral crises such as third-world debt, settlement of refugees, establishment of human rights, prosecution of war crimes or creation of ecological law. Perdurance of judgment and forgiveness engendering condemnation yet negotiation is the divine way with humanity. From the shadowy origins of the Decalogue in Abrahamic wandering, empirically refined in enforced labor in Egypt, in Exodus, into precise formulation in Mosaic guidance and at Sinai, it is the Palestinian settlement and the historical crisis of Northern and Southern Kingdom history that finally gives decisive shape to the ethical tradition. The severe and serene monotheism of the Northern Kingdom joins with the Judean awareness of ancient near-eastern law in the crisis of the fall of the north and the Josiahan reform in the south in the eighth and seventh

121

centuries. Gathered from these two sources in the memorial consciousness of Israel, the akedic and mountain-of-God tradition, as these recall Moses' memory and the human justice customs at the city-gate tradition where human conflicts are mediated, the binding recollections of the people of Israel are melded into an ethical heritage for the ages.

From this critical axis-time the history winds backwards and forwards. The Decalogue tradition can be traced on the following line:

Old oriental precursors

Patriarchal roots

Sinai

Confederate judges

Prophetic period

Deuteronomic reform

Priestly period

Qumran

John the Baptist

Jesus

Early Church

Old Oriental Precursors

Since the dawn of civilization in Africa, Northern Arabia and the Western Orient, a cultural, juridical and religious development had occurred that laid the groundwork for the Decalogue. When people evolved from hunter-gatherer migrants and began to live in cities, make economic transactions, establish properties, adjudicate interests and differences, not long after the withdrawal of the last ice age (c. 10,000 BCE), codes and customs arose which presaged the Hebrew Decalogue. In the Babylonian *Surpu*, we find a list of incantations chanted in catechetical form by oracle priests:

- Has he done injury to a god or goddess?
- Has he dishonored his father or mother?
- Has he used false weights?
- Has he accepted unjust recompense?
- Has he gone into his neighbor's house?
- Has he drawn near to his neighbor's wife?[73]

---

[73]H. Grossman. *Altorientalische Texte zum alten Testament* Second Edition, 1926, p. 324ff.

Excretory texts from Egypt display in similar ways a catalogue of divine-human expectations for the life of justice that were likely extant perhaps as early as 5,000 BCE. The funerary texts of the Egyptian Book of the Dead show striking similarity to the Decalogue, even to the Matthew version of Jesus' apocalyptic rendition (Matthew 25).

> Then the King will say to those on his right hand, come blessed of my father, take your place in the kingdom prepared for you from the foundations of the world for:

- I was hungry and you gave me food
- I was thirsty and you gave me drink
- I was a stranger and you welcomed me
- I was naked and you clothed me
- I was sick and you came to me
- I was in prison and you visited me
  Matthew 25:34-36

Hittite treaties of the second millennium BCE and Hammurabi's law code (circa 1800 BCE) show affinity to the Decalogue. The Hittite and other ancient Suzerain treaties exhibit a similar format: a historical preamble, conditions of covenant (*imperativa* and *prohibitiva*), and a covenant pledge or oath. The resemblance is striking:

- I am the Lord your God who led you out of Egypt
- You shall have no other Gods...
- You shall serve the Lord and swear by his name
  Deuteronomy 6:13

Records of ancient Mari negotiations and transactions, like Hammurabi's exquisite code of justice, set clear precedents for the Decalogue.

Patriarchs

In the time of the Patriarchs, other precursors are found. For example, the neighbors of Abraham and the nascent Hapiru, including the Midianites and Kennites, practiced elaborate sabbatarian rhythms that involved farming, animal herding, mining, and occasionally the banking of the blacksmith fires. All these rituals portend norms in the Decalogue.

Sinai

Obviously, the Sinai experience is historically formative to the Decalogue. The Hebrew people have already coalesced into a somewhat cohesive religious, even ethnic, community. They have been forged into a common identity by coerced labor and by the overwhelming and constitutive experience of the Exodus. Now in the Sinai desert, under the leadership of Moses, as the people enact an ancient "mountain of the gods" theophany, entailing spiritual and moral reconstitution, they are further defined and destined in a way that will forever mark their existence.

In Martin Buber's brilliant exposition of *"Die Worte Auf Den Tafel"* in his epic study of *Moses*, he critiques Goethe's Strasbourg theses (1773), which noted the "cultic" context of Exodus 34 and led Goethe to affirm a provincial, parochial and ultimately Christian interpretation of the Decalogue.[74] Buber sees the historical encounter at Sinai as decisive and universally significant. The world populace heretofore and forever after is epitomized and represented in this recently emancipated slave-band, now to be constituted as God's holy people in the world. Here a new humanity is being formed, one that will transfigure universal history towards justice, righteousness and peace. For Buber, the radical meaning of Sinai is a break with the vestiges of Egyptian idolatry and a decisive spiritual and ethical redirection as a God-possessed people. Buber rejects the notion that reigned from Goethe to Wellhausen that we have here an *"Israeltische catechismus."* Nothing so impersonal, provincial and routine, he claims. We have here direct and personal address, the attribution of *"du,"* (thou) to an historic "FEW" who hold in their Abrahamic destiny the universal "MANY". It is a searching, alldemanding, all-gracious encounter.[75]

Sinai, as we will see, is reenacted in Pentecost. It is the festival of Succoth. The ten tongues of fire descend in the Spirit's wind on the seventy. Just as a portion of His Spirit is given to Moses' seventy charismatic elders who are sub-judges (Deuteronomy 1:16, Numbers 11:16 ff). The decisive theophany of Moses and the people is now reconfirmed in Peter's preaching as Israel's consummate destiny to offer spiritual blessing to the world is fulfilled in the Messiah who died and rose again.

Whether it was a sudden and dramatic awakening or a gradual growth in God-perception, ethical awareness and responsibility, the Decalogue acknowledges that each generation must be taught anew and each person in his or her freedom must personally and communally renew the covenant. There is what Buber, after Kierkegaard, would call the existential moment, the radical break and occasion of insight when all is examined, free choice is demanded, and thereafter everything is different.

As the Israelite people settle down in a new homeland, new historical crises await them. The challenge of alien, corrupting peoples with strange gods and customs requires constant rehearsal, even intensification and exaggeration of its historic ethical constitution. Pagan and idolatrous belief and practice among the

---

[74] Goethe's *Werke Auswahl in 16 Bäden.* Leipzig: Reclams Ausgabe, Vol. 7, 1910, pp. 146-152.
[75] Martin Buber, *Werke* II Band: Köselverlag, Mu☐nchen, 1964, p. 151.

neighbors serve to sharpen and focus Israel's spiritual and ethical charter. This corporate saga of a people is a paradigm of the pilgrimage of each person who will ever live. Morality concerns the one and the many. Deliverance from bondage, disclosure of deity, cleansing from idolatry and immorality, constitution and commission of new humanity — this is living theology. Hebrew iconoclasm introduces a radical new faith into human history. If all impediments are removed, this faith believes, the living God will autonomically become known.

Judges

Roughly at the same period of history, we find an ordering of the common life, a period of judges and civil law, a period of spiritual cult and ordered shaping of moral life styles. Apodictic law yields more to casuistic customs in such times. Judges and "lesser judges" sit at the gate and mediate concrete instances of wrong, injustice and dishonor. In this pre-monarchic period, say 1100 BCE, the code of behavior that is the Decalogue was hammered out, refined and applied in particular cases.

The festivals of this period, especially the festival of New Year and the periodic seventh year renewal, offer occasions for annunciation and recitation of the ethical charter. These seasons of confession, cleansing and recommitment at Shechem, for example, when the confederated tribes gathered for covenant renewal, were times when the Commandment/curses were chanted by the people (Exodus 34). If the sitting pastor/prophet/magistrate worked out particular ramifications of Decalogue for individuals, adversaries or families, the whole people in tribe-transcending solidarity pledged fresh vocation to the divine mandate. Joshua 24, for example, tells the story of this ritual of spiritual and ethical renewal. The act of election and exodus are remembered. The recall from other loves and loyalties is effected. An ardent new beginning is undertaken. Just as the prolonged amnesia of decades, even centuries, was chastened in King Josiah's Deuteronomic reform, so, in this period of judges and tribal festal celebration, six years of wrong-doing and wrong-going were chastened by fresh attention to Decalogue.

Prophets

In one way, the entire prophetic plea is such a recall to faith and rectitude. "Thus says the Lord"— In the prophets of Israel and Judah from the shadowy mists of Samuel in the tenth century, through Amos, Hosea, and the eighth century prophets of Israel, Isaiah in Judah through Jeremiah and Ezekiel before the fall of Jerusalem (587 BCE)— all exert a call to "get it right again." The instruments of remonstrance and renewal are Decalogue, covenant, and whatever broader body of Torah was then extant. Ezekiel 18 is a vision and oracle of the prophet received roughly concurrent with the Babylonian siege of Jerusalem and the region by Nebuchadnezzar and his royal family (587 BCE). The prophecy in turn is an offered vision and oracle to the people that predicts judgment and hope. The oracle is fashioned around the Decalogue and its elaborate ethical substance.

> All souls are mine...the soul that sins shall die (Ezekiel 18: 4) The soul shall live who
>
> -does not lift up his eyes to idols
> -defile his neighbor's wife
> -does not oppress anyone
> -commits no robbery
> -gives bread to the hungry
> -covers the naked with a garment
> -does not exact interest
> -executes justice between people
> (Ezekiel 18: 5-9)

Deuteronomic Reform

During his reign as king of Judah 639-609 BCE (II Kings 22 h.), Josiah recovered the Decalogue and covenant code and ethically renewed the life of the community. The renewal is linked to the prophetic ministry of Jeremiah. The event is shadowy, but apparently the priest Hilkiah "found" the lost book of the law in the Jerusalem Temple. In any case, this second-law-reform was a decisive ethical moment in the history of Israel. The common life of the people of Judah (heirs of now dispersed Israel) is now purified and made just and fair under the guidance of the Decalogue.

Exile/Priests

The most salient period of faith/ethics formulation for the people of Israel and Judah is the exile. The emergence of the priestly and synagogue tradition followed by the restoration, with its attempt to reclaim land and governance along with revived Torah, reinvigorated cult and rebuilt temple, all sought to refocus common life in the Decalogue. The stress of Hellenistic, then Roman, occupation exposes the moral vacuum and strengthens the yearning for an almost forgotten faith and justice. When the temple, land, and cult are in place and the theocratic state and law is established, routine sets in. In periods of exile, persecution, even underground resistance (Judas Maccabeus, c. 160 BCE), we may assume the Decalogue bore a vital witness, sustaining the people through the horrors of death, refugee expulsion and assimilation. It then animated faith and godly virtue through each crisis. The Nash papyrus, the earliest text we have of the Hebrew Bible, has the Decalogue and the Shema recited together (c. 300 BCE?). The Nash papyrus show that normative Judaic culture, by the second century BCE, is guided by piety reflected by the Shemah: "Hear oh Israel—The Lord our God is one..." ("unification of the Name"C-3) and ethics as reflected in the Decalogue. The tumultuous religio-moral crisis that would change human history in the next three centuries exemplified by John the Baptist, Jesus, Peter, the Apostles, and finally Paul would sustain this synergy of piety and morality.

Faith in its very essence contained this way of life and the work of life. The way of Israel now finds its universal destiny in the *Pax Romana*.

The Succoth festival of Booths (Deuteronomy 16:13, 16) or the festival of weeks (Deuteronomy 16: 9-10) was the occasion of celebration of the covenant and receipt of the law. For the Essenes and probably John the Baptist this was the central act of devotion. Jesus comes up to Jerusalem for this festival celebrating the conjunction of piety and morality—of faith and life. (Matthew 9:53, 16:21 Luke 2:41 John 12:12). It becomes the birth time of the church at the Jerusalem Pentecost (Acts 2:1) and Paul hastens back not to miss this central *liturgos* of his people (Acts 20:16, I Corinthians 16:8).

The "Decalogic" meaning of Pentecost, the Christian celebration of receiving the Holy Spirit, contributes to our restoration of the biblical and Judaic grounding of Christian faith and ethics. The truth of the event is conveyed through the vehicle of Jewish mystical numerology. Twelve disciples or tribes, 10 commandments and seventy disciples are involved. The second chapter of Acts is preceded by the reinstitution of the 12 apostles after Judas' preordained betrayal (Acts 1:16).

The full complement of twelve tribes and twelve gates to the Holy city is restored. Now, on the day of Pentecost, the ten words in flames and tongues descend in 7 day portions on the seventy (or 120) evangelists (Luke 10: 17 Acts 1:15). The appropriation of mystical numerology conveys the perfection of the mosaic and Christic covenant. Eden has been renewed, Babel reversed and the focusing from all the nations of a particular people, Israel is now universalized in all the gentiles as Abrahamic destiny is renewed. Let us review this sequence.

John the Baptist and the Law
Recent scholarship has raised the possibility of the Baptist's relation to the Essene community that withdrew to the shores of the Dead Sea as the ultimate confrontation with Rome drew near. The currency of the law in John's ministry is hotly debated. He certainly is the zealous ethicist going to the wall and losing his head by condemning the illicit marriage of Herod, the tetrarch of Galilee. He also pronounced ethical judgment on "all the evil things" that Herod had done (Luke 4:19). Today in Sebastea (Samaria) you can see the ruins of Herod's palace where Salome danced and demanded that John be beheaded. Well authenticated is the rock-pit where he was imprisoned.

I've wondered recently whether John's conversation with the crowds, tax collectors and soldiers (Luke 3:10-14) is not Luke's report of a reprise of the Decalogue:

> share coat and food c.f. Ezekiel 18:4 ff (oracle on Decalogue)
> collect only what is due C-8, -9, -10
> rob no one by violence

no false accusation C-3, C-9
be content with your wages C-8, C-10

As we review the brief notes that the Gospels give us of John's life and ministry we are impressed with the qualities of prophesy and moral teaching, although Matthew and Luke raise the perplexing notion that the "law and prophets" pertained until John and were then superseded by "The Kingdom of God" (Luke 16:16, Matthew 11: 13). John's ministry calls for people to repent (moral regeneration) and enter" The Kingdom" through preaching/repentance as represented as a "violent" entrance (Matthew 11:12, Luke 16:16). He calls "the brood of vipers" who seek "to flee from the wrath to come" and admonished all to "bear fruit worthy of repentance." What repentance and re-centering could he be calling for other than the righteous life of the Decalogue?

When Jesus announces that The Kingdom of God is at hand, as evidenced by the miracles and healings, he is surely showing that eschatological judgment draws near, that we are called into account for our lives and that the time of fruitful ethical responsibility is ready. God's way of life is now evident and prominent and we are to live up to it in both piety (*eusebia*) and performance (*justitia*). The picture emerging to contemporary scholarship of Judaism at the time of Jesus, of James and Jesus' family, of Jewish Christianity and the Essenes, all point to a time of total synthesis of law and Gospel.

Qumran

By the time of Jesus and the Qumran community, we find the body of commandments vital, informative and central. We can safely assume that Jesus was instructed in Decalogue at home and in the synagogue. Much of his brief ministry and his instruction is devoted to recapturing the essence of Decalogue righteousness, of recalling the wayward from apathy, the poor from discouragement, the Pharisees from self-righteousness, the demoralized to morale. His ministry reached out to the complacent and lethargic house of Israel, calling them back to renewed covenant faith, salvation from sins (violations of Decalogue), and righteousness in the walk with God. Recent discoveries disclose that Qumran teachers of righteousness wore phylacteries with the ten words inscribed on the frontal head piece. Decalogue was personal, public and pervasive in the first centuries BCE and CE.

John the Baptist and Jesus himself may have been associated with or come under the influence of the Essenes (Hasidim: Holy Ones). In their disciplined monastic communities, they followed Torah and Decalogue with great rigor. They refused to make any oath in God's name (**C-3, C-9**). Their rituals held in deep reverence the ancient laws. They advocated strict observance of the Sabbath. They were prohibited from making weapons and were profoundly pacifistic (**C-6**). We may wonder at the fate of these communities under Roman assault, especially the Qumran community, as we view the history of neighboring Masada. The tenure of the Qumran community may have been approximately from Judas Maccabeus 140 BCE - Roman Denouement 73 AD. The community reserved the death penalty by 100 Judges for blasphemy (**C-3**) (Josephus). Even in the face of Roman torture, they refused sacrilege, even for the slightest abrogation of the law. The new evidence of Qumran attests to the high importance of Decalogue in first century Judaism and in the ethical consciousness of John the Baptist, Jesus, and Paul.

Jesus and the Law

In a provocative phrase in his letter to the Galatians, Paul takes a deep element of the Jesus tradition and his own gloss: He was born under the law (4:4) to redeem those who were under the law (4:5). Weaving into one affirmation the radical traditionalism and dramatic release of Jesus' rendition of God's Way for Israel and the world, Paul acknowledges the apostolic tradition that Jesus was circumcised, raised devout and observant, before becoming a teacher of Torah. As he will later affirm in the letter (6:2), rather than repudiating the law, Jesus offered the world "the law of Christ." The primitive church of Pentecost believed that Jesus was the Messiah of Israel, and the Savior of the Gentile world. To establish this composite truth, the preacher-evangelist-historians appropriated the Jesus sayings and deeds, the parables and miracles to ground a provincial and universal redemption. The witness of Jesus is entirely resonant with the law.

That Jesus submitted to the baptism of John, that (perhaps is even implicated in the Qumran "teacher of righteousness") he said that not the smallest particle will be omitted from the law (Matthew 5:17) and that he expounded the inner meaning and outer performance of "the way" on Beatitudes Mountain just near the Capernaum base of his Galilean ministry, makes us re-examine the question of Jesus and the law. Can we see in this life and witness something other than what we see through the eyes of Paul, especially Paul through the eyes of Luther? In this section we will be guided by the thought of the great Oxford Jesus Judaists — E. P. Sanders and Geza Vermes.

In two books, *Jewish law from Jesus to the Mishna* (1990, SCM Press: London) and *Jesus and Judaism* (SCM Press, 1985) E. P. Sanders sketches the life and work of Jesus with respect to the law as reported by the Gospel writers. Sanders' views can be summarized as follows:

> He finds a via media between E. Schweizer (Jesus broke law and was
>> killed for it) and G. Vermes (Jesus adhered to law at
>> all points).
> Jesus was more a charismatic prophet (Thiessen) than a
>> charismatic magician-healer (Crossan)
> That Jesus offered the kingdom to sinners ("Those outside
>> law") does not obviate his adherence to law.

"Let the dead bury the dead" is a one time commission to
        discipleship not abrogation of (**C-5**)
Prohibition of divorce (e.g. Matthew 19:3-9) is radical
intensification like the Covenant of Damascus and not
        a departure from (**C-7**).
Jesus recapitulates the intent and content of Sabbath law
            involving no work, but that necessary for life and
            divine service. He detracts from the post second
            temple
tendency to exaggerate and elaborate Sabbath
            commands.
Jesus affirmed plucking grain (Mark 2:23-28) and heals
the
            man with the withered hand (Mark 3:1-6) on the
            Sabbath because the disciples were more than a
            days
            walk from food and it is lawful to "do good"
            (affirm health and life) on the Sabbath.
Food, fasting, and hand washing (purity) and tithe and tax
            laws, though crucial, are beyond the range of the
            Decalogue which is our focus.
Jesus does not transgress blasphemy law (**C-3**) in
            pronouncing forgiveness of sins because it is
            announced
            in the passive "your sins are forgiven" (Mark
            2:5-7).

In responding to the Sanhedrin's interrogation the morning of his crucifixion his response to "are you Christ" is ambiguous, "you say that I am" (Luke 22: 67). Even in Mark and Matthew's stark "I am" there is a question of whether affirmation of being "The Son of God" or "The Christ" is blasphemy.

Jesus affirmed the Shema-Decalogue-Great command couplet or summary (Mark 12:28-34) and firmly advocated Philo's summary of the imperative to love God and humanity. He even affirms the *teffilim (Phylakteria)*, the capsule carrying of the commands, although he cautions against exaggeration (Matthew 23:5).

Speaking from his own Judaism, Vermes insists even more strongly on the nomian (law-grounded) witness of Jesus. The whole affirmation he claims is gathered into Jesus' remarks on the oath (**C- 9**):

The Israelites acceptance of the Ten Commandments was signified, according to Rabbinic sages by a sole yea, or yea yea, nay or nay nay.[76]

---

[76] "Mekhilta" quoted in Vermes, *The Religion of Jesus the Jew,* p. 35.

Jesus, like his slightly later Alexandrian contemporary, Philo, had a balanced view of the righteousness of God—an equipoise of innerheart faith and outer behavior. In Matthew 15:17-19 Jesus is embroiled in a controversy with the Theological-lawyers over eating unkosher food with sinners, without washing hands. He seems to be talking of the Ten Commandment Tableau:

> Whatever goes in by mouth passes into the stomach and so is discharged into the drain. But what comes out of the mouth has its origins in the heart; and that is what defiles a man. Wicked thoughts, murder, adultery...perjury, slander...
> (G. Vermes translation)

To summarize our view of Jesus and the law we quote C.H. Dodd who argues

> "that Jesus himself is the "creative mind" that recasts and goes to the authentic core of Judaism's ethical theology"[77]

We conclude this section on Jesus and Decalogue with some passages at the end of Vermes', *Jesus the Jew*. Joseph Klausner wrote in the final paragraph of his famous book, *Jesus of Nazareth*, published in its original Hebrew edition exactly fifty years ago:

> In his ethical code there is a sublimity, distinctiveness and originality in form unparalleled in any other Hebrew ethical code. The positive and constant testimony of the earliest Gospel tradition, considered against its natural background of firstcentury Galilean charismatic religion, leads not to a Jesus as unrecognizable within the framework of Judaism as by the standard of his own verifiable words and intentions, but to another figure: Jesus the just man, the zaddik, Jesus the helper and healer, Jesus the teacher and leader, venerated by his intimates and less committed admirers alike as prophet, lord and son of God.[78]

Decalogue and Pentecost
Another illustration of the Holy compact:

> It is the day of *Shavuot* festival in the year 29 CE. Again, as out on Sinai centuries ago, a sound and a mighty wind, and the tongues. Peter rises while it is yet the wee hours of morning. "Inebriated at this hour?", he objects: "Indeed, these are not drunk, as you suppose, for it is only nine o'clock in the morning. No, this is what was spoken through the prophet Joel: In the last days it will be, God declares, that I will pour out my Spirit upon all flesh, and your sons and your daughters shall prophesy, and your young men shall see visions, and your old men shall dream dreams...Then everyone who calls on the name of the Lord shall be saved" (Acts 2:15ff).

---

[77] C.H. Dodd According to the Scriptures: The Sub-Structure of New Testament Theology London: Collins, 1952, p.110.
[78] *Jesus the Jew*, p. 224-225.

Pentecost was a celebration of Sinai. It was the feast of *Shavuot*. From the deep recesses of mosaic and monarchic history for perhaps twelve centuries, this celebration reenacted the receipt of the law. The divine Presence, Word, and Spirit, which constitutes and inspires a people was the meaning of the event. Psalms such as 50 and 81 reflect this assembly which now becomes *Yom ha-qahal*—"the day of the assembly." In this festival, the people gathered to hear the word and will of the Lord expressed in the Ten Commandments (Deuteronomy 9:10; 10:4; 18:16). It was a festival of cleansing (Exodus 19; Genesis 35:1-3) symbolized by the shofar, which signaled the people ready to receive and recite the oath. When the feast called Pentecost came around, the entire city and countryside crowded round the temple in Jerusalem. It was homecoming:

> Parthians, Medes, Elamites and residents of Mesopotamia, Judea and Cappadocia, Pontus and Asia, Phrygia and Pamphylia, Egypt and the parts of Libya belonging to Cyrene, and visitors from Rome, both Jews and proselytes, Cretans and Arabs...(Acts 2:9-11)

It was the reversal of Babel for:

> ...we hear, each of us, in our own native language. (Acts 2:8)

In Acts 20:16, Paul attempts to reach Jerusalem — leaving Philippi and passing over Ephesus in order to be in Jerusalem for *Shavuot*. In a manner similar to Judas Maccabeus' return for the Decalogue renewal before marching out against Gorgias the governor of Jamnia (2 Maccabees 12:31-32), for Paul the *Shavuot* which celebrates the Decalogue is the central enactment of faith.

The tongues and flames resting on the heads of each at Pentecost reenact the decisive and constitutive theophany at Horeb:

> All the people saw the voices (*qoloth*) and the flames (*lapidim*)...
> (Exodus 20:18)

The Sinai word, according to the Targum, is divided into seventy tongues so that it might reach all of the nations (seven tongues for each of the Ten Commandments). As in Numbers 11, the Holy Spirit of God comes to rest on all the elders and they become leaders of the congregation.

So the birth of the Church occurs on the day of Decalogue renewal. The historic fall of Babel into bewilderment, confusion and calumny is reversed. A new cosmos of spirit and right arises. The bestowal of divine Spirit and the animation of the global mission of God's people is anchored in the Decalogue. Now creation's pattern will be reversed. Just as one people of all nations on earth was found by moving from the outer edges of the earth to the center of the earth in Jerusalem and Judea, so now a witness shall proceed from Jerusalem, Judea, and Samaria to the Gentiles back out at the farthest edges of the earth. Now at exactly the place where the inception for the chosen and holy people began, its consummation begins.

Decalogue and the Great Commission

...walk in God's law (Torah), which was given by Moses the servant of God, and to observe and do all the commandments of the LORD our Lord and observe his ordinances and statutes. (Nehemiah 10:29)

go therefore and make disciples of all nations, baptizing them in the name of the Father and of the Son and of the Holy Spirit, and teaching them to observe everything that I have commanded you. And remember, I am with you always, to the end of the age.
(Matthew 28:19-20)

The story is the same: tongues, nations, Decalogue. Christian exegetes usually give it short shrift:

...everything that I have commanded you.

A need had arisen to repudiate and redefine Judaism among the apostolic community. Apostolic preaching soon took on an equal authority to Hebrew scripture. Though Jesus and the apostles were all Jews, an anti-Jewish sentiment sets in among those who compose and redact the Christian testament.

The Christian hang-up with the law stems not only from its chronic anti-Semitism, but with the radical grace-law juxtaposition that Martin Luther reads back into Paul, the Apostle. Again, to summarize E. P. Sanders, we find quite a different picture when we consult Paul directly in light of his own Judaism.

Paul and the Law

Luther may be forgiven. He was reacting against a late medieval Roman ethical and legal casuistry that trivialized and abused religious law just as late Second temple Judaism had. Paul's evangelical/ethical mission to the Gentiles was complicated by perceived difference from Jerusalem "pillars" (Galatians 2:6) in their allegiance to the Torah and a real difference with the hyper-Judaizers in both Asia Minor and Greece who believed that only Torah observance offered eschatological salvation ("false brothers" Gal. 2:4). The eventual authorization of his ministry by Peter, James and the Jerusalem leaders and the rejection of the radical legalizers placed Paul at the normative center of Biblical faith. Luther also had to grapple with a very complex Pauline theology of law and ethics. E.P. Sanders is again our expert. His analysis of Paul and Jewish law follows these lines:

- In Romans 5-7 Paul articulates the doctrine of *hamartia* (sin). Sin reigned in my body, consigning it to death 5:21-6:12). Sin found opportunity in the commandment, "wrought in me all kinds of covetousness" (7:8) and by the law "killed me" (7:11).

133

- The law of sin which reigns in my body and is *thanotropic* (driving toward death) is stimulated by the commandment. Yet it works against the "law of God" (7:17-23).

- The enticement and excitement of life and death, guilt and grace is provoked as the commandment confronts my being where the law of sin and law of God contend.

- Paul is here invoking the inner crisis of spirit found, for example, in the biography and psalms of David (e.g. Psalm 51). He rightly sees that the struggle to be and do God's will is beset by a contrary spirit and will.

- Deliverance from this body of death and from the commandment as condemnation not liberation is found in the saving God who effects righteousness in us.

- We are made righteous by faith.

- Paul's doctrine of law and sin, grace and redemption radiates from the existential into the societal and cosmic. Jew and Gentile, slave and free, male and female are embraced. The whole creation groans in travail; subjected in hope - it awaits its redemption.

- The concourse of Gospel and Kingdom has penetrated the cultures of Syria and Asia Minor, Greece and Italy. The Hebraic essence is now radiating throughout the Hellenic *Oikumene*; a new global community is being fashioned where Jew is joined by Gentile, even Barbarian.

- The twin pillars of Judaism; covenant election and law are sustained.

- While the law does not give life lest one neglect to die to sin in Christ, it is holy, just and good. (Romans 7:12). The law leads to neighbor love as its entire fulfillment (Galatians 5:14). Paul reasserts the commandments on adultery, murder, theft, and covetousness (Romans 13:8-10)

- (C-1) no other gods—Paul adamantly rejected the surrounding idol cults in Asia Minor (Ephesus) and Greece. "Shun the worship of idols...the cup of blessing which we bless is it not participation in the blood of Christ?" (1 Corinthians 10)

- While the law pertains for Israel it was tutor (*paidagogos*) until Christ came. Now faith induces righteous behavior, good works do not achieve righteousness.

- For now we are to live blameless, behaviorally sacred lives fit for the Lord's coming. For this purity that shuns idolatry, porneia, covetousness and the like, the law (Decalogue) is a sound guide.

Decalogue in Contemporary Jewish Texts

The significance of Decalogue for Jesus and Paul is further illumined if we consult the parallel literature of contemporary Judaism. We noted earlier the Jewish apocrypha (200 BCE – 100 CE), pseudepigrapha and Philo (20 BCE - 50 CE) acknowledge that the unique title Son of God is attributable to one who embodies perfect righteousness "father to the fatherless, husband to the widows..." (apocrypha of Solomon). In these same texts the Son of God is the one who perfectly obeys the Decalogue. (see Vermes, *Jesus the Jew* p. 194ff).

One finds two streams in contemporaneous Jewish ethics; one concrete, one mystical. The more concrete the mood of a particular tradition of literature the more casuistry is found. Particular concrete cases are argued and adjudicated. In Paul's "arguments" with the Jewish scholars at Thessalonia, Phillipi, Ephesus and Athens, he takes this decalogical approach. The mystical, or apocalyptic traditions are opposed to these historic-pragmatic renditions seeing divine law as eternal and non-negotiable.

In the important book *Israel and Humanity*, the great Jewish Philosopher Elijah Benamozegh reflects in part III on the law on this mystical character of Torah and Decalogue. Human law must be a reflection of divine law. The Logos connects human rules with the ontological and cosmic divine law. God (who himself wears the phylacteries with the vellum texts of Decalogue and Shema) himself practices the perfect righteousness that he expects from people. God lives out justice, love, peace, holiness and forgiveness. The being of God is, indeed, the ontic epicenter of these principles. Humans, as they follow or portray God, are themselves *SEFER Torah*, books of law. Now Jesus in John's Gospel says "If you love me you will keep my commandments." (John 14:15). We are to collaborate with God in public life to enact the commandments. Public policy should show that we are on the same track with the divine will. Eschatological apocalyptic and mystical Judaism (very close to John the Baptist and Jesus) had the following tenets:

- People are *imago dei*—we are to practice God's righteousness (to be Godlike).

- The intelligible (perceivable) pattern of righteousness in the world is through Logos: Decalogue.

- One perfectly righteous will be Messiah and Son of God.

- Human righteousness alone will bring about messiah and the day of the Lord.

Decalogue in Early Church History

The Decalogue is widely used in earliest Christian writings: Didache, Irenaeus and Clement of Alexandria, Tertullian, Jerome and Augustine, all fathers of the Latin church, believed that the divine precepts of the Decalogue were engraved on human hearts prior to the exposition at Sinai. These were imprinted in the heart by the Spirit (Jeremiah 31:31). They affirmed the Pauline etiologic doctrine and the Jeremian eschatologic doctrine:

> What can be known about God...is plain to them since the creation of the world. (Romans 1:20ff)

> I will write my law on the tablets of their hearts. (Jeremiah 31:33)

These church fathers therefore positioned the Decalogue central in the catechetical, homiletical, and liturgical process. By Augustine's time, the Decalogue was a catechetical tool to distinguish orthodoxy and orthopraxy from Manichean teachers who claimed that the world was the work of evil powers. Again in the ninth and thirteenth centuries, seasons of moral revival and renewed faith, the Decalogue appears prominent.

The religious history of the Decalogue establishes the point that humans at their most self-conscious and conscientious moments and God in seasons of revelation, historic action and spiritual renewal, together seek the bridges of decalogic dialogue and collaboration. From Moses' furtive introduction of this new way to a confused, wandering people in the Sinai desert through the time of the judges in sabbatical renewal and rededication at Shechem or Shiloh, in the piercing vision and voice of the prophets, in Jesus' day through synagogue recitation and elucidation (e.g., Sermon on the Mount), the Decalogue is always seen as God's preferred pathway of return and fulfillment. As we saw, through worship-centered catechesis in Augustine and other early church leaders, through its centrality in instruction and liturgy in Luther, Bucer, Calvin, and the Protestant Reformation, through Cranmer, who placed it central to the *Prayer Book*, and Heidelberg, which made it the architecture of the catechism, the Holy Text continues to portray the concerned love of God for people and the worshipful desire of people to make their lives right before God, creatively concordant with his purposes in the world. In this light, the Decalogue is a trustworthy expression of the Word and Will of God and the ground of a palpable and relevant human ethic. It embodies biological givens, sociological norms, and philosophical truths. It is true because it is God's Word. Because it is true, it is God's Word.

Summary

Gerhard Von Rad summarizes our findings to this point. He shows that the historical and narrational setting of the Decalogue—the golden calf escapade (Exodus 32), which undergirds C1-C4—and the Garden of Eden through Cain's criminal episode (Genesis 1-4), which undergirds C5-C10, show the law to be essentially about disrupted and reconstituted friendship and love (*hesed*) between humans and God. This binding affection and constancy is the basis of covenant in Judaism, Christianity and Islam. Von Rad rehearses the story:

God created the world and man. After the destruction of the corrupt human race by the Flood, God gave to a new human race laws for its self-preservation, and, in the covenant with Noah, guaranteed to it the outward continuance of the world and its orders. He then called Abraham, and in a covenant, which he made with him, promised him a great posterity, a special relationship to God and the land of Canaan. The first promise was fulfilled in Egypt, when the patriarchs grew into a people; the second was fulfilled at Sinai, when with a fresh covenant Israel received the regulations for her community life and for her intercourse with God; and the third was fulfilled when under Joshua Israel took possession of the land of Canaan. Thus, by means of the covenant theology, the entire mass of the hexateuchal tradition was set beneath a three-fold arch of prophecy and fulfillment. Initially, there were only the patriarchs: they were not yet a people, they have not entered into the promised special relationship with God, nor do they possess a land. Then, from the patriarchs a people come into being; but it is without the special relationship with the land. And finally, in what is perhaps the most exciting period, Israel, which is entirely ordered in one direction only, that is towards Jaweh, towards the last promise, the land of Canaan.[79]

Von Rad also shows convincingly how the Decalogue became imprinted in Israel's moral consciousness through the memory of historical events, mediated through a narrative tradition, celebrated in cyclic festival. The Feast of Weeks, or harvest feast, is the commemoration of the settlement. Here thanksgiving is offered for salvation and enduring providence. The Feast of Booths commemorates the Sinai confrontation with Yahweh.

Each festival involved four elements: preparatory hallowing, drawing near of the assembly, theophany and communication (recitation of divine demands), and a concluding sacrifice to seal the covenant. The law, in other words, is inextricably bound up in worship and confession of sin. Celebration and confession issue in forgiveness and restoration of the people. Calvin, then Cramner in the *Prayer Book*, rightly places the Ten Commandments at the head of the approach and confession phase of the liturgy.

Shariah and Decalogue

Al-shari'ah is the Arabic phrase for the way of faith and life in Islam. Much like the Hebraic derivation of *Torah* (walk, way), the word originally refers to a path followed by camels to the water oasis. Like the pathway of life in its sister Abrahamic precursors, Judaism and Christianity, this path leads faithfully through one's time in the world on into eternal life. As in these sister faiths, *shari'ah* perpetuates the synergy of the Decalogue and summarized in the great biblical couplet "love God with all your being and the neighbor as self."(Leviticus 19:18, Matthew 19:19).

---

[79] Gerhard Von Rad, *Old Testament Theology,* Vol. 1. New York: Harper & Bros., 1962, p. 135.

Out of the perceived divine revelation inscribed in Muhammed's words and *Quran* an enlarged body of law has emerged across the centuries. *Shari'ah* obliges and blesses both faith adherents within the last judgment and governments in the penultimate divine judgment of history. Both personal duty and public responsibility are prescribed in *Shari'ah*.

Ibadat are the strictly religious duties—obligations to God. Here we have rules about worship and observations especially the cardinal five precepts of prayers (*salat*), pilgrimage to Mecca (*hajj*), fasting during Ramadan (*sawin*), payment of alms for the poor (*zakat*) and confession of faith (*Shahadah*).

The other main *Shari'ah* category is *mu'amalat*, which pertains to the relations and interactions among persons. Marriage, divorce and inheritance laws emerge here leading toward the more profound decalogic principles of adultery, killing, stealing, lying and perjury in terms of social obligation. Muslim civil, criminal, economic and environmental law coalesces at this point. Rules which are suggestive or recommended evolve toward the mandatory as sanctions intensify. In Northern Nigeria today, for example, societal *shariah* struggles with several cases: execution by stoning (after giving birth) of a woman who conceived her baby in adultery (forced); homosexual males censured; and a case of hand amputation for stealing in the market place. In all jurisdictions of Muslim dominance, a greater severity is found than in more pluralistic settings.

Though a lively debate ensues between Western and Islamic scholars as to whether Islamic law emerges *de novo* or evolves from the cultural traditions within which Islam emerges—Romano-Byzantine, Jewish and Christian Canon Law—this seems irrelevant to the *prima facia* self evident fact that *Shari'ah* resonates with the Mosaic, Levitical and prophetic biblical heritage.

The ethical and legal heritage of Islam follows therefore the general contours of Judaism and Christianity as the law of Muslim countries, say Egypt or Pakistan, is much like that of Israel or America, with one caveat. During the present historical crisis whose epicenter is the Israeli/Palestinian conflict and is called the "war on terrorism" and is characterized by belligerent Judaism, paranoid and crusading Christianity and militant Islam, fundamentalist Islam in places like Iran, Taliban, Afghanistan, and Northern Sudan or Nigerian takes on an aberrant hyper puritanical character. The contrast of *Shari'ah* with this intensification and exaggeration in some Muslim nations over against a secularized, materialized and morally libertanical ethos in Western Europe and America. This clash of civilization makes for evocative culture wars. The thesis of this section of our work on the Abrahamic "Way of life" is that reconciliation, justice and peace can only ensue when the decalogic impulses, religious and public—impulses to faith and iconoclasm, to fidelity and nonviolence, to reverence and honesty, to compassion for the poor, veracity and to respectful reciprocity—illuminate within and radiate without all nations of Abrahamic heritage.

Implications of the Decalogue

The Decalogue has a decisive place in this pervasive theological history of Israel. It is a quantum leap from the nature gods of the ancient Near East still lingering in the geological tumult of Mt. Sinai to the god of the mountain now reminiscent of Pharaoh Iknaton's singular solar deity to the God who speaks, companions, leads and befriends as a father—YAHWEH. Now Yahweh assumes the already perceived preeminence of a "High God" above all gods. But this "High God" is not aloof and apathetic, as were most oriental and Mediterranean high gods. Yahweh is active, troublingly concerned, fiercely committed to justice on earth, involved, demanding singular devotion, going somewhere. From this theology, a clear and rigorous ethic emerges. The parochial demands of the familial deities, e.g., "the Shield of Abraham," now yield to the strong universal ethics expressed in Israel's conscience as Noahic and Mosaic codes, and in particular in the Decalogue.

Reaching into Noachian memory, later rabbis postulate a singular moral law for the whole world that coalesced in the epochal events of global sin, flood and cleansing embodied in the story of Noah. The themes of Noachian ethics seem to be these: mandate to monotheistic loyalty, filial and parental love and respect for nature. These are pronounced against the background of prohibitions of blasphemy, killing, stealing, adultery and cruelty to animals.

This shadowy conviction from the mists of prehistory is consonant with the theological myths and received moral wisdom of cognate cultures throughout the ancient Near East. Israel's moral vision corresponds with Sumerian cosmogony, Egyptian eschatology and Hittite covenant. Now this genetic heritage becomes sharply defined and historically grounded in the Ten Commandments. A refreshing new study by Jack Miles[80] describes the setting:

> On the third day, as morning dawned, there was thunder, and lightning, and a dense cloud upon the mountain, and a very loud blast of the horn; and all the people who were in the camp trembled. Moses led the people out of the camp toward God, and they took their places at the foot of the mountain. Now Mount Sinai was all in smoke, for the Lord had come down upon it in fire; the smoke rose like the smoke of a kiln, and the whole mountain trembled violently. The blare of the horn grew louder and louder. As Moses spoke, God answered him in thunder. The Lord came down upon Mount Sinai, on the top of the mountain, and the Lord called Moses to the top of the mountain, and Moses went up. The Lord said to Moses, 'Go down, warn the people not to break through to the Lord to gaze, lest many of them perish. The priests also, who come near the Lord, must stay pure, lest the Lord break out against them.' But Moses said to the Lord, 'The people cannot come up to Mount

---

[80] *A Biography of God.* New York: Knopf, 1995, p. 115. Jew, Christian and Muslim.

Sinai, for You warned us saying, "Set bounds about the mountain and sanctify it." ' So the Lord said to him, 'Go down, and come back together with Aaron; but let not the priests or the people break through to the Lord, lest he break out against them' (Genesis 19: 16-24).

Global Implications

Today we seek to articulate and activate a global ethical code that is binding on all persons and nations. The laws of the seas emerge in the late Renaissance. The Hague Conventions in the early twentieth century affirm the rights of prisoners and refugees. Nazi generals and physicians are convicted of crimes against humanity in the Nuremberg proceedings. The United Nations condemns, then sends peacekeeping personnel in the face of genocide in Bosnia and Rwanda. Part of their mission must surely be to bring to justice those guilty of war crimes. This is the rightful legacy of the Decalogue.

As a world conference on population convened in Cairo in 1994, we saw two responses to Noachic and Mosaic ethical teaching. Curtailing population growth was thought to be necessary to alleviate human misery, death and eco-destruction: faithfulness to ethical law. Other voices, especially within the conservative expression of Abrahamic and Sinaitic faith (Vatican and Islamic scholars), said that contraception and abortion may be transgressions and that promiscuity, adultery and homosexuality may be at variance with the norm of monogamous, procreative union. Again, response to Decalogue. A perfect 10 hovers in the background.

Before beginning an exposition of the Ten Commandments, several other fundamental implications help to clarify the nature of the ethical theology implicit in the Decalogue.

The code enhances freedom within human history. "No other gods" condemns all tyranny over the mind and soul. "All other gods" must be dismissed, claimed Bonhoeffer, for humans to come of age and be free. Erich Fromm discusses the awesome freedom of the text, "They shall be like gods," an implication of "No other gods."[81] "Do not steal" honors autonomy and freedom of expression. The Sinai Charter seals the liberation offered in the Exodus. If moral excellence does not accompany political liberation, we await only greater tyranny and bondage. Freedom itself is ambivalent if it lacks clear direction.

> Me this freedom tires,
> If I feel the weight of chance desires.
> Wordsworth, "Ode to Duty"

Today freedom is erupting around the world. In 1980, of 120 nations in the world, 97 were dictatorships or other single party systems. Since then, especially

---

[81] Erich Fromm, *You Shall Be As God.* New York: Holt, Rinehard and Winston, 1960.

with events in the Soviet Union, Eastern Europe and Africa, numerous nations have become popular democracies. The problem is that this exuberance has become the occasion for violence and greed. Eastern Europe, for example, is now a hotbed for gang violence, drug abuse, infant mortality, and gun mortality. Degradation is one of the diseases of freedom.

Decalogue righteousness binds people from freedom into responsible community. In the Decalogue, law is seen as binding obligation sealed in the covenant relationship of people with God. The broad divine bequest of Torah, a treasury including the Code of the Covenant (Exodus 20-23), the Deuteronomic discovery (Deuteronomy 12-26), the Holiness code (Leviticus 17-26), and the Priestly code (Leviticus 1-16) all intertwine in the fabric of an endearing and obliging relation of people to Yahweh. The radical implication of the preparatory and historical material that we have reviewed thus far is that the human race has met a new kind of God—an ethical being. Yahweh is one who says and does righteousness. No longer a passive and immutable force, now God is one who lives, knows, hears, speaks, acts, watches, blesses, regrets, delights, punishes, forgives, and loves. God is like us or better, fashioned, as we are *Imago Dei*, we are like God. Such a living God gives different grounding for the moral life.

SHEMAH is the word. Hear, O Israel. Jaynes was correct in his speculation about the evolution of the bicameral human mind.[82] For millennia of human evolution, before language developed, we heard voices. God is like a mother or father. God utters sounds with meaning. Grace itself is the onomatopoetic cry of a mother camel for its child lost in the desert. We are equipped by nature to hear and imprinted to understand.

Ethics is therefore a prophetic and proleptic phenomenon: God holds before us something new, offering a better way. If God is one who speaks and acts, we are addressed toward something different. Yes, we are affirmed in and of ourselves. Yes, we are invited toward our possibility. This is the essence of speech, word, command of God. Torah, word and will of God, is the structure of consciousness, activity, and being toward which we are invited. This is the root of spiritual phenomena, like sin and grace, judgment and mercy, disappointment and acceptance, fresh beginning and pilgrimage.

But something has gone wrong in us and in the world, because God holds behind and before us another reality which in creation prompted the saying "Look, it is good." Part of human distinctiveness, *Imago Dei*, is the sense that we go wrong and we could be different. If either honesty or hope betray us, we are left bewildered.

---

[82] Julian Jaynes, *The Origin of Consciousness in The Breakdown of the Bicameral Mind*. Toronto: University of Toronto Press, 1983.

Edna St. Vincent Millay offers the truth in her sonnet:

> Wisdom enough to teach us of our ill/ is daily spun; but there exists no loom to weave it into fabric.

And the Russian poet Yevgeny Yevtushenko:

> There can be no rebuilding without rebuilding memory, and without rebuilding monuments to those who built us.

Decalogue is the loom and building. Here conviction of sin achieves its purpose in redemption of being.

The Ten Commandments, recall and departure toward new being, remind us that God speaks and listens to us, comes through to us, deals with us directly. This is the basic implication of Yahwism, of Torah (instruction). As I write, it is the beginning of the Jewish high holy days. Israel's three million Jews, America's 5.5 million, and the roughly two million dispersed elsewhere throughout the world celebrate Rosh Hashanah, the Jewish New Year, and Yom Kippur, the Day of Atonement. The central prayer of the holy days reminds the faithful that Yahweh is one who is involved with us. The bedrock prayer claims that during this season God is determining who will live and who will die, who will prosper and who will not.[83] The conviction that God is at work within us effecting his will is a blessing coming toward human life from Sinai.

A Final Word about Word

The concept of *dabar*, speech or word, is a gentle word that we erroneously translate as "commandment." The law is more a gentle invitation, a tutor. It is like a father teaching his son to walk. Hosea says, "When Israel was a child I loved him...out of Egypt I have called my son." *Dabar* is utterance. It is address, direct, face to face (cf. Numbers 12: 1 ff). The word at Sinai was too awesome and terrifying to hear directly. It had to be mediated through Moses. It was not the tedious and trivial word of later rabbinical elaboration. It wasn't the tiresome clichés and shibboleths of a thousand ranting preachers. His word was truth. Like Jesus on his Sinai recapitulation in the Sermon on the Mount, "He spoke as one with authority—not as the scribes." (Matthew 7: 28-29)

Both qualities of the divine being with us, communication and covenant, convey affirmation and expectation. The very fact that God approached us—found us worthy or needy of care—is itself an enormous compliment. Interest establishes our dignity. God's grace ennobles our being. The etymology of the word grace in Hebrew signals this searching and saving yearning. God's attention presumes that we are kings and princes. God's coming is also disruptive. It calls us into question. It asks after our loyalties, our secret thoughts and intentions, actions and directions. Yahweh is not only a proximate and passionate God, as Andrew

---

[83] The New York Times, Sept. 1, 1994, p. B-98.

Greeley poses in his very good book, among many not so good books on the subject.[84] The God of the Decalogue searches us out, finds us, straightens us out, and makes us whole. God beckons us with personal and communal specificity.

Conclusion: What is the Decalogue?

Are the Ten Commandments a theological necessity? Are they biological evolutionary impulses that ensure survival, adaptation and generativity, naturally encoded like RNA or DNA? Are they sociologic, embodying custom gleaned over millennia by painful trial and error as those modes of conviviality, which keep communities viable? Was *vox dei* really *vox populi*? Surely stealing and killing destroy the fabric of society. Is the code basically encoded rational wisdom? Empirical common sense, winnowed wisdom, universalizable moral principles? My study of the Decalogue leads me to offer the appraisal that they are not sublime human contrivance, nor are they divine dictation. Both the historicalcritical rendition of their relativity and the fundamentalist rendition of their transcending objectivity are only partial truth. The Decalogue, like Torah more generally and Scripture in particular, are human worshipful response to divine encounter and endearment.

I have argued that both claims about the divinity and humanity of the Decalogue are true. I shall attempt to show in this study that the moral capacity in humans is the divine presence by virtue of *imago dei*. Human moral capacity does not exhaust and exhibit ethics because of the severe limitation and misdirection of human life. Full moral realization is only possible in and through God. Similarly, God has not chosen to give will and purpose to creation except through the structures of human conscience, reason, emotion, biology, social custom, and law. In sum, I subscribe to the view that Yahweh etched them—again and again (Deuteronomy 4: 13, 9: 10).

Excursus

On this thus-far heady trip—the first of occasional diversions—remarks on the human condition. I sit this evening in a low class Greek/Turkish fast food joint near the train station in downtown Strasbourg. It has just come to me that I have not seen a policeman all day, all week for that matter. Yes, they may be in plain-clothes, or hidden in cars or offices, but they are not evident and certainly not omnipresent as in my hometown—Chicago. I doubt if Chicago's 50,000 strong force could be marshaled in all of France, outside Paris. It leads me to ask if people need the law. What makes people go wrong? Was the Apostle onto something when he implied that the law was incentive to break the law? There are many shady characters here on the streets—*clochards*, they are called. They appear to me to be the profoundly homeless—what the Brits call living "in the rough." These guys (and regrettably a few women and children) are really rough. Tough red skin, scraggly beard (like mine). They sit in their bedraggled rags on the steps of buildings, often with their mangy dogs, often with a bottle

---

[84] Greely, Andrew, *The Sinai Myth.* New York: Doubleday, 1972.

up the sleeve. Who are they, the lost? the lawless? the morally destitute? the outcasts? Are these those for whom The Decalogue was finger-etched? Are these those for whom Christ came and loved, and died? For these, did he become way, truth and life, even amid festering degradation and death? Some prostitutes circle outside in the February evening mist. Is this the adultery Moses described, that Jesus strongly Chastened?

What is the *conditio humaine* addressed by Decalogue and the law of love? It is my hunch that the disrepair and misdirection of our lives is expressed in a subtle blend of being and action—beingestranged and in action-misguided. In old Alsacian word play wellknown to Luther and Bucer, we are lost in a singular furtive display from Gott und Gut. And we'd stay lost had not the call gone out, the word found us, the way and path—drawn us. Ten easy pieces—sure! Surely there is breach this night here in this place. Theft, blasphemy, lust if not adultery, hate, if not murder. Yet the One who comes keeps coming. The royal law of love persists as touchstone, teacher, transformer. The resolution is the same—a weary warrior stumbling down Sinai with tablets in his arms or Godself coming down the stairs of heaven to a cowstall in Bethlehem with a babe in his arms. And there at the base, what a party!

I. No Other Gods: A Theology of Idolization

Gott ist mein führer.
Pastor Martin Niemoller

I have sworn on the altar of God, eternal hostility against every form of tyranny over the mind of man.
Thomas Jefferson Letter to Benjamin Rush (1801)

No man can serve two masters; for either he will hate the one
and love the other, or he will be devoted to one and despise the
other. You cannot serve God and mammon.
Matthew 6: 24

"Ten Suggestions"
Ted Turner

We returned to our places these kingdoms,
But no longer at ease here in the old dispensation,
With an alien people clutching their gods.
T.S.Eliot "Journey of the Magi," 1927

Incursus

While dad reads the technical section of the newspaper, his faithful son, Pavel, glances at the obituaries on the back page. "What is death?" the ten year old asks his father. "The heart stops, respiration and circulation ceases and then the brain dies," dad responds. "But why, what does it mean?" asks Pavel, "Isn't there a soul?". "There is no soul," papa autonomically retorts. "Your father learned to measure," the boy's aunt comes '*deus ex machina*', "now for him only what can be measured is real. But for you, dear Pavel, God is simple to faith."

Krzysztof Kieslowski's The Decalogue (1988), an epic film achievement, begins with a moving study of a computer buff - technophilic father- a linguistics professor- who lives in a Warsaw apartment complex with his trusting mimetic son, who has even programmed the door locks and bath water with his own computer virtuosity.

The child has received new skates for Christmas. "Can I go out and skate?" he pleads. Together father and son calculate the thickness of the ice on the nearby lake by entering the temperature for recent days. "The ice will support 257 kilos per square meter," dad assures Pavel. One afternoon he himself walks and jumps on the ice to test it, scarcely noting the haunting blonde figure of a man who, like Alfred Hitchcock, will appear in all ten films, sitting at lakeside by a fire.

The inevitable consequence of his false faith and devotion falls on a gray afternoon when Pavel fails to return from an English lesson. A neighbor, whose son is also missing, cries out "He told me your calculations showed it was strong enough." "Calm down" says the now shattered, icy facade of the father, "the ice could not break." Even as the fire department and emergency vehicles rush to the scene, papa is on his cellular intercom calling his lost son who is even then being dredged from the lake.

He stumbles into the cathedral, looks up at the black madonna, tears trickle from her eyes and down her wooden face. He pushes the altar down and then collapses at the feet of the baptismal font. He reaches in and withdraws a disc of ice and with this searing stone he consecrates his forehead. One feels the redemptive tone of Kieslowski's art and of the Decalogue's perennial spiritual power. The founding is lost and one long lost may be found as both are swept in to the enigmatic divine drama of judgment and grace. "What does life mean?" the young child asks as he dwells on the frozen corpse of a trash dog. "to leave an influence in the world" says the father, and echoing Verdi's Otello, "after death...nothing." A lasting and liberating influence has been left in the world. From its foundations to its fulfillment the Decalogue captures that secret law that is light and life (Psalm 119:105).

Introduction

On each Commandment we will organize reflection around four topics: text, tradition, theology, and today. Each word condemns and commends. The first word condemns idolatry and commands faith. In forbidding acknowledgment of other gods we are given over to loyalty to God alone. Shunning the vice of moral voyeurism, we live in the virtue of reverence. There is no more decisive ethical principle to have entered human conscience than the first commandment. It sears falsehood and extols truth. It rightly anchors trust by forever negating selling the soul short. It is the cornerstone of freedom.

The cornerstone of the whole structure of human ethics is our responsibility to God, the Giver of All. All inter-human responsibility rests here, in this personal ethical charter to mankind, God first becomes real to His people. Revelation and relationship precede requirement. In the logic of ethics, relation precedes intention, which, in turn, precedes action.

Text

The text heralds the existence of God—the one and only God. At the most rudimentary level it repudiates atheism and agnosticism. It commands belief in God. Ancient Semitic language is not about laying out options. Ted Turner knows this. This is an apodictic text—it commands belief. God is introduced as deliverer, not creator. That doctrine implies something far more serious than suasion toward assent.

> AND GOD SPOKE THESE WORDS, SAYING, I AM THE LORD, YOUR GOD, WHO DELIVERED YOU FROM OPPRESSION IN EGYPT. YOU SHALL HAVE NO GOD BUT ME.
> (Exodus 20:1-3)

Verse 1: Heb. *anochi* The source of power, life, consciousness, personality, moral purpose, ethical action. Aniconism is the reason for the empty cherub throne over the ark.

Verse 2: God is liberator, giver and securer of freedom, no slavery is tolerable. God wills to bring liberty and justice to world history.

Verse 3: No being or power shall be interposed between God and a human person.

The preface and Commandment can be translated from the Hebrew three ways:

- I am Yahweh, your God...
- I Yahweh, am your God...
- Besides me, Yahweh, your God, who brought you out of the land of Egypt, you shall have no other Gods.

The setting of the text is commemorative celebration of deliverance. The words are hearty and defiant.

> ...there will be no God in defiance of me (*al pene*).

The same words are used in Genesis 16:12 in the promise made to Ishmael,

> ...he shall dwell over against his kinsmen

146

The text does not presume monotheism, in fact it acknowledges the existence of other gods—these shall not usurp or displace Yahweh's sole authority for Israel. The ethos is therefore more one of monolatry.... you are surrounded by a dazzling array of competitors, tempters and pretenders. Therefore, you shall not be lured away by other gods. Idolatry itself is an ethical phenomenon. Conviction, commitment and character go together. Yahweh's zeal or jealousy is the ground for our reciprocal zeal and zealotry. God's word calls us to a passionate, discerning, dividing, distinguishing loyalty in the first three words:

> ...no other gods
> ...no carved or constructed substitutes
> ...no carrying around the name lightly, flippantly

The enduring cultural contribution of perceiving the character of God as righteous, as a concerned and calling creator, as a wordbearing and word-giving being and not just a brute force, even just a law giver, is to order human life humanly, justly and lovingly. Jack Miles summarizes:

> What counts, is that in one way or another, moral values shall have been placed above the other values that human beings properly recognize: power, wealth, pleasure, beauty, knowledge...the list is long. All these goods of human life must somehow be gathered into a single perspective and ranked and moral goodness must be assigned the top rank.[85]

This for Miles, is the genius of monotheism or monolatry as a human achievement (apperception: P. Lehmann)—the gift of divine selfdisclosure. The acknowledged reality of God gives human life the possibility of honor and respect.

Tradition
> If gods are no more in the earth, then we ourselves are gods.
> -F. Schubert, Die Winterreise

The two-fold yield of **C-1** "no other gods" and "having a God" (Luther) has shaped a course of theological history that has erupted in violent iconoclasm and cleansing Puritanism, coercive demagoguery and respectful, reserved faith. Luther's provocative phrase in the *Grosser Katechismus* is instructive:

Q: Thou shalt have no other gods
        What does this mean?

A: We should fear, love, and trust in God above all things.
        (Shorter Catechism, 1:1)

Q: ...what does it mean to have a god?

---

[85] Miles, Jack, *GOD: A Biography*. New York: Knopf, 1995, p. 110.

A: A God means that from which we are to expect all good and to
which we are to take refuge in all distress . . . to have a God is
nothing else than to trust and believe Him from the heart
that...upon which you set your heart and put your trust...is your
God.
(Larger Catechism 1:1)[86]

"To have faith and to have a god is one and the same thing" writes H. Richard
Niebuhr "faith in Gods and in God"[87] In the anguish, anxiety, and assault of life,
our theology is laid bare. There and then we find who we believe in and in
whom or what we ultimately trust. In true Lutheran spirit, Tillich says that our
ultimate concern is our God. "Have no other gods" may be much easier than
"Having a God," The hymn "Blessed assurance, Jesus is mine" doesn't ring as
well as the more biblical truth, "Blessed disturbance, I am his." Loyalties, like
deities, are more or less all- consuming. We can take or leave a steak dinner, a
new jacket. A job is another matter. And one's nation, one's spouse and family,
one's life? Luther finds it all expendable.

Let goods and kindred go.
This mortal life also...

(Nehmen sie den Leib,
gut, ehr, Kind und Weib)
(A Mighty Fortress, 1529)

For us, gods are not shaped or shattered so easily. Having a God may be life's
most formidable challenge. Unless, that is, the old Hebraic notion is true that we
need not name, claim and define God, but merely let go and let God. An
intriguing feature of Yahweh, the unutterable One, the nameless One is that once
penultimates are shattered, theophany occurs, God appears. Knowledge of God
may simply mean not being full of ourselves.

A turning point in western theology and political philosophy, a decisive moment
influencing John Locke and all democratic theorists, is found when John Calvin
also turns to the Decalogue. All human tyranny and kingship stalls before
democratic forms. He refers to C-1 three times in the *Institutes*. These references
correspond with his three uses of the law: conviction of sin, constraint of evil,
consecration in faith (Pedagogic, politic, didactic function). In Book I on
knowledge of God, the creator, Calvin develops in Chapter X (p.96ff.) the
argument that scripture has set the true God alone over all the gods. This means
cutting away from nature. Though God's power, even knowledge, is conveyed
in and through the creation, the doctrine of commensurate deity or pantheism,
clear and compelling awareness of God, comes not from the things which are

---

[86] *The Lutheran Confession: A Harmony and A Source Book,* ed. Neelak S. Tjernnagel.
Evangelical Lutheran Synod, 1979, p. 1.
[87] *Radical Monotheism*, p. 117-199 Louisville Westminster, John Knox Press, 1960.

made but through the living word; through face to face conversation. The creation of the world, however resplendent, does not "mount up to Christ the mediator" (I, x, 1. p. 97). Juxtaposing C-1 with Romans 1, Calvin writes, God is as "he declares himself in his word" (I, x, 2, p. 98).[88]

> "Scripture...to direct us to the true God, distinctively excludes and rejects all the gods of the heathen, for religion was commonly adulterated throughout almost all ages." Then conceding to Paul in Romans I, "Indeed, it is true that the name of one God was everywhere known and renowned. For men who worshipped a swarm of gods...whenever speaking from a real feel of nature, as if content with a single God, simply used the name "God" as Justin Martyr...wisely noted in a book God's monarchy" (I, x, 3, p. 99).

Yes, God is vivid in nature and natural conscience, but "no other gods" ultimately means that God's holy being and will is firmly known, not in creation's splendor but in God's commanding word.

In Book II on knowledge of God the Redeemer, we find Calvin's exposition of the Ten Commandments, including C-1. The law in its first function has disclosed true godliness and the terrible desolation of our lawlessness. It leads us toward the mediator. Now, exposing the positive, redemptive function of the law, Calvin shows how law, especially C-1, holds us in true worship and suppresses the currency of wrongdoing in the world. When Luther, Calvin, or John Knox call on the state to enforce true worship, they invoke C-1. Calvin writes:

> "Claiming for himself the lawful power to command...he calls us to reverence his divinity (no other gods)." (II, viii, 1 p. 367)

God's way may only be to lead us part way. As for example in C-6 by "half commandment" or "*synecdoche*," God intimates his positive will (that we hold the brother's life dear and precious) by negative constraint (that we not hurt or harm a brother unjustly). This partial measure, where the law of controlled evil presages the law of affirmed good, is given in order to hold the world together.

Example: The morning's news (September 7, 1994) carries a tragic story from Russia. As the population-environment conference convenes in Cairo, it is disclosed that dirty air, poisoned water, industrial waste, and radiation contamination has despoiled the land of Russia to the point where infant mortality has risen 15% and life expectancy has dropped to where the average male will not live to see retirement.[89] The frantic race for "development" it seems has decimated life. Along the lines of Calvin's moral analysis constraint of the sin of exploitation and degradation should have been imposed by law,

---

[88] Calvin, John. *Institutes of the Christian Religion.* Library of Christian Classics, ed. John T McNeill, London: SCM Press, 1960. Hereafter cited as *Institutes.*
[89] *The Chicago Tribune,* Wednesday, September 7, 1994, Sec. A, p. 1.

even though the positive values of love of the natural world and respect for fellow humans were not, at that moment, viable. Calvin put it this way:

> When the first foundation of righteousness (the worship of God)...is overthrown, all the remaining parts of righteousness, like pieces of a shattered and fallen building, are mangled and scattered (Institutes, II, viii,11 p.337).

In other words, there is law that flows from concordant wills, there is law that flows from good intent, and there is law that flows from having your arm-twisted. The law holds life together until we can get back right with God. Beyond legal restraint of evil, C-1 for Calvin is also in use two, the gentle leading of the tutor. It is the invitation of God's "sweetness in redemption." God first shows himself to be the one who has the right to command and to whom obedience is due. Then in order not to seem to constrain men by necessity alone, he also attracts with sweetness, by declaring himself God of the church. "I will be their God, and they shall be my people" (Jeremiah 31: 33; Institutes ii, VIII, 14 p. 380).

Finally, in Book III on "the ways in which we receive the grace of Christ," in Chapter 17 Calvin speaks of the concordance of the promises of law and Gospel. Again Calvin quotes Jeremiah as the prophet alludes to C-1:

> If you direct your ways and your efforts aright...nor walk after strange gods; if you execute justice between people and not oppress the poor then I shall walk in your midst...(Jeremiah 7; Institutes III, xvii, 1 p. 803).

The royal freedom afforded by the Law of Moses and the law of Christ promotes the life of justice because of its singular, transcending devotion. The life of deepening justice and love is the walk with God in this life of holiness and consecration. The blessing of sanctification and companionship. "I am with you always."

What general lessons can we draw from Calvin's thoughts on the three-fold function of the law as illustrated in this interpretation of C-1?

First, sound theological priority establishes the ethical life on solid bedrock. The validity of the good can only be anchored in the reality of God. We learn this as he anchors the seven ethical stipulates on the three theological stipulates. The second inference from C-1 is like the first. The heart of divine purpose in the world is an ethical project of repair and restitution. Unlike the static Parmidian being of the god of Greek philosophers or the capricious, easily-cajoled spirits and demons of primitive fear, Yahweh is a moral God. God's purpose is simply to do a good thing in and through the creation of the world and with the collaboration of humankind. Creation is to be made good and whole. Sin is misdirection and alienation from moral purpose and possibility. Redemption is turning away from evil toward good. Christ's messianic work with the human family is to receive us back from our wayward paths of harm to the healing paths of love. Salvation is the forgiveness of sins. All of the other renditions of the theological drama of the life in the world—seeing it as metaphysical, ontological, or existential—are found wanting because the background theologies are not ethical at heart. C-1 conclusively shows that ethics not grounded in theology is arbitrary and inhuman, and theology without ethics is illusion and danger. These twinchecks against the idol of other gods and the idol of human works, captures the essence of C-1 as interpreted in terms of Calvin's first two uses of the law. The third sense of the law is announced in the New Testament when John writes, "The law was given through Moses; grace and truth came through Jesus Christ" (John 1: 17). Or again in John 15—"If you keep my commandments you will abide in my love" (John 15:10). As C-1 recognizes it, the life and heart given over to God in obedience and love is the starting point of righteousness. Law functions in the believing life in terms of edification and sanctification to create moral power or virtue in a person's life.

The moment in the history of theology that rivets my imagination these days is the critical period from 1538 to 1541, when Calvin was banished from Geneva and joined Bucer at Strasbourg. Critical understandings of church and state, of the meanings of C-1, were fashioned at this time. Dramatic new understandings of personal, spiritual and communal devotion were fashioned. The political influence of these changes in Alsace and Switzerland, and subsequently in England, Scotland, Holland and America was far-reaching.

Moving to the modern era, one of the most moving appropriations of C-1 in the confessional tradition of the church is the Barmen Declaration. Written on the eve of the Second World War by Karl Barth and the confessing church during the *Nazizeit*, the confession cries from the beginning to end, "no other gods."

> I. Jesus Christ, as he is attested for us in Holy Scripture, is the one Word of God which we have to hear and which we have to trust and obey in life and death.

Note the affinity with Luther's treatment of the first Commandment and the opening clause of the Heidelberg Catechism. The architecture of Barmen is similar—affirmation then caution.

> II. We reject the false doctrine, as though there were areas of our life in which we would not belong to Jesus Christ, but to other Lords...

Again Heidelberg is in the background as in C-1. "No other gods" now directly means allegiance to the Hitler State and the co-opted *"Deutschchristen"* state. Like Jewish history, the Christian saga is ennobled by moments when the sheer affirmation of the reality of God is sounded, when the knee bends to no subordinate devotion, when even in the face of death a life cries out "...no other gods."

- Jesus before Pilate
- Stephen before the High Priest and synagogue freedman
- Polycarp before the Roman counsel at Smyrna
- Joan of Arc before Beauvais at Rouen
- Luther before the Diet of Worms
- Cramner before Queen Mary
- Bonhoeffer before Hitler

When Pastor Tokes in Hungary/Rumania or Vaclev Havel in Prague stand against authorities in the singular power of God, we see the enduring influence of the first commandment. The ultimate grounding of one's devotion and action in God is the surest anchor for one who seeks to do "what is right." The command mitigates against all tyranny. All other expediencies short of God— survival, security, reputation, gain, —finally yield sway when all is at stake. A collective people cannot live the command in life or death circumstances. The closest any group or nation has come are the pacifist Amerindian tribes, the Armenians before the Turks in Anatolia or the Jews before the third Reich. The biblical tradition lives on through catechisms, creeds and declarations. It also proceeds into the world through the beliefs and actions of people. Let us now turn to some of the theological-ethical ramifications of C-1. We will then finally turn to some implications for today.

Theology

Some scholars like Joy Davidman[90] and Calum Carmichael[91] argue that the eventually-settled text is set after years of violation of the specific stipulates. Davidman contends that the theological sense of the Commandment "Do not kill," for example, is an acknowledged awareness of the fact that we tend to kill, harm and otherwise do violence to one another all the time. The Commandments, as it were, say this,"you are, therefore you shall not." Carmichael finds in C-1 a response to the incident of the golden calf (p. 28). In Exodus the people offer the false claim to Aaron, who is smelting the idol:

> These are your gods, O Israel who brought you up out of the land of Egypt.
> (Exodus 32: 4,8)

It is also retroactive response to the golden calves later set up at the religious shrines of Bethel and Dan (I Kings 12: 25-33). These authors are correct to note that the first God commandment says something about both God and humans. As we will see with the next word, humans are always about construing God in human image, much as God makes people in God's image. Despite the ubiquity

---

[90] *Smoke on the Mountain.* Louisville: Westminster/John Knox Press, 1985.
[91] *The Origins of Biblical Law.* New York: Cornell University Press, 1992.

of this mirroring and manipulating tendency, C-1 affirms the radical freedom and separateness of God from all human construction and creativity.

God remains free and sovereign, not to be coerced. God's first demand is for singular loyalty. It is surprisingly free of definition. There are no strings attached, no details given—only a simple prelude of great deeds of deliverance.

> I am the Lord your God
> I delivered you out of Egypt
> You shall interpose no other gods between us....

The first theme of C-1 is the saving God who now says to us what that awesome deliverance means.

The actual name of the God of Sinai, says W.F. Albright, is *YAHWEH ASER YIWEH*. This God is the only God; the one who brings into being whatever comes into being. This is Yahweh—I Am Who Am—in the old Creed and Latin Bible—*EGO SUM QUI SU*. Luther's words are more faithful to the Hebrew:

ICH WERDE SEIN, DER ICH SEIN WERDE.

I will be the one I will be. God is the full expression of all we put into three poor human words: act, will, and being. In Exodus 23:19, a companion text to the Yahweh text says:

> I will be graceful to whom I will to be graceful
> I will show mercy on whom I show mercy.

The verb senses of both the Hebrew future tense and the Greek passive participle connote dynamic movement. God is not passive and abstract. Though not limited in any sense by space and time, God is a living God- with all that means in terms of being in nature and history. "Look—I am doing a new thing—do you perceive it?" (Isaiah 43:19). In biblical verbiage, it is best to say:

> "I am who I am becoming" (Exodus 3:14, 15)
> "I am being saved" (I Corinthians 1:18)

Such a God is effective and engaging. Efficacy is the characteristic of God's ongoing work in the world. God heals, makes right, restores, makes whole, renews and fulfills. God does well. God fashions Shalom. Engagement is the mode of God's activity. God's being and doing is cooperative, co-creative, participatory. There is an ethical flow going on, cleansing our evil, refreshing our good.

False Gods

The obverse of establishment is elimination. For Yahweh to reign unrivaled all other gods must cease to be. As John Milton sang on the "Morning of Christ's Nativity" (1629), there is a certain sadness in this *Götterdämmerung*:

> The horrid clang as Mt. Sinai rang...
> Nor is Osiris seen
> In Memphis grove or green,
> Trampling the un-showered grass with lowings loud
> He feels Judas' land
> The dreaded Infant's hand;
> The rays of Bethlehem blind his dusky eye.

A liberal and tolerant age such as ours especially chafes in the presence of such monistic and imperialistic spirit. The variety of perspectives and values, all derivatives of the plethora of ultimacies which people own, provides a rich and colorful ambiance for living. Dr. Casauban in George Eliot's *Middlemarch* has spent his entire scholarly life showing the commonality of all of the world's myths. No one has had the heart to tell him that the Germans had already done the research. Life is more interesting with a range of options. Swinburne reproached the "Pale Galilean" for displacing so many exotic things. There is a certain harsh and predictable ethos that comes with secularization, what the Germans call *Entmytholizierung* or *Entgötterung*—the wiping away of the little fakers. Science is now possible. There are no more erratic impulses in nature. Yet mathematics, science, and certainly technology is of such boring regularity.

In ethics, the iconoclasm of C-1 stifles promiscuity and fosters homogeneity and orthopraxy. There is a singular right way. It happens to be our way. All people had better subscribe and conform. But is this plea of the pagan and anticlerical not merely a caricature of the ethic and underlying theology of the twin mountains of Sinai and the *Bergpredigt*? In this emblazoned, yet endearing, composite message, we are asked to forsake those deities which cannot refresh and enlarge but which can only diminish our spirits because they are penultimate and irrelevant. These vitiate the good way, the good truth, and the good life which alone vivifies. God does not take redolence and fragrance from us. The God who knows us and redeems us in Christ—also in Him—freely gives us all things (Romans 8:32). In authentic biblical faith, the law is the light, the delight of life. The first road is less traveled. In biblical imagery, the light of the two ways of life is sketched from Elijah to Didache. C-1 asks us to abandon our fantasies, illusions and projections and return to the truth of God. Freud noted that our projection of some protecting and providing deity alleviated responsibility and muted joy. The god of Jane Russell, "A Cosmic Sugar Daddy," is too saccharine. Tchaikovsky's "Kingdom of Sweets" in the Nutcracker can become a scary and bitter place. Freedom is reality, not fantasy. Reflecting on the therapeutic meaning of "no other gods" and on the transcendent focus of the psyche, Ann and Barry Ulanov write in *Religion and the Unconscious*:

> By directing allegiance to an extra-mundane authority, religion provides the individual person with a frame of reference that transcends the mass-mindedness of modern society. Such empirical awareness of an intensely personal reciprocal relationship between one's self and the otherness of this otherworldly authority protects the individual from submersion in the mass. It provides the basis of individual freedom and authority.[92]

Many of the treacherous self-deifications and projected ideologies of the mind and heart are simply prejudices. Obsessed with such an *idee fixe*, such absolutisms and apotheoses of the human will, we shape God into our own images. Refusing to acknowledge God's pre-eminence and the derivative requirement of human love and justice, we turn others into objects of contempt and discrimination. In his blunt Brooklyn way, Archie Bunker runs roughshod over the Commandment with his neighbor, George Jefferson:

Archie: You an atheist?

George: No, I believe in God.

Archie: That's nice. Interestin', too! I mean how the black people went from worshipin' snakes and beads and wooden idols...all the way up to our God.

George: What do you mean, YOUR God?

Archie: Well, he's the white man's God, ain't he?

George: That ain't necessarily so. What makes you think God isn't black?

Archie: Because God created Men in his own image, and you'll note I ain't black.

Redirecting attention and understanding to God is the only way to avoid objectifying and dehumanizing others, thereby destroying their subjectivity. Closely related to the iconoclastic mood in spiritual life, the mood of humility in the ethical life, like the cathartic mood in the psychic life, is the political mood defying any tyranny over the human person. The Reformed catechisms, which tend toward tyrannicide and popular democracy over monarchy, anchor this allegiance in **C-1**.

The history of Israel until its ancient destruction, exile and dispersion was one of oscillation between loyalty and idolatry. Idolatry usually took the form of sell-out to some comfortable tyranny over mind, heart, and devotion. The golden calf was smashed at the foot of Sinai, but it continued to be enshrined, especially in Ephraim, long after Moses. After Baal was overpowered at Mount Carmel,

---

[92] Ann and Barry Ulanov, *Religion and the Unconscious*. Philadelphia: Westminster Press, 1975, p. 216.

Elijah slew his prophets by Brook Kishon. Yet Elijah was soon on the run; it remained for bloodthirsty King Jehu to wipe out the House of Ahab, feed Jezebel to the dogs and eliminate Baal worship from Israel. Even then we remember Jehu's seduction of the wife of Hosea. And down to our own history—the house has not yet been swept clean. From the time of Abraham until our own, little gods are always tucked away in the knapsack.

In Mother Russia early in the twentieth century, in the heart of Byzantine Christendom, other gods would dethrone the Lord and enthrone a demi-god that would last 80 years. And then in the land of Luther, that land so exquisitely purged of the pagan thought and ritual so that even Rome acknowledged the validity of its Reformation, Germany itself in the early mid-twentieth century became a new demi-god as a new worship took hold and the curtain of inhumanity descended. Elie Wiesel's *Night* ensues. And, even as Pastor Bonhoeffer hangs on Flossenberg's gallows, the voice of Pastor Niemoller is heard, crying *"Gott ist mein Führer."* "We reject the false doctrine that the state should or can beyond its special task become the sole and total order of human life, thus fulfilling also the Church's vocation": so confessed the Synod of Barmen in 1934.

The principal social and political yield of C-1 has been the challenge to tyranny. Jews and early Christians in their turn refused to acknowledge the Roman Emperor as *Kurios*. John Wycliff lectured on this in fourteenth century Oxford, decrying the tyranny of church and state and planting the seeds of reformation. Jan Hus, Tyndale and Cramner continue the tale. The State, even the sacral state, is not God.

Today

Which leads us to today. Reflecting on the wonderful antinomy in Luther's larger catechism of "Having no other gods" but "Having a God," Paul Lehmann reflects on the nature of concentrated iconoclastic, monolatrous faith in God. He finds two human ways to perceive and politically construct the world both in defiance of God's law and God's kingdom. Though these construals are inevitable, they are both in error. We wish the world to be shaped in *hierarché* or *egalité* and do our best to make it one way or the other. The ancient autocratic and modern feudal structure is one pathway. The way of the French Revolution is the other. Both defy the Lord God of history who, at will, lifts up and casts down. We seek a world either ordered, valenced and subordinated or one radically undivided, unorganized and unordered. In the divine schemes of apperception of the divine, as Lehmann would call it, *hierarché* and *égalité* are ways that we construct the world without God. Authority or freedom is a way we position ourselves over against God—the kind of interposition condemned in C-1. Here we seek to give ourselves position, standing. And the warnings of Eden's Garden echo throughout the annals of history, "They shall be like gods."

Jack Miles sharply draws the implication of C-1 by observing that God—the one whom the bible biographs—gradually becomes more unitary and ethical.[93] Miles may be right, but is it not rather the case that humans, gradually chastened through cultural evolution, have become less interposing and more disposed to hear and respond to one whose character and will is justice and love? The first commandment will always haunt us. Its sheer and radical cue to acknowledgment, then belief, then love, then service is the genius of human theology, philanthropy and of humankind's sublime and solemn victory over destruction and death.

Self

The drama of the first commandment transpires primally in the soul of each person. Who am I? *Cogito, ergo sum.* The paradise narrative speaks of an immediate relation with God, unmediated by estrangement, unsullied by shame. By the time of Moses, a painful distance had fractured this intimacy. Humans cannot bear to see the face of God. They can't even endure the face that has seen the face.

Today, as depicted in Boissan's painting *"Printemps"* in *Quatre Saisons* in the Louvre, we have been expelled from such dreaming innocence of intimacy and immediacy as we enjoyed in the garden before succumbing to delectable freedom and autonomy. The search to discover the self has followed psychoanalytic, political and philosophical paths. In each case the "know thyself" has failed since, as Calvin showed, true knowledge of self is intertwined with knowledge of God.

Sacred Community

As we noted earlier in this chapter in the section on the Barmen Declaration, apotheosis of the self, the breach of C-1, can corrupt the church and interpose it as a foreign, competitive god that distracts the loyalty of people who rightfully belong to God alone. Nothing is more insidious than "other gods" usurpation of rightful sovereignty in the house of faith itself. The revolutionaries of the sixteenth century changed the modern world of spirit by orienting the church to God's word. When Scripture replaced ritual, sacrament, hierarchy and all other primacies as the center of ecclesial life, a constant corrective to disorienting religion was set in place. When the living word—preached, written and studied—chastens religiosity, the chances are enhanced for *verbum dei* and *visio dei* to sustain our life.

Society

Political entities can seek to stand beside or even displace deity. Nationalism, especially pagan hyper-nationalism such as we saw in Germany, Italy, and Japan in the mid-twentieth century, inclines in this direction.

---

[93] *Ibid.*, p. 110, 111.

Similarly, collectivism, when joined to totalitarian structure and propaganda, can distort the channels of free communication of truth and the rightful lordship of God over people. When social systems seek to dominate the soul, require undivided loyalty and be revered, even worshipped as god, they usurp their rightful authority and corrupt the integrity of selves, sacred communities and society itself.

Freedom and Human Rights

The first commandment provides the philosophical ground for several prized values, including religious liberty, freedom of conscience, the right of civil disobedience, and the broad spectrum of human rights. Religious liberty and its concomitant public policy commitment to religious toleration is grounded in the fact that no person or group can be coerced to some devotion or worship. While the question of religious observance in public settings (school prayer, religious symbols in the town square, etc.) remains controversial, the abiding norm is that God alone reigns in the conscience and no human imposition can displace that authority.

Freedom of conscience, related to free speech, free press, etc. and its active expression in conscientious objection and the right to civil disobedience, flows from the same "Higher Law background to the American Constitution." (Corwin) rooted in the Decalogue and first commandment. The human ethical principle of sanctity of soul and conscience is grounded in the divine principle of unhindered access to those same faculties. Humans are worthy of ultimate respect by virtue of *Imago Dei*. A modest and restricted mandate on issues of advertising, education, indoctrination, media influence, ideological requirement and political loyalty also flows from this theological verity and derivate ethical value.

The broader field of human rights also finds substantial support in the societal yield of the first commandment. The two-fold premise that God wills human fulfillment and that fulfillment comes through certain rights: worship, education, movement, justice, health, etc., and that humans tend to expropriate and violate these rights is the **C-1** architecture for all documents on human rights. While these premises of human possibility and human sin are not explicit in secular, public charters they are obviously implicit. They are "endowed," "inalienable" from "The Creator": **C-1**.

Excursus

We've frequented this restaurant for years. Each time we come to Strasbourg, the old Brasserie under the cathedral has been a great place for *tarte flambé* or *steak, frites* and *salade*. Tonight, as always, it is filled with young people. One can only wonder, what are their gods? What things do they hold dear? What do they live for? What interposing ultimacies turn them off? Students—aspiring to a career, to make a living, have some fun, have a family, make some difference before it all ends. Their age may make them selfreflective. Their music is intense, erotic, angry, yet open to meaning. Their films celebrate comedy and irony, revel in mystery, intrigue, rescue, survived suspense and violence. Or are these perhaps the bimillenial "organization kids" at Princeton who, in David Brooks' interesting essay in the Atlantic monthly, when asked about moral questions… "would flee such talk and start discussing legislative questions.[94]

Was Augustine right: was sacrament visible word? What is their sacrament? What is their Gospel? Law? Values are certainly configurative (from comtemporaries) rather than post- figurative (from elders and authority, to borrow Margaret Mead's category). In the end, peer pressure prevails and their lives will be lived out on a fairly flat strata of experience. We find little heroism in these days of affluence and comfort. Yet they are poor in their own way and will suffer as persons of all conditions in all generations suffer sickness, trembling disappointment, loss of love, grief, pain and death. The Westminster Confession offered "Man's chief end is to glorify God and enjoy Him forever", and Heidelberg seconded: "My only hope in life and death is my faithful savior, Jesus Christ." All are after Luther's "Have no other gods," but "Have a god." Yet tonight the young people seek to rub shoulders, to laugh and sigh with friends, to lift the stein and pass a few hours, and I'm here with them. Perhaps when we depart into the evening's chill and light snowfall, we will ask together the question of C-1: "what's it all about?"

II. Mirrors and Images: A Theology of Imagination
Mirror, mirror on the wall, who's the fairest one of all?
-The Wicked Witch in Snow White

> Then Jesus and the disciples went away to the village near Caesarea Philippi. On the way he asked them, 'Tell me, who do people say I am?' 'Some say that you are John the Baptist,' they answered; 'others say that you are Elijah, while others say that you are one of the prophets.' 'What about you?' he asked them. 'Who do you say I am?' Peter answered, 'You are the Messiah.' (Matthew 8: 27-29, Good News Bible).

Paul writes to the Church at Corinth of the way in which they are living letters to each other:

> It is clear that Christ himself wrote this letter and sent it by us. It is written, not with ink but with the Spirit of the living God, and not on stone tablets but on human hearts.

> We say this because we have confidence in God through Christ. There is nothing in us that allows us to claim that we are capable of doing this work. The capacity we have comes from God; it is he who made us capable of serving

---

[94] David Brooks. *The Next Ruling class; Meet the Organization Kid.* The Atlantic Monthly, April 2000, p. 53.

the new covenant, which consists not of a written law but of the Spirit. The written law brings death, but the spirit gives life.

The Law was carved in letters on stone tablets, and God's glory appeared when it was given. Even though the brightness on Moses' face was fading, it was so strong that the people of Israel could not keep their eyes fixed on him. If the Law, which brings death when it is in force, came from such glory, how much greater is the glory that belongs to the activity of the Spirit! The system, which brings condemnation, was glorious; how much more glorious is the activity which brings salvation! We may say that because of the far brighter glory now that the glory that was so bright in the past is gone. For if there was glory in that which lasted for a while, how much more glory is there in that which lasts forever!

Because we have this hope, we are very bold. We are not like Moses, who had to put a veil over his face so that the people of Israel would not see the brightness fade and disappear. Their minds, indeed, were closed; and to this very day their minds are covered with the same veil as they read the books of the old covenant. The veil is removed only when a person is joined to Christ. Even today, whenever they read the Law of Moses, the veil still covers their minds. But it can be removed, as the scripture says about Moses: "His veil was removed when he turned to the Lord." Now, "the Lord" in this passage is the Spirit; and where the Spirit of the Lord is present, there is freedom. All of us, then, reflect the glory of the Lord with uncovered faces; and that same glory, coming from the Lord, who is the Spirit, transforms us into his likeness in an ever-greater degree of glory. (II Corinthians 3: 3-18: *Good News Bible*)

Now we see through a mirror vaguely; then we will see face to face. (I Corinthians 13: 12)

When the Lord spoke to you from the fire on Mt. Sinai, you did not see any form. For your own good, then, make certain that you do not sin by making for yourselves an idol in any form at allwhether man or woman, animal or bird, reptile or fish. Do not be tempted to worship and serve what you see in the sky-the sun, the moon, and the stars. The Lord your God has given these to all other peoples for them to worship. But you are the people he rescued from Egypt, that blazing furnace. He brought you out to make you his own people, as you are today. Because of you the Lord your God was angry with me and solemnly declared that I would not cross the Jordan River to enter the fertile land which he is giving you. I will die in this land and never cross the river, but you are about to go across and occupy that fertile land. Be certain that you do not forget the covenant that the Lord your God has made with you. Obey his command not to make yourselves any kind of idol, because the Lord your God is like a flaming fire; he tolerates no rivals.

Even when you have been in the land a long time and have children and grandchildren, do not sin by making yourselves an idol in any form at all. This is evil in the Lord's sight, and it will make him angry. I call heaven and earth as witnesses against you today that, if you disobey me, you will soon disappear from the land. You will not live very long in the land across the Jordan that you are about to occupy. You will be completely destroyed. The Lord will scatter you among other nations, where only a few of you will survive. There you will serve gods made by human hands, gods of wood and stone, gods that cannot see or hear, eat or smell. There you will look for the Lord your God, and if you search for him with all your heart, you will find him. When you are in trouble and all those things happen to you, then you will finally turn to the Lord and obey him. He is a merciful God. He will not abandon you or destroy you, and he will not forget the covenant that he himself made with your ancestors. (Deuteronomy 4)

Introduction

Images and reflections, idols and personifications. The relevance seems remote to an ethical theology today. Yet that ancient contemporary world of the Egyptian detention, the Sinai experience and the settlement of Palestine was one bursting with deities and idols. Despite Iknahton's monotheistic revolution in Egypt, there were still the gods of river and moon, dog, cat, crocodile. In Canaan, Baal and Astarte were alive and well along with myriad *Kadoshim* (Holy Temple prostitutes). Cosslett Quin summarizes:

> Into such a swampy forest of pagan religion, with its towering trees and flowering creepers, its monkeys and birds of paradise, its sweet fruits and swift poisons that look no less bright and sweet, its snakes and crocodiles and slime came the children of Israel. Their lungs were still full of the pure dry desert air. Their ears still echoed the Word of Sinai, "I am the Lord thy God", and the "Thou shalt's and the "Thou shalt nots" which had come out from amid the lightning and thunders. Would the swamp swallow them up into its life and fragrance and corruption? Or would they be able to drain, clear and inhabit it?[95]

The austere desert is associated with Decalogue, the steamy city with debauchery. Jacques Ellul spoke of "La Cite" as the place of God-abandonment. Life today is similarly succulent. The spiritual simplicity and ethical austerity of the Sinai then and now do not come easy to people soaked with options and surrounded by enticements. If C-1 is about the divine expression into human reality making all pretension impotent, then C-2 is about the human expression of thoughts and arts toward the divine ultimacy. The commands therefore are closely linked. We humans are *Homo Religiosis*. We inevitably worship and serve something or someone. Every human being believes in some ultimate reality and behaves in accord with some normative vision. The confluence of C-1 and C-2 therefore provides the architecture to assess the theological and ethical edifice of our lives. Our gods can be self, nation, prosperity and race. Our passions can be narcissistic, nationalistic, acquisitive, and prejudicial. The message of C-2 is that all our gods are too small (J.B. Phillips).

Some commandments obviously reflect the backdrop of the paradise garden and East of Eden memories. Cain and Abel is obviously in mind in C-6, "You shall not kill." C-1 through C-3 seems to evoke the Garden of Eden motif of a primal competition between humans and God. Coveting may allude to the allure of the

---

[95] *The Ten Commandments: A Theological Exposition*. London: Lutterworth Press, 1951, p. 52.

garden trees. Again think of Boussan's first of Four Seasons in the Louvre or his contemporary, Michaelangelo's *Temptation Garden* in the Sistine Chapel. C-2 is a vivid reaction to the Golden Calf episode (Exodus 32). The calf was a popular regional deity, combining ostentation, fertility, and sacrifice. So persuasive was the symbol that it persisted in the tribe of Ephraim and at Bethel and Dan long after the Mosaic iconoclasm.

In order to trace the theological and ethical significance of the *Bilderverbot* for us today, let us continue our sequence whereby we examine the text, then follow with analysis of tradition, theology and the commandments' meaning for today. In all of the archaic legalethical systems, the Noachian heritage in Semitic tradition and the Egyptian heritage in the Book of the Dead, for example, a primal wrong is blasphemy—presumption against and failure to extol the God. To insult the being or action of God, defaming, displacing, or disavowing the power of God, denying the existence or denigrating the efficacy of God is the primal violation embodied in C-1 through C-3. Refutation of the great "I am" is simply "You're not." The Garden rebellion is simply doubt. "Did God say?" "You shall not die." "No other gods," "no idols," "no misuse of the Name," are a composite affirmation of the positive and absolute reality, integrity, singularity, and authority of God.

Of course we find in the commandment a vestige of the primitive superstition and identification of the spirit and object found in the voodoo doll, or other castings or carvings such as Sumerian fertility goddesses. The conviction behind these idols, amulets, or seraphim was that you could control, cajole, or harm the being or spirit represented by the model.

Yet something novel is occurring in this Sinai dictum. Yahweh, this strange and intrusive new God, heretofore unknown, comes into sharp relief at Sinai. This God is not like the precursor deities, even the compelling monocrats who were still somehow commingled with fertility, bane and blessing, sun, moon or stars, trees or animals. This new God stands behind and above creation and is profoundly and caringly involved in things that happen to people and nations. Though still a God whose power is manifest in nature, Yahweh is more rightly described as a God of history. God is intimate to creation and to his creatures but it is a mysterious or sacramental presence; first you see it, then you don't. God is not enmeshed in or immersed in the matter. In the acute understanding of iconography represented, among others, in the Greek, Russian and Armenian tradition, the icon is not the god in any material sense—but the divine Spirit can shine through the image as the eyes of faith see through the very common physical object, picture, or form. It is sacrament. Like the stained glass rose window of Chartres Cathedral, it radiates a story, yes, and a presence from beyond. It is the faith story of the people of God that irradiates and illumines an icon. Gerhard Von Rad observes:

> Nature was not a mode of Yahweh's being; he stood over against it as its Creator. This then means that the Commandment forbidding images is bound

up with the hidden way in which Yahweh's revelation came about in cult and history...The Yahweh whom Israel was so strictly forbidden to worship by means of an image was still the same Yahweh by whose hidden action in history she was continually kept in suspense.[96]

The profound irony of biblical faith is that the image-busting and iconoclasm so prominent at the inception of the Yahweh covenant and so intense, especially at historical moments of orthodoxy and orthopraxy, itself relies on the mediating efficacy of two icons: human persons (*imago dei*) and Jesus the Christ as God's self expression, "the image of the invisible God" (Colossians 1:15). Unless you believe that deity is pure oblivion, some kind of iconographic imagination is necessary to depict faith. The same people who warned against images as impeding the true knowledge of God rely on two images as essential to that conduit—the human soul as a divine casting, carved out in the image of God, and the God incarnate as image that has at last penetrated the veil of alienation (Hebrews 10:1). God's image, as Karl Barth suggests in his reflection on Genesis, is the man/woman relation. "Woman is the mirror image of man," says Hildegard of Bingen, "in whom the whole human race lay hidden." In this reciprocity the divinity/humanity of God is represented. Yet something is wrong, something is missing in the very act of representation. A photo or painting never even approximates the real thing, unless it is Van Gogh's "Field of Purple Iris" or Monet's "Pond of Lily Pads." As the Sioux Indian woman looking on Mt. Rushmore, South Dakota, bewailed the white man's iconography:

I feel like it's a desecration—to have to carve those heads is an insult to the storm gods—they can do the carving themselves—they came here and took everything from us.

There are iconic and aniconic idols. The Mt. Rushmore heads—Jefferson, Washington, Lincoln, and Roosevelt—are icons; the natural mountain, and in some sense the new great horse being carved in Dakota, like the chalk horse in Uffingham in Southwest England, are aniconic nature forms. Aniconic forms are not as selfimposing. (Was it Reagan or Rockefeller who commented when viewing Mt. Rushmore, "I'd like to be a part of that?")

A colleague calls these explicit and tacit transgressions. Sometimes the sin is silly: the primitive African fertility statue with gross counterbalancing bosom and buttocks. The heaven above and the earth beneath—add Esther Williams and we've got the water under the earth or a fish called Wanda.

Text

YOU SHALL NOT MAKE YOURSELF IMAGES OR ANY RESEMBLANCE OF THINGS IN HEAVEN, ON EARTH, IN THE UNDERWORLD, OR IN THE SUBTERRANEAN WATERS. YOU SHALL

---

[96] *Op Cit.,* p. 218.

NOT BOW DOWN TO THEM, OR SERVE THEM; FOR I AM A JEALOUS
GOD...
(Exodus 20: 4, 5)

The verse expands the textual intent of C-1. When worship of the one true God
is forthcoming all is well and good, only now that devotion is expressed through
inadequate symbols or imagination. Depictions are incapable of bearing deity.
Worship, yes, but not the wrong way. Glory, praise and service must be direct
and unmediated. Thus, the offense to Judaism of Jesus, the image of the
invisible God (Colossians 1:15).

The exotically crafted creatures of Egypt must come to mind. Great birds, dogs
(*Anubis*), the marsh and water creatures: hippos and alligators. Nostalgia must
be rejected, for here and now in Yahweh's train comes a new mandate, a new
project.

"For I am a jealous God." Originally the word *Kanna* suggests one who has
been injured or hurt. When one invests in a people, singles them out from among
the nations for a special favor, blessing and opportunity, rejection or displaced
devotion wounds the One who cares so deeply. The image here of husband,
parents or lover expresses possessiveness in the best sense, and recalls Hosea.
God's love for us and our love for God is close to the essence of Judaism.

The point of the commandment is not to discourage arts and crafts, but rather
not to indulge the cults these images and idols represent. The text, in other
words, repudiates other loves, other ways of life, other settlements of faith.

Textual History
The commandment traces a moving legacy through Hebrew scriptures. Here
are some of the touchstones:

- Exodus 34: 17—cast idols illicit in cultic code.

- Deuteronomy 6: 14—now applied to foreign gods, eg. Canaanite
  deities.

- Leviticus 19: 4—a dimension of moral and ritual holiness.

- Jeremiah 43: 13—recollection of Yahweh's iconoclastic fury
  toward Egypt.

- Hosea 3: 4, 10: 1, 2—Yahweh's good inheritance will have no
  need of idols, pillars.

- Psalm 73: 20—Yahweh despises their images.

- Ezekiel 7: 20, 16: 17, 23: 14—Images are abominations to the
  Lord.

- I Kings 6:23ff., 29, 7: 25, 29; II Kings 10: 26, 27, 18: 4— when objects of religious art glorify God they are honored. When they themselves are venerated, they must be banned.

In further tracking C-2, the New Testament continues the iconoclastic mood though, unlike Maccabean Judaism, it extends honor to the Roman Empire. The Roman coin reminds us of two loyalties.

- Acts 7: 41—In Stephen's majestic sermon, he recounts the episode with Moses, yet God's persistent love for his people.
- Romans 1: 23, 26-31, 2: 22—The perishable images of human construction are contrasted to the image of God on the son—true and connective in Tillich's sense of symbol.
- Revelation 9: 20ff.—The destroying sixth angel comes in judgment to those who have given over their lives to serve idols.

The textual tradition places great weight on the crafting of alienating or diverting images or idols. These are soundly condemned because they distort knowledge and devotion and lead us astray. Idols and images are tantalizing lures to the imagination. They fascinate and rob God of proper devotion. They also harm the human spirit by anchoring trust and direction in non-living entities that fail to comfort and mislead. They can't do it, come up empty, and are not worthy substitutes for God alone.

Tradition
Early Christianity
When one tours the environs where early Christianity took hold, you cannot miss the impact of early Christian iconoclasm. In the western coast of Asia Minor and in Greece, for example, the turmoil-filled centuries between the second CE and seventh (the rise of Islam) are marked by the following movements:

- Ancient Greek and Roman temples are identified as places of worship.
- The ancient figures, columns, statues and depicted mosaics are obliterated in iconoclastic fury.
- In Constantinian and Justinian establishment the old pagan sites, together with the Christian holy places are baptized and re-consecrated.
- They are dismantled again in the Islamic iconoclasm.
- Finally they are reconstituted in the modern settlements.
- This is true in Jerusalem, Bethlehem, Nazareth, Pergammon, Ephesus, and elsewhere.

- The sheer force and fervor of the unmediated God, one known in the intimacy of the devout soul and conveyed in sacrament and ritual alone explains the enormous energy given to dismantle the "graven images."

Beneath the exuberant religious art and statuary of the early renaissance in Europe a similarly severe spirit of iconoclasm can be felt. The catechisms of the sixteenth century press hard on C-2 in order to safely lead children and converts from the false loyalties that abounded so in that demoralized world back toward the living God. In catechesis and liturgy Luther, Bucer, Calvin, Zwingli and the rest seek to sternly warn parishioners against erroneous worship. In Calvin, for example, rightful worship is itself a censure of idolatry. A false and empty way of worship, piety and prayer had set in during the formalism and nominalism of the late middle ages. Faith was a "name only" business and did not claim one's total life. The problem, of course, with the sixteenth century Protestant polemic is that there actually was spiritual vitality in Roman Catholic worship and piety, and not all Protestant worship was vital and lifechanging. The Protestant diatribes against the "idolatrous mass" were necessary for pure word and worship of authentic Catholic faith to be renewed, but they should have looked in the mirror.

The issue of idolatry was a central concern of Bucer and Calvin's reform. Luther was less animated to transform liturgy or sacrament. The mass for Calvin was an abomination—the human construction of God-offending gibberish, superstition and pagan idolatry. For Calvin, the purpose of human life is to know, worship, and serve God aright. Disorienting worship makes such human fulfillment impossible.

If the whole purpose of human existence is to honor God—*Soli Deo Gloria*—then authentic worship is the precondition of being truly alive. In his 1543 treatise *"On the Necessity of Reforming the Church,"*

Calvin writes in words pervaded by C-2:

> If it be asked then, by what things chiefly the Christian religion has a standing existence amongst us, and maintains its truth, it will be found that the following two not only occupy the principal place, but comprehend under them all the other parts, and consequently the whole substance of Christianity, viz, a knowledge first, of the right way to worship God; and secondly of the source from which salvation is to be sought. When these are kept out of view, though we may glory in the name of Christians, our profession is empty and vain.[97]

The church, as then constituted, couldn't deliver. It impeded salvation. It interposed idols between humans and God. Pagan idolaters in antiquity clung tenaciously to their altars, entangled entrapment and magical hold on people.

---

[97] "De necessitate reformandae Ecclesia," (1543), *Calvin Opera* 6:459.

They had to try to prove, like the Baal prophets on Mt. Carmel, that they could deliver the goods, that their rituals were efficacious. Protestant worship, emphasizing God's word in living sacrament, restored this selfvalidating efficacy to God's self-giving and comforting (strengthening) embrace of His people. Yet, even *Protestant worship* would forever be haunted by new idolatries: the book, reason and conscience, penultimacies of ego and culture elevated to ultimacy.

Extracts from Calvin's (1536) and Bucer's (1537) catechism emphasize this point in another sector of societal and church reformation, that of the demoralized and redirected and renewed person. If Bucer and Calvin had strong administrative (ecclesial and political) instincts, Luther's were those of personal sacrifice and existential rigor. What transpires in the human spirit, in the inner soul when the self is divided between greater and lesser gods or the ultimate God and penultimate impressions or imaginings (C-2)? Bucer and Calvin accent the point of Luther's catechism of undivided attention that alone saves and sustains. The accent of C-2 in the 1536 French catechism is that condemning judgment (the long afterword of the commandment—judgment to the fourth generation) is always counter-balanced by irresistible searching and saving grace of forgiveness.

Q: Why does he here say a thousand generations (forgiveness), whereas, in the case of punishment, he mentions only three or four?

A: To intimate that he is more inclined to kindness and beneficence than to severity. This he also declares, when he says he is ready to pardon, but slow to wrath.
(Exodus 34: 6, Psalm 103: 8, 145: 8).

For Calvin, knowledge of God, which is associated with knowledge of self (Bk. I, Institutes), is inextricably bound to authentic worship, which is safe guarded by C-2. Bucer accents the same point in the 1537 catechism (my translation).

Q: What does the Lord intend in this commandment?

A: That I not place the majesty due God only on picturesor other gods, but that in all knowledge, belief and devotion, I focus on God in spirit and in truth.

In a companion prayer to this phase of the Decalogue Bucer offers: "only thus can my heart and conscience remain free." The Scots and Heidelberg Confessions emphasize strongly the iconoclastic impulse, given the mania for depiction that verged on idolatry in the late medieval Roman culture of the Pfalz and "Heather" Scotland. Barmen is focused on the same point, as both state and church are lifted up to entice imagination and loyalty.

Theology
This leads to a discussion of the theological meaning of C-2. The continuing theological challenge of C-2, as Shubert Ogden or James Gustafson has shown, is to better square our misshapen fabricated concepts with the reality of God. C-2 is a religious commandment. Behind it is the threat of idolatrous worship or piety grounded in false imagination. Its primary burden is the theological. A range of theological meanings is borne on C-2. If God is the only true God and the source of all truth then all other gods are human projections. If God is a moral God then to follow any spurious 'other' is misleading and dangerous. Cardinal to the theology of C-2 is the notion that God is beauty. The *summum bonum* of the Greeks was the true, the good and the beautiful.

> That beauty which penetrates and clasps and fills the world.
> (W. Wordsworth)

The psalmist (29:2) sings of the beauty of holiness which evokes our worship. William Blake once remarked, "There are three powers in man of conversing with paradise—poetry, painting, and music."

The Pythagoreans believed that three human endeavors penetrated the veil and touched the infinite and eternal: mathematics, music, and theology. If, indeed, certain human expressions have this transcending capacity to touch the divine realm, can they be condemned as "graven images?" If not, then touching the divine not to bring God down, to construct and define, but to lift us up to God is a noble gesture. For this reason, the less Puritanical and less iconoclastic of the Reformed creeds (e.g., Calvin) make a point not to condemn the plastic arts and painting.

A theology of beauty will lead us to express and fashion praise of holiness in music and poem, painting and sculpture. This all becomes faithful representation because, like the Tiffany stained glass of the Ascension at the beautiful Second Presbyterian Church of Chicago, which I have served as a pastor, it mediates and radiates divine glory.

In another sense beautiful forms, pictures and stories convey theological truth. James Gustafson writes of the aesthetic power in his own Scandinavian Reformed tradition:

> Novels, drama, poetry, music, and graphic arts have powers of illumination for many people that the abstractions of philosophers and theologians do not have. Certainly, then, such aesthetic representations have a religious significance. One can be affected by undisturbed concentration on, and absorption of, Bach's St. Matthew Passion in a way that is not only aesthetic but deeply religious, and certainly one can be more moved in this way than by reading a theological treatise on the atonement. For all its anthropomorphism, Michelangelo's depiction of the creation of the ceiling of the Sistine Chapel can evoke a deeper religious as well as emotional response than a rehearsal of the arguments about

creation out of nothing. Stories, narratives, metaphors, similes, and other aesthetic presentations of life, no doubt have formative powers in the development of coherent and meaningful outlooks on life.[98]

There is, therefore, also a theological-ethical meaning to C-2. If an authentic relationship with God involves not contorting divinity into our own shapes but being shaped by its grace, then the ethical life is the imagery and way by which we are transformed by spirit rather than conformed to world. (Romans 12:2) We are inevitably being shaped and sculpted according to some design. Some process of formation is shaping each of us all the time. We are either in shape or bent out of shape. As the Genesis narrative and Jeremiah movingly depict, we are sculpted from the mud of the earth into icons, images of beauty. Into what mold are we being cast? This is the question of character and virtue, which, along with specific acts and deeds, is the substance of ethics.

The second Commandment wisely counsels that the life of righteousness is the life free of disorienting encumbrances, "no false idols." In Graham Green's story "The Fallen Idol," he depicts the perennial icon as one in which more is invested than it can deliver. We have been love-bound and trust-bound to a jealous God. Though crude in anthropocentric imagery, this is the best we can do to describe the ligature of devotion, discipleship, and directionality that a concerned, non-apathetic God desires for our fulfillment as persons.

Worship, "our reasonable service," is the act of ascribing worth and acting in loyalty and common cause. Without ethical action worship is vacuous. Without worship, ethics is ill-informed. Conformation or transformation to the world (idolatry) or to God (worship) is being fashioned (sculpted) in concordance or contradiction. Proving what is good, acceptable, and perfect (Romans 12:2) is the construction of our lives into God's will. The prayer of Archbishop William Temple captures this imagination.

> Worship is the submission of all our nature to God. It is the quickening of conscience by his holiness; the nourishment of mind with his truth; the purifying of the imagination by his beauty; the opening of the heart to his love; the surrender of will to his purpose—and all of this gathered up in adoration, the most selfless emotion of which our nature is capable and therefore the chief remedy of that self-centeredness which is our original sin and the source of all actual sin.[99]

Morality, as German philosophers would say, involves being, being with God and being for others (*Miteinandersein*). Existential, eternal, and ethical being and belonging ground the good life. This threefold commitment is easily distorted and deviated. It requires strict concentration and fidelity. Any liaisons,

---

[98] *Ethics from a Theocentric Perspective*, Vol. 1. Chicago: University of Chicago Press, 1981, pp. 29, 30.
[99] William Temple, *The Oxford Book of Prayer*. Oxford: Oxford University Press, 1985, p. 3.

dangerous or benign, can disrupt genuine moral passion that is the will of God. To keep the mind and heart clear and free for belief and justice we must, in the words of Gabriel Vahanian, "Wait without idols."

Tillich after Anselm argues that God is "being itself"—which is a non-symbolic statement; it doesn't point to anything else. The most telling abrogation of C-2 is to make God into an object. Forsaking the mystery, we persistently try to objectify the being and willing of God. In James Gustafson's words, we "make God an object alongside of other objects in the world."

But we do and must picture God and God's purposes in order to perceive and act in response to God's being and will. Tillich offers the ancient Greek idea of *analogia entis* as a guide. If we call God, "shepherd, father or king," we do not fall into the trap of idolatry if that symbol is lifted up into the holiness of God.

> If a segment of reality is used for a symbol of God, the realm of reality from which it is taken is so to speak elevated into the realm of the holy. It is no longer secular. It is theonomous.[100]

Theonomy then becomes prophecy, reception of divine will, a God word or God law. God's people in the world are called to be prophets to one another. The prophet tears down in order to build up. The prophet is an idol buster. The moral counselor exorcises false images and illusory projections—false idols. Counseling, perhaps even psychiatry, is helping us become straight again after having been bent by some injustice in life. The purpose of catharsis is edification; putting one's life back together. The politician, if free from the false idols of expediency and true to that vocation, disabuses tyrants and defuses propaganda, refuses to hear *vox populi* as *vox dei* and honors the weak and vulnerable in public policy. In the words of Mary's Magnificat, a true leader is one who takes down the mighty in order to exalt the humble. At its best this is called democracy. The teacher, attorney, business person, and parent each live out iconoclastic duty as part of his or her responsibility in that particular path of life and history which is his or her destiny (vocatio). They do this in order to help build lives. Iconoclasm goes hand in hand with creation.

Excursus: Hand-made

> ...Not the labor of my hands, can fulfill thy law's demands.
> ...Nothing in my hands I bring, simply to thy cross I cling.

The heart of a Christian theology about idolatry is that we are freed in the Gospel of the responsibility of "*Handeln*," of fabricating, making everything ourselves, the world, our ultimacies. Now our handiwork, the labor of our own hands, can be exerted instrumentally rather than idolatrously. As with the Greek

---

[100] Paul Tillich, *Systematic Theology,* Vol. 1. Chicago: University of Chicago Press, 1951, p. 241.

icon, divine workshop can shimmer and shine through our own draft and craft. In the Hippocratic ritual of "laying on of hands," stark contrast is drawn with the biblical theology of blessing. In Hippocrate's treatise Holy Disease (Epilepsy, Seizure, etc.) he implies that in the "hands" of a doctor no external or internal power, healing or destructive, can "get hold of you." "You're in our hands now, you're safe." The divine benediction or the Ephesian elders laying hands on Paul is rather a blessing conducive to holy energy and benediction.

In Athens (Acts 17:24), Paul claims that the creator does not dwell in structures made "with human hands." In Christ's new creation, *acheiropoietos* (not made with hands) displaces the old usurping mode of creativity, *cheiropoietos* (made with hands). Just as Jesus, like an authentic iconoclastic prophet, foretold that in his own body (*Imago, Icon*) he would destroy the temple and recast another, "not made by hands" (John 2:13ff, Mark 14:58, Acts 7:48) So Paul looking on Athens' Acropolis with its Parthenon and Erechtheum sees the city "full of idols," and preaches the cosmic recreation of Christ's resurrection form. The majestic construction of the Torah, and the majestic Athenian project of thought and form are now given renewed form. Legal artifact, i.e. circumcision ("made in flesh by human hands" Ephesians 2:12, Colossians 2:11) is displaced by the circumcision of Christ, not made "by hands." We now have a temple made by God "a house not made with hands, eternal in the heavens." (II Corithians 5:1) The authentic way (road, fashion) of God is given. Torah is renewed.

In Christ's completed creation we appreciate that God has fashioned creation so that Torah fits. God tears in order to heal, prunes to allow fruition. God has constructed conscience so that Torah forms its architecture. The template of moral structure that organizes all of reality is the law which is light and life (Proverbs 6:23). The expectation toward and inclination away from God forms the axis point of the good. This moral law in creation corresponds to the inner capacity fashioned in the engraving of the spirit where hearts of stone are carved out to be sculpted by the residing law into the soft fleshy hearts within (Psalm 37:31, Ezekiel 11:19ff).

Augustine's prayer captures this divine iconography, where a God-shaped vacuum is filled by the precisely made-to-fit-in dwelling presence. It captures the mood of C-2.

"Late have I loved Thee, O Beauty so ancient and so new; late have I loved Thee: for behold Thou wert within me, and I outside; and I sought Thee outside and in my unloveliness fell upon those lovely things that Thou hast made. Thou wert with me, and I was not with Thee. I was kept from thee by those things, yet had they not been in thee, they would not have been at all. Thou didst call and cry to me to break open my deafness: and Thou didst send forth Thy beams and shine upon me and chase away my blindness: Thou didst breathe fragrance upon me, and I drew in my breath and do now pant for Thee: I tasted Thee, and now hunger and thirst for Thee: Thou didst touch me, and I have burned for Thy peace."[101]

Today

The second commandment carries special relevance for our day. We live in an age of divided selves, a contentious church and a fractious society. All of these manifestations of disorder and disorientation can be traced to abrogation of C-2. Healing can only come in renaissance of decalogic discernment.

Even before the dawn of Hebrew scripture, a cleavage in the human spirit was felt. "Choose this day who you will serve," cries Joshua. "As for me and my house, we will serve the Lord." C-2 addresses an ancient temptation and human tendency before a parting of the two ways.

Didache, a most early Christian catechism (c. 100 CE), is grounded in the juncture and the points of departure it enunciates. There is the Way of life (Torah, way) and the way of death. A memorable poem by Robert Frost depicts the two ways:

> Two roads diverged in a yellow wood,
> And sorry I could not travel both
> And be one traveler...

The integrity of the human self is constantly tempted of being torn into a divided self. We are either of one piece or schizophrenic (many). Resistance to the schizoid or diabolic (split, torn-apart) must be vigilant so that the authentic (symbolic/knit together) self can thrive.

As Scottish psychiatrist Ronald Laing has shown, the divided self is characteristic of contemporary persons. We have achieved some measure of immunity against suffering and death, yet we cannot evade our finitude. We have secured powerful ingredients of the good life yet pain, alienation and failure haunt us. The very presence of great possibility sets us up for disappointment. Even the pervasiveness of constant visual and audial stimulation (media) and erotic pleasure leaves us unfulfilled. Relationships cannot bear the expectations with which we invest them. Themes touched on in the inter human commandments—sexuality, violence, property and envy— illustrate the psychic and emotional truth of the theological commandment of worthy focused imagination (C-2).

Modern Depiction

In recent years, mainly through the influence of my wife Dr. Sara Anson Vaux, a scholar of literature and film, I have been challenged to think theologically about the new arts of visualization, especially the film. My rather simple, initial reaction is that great films; Bresson's Diary of a Country Priest;

---

[101] St. Augustine, *Oxford Book of Prayer*, p. 65.

Bergman's Winterlight, Stone's Platoon, and others, are in the sacramental tradition of enacting (visualizing to sound, touch, and taste), transcending matters of spiritual and moral insight. Augustine called the sacrament "The Visible Word." Even the great Jesus films; Jesus of Montreal (Arcand), The Gospel according to Matthew (Pasolini) and The Last Temptation (Scorsese) do not so much strike me as idolatrous or sacrilegious, but as iconic attempts to convey ultimate meanings, convictions and commitments. Of course idolatry is rampant. The pervasive defacing of the human body and love in our obsessive and abusive sexuality and violence is reprehensible whether it is MTV or MGM. The deep theological meaning of word, presence and sacrament in literature and film is that icons that portray ultimacy or the reality of God-self must be transparent, and conducive, i.e., not pretend to usurp God. They are symbols who, like John the Baptist, point to the One who is to come.

Food Offered to Idols: Sepsis and Carcinogenesis

A most difficult theme of this study comes early on and is cognate to the issue of idolatry. Jesus' ministry stumbles hard into scribal and pharisaical understandings of the law on this cache of matters:

- eating with sinners (Luke 5)
- not washing hands before eating (Mark 7:14-15)
- declaring all foods clean (Mark 7:19)

Jewish law held that:

- only a certain range of animals may be eaten:
    - those who "chew the cud" and have cloven hooves
    - fish with scales
    - the main fatty portions of animals, and their blood is forbidden, birds of prey, etc.
- animals that had remaining blood are forbidden
- animals that had been sacrificed to pagan idols are forbidden
- oil or wine that may have been contaminated by pagan libation are forbidden.

While these kosher, commensual and purity laws are not highlighted in the Decalogue, they are central to the "Noachian" essence of divine command (Genesis 9), and the version of that summary that becomes the basis for the settlement on the "required law" for Gentiles at the Jerusalem Council in Acts 15. They are also highlighted in the Edict to Antioch authorizing Paul's exception of the circumcision requirement, and the essence of law that Mohammed and Muslims were ready to accept in their dialogue with Medina's Jewish community in the seventh century C.E.

173

The purity of the food supply, and kosher law, is of course, based on sound public health principles in an age when we know as much about contamination and infection as we know today about carcinogenesis. These practices must have been grounded in centuries of trial and error experience. We know that sepsis—microbial infection—is the ground of contamination, and the broader vector of disease and death in the creation. The microbial bed of creation draws all life toward death and dissolution. Protecting oneself and one's community from premature and unnatural infection was a requirement of life.

The theological notions behind these monumentally important laws are the principles: (1) that God is life, (2) God does not kill and (3) that humans are the glory of God. Father Elias Chacour, the priest of Ibilin, Galilee, was the first Palestinian Catholic to receive a degree from Hebrew University. He writes in words which he inscribed in a book to me in the summer of 1996:

> God does not kill...God does not kill the Ba'al priests on Mt. Carmel or the inhabitants of the ancient city Jericho. God does not kill in Nazi concentration camps...or Palestinian refugee camps...or in any field of battle. Wherever there is killing or oppression, it is we who do it in the name of God. God does not kill...God gives life.[102]

A Judaic version of life's concourse and destiny, one which Jesus lived by and taught, held that the power of evil drew life toward sickness, madness, sin, and death. The life-giving healing power of God, expressed in the charismatic ministry of Jesus, the disciples, and Paul, for example, contended with these demonic powers and delivered persons through salvation and secured then through prophylaxis, health and sanity, grace and life. Torah and the commandments are in this sense the light of life.

In John Calvin's exposition of the world of nature as it becomes the theatre where God displays his glory, nature is fragile and precarious, always on the verge of collapsing back to dissolution, chaos, non-being. This world of nature is upheld and maintained in coherence only by saving grace. The commandments, especially the initial great God commands, contend against chaos for cosmos.

> ...God, who commanded light to shine out of darkness, has shined in our hearts of giving the light of knowledge of the glory of God in the face of Jesus Christ. But we have this treasure in earthen vessels that the excellency of the power may be Gods' not ours. (II Corinthians 4:6-7)

Sexuality and Idolatry

---

[102] Elias Chacour, *We Belong to the Land*, San Francisco: Harper Collins (Pickering) 1992, p. 163.

The impending chaos, ever impeded by command, is also found in the realm of sexuality. Another special topic on this point of the personal meaning of C-2 relates to sexual deviation. The Apostle Paul in Romans 1-3 speaks of the conjunction of idolatry (distraction of the divine-human relation) and immorality (deviation from ethical righteousness). Forsaking the worship of the true God, humans turn to unworthy associations. Is it possible that homosexuality, therefore, certainly addressed in these opening chapters of Romans, is sinful only when it is joined to idolatry? Just as it is worth exploring whether baptism bears on homosexuality, its relationship with idolatry might prove salient. It may be that non-idolatrous expression of homosexuality is chaste in the eyes of God. If love of God and neighbor is not violated, such persons and such relationships may be whole and well. Though I was the author of the 1978 document of the Presbyterian Church denying the right of ordination to "outward practicing homosexuals," twenty years of reflection, experience and prayer have led me to believe that homosexual being and practice, when chaste, monogamous and loving, can be in accord with the law and will of God.

The liberated self, the Exodus or Easter self, is one on the Way. Here one leaves the debilitating and oppressive past. "Who loves father or mother, brother or sister more than me...is not worthy of me...(straight out of C-1, C-2). "...let the dead bury their dead...come and follow me"—The Lord Christ exemplifies Yahweh—one who leads his people into the yet-to-be-redeemed unknown. God's leading of unitary selves is purposed by the same prophetic dialectic of C-2; to destroy idols (e.g., fight injustice) and open pathways, which is peace. He is our peace, who has broken down dividing wall of hostility (Ephesians 2:14).

The contemporary church is contentious. Parties tear at the purity, peace and unity of the sacred community. From the Reformation onward, constant schism has afflicted the church. Every man now sits under his own fig tree and each creates his own denomination. The price of exuberant freedom is endless elaboration. In the old Soviet Union and the Communist world today, freedom has become fractious. Chechnya revels in independence. Croatia and Bosnia seek independent existence after the collapse of Tito's coalesced, pluralistic, and communistic union.

Today the church is embattled by moral divisiveness. This can be specifically traced to failure of obedience to C-2: disagreement over abortion, women in ministry, homosexuality, prayer in schools. These issues raise again the decisive import of C-2. We are not to imagine and honor extraneous, heteronomous entities. When we conceive and worship ideologies, causes, false portraits of salvation, or exaggerated self-generated concepts, we divert concentration and community from the true God and that way which is unity and peace. When we elevate relativities to ultimacy, we cause havoc.

In the year 1996-97, the American Protestant churches entered a new season of potentially debilitating disunion. The issues at stake were homosexuality and

175

ordination. Reflecting a renewed culturewide concern about sex ethics in general—adultery, promiscuity and the like—C-7 in particular was being taken down from the shelf and dusted off. For now let it be said that the fatal flaw on both extremes of argument seems to be an idolization, a sacralization of some mode of being or being-together. The homophobic community cannot find place for same-sex affection, union and full civil and ecclesial rights for persons who identify themselves with homoerotic sexual preference. The gay-liberation community seeks to make its lifestyle normative, which probably arises as an exceptional pattern in nature and history rather than a norm. C-2, and as we will see C-7, opens up another option, of allowing limited alternate expression, even ordination, celebrating church membership, and blessing unions (see actions of the United Presbyterian General Assembly, Summer 2001), without normalizing the life style and degrading the normative pattern of male-female mating, child-bearing and family life. This latter good is affirmed throughout the Ten Commandments, especially in C-2, C-3, C-5, C-7, and C-10.

Diversity in unity would seem to be the ecclesial schema implicit in C-2. When sects and divisions are not accorded ultimacy, but all are held subject to the overarching Lord of all, false and fractious imagination then yields to God's truce and shalom.

Finally, today we note a terrifying injustice, brokenness and insoluble alienation among the segments of the society. The common good is nowhere acknowledged and the communal covenant is lost. The rich rush forward into ostentatious affluence, while the middle class stagnates and the poor increase in misery. Western nations, especially the United States, are rapidly coming to resemble "banana republics," where walled and policed cities of the rich on the hill fend off the desperately poor peasants clamoring down in the valley. In the last economically vibrant decade in America (1985-95), 100 percent of the newly generated wealth went to the top 10 percent of the people—most to the richest 1 percent.

Racism, ageism, sexism and tribalism (ethnocentrism) of all sorts abound and fracture the society. We have been reduced to a plethora of interest groups, each affirming its own rights and prerogatives against all others, all with the aid of our ubiquitous, modern, self-appointed gate-judges: lawyers.

The idolization of tribe, like that of the self, leads not only to social disintegration but also to violence and ultimately to selfannihilation. Recent reports, for example, on the status of African- Americans show that 25 percent of black men in the second and third decades of their lives are under detention or supervision by the criminal justice system. Drugs, violent crime, domestic strife, unemployment, under education and AIDS decimate the community. Were it not for the pathologically exaggerated birth (and infant mortality) rates in this community, the claim that the black-male ought to be listed as an endangered species would be credible.

How is this a violation of C-2? In our imagination (prejudice) and idolization (discrimination), we have fashioned an intervening god (false image) of white supremacy that restricts the full opportunity of this minority community to fully participate in the society. In a word play on C-8, we have blackmailed the black male and our treatment of women and children is also atrocious.

Again, the rich world of diverse persons, languages, families and tribes is a reality to be celebrated within the dominion of the God who is calling all peoples and nations up different pathways to the Isiainic Zion of arbitration and peace. To absolutize oneself or one's own, to demonize the other, is to violate the spirit of C-2, subvert the concensus of salvation, and thereby threaten life on earth.

Excursus

The ultimate idolatry is narcissism. Gazing in the mirror or pool in self-fascination is the all-too-pervasive detour from faith. The extreme arts of asceticism and monasticism, subduing selfconcentration and focusing attention on God alone can be understood as sustaining measures of **C-2**. It would seem that the telling twist on this point is the fact that we discover God in knowledge of the other. The human person served in justice and love is the divine icon, the Christ incognito (Matthew 25). I see the wonder of God in the eyes of our exuberant granddaughter. I saw the wisdom of God in the aging glance of my parents. I see the pain of Christ in the clochard sitting on the sidewalk outside our apartment, in the trembling Iraqi child as American bombs drop, in the poor black mom who trudges with her baby in Chicago's freezing greydawn to Cook County Hospital. I glimpse the glory of God even in its disguise in earthen vessels. Jean Val Jean's song in the musical Les Miserables captures this aniconic grace: "Who loves another has seen the face of God."

III. What in God's Name? A Theology of Linguistics
"Sticks and stones may break my bones but names will never hurt me."
Perennial Kid's dubious Wisdom

"I swear to God and hope to die!"
Classic prelude to really big lies

"Are you Coach Krzyzewski?...Yes, I am!"
"I'm Tiger Woods!"
Popular TV ads of impostors

Again you have heard that it was said to the men of old, 'You shall not swear falsely, but shall perform to the Lord what you have sworn,' But I say to you, Do not swear at all, either by heaven, for it is the throne of God, or by the earth, for it is his footstool, or by Jerusalem, for it is the city of the great King. And do not swear by your head, for you cannot make one hair white or black. Let what you say be simply "Yes" or "No"; anything more than this comes from evil. (Matthew 5: 33-37)

- I have not blasphemed a god.
- I have not done violence to a poor man.
- I have not done that which the gods abominate.
- I have not defamed a slave to his superior.
- I have not made anyone sick.
- I have not made anyone weep.

    Cognate commands to C-3 in the Egyptian Book of the Dead

Paul recalls C-2 and C-3 writing to the Church at Phillipi:

> Have this mind among yourselves, which is yours in Christ Jesus, who, though he was in the form of God, did not count equality with God a thing to be grasped, but emptied himself, taking the form of a servant, being born in the likeness of men. And being found in human form he humbled himself and became obedient unto death, even death on a cross. Therefore God has highly exalted him and bestowed on him the NAME which is above every NAME, that at the NAME of Jesus every knee should bow, in heaven and on earth and under the earth, and every tongue confess that Jesus Christ is Lord, to the glory of God the Father (Philippians 2:5-11, KJV).

> Salmon Rushdie is guilty of the crime of blasphemy...
> Fatwa of Hezbollah (The Party of God)

Incursus (C-3)

Again the carcass. A rabbit has been dropped from an upper floor apartment onto the hard cement of the Warsaw housing complex. Can one fail to remember the human carcasses carted away fifty years ago from the nearby ghetto(Auschwitz) during Hitler's occupation? The young wife, Dorota Gelle, lives in an apartment near the doctor. Their only previous encounter came when she ran over and killed his dog. "It should have been you," she warned him as she shaped her Faustian wager. Her husband was dying with cancer. She was three months pregnant by another man. She sought to extract from the doctor that transcending yet impossible assurance that her husband would die, so she would not have to abort this baby. "If my husband lives I can't have the baby". She finally extorts the oath; "do you swear?" "I swear." Yet the young husband miraculously survives.

> ...Do not swear (by God's name)...the third commandment.

"Do you believe in God?" she asks the old doctor. He had lost his family, to the bombs of war. He remembers having just talked with his baby who called, "qu, qu, da, da" on the phone. Like Madeline in Giordano's opera *Andre Chenier*, he

178

returned to find a crater where his home had been. "I have only enough faith," sighs the weary doctor.

Kíeslowoski's strong character studies prevail in his films as he ponders C-3. To swear or name is to put one's character on the line, to place one's being bound to God's. It becomes commitment that moves heaven and earth.

"I know you can't understand how I can love two men," Dorota tells the doctor. This is the heart of the crisis—divided loves and loyalties...

"You shall not take the Lord's name in vain!"

Introduction

C-3 continues the Yahweh affirmation and the condemnation of every pretender and distraction. That is the spirit of C-1 and C-2. The import of C-3 is to rule out the way humans seek to define, confine, and defame the Lord through the power of the word. C-3 sharpens responsibility in the wordsmith and worshipper. "What's in a name?" Enormous manipulative power, that's what's in a name. After all, whoever calls on the name shall be saved (Acts 9:21). Words increase and intone the power to save and damn. In primordial meaning name touches power. Adam names the animals and assumes dominion. Martin Noth comments:

> Anyone who knows a divine name can make use of the divine power present in the name to effect blessings and curses, adjurations and bewitchings and all kinds of magical undertakings.[103]

The linguistic command takes seriously the power of word in God in human thought and speech. Noam Chomsky in his massive scholarly corpus on linguistics has shown the neurological grounding and creative power of human language. In anthropologic perspective, we are like God with freedom and power through word to designate, comprehend and change reality.

God is available to the world and to his particular people. God is not available for abuse. There is a limit to how we claim and use God's power. Is it wrong to invoke Yahweh's name to curse another person or conjure up evil spirits to overpower another? To curse or defame another person falls within the range of blasphemy because the divine image of a person manifests the divine presence. To call one by degrading names is not only to insult and wound that person, it is to assault the One who gives being and life to that person. We are to invoke life and blessing from God and evoke these gifts in and through one another.

We are to draw from God and to hold out to one another the name and grace of joy, forgiveness, and hope, not the curse of condemnation and damnation. Because of the fragility of the human mind the flippant phrase, "damn you," has

---

[103] *Exodus*. Philadelphia: Westminster Press, 1962, p. 163.

been twisted to cast many thousands into perpetual insanity by the fear of eternal damnation. The opposite of curse is confession. Curse closes the door to grace. Confession conducts grace.

> Who believes in heart and confesses in words...shall be saved. . .
> (Matthew 10:32, Romans 10:9)

The curse impedes and degrades. Following reflections on background and text we will explore the theological and ethical meaning of C-3.

Text
"You shall not lightly utter the name of God"

is the textual intent of this command:

DO NOT BLITHELY THROW OUT THE NAME OF GOD.

The name of God, YAWEH, is unutterable. The tetragramm, which we erroneously articulate as Yaweh or Jehovah, is meant to caution humans from flippantly dealing with the power of the divine. Just as touching the Ark runs the risk of electrocution, so uttering the unutterable word risks all the fury and creative effect of the divine presence. God is holy. God's name is therefore holy. This is not a magical superstition. Rather, it takes seriously the word-being and word-acting character of God. Within the divine milieu, Word makes things happen.

The rabbis felt that this commandment meant that we were never to attest anything false with the name of God. Attestation in the name of God is the guarantor of the truth of the words to follow. All law is based on this association, as attested in oaths before testimony. The text forbids false or flippant oaths—any taking of the name lightly or to no effect. We do not drop the name of God in commonplace conversation.

The text has also been often taken to forbid evil prayer or sorcery. An invocation or benediction is to be offered only with utmost seriousness. The Hebrew scripture tracks the command as follows:

- Leviticus 18: 21, 19: 12, 20: 3, 24: 16—The holiness code associates speech, with sanctity, with God. Ritual itself is holy work to atone for the profane in normal life.

- Deuteronomy 5: 11, 14: 23—The presence of God is designated by the name.

- Psalm 24: 4—The holy hill can only be approached by persons with clean hands, pure hearts...Those who do not swear deceitfully.

- Isaiah 29: 23, Jeremiah 44: 16ff., Hosea 10: 4, Amos 6:10—In all the prophets the conspiracy against the Lord and the injustice toward others begins with false speech.

Tradition

Jesus only appeared once in a court of law. The high priest adjured him by "the living God" to answer if he was the Messiah, Son of David. Jesus answered affirmatively with an oath perhaps using the Aramaic *"gebhurta,"* "power," to avoid mentioning the divine name (Matthew 26: 63, Mark 14: 62). In the rabbinic practices of Jesus' time, a detailed and manipulative casuistry had superceded the high legal-ethical obedience of Shechem festival or Solomonic judgment. As James Aitken writes in an excellent older study on the Decalogue:

> Christ had to deal with a state of society in which the Scribes had taken all solemnity, all honesty, and all utility out of oaths by the jugglaries of a subtle casuistry so that men sought for forms of oath out of which they could legally extricate themselves, and avoided those forms which alone were binding...[104]

A rich array of meanings is found in the New Testament represented by the following passages:

- Matthew 9: 3—Jesus heals the paralytic. The power of the name becomes the power of exorcism and healing. The Scribes condemn this as blasphemy.

- Matthew 1: 23, 10: 42, 24: 9, 28: 19—At many points (birth, service, persecution, preaching and baptism), the ministry of Jesus is marked by the name.

- John 10: 31-39, 19: 7, 14: 14—The offense of self designation with the name (and power) of God is blasphemy to "the Jews." It is also the ground of evangelism and power.

- Acts 2: 21, 2: 38, 3: 16k 4: 12, 5: 41, 9: 16, 10: 43, 16: 18, 21: 13—The vast apostolic project all takes place.

- "in the name"...The apostolic ministry in essence is an expression of the Pentecost power of the name.

- Pentecost is the association of word, command, wind, fire, spirit and commission. The linguistic confusion of Babel now becomes the linguistic clarity of the Pentecost.

- Ephesians 1: 21, Philippians 2: 9-10, Colossians 3: 17, Hebrews 1: 4—The Pauline ministry mediates Christ's power by invoking the name. The positive implication of C-3 for early Christians must have been the obligation to utter the name of Christ when the spirit of God presented an evangelistic opportunity.

---

[104] James Aitken, *The Abiding Law.* Edinburgh: Oliphant Press, Anderson and Ferrier, 1899, p. 61.

- Revelation 2: 3, 3: 12, 13: 6, 16: 9, 19: 13—The name is the Word of God.
  All metaphors and symbols of the apocalypse point to this central truth.

Letter would eventually displace spirit. When one thinks of the Watergate or Irangate proceedings, or O.J. Simpson's trial, it must have been a day much like our own.

> Earth is sick
> And heaven is weary of the hollow words
> Which states and kingdoms utter when they talk
> Of truth and justice.
> (W. Wordsworth)

The cultural tradition of C-3 helps to illuminate its character.

Some scholars feel that the substratum of the third commandment originates in ancient society, when the household was the fundamental religious unit within the broader context of the tribe. When the father was the priest of the household, the primal cry may have been, "When you come home, don't come home emptyhanded!" As priesthood was transferred to the larger tribal and national entities, the meaning of taking the name in vain, "coming up empty," was applied to the divine name. In Exodus 23 and 34 we find elaborate instruction for the feast of unleavened bread, which must recall the ongoing ancient Shrine festivals of Israel when sacrificial feasts served as events to commemorate deliverance and rehearse the covenant. These liturgies ended with the words, "Never come to worship without bringing an offering" (Exodus 23:15, 34:20).

Worship at the shrines appears to have been threefold—the evocation or ascription of the name, the presentation of an offering, and the bestowal of blessing. This manifold gesture, *in toto*, constituted the renewal of the covenant and the appeasement. To call down the blessed power of the name without offering the commensurate sacrifice and dedication of life was empty, vacuous, and hypocritical. Naming the name without giving the gift was profanity, words devoid of deeds. If you don't have the goods when you call on the name of Yahweh, you will be blown away. This seems to be the meaning of the confrontation of Elijah and the prophets of Baal on Mt. Carmel.

Yahweh's name was solemnly invoked in many Hebrew names. Jochebed, (The Lord is Majesty), Jerohoam, (The Lord Have Compassion), Elijah, (The Lord is My God), Obadiah, (Servant of the Lord). To say nothing of Joel or Joe. Antique oath formulas evidence the ubiquity of the presence of the practice of invocation, interdiction, and benediction.

> May the life of Yahweh God kill me. Yahweh be a witness between you and me (Matthew 26: 63).

182

Today we enjoin action with the words, "By God," or, "For God's sake." Numbers 6 recalls the period that unfolds from the time that the common religious and moral life of the coalesced tribes focused on the Mosaic legislation under the judges and kings until the age of the pre-exilic and exilic prophets. The passage recalls another response to the ethical impact of C-3. Priests in the train of Aaron are directed to invoke the divine name in blessing culminating in the invocation of the High Priest on the Day of Atonement, first audibly, then under his breath. The Lord said to Moses,

> 'Say to Aaron and his sons, Thus you shall bless the people of Israel: you shall say to them, 'The Lord bless you and keep you: The Lord make his face to shine upon you and be gracious to you: The Lord lift up his countenance upon you and give you peace' "So shall they put my name upon the people of Israel, and I will bless them' (Numbers 6: 23-26).

By the time of Isaiah, Israel is struggling against Assyria after the death of Sargon in 705. Courting the power of Egypt the name of God has come to signify Godself.

> Behold the Name of God cometh from far
> Burning with anger, and in thick rising smoke
> his lips are full of indignation, and his tongue
> is a devouring fire.
> (Isaiah 30: 27).

By the time of Ezra and Nehemiah, the return and restoration, Torah and covenant had taken the form of written text and the word of the Lord itself was normative for faith and ethics. Out of an awestruck reverence the book of Esther evades using the divine name. As we will soon see in those collations of scriptures in forthcoming centuries the image (C-2) and name (C-3) of Yahweh has become graphic and obedience has taken on something of a literal form. Judaism, which had heretofore avoided using the name of God, now both sharpened that prohibition and found myriad modes of circumvention. Should the Hebrew Bible be translated into Greek? For Palestinians, how should the Aramaic language refer to Yahweh? The names for Yahweh proliferated: *Adonai Mar, Kyrios, Dominus*, Lord. And the Commandment persists, "You shall honor, not defame, the divine name."

When Jesus' mountain sermon recasts the message of Mt. Sinai or in the same vicinity models the prayer of the ages, "Hallowed be thy name," (more in Part III) we are encouraged to economy of speech. It is a solemn reticence to invoke the divine name and power and simple trust and insouciance toward life that knows that each hair of our head is numbered (Matthew 10: 30). Despite Dennis Rodman or Mike Piazza, even with Clairol we cannot change the color of one hair or alter in any rudimentary way the crown of glory, which is *imago dei*.

And Paul, who often swore in the sense of assertion not defamation, elucidates biblical wisdom about C-3 in the letter to Philippi (4:8):

> Finally, brethren, whatever is true, whatever is honorable,
> whatever is just, whatever is pure, whatever is lovely,
> whatever is gracious, if there is any excellence, if there is
> anything worthy of praise, think about these things.

As Cosslett Quin incisively wrote:

> ... the name of God is the compendium of His Revelation, the very point and edge of His Word.

In the Christian centuries when realism was the prevailing linguistic and philosophical premise, words were felt to be imbued with supernatural power. In the modern world, especially after the rise of nominalism, we tend to see words as "names only" or as symbols pointing to reality but not themselves bearing that reality.

Luther's discussion of C-3 is interesting at this point. Luther felt that there were times when speaking truth earnestly and honestly required profanity. To lie is the violation of this mandate.

> We are to swear truly when such is demanded. The Lord's Prayer is a total enactment of taking the name.[105]

John Calvin also emphasizes the importance of swearing by God's name to attest to truth "...when a matter is of great importance...to maintain mutual love and concord, it is imperative to swear by God's name."[106] For Calvin, every thought and word should be offered with the intent of bringing God honor. In Bucer, the subtle connection between civil, ecclesial and spiritual meanings is felt. The third commandment is given for the express purpose of enlarging the majesty of God. "I will (in all things) confess and praise my God." Bucer is concerned to fashion the Christian commonwealth where the law of God informs and ethically orders civil society. For *Regnum Christi* a good commonwealth to ensure in this world, the poor and presence of meaning, ultimate and penultimate must abide.

Islam on Commandments 1-3

Muslim renditions of C1-3 go to the heart of the intolerance and belligerence that is ill-founded adherence to the first commands. They also express the spiritual and moral genius of Semitic monotheistic monolatry.

---

[105] All references to Luther's *Larger Catechism* are from Neelack S. Tjernagel, *The Luther Confessions: a Harmony and a Sourcebook*. Evangelical Lutheran Synod, 1979. Hereafter cited as LC.

[106] Calvin, John, *Catechisms of the Church in Geneva,* Grand Rapids:Eerdmans Press, 1958, p. 60.

The ideological groundwork of the Madrasas (Koran schools) and the Al Qaeda liturgy is that idolatry and blasphemy threaten the home of God (Allah) in the world. Diaries and documents found in Afghan caves tell of pledges to "kill the apostate" (violations of the imperative to believe—C-1). The ideology makes two grievous mistakes: (1) it identifies the two parental and sibling Abrahamic faiths as sources of this atheism denouncing the reality that they confess the same name (C-3). (2) Rather than trusting the divine will and God's judgment in history, it takes the duty of fidelity and purification into its own hands, then yields that responsibility into the corrupt hands of its own political movements: Taliban, Al Qaeda, Hamas, Egyptian Jihad, etc. Yet we agree that domination by a heretical Western faith based on money, power, materialism and secularism is an abomination.

Since the days when America first undermined the Muslim fabric of life in Iran in the 1950's and 60's and propped up the secularist Shah who sponsored the worst of Western values, we have contributed to this conspiratorial theology which marked the regime of Ayatollah Khomeini and other passionate religious Muslims in the lands of Arabia. Our endorsement, even fabrication of quasi-secular regimes throughout the region, regimes which opposed both Islamic fervor, and the imposition of Shariah as legal system on the one hand and human rights and participatory democracy on the other, all in our craving for cheap oil and political hegemony, was also a mistaken public policy and an erroneous reading of the theological ethic of the first (God-adherence) commandments.

One caveat. I believe that part of the appropriate theological destiny of America and the Christian West in world history is the extension of economic opportunity and prosperity into impoverished areas. I celebrate President Bush's call on January 2002 (State of Union Address) for a "freedom corps" and an amplified Peace Corps to send thousands of volunteers into the needy world to, as he says, "love the children"—to educate children, shelter the homeless, heal the sick, clothe the naked, liberate the oppressed and bring good news to the poor. While my theology is strongly critical of substitutionary materialism for devotion to God alone, I believe that a particular burden of our history (through the Anglican and Puritan faith history) is to generate wealth in the world, to stimulate its entrepreneurial ethos and distribute that derivative wealth equitably. John Calvin's ethic of the rich and the poor is to give back and to share. If this is the case then part of the spiritual and ethical vocation of the West is to challenge the hoarding and concentrating of wealth both in America and Arabia. We need to rephrase both the radical Islamic and pagan Western construals of economic vocation. Equal and just economic opportunity requires, as another important war theorist George Landes, *The Wealth and Poverty of Nations,* says, both freedom and social responsible policies of taxation and wealth distribution.

Osama bin Laden saw the war as strife against "unbelief and unbelievers." The Taliban's destruction of the colossal ancient Buddhas was a symptom of an iconoclasm which reminds one of Jewish iconoclasm against Hellenic monuments, early Christian destruction of Greco-Roman temples and statuary, the Crusaders trashing, even of Hagia Sophia-Constantine's church in Istanbul. Islam's sometime virulent destruction of Christian sites, and Henry VIII's, then the Puritan's destruction of the beauty of England's lovely cathedrals continue the travesty.

The issue of iconoclasm is complex. In rigorous Semitic sensibility any artifactual simulation of the divine is suspect. It could be argued in terms of radical irreplicability mimesis that not only buildings and statues, sanctuaries and scriptures, but even theological texts are human constructs and therefore incapable of bearing the divine. Nothing penultimate ought to be invested with divinity (*Finitum non capax infinit*). The dilemma of this view is that the iconoclast himself presumes the veracity and divine authority of his own construal of the truth and of his own designation of the other as inferior and "corrupt."

"Defending the faith" has proven historically to be the prime religious value in offensive and defensive war. "To insure a home for the divine presence (name)" is the essence of Israel's Holy War in first millennium BC Canaan. That the "Name of Christ" not be obliterated from the earth animates the Crusades, especially the campaign against Jerusalem (securing Constantine's and Helen's churches including the Holy Sepulcher in Jerusalem and the Church of the Nativity in Bethlehem). Osama bin Laden's December 2001 tape heralds the "Blessed terrorism" of the period surrounding 9/11 as contesting "the crusade of America and Israel against Islam." In the Reformation and in the religious wars and Cousins' Wars, this C1-3 value is expressed as demand for religious freedom. Across the millennia thousands have died that 'the Gospel be preached and lived."

The dilemma surrounding the God-war commands (C1-3) is finally the quandary of modernity/post-modernity. Is there objective and universal reality and truth or do we only have relativity and refracted insight (what Plato called *doxa* – opinion).

Theology

As with each of the commandments, C-3 unfolds layers of meaning. In theology it ranges among the themes of word and spirit, power and authority, sin and grace. It deals with the virtues of scrupulosity and reverence. It subsumes behaviors from nominal speech, to oathtaking, blasphemy and empty, word-only worship. Ethically, C-3 spans transgressions from small indiscretions to unforgivable sin. It deals with profanity and perjury, promise keeping and betrayal, vows of all sorts from baptism to marriage, with practices from magic and blasphemy to prayer and worship. The commandment is rich as it embraces a range of theological and ethical implications and ramifications.

The genius of C-3 is found in its insight into the nature of God and man. Yahweh is energy. Humans are receptors and transmitters of power. There is no power (*exousia*) on earth unless it comes from above. The point of the third commandment is that God's zeal must be reciprocated by human expression. When humans violate the divine relation by abusing the presentation or by bringing faithless worship they "take the name in vain." Remember Gladstone's words: "The Creed of the English is that there is no God and that it is wise to pray to him from time to time." Taking the name in vain. God's being and power is the direction of human righteousness and virtue.

Empty, vain, meaningless, and impotent. In the chaos that preceded the word-directed cosmos of the creation, all was empty, dark and without form. The prophets condemned Israel's vain and sterile worship—(Bring me no more vain offerings—they stink! Isaiah 1:13). The apostle Paul counsels that without love our words are vacuous, without divine melody they become a clanging gong or a tinkling cymbal (1 Corinthians 13:1). Throughout biblical history shallow ritual, empty words, profanation and otherwise trivializing divine power are all condemned in the enduring spirit of C-3. These all constitute violations of the divine name. People of faith live by and die for "the name." For we who belong to Israel and new Israel are people of the name.

> "Thus says the Lord: I will give then my everlasting name— it will not be cut off " (Isaiah 56:5).

> "I come in my father's name." "What I do I do in my father's name"..."to those who believed in his name...He gave power" (The Gospel of John).

The positive commendation of C-3 is that not to be in touch with the name is to be devoid of being and power.

The third commandment is a theological lesson in the doctrine of word and spirit. God's address to the world is found in the ingratiating spirit. *Ruach elohim* hovers over the turbulent waters of creation. Ezekiel speaks of the new spirit within, which is engraved law. Jesus sends that same wind that blows where it wills (John 3: 8) as the Pentecost bestowal. The spirit of God writes divine word on our hearts (Ezekiel 36: 27), illumines a scripture (II Timothy 3: 16, 17), and itself prompts within us the life of faith and goodness (Romans 8). Blasphemy, evacuating or emasculating the name, invalidating the word, is the sin against the Holy Spirit, grave, perhaps unretrievable. When one is animated by Jesus' Spirit, profanation is impossible: "No one speaking by the spirit of God can curse Jesus and no one can confess Jesus as Lord but in the spirit" (I Corinthians 12:3). Spirit descending evokes confession ascending.

From the moment Jesus was baptized by John and the Spirit at River Jordan, God can only mean mystery. This motion is expressed in a remarkable passage from Cosslett Quin:

Baptism commits God, and therefore also commits you. You must utilize God's gift there given, and release its latent powers. Baptism is the laver of regeneration, therefore your conversion is demanded by it. Baptism is an assurance, therefore you mustbelieve on the warrant of your Baptism. God has made you His child, therefore you must strive to behave like a child of God. He has introduced you and incorporated you into the Body of Christ, made you a part of the Temple of His Spirit, therefore be what you are. He has made you an inheritor of the kingdom of heaven, a present possessor of that great Not-Yet that came in Christ, and is coming on earth, and yet will not be perfected till the last day; you must be therefore one of those who look for the coming from heaven of the Savior. 'He that believeth not shall be damned.' [107]

This passage explicates an inner meaning of C-3. God's gift to us evokes either blessing or curse. It causes reception and transmission or refusal and blockage. "Who is not for me is against me" (Matthew 12: 30). To be baptized and confirmed into Christ's family is to honor the receipt in holy gratitude - an act of assent.

The notion of word and spirit as understood by the science of linguistics is the verbal act whereby transcendent and moral meaning is translated into speech and deed. The reality of God and God's moral will for human life is conveyed into the minds and mouths of persons. Humans then either think, speak or do good or thwart that communication. The third commandment commends the transmission and condemns the retardation of that word and spirit. C-3 is the charter of creative word, work and worship, the linguistic imperative. "Words are the single starts coming from people" (Jimmy Santiago Baca).

The God-self introduced in the Mosaic covenant—Yahweh by name—is a communicative being. While the Parmidean static divine being might be derived from the "I Am" of Exodus, the God the world meets at Sinai, then on the Sermon Mount, is a God going somewhere. "I will be who I will be", "Blessed are the meek, they shall inherit the earth." A God is now known who not only leads but who speaks, listens, commands, guides, directs.

In very poor analogic language, which is all we have to describe ultimate and moral power, most essentially God is one who takes persons and peoples who are willing to follow into a new and better realm. God transforms His avant-garde people from oppression to liberation, from exploitation to justice, from death to life. The intent of this word-animated phalanx is to live no longer to self but to him whose way is to transform the world. We are people of the name— the Way.

God is alive, a good parent, a kind and inspiring father, a mother who nurtures and is to be emulated, or like a good shepherd, that is a king, a public leader,

---

[107] *Op Cit.,* p. 97.

teacher or minister whom we trust and follow because we know we are safe in journey and that all "will come round right."

The issue therefore is where does God lead? What kingdom (to use an almost irretrievable metaphor) does God will to create for the world? What are the qualities of the new state of affairs, the "realm" envisioned by the redeeming heart of God? What are the ethical ramifications of C-3?

In Jewish thought, ethics rests on character, which is grounded in Torah faithfulness. When one lives as a receptor of divine word and spirit one either enshrines or stifles the divine impulse. For the Jew, religion is primarily ethical and communal. Religion is either authentic and ethical or superficial and vain. Hebrew consciousness sees the person as the *ZEDEK YAHWEH* (one righteous and sincere) or an *AWON* (twisted). Human faith and life either converts or perverts the divine message. One's moral life in community expresses the word of God in virtue or in vacuity. We take the Lord at his word or take the name in vain.

Ethical implications of C-3 include values and sanctions concerning worship, perjury and profanity. Should prayers in public schools be encouraged or banned? Is this controversial activity one of empty words, of taking the name in vain, or is it reverential duty? Gordon Allport of Harvard offered research into religious practice that has illuminated C-3. His research was stimulated by the observation that persons who scored high on the scale of religiosity (practices including church attendance) were also likely to score high on measures such as prejudice, discrimination, and bigotry. This starting point led him to develop an instrument to study religious ideas and habits according to their extrinsic or intrinsic validity. Those who inclined toward extrinsic religion tended to "use" religion, to go through the motions, to render its substance empty. They take the name of the Lord in vain.

Both C-3 and C-4 bear on our life of worship. Our words and work constitute the imputed worth of God offered by our lives. If our worship is frivolous and hollow, we defame the divine name and power. Bar and Bat Mitzvah are vows. Baptism, as already noted, confirmation, marriage, eucharist and ordination all are rituals that take the name with particular worship.

The temple in Jerusalem, writes Edwin Poteat, was a court of justice and a court of song. David's instruments sang out. Four thousand priests attended the music. Six thousand were judges. Poteat continues:

> "If the impulse to worship is awe and gratitude, the defeat of worship is stereotype."

False, hollow, or routinized worship bores, offends, and defames the name. Similarly, pop and trendy worship trivializes the might, beauty and subtlety of God and the finer instincts of the human spirit. It is easy to see and feel when worship is dead or vital, even the "noise of solemn assemblies" is hollow (Amos 5:23). Promise-making and promise-keeping and the proscription of perjury and profanity are other imperatives imbedded in C-3.

Today

Though living each moment "in the name" is the root mandate, we can examine the present day implications of C-3 by briefly mentioning three derivative themes: promises, perjury and profanity. Herod was not the first or the last to make a promise he would regret. When he swore to his stepdaughter and vowed the head of John the Baptist, cosmic evil commensurate with Judas's pledge for 30 silver pieces was committed. In two foolhardy promises two bent figures brought to a close the earthly ministry of the greatest name born of woman and of "the name above every name." Here specious promise is of the order of blasphemy and unforgivable sin. Yet as we saw in Part I, "it pleased the Lord to bruise him...He will see the victory of His name" (Isaiah 53).

Kant found in promise-keeping a mandate of practical reason. The moral universe requires this categorical imperative. Aristotle and the teleologists see truthfulness as fulfilling virtue in our nature. Utilitarians calculate consequences. Scottish common-sense philosophy from the old Adam Smith to the new, says it pays off, brings dividends. Divine command theory rests obligation on the expressed word. Spirit and the will of God find repose and response in the receptive human conscience.

Perjury is an oath supporting a lie. In court we swear to "tell the truth, the whole truth, and nothing but the truth...so help me God." This is a throwback to a world where divine help and harm, punishment or blessing was palpable. When the fear of God shaped thought and action, this vow or oath not only was understandable but also may have encouraged truthfulness. Today, though still bearing great currency, its principal import is to ground the legal countercharge of lying under oath. In a system that is more and more shaped by deceptions, technicalities and adversarial language, the metaphysical power of this C-3 grounded stipulate should always be renewed.

Profanity today has become commonplace. Like Luther, the producers of the Sopranos protest that profanity is the cost of reality. The proscription seems irrelevant and petty. Guardians of the divine name have always bemoaned unholy speech. Listen to the Minister of Dundee.

> The use of profane language is notoriously a sin of the street. We can hardly pass the mouth of any of our lanes or any corner frequented by loungers, without having our ears offended and our whole soul made to shudder by the way in which every sentence uttered teems with the unholy use of names to us most sacred. Polite society has happily cast out the offence, though it has done so rather by branding it as unmannerly than by frowning upon it as irreverent; but the foul-mouthed language of our lanes and alleys tells us where the spirit of blasphemy has found for himself another home. And from that home, where

the politeness and decencies do not cause their wit to run, only the spirit of a reverent religion as it is in Christ will ever cast it out. That is the Church's work; and you will find it across the lane from where we now worship.[108]

John Bunyan, a holy pilgrim, regretted that, "I knew not how to speak unless I put an oath before, and another behind, to make my words have authority." God's word in holiness is divinity. Man's word in profanity is anti-word. That is its gravity and sadness. The first three Commandments form a matrix of meaning for the good life. Harrelson summarizes:

The first three Commandments focus together upon Yahweh's exclusive claim upon the people for whom these Commandments were binding. All have in view the preface telling of Yahweh's gracious act of deliverance from Egyptian slavery. All presuppose the love and grace of the God who places these demands upon them. And all drive home with vigor the fundamental necessity for God's people to observe these prohibitions. No penalties are stated. There is lean, clean brevity of speech. God simply lays down the basic kinds of human activity that are not permissible, not tolerable, by any means to be done. To add threats would be unnecessary and would weaken the force of such a lean and astringent set of prohibitions. Where in all the Hebrew Scriptures do we get a clearer picture not simply of what the God of Israel will not tolerate from his creatures but also of the very character of this God? God, the deliverer from Egyptian bondage, will not have people lavish upon him their gifts of gold and silver and jewelry and other bounties in an effort to placate him, or buy him off from demanding righteousness of them. God will not let them use the unmistakable power that they have through knowing his name to do harm to their enemies. God remains the determiner of how the power inherent in his name is to be used. And God will not permit them to make images of him from any goods of earth, for nothing in all the earth can adequately show his true nature and character. Human beings are to live and act in such a way as to enable other human beings to know more and more about the nature and character of God. If people want to know more about the God of Israel, they should be able to look to the people redeemed from bondage in Egypt and find out about that God.[109]

C-1 through C-3 demand of wilderness nomads unequivocal and undivided allegiance to Yahweh. C-4 now begins to apply obeisance theology to obedience ethics.

Today, the linguistic commandment takes on fresh power and meaning. At the personal level, words shape our being. Harmful words can trigger gnawing doubt and self-recrimination. The kindly word or compliment can transform one's existence and instill strength. When words are joined to thought, conformation of being occurs. In Christian confession, saying the word "Christ

---

[108] James Aitken, *Op Cit., p. 64.*
[109] Walter Harrelson, *The Ten Commandments and Human Rights.* Philadelphia: Fortress Press, 1980, pp. 76, 77.

is my Lord" miraculously makes it happen. One suddenly finds oneself confirmed in faith and conformed in being. The self is the creation of auto- and hetero-linguistics. The self is also the creation of the living God.

The words saved and damned and the privilege or oppression attached to each show the power of name designated status. To own or disown the name of Jesus could mean life or death in the early centuries of persecution in the Roman Empire. Years later the name Jew, Baptist, Hugenot or Puritan could mean gallows, guillotine or the fires of Smithfield or Salem.

"Take the name of Jesus with you." In some Southern Baptist cities, being in the business directory of the "saved" can prove profitable. The "damned" or outcasts can not only be banished, their shops can be shattered on some *Krystallnacht*. The terror of madness, castigation or stigmatization can indelibly mark and disgrace, the God-given being of the one cursed.

Today labels like "the poor," "the ignorant," "the sick" can be occasions for isolation and expulsion or extraordinary gestures of care. Talcott Parsons wrote of the "sick role," the privilege of disengagement and passivity accorded one who was "sick." Today's HIV status is a stigma, as is having the carrier (non-sick) status with some genetic diseases. A person can have recessive trait for sickle cell anemia or Tay-sachs disease. In the future a wide range of disease entities may lead persons to be labeled deficient in some manner and ostracized. When we join labeling and stigmatizing with designation cards, arm-bands forehead marks, tatoos or computer records, new meaning is brought to the question: "What's in a name?"

The meaning of C-3 is that we are noticed as we are designated by *dabar*, by God's language. The essence of our identity is being named, being noticed. God, who knows us by name calls us in person to be his own. The name which is our new being is bestowed as knees bow and tongues confess Jesus as Lord.[110] That name above all names.

Excursus

The *Fasching* weekend in Germany is a great mid-winter festival. Revelry redounds even as rain and snow abounds. Everyone suits up in fantastic costumes: dragons, cowboys and even Dennis Rodmans (with green hair), were seen yesterday in Rudesheim on the Rhine. My dear wife, Sara, sits this morning at Frühstuck with our family friends, the Hahn family, who live in Hildegard's old town, Bingen, on the Rhine. She struggles to put together sentences *auf Deutsch*. I grow weary at the tedious exercise and excuse myself. But I commend and admire her. She struggles much more than I do to stand out, to be noticed, to get through, to communicate. I prefer to slide into the background, to go unnoticed and avoid, God help me, the terror of someone calling my name. I

---

[110] *Op Cit., p. 67.*

get along, *auf Deutsch*, but in France I am terrified that some colleague professor will call me out, name me and linguistically confront me with what is my own *Muttersprache*, my *langue familie*, a gentle and lovely language which I scarcely comprehend and in which I barely can communicate.

The experience of being in a foreign land is liberating for me, however. It forces humility in its humiliation. Of necessity, you become a child again. An anonymous child. The broad pretense and status of all you have become back home is stripped away. No one calls you professor, or doctor, or—thankfully—reverend. You have been denied your names. Here, nobody knows who you are. No one knows your name. The array of designations, opinions, estimations, and yes, misunderstandings, jealousies, subtle alienations and distances, all are shorn away like a dog I saw last week in le Gare, Strasbourg, shaved bare to the skin. Most of us need the comfort of Cheers pub in Boston—someplace where "everyone knows your name."

I remember now my first trip home to *Vaterland*, Europe. We came by boat in the nineteen-sixties—a ten-day trip as I recall. A great delight to travel on this student ship. As we crossed, we sang the protest songs of the sixties. Although the Kennedy boys and King were still alive in 1960, we sang one spiritual that tore at my heart even then, and much more, later.

> There's a man going round takin' names
> He took my daddy's name-now wasn't that a shame
> He took my mamma's name
> He took Abe Lincoln's name
> There's a man going round takin' names.

IV: Holiday: A Theology of Rest

Observe the Sabbath and keep it holy, as I, the Lord your God, have commanded you. You have six days in which to do your work, but the seventh day is a day of rest dedicated to me. On that day, no one is to work—neither you, your children, your slaves, your animals, nor the foreigners who live in your country. Your slaves must rest just as you do. Remember that you were slaves in Egypt, and that I, the Lord your God, rescued you by my great power and strength. That is why I command you to observe the Sabbath (Deuteronomy 5:12-15).

> Hear this you who trample the needy and destroy the poor of the country. You say to yourselves, "We can hardly wait for the holy days to be over so we can sell our grain. When will the Sabbath end so we can start selling again? Then we can overcharge, use false measures, and fix the scales to cheat our customers." (Amos 8: 4-5)

> Jesus was walking through some wheat fields on a Sabbath. As his disciples walked along with him, they began to pick the heads of wheat. So the Pharisees said to Jesus, "Look, it is against our Law for your disciples to do that on the Sabbath!"

And Jesus answered, "Have you never read what David did that time when he needed something to eat? He and his men were hungry, so he went into the house of God and ate the bread offered to God. This happened when Abiathar was the High Priest. According to our Law only the priests may eat this bread— but David ate it and even gave it to his men."

And Jesus concluded, "The Sabbath was made for the good of man; man was not made for the Sabbath. So the Son of Man is Lord even of the Sabbath."(Mark 2)

Now God has offered us the promise that we may receive that rest he spoke about. Let us take care, then, that none of you will be found to have failed to receive that promised rest. For we have heard the good news, just as they did. They heard the message, but it did them no good, because when they heard it, they did not accept it with faith. We who believe, then, do receive that rest which God promised. It is just as he said,

'I was angry and made a solemn promise: They will never enter the land where I would have given them rest!' He said this even though his work had been finished from the time he created the world. (Hebrews 4)

Judaism is a religion of time, aiming at the sanctification of time.

Abraham Heschel

Incursus

Sabbath day is Christmas Eve. "It's difficult to be alone on a night like this". The young woman had been the mistress of the husband of a young family. He plays Santa Clause for his family then excuses himself for a long night taxi ride through the deserted streets of Warsaw. As the night proceeds he confirms his marriage and family and the young woman finds resolve to live on.

Sabbath is the rhythm of work and love which Freud found to be the *raison d'etre* of human living. Return and rest, is the composure of our existence in meaning.

At dawn he returns home:

"Eva?" his wife asks.
"Yes, Eva."
"You'll be going out again evenings?"
"No."

Kieslowski has glimpsed the drama of waywardness and homecoming among the striving souls in the bleak Warsaw apartment block. Apocalyptic "that day" has modulated into the plaintoff advent of Christmas Eve and in Michael Wilmington's words on Kieslowski's work:

This overwhelming psychological and spiritual epic for our time - faces the darkness (and) sends out a song against the Storm.
(Chicago Tribune, Friday March 22, 1996)

The orthodox community on the near Northwest side of the old city of Jerusalem is aiming at the same target. They want to close the Nablus/Ramalah highway on Shabbat. The demonstrations have gotten cruel. Ambulances, police and fire vehicles could not pass through (although sabbath law allows for life-saving and welldoing). But what of those Israeli business leaders who seek recreation (sabbath) who are returning sabbath evening from the beaches around the sea of Galilee or Haifa? What of those who must labor under stress of another hour to get home?

Introduction

In my library I have a model, a rubber idol, if you insist, of Homer Simpson, and, of course, his irascible son, Bart. I have him decked out as a Scottish clergyman with scarlet robes and tabs. Like my children, I guess I've always appreciated Homer's sacrilege and the fact that Bart's such a crummy kid. As W. C. Fields said, "no man who kicks dogs and hates kids can be all bad." In a recent episode of the Simpsons, Homer has been dragged reluctantly to church on Sunday. His Sabbath rest is pro football. The church service heats up, so does the game which he is listening to on his walkman transistor radio. The game comes down to a big field goal. He listens: It's up, it's up! IT'S GOOD! He jumps up, shouts, rising with two arms stretched like Notre Dame's touchdown Jesus. From that moment on, irreverent Homer becomes the chief holy roller in the congregation. "It all began with a baseball game," goes the old saw, "In the big-inning."

Karl Barth, the German Reformed theologian who has offered the world the most massive systematic work since Calvin, Luther, and Aquinas, begins his Church Dogmatics exposition on the creation with a section on "The Holy Day." Holiness, or God portrayal, is the design for human life in the cosmos. In excellent studies Abraham Heschel and Jurgen Moltmann offer profound insights into the meaning of Sabbath. "It is the Sabbath which blesses, sanctifies and reveals the world as God's creation"[111] Following the powerful and gripping words of the Decalogue making God's exclusive claims, we now turn to the moral tableau. Here we find spread before us the ethical charter, which builds on the underlying theological foundation. Here we are given the basic institutions and orders, which form the fitting human response to God's grace and deliverance.

Sabbath is the first of these regulations or celebrations. Here the dynamic antinomy of work and rest is founded. Here the oscillation of worship and enterprise is grounded in the cosmic belief that like the creator, on one day in seven we too need to stand back and sigh, "It is good, very good."

---

[111] Jurgen Moltmann, *God in Creation*. London: SCM Press, 1985, p. 6.

Text
Remember the Sabbath, Keep it Holy

Remember. The tradition is not only of the people. The Rabbis celebrate the eternal sabbath by offering the kaddish prayer. Sabbath has as its root the idea of stopping work. *Mishna* enumerates 39 categories of work that are to be discontinued on the Sabbath. The tension with Jesus teaching and Sabbath work (Mark 2) must be seen against this background. The entire estate, entourage and community, even the animals, are to be blessed by this relief—by this commandment which is life (Leviticus 18: 5). The Sabbath is endowed with recuperative, healing and holy power. From the punctuation of rest in the creation itself (which Darwin, Copernicus, Newton and Einstein do not allow), this rejuvenating pause is derived.

The Sabbath mandate does not arise in a vacuum. Life in the ancient world was seen in its rhythmic quality. On a regular basis, often in a 6 and 1 cycle, crop yielded to fallow, business to market, toil to celebration. Ugaritic practice seemed to follow this sabbatical rhythm of days and years. Another precursor of C-4 with which Moses was familiar seems to be the patterns of work among Midianite and Kennite miners and smiths. Iron age forgers cooled their hearths in gratitude for the gifts of fire and iron. Responding to lunar cycles, Assyrian and Babylonian calendars set aside the seventh day for withdrawal from work. A Babylonian fragment from the great Hammurabi period (c. 1800 BCE) designates the 7th, 14th, 21st, and 28th day of the month as a pause when:

> The shepherd of the great nations shall eat no roast flesh...The King shall not mount the chariot...The physician shall not lay his hand on the silk. [112]

Paul Lehmann notes that desert nomads in empirical wisdom would return only in long intervals to an oasis, giving it time to "catch its breath."[113] Work and war, even shepherding and healing deserve pause in the great cosmic project. Today stock markets are open 24 hours a day. As Paris and Frankfurt close, New York opens. In this day of the information superhighway, the one who really would stay on top of things will be at the monitor day and night. Because of this temptation to frenzy in this law, the common life was also viewed in its moral quality. Sensing with awe and wonder the provision of bounty and blessing, sometimes precarious days of ill omen, taboo days, days of appeasement of natural and supernatural powers punctuated the day-to-day routine. In Babylonia, for example, such days were inauspicious times to venture out, begin journeys, lay wagers, or otherwise provoke the world with creative or innovative demands. Like the great manager, *Deus ex Machina*, there is a time to hold back.

From the dawn of time, aggression or activity has been associated with guilt and remorse. Condemnation was received from the "powers that be" for laying

---

[112] Edwin Poteat, *Mandate to Humanity.* Nashville: Abingdon, 1953, p. 22.
[113] Lehmann, *Op Cit., p.74.*

heavy hands on the world. Conversely, detachment, receptivity, and rest were thought to please the gods. The *via negativa* seemed to be the positive way of life. All that was necessary for *Shekinah*, the appearance of God, was the elimination of all other gods. Moral righteousness was simply refraining from harm. Desisting from work was, *per se*, the presence of Sabbath rest.

Deep in the recesses of history among many peoples we find sabbath observance. Like day and night, the rhythm of activity must be punctuated by withdrawal and reprieve. It remains for the Hebrew people to sanctify the pause. Now it becomes a day for holy remembrance, reconstitution of piety, thanksgiving.

The textual history reveals the full-orbed meaning of Sabbath:

> And on the seventh day God finished his work which he had made; and he rested on the seventh day from all his work which he had made.
>
> ...And God blessed the seventh day and hallowed it; because on it he rested from all his work that he had created and made (Genesis 2: 2-3).

> God slumbers not nor sleeps (Psalm 121: 4).

> If you turn back your foot from the Sabbath, from doing your pleasure on my holy day, and call the Sabbath a delight and the holy day of the Lord honorable; if you honor it, not going your own ways, or seeking your own pleasure, or talking idly; then you shall take delight in the Lord, and I will make you ride upon the heights of the earth; I will feed you with the heritage of Jacob your father, for the mouth of the Lord has spoken (Isaiah 58: 13, 14).

> Now that day was the sabbath. So the Jews said to the man that was cured, "It is the sabbath, it is not lawful for you to carry your pallet." But he answered them, 'The man who healed me said to me, 'Take up your pallet and walk.' They asked him, 'Who is the man who said to you, "Take up your pallet and walk?" ' Now the man who had been healed did not know who it was, for Jesus had withdrawn, as there was a crowd in the place. Afterward, Jesus found him in the temple, and said to him, 'See, you are well! Sin no more, that nothing worse befall you.' The man went away and told the Jews that it was Jesus who had healed him. And this was why the Jews persecuted Jesus, because he did this on the sabbath. But Jesus answered them, 'My father is working still, and I am working'
> (John 5: 15-17).

The context of the Sabbath commandment is set vividly in Edwin Poteats's summary of the "Mandate to Humanity."

> In the sixteenth chapter of the book of Exodus we come upon the children of Israel forty-five days after the night of their escape. The abortive efforts of their Egyptian pursuers to overtake them had allowed them time to make temporary bivouac, but it had also given them time to think over their predicament and to decide that liberty was not a universal blessing. Their discouragement was

deep; hunger had dampened their enthusiasm for freedom. Death at the hand of Yahweh in Egypt was preferable to life under the guidance of Moses in the wilderness. Water was scarce and brackish; food was meager, and foraging was hard. It was Moses' fault, and there was no lack of voices to tell him so. The murmuring of the people frightened him, and he called on Yahweh to protect him. Yahweh showed him a tree, which he cast into the bitter water and it was sweetened. Bread and meat in the form of manna and quail were promised, and when they miraculously appeared, 'they gathered...every man according to his eating' (Exodus 16:21). This sort of thing deserved a celebration, so Moses told them: 'This is that which Jehovah hath spoken, Tomorrow is a solemn rest, a holy sabbath unto Jehovah...See, for that Jehovah hath given you the sabbath, therefore he giveth you on the sixth day the bread of two days; abide ye every man in his place, let no man go out of his place on the seventh day. So the people rested on the seventh day.' (16:23. 29-30.) It is interesting to observe that this time it was not Yahweh who needed the rest but the people.[114]

The Exodus rendition of C-4 and that of the Deuteronomist lay out the two purposes of the Sabbath custom.

> Remember the sabbath day, to keep it holy. Six days you shall labor, and do all your work; but the seventh day is a sabbath to the Lord your God; in it you shall not do any work, you, or your son, or your daughter, your manservant, or your maidservant, or your cattle, or the sojourner who is within your gates; for in six days the Lord made heaven and earth, the sea, and all that is in them, and rested the seventh day; therefore the Lord blessed the sabbath day and hallowed it. (Exodus 20: 8-11)

> Observe the sabbath day, to keep it holy, as the Lord your God commanded you. Six days you shall labor, and do all your work; but the seventh day is a sabbath to the Lord your God; in it you shall not do any work, you, or your son, or your daughter, or your manservant, or your maidservant, or your ox, or your ass, or any of your cattle, or the sojourner who is within your gates, that your manservant and your maidservant may rest as well as you. You shall remember that you were a servant in the land of Egypt, and the Lord your God brought you out thence with a mighty hand and an outstretched arm; therefore the Lord your God commanded you to keep the sabbath day. (Deuteronomy 5: 12-15)

Tradition

The biblical tracing of Sabbath is instructive for our deepening understanding.

- Exodus 16: 23-29, 31: 13-16, 35: 2-3—The establishment of this day reenacts creation and deliverance. It is to be integrated and protected in the public calendar.

- Leviticus 19: 30, 23: 3-38, 24-26—The purpose of reverence to God and the derivative honoring of life is emphasized in the priestly and holiness writing.

---

[114] Op Cit., p. 122.

- Jeremiah 17: 21-27—loss of Sabbath holiness reflects a deeper alienation of people from God.

- Hosea 2: 11, Amos 8: 5—When the formal ritual of the Sabbath supercedes its spiritual and ethical intent, it is hollow ritual.

In the New Testament this spiritual-moral intent of Sabbath law is amplified:

- Matthew 12: 1-12, Mark 2: 27, 28—Jesus recasts law in terms of its allowance to help and heal.

- Mark 1: 21, Luke 4: 16, 13: 10, Acts 13:14—The Sabbath is the day of worship, scriptural interpretation, teaching, wrestling with scripture, attending the divine Word.

Jesus and the Sabbath Controversy

Jesus' healing on the sabbath of the man with the shriveled hand (Mark 3:1-6 and parallels) and Luke's record of the healing of the woman with scoliosis (curved spine) and the man suffering from dropsy (Luke 13 & 14) were disturbing, provocative, some say intolerable, to the strictly observant and the overseers of that observance. Mark 3:6 explicitly states that sabbath breach was a direct cause of the crucifixion. One senses in the Gospels a momentum or at least an excuse to stop this healer-exorcist before it goes any further. The rabbinic casuistry of the day seems irrelevant in light of this mania to stop it. In any reading of law the saving of the body, even a part of the body (circumcision), certainly saving a life, supercedes the temple and Sabbath commands. The rabbis held that a fallen sheep may be lifted out of a pit and a distressed son or even an ox must be pulled out of a well on Sabbath (Matthew 12:11- 12, Luke 14:5)

Even more problematic than healing and helping was working—in this case plucking and hand grinding corn or wheat (Mark 2:25-26 and parallels). Was the good of nourishment sufficiently overriding to violate sabbath? Where does hunger become health and lifethreatening? Vermes finds Jesus' behavior well within the parameters of orthopraxy, unless that is, certain petty legalists were inflamed by jealousy and fear, and were looking for an excuse to be rid of Jesus. E.P Sanders in fine Oxford tradition, also finds a tempest in a teapot. There was no substantial conflict, he claims, between Jesus and the Pharisees with regard to Sabbath. The *Habarim* then and today took on supererogatory righteousness and often resentfully laid rigor on others, that they themselves shirked.

In my view, Jesus did not exhibit what Bultmann and other antinomian exegetes call a "sovereign freedom over the law." He took the righteousness of God in full seriousness to its deepest kernel of meaning. The Sabbath is God's healthful provision for rest, worship, rightful perspective on work, refreshment and focused devotion to God alone. These principles are awesome and inviolable. One can see why Philo, Josephus and the wide mystical tradition of Judaism and religion itself ascribes eternal verity to Sabbath and the other God commands, as the humanistic tableau of the decalogue. The Sabbath tradition is reinstated in the Reformation. The renewed emphasis on law, on the chosen people and a design to transform public life again creates a Sabbatarian consciousness. The doctrine that holy orders vicariously enact Sabbath for the populace is challenged and rigorous adherence from the laity is again called for.

Luther accents two tasks: *Feierabend machen* and *Heiligen Abend geben*. Ceasing work and causing to celebrate are the two impulses born in the commandment. These two sides of the coin correspond to the positive and negative imperatives in the first three commandments and to some extent to all of the ethical commands. Luther accents the labor that is possible on the Sabbath, attending the word and edifying the soul by the spiritual exercises (like reciting and reflecting on the Decalogue). The Word of God is the sanctuary for true repose, true Sabbath. In his ever-interesting way, Luther condemns both the indulgent and the prohibitionist violations of Sabbath.

> Therefore not only those who sin against this commandment who grossly misuse and desecrate the holy day, as those who on account of their greed or frivolity neglect to hear God's word or lie in taverns and are dead drunk like swine; but also the other crowd, who listen to God's word as to any other trifle, and only from custom come to preaching, and go away again, and at the end of the year know as little of it as at the beginning.[115]

For Calvin, the Sabbath command is somewhat downplayed, although it certainly stands out in the Puritan branches of Calvinism. He finds it useful for three reasons: spiritual rest, preservation of church policy and the relief of workers (especially indentured servants). The Sabbath was to be an occasion for replenishing the spirit. Remember the ritual of Sunday in the Presbyterian Manse in Montana of Norman Maclean in the book and film *A River Runs Through It*. Beginning with the Saturday evening bath, a time of sprucing up, getting ready, listening and learning, sharing and delighting in God, marks the day of reprieve. Calvin's social conscience is also sharp in requiring the relief of those who are under the employ or authority of others.

> ...you will set aside wordily and extraneous things (*weltlichen und vergenglichen*) to rivet attention on the spiritual. Already the press and acceleration of a new day of commerce, work, industry and business is being felt.[116] (Bucer)

Theology

God needs a break. As God's handiwork and coworker we need a break. Those who do our work need a break. The animals and fields need a break. "Give me a break" may be the primal plea of the beast of burden and the

---

[115] *LC*, p. 8.
[116] All Bucer references are from the German edition *Deutsche Schriften*, ed. R. Stupperich. Gutsloh and Pris, 1960. See note 14.

proletariat from the dawn of employment. The Habiru were slaves in Egypt. They were locked in bondage to the enslaving drudgery of no-exit and oppression. Humanity was representationally liberated in Exodus and universally liberated in Easter. Now we are given an obligation to bestow sabbath release and rest to the world, especially on those who do its dirty work. Bertrand Russell said, "There are two kinds of people in the world: Those who move dirt from one place to another and those who tell them to do it". In the twenty-first century, one portion of the world is people being emancipated from work as toil under the impact of technology and leisure. Another portion of humanity is enfolded in very hard labor. Even if Sundays and Saturdays cannot be freed up in our ravenous consumer world, we must find alternate rhythms of rest. Sabbath means compensation, rest, and provision of security when work is done. The labor movement in the twentieth (now twenty-first) century and the recent repositioning of economic vitality into the developing world is nothing less than the Sabbath compensation.

One of the most famous paintings at Chicago's Art Institute is Georges Seurat's A Sunday on La Grande Jatte. It is the masterwork of the school of pointillism. One is impressed by the blissful, pastoral scene of trees and flowers, gentle breezes and waters, couples and families strolling with parasols. Animals and children play blissfully on the grass. But the pointillist style is shocking and prophetic like the commandment. The thousands of minutely and accurately placed dots show the belabored tedium that lies behind such laborless bliss.

Earlier in our life we lived in Riverside, Illinois. This first planned suburb in America was designed by Frederich Law Olmsted and his partner, Calvert Vaux. While they were designing Central Park in rapidly industrializing New York City, the team was called to build this pastoral oasis in Chicago at precisely the time that Mrs. O'Leary's cow (wrongly maligned) kicked the lantern and firecleansed that wooden shanty-town (1871).

Behind all pastoral peace is toil and labor. The injustice of inequitably distributed work always lies behind Sabbath rest. For the comfortable to rest by their warm stoves on Sunday afternoons, the miners must go into the hole and dig coal on Monday. For the fine silk and linen laces to bedeck the affluent at church on Sunday, poor children had to work lethal and joy-robbing hours in the factories of nineteenth- century England. Behind the cotton finery in Sunday service in the old South is the backbreaking sweat of the slaves in the fields.

Thomas Jefferson understood the awakening of justice, which must precede rest. "I tremble for our nation when I remember that God is just. His justice cannot sleep forever."

Among the many other passages of sabbath rest that could be chosen for a textual chronicle, the final one I have chosen is from Hebrews. By the time of the Gospel the putative jealousy and retribution by which sabbath God is described by the Hebrew writers has been transformed into a sublime and irenic gift. Now Sabbath and rest are related to the dynamics of faith. Faith is repose in the Godly work of sufficient salvation. The ultimate sabbath rest is release from the burden of life , there in heaven.

Ultimately Sabbath is the good death. With the metaphor of the febrile deathbed from pneumonia, Cardinal John Henry Newman wrote the blessed prayer for the English Prayer book:

> Lord, support us all the day long of this weary life until the shadows lengthen and the busy world is hushed and the fever of life is over and our work is done. Then in thy mercy, grant us a safe lodging, an eternal rest and peace at the last. Through our Lord, Jesus Christ.[117]

Shabat, Christ's accomplishment on the day of resurrection, God is displayed in the One through whom the work of worldmaking was done (Hebrews 1:2). This same One is now the heir to all things (1:2). The consummation of all created reality when this blessed sphere of visitation is reabsorbed back into the pinpoint black hole where God's original intention big-banged, this will be the ultimate sabbath rest.

Hebrews lays the foundation for a sabbatical theology. God's exclusive claims (C1-C3) based on God's rescue of humanity from our disorientation in freedom now ground cosmic orders of faithfulness. Work and leisure, family and fidelity, safety and law, property and non-insinuation into another's world, now round out the compendium of faithful ethical response to God's deliverance and adoption.

Abraham Joshua Heschel outlines the principal themes of a theology of Sabbath:

> Sabbath is Menuhah, a day of happiness, stillness, peace, and harmony. In the words of an ancient Jewish catechism: "What was created on the seventh day? Tranquility, serenity, peace and repose."[118]

Sabbath is an eternal equipoise between this world and the world to come. In the words of the hymn, sabbatarianin its recurrent rhythms and reminiscent of Augustine's *Coram deo*:

> My spirit longs for thee within my troubled breast,
> Though I unworthy be, of so divine a guest
> Of so divine a guest, unworthy though I be,
> Yet has my heart no rest, unless it comes from thee.
> Unless it come from thee, In vain I look around,
> In all that I can see, no rest is to be found

---

[117] *Book of Common Worship*. Philadelphia: United Presbyterian Church, p. 214.
[118] Abraham J. Heschel, *The Sabbath*. New York: Farrar, Straus, and Young, 1951, p. 22.

No rest is to be found but in thy blessed love,
O let my wish be crowned, and send it from above.
John Byron, 1773

Today

Sabbath is the inexplicable serenity of the valley of the shadow. The still waters of Psalms 23 are *menuhot*—the green pastures—*menuha*. In Heschel's words, "Sabbath is the sharing of holiness at the heart of time, a moment of eternity."[119]

Sabbath is light irradiating the dark world.

> Six days a week the spirit is alone, disregarded, forsaken, forgotten. Working under strain, beset with worries, enmeshed in anxieties, man has no mind for ethereal beauty. But the spirit is waiting for man to join it. Then comes the sixth day. Anxiety and tension give place to the excitement that precedes a great event. The Sabbath is still away but the thought of its imminent arrival stirs in the heart a passionate eagerness to be ready and worthy to receive it.

> Then the Sabbath candle is lighted and "just as creation began with the word 'Let there be light,' so does the celebration of creation begin with the kindling of lights.

> And the world becomes a place of rest. An hour arrives like a guide, and raises our minds above accustomed thoughts. People assemble to welcome the wonder of the seventh day, while the Sabbath sends out its presence over the fields, into our homes, into our hearts. It is a moment of resurrection of the dormant spirit in our souls.[120]

The Sabbath commandment begins the tablet of moral wisdom. The original demarcation may indeed have been 3 and 7. Great controversy, which we will not deal with, has for millennia attended the task of establishing and balancing the Decalogue text. C-4 is about sanctity or holiness in life. It is about community restitution and revitalization. As long as the Hebrew people continued their walk with Yahweh, as long as they remained true and faithful to the God of their deliverance, their moral sensitivities, their fellow feeling, their impulses of justice and love became more acute.

Ethics followed from this sensitization. In Sabbath we know that we are not self-made and that we have not made the world. Both our being (existence) and our becoming (ethics) is a divine work. God is bringing about his purposive will in the creation. From the raw material of earth's beginning God is fashioning a new heaven and new earth. We are invited along as co-workers.

---

[119] *Ibid.*, p. 65.
[120] *Ibid.*, p. 66.

Our reasonable service is not only living sacrificially (Romans 12:5) but living serviceably. Our service is to care for the earth. Our *abodah* is to work for what Teilhard calls the building of the earth (*dominium terrae*). Our work is to be spirited not slothful. It is sacramental; "those who don't work, don't eat" (2 Thessalonians 3). Work is to be reverential and contemplative, drawing from earth's resource its inherent provision. Earth's mission, aside from its inherent beauty and life for its own sake, is to offer food and warmth, embellishment and enterprise, life in abundance for all from whom God has given or ever will give or draw breath.

Humanity's most serious violation of *Sabbatgebot* is our compulsive and consumptive way of life. In a massive life-long program of research, Max Weber has shown how spiritual orientations and commitments shape economic activity. Judaism and Protestantism have generated enormous economic enterprise. The impulse to work in C-4 loses its moral excellence when it becomes compulsive, all consuming and exploitative. Amid this mania the imperative to rest deteriorates into lassitude and laziness. The capitalistic ethic errs on issues of justice and concern for the poor. The socialistic ethic errs on issues of incentive, initiative and freedom.

One wonders what kind of world is being fashioned today on the foundations of sixteenth century Calvinism and derivative capitalism. In the high-energy, high technological section of the world— Europe, America, Japan, Israel, South Africa and now Indonesia, Korea and other nations—work consumes much of the day and night of both man and wife in most households. The banks and markets are open around the clock in most of these societies. Our host in Paris returned home at 10 PM the day of our arrival. He works in Paris and London for a New York-based bank, which often requires his attention far beyond that other basic daily rhythm of work and rest. When we invented clocks and lights in the modern world and could prevent the world from ever becoming dark, we assaulted the very rhythmic structure of work and rest.

Today, in Europe, there are many unemployed. British and French elections in 1997 reflected the ire of the population. Many overwork while some underwork. Why? Then there is retirement. Millions of octogenarians and centenarians, still vital and competent, are farmed out to an enforced and resented retirement. Why can't we work less time per day early in our lives, especially when children need our attention, spend less time then in school and work and extend the span of learning and working into our later years? The new industrial, free enterprise, competitive world economy needs to be refreshed by some reawakening of *shabat*.

Secular Meaning of Sabbath

The temporal and spatial meaning of Sabbath must be recovered if we are to regain sanity and humanity in this global economy, ecology and *oikumene*, which is the environment of our life. To find a time and place of replenishment is vital for a rushing world that is pressing its resource-bed to its outer limits. The seas need to rest along with the global aquifer network. The Hebrews believed that only God-water (rain) could be used for vital cleansing. We are siphoning off nature's natural water cycle in the Great Plains and Rockies basin to saturate the now exhausted fields of California. The Eastern European aquifers are near death. The Dead Sea in Israel is receding to the point of calamity as the Jordan's fresh water is siphoned off for fields and settlements. Need we mention the rainforests of South America or Africa's fragile terrain?

The species of life and nature more generally desperately needs Sabbath. In the last fifty years 70% of the species of birds, insects, other animals, even plants have become extinct in Hawaii. Again Eastern Europe is an ecologic wasteland. Woodlands and wetlands worldwide are under assault in our ravenous entrepreneurial age. How shall we sustain both the Sabbath of undeveloped nature and of employment and livelihood?

Conflict between peoples needs a Sabbath. Can we call a Jubilee hiatus between Chicago's street gangs? Among Israelis and Palestinians; Turks, Iraqis and the Kurds; Tutsi and Hutu; Catholics and Protestants in Ireland; Muslims, Jews and Christians? Jesus' rather original construal of Decalogue in the Sermon on the Mount is instructive: Blessed (happy, at peace etc.) are the poor, the merciful, the peace-makers, the meek—those who will and deed Sabbath into the world.

Another ethical implication of C-4 is the question of a refusal to accept death. The New Testament equates anxiety, acquisitiveness and the fear of death.

> I will build bigger barns—settle back and take my ease. Fool—this night your soul is required of you
> (Luke 12:20).

Jewish and Islamic Sabbath is designed to effect a godly and goodly transfiguration of the world. The Christian construal as otherworldly and world-negating is the result of its tragic anti-Semitic turn. Semites view the transformation of secular life as Sabbath duty. For those peoples there is no separation of God and life, Church and state. They are correct theologically and ethically. We are to transform this earth-its institutions and vitalities - after the impulses of the divine spirit and the imperatives of decalogues. Akedic strife in the world is the enterprise of provoking the demonic as we invoke the kingdom-Sabbath rest/work.

Sabbath rest is ascetic pause. Rather than exulting in *Gute, Ehe, Kind und Weib*, we let goods and kindred go. It is not possessions, which enable us to take our ease. Not even the dearest possessions of family can give us rest when all is taken from us in death. *Askese*, insouciance, or Sabbath rest is of God. Holding on, demanding more and more life supports, consuming more and more resources so that enormous wealth is consumed in terminal life prolongation amounts to diminishing the life prospects and the fundamental rights of others. This is unwillingness to receive God's sabbath rest, which is delight and peace.

Today, Sabbath, is NFL games, croissants and the *New York Times* on the balcony, Sunday in the park. Does the question of life's meaning, the reality of God and the moral imperative ever cross our minds or have these been displaced by some endless distraction? Perhaps the old diction still pertains.

Vacate et videte—Be still and know.

Excursus

We're still on sabbatical. Today, we return from Catholic mass in the small village of Weiler, near Bingen. The priest offered a *tour de force* this morning that parodied all of the foibles of our life. The insidious comparisons we make. The not so subtle put-downs, the perennial tensions of *Mann und Frau, Frau und Mann*—and the church—priests—and our petty gripes and excuses. At the end of the fifteen minute-long poem, to his suprise, the young priest, Father Daun, was given a strong ovation. A full house in the church. I thought of Bernanos's troubled *Curé de la Campagne or Black Adder* (Rowan Atkinson) as the priest fumbling with names in *Four Weddings and a Funeral*. "...do you Alasdair, William, Syngen, Arnold ,Whitehouse take...?" But this service was less raucous and had more decorum and solemnity than theirs. I thought of my own last communion service at Garrett-Evangelical when I reconstructed the early Bucer-Calvin liturgy with the Decalogue preceding the Eucharist. "Solemn," one said, respectfully. This service also had a gentle, forgiving and joyous mood. The congregation in Germany was mostly widows and younger women, though a small cadre of townsmen and children were present. More typically, in Catholic and Protestant Europe, today, as in Chicago, New York or San Francisco, Sunday sacrament is croissants, cafe latté and *Le Monde, Suddeutsche Zeitung* or *The New York Times*. That pause will at least tide you over in Sabbath ease until the vicarious tribal-warfare begins at noon—the NFL.

It is *Fastnacht Sonntag*. Tuesday in the Latin world will be Mardi Gras, then Ash Wednesday. This revelry before Lent is also anchored deep in pre-Christian history. Carneval or some other latewinter ritual was a moment of Sabbath suspension that overturned all order and regularity.

Remember the Sabbath day and keep it holy! The narrow meaning, under the obtuse reflections I have offered on work and rest, is simply "go to church." Here we designate ourselves as believers (C-1), those who seek singular devotion (C-2) and holiness (C-3). It is not particularly dangerous anymore to show up, to be seen and named—even in China—perhaps North Korea or Albania? It may appear a bit *komisch* and old-fashioned to the young people, who still sleep off late and live Saturday nights. We are certainly liberated in the West today from Sabbath Blue laws, or Calvin's patrols checking out anyone who stayed home from service in sixteenth century Geneva. Didn't they find the Unitarian heretic Dr. Servetus absent one Sunday morning?

I yearn for a renewal of *Christenheit* and *Christenzeit*, when the whole people converged in faith on the small church in the mountain village on *Weinachtsabend*. I see the snow in the Tannenbäume and an simple new tune coming from the small organ of Franz Grüber. It is such a *"Stille Nacht, Heilige Nacht."* Could a new public faith arise amid our secular, distracted world? One now consensual, not coerced? God only knows. For now, Sabbath rest remains hard work for some, sleeping-in for others. And the commandment stands—a haunting reminder of what once was—or someday might be.

V. Family Values: A Theology of Conviviality

Parenting is a special responsibility. If your conscience doesn't make you do right for your kids the law should.
Al Hofield, Perpetual Chicago Political Candidate,
Proposing that the social security numbers of both parents go on a child's birth certificate.

Children begin by loving their parents; after a time they judge them; rarely, if ever, do they forgive them.
-Oscar Wilde, A Woman of No Importance

A man shall leave father and mother and cleave unto his wife.
(Genesis 2:24)

Your mother wishes to speak to you."
"Who is my mother...who are my brothers?"
"These (my disciples) are my mother and my brothers. Whoever else does the will of my father in heaven is my mother, my brother, my sister."
(Matthew 13: 46-50)

The same harsh, family negating ethic may be the reason that Paul also deletes C-5 in Romans 13: 8ff.

If any man come to me and not hate his father and mother and wife and children, brothers and sisters, yes even his own life, he cannot be my disciple.
(Luke 14: 26)

We must hate...Hatred is the basis of communism. Children must be taught to hate their parents if they are not Communists.
-Lenin, to the Commissars of Education, 1923

Children shall rise up against their parents.
(Matthew 10:21)

Children, obey your parents in the Lord: for this is right. Honor thy father and mother (which is the first Commandment with promise) that it may be well

with thee, and thou mayest live long on the earth. And, ye fathers, provoke not your children to wrath; but nurture them in the chastening and admonition of the Lord.
(Ephesians 6: 1-4)

Behold, I will send you Elijah the prophet before the coming of the great and dreadful day of the Lord: And he shall turn the heart of the fathers to the children, and the heart of the children to their fathers lest I come and smite the earth with a curse.
(Malachi 4:5- 6, the last words in the Hebrew Testament)

It is true...that parents could attain salvation by training their own children...Here right before you are the hungry, thirsty, naked, imprisoned, sick, strangers...God makes your own house a hospital (and a little church) . . and sets you over as chief nurse to give them good words and works...that they may learn to trust, fear and hope on God...to honor His name, not to swear or curse, to mortify themselves by praying, fasting, watching, working...attending worship, listening to God's word, keeping Sabbath, learning to despise temporal things, bear misfortune calmly and not fear death, nor love this life.
-Martin Luther, Treatise on Good Works, 1520

Incursus

Dekalog Cztery takes place on Easter Monday. It is the day of awakening. The dawn of ever-aftering. Father and daughter compose Kieslowski's tale about family. It begins with a sealed letter from her mother, who died when she was 5 days old. She has known of the letter for years. On the face it reads "to be opened after my (the Father's) death."

"I planned to give it to you when you were 10," says the father to the young actress. "But you were too little."

"I planned to give it to you when you were 15," "But you were too big."

The daughter, who has been schooled in post-modernism, says she has been taught theatre training to search for "The hidden Meaning." She has not been able to authentically relate or love her father with this uncertainty in the background.

"When I'm with a man I'm not with him at all." "I always feel guilty."

Is the man really her father? He has raised her and cared for her well, yet doubt persists.

Decalogue, *Vaterunser* and Creed all begin with the forceful fatherly affirmation. As throughout time young women come of age, and as in our era we begin a long overdue emancipation and find a long lost equality, we wonder about the divine meaning of father/daughter.

Freud spoke of the complex connection. Experience bears out the intimate, yet conflicted, association. Could it be that humanity, and the cosmos, can find renewal in our time only as this worldhealing paradigmatic shift is effected and equality relation is established.

Finally, the daughter cries out "Dado!" Together they burn the letter they never read. Love is sufficient.

Honor Thy Father and Mother
Introduction

Following Augustine, Luther began the second table of the law with C-5 in our scheme, the fourth Commandment in his; honor your father and mother. Making a clear shift from theology to ethics, from faith to works, this commandment in Luther's theological ethic is the transition from table 1 to table 2. Now that singular allegiance to God has been established, the still-feudal priest and *Hausvater* now asks what is appropriate authority of and honor to our superiors, in the first case, our parents. After that, would follow obedience to the church and state, both loyalties incidentally implied in the Commandment to honor one's parents. After this commandment, the tablet would proceed to define our rightful relations and orders with the neighbor; beginning with the neighbor and spouse.

Rudyard Kipling tells the story of this commandment in his tale of the baby elephant that asks how he got the long trunk. As a baby with a short pig's snout he was told by his parents not to drink from the crocodile's pool. The teenager inevitably could not resist the temptation to check it out. As he dipped his face into the pool the crocodile latched on. When the little elephant tried to pull away his snout was stretched and stretched until it became a trunk. He survived, it was said, and lived so long because he learned at last to honor and obey his parents.

The morning news carries another poignant story pertinent to the commandment. It seems that several killers are loose in South Africa. In recent months, violent elephants have killed a dozen rhinos. Another two rhinos were also found dead—one died from starvation after the death of his mother—the other was ravaged by lions as he tried to defend its mother's body.[121] All the commands, as Konrad Lorenz has shown, have natural bearings. In this case, C-5 is rooted in the biological nature of animal filial piety.

Sustenance and support, obedience and honor, loyalty and sacrifice—the fifth commandment. The human cultural background illumines the mandate. In the ancient Orient and near Near-East, filial piety was a strong obligation and virtue. By the time the Confucian tradition emerge s in Asian history a long legacy has developed of children honoring parents as long as they live. The communities of Asians who now live among us in the West also venerate their elders, to our

---

[121] *The Chicago Tribune*, October 2, 1994, Sec. 1, p. 19.

dismay and instruction. Judaism is deeply steeped in the same ethos. It is no accident that the Chinese and Jews are among the most longevous peoples on earth. In Judaism, according to Josephus, C-5 is the last Commandment to address our duty toward God. The seriousness of filial piety and parental responsibility is reflected in the connection of this mandate with obligation to God-self. At various places in the ancient world, parents could sell their children as chattel into slavery or condemn them to prostitution. The Greek and Roman father could refuse to "name" a newborn, and expose the child if he was deformed or she was a female. When we review the shadowy event represented in Abraham's ready sacrifice of Isaac in Genesis 22 we realize the ultimate measure of parental betrayal in Canaan and elsewhere. A new way of mutual respect and love between parents and children was charted as Israel confronted Yahweh, whose holiness required awe-filled honor and love in every relation and whose righteousness expected fidelity in all events.

Text

Each one (here first father) is to be reverenced and respected. In Leviticus (19: 3) mother comes first, as it should be. Labor (C-4) is her burden and nursing, watching, caring and grieving. In most ages, childbearing has dramatically cut short the life expectancy of women. In many species the father cuts out and moves on with seeming disdain for, or abandonment of, the young. He kicks offspring out of the nest to let them fend for themselves. He is the Darwinian survival mechanism personified. Kieslowski's caring Dad and Bill Cosby are worthy exceptions to the pattern. Yet, in life and beyond, both parents are to be honored. The Asiatic instinct is here intact. The contradiction of C-5 with C-1 and C-2, in bestowing honor on earthly beings, is explained by the rabbis in that parents share procreative power with God.

The textual history of C-5 illumines its meanings. In the Hebrew bible, children are instructed to filial piety and obedience to parents. Contempt and disobedience fall under severe sanction.

In Deuteronomy the brutal side of this expectation is laid out in a seldom, if ever, implemented sanction.

> If a man has a stubborn and rebellious child, one who will not obey the voice of his mother and father, one who is unrepentant after they chasten him- He shall take the child to the elders of the city- Record their complaint- He is a glutton or a drunkard- The elders shall then stone him to death. (Deuteronomy 21: 18-21)

This intensification of the parental command is harsh, severe and unacceptable. Jesus could not condone it. Even *Shariah*—Islamic law—which most rigorously expresses the severity of Semitic law— would not follow this justice. Of course, today we go to the opposite extreme and kill our children, softly, with kindness. In the centers of libertarian indulgence—especially in the Western world—

210

gluttony and drunkenness almost sound like the common description of a teenager.

Radically overriding the spirit and counsel of this law is the spirit of Hebrew Scripture: "As a father is merciful to his children, so the Lord is merciful to those who fear him" (Psalm 103:13). Remember also Ezekiel, where God cares for Israel as a child in the nursery (2:9).

One senses in the fifth commandment a link with the fourth. It obviously addresses adults as they ponder obligation to their aging parents. When our elders become old and frail—when they enter into the Sabbath of their existence, we are to afford rest and respect, support and care. Parenting and honoring the folks are hard Sabbatarian work. The commandment commends us generally to defend and uphold the lives of the weak and vulnerable. In the late twentieth century our elders are not only poor and exploitable, but they also constitute a powerful political voting block, often luxuriating in Florida while a younger generation is crushed by taxation to support the social security system. We need to be reminded of the reciprocal nature of this command—parents to children—children to parents. With these plaintive prophecies Hebrew testament ends and Christian testament begins. (Malachi 4:5, Luke 1:17).

> And He shall turn the hearts of the fathers to the children and
> the hearts of children to the fathers...Lest I come
> and smite the earth with a curse.

Life itself does not bestow dignity on old age. Functions fail and we become decrepit. Psalm 90 sets down the lifespan (70-80 years) and the sobering counsel is that its days will be labor and sorrow. Youth ought to be hopeful rejuvenation and not grief to their elders. Yesterday I saw a bent-over old man out for an obviously painful arthritic walk. A little boy came along on a bicycle. The old man's eyes lit up and a smile crossed the weary brow—life and legacy will endure. The world will go on after me and all is good. This is God's akedic mystery and will. Additional nuance is given the text with cognate passages in Leviticus 19: 3:

> You shall revere mother and father and keep my Sabbaths,
> I the Lord am your God

And the detailed passage from Ecclesiastics (3: 1-16 Jerusalem Bible) gathers the composite wisdom of the ancient near East.

> Children, listen to me your father, do what I tell you, and so be safe; for the Lord honors the father in his children, and upholds the rights of a mother over her sons. Whoever respects his father is atoning for his sins, he who honors his mother is like someone amassing a fortune. Whoever respects his father will be happy with children of his own, he shall be heard on the day when he prays. Long life comes to him who honors his father, he who sets his mother at ease is showing obedience to the Lord. He serves his parents as he does his Lord.

211

Respect your father in deed as well as word, so that blessing may come on you from him; since a father's blessing makes the houses of his children firm, While a mother's curse tears up their foundations. Do not make a boast of disgrace overtaking your father, your father's disgrace reflects no honor on you; for a man's honour derives from the respect shown to his father, and a mother held in dishonor is a reproach to her children. My son, support your father in his old age, do not grieve him during his life. Even if his mind should fail, show him sympathy, do not despise him in your health and strength; for kindness to a father shall not be forgotten but will serve as reparation for your sins. In the days of your affliction it will be remembered of you, like frost in sunshine, your sins will melt away. The man who deserts his father is no better than a blasphemer, and whoever angers his mother is accursed of the Lord.

The textual history of C-5 flows into the Gospel's depiction of Jesus, who gathers children in love to himself, showing that "of such is the Kingdom of heaven" (Mark 10:14). In the parables we learn of good fathers, waiting fathers (Luke 15: 22) and the greater God and father of Jesus to whom we pray for daily bread and protection from temptation, whose name is to be kept holy (Matthew 6: 9).

The biblical pathway of C-5 has many signposts:

- Leviticus 27: 7—implies that the aged parents who live within the Israelite family are to be treated with kindness, not forced to leave the house (even if they have Alzheimers) or deprived of food (shelter, warmth, health care) etc, and are not to be forced as were pagan precursors to voluntary deaths (ice floats or cold winter night exposure).

- Proverbs 19: 26, 20: 20—To put one's parents away or do them violence is to bring reproach and disgrace on oneself.

- Deuteronomy 21: 18-21—this troubling text is another way of affirming respect for *pater, mater,* and *familis.*

- Hosea 11: 1ff., Isaiah 1: 2ff., Micah 7:5f.—The dissolution and apostasy that brought on the destruction of the increasingly urban culture of the Northern Kingdom in the

- 8th and 7th centuries B.C. was in part attributed to "bad sons" and the breakdown of family honor and affection.

- Matthew 15: 5, 19: 13—dishonoring parents is to "void the word of God."

- Mark 7: 11—Tradition, custom, the "in thing" is never to abrogate the parental commandment.

- Ephesians 6: 1-4, Colossians 3: 20, 21—are lovely elaboration's of the reciprocal obligations of honor between parents and children.

- I Timothy 5: 4—A pre-eminent priority in our lives as we become adults in the world and mark our own way is to provide for our parents.

For rock stars and professional athletes, this comes easily. For many today, children remain abjectly dependent on their aging parents. A society should not tolerate this disgrace.

Jesus and the Family

As a true son of the second temple, Jesus focused his ethical teachings on the Decalogue. In Mark 7:9ff (Matt 15:1) he chastises a group of Jerusalem Pharisees that he meets in Galilee stating that they elevate the *qorban* rule (a donation to the temple derived from C-5) above filial support of parents:

> Moses said 'Honor your father and you mother; and He who speaks evil of father or mother, let him surely die; ' but you say, 'If a man tells his father or his mother what you would have gained from me is Corban (that is given to God) then you no longer permit him to do any-thing for his father or mother'...you make void the word of God through your tradition...

In light of this text, what do we do then with several unmistakable slights to parents where Jesus seems to further the departure ethic of Genesis "...For this reason a man shall leave father and mother..."? When Jesus tarries behind at the Jerusalem temple when the family is up for Sukkoth, they return irritated after he is missing three days. They find him in the temple "questioning and listening, understanding and answering" (Luke 2:46, 47).

> "Son, why have you treated us so?"
> "...did you not know that I must be in my father's house?" (2:48, 49)

Then the return to Filial piety:

> "...He went down with them and came to Nazareth and was obedient to them"
> "...Jesus increased in wisdom and in stature and in favor with God and man."
> (2:51, 52)

We have cited the other passages:

> "who is my mother and father?" (Mark 3: 35)

> "Whoever comes to me and does not hate his own father and mother...cannot be my disciple"
> (Lk 14:26)

> "Let the dead bury the dead" (Lk 9:59, 60)

I concur with E. P. Sanders who holds that Jesus is not obviating or vacating the fifth commandment in these passages, but rather accenting the radical nature of the call to discipleship.

> "If anyone would come after me - Let him deny himself, take up his cross, and follow me..."

"The call to discipleship," writes Sanders "...overrides other responsibilities." "...it supersedes the requirements of piety and torah."122[122]

Vermes believes that here, his respected colleague Sanders has overreacted. He feels that Jesus would have honored the immediate filial grief and obligation of a son to "bury the dead" and care for his father's affairs. Jesus' radical call may have come when, after prolonged grief—or unwillingness on the son's part to move on—he issued the discipleship imperative. In light of Jesus' consistent adherence with Decalogue this interpretation makes good sense to this author.

Islam and Family Law

A young expectant mother in northern Nigeria is condemned to death by stoning after she has weaned the baby who was illicitly conceived. The mother of suicide bomber, Muhammed Atta, claims that he honored family and the family of God in his "jihad martyrdom" of 9/11/2001. Treatment of women including subservience, education of children, especially girls, are among the cache of controversial issues arising from the confrontation of the Jewish-Christian view with Islam at the turn of the century.

Fazlur Rahman argues that the thrust of biblical, Judaic, Christic family values is essential to Islam. The impulses of the Decalogue is reflected in Quran and in Muslim heritage as it extols the dispositions of mercy and care for women, children, orphans, widows and the basic lineaments of family loyalty and extended family life. These committments must find expression in the modern world where they are more critical for the fabric of life than ever before.[123]

Commandments 4-5 in Islam

These commandments governing observance of the Sabbath, work and rest in general and familial piety, also impinge on the war of/on terrorism. In 1998, Osama bin Laden cried out against American violation of the Muslim sacred place and holy family. In the *New York Times* Andrew Sullivan quotes him:

> The call to wage war against America was made because America has spearheaded the crusade against the Islamic nation [family] sending tens of thousands of its troops to the land of the two holy mosques [Sabbath] over and above its meddling in its affairs and its politics and

---

[122] E.P. Sanders, *Jesus and Judaism* London: SCM Press, 1985, p. 253, 255.

[123] Fazlur Rahman, "A Survey of Modernization of Muslim Family Law" *International Journal of MiddleEast Studies,* (1980), 451.

its support of the oppressive, corrupt and tyrannical [C-1] regime that is in control.

Sacra familia, terra sancta, and sanctuary are complex doctrines in the Abraham faith communities. Your house of worship and home are to be inviolable citadels of faith, nurtured and protected with one's love, service, even life. Here faith, hope and love are born and transmitted. Yet these two doctrines also retain an ancient Bedouin element. Related to ancient near-Eastern hospitality, sanctuary requires the hosting and safeguarding of the stranger, sojourner, even the enemy. Obviously President Bush's indictment of harboring "terrorists" is problematic as was the policy of his father of 'busting' American churches offering sanctuary to Nicaraguan exiles. In Bethlehem's Church of the Nativity and Christmas Lutheran Church, sanctuary has been violated by the Israeli incursion of April 2002.

The theological doctrine, ethical obligation and political duty of C-4 and -5 are born in the startling assertion "the earth is the Lord's" (Psalm 24:1). Defending the motherland is an impulse to sustain not only the microcosm of the family and tribe and the cosmos of the nation, but the macrocosm of the wide world. The Abrahamic doctrine at stake is "angels unawares" (Hebrews 13:2). In receiving the visitor, one entertains God disguised as the neighbor.

> When did we see you hungry and feed you,
> naked and clothed you,
> in prison and visited you?
> Inasmuch as you did it unto the least of my brethren
> you did it to me...
> (Matthew 25, after Egyptian funerary texts)

Just as America's finest destiny is opening itself up, Emma Lazaruswise, to the "tired and poor, huddled masses yearning to breathe free," all nations of the world in *dar al Islam,* in Christendom and in '*aretz Israel* must be havens and hostels to the diverse families of the world. This is the epitome and epiphany of Abraham's faith enfolding "all nations of the world."

The tradition of C-5 also is rich and varied: Luther's teaching paves the way for respect and solidarity in family values. Parents are representatives to us of God.

> However lowly, poor, frail and queer they may be, dad and mom are God's gift to us.[124]

Similarly Calvin,

> All authority is instituted by God for our sustenance and edification. Parents are the primal setting of Godly authority.

---

[124] LC, p. 9.

Bucer, like Luther and Calvin, also adds the community and state as proper authorities (Romans 11) instituted on our belief for our good.

Theology

Let us now build on this textual foundation a theology of conviviality, and familial solidarity. In one sense C-5 properly belongs on the theological tablet. The appeal is for the nascent generation to perpetuate the faith of the senescent generation. The word "religion" means to be bound (ligatured) back to the formative truths, visions, ideals and behaviors that constitute the tradition in which we stand. Religion enfolds us in an *ethos* (stable, *habitus*). Jesus honored the God of Abraham, Isaac and Israel. The eternally living God was the God of the living. The patriarchs and the matriarchs of faith still live in the memorial presence of God (Acts 8). Our parents in faith were progenitors of the covenant. We now regenerate that same bond. Yes, faith is an immediate personal relation to the living God. The faith of our parents must be appropriated and become our own faith. But something about faith is irresistibly generational and generative. In our age we have come near to forgetting this.

Our faith is not *de novo*, disconnected from the heritage. "The promise is to you and your children even as many as the Lord God shall call" (Acts 2: 39). We are saved and blessed in solidarity with the generations. The promise and the kingdom, the ongoing substance of faith, is trans-generational. The heresy of modern Western cultures, especially Protestant cultures, is the belief that every person and every generation must reinvent itself. "When you come of age, leave home for college, go out on your own, you have to choose your own God, your own beliefs and values, your own priorities and way of life." Though there is some truth in this pilgrimage ethic (recall the story of Ruth), severed in rude autonomy from preceding and proceeding life we become atomized, isolated islands. The doctrine that one is separable from parents and tradition is as insidious as that which says we are inseparable and indistinguishable. We become authentic as we recapitulate our roots within new circumstances.

The correlated truth to continuity is creativity. Law and Gospel says, here is the way, truth and life—you must receive it and show it, lest it disappear from the lineage. Jesus' words on this acute responsibility seem harsh. "You must hate your family—even your own life—to be my disciple." We are not even to tarry to bury our father, but to follow (Matthew 8: 21). Abandonment of family in favor of new family is implied in the Jesus ethic. "If you love those that love you, what reward have you?" (Matthew 5: 46). We are called to belong to a new transgenetic, transgenerational, transnational family. We are to honor our seniors as a community not only our biological parents. Providing them security and provision for needs in their seniority is our responsibility toward all elders. While veneration of one's own dear parents is primal—we must extend such honor to all who have sustained our life and faith in the world and whose inheritance makes us who we are.

216

One of the deepest truths of theology is that humans bear back the divine image in regard for their progenitors and bear forward the divine image in the commitment of procreation. "Adam beget a son in his likeness, after his image and called his name Seth" (Genesis 5: 3). Generativity in both directions is the glory and guilt of our existence.

George Eliot tells the genetic tale of Adam Bede and his resemblance to his mother:

> Family likeness has often a deep sadness in it. Nature, that great tragic dramatist, knits us together by bone and muscle, and divides us by the subtler web of our brains; blends yearning and repulsion; and ties us by our heart-strings to the beings that jar us at every movement. We hear a voice with the very cadence of our own uttering the thoughts we despise; we see eyes—ah! so like our mother's—averted from us in cold alienation; and our last darling child startles us with the air and gestures of the sister we parted from in bitterness long years ago. The father to whom we owe our best heritage—the mechanical instinct, the keen sensibility to harmony, the unconscious skill of the modeling hand—galls us, and puts us to shame by his daily errors; the long-lost mother, whose face we begin to see in the glass as our wrinkles come, once fretted our young souls with her anxious humors and irrational persistence.[125]

Alienation and reconciliation abide at the crux of this commandment. With this relation, as in Eden's garden, our freedom and autonomy prompt us to deny where we came from and to whom we belong. We wish to be self-defined, self-willed and selfdetermined. We chafe at the fact that we proceed from a father and heavenly father. "I just want to be my own person;" this is the perennial human ambition.

The commandment also invites us to celebrate our origins and obligations. We are built to be strong bridges between generations, however troubled the undertowing waters. We come from God and proceed toward God and that origination and destination is the spiritual genius and moral direction of our existence. Our parents cared enough to receive our life, take care of us a little while and then turn us over to our independent ways and futures. We live on in thankful memory called love and trusted venture called hope. Genesis-owned becomes integrity-lived.

There is also a political dimension to the theology of C-5. In the Scots Confession of 1560, a document that has changed the history of the world, we learn a posture of political allegiance tinged by watchful scrutiny wherein we are called

---

[125] Quoted in Henry Sloane Coffin, *The Ten Commandments*. New York: Doran Co., 1915, p. 95.

> To honor father, mother, princes, rulers and superior powers, to love them, to support them, yea to obey their charges—no repugning to the Commandment of God—to save the lives of innocents, to repress tyranny, to defend the oppressed...
> -Scots Confession of 1560, Article XVI

As with the first commandment, the fifth condemns all forms of idolatrous totalitarianism while honoring duly constituted systems of government. We are to honor and love our officials as we do our parents. Legitimate political authority in terms of this Commandment is protection and affirmation of the vulnerable. "Save the lives of innocents," "defend the oppressed," and govern within the parameters of the moral law is embodied in the Decalogue and the derivative bodies of constitution and legislation. This is the public trust. Public authorities function legitimately only within the will and Word of God. The residue of the polemical C-5 ethics of Calvinism can be found throughout the world in systems of liberty, democracy and tyranny.

Identifying earthly authority with the eternal authority has proven throughout history to be a bane and blessing. It has propped up abusive rulers with the mystique of divine-right. Conversely, it has fashioned a political ethic, which grounds justice and righteousness. It sets a noble standard for rulers to live up to.

Today

The ethical system that emerges from C-5 has the same equivocation. Conditional esteem is the moral disposition grounded in this command. As with the filial piety of the Confucian tradition, we honor parents or others in authority as they are worthy of that respect. The Commandment implies a constellation of family values along with a range of parental and filial obligations.

The family unit is extolled and strengthened by this mandate. Despite all the abusive potential, all the possibilities of familiaritybred- contempt (even Jesus was without honor in his own province), despite the frightful potential for alienation and pathogenesis, the family is given a place of nobility, profound esteem and sacred honor. The family, nuclear and extended, is a bulwark of love, acceptance and support against centrifugal and centripetal tendencies in human arrangements. In Luther's words it is the bulwark against fear, want and the demonic. The temptation toward isolation and a "do your own thing," "go your own way" ethic is prevalent in modern American families. Each family member is too busy to ever be together with the others. The sad spectacle of too many African- American families, fueled by unjust economic and employment patterns, where the father, if around at all, circles in some far-distant orbit, exaggerates this pattern of disarray common to most family groups.

Parents, Children and Western Culture

Returning for a moment to the "disdain of parents" passages. In the radical call to discipleship and the likewise radical call to conscience and autonomy in the Western tradition, e. g. Luther, Locke, etc., there is a certain spirit of freedom that loosens the ligature of the parent-child bond. The abandonment by parents of their children and the assignment of parents to neglectful nursing homes by their children, so rampant in the modern West, is a sign that such freedom has gone amiss. Many young families today have to decide whether a two-career, affluent lifestyle supersedes concern for mom and dad to the point where they must be relegated to a nursing home. Dinner and theatre once a fortnight, the education of children (now $40,000 + a year in elite colleges), a reliable retirement fund for health crises, etc. These values assume preeminence. In other words, we have come to face the tough kind of conflict that Jesus must have faced with the man looking after his father's funeral. Are you willing to forego braces for the kids' teeth or an education at Northwestern University in order to care for mom and dad? Certainty when the filial obligation for parents is generalized to elders as a group and the crunch comes with higher taxes for expanded social security and publicly-funded geriatric care, the priority becomes clear:

Look out for number one!

If autonomy and personal gratification ethics are irresistible in the evolution of human morality and if Francis Fukiyama is right that capitalistic and entrepreneurial freedom is the forward wave of history, not to be denied, then the only hope against final degeneration of the family is a renaissance of YAWEH faith and Decalogue righteousness. We need Elijah or John the Baptist (not Televangelist Bradshaw or Family-Values Dobson) to turn the hearts of the fathers to the children and the hearts of the children to the parents. "Lest (He comes) to smite the earth with a curse."

The kibbutz in Israel at best or Branch Davidian, the Swiss order of the Solar tradition, or the Leninist commune at worst, are examples of incestuous familial clumpings where personal development may be stifled by collective coercion and expectation and where the ethics of surveillance and betrayal may displace those of enhancement and trust.

The 'good' (my rationalization) family is one animated by spirited word. When parents, especially mom, talk and read to children, they flourish. When talking and listening—communication—is vibrant, growth and security ensue. The child is able to move out in confidence toward the world. Autism or nonverbal existence becomes sad and dangerous. Alienation leads to autism, silence and violence. Infants develop their interactive capacities, their competence in life in the parental-child dialogue, the generational dialogue and the societal dialogue. "Train up the child in the way he should go and when he is old he will not depart from it" (Proverbs 22:6).

From the child to parent and grandparent, an obligation is set in C-5 to care and provide care of one's aging and dying. The economic system, social security and health care apparatus, the housing and transportation arrangements of our common life all have taken enormous strides toward elder respect in the modern world. In these days of rapidly diminishing public welfare we need to hold the line and seek improvement. Even in the affluent world, poverty is concentrated in the very old and the very young. The judgment of God expressed at the end of the Hebrew Testament and the opening of the Christian Testament is even with us:

> Behold, I will send you Elijah the prophet before the great
> and terrible day of the Lord comes. And he will turn
> the hearts of fathers to their children and the hearts of
> children to their fathers, lest I come and smite the land
> with a curse (Malachi 4:5, Luke 1:17).

Excursus

I have learned the truth of C-5 from my wife, Sara. She embodies all that a child, and especially a parent, should be. Fortunately, for me, she covers my multitude of sins on this mandate. Her honor for her parents and her attendance to their needs as they grew old and approached their deaths superseded all other values in those days. As my own parents entered that dark valley of shadows, I sought to be half as true.

But I've admired most her way with our children. She always loved to be with them and read to them. They were her contemporaries and friends. Day in and night out she delighted in their presence. Strolls to the park, playing in the sand-box, bathing and dressing, walking the floor at night when they cried, nursing their hunger. Much of her own promising career (Ph.D in comparative literature) she set aside for a while to be with them. She started them in music, in languages, in cooking. She was so good that my persistent absence was forgiven. All four children erroneously think that I did a good job. She covered for us both.

No wonder "her children rise up and call her blessed!" (Proverbs 31:28)

VI. Natural Born Killers: A Theology of Life

You shall not kill.
(Exodus 20: 13)

"You have heard that it was said to the men of old, 'You shall be liable to judgment.' But I say to you that every one who is angry with his brother shall be liable to judgment; whoever insults his brother shall be liable to the council, and whoever says, 'You fool!' shall be liable to the hell of fire. So if you are offering a gift at the altar, and there remember that your brother has something against you, leave your gift there before the altar and go; first be reconciled to your brother, and then come and offer your gift. Make friends quickly with your accuser, while you are going with him to court, lest your accuser hand you over to the judge, and the judge to the guard, and you be put in prison; truly, I say to you, you will never get out till you have paid the last penny."
(Matthew 5:21-26)

Incursus

"The law should guide human behavior."
"People invented the law to control others."
"People will either observe or break it."
"As we question more and more what, if anything, life means, the law must amplify."
"Since the days of Cain no punishment has been adequate."
[Lawyer's Bar Exam]

Like *Dead Man Walking* (Sean Penn or the Green Mile), Kieslowski's treatment of Do Not Kill deals with a murderer, an advocate, and the issue of capital punishment.

The killer is brutal by nature and nurture.

he scares away the pigeons being lovingly fed by an old lady he pushes a carefully dressed young man into the swill in a public latrine in brutal calculated premeditation he kills the fat old cab driver even at the end he asks his lawyer, to place him, not his mother, in the one remaining family grave plot.

But Kieslowski will not let us brutalize the youth. Like Timothy McVeigh he has a soft likable human side. He carries around the confirmation photo of his beloved sister who was run over with a tractor by his drunken friend.

Complexity compounds: The taxi driver is also Mr. Nasty to anyone and everyone. He startles the little dogs as they cross the street. He speeds away from an injured man needing to go to the hospital.

Kieslowski's shades of good and evil are always blurred. Like devilsticks, the evil rod is always split and drawn apart.

As the young killer is led away to the armored transport vehicle he looks up as his lawyer calls to him. "When you called my name, I cried," he tells him as he is about to be executed. "No one ever called my name before."

In Deadman Walking, the Catholic Nun sister, Helen Praejan, attends to Matthew, the white supremacist, who has also been part of a brutal killing of two young people. She looks after his needs—caring for his mother, contacting a lawyer to at least seek life rather than the death sentence. In long and honest dialogue she seeks to bring him to honesty and moral repentance. Finally the appeal for clemency is denied and he faces his accusers before the lethal injection table. "Matthew," she demands, "did you kill that boy?" Finally he breaks down and cries bitterly, "Yes, I killed him." "Matthew," the Sister shares, "You are now a child of God." "No one has ever called me a 'child of God' before." He sobs as he is led away. With her hand on his shoulder she reads from Isaiah:

221

> "Fear not, for I have redeemed you, I have called you by name; you are mine. When you pass through the waters I will be with you. When you walk through the fires you will not be harmed, for I am your God."
> (Isaiah 43:1-3)

"Execution is the opposite of baptism" comments sister Helen Praejan, the author of the book, Deadman Walking. In the covenant of life, killing excludes, loving includes C-6 killing sustaining resorts to C-3 cursing/naming.

Both films finish in a non-Kieslowski color purple, redemptionpathos, and regality. Kieslowski's film ends out in the misty Polish meadow at dawn. The young lawyer cries out against the death penalty and law itself "*YEN NAVIDNE*" (I abhor it!)

Text

The Hebrew root means either to kill or to murder. The image of God in human beings makes murder blasphemy. Human blood spilled cries from the earth to God. God gives and takes away life. The prerogative is not shared. In Hebrew convictions, even the "justifiable" homicides—capital punishment, self-defense, war, etc—are offenses, not cause for celebration. Willful murder is the focus of this commandment (*razah*). Non-culpable homicide is also covered by the word as in (Numbers 35: 11, 27, 30, Deuteronomy 4: 42) where the powerful prohibitive conveys the positive imperative of the sanctity of human life. The biblical concourse of C-6 shows its dramatic meaning:

- The silent horror of the Genesis stories, Cain and Abel in particular, are now followed in the bible by a bloody pathway beginning with the plagues in Egypt, the drowning of the Egyptian pursuers and the victims of the conquest. The beginning of monarchy with Saul, David and Solomon is also replete with killing. The commandment (C-6) seems to have been lost in the sand at Sinai.

- I Samuel 2:6 summarizes the saga: the Lord gives life and kills.

- Leviticus 24: 17-21 begins an enumeration of the penalty to be exacted for different killings.

- Matthew 10: 28, 17: 23, 21: 35-38, 23: 34-37 and other passages note the severity of human killing against the peace of God but also see divine providence working at a deeper level.

- In Luke, John and the Acts, one has the clear impression that God uses murderous human violence to accomplish his will.

- In Paul (Romans 11: 3, 2 Corinthians 3: 6) etc. again death is laid against the serene background of sacrifice and redemption.

Tradition

In the deepest historical recesses of Hebrew moral memory, we find conviction finally codified by the exile priests. Here is the ancient proscription of blood revenge which stands even in the primal Noachian covenant

> And God blessed Noah and his sons, and said to them, "Be fruitful and multiply, and fill the earth. The fear of you and the dread of the earth, and upon every bird of the air, upon everything that creeps on the ground and all the fish of the sea; into your hand they are delivered. Every moving thing that lives shall be food for you; and as I gave you the green plants, I give you everything. Only you shall not eat flesh with its life, that is, its blood. For your lifeblood I will surely require a reckoning; of every beast I will require it and of man; of every man's brother I will require the life of man. Whoever sheds the blood of man, by man shall his blood be shed; for God mademan in his own image. And you, be fruitful and multiply, bring forth abundantly on the earth and multiply in it."
>
> (Genesis 9: 1-7).

God's fundamental will for the earth is that life should flourish and not perish. The ancient code is also reflected in what may be the root text of C-6: the ritual curses recorded in Deuteronomy 27. This text reflects an ancient reenactment and recitation of the covenant at Schechem or Mt. Gerazim, the Samaritan Sinai.

And Moses charged the people the same day, saying, "When you have passed over the Jordan, these shall stand upon Mount Ger'izim to bless the people: Simeon, Levi, Judah, Is'sachar, Joseph, and Benjamin. And these shall stand upon Mount Ebal for the curse:

> Reuben, Gad, Asher, Zeb'ulun, Dan and Naph'tali. And the Levites shall declare to all the men of Israel with a loud voice:
>
> 'Cursed be he who slays his neighbor in secret.' And all
> the people shall say 'Amen.'
>
> 'Cursed be he who takes a bribe to slay an innocent
> person.' And all the people shall say, 'Amen.'
> (Deuteronomy 27: 11-14, 24,5).

Jesus and Killing

In the *locus classicus* New Testament passage Jesus is not vacating or excusing C-6 when he says "you have heard it said of old, but I say to you." It is unimaginable that Jesus or Paul would say that "do not kill" was a feature of rabbinic or pharisaic legalism that could now be set aside. And as we listen further to the Sermon on the Mount we see that the strictures are not loosened but rather tightened. Jesus goes to the root cause of murder, the silent brooding hatred and violence of the killing-will. Anger may be the beginning, then verbal abuse, then the secret thought. Desire, intent, then act is the biblical progression. The murderous intent, as Kieslowski depicts, begins long before the culminating act.

Vermes takes us to the heart of the Judaic spirit of C-6 from the Tannaitic Midrash:

> Lest innocent blood be shed...and so the guilt of bloodshed be upon you...But if a man hates his neighbor, and lies in wait for him, and attacks him...On this account it has been said: A man who has transgressed a light commandment will finish by transgressing a weighty commandment. If he has transgressed You shall love your neighbor as yourself (Lev. 19:18), he will finish by transgressing. You shall not take vengeance or bear grudge (ibid), and You shall not hate your brother (Lev. 19:17), and that your brother may live beside you (Lev. 25:36) until he comes to shedding blood.[126]

Whatever the cultural and cultic background by the moment of the Mosaic revolution, the conscience of a people is prepared to hear the voice of God and to receive *mizvot* which will forever after guide personal and public life. The long legacy of C-6 spans homicide law, to holy war crusades, to suicide. Specific stipulates that allow acts of capital punishment in the name of justice, such as John Wayne Gacy's execution, are faithful allowances to violence in the name of peace.

In the larger catechism, Luther dwells heavily on Jesus' intensification of the killing commandment in Matthew 5.

> We must not kill, neither with hand, heart, mouth, signs, gestures, help or counsel.[127]

The serene acceptance by Jesus of his death at the hands of Roman authorities and by reason of Jewish law imprints deeply Luther's analysis of C-6. Luther's quick resort to lethal force to quell the peasant's revolt shows that he also believed that rightful and necessary killing was conscionable within this mandate.

Calvin's answer to one query on C-6 illumines a use we find in his social ethic and that of Bucer and other Reformed creeds that is rooted in Luther and ancient Catholic tradition.

> ...The Lord, by condemning hatred and restraining us from any harm by which our neighbor may be injured, shows at the same time that he requires us to love all men from the heart and study faithfully to defend and preserve them.[128]

Holy war is almost endorsed anew in the Reformation. It may be necessary to kill some people, in other words, to purify a land, or pacify rebellion, or resist the Turks. The Calvinist spirit allows the hounding down and execution of

---

[126] Quoted in Geza Vermes, *The Religion of Jesus the Jew*. Minneapolis: Fortress Press, 1993, p. 31.
[127] LC, p. 16.
[128] 1536, p. 64, 65.

Servetus. It condones the beheading of King Charles I over Oliver Cromwell's signature.

There is a certain love of killing for righteousness' sake that marks the Protestant, Catholic and Dissenter wars of the sixteenth and seventeenth centuries. The prohibition is almost construed into an imperative. You pleased God and furthered God's will and kingdom by killing his supposed and your actual enemies. It takes the anticlerical, secular peace in the eighteenth century to finally end the religious wars. Regrettably, in modern times, the same religious killing has resurfaced with greater venom ever known to Catholics or Protestants. But thankfully, killing even a God-enemy and paying with your life has receded as an act of martyrdom in Judaism and Christianity (an unfortunate residue remains in Jihadic Islam).

The one bright shaft of light throughout the dark night is the gentle witness of some pacifist groups such as the Quakers, Mennonites, and peace churches. Faithful to C-6 and to Christ's nonretaliation even to death, they retain a witness to the enduring ethical power of C-6.

Commandment 6 in Islam

To ignore or flaunt divine and natural law by asserting superiority over it or unwillingness to submit to it by reason of power, sovereignty or authority over it, strikes fear into the heart of others. To breach such instruction (Torah) is to menace others. To kill, rape and pillage is to terrify the world. This section of our exploration of the war on terrorism is the most difficult. Its theme is the most subtle and nuanced. To kill in war and under threat involves profound issues such as:

- killing civilians (either collaterally or intentionally)
- assassination
- combat mortality itself

Let us explore the morality of these issues within the current context.

Initally we must note a sequentialism implied in the unfolding of our thesis. Basic to the modes of moral law and ethical principles of the Abrahamic tradition (Torah, Christian ethics, *Shari'ah*), is the process and momentum flows in this way:

- "the fruit was pleasant to the eye"
- "the serpent beguiled me"
- "I ate it"

Similarly with killing, meditation precedes intention which proceeds to action. When *Madrasas* (Koran schools) in Afghanistan and Pakistan enjoin suicide-assassination as Holy Law, they violate this cardinal command of Allah.

Though initially each Abrahamic faith movement (*hegira*) involves terror, violence and killing, both defensively and offensively, to protect and establish the faith, the movements are deeply and normatively more irenic than bellic. The 'conquest' in Canaan probably was no such thing and we know that even though Solomon's realm could have been an empire, it settles into a provincial kingdom. Like Moses, Jesus' appearance in the world is accompanied by infanticide. (Exodus 2:15, Matthew 2:12) The early church is so dispossessed of this world that even three centuries after apostolic times, Constantine's state, even to Augustine, verges on pagan audacity. Though Mohammed's *hegira* begins with the sword, ostensibly to protect the nascent revelation, his final trek to Mecca is weaponless, placing himself at the mercy of his adversaries.

Despite this peaceful norm at the center of the three faiths, crises and threats seem to turn the embracing political structure and even the faith movements themselves hostile and violent. In the 1930's a tendency emerged in Islam which turned many persons—Mullahs and zealous laymen—radical and aggressive. In 1948-50, Israel is planted in Palestine, and America overturns Mohammed Mozedeh in Iran and plants the Shah. In Egypt in the 1950's and 60's, the radicals were jailed, tortured and executed in their homes for their venom against Western influence and their desire to replace their regimes with Islamic states. These extremists, like the Egyptian Jihad in 1981, assassinated President Anwar Sadat, whom the West saw as a new peace and justice Pharaoh. (Throughout this section I am indebted to the essay by Robert Worth, "Justifying Murder: The Deep Intellectual Roots of Islamic Terror," *The New York Times*, October 13, 2001, p. A 13, 15)

After that stadium massacre which killed Sadat, a document found called "The Neglected Duty" provided theological justification for suicidal assassination because the ruler had abandoned Islam. Like some Puritan documents (even the American Declaration of Independence: "The people have the right and duty to abolish that government"), tyrannicide was justified as duty to God and the people.

Al Qaeda emerges out of the Islamic Jihad movements which spring up in the 1980's and 1990's throughout the Middle East and Western Asia. Osama bin Laden's worldview finds even deeper resource in a version of otherwise liberal and magnanimous medieval Islam which had turned defensive against the Spanish Inquisition and Mongol hegemony. *Salafiyya* sought to purify Islam to its seventh-century origins from the corruptions of idolatry. It must be remembered that both Judaism and Mohammedism have a strong anti-idolatry tenor in their origins. Like Israel before and Islam after, Christianity is a movement to purify YAHWEH faith from an "idolatrous and adulterous generation." (Mark 12:39) The official *Wahhabi* ideology of Saudi Arabia is this version of purging, Puritan cleansing, restoration and strict adherence. Regrettably, the Saudi and other affluent Emirites which adopted this theocratic program missed its prophetic fury against injustice and neglect of the poor.

Major literary influences on radical Islamic Jihad, Al Qaeda and Osama bin Laden were Sayyid Qutb who wrote *Signposts on the Road* (1964) and Agdallah Azam, a Palestinian who was killed by a car bomb in 1989. Such thinkers influenced the former rich Saudi playboy by transforming the Islamic stipulate against killing a fellow Muslim, now finding it acceptable., even honorable, to kill them if they were Jews, Christians or pseudo-Muslims. The thought forwarded was that an official within *dar-al-Islam* who is not Muslim is a positive threat to social and spiritual integrity in the nation.

The main theme of the killing document of Hussain is that killing is authorized by the presence of oppression (*fitna*). The major difficulty already evident is that liberty-grounded peoples likeAmerica and Israel do not think of their presence or influence in cultural phenomena like secularism, democracy and capitalism as oppression. So we continue. For Hussain's reading of Quran, oppression is "worse than killing." "While killing is evil, yet it is enjoined to crush a bigger evil." Here we have a utilitarian addendum to the actual command "do not kill."

Finally, there is reward for killing oppressors. "Those who sacrifice their lives for the cause of Allah get an exalted eternal life immediately, and are called martyrs (*shaheed*)."[129]

The argument of justifiable homicide at the political and theological level remains problematic. Was the judicial murder of King Charles I (1649) by the Puritans warranted? Were the conspirators in the aborted July 20, 1944 movement to assassinate Adolf Hitler justified? Bonhoeffer, Dohnanyi and my teacher, Helmut Thielicke, struggled with this issue. It is the same genre of issue as the justification of the instant killing of 100,000+ Japanese civilians with the atomic bombs at Hiroshima and Nagasaki. Does the greater good of end of war (Truman) or relief of oppression (bin Laden) justify the killings?

The persuasion of the particular thesis I am putting forward is that these acts of so-called "redeeming death" are not justified. For two reasons: (1) the ethic rooted in the reality of God reserves lifeand death-dealing to God alone. From human calculations such acts may seem to be good and helpful. But in the divine purview, which sees beyond the exigencies of the moment and of human passions, all killing is blasphemous and evil. (2) Even in terms of human consequences, such acts always set in motion a cycle of reprisals.

---

[129] "Two Views: Can the Koran Condone Terror?" *New York Times,* October 13, 2001, p. A 15.

Osama bin Laden's first videotape mentioned one American atrocity in particular—the nuclear bombing of Japanese civilians at Hiroshima and Nagasaki. In biblical ethics, a killing must be commanded by God. All other killing is outlawed. The philosophical justification of homicide in capital punishment, war, self-defense and abortion are rational, but theologically sinful. God's call to Abraham to offer Isaac is the paradigm. If righteous and moral war, say of the U.S. Civil War against slavery, or World War II against Hitler, is justified, that justification provides allowances for killing, though it remains full of remorse and repentance.

In addition to this theological and pragmatic premise, our thesis adds yet another dimension which forbids intentional killing. Joining *akedah* to Abraham in the moral structure of reality argues that salvific (redemptive) death has occurred with finality in the being of God. The meaning of Messiah (The Anointed One) in Hebrew and Christian faith and of the sacrificial lamb in all three expressions of the heritage is that the sin of the world and the burden of righteous recompense (judgment) has ultimately become a divine act. There is no longer necessity for humans to take justice in matters of life and death into their own hands. We will develop the meanings of this, albeit marginal thesis, as we go along, especially with further reference to Jack Miles, CHRIST: A Crisis in the Life of God. For now we note that the sublime metaphysical and eschatological realities of forgiveness and peace militate against the necessity of terrorism and war. Realism vis-à-vis the enduring stupidity and violence of humanity will always counter-mitigate this transcending reality, offering the remote possibility of a holy passion of justice.

Theology

The theology of C-6 is the doctrine of the Image of God in persons and the derived doctrine of the sanctity of human life. The background story is troubling as all get out. God is ticked off by Cain's offering—sprouts instead of sushi. Miffed at being slighted, Cain goes after his brother, the favored Abel—knocks him off and buries him in the sand. Yahweh calls out at the sight of the trickle of blood on the earth, with the haunting question—"Where is Abel your brother?" Then follows the violent and apathetic response of the ages, "Am I my brother's keeper?"

It seems to be an archetypal story. It says something about the fratricidal impulse and homicidal inclination in all of us. It also searches out the dynamics of sibling rivalry and of trying to please God apart from generosity and human kindness. The passage of God's gentle counsel is moving:

> The Lord had regard for Abel and his offering but for Cain and his offering he had no regard. So Cain was very angry, and his countenance fell. The Lord said to Cain, 'Why are you angry, and why has your countenance fallen? If you do well, will you not be accepted? And if you do not do well, sin is crouching at the door; its desire is for you, but you must master it' .
> (Genesis 4:5-7)

Recollection of the prodigal son, in this case the older favored brother, grumbling, resentful, bitter, privileged. The wayward son is welcomed home—undeserved favor for the lost rebel. In both stories, the same understanding father—the same long-suffering, ever-welcoming God. Why this brooding bitterness? Is it the old tension between the farmer and cattleman? What is the deeper message of hatred, insecurity, and meditated or unpremeditated murder? All we know is that, as in the Fall, the Genesis writer brings genius out of disgrace.

The offspring of this marked man was Enoch the city builder and then Jabal, Jubal, and Tubal, founders of the commodities, arts, and crafts. Fall becomes ascent. Curse, creativity. Yet all perdures through history, as human's anguish in a brutal alienation from nature are robbed of their original bliss.

Abel's blood stains the earth. The clay from which the images (statues) were first molded now turns sour. Never again will the ground (*adama*) yield unless you put DDT to it and with DDT, the endless cycle of technological fixes. Otherwise, mother nature will destroy us. Now humans wander restlessly on the earth—like the Babylonian Noah, old Gilgamesh, or Cain and the prodigal, we are condemned to an alienated pilgrimage—a quest—ever searching for our home, which is peace.

Underneath it all, is the profound irony—Moses the putative giver of the law " you shall not kill" is himself a murderer. He struck down the Egyptian and buried him down in the sand—but you can't hide a man in mud. Blood cries out. Murderous intent and act, it seems, are part of the human condition. The tendency toward self-neglect and destruction, toward apathy, even antipathy with others, toward selfishness, xenophobia, fear and desire to be done with different people and groups, are all part of our nature. Killing is ubiquitous in the human emotions and human experience. There may be something suicidal, homicidal, fratricidal, patricidal, ecocidal, even deicidal, in all human beings. What Freud called *thanatos*, that mysterious mortal impulse, may be ingrained in our very being. Biblical theology acknowledges that our unredeemed lives begin in rebellion toward God's will and animosity toward our fellows. We shrink from life (*l'hayim*) and resent it in others. Our death instinct (*Todestrieb)* ends in our own demise in the irrefutable Deca-logic. We tend to usurp God's lordship over our existence, which includes the trust in which God places others to our hearts. Part of our creaturely rebellion is our despising all of life, even our own. The law of God expressed in covenant and command holds our negligence and violence in check through God-sanctioned structures like the state, the apparatus of justice and punishment, the coercive force toward non-violence, the goods of family and community, the civilizing effects of education and society and the redeeming effects of the church. God marks us with the protective stigmata of the sign of Cain, which is now the cross of Christ that protects humanity from self-destruction. The new covenant of non-revenge in (Matthew

5 :38, 39) sets the stage for a positive urge toward reconciliation and redemption as "do not kill" mutates into "do good." Now we are instructed, "If our enemy is hungry, feed him" (Romans 12: 20-21). But he will live again to kill you"... we recoil...exactly.

Oliver Stone is right, in part, the thesis of his films Platoon, JFK, and his latest Natural Born Killers is that we are not natural born killers, but rather humans in rebellion against our peaceful, reconciled nature by God. Biblical anthropology finds the human condition under the fall to be vicious and violent, even in its subtle refinements. We all kill and die in our sins and by virtue of the sin of the world let loose that cosmic evil into the world through our perpetual complicity in original crime. When Stone says that we all kill or will be killed, it is not that God wants it that way, but that we affirm the reign of death in nature and history. We cause disease and reap the harvest of nature's reaction to our aggression. The law brings death to the life-world and to the human spirit. "Our feet are swift to shed blood. Destruction and misery is our way, not the way of peace" (Romans 4:15). But Christ died for the sin of the world. He bore in his crucified body the sickness of the world, the violence of our life, the deserved death of humanity and the cosmos. In Christ crucified and resurrected, the world is restored to its peace. He brings "life and immortality to light through the Gospel" (2 Timothy 1:10). "The dividing wall of hostility is breached as he is our peace" (Ephesians 2:14). Now we are given to the world to uphold life in love. The old order of sin and death has been displaced by the order of grace and life. "We know we have passed from death to life if we love the brethren" (I John 3:14).

Today

The classic cases: capital punishment, abortion, and euthanasia, point to the root complexity of C-6. Can killing ever be ·good? Is it permissible, even purposeful in the deeper patterns of providence, or is Elias Chacour right—"God does not kill!" The question is problematic for Israel since the Exodus and *landnahme* (taking of Palestine for a homeland) involved killing. Holy war in Israel becomes killing mandated by God. This complexity is compounded as the Gospel writers and evangelists of the primitive church take the Abraham-Isaac sacrifice as the paradigm to interpret Jesus' saving death on the cross. (John 8, Hebrews 11:17). The deepest mystery of biblical faith is that death is woven into life.

Excursus

In the many years I have served in the medical school and hospital, the most profound divergence of views I have witnessed have been those between the Christian and the Jewish view of death and killing. Persons of Jewish faith and culture are widely represented in medicine. One finds in this religious and even cultural consciousness an energetic commitment to life, health, and some reticence to accept dying. Fortunately, in my view, the respect for person's freedom of choice and the honoring of wholeness, strength and vitality in the tradition mitigates against "cadaver medicine." When I dialogue with these colleagues on the medical faculty, for example, about the Christian view of death, life after death, or what the saving-death of Jesus Christ meant to patients, Jewish colleagues resist an easy willingness to allow persons to die. Even some sympathy with suicide and assisted dying when surviving seems grotesque, sounds an alarm.

Add to this the fact that my colleagues in feminist-liberation theology are now raising serious theological issues about the father-God giving the son over to death, and I have come to the conclusion that the theme of welcome death in Christian theology must be reexamined.

Of all the stipulates of the Decalogue, the one most needed today is C-6. We have nuclear capacity to liquidate all life on earth as we did in microcosm at Hiroshima and Nagasaki. We have weapons of mass destruction and primitive killers. Millions of land mines made in America and China now infest the ground from Cambodia to Bosnia.

Death and death dealing has become a modern obsession in developments like Dr. Kevorkian, our abortion culture, teenage suicide, euthanasia and stem cell medicine. We have quite completely lost the tenor, temper and theory of C-6. Why live? Why not kill? Are we "natural born killers?" (Oliver Stone, Joy Davidman) or as socio-biologists proffer "is there altruism in our genes?"

The personal, familial and social imperative to honor life and to affirm its sanctity may at last be breaking out around the earth. I am impressed at the imprint of the women's movement. We are not giving women and children over to death, the way the human race has for millennia. We seem willing to not only accept but celebrate difference. People bring different ethnicities, skin colors, languages, even faiths to the table of the world and we start to revel in the diversity. The bitter saga of genocide, though painfully present in our cyber-aware world, is at least now conscious and therefore unconscionable.

The commandment seems to focus on the danger of taking the law into our own hands. In numerous situations, private actions, apart from public consent, can bring an end to life. Killing children in the cities is a terrible arrogation of power toward the weak and disenfranchised. Young punks killed basketball star Ben Wilson. A gun in the night removes murder from all public cognizance. In this sense abortion and euthanasia may be more acceptable and ethically licit if they are done publicly in the light of day. Even in Holland,though sanctioned by law, persons are euthanized in semi-official ways, fully witnessed and endorsed by family and physician. In the U.S., we are inevitably moving toward an acceptance of suicide and assisted suicide in the face of desperate terminal disease. This may be affirmation, not violation, of the commandment.

VII. The Love Commandment: A Theology of Sexuality

"It appears that two wrongs make a right."

"In the military it appears that adultery is a crime...that seems somewhat outmoded."
(the aborted careers of Airforce Pilot Kelly Flynn and Joint Chief designate General Joseph Ralston)
Bob Shiefer, CBS News, Sunday morning, June 8, 1997.

I no longer find her (Nicole Kidman) attractive.
Tom Cruise.

There's trouble in the house of Windsor. Charles says that he never loved Diana."If they can't be reconciled," says the bloke on the street, "give them a divorce."
The Prince of Edinburgh, keeping that traditional stiff upper lip, replies: "The monarchy is intact!"
-CBS Evening News, October 18, 1994.

'You heard me—if she's with another man, I'll kill her.
O.J. Simpson as quoted in Faye Resaiek and Mike Walker,
Nicole Brown Simpson: The Private Diary of a Life Interrupted, 1994
(pre-trial).

Towson, Maryland:
A man who shot his wife to death after catching her in bed withher lover drew 18 months in prison from a sympathetic judge in what women's activists say amounts to giving spouses a license to kill.
Racine Journal Time, October 19, 1994, p. 1

That was another little goof of mine [like ostriches and avocados (seeds too big)]. Shame, I don't know why we needed shame.
George Burns as "God" to Jerry (John Denver) in the film *Oh, God* as he speaks to Jerry in the shower.

Roman Catholics who divorce and remarry may not receive communion unless they get annulment or abstain from sex with their new partner.
Vatican Letter to World Bishop October 14, 1994.

Paul Hill, a former Presbyterian minister, was convicted on two counts of first-degree murder of Dr. Brittom and Mr. James Barrett (administrator) outside the Pensacola Ladies Center (an abortion clinic).
Pensacola, Florida:
(November 2, 1994 executed 9/03)

B: "Thou shalt marry Holden. I declare it, I decree it."
S: "You're sounding tiresomely biblical!"
Alan Alda as *Bob*.
Goldie Hawn as *Steffi*.
In Woody Allen's film, Everyone Says I Love You

Incursus

> Kieslowski has always insisted that Dekalog was not a religious film, "I simply wanted to show that life is complicated, nothing more." "The films are about...the diversity of failure that humans suffer as they try to give and receive love."
> Ray Pride "Thou Shalt Not Forget"
> Windy City News, March 21, 1996 p. 42

Awakening love is the theme of DEKALOG 7. The 19-year-old Tomec delivers milk at dawn, clerks in the provincial Post Office by day, and with spy glass at his window by night peeps, á la Alfred Hitchcock, at a beautiful woman across the apartment complex as she undresses, receives guests, and makes love.

His passion is physical, not platonic, yet it is strangely disembodied; a longing for care. He is an orphan, living with an older woman whose own son had run away. When his beloved gently offers to lead him to love he demurs.

> "Do you want to kiss me?" — "no"
> "Do you want to make love to me?" — "no"

When he falters in the actual encounter, he razors his wrists in a failed suicide. In tones and moods reminiscent of Red (Kieslowski's drama of hell) as he bleeds out, again his paramour plays to him. Now, her maternal love is represented in the milk in bottles, which spills out on the table.

> "I love you" Tomec says, "There is no such thing," she replies.

In the final scene he has come of age (life and love, suffering and near-deaths, have worked their good, though excruciating, will).

> "I'm not peeping at you anymore."

Kieslowski has glimpsed the impulses of the human heart. The longing, the reticence, the attraction, the short fall, the exuberance, the endings found in every beginning. In knowing the human condition, Kieslowski knows the Bible. Not a torrid drama of an illicit affair, not youthful promiscuity. In the commandments wisdom, adultery is about violation of love offered in trustful fidelity, Hosea's *hesed* is proportionate and prioritized commitment, affirmation of the other (all within the divine mystery).

Introduction

As with each commandment this one begins with an application which is strict and restricted. No sexual relations with the wife or fiancée of another man. It is rudely gender specific at its technical core. Yet, however terse on face, as history unfolds, its meanings have become general and wide-ranging. Across biblical and Christian history, this word we call the seventh commandment becomes the foundation of an elaborate sexual ethic extending to monogamy, marriage, divorce, promiscuity, prostitution, pornography, pederasty, rape, incest, homosexuality, bestiality, masturbation, sado-masochism, contraception, cloning, abortion, surrogacy, sterility therapy, imaginative fertilization, gestation. This saga of sexual identity and activity is obviously one of profound human complexity—the source of wholeness and bewilderment; of satisfaction and estrangement. It has thrown families, communities and societies into moods of indulgent libertinism or harsh Puritanism, vicious extremes bracketing the normative virtue.

Beyond all the ramification and complexity, the word is simple. It concerns relationships. It is about love and loyalty, the most important qualities of human association. Sex is problem and crisis because of something that happened in the history of the human soul and of society. From something natural, joyous and mimetic, sex became a matter of anxiety and alienation. Some say that war and violence as well as creativity and concord find their source in sexuality. A study of comparative culture, of the texts and artifacts of human history and of the unfolding development of the human psyche, suggest a time when we were not so hung up. The fall may thus have empirical verification. For certain we have moved in this realm from is to ought. We feel a distance between what "is" and what "should be." As Genesis suggests, sex has become a moral experience.

The evidence of the primitive and ancient world suggests that sex was a human power and experience that resonated with the fruitful rhythms and sacred mysteries of the world. It was good and natural, celebrative of the ongoing fecundity and creativity of nature. Divine co-creativity was manifest in human sexuality— hence the word: procreation. By the time of the great empires and civilizations of the ancient near East, a severe and austere rendering of sexual activity had come about. With the dawn of conscience sex becomes problematic. The death penalty accompanies adultery in several ancient near-Eastern cultures. Abortion is punished by impaling the woman in second millennium Assyria. Again, harsh patriarchal bias, even if we accept the rectitude of the canon. Perhaps the precious sacredness of the loved one and the fruit of the womb had to be protected from the all-too-prevalent assault and danger. Perhaps men, especially familial and tribal brotherhoods, had to protect their possessions. Whatever the prehistory and cultural precedent, by the time the mosaic covenant is promulgated, we find a finely honed sexual ethic. This is developed in some tension with the more relaxed and unbridled sexual practice of Fertile Crescent neighbors like the Caananites and the licentious customs of Greece and Rome. The rigor of the biblical ethic of sex can be traced in the textual history of the Seventh Commandment.

Text

Adultery is an "execrable and God-detested wrong-doing," wrote Philo. He speaks the fervent, somewhat desperate ethos of first century Jewish-Hellenic culture where sexual practices alien to the faith were as strong perhaps as when

Israel first coalesced in Canaan. Here, in the face of numerous fertility cults and blatant erotic rituals, the cultures exuded sexual idols, feminine goddesses and fertility orgies. In ancient Greece and Rome, practices similarly offensive to sexually chaste Judaism were widespread—promiscuity, pederasty, infanticide, and adultery. Possessiveness and protectiveness of the marriage covenant in Israel intensified as acculturation spread during the Hellenistic diaspora.

Infidelity profanes the holy covenant, which is the closest earthly approximation to God's holiness. The sacredness and inviolability of the home and family is an ethical theme, found in various ancient cultures, that is given absolute centrality and preeminence in Judaism. No culture so honors home and family life. No culture so honors and respects the woman. That the intensity of respect borders on patriarchal possessiveness and contributes to the subordination of women, are problems in Judeo-Christian history that must be addressed. The underlying attribution of sacred honor to the woman, marriage, sexual fidelity, raising children and family life must be affirmed, along with our modern feminist and liberationist values, which arise within that same ethos.

The verb *na'af* denotes sexual relations with a married woman by anyone but her husband (Leviticus 20: 10, Jeremiah 29: 23, Ezekiel 16: 52). This anthropological basis of patrilineal societies, of course, is unequally unjust toward women from the perspective of modern democratic and egalitarian rights. It should be stated that the respect for the woman and the inviolability of the marriage contract provides the basis for what will become the emancipated marriage of contemporary Christian experience. Here fidelity is required of both husband and wife.

The prohibition of adultery is part of a larger textual history that includes Leviticus 18: 6-17, and 20: 24 which prohibits sexual relations within the extended family: adultery, incest, sodomy, intercourse with a menstruating woman and other prohibitions. Primitive genetic knowledge and hygienic customs are intertwined here with the rigorous restrictions on what must have been (and are today) extremely aggressive and ubiquitous drives and desires.

Mowinkle finds the Decalogue in miniature imbedded as the holiness code in Leviticus 19.

The mini Decalogue (actually 13 commands) in Ezekiel 18: 5ff. again accents these sexual stipulates. We can assume that the assault on marital fidelity was intense at this period of Israel's history.

We have here an interesting continuity and affinity with the first commandments. There we are to give and not withhold that attraction, praise and worship that belongs to God. Here in C-6 through the end of Decalogue we are not to take away that which belongs to the partner.

One wonders at the significance of placing the commandment on adultery before the one on killing in the Nash Papyrus. The oldest extant text of the Hebrew bible (date c. 200 BCE) has the Decalogue and Shema (Hear, O Israel) in tandem. Philo's *De Decalogo* also has this order. If this manuscript rightly conveys earlier traditions, could it be that intact divine adoration, Sabbath loyalty, family solidarity and marriage were seen as a bulwark (Luther) against the tendencies toward destruction and dissolution conveyed in the first few commandments? The God-ward tableau may be coherent whole, setting precedent and precondition for the human-ward table.

The strict meaning of C-7 is that a man may not intrude in the marriage of another man by seducing his wife. Though women have often been condemned or stoned for the act of adultery (John 8), here the emphasis seems to be on the culpability, at least coculpability of the male. Evidence for this is found in Leviticus 20: 10 where both the adulterer and adulteress are to be punished.

Short formulations of C-6-8 are found in Hosea 4: 2, Jeremiah 7: 9, Leviticus 19: 11 and Job 24: 14-15. Jeremiah seems to rely on the Hosean tradition of Decalogue teaching. Jeremiah's capsule summary (7: 9) places C-6 at an interesting hinge point between theft and murder and profanity and idolatry. The connection in a structure of justice in terms of the thesis of this book is the reciprocity of theology and ethics.

Another textual reflection would point to the ubiquity of such transgression, the understanding God has of our frailty in this realm and of the opportunity for forgiveness and new life. The spirit of Jesus' teaching on adultery and divorce conveys this temper. When we look at Genesis 38 or Judges 16, we see that sexual relations of a man with unmarried women or with an unmarried daughter of another family, while offensive, are not considered adultery.

The textual roots of C-7 are like C-6 in reflection on the Cain-Abel narrative of the creation sagas. These were appropriated into the Mosaic, Davidic, Prophetic and Deuteronomic phases of Israel's ethical history. Cain (now fratricidally alone) is the first person to be married. Adam and Eve were created, taught the rabbis, anticipating marriage. Now, in generations subsequent to Cain, a man will leave his father and mother, cleave into his wife and they shall be one flesh (Genesis 2). Cain not only offended God, the giver of spiritlife, in executing Abel, he dishonored his parents. The covenant of familial integrity is shattered.

We have mentioned much of the biblical trajectory of the command. Other passages which fill out the textual tradition include these:

- Proverbs 6: 32—adultery is foolish, self-disregard.
- Jeremiah 3 and 29—By analogy speak of Israel's backsliding away from Yaweh as adultery.

- Matthew 5: 32, 19: 19, 5: 27, 28, 19: 18 (moichaomai, moicheo) —
  is strongly condemned throughout the New Testament of Romans
  2: 22, 13: 9, James 2: 11, Revelation 2: 22.

Jesus on Adultery and Divorce

Here again Jesus enforces, amplifies, and goes to the heart of the
commandment. It is the inner ascetic spirit and psychology of the laws that Jesus
invokes in the Sermon on the Mount. (Matthew 5:27- 30) In numerous places
the Dead Sea Scrolls speak of the "lusting of the eyes" or "walking after the
lusts of the heart and the eyes." Jesus is invoking familiar hasidic or essenic
metaphors.[130]

In practical terms his words point to the continuity of intention and action.
Thought, will and act are a continuum for good or evil. Paul extends this aspect
of living well by pleading with the Corinthians, as they bathed in an
environment much like ours, constant in sexual temptation and seduction: "To
bring into captivity every thought to obey Christ" (II Corinthians 10:5). A
trained discipline of thought and will best serves the one who seeks to live in
God's "Way".

The same teaching ensues on divorce. Divorce is a sub-theme of adultery in
Jesus teaching and the way in which Matthew has structured the Gospel. Like
the essenes in the Damascus Document (4:21), Jesus saw marriage as given in a
divine principle, an indelible union, grounded in the metaphysical union of God
with persons in the world. *Imago Dei* is the juncture of divine presence in the
world. *Porneia* defaces the image. When John the Baptist confronted Herod on
his liason with Herodias, his brother's wife, it had an absolute finality and
judgment, as attested by the outcome. Jesus is obviously identifying with the
rigorous apocalyptic school of moral interpretation of C-7 and not the more
lenient Hillel school (Matthew 19:3).

YOU SHALL NOT VIOLATE THE MARRIAGE RELATION

Sketching the biblical development of C-7, consider the following theses:

- Human beings are made for marital fellowship. It is not good that
  man be alone—I will make a help-mate for him (Genesis 2:18ff.).
  Ish and *Ishah*: the two have become one.

- We are surrounded by invitation to seduction away from chastity
  and fidelity. Joseph's master's wife eyed him and said "lie with
  me." Joseph said, "no"—She seized his garment, kept it and lied to
  her husband that Joseph had seduced her and he was cast into
  prison (Genesis 39).

---

[130] Geza Vermes, *The Religion of Jesus the Jew*, Minneapolis: Fortress Press, 1993, p. 32.

- Men and women feel and act-out desire even with persons who are married to another. David sent Uriah the Hittite to the front where he would be killed and took his wife, Bathsheba (2 Samuel 11, 12).

- Love and attraction can grow cold. When a man takes a wife and then finds blemish or fault in her, he shall offer her divorce papers (Deuteronomy 24: 1).

- Marriage is meant to be deeper than appearance and feeling. Moses let you divorce, said Jesus, but from the beginning it was not so . Haven't you read that God made them *Ish* and I*shah*, man and woman—and that for this reason a man shall leave his parents and home and go with his wife. Whom God has thus joined, men should not break apart. Divorce is wrong except for adultery (Matthew 19: 3-12).

- Outward and bodily faithfulness is not enough. Even sexual fantasy can damage chastity in the subject and infidelity in the object. "Who lusts in his heart has committed adultery." "If your eye offends you, remove it" (Matthew 5: 28-29).

- Love and mutual respect bind the conjugal relation. "Submit yourselves to one another in the fear of God. Wives, honor your husbands. Husbands, love your wives" (Ephesians 5: 21-25).

- The ubiquity of sin and the complicity of us all in the sin of the world should lead us to love the sexual sinner through to repentance and new life.

They went each to his own house, but Jesus went to the Mount of Olives. Early in the morning he came again to the temple; all the people came to him, and he sat down and taught them. The scribes and the Pharisees brought a woman who had been caught in adultery, and placing her in the midst they said to him, "Teacher, this woman has been caught in the act of adultery. Now in the law Moses commanded us to stone such. What do you say about her?" This they said to test him, that they might have some charge to bring against him. Jesus bent down and wrote with his finger on the ground. And as they continued to ask him, he stood up and said to them, "Let him who is without sin among you be the first to throw a stone at her." And once more he bent down and wrote with his finger on the ground. But when they heard it, they went away, one by one, beginning with the eldest, and Jesus was left alone with the woman standing before him. Jesus looked up and said to her, "Woman, where are they? Has no one condemned you?" She said, "No one, Lord." And Jesus said, "Neither do I condemn you—go and do not sin again."(John 8).

°Sexual liaisons are not innocent and incidental, they implicate and identify. When one is joined intimately with another body, he becomes one with that being. Adultery is therefore of the order of idolatry as love is of the order of faith.

238

The immoral, idolaters, adulterers, sexual perverts, thieves, the greedy, drunkards, revilers, robbers will not inherit the kingdom of God. And such were some of you. But you were washed, you were sanctified, you were justified in the name of the Lord Jesus Christ and in the Spirit of our God.

'All things are lawful for me,' but not all things are helpful. 'All things are lawful for me,' but I will not be enslaved by anything. 'Food is meant for the stomach and the stomach for food'—and God will destroy both one and the other. The body is not meant for immortality, but for the Lord, and the Lord for the body. And God raised the Lord and will also raise us up by His power. Do you not know that your bodies are members of Christ? Shall I therefore take the members of Christ and make them members of a prostitute? Never! Do you not know that he who joins himself to a prostitute becomes one body with her? For, as it is written, 'The two shall become one flesh.' But he who is united to the Lord becomes one spirit with him. Shun immorality. Every other sin which a man commits is outside the body; but the immoral man sins against his own body. Do you not know that your body is a temple of the Holy Spirit within you, which you have from God? You are not your own; you were bought with a price. So glorify God in your body.
(I Corinthians 6: 9-20).

Tradition

Building on this extensive overview of the textual heritage, let us now see how C-6 has been appropriated by the tradition. We offer a more extensive analysis of this commandment in its cultural history because it has been so variously interpreted. What John Kraus has called a "stream of debris," which has carried along the biblical tradition, includes the pathologically sensual influences of Egypt and Canaan, the body negating influences of Persia and Greece, the Puritanical influences of Assyria and Babylonia and the strangely intermingled erotic and neurotic influences of the dozens of ancient Near-Eastern cults, which impinged on early Christianity.131[131]

The first stop on a journey along this circuitous route is found in the early church. An ambivalence present in late Judaism, e.g.., celibacy among the Essenes, marks the earliest Christian era. On the one hand we find the traditional Jewish honoring of the body, marriage, family life, procreativity and delight in human sexuality. On the other hand, an ascetic spirit has set in that counsels celibacy. Rabbis as early as the Babylonian exile, Talmud and Yeshiva (5th century BCE), accept the single, celibate life for sake of work toward the kingdom of God. Like the Essenes, Jesus enters into this life pattern (the issue is complicated and unresolved for John the Baptist, Peter and the disciples, the Lord's brother[s] and Paul).

The early church fathers within Greco-Roman culture affirmed the Decalogue ethic we have reviewed of the indissoluble marriage, reciprocal duties of spouses, purity of heart and fidelity in conjugal commitment. Within Greco-

---

[131] R. Bultmann, *Urchristentum* (Primitive Christianity).

Roman culture sexual practices were rampant that offended Jewish and Christian conscience. These included promiscuity, pederasty, infanticide, abortion, divorce and homosexuality. Ascetically extreme groups such as the Encratites, Gnostics, Montanists and Novatians arose to separate the sacred community from these offenses.Clement of Alexandria (150-215 CE) fought against Gnostic tendencies to denigrate marriage and extolled both the procreative and conjugal love purposes of the family. In Ignatius of Antioch (35- 107 CE) and at the Synod of Elvira the *sacramentum* of Christian marriage is viewed as an analogue of the relationship of Christ and His church. We also begin to see the problematic notion of the religious priest married to Christ and the church through the same analogy.

In Augustine, the conjugal act is a duty, helpful to health and happiness. It is free of sin since, it bears the possibility of procreation (the problem of sexual transmission of inherited sin is a problem here). Yet because of his own playboy past and the influence of body-negating Manicheanism, Augustine also contributes to a theology of shame and guilt about sexuality and body that haunts Christendom down to the present.

It is this heritage that the Reformers inherit and struggle with. Bucer is one of the first priests in the Southern Germany-France of the sixteenth century to marry (1522). He was followed by Luther in 1524. The renaissance of faith that we call the Reformation and Catholic Counter-Reformation (proceeding from St. Francis through Thomas Aquinas to Erasmus and the Catholic reformers) drew together liberating change in the mass and marriage as one package of covenant renewal centered in the Decalogue. In Luther's (1529) *Larger and Shorter* Catechism we see reflected some of his own Wartburg turmoil kindly resolved in his marriage to Katerina. The commandment not to kill (to destroy a person or self-in-person) is followed by concern for "...the person nearest him, or the closest possession next to his own body, namely, his wife, who is one flesh and blood with him."[132] God created and sanctioned (blessed, sanctified) marriage "...that they should live together, be fruitful, beget children, and nourish and train them to the honor of God. God has "wrapped up" all there is in "the world for us in marriage" (p.17) [*dazu alles das in der welt ist, darauf gewand und ihm einige tan*].[133]

Calvin, despite his French roots, is not nearly as "jolie" and "menschlich" in these matters as is Luther.

Q: Explain the substance of the seventh commandment.

A: That all kinds of fornication are cursed in the sight of God.

---

[132] LC, p. 17.
[133] LA, p. 11, vol. 30.

A: ...our bodies and souls are temples of the Holy Spirit, therefore we must be chaste in heart, mind...as well as body.[134]

Bucer focuses on the lure and temptation.

Q: You shall not seduce or be seduced (*unkeusch*), then follows the example of David and Bathsheba.

A: I must seek to suppress the evil lust of the flesh that is in me, rather serve my neighbors with integrity and character (*zucht in Heiligkeit*). I will seek to be a holy child of God in all that I do: eating, drinking, dressing and living.

The passion to protect the chastity of children, especially the chastity of their minds and impulses, seems to be strong in the Reformed catechisms of the sixteenth century. After a decade of MTV and erotic videos and music (the best we moderns can do in inculcating sexual ethics), one sees a certain virtue in these, admittedly severe teachings.

The Protestant theological ethic in the Reformed tradition assumes one important footnote in Karl Barth's neo-orthodox theological system and his restatement of Christian orthopraxy in the sexual ethic. The earliest words in human speech, Barth notes, are ma and da (*am und ad, auf Deutsch*). The mating and bonding of parents is the crucible that makes the world safe for children to enter, to thrive and to grow. The sexual union is the divine allotment for life so that God glorifications may proceed in the world. Mating is the divine mandate implicit in the Word of God in creation. Barth was so struck by this biblical covenant that he affirms *imago dei* in the act and covenant of man-woman being together. In the words of Mozart's *Die Zauberflöte* (which Barth loved), *mann und weib, weib und mann* is the joyous gift of the creation.

On this foundation of text and tradition we can now fashion an ethic of sexuality as a building block of our ethical theology.

Theology

The biblical legacy is one of freedom and covenant, full of care and caution, forgiveness and earnestness. What theology can we derive from this biblical material? First, sexuality unites us with the mystery of creation. To know another in sexual intimacy, *yadah* , is like God knowing us. It is the same Hebrew word. This biblical norm is grounded in the ancient world where sexual intercourse was not only a participation in the divine-human intercourse, it was reenactment of the act of creation. The ongoing activity of procreation was a feature of divine creation. In the deeper recesses of prebiblical history, sexual intimacy was experience whereby persons entered ecstatically into the realm of the gods. Human intimacy, love, and procreation mimic the sustaining care of

---

[134] 1536, p. 65.

the gods for heaven and earth. The fecundity of the marriage relation was recreation. Sex was a high, a moment of transcending experience. In our day when premarital and extramarital intimacy is so widespread, the ecstasy of this primal experience may be diminished. Sex is a bond of self-giving, sacrificial love. It transmutes self-pleasure into responsibility for another.

This primeval fantasy undergoes radical transformation in biblical history. In Genesis, attraction, passion and delight are well and good, yes! But they are also transected by the cloud of shame. In the Garden of Eden the primal pair knew they were naked—jubilant fecundity soon becomes the toil of childbirth. Sex was removed from the mystical and mimetic realm to a zone of danger and judgment. We no longer participate in a creativity by which God renews the earth; sexuality is transposed to a realm of temptation, obligation, suspicion even taboo.

We can reflect on the issue of sexuality, shame and ethics with the help of Dietrich Bonhoeffer's *Ethik*. Is the residue of guilt and shame that is often the concomitant of sexuality in the Western tradition the legacy of unfortunate associations and negations in Jerome, Tertullian and Augustine, or is there some meaning and value to the phenomenon of shame? In the center of his ethic, Bonhoeffer relates the story of temptation in the garden of Eden, the experience of exposure and shame, the covering of the genitals and the lure of good and evil, symbolized by the accessible tree of moral knowledge and the quarantined tree of life.

Bonhoeffer offers the thought that these biblical texts reflect on the fundamental experiences of being alienated in the world in part because we are beings who know good and evil. "Shame", "Shame and conscience" and "a world of recovered unity" are the sections with which Bonhoeffer develops the point. Human experience is always one of alienation from this primal status of who we were meant to be. Here and now we are driven, torn, blown in all directions without guides or rudders through the course of life. We live therefore in constant concupiscence and shame. Yet these urges, impulses and imperfect yearnings are signs of eschatological hope. We strive toward, hope for and work seeking a world where the unity, love and honor (non-shame) of paradise is restored.

Though unmarried, Bonhoeffer shares this profound insight into marriage and the blessing of C-7 in this passage from the ethic:

> If I love my wife, if I accept my marriage as an institution of God, then there comes an inner freedom and certainty of life and action in marriage; I can no longer watch with suspicion every step that I take; I no longer call in question every deed that I perform. The divine prohibition of adultery is then no longer the centre round which all my thought and action in marriage revolves. (As though the meaning and purpose of marriage consisted in nothing except the avoidance of adultery!) But it is the free honouring and the free acceptance of

marriage, the leaving behind of the prohibition of adultery, which is now the precondition of the fulfillment of the divine commission of marriage. The divine commandment has here become the permission to live in marriage in freedom and certainty.[135]

In the commitment of marriage, another norm ensues: now a man and woman are joined as fellow journeymen across life—leaving father and mother they cleave to each other. Family, for Luther, becomes the bulwark against anxiety and the threats of the world.

Woman is now in a protected relationship. Not only is the terror of the world, the ever-presence of violence, seduction and strife abated if not removed, but the chaos of family disintegration as perpetual threat is relieved. Succeeding the ancient drop-by husband and father and preceding the contemporary drop-in husband and father, we find in biblical tradition *pater familias*-a strongly protective and paternalistic husband and father. This is not without problems. Adhering to this paternalistic notion, the commandment has led to a sad cultural history. The Hebrew scholar H.J. Kraus is correct when he says "Since earliest times the interpretation of the adultery commandment has carried along with it in the stream of tradition the debris of culturally conditioned ideas and concepts which to some extent already silted over the true intention of the biblical directives in marriage."[136] This debris and silt which buries the treasure includes such ideas as these:

a)   the idea of marriage as property relation in which the husband is owner (Baal) who rules, decides.

b)   the idea of marriage as a "tabu zone" where laws of discipline and order prevail; an unbiblical hostility to sex (especially in middle ages) prevails.

c)   an attitude of moralistic and legalistic strictness, where Pharisaic self-righteousness seems obsessed with sexual sin. This was seen, for example in the march on Selma, when local Alabama newspapers focused attention not on the issues of racism and Civil Rights but on the fantasized "hanky panky" that was thought to have gone on in the marcher's tents (especially those of the Catholic Priests and Nuns).

The grounding of a biblical theology of marriage is celebrative, profoundly respectful, convivial and very serious about the relation. Especially today, when 30% of the children born do not have a resident father and their birth does not proceed from a solemnized marriage. Those who take on this relation with its tough requirements deserve society's honor and support. The man-woman relation is the basic model for co-humanity in the world. Without one another, we are only shadows of human beings - "ghosts" in Karl Barth's phrase. Karl Barth is at his best when he reflects on these matters in the anthropological

---

[135] Dietrich Bonhoeffer, *Ethics*. New Your: Macmillan, 1965, p. 67.

[136] Kraus, H.J., *Reich Gottes*. Neukirchener Verlag 1975, p. 359.

volumes of the Dogmatics. Karl Marx, I believe, is also on target as he reflects on the anthropological, political, even cosmological truth of this command.

> The immediate, natural, necessary relations of person to person is the relationship of man to woman. In this natural speciesrelationship, the relation of the human being to nature is immediately to the fellow human being.... It is possible to judge from this relationship the entire level of development of humanity...This relationship also demonstrates the extent to which the human being's needs have become human needs, hence the extent to which the other, as a human being, has become a personal need, the extent to which, in existence at its most personal, the human individual is at the same time a communal being.'[137]

The sin in every commandment is straying from a rightful God-relation. This deviation from the way, disorients the self-relation and human co-relation. Quin summarizes:

> To the prophets the spirit of idolatry is the spirit of fornication and adultery. In practice heathen rites were associated with sexual orgies. But the meaning goes deeper. We are all adulterers in more than merely the sexual sense. It is true even of the imagination. Even Dante's picture of pure spiritual love at its highest was inspired not by his wife Gemma Donati, but by Beatrice Fortinari, a comparatively distant acquaintance. How often we do what David was blamed for by Joab. We love our enemies and hate our friends, we neglect our actual duties, and go a whoring after things that are none of our business. We are charming to strangers and fiends in the home circle. We are dull about our own job, and excel (in imagination) in every other. We hate the place we are in, and long to be somewhere else. We hate the old and love the new and seek like the Athenians for some new thing.[138]

Today

Three telling and crucial ethical issues among many illustrate the lasting relevance of C-7. Though we could discuss abortion and promiscuity, invitro fertilization, stem cell medicine and serial monogamy all under the umbrella of this commandment, let us focus illustrative analogy on three problems that pertain to self, sacred community and society. I choose the issues of gender, homosexuality in the church and family integrity.

After having served for 25 years of my career in a medical setting, I have had the privilege recently of coming into a theological faculty. While in medicine and science, the issues of gender difference, the place of women, and the theoretical and practical problems that these concerns generate are not as significant as they should be. In the Seminary, they are paramount. A mathematical theorem has absolutely no respect for gender, and while women have been discouraged from making careers in math and science, there is absolutely nothing in the discipline or culture of science that discriminates on

---

[137] Karl Marx, in Quin, *Op Cit.,* p. 30.
[138] Quin, *Op Cit.,* p. 32.

this quality. In theology and ministry, however, the issue is quite different. Our seminary, along with most main-line Protestant centers thoughout the world, has opened the doors wide to women, while Judaism, Eastern Orthodoxy and particularly Roman Catholicism share strong reservations about women in theology and pastoral practice. Protestantism, much like medicine in Russia, is rapidly becoming a feminized profession. As the father of two daughters, I celebrate this. I am concerned, however, that we keep an appropriate balance of men and women in ministry so that we not allow ourselves the insidious opportunity to down-size and cost-cut, saying it is "just a woman's profession." This seems already to be happening in American ministry and medicine, especially in small church pastorates and in the primary care fields of internal medicine, pediatrics and family practice.

Part of the provocative and exciting atmosphere of my present post at Garrett-Evangelical Theological Seminary is the presence of an important circle of women theologians, including one considered by many to be the best, Rosemary Radford Ruether. At the height of a remarkable career, Ruether has now completed her *Magnum Opus*, a systematic and historical study of women and theology.[139]

Ruether recently fell upon criticism (nothing new to her) for her leadership in a chapel at our seminary, where a prayer was offered to the goddess Asharte (the consort of Baal). The detractors who have attacked her and our seminary have been lying in wait in the woodwork since a provocative meeting some years ago in Minnesota that was called the "Sophia" ("Reimagining") conference. This meeting, with women delegates from all denominations, sought to celebrate the vitalities and gifts that women bring to the church. The misinformation that came from this conference caused considerable consternation and uproar in the church.

Though I fall more on the conservative-evangelical side of the Protestant theological spectrum, I write, believe it or not, as a fully committed feminist theologian. To do otherwise in our home with Sara, a feminist theologian and literature-film analyst, and two daughters Catherine and Sarah, firmly in the movement, would, of course, be foolhardy. But even without such encouragement, I would solidly endorse the project of Ruether and colleagues for the following reasons:

1) They restore orthodoxy to theology. Any careful reading in the history of theology shows that we have twisted what are gender-free biblical origins into a patriarchal tradition that is quite alien to the spirit of Judaism and the biblical heritage. The radical innovation of the Sinai tradition is that all persons—men, women and children—are free and

---

[139] Rosemary Radford Ruether. *Women and Redemption: A Theological History.* Minneapolis: Fortress Press, 1998.

responsible beings before God. Each is held in high esteem because God loves, has rescued, liberated and wishes to redeem and grow in faith of each one—man, woman and child. As my colleague here at Strasbourg, Jean-François Collange, has shown in his corpus, the human rights of all people are firmly rooted in the Hebraic tradition of law. God is not gender-specific. Metaphors that include mother, wisdom, wing-protecting bird, mother-camel searching for lost son, all convey the female attributes of God. That fatherly, kingly, lordly metaphors predominate in God pictures is an accident of history for these alone could be understood on the patriarchal phase of human history that prevailed from the 5th millennium BCE to the 2nd millennium CE[140]

2) Feminist theology also restores orthopraxy. As we have seen throughout our study of the ethical structure of biblical faith, focused in the Decalogue, persons, irrespective of gender, are held dear and held responsible before God. Indeed each command has some special meaning for the feminist, liberationist cause. No other gods-including feminine consorts are tolerated. God, godself embraces the entire human family. No idols, fertility icons or belligerent chauvinist figures will be tolerated. The divine name will be honored and not blasphemed. Here the inclusive language concerns find solid ethical grounding. The name of God ought not to be gender-specified. Where possible, we should write hymns and cast liturgy in gender neutral language. My colleague, Ruth Duck, a major hymn writer and liturgical scholar, has made important contributions on this issue. To take the name of God with reverence we must honor every name under heaven- men, women, children, elders, animals- all participate in the grace of sharing the divine name, presence and power. Women's liberation is necessary to fulfill the structure of ethics envisioned in the Decalogue. Family life is here honored, killing (often a male obsession) can cease. The dignity of love and committed marital relations can be rejuvenated. Nurturing homes can be re-established. And the final three mandates of envy, false accusation and coveting are less liable to fracture human community when gender equality and full access to social process is achieved.

3) Women in ministry also make possible orthosacrality. The gifts of ministry are distributed throughout the church without respect to gender. The offices of teaching, preaching, pastoring, and serving must not only be given to all but must have full participation from both men and women to be full-orbed and complete. Word and sacrament are distorted when offered in a gender-biased fashion. In male dominated

---

[140] Collange, J-F., "loi" in *Encyclopedie du Protestantisme,* Geneve: CERF/Labor et Fides, 1995, p. 903ff.

church life, the word tends to be more power-obsessed than love-chastened. The sacrament can be more judgmental than healing. The pastoral arts can be more legalistic than liberating.

The church has always been kept alive by women, officiated by men. Perhaps this pattern will change in our time, perhaps not. We are learning much these days about male and female catechesis, confirmation and coming-of-age. There are decisive gender differences which need to be honored in a healing and wholesome social order. There are times and places to accent differences—to be together as women or men. There are times to associate across gender, age, linguistic and ethnic particularities. There may be important role differentiations although, it seems to me, that making science and humanities, arts and crafts, sports and military service, heavy work and house work completely gender unbiased is generally a good thing, harvested in that seedbed ground of human rights, the Decalogue.

Ruether's project, in other words, is evangelically faithful. It is restoring, or better, receiving of the theological and ethical imperative of the biblical tradition that too long has laid latent and oppressed by the prevailing male-biased system.

Homosexuality and the church, as I have intimated throughout this book, may be the most provocative issue of C-7 to confront late twentieth century society. I have been over and over these issues for three decades since I was placed on the commission of the Presbyterian Church in the US in 1976. We were given the assignment to formulate the church's position on the ordination of practicing homosexual persons to the ministry. In times of sexual threat from competing and licentious life styles in cognate cultures, scripture and tradition have come down quite hard on this issue. The holiness code's rendition of the Decalogue construes it primarily as a sexual and familial mandate. The Didache, an organ of early Christian catechesis and its appropriation of divine word and command for behavior, strongly accents sexual purity and constancy. In an early exumenical council of the Christian Church in 309, in Elvira, Spain, 42 of 80 canons adopted dealt with human sexuality. Today conservative and evangelical bodies-especially Jewish, Islamic, African, Asian and Hispanic respond cautiously to sexual and gay liberation.

The issue rises as to whether these moments of orthopraxy posed against threat are normative in the fullest sense. Since ethical, ecclesial and pastoral issues intertwine, we will have to deal with the way in which the Decalogue, the sacraments of baptism and eucharist and pastoral care for wounded and oppressed persons, intertwine on this issue. Paul Lehmann raises the provocative concern as to whether baptism of persons who later become homosexuals should in any way influence our views toward church membership and ordination. If there are biological foundations involved in homosexuality, is this not the being and mode of being that has been consecrated to God in baptism?

Ethics, ecclesiology and cure of souls intertwine in one synthetic and sympathetic reality in the church. The classical concern to maintain the peace, unity and purity of the church (Ephasians 4: 3-13) is the imperative of church order flowing from the impress of Christ's holy spirit as spirit enlivens the church, conduits God's word to the people and brings to remembrance "the things of Christ." This impulse draws together the ethical, ecclesial and pastoral dimensions of life. The imperatives that emerge from the conjunction regarding homosexuality would seem to be:

- a recognition that homosexuality is a part of the natural evolution of the human species.

- a recognition that persons of this sexual preference are experiencing calls to Christ's ministry in our time.

- a conviction that accepting, even celebrating this exception to human intimacy will not compromise the norm of male-female mating, marriage, child rearing and family building.

- full recognition of civil and human rights for gay persons and forceful rejection of discrimination and harassment.

- profound sympathy, support and care for homosexual persons.

- decriminalizing for now the matter of ordination to church office so that ecclesial and parochial dynamics might shape what mode and measure of ministry by and for the homosexual community is to emerge in the church. (the 2001 Presbyterian and 2003 Anglican concerns move in this direction).

Ultimately celebrating full church membership, participation, and celebration of sacred unions of gays, and acceptance into Holy orders is called for.

In the summer of 2003 several main line Protestant churches, Episcopal, Methodist and Presbyterian, among others, revisited the issue of ordaining homosexual persons. They decided, again, whether to revise present restrictions against ordination, maintain these or more toward some non-committal state. My convictions, based on the summarial love command of the New Testament counter balanced by C-7 in Decalogue, led me to advise the churches to withdraw both prohibitions and encouragements and see what practice would emerge in the church. In my own church, the Presbyterian 2001 marked a turning point toward inclusivity and full privileges. I have argued for the same position on physician-assisted suicide, contending that the absence of law is to be preferred over restrictive or conducive legislation.

I expect that natural pathways of service and need will coincide in the impress of God's spirit. I am appealing now to my doctoral students in Theology and ethics to ground homosexual equality in ministry in Ethical (Decalogue) and Evangelical (Gospel) imperatives. To date, certain congregations in all

Protestant denominations have designated themselves to particular service by and to the gay community. "More light" congregations among Presbyterians, and "reconciling congregations" among the Methodists, join Metropolitan churches to explore specified ministries. From Jonah's ministry to foreigners to Paul's mission to the Gentiles, with certain suspensions of Kosher law, in medieval ordination of lepers to particular service, the church has often experimented with peculiar vocation. I respectfully offer that such creativity of ministry is now called for.

Finally, some reflection on sexuality and family life in the modern West. Our culture, Western Europe and America in particular, has pioneered a sexual liberation and life style very much born in the ethos of the renaissance and reformation, that era that celebrated the liberated conscience. Today it is often said that we are seeing the sad aftermath of such liberation in our-of-wedlock births, sexually transmitted diseases, divorce, domestic violence and the disintegration of family.

Not so, says a new study (1999) by the University of Chicago, where it is reported that the age of sexual liberalism is far less flamboyant than the Jeremiads have thought. The incidence of promiscuity, adultery, pederasty and voyeuristic homosexuality is far less than we have been led to believe. Most people, the study shows, believe in the basic purposes of marriage; procreation and mutual support and affection.

- 84% of those interviewed strongly disapprove of extra-marital relations.
- 96% have been faithful in their marriages over the last 12 months.
- over a 25 year span, 80% of females and 70% of males have been faithful.[141]

In sum, sex within marriage is better.

Excursus

During the mid nineteen-nineties a major book and film to captivate the American imagination was *The Bridges of Madison County*. It is the story of a middle-aged American housewife on a farm in Iowa. She (Meryl Streep) was born in Italy, married to a G.I. after the war and settled into a temperate but bland existence for several decades: meals, raising kids, doing the farm chores. It is a conventional, unexciting world punctuated on occasion by Grand Opera on the radio. One weekend, while the husband and children are away showing cows at State Fair, a National Geographic photographer (Clint Eastwood) drives his pick-up truck into the rural Iowa countryside to photograph the covered bridges of the county. They meet and enjoy a brief but poignant love affair. The

---

[141] E. Laumann, et al, *Sex in America,* reported in the Chicago Tribune, April 10, 1999.

dialogue explores all of the issues of our day: postponed and disappointed dreams (and fantasies), alienation, sadness and broken marriages, romance, acceptance and love. The film is an excellent treatise on C- 7. In an age where fidelity, mutual support, and creative living amid mundane experience is caricatured in music, magazine, TV and film as the colossal bore, we need to be recalled by the simple grace of one like Luther who shows us that daily bread, love and blessing and not persistent enticement and excitement, is the real delight of life. C-7, in other words, has it right.[142]

VIII. Taking Care of Business: A Theology of Property

'I wasn't stealing. Just moving funds around.'
-Judah, in Woody Allen's film
Crimes and Misdemeanors.

Magnum imperium, magnum latrocinium.
-Augustine

Our masters taught: You shall not steal! The
scripture is speaking here of the theft of
human beings.
-*Sanhedrim, Talmud* 865.

God wills that there be equality among us.
That is, none should have too much and
none too little.
-John Calvin *Commentary on II Corinthians.*

Do not lay up for yourselves treasures on
earth, where thieves break in and
steal...Where your treasure is there your
heart will be also...you cannot serve God
and mammon.
(Matthew 6: 19ff.).

'I have no morals when it comes to money. None of us can afford to."
(Business manager in the Big Ten Athletic Conference)

Robin Hood stole deer from the King's preserves to feed poor foresters. For Karl Marx, it was right for workers to take their share from owners. Back as President of Haiti, Fr. Aristide believes the same. Can it be long until he is exiled to Africa?

The prophets condemn the exploitation and expropriation whereby we hoard, rob, concentrate capital, focus injustice, defraud, oppress and ignore pleas for help, all in the face of God's adequate provision for all life in the world. The

---

[142] See William Lazareth, *Luther and the Family.* Philadelphia: Muhlenberg, 1960.

sacrament of death into life, the akedic sacrificial mystery focuses on one who in command loyalty laid down life to perpetuate the seed of humanity and one, who though rich became poor for our sakes. Stealing is a most subtle contradiction of sharing, which is how life was meant to be lived. Stealing is a most subtle, even morally troubling commandment. The poor may actually be taking back from the rich what the rich had taken from them in the first place. Stokley Carmichael cynically noted that when the missionaries come to Africa, "we had the gold, they had the bible. When they left, we had the bible, they had the gold." Another subtlety: The *mitzvoh* about stealing is an intense affirmation of property rights. Capitalism and private property find their justification in Torah. But what does private ownership mean in a world where God, not humans, owns all?

I stole another bike at Maxwell Street the Sunday it closed—$20 for my big pink roadster. I should have paid—well at least $21. I'm sure it was stolen, like my three preceding bikes. Maxwell was an elaborate recycling center. Anything you lost on Saturday throughout Chicagoland could usually be found there on Sunday. One early Sunday morning, the custodian discovered the great pulpit chairs missing from nearby Holy Family Church on Roosevelt. Street wise, he quickly slid into the crowds down the onion drenched sausages on Halsted Street onto Maxwell Street, where be bought back the chairs in time for the Sunday service. What a deal—thousands of dollars in giant ancient liturgical thrones—$50, I think. Indeed the unwritten moral code on Maxwell Street is if you find something that you can prove is yours, 1/2 price—no questions asked!

> Is it Al Jolsen I hear singing?
> Another day, another deal,
> another buy, another steal,
> another season, another reason for making whoopie!

Another memory from the closing Sunday of the Maxwell Street market: the famed open-air festival in Chicago's impoverished West Side was the scene of unusual reverie tinged by sadness. For over 100 years, the conglomerate of antiquities, vendors and junkers had peddled their wares between Roosevelt and 16th Street, Halsted and Peoria Avenues. Today, as thousands milled in the tamale savor in the Mexican food sector, a lanky black youth came running through the crowd. In his hands, a hot VCR. On his tail, but falling behind rapidly, were short, stocky Hispanic merchants. Later, I heard a Yiddish shoe seller say to the smiling African woman in the next stall, selling toothpaste, "You...god...make this rain?" "Yeah. I prayed for rain," she beamed. I bought that bike for $20, bid down from the asking price of $25. I left the $20 with the Cuban gentleman, trusting he would still be there after I made my rounds. Later I met my good friend Hans Morsbach at his Hyde Park Medici restaurant. Trying to interest him in our new Center for Ethics, I asked him what the moral issues were for him in the business. "Tax ethics," he said. "I play it straight and pay tax on my Mexican employees! My competitors don't." Honesty, trust, don't steal, the every day world of C-8.

251

Dateline Chicago, January, 1996: The two perpetrators were 10 and 11. They hatched their plot as they walked home from school to the south side Ida B. Wells public housing project. As they passed a candy store, they told 5-year-old Eric Morris to steal some candy. He refused. Was it fear he'd get caught? Was it some primitive and natural conscience about taking things that aren't yours? Had he heard mom or the preacher say the command, "You shall not steal?"

Angry at Eric's refusal, they took him up to an abandoned 14th story apartment and with each boy taking one leg, they dangled him out of the window. Still he refused to steal. They went and got Eric's 8-year-old brother Derrick, kicked out the window from the vacant apartment and told both brothers to go and steal for them. They refused. They then dangled Eric out of the window again, this time by his wrists. His brother, Derrick, tried to rescue him. He took Eric by the hand and the other boys let go. As Derrick desperately tried to pull him inside, the 11-year-old bit his hand. Eric plunged to the ground. He was declared dead from massive head injuries at Wylers Children's Hospital (1994).

In a precedent-setting case, the two boys accused of the crime, then 12 and 13, were sentenced to jail for the murder, amid great debate of whether they should be locked up or placed in a center for therapy and rehabilitation. Now 15, the kid killer has been given a long sentence in adult confinement.

Incursus

Kieslowski has it right. "Kidnapping," is the theme of the commandment "Thou Shalt not steal." With the story of Joseph and his brothers in the background, the biblical command moves from a narrow technical meaning of the kidnapping of a Jewish brother, to the generic condemnation of kidnapping, and on to slavery and oppression of any sort. Kieslowski is intrigued by the personal and familial meaning of this value. Malka had her baby as an immature 16 year old. Her mother, who had rejected Malka and could not have other children, now became mamo to Aika. The six year old girl now accepts her mother as an older sister and grandmother as mom, who had even breast fed her as a baby. Malka seeks to muster the energy to leave for Canada with the child. She fails.

"I hate her" she howls at her mother, "can you steal something that's yours?"

The little daughter cries out in her sleep. The film ends as the train departs as her young mom finally leaves in desperation. Aika runs toward one she could never call "mamo," but it's too late.

Introduction

Ancient Near Eastern law focuses on proper recompense. One caught stealing must make full restitution, including injury. In Hammurabi's code, we realize that losing and eye or a limb, a cow or a dog, requires not only the return of the property, but recompense for the wound. Our laws today are fascinated with catching a thief, not with compensating the victim. We have lost the ethical spirit of Israelite law. Only in Hebraic justice do you find the full drama of guilt, repentance, return, atonement and peace. Yet this fall is paradoxically an ascent.

The background of C-8 is the paradise garden. Adam and Eve lived on the estate in bliss and security until they ate of the tree of the knowledge of good and evil. They stole something that was Yahweh's—the forbidden fruit. Now shame, not security, marks their existence. They had taken wrongfully what belonged to another.

I remember as a very young boy, say seven years old, looking over the fence at our home on Long Island, toward our back neighbor's home. The had a lovely peach tree trellised against the garage with a glorious fruit that grew and was more beautifully orange colored each day. Every day, I would admire it more and more. Finally, unable to restrain myself, I slipped over after dusk and took a peach. It was hard, fuzzy and tasteless. I knew for the first time, I think, the reality of temptation, of incessant fascination for the forbidden, of shame and the bitter taste of wrong-doing. Like the child, Augustine with his apple, Richard Baxter in the forbidden orchards, or later Robert Oppenheimer with his bomb, I had known sin.

In the ancient Near Orient as throughout Indo- European society, the hunter-gatherer phase of history had yielded to tribal culture, which also involved cattle rustling, stealing, raping of women, and raiding of crops and possessions. For the Israelites, theft was a tort, not a crime. Restitution was made as fairly as possible. If an ox gored a beast from another's herd (Exodus 21: 35), the carcass was sold and the proceeds divided. Ancient Near Eastern ethical legal doctrine required either proportionate recompense—an eye for an eye (Hammurabi), or appropriate damages, e.g., fourfold recompense for a killed sheep (Exodus 21: 37). A thief who was too poor to pay the required damages (Exodus 22: 26) was himself sold.

Already we see the disproportionate terror of this commandment on the poor. Those desperate and without resources may be required to beg or steal. Actually, in a subtle ramification of this command, mendicant life, begging, is a privilege. The Franciscan orders, even the young Luther as an Augustinian monk, begs for his food as *Imitatio Christou*. Neglecting this insight of the blessed privilege of the poor, we have created a criminal culture. In the affluent world minority and poverty culture most often take from the rich in order to survive, feed one's own, pay the rent, etc. In western societies, especially the U. S., the jails are filled with poor men and women who have somehow violated our property or violence standards. High religion and noble ethics is sensitive to this point. They exhibit particular mercy and exoneration toward the desperate poor. Literature, poetry, art, and music similarly offer this prophetic message of understanding and forgiveness. In Victor Hugo's *Les Misérables*, for example, the strict legalist policeman, Javert, hounds relentlessly the simple man Jean Val Jean who stole a loaf of bread to feed his starving family in the harsh days of the French restoration. Here again we see the Hebraic sympathy that leaves the edges of the crop fields unharvested for the poor. Since human ethics mimic God, we ought to generously care for the poor, giving them more than they need to just get by so they can in turn give to others and retain their philanthropic dignity.

Text

> When the wife of Uri'ah heard that Uri'ah her husband was dead, she made lamentation for her husband. And when the mourning was over, David sent and brought her to his house, and she became his wife, and bore him a son. But the thing that David had done displeased the Lord.
>
> And the Lord sent Nathan to David. He came to him, and said to him, "There were two men in a certain city, the one rich and the other poor. The rich man had very many flocks and herds; but the poor man had nothing but one little ewe lamb, which he had bought. And he brought it up, and it grew up with him and his children; it used to eat of his morsel, and drink from his cup, and lie in his bosom, and it was like a daughter to him. Now there came a traveler to the rich man, and he was unwilling to take one of his own flock or herd to prepare for the wayfarer who had come to him, but he took the poor man's lamb, and prepared it for the man who had come to him." Then David's anger was greatly kindled against the man; and he said to Nathan, "As the Lord lives, the man who has done this deserves to die; and he shall restore the lamb fourfold, because he did this thing, and because he had no pity." Nathan said to David, "You are the man."
> (2 Samuel 11: 26- 12: 7)
>
> Will a man rob God? Yet you have robbed me? You ask where have we robbed God? In our tithes and offerings.
> (Malachi 1: 6ff.)
>
> Many have sinned for things that don't matter. A nail that seeks to multiply gain will turn his eye away. A nail will stick fast between the joining of stones; and sin will thrust itself in between buying and selling.
> Ecclesiates 27: 1-2.
>
> Blessed are the meek, they will inherit the earth.
> (Matthew 5)

In addition to the tree of the forbidden fruit in the garden, the story of Joseph and his brothers is implied (e.g.. Exodus 21: 16). Leviticus 19: 11 adds the elements of thought and will, joining "no deceit" to the structure of the mandate. Deception and the lie are part of the act of misappropriation.

- Luther and many rabbinic authorities see the connection between stealing and coveting. For Luther, C-8 is "directed against envy and loathsome avarice."

- The verbs *hamed* and *hitawwa* both mean to desire and covet, Wanting, taking, and robbing is seen as a continuum of violation.

In Joshua 7: 21, in Achan's confession of guilt, he says: 'I coveted them, then I took them (the booty).'

This is usually the movement. One thinks of the frightful state of affairs in Bosnia or Jerusalem in 1995-6, where homes lived in for decades and centuries were coveted and seized with official sanction and no recourse. Of interest are the properties confiscated decades ago by the Nazis under emergency laws, now finally, in some rare situations being returned to the original (Jewish) owners after residing for decades in the hands of other persons.

> Exodus 34: 24—the irony of the occupation of Canaan, and of all forceful occupation is that "*Landnahme*," seizing land is for Israel right and good and the subsequent protection of God or the state is that none other will covet your land.

As long as a covetous mind is still around, the threat of stealing is present. One wonders about the present ethical consciousness of the poor in America. They have been schooled in the injustice of their plight, encouraged to envy what others have, and yet we wonder why a culture of theft has arisen. When underlying injustice persists, e.g.. exploited labor on which wealth is built, is it not justice that the wealth be envied, desired and in some way be taken back, if only in the form of graduated taxes? The awareness that my wealth is built on the toil of others is remote to our contemporary consciousness. It comes to life in the spiritual animation of a disturbed conscience.

> Exodus 21: 16, Deuteronomy 24: 7—texts that contend the focus of the command to be slavery or kidnapping.

Though the eighth commandment has come to mean prohibition of theft of any kind, especially of property, its original meaning was the prevention of man stealing—of kidnapping. In Exodus 21: 16 and Deuteronomy 24: 7 we read:

> ...He who steals a man and sells him or if he is found being held they should be put to death.
> (Exodus 21: 16)

The story of Joseph floods to mind:

> If a man be found stealing one of his fellow Israelites and then selling them, then they shall die. You shall remove this evil from your midst.
> (Deuteronomy 24: 7)

The theological meaning of the text is that Yahweh protects persons as his own. God will not allow us to be snared away. The theological imperative therefore condemns carrying off human beings. Slavery, oppression of all sorts and ultimately exploiting or subjugating human persons for another's benefit is forbidden. C-6, 7, 8 are similar in their emphasis on being cut off and lost from

God forever. Those who succumb to murder, *porneia*, or kidnapping are removed from Yahweh's enthralling orbit. In the words of Jude, they become wandering stars for whom is reserved the "blackness of darkness forever" (Jude 5: 13).

The Septuagint, in Deuteronomy 24:7, translates the Hebrew word for theft as (*katadunasto*), which connotes exerting power over another. It is to oppress, dominate, exploit someone. Targum translated the word to "merchandise someone." To reduce a human being to a commodity of exchange is to trash that person.

> If the event of eating the forbidden fruit—taking what is not yours—is the recollected primal sin in C-8, the ensuing litany of blame—the woman, the serpent—sets us up for C-9, false and misleading witness.

> Building on the preceding commandments, the rabbis claim that C-8 affirms the "sanctity of property" and that it therefore forbids every illegal acquisition of property by cheating, embezzlement, forgery or foreclosure. The nature of property as temporary possession requiring good stewardship is the Hebrew concept behind the commandment.

An array of texts points up the various nuances of the ethical obligations. Other landmarks of the use of C-8 in scripture point to further meanings:

> Genesis 31: 19-39—This classic story of righteousness, stealing and belonging contains all of the elements of an ethic of theft. Jacob has been wronged by Isaac and deceived by Laban. He steals away with what is rightly his, including expropriated household goods. The great settlement and benediction at the pillar Mizpah forever marks the boundary of one's property from another. The Israelites, we recall, took with them the goods of Egypt when they were liberated.
> Proverbs 6—Recasts the Decalogue in terms of household and civic ethics.

C-8 is strongly applied even in the face of justifiable reasons. Do not men despise a thief if he steals to satisfy his appetite when he is hungry? And if he is caught, he will pay sevenfold; he will give all the goods of his house (Proverbs 6: 30, 31). The common custom and law exacts not only rightful recompense, but the deterring compound. Wisdom and prudence avoids this outrage.

> Obadiah 5 and Zechariah 5: 3 show that stealing and concomitant vice-deception, envy, and acquisitiveness all numb the spirit and mitigate against justice.

> Romans 2: 21, 13: 9, Ephesians 4: 28—Integrity of ethical action means not only speaking but doing the right. Honest work and just wages will obviate the need for anyone to covet or steal.

Tradition

The minimalist tradition of C-8 (theft of property with the accompanying covetous and envious spirit) and the maximalist tradition (kidnapping, slavery, oppression and exploitation) have shaped a certain kind of legal, economic and social order in the societies where biblical ethics and the Christian ethical tradition has shaped public life.

Luther, who some would say stole the church wholesale from Rome and placed it in the hands of avaricious German princes and merchants, dwells on C-8 in its personal, interpersonal and societal effect.

> Q: What does this mean?
>
> A: We should fear and love God that we may not take our neighbor's money or property, nor get them by false ware or dealing, but help him to improve and protect his property and business.[143]

The progression of that which is sacred, valuable and to be honored continues. After self and spouse comes what teens call "one's stuff." This combination of few books, a massive stereo, a stack of CDs and an impressive closet of clothes has been earned by one's hard work (or father's generous allowance). It is inviolable; one safeguards it with gusto. In later years it becomes one's home, car, bank account, stock portfolio and pension fund. Defying the obvious truth, so explicit in the life and teaching of Jesus, that you "can't take it with you" we protect, assemble or hoard an ensemble of property and estate and guard it with threats and dogs and guns. Luther, as always, extended the interpretation of the commandment:

> ...to steal is not only to empty our neighbor's coffer and pockets, but to be grasping in the market (maximized profits), in all stores, booth, wine and beer cellar, workshops...wherever there is trading or giving or taking money."[144]

Further,

> ...there are also swivel-chair robbers, not pick-pockets or sneakthieves who snatch away the ready cash, but who sit on the chair...great noble men, honorable, pious citizens who rob and steal under a good pretext."[145]

As in our day, Luther knew the more serious "white collar criminals." He also understood systemic theft and crime. If our estate, wealth or success is built on fraud, theft or exploitation, the wrong will come round to haunt us (Luther believed in an underlying natural law that was resonant with and derivative from the Decalogue). When the pastor thought he could exact a reduced rate from his

---

[143] Luther, Martin, *Smaller Catechism,* p. 20.
[144] LC, p. 20.
[145] *Ibid.*

auto mechanic, when having his car repaired, he claimed, "I'm just a poor preacher." The mechanic retorted "I know, I heard you last week." Reminiscent of Augustine—great wealth—great theft, Luther falls back on basic cause/effect justice:

> ...If you steal much, depend on it that again as much will be stolen from you; and he who robs and acquires with violence and wrong will submit to one who shall deal often the same fashion with him.[146]

The great film *Wall Street* depicts this inevitable process as illgotten gain, eventually comes around to reclaim itself and reduce the Ivan Boskys, Mike Milkins and Nick Leesons to penury. Calvin is not so harsh on commercial profit. He sees creative industry, even investment as resources to be properly and wisely stewarded. Like the manna in the wilderness, God will provide resource. We are to turn it around in human service and help it abound as it graces life and builds the world.

> Q: What must we do to obey this commandment?

> A: Let every one have his own in safety.[147]

and Bucer:

> ...I will always look out for the good of my neighbor.

Here, Bucer sides with the ethical imperative that Luther developed, i.e. goods are given for the sake of serving the neighbor. The tradition of C-8 has been to fashion a society and economy that generates wealth and possessions, circulates currency and resources, and more or less adequately distributes wealth and cares for those who fall through the entrepreneurial cracks and cannot make a living wage for themselves or their family. The great economic systems of the modern era: capitalism, socialism and communism pose different schemes of caring for the misfortunate in our midst. The basic imprint of C-8 on social ethics is to affirm the right (righteousness) of earning one's livelihood, establishing one's home and contributing to the general welfare with the overflow after essentials. The concourse of this "Protestant ethic" throughout the modern world has rapidly improved both individual and common wealth, but it has not been without great disparities.

Today

Helmut Gollwitzer has reflected on the economic ethics of the Christian tradition and on our concern for the poor. In his *Die Reichen Christen und der Arme Lazarus*,[148] he argues that fundamental to the Christian concern for the

---

[146] *Ibid.*, p. 21.
[147] 1536 p. 65, 66.
[148] Munchen: Kaiserverlag, 1969.

poor in the world is the mounting of a prophetic critique before the capitalist society calling it to its responsibility in justice to attend the needs of the poor. The most richly blessed nation in the world is now condemned as a rogue nation throughout the world for having been the sole negative vote on the Kyoto ecology protocol, the biological weapons convention and the landmine treaty. "To whom much is given, much will be required" (Luke 12:48). The only alternative to such prophetic action is some kind of endorsement or baptism of the exploitative system or some kind of revolution, which ultimately harms the perpetuators as well as the innocent. Creative prophetic action within the free enterprise system offers the best hope for real improvement for people.

Recent studies have shown that of the enormous upsurge of wealth in the United States in the 1980's, 100% went to the top 10% of the population. In 1983, the top 1% of the population owned 33% of the wealth. By 1989 it was 39%. The top 20% of Americans has net worth sheets valued at $300,000. The top 5% were at $800,000, the top 1% were at $3,000,000+. The robust growth of new capital being created in the world, especially in the West, comes to reside in the estates of fewer and fewer people. What are the societal consequences of this "theft" by the big boys in swivel chairs?

In 1995 NISSI (the National Institute of Social Science Information) published a working paper on "Poverty and Crime in the Inner City" which came to the following conclusions:

1) Disinvestment in American cities forces residents to turn to crime.

2) Economic changes in the 1970's and 1980's penalized innercity blacks.

3) Isolated urban communities (such as the homes of "Yummie" Sandifer and Eric Morris) are caught in a cycle of decline.

4) Drug dealing becomes the replacement economy.[149]

As we unpack this frightening report we see the extent of our societal violation of C-8 in the American cities:

1) In the real world of urban economics, living zones are either spheres of investment or disinvestment. If there is investment stability, prosperity is forthcoming. If there is disinvestment, disintegration follows. Toronto sociologist John Hagan comments, "we acquire at birth and accumulate through our lives unequal shares of capital that incrementally alter and determine our life chances. We acquire this capital through structural and cultural as well as genetic processes, as members of social groups as well as members of biological families" (p.1). Resources such as physical capital (buildings), human capital

---

[149] *NISSI,* Poverty and Crime in the Inner City, January 6, 1995

(education, skills), social capital (access to funds, family) and cultural capital (cache of attitudes and beliefs) are either amplified or diminished in communities. The "disinvestment" of such resources, rapidly occurring in America's inner cities, comes about through events such as racial segregation (block busting, moving factories), racial inequality (loss of manufacturing jobs) and the concentration of poverty.[150]

2) The theft is not deliberate but coincidental with economic changes of the 1970's and 1980's. In these decades, our economy shifted from a goods to a service producing economy and the labor market split into low and high wage sectors. Unskilled workers were now cast into the pits of economic deprivation. Wilson shows that:

- in 1964 88.8% of black men had jobs.
- by 1984 it was 66.2%.
- In 1994 only 58% of black males in America were employed. To further illustrate this impact of white and middle-class black flight on urban blacks in particular, Wilson cites statistics about 77 communities in Chicago:
- Of the 8 high poverty areas that existed in 1970, 6 went from high to extreme poverty in ten years and one went from an extreme poverty rate of 44% in 1970 to 61% in 1980. Wilson says that this increase is due to "the large out-migration of nonpoor blacks" since the total number of poor blacks remained constant in these areas.
- The total population of the city decreased by 11 percent from 1970 to 1980, but the number of poor people increased 24 percent. Seven non-poverty areas in 1970 became impoverished with the out-migration of nearly 185,000 whites and non-blacks by 1980. The total number of poverty areas increased from 16 to 26, and the number of extreme poverty areas grew from 1 to 9.
- Unemployment rates of at least 15 percent affected 5 communities in 1970 and 25 in 1980. Of these 25, 10 predominantly black communities had unemployment rates of at least 20 percent.
- In neighborhoods with few employed families, Wilson says "people experience a social isolation that excludes them from the job network system" that exists in more prosperous communities.

---

[150] Wilson, William Julius, *The Truly Disadvantaged.* Chicago: University of Chicago Press, 1987.

- As a result, these low-income neighborhoods are plagued not only by unemployment but also by criminal activity and substandard schools, making the area even less attractive to outsiders.[151]

The primal theft initiates a circle of theft that, as Luther predicted, comes back to haunt the original thief. How? In the first place, drug abuse and the consequences for the health care and criminal justice systems take back the tax dollars from the dominant society that allowed the disinvestment to occur in the first place because of the diminished ethical concern for the neighbor. A natural retributive justice sets in with a vengeance when the apodictic justice of Decalogue and the law of love is abrogated.

The other price we pay for past theft (oppression and exploitation of persons) is present kidnapping of two kinds. Sometimes the actual child of a wealthy family is kidnapped, even killed, as ransom is sought. Then there is the insidious process of kidnapping minority children: Amerindians, Asians, and Africans by the wealthy. Much more common is the process by which we mansteal young black males and place them in jail (our hidden places of removal). Studies in recent years have shown that approximately one third of black males between 18-30 years old are in prison, on bail or in some way under supervision of the criminal justice system. This kidnapping also steals from the negligent society, since it costs the society roughly $50,000 per year per inmate for the incarceration.

I have a seminary classmate who is Dean at General Seminary in New York City who conducts a Master's degree program at Sing Sing prison in Ossening, New York. The program is one of the strongest of the seminary, not only because of the theological insight and acumen of the participants. The captive audience is the dream of every professor. Most of the candidates for degree are long-termers or "lifers." They have come to struggle with notions of good and evil, sin and grace, freedom and fate, guilt and forgiveness, more deeply than most of us going about our business on the outside. What motivates the criminal? Dostoevsky asks this question his novels. The good we seldom achieve and the wrong we so readily succumb to is usually entangled in a web of fault and responsibility. How did our inner-city modern societies get that way. Was the transition from rural to urban America, from industrial to service economy inevitable? Or was human greed and violence, apathy and disdain involved?

God taught Moses the Decalogue and God sent Jesus to die for the sin of the world because of the tangled skein of sin and guilt that gripped the world and the difficulty, verging on impossibility, of finding a way out. The morally regenerative salvation of Christ and the good guidance offered by the Decalogue-woven into the prime metaphor of biblical faith-Akedah offers us, not escape, but a way through.

---

[151] *Ibid.*, p. 39-46.

Good news is about captives set free, imprisoned ransomed, death-sentence reprieved, dead raised. C-8 "Do not steal" goes to the very heart of this matter.

Theft's injury to the self is the uneasy hold. When we are overly possessive, we cling tenaciously to what we have, afraid that we don't deserve it, that it will be taken away. Only the maniac can shout with a Napolean or Hitler, "It's mine, all mine." It may be the case that even legally permissible wealth and acquisition feels tenuous to the soul "that comes naked into the world" and leaves the same way. "Take your ease," "you've got it made," said one to himself that night— having filled barns and silos we assume with the rightful increase of his work. Yet even here "this night, your soul is required of you" (Luke 12: 20). Jesus encourages his followers to take along little on their mission, not be encumbered by possessions on life's way (Matthew 6: 8ff.).

Helmut Gollwitzer, to whom we have briefly referred, has written of the Lord's Supper in Calvin and Luther. It interests me that this theologian, so concerned with poverty and the needs of others, begins with the Lord's Supper. Why did the Reformers place the Decalogue before the Eucharist when they revised the mass? Does the table somehow call us to fellow accountability? Has the deliverance and destiny, the death and new life we commemorate at Passover and communion something to do with virtue and moral action, with who we are and how we're doing? The sacred community is entrusted with a great treasury. We must not hold up and protect it. It must be opened up for all to take freely- "this is my body, my blood—take, all of you, eat and drink."

Salvadore Dali's Last Supper flashes before my mind. It is portrayed, as is his Crucifixion, before the arch of the cosmos. It makes you think of the cosmic theft, the exhaustion of energy that transpires for the organization of life to ensue. Yet the last supper is more disentropic than entropic. The airy open windows say that all that is taken away from here, even my life will be replenished and refreshed by inexhaustible wind—that blows where it wills (John 3: 8).

Excursus

We have a lot of stuff: A library of 2000 volumes, like most, largely unread; a home with marginal equity value over our mortgage and educational loans; some sadly depleted savings, some stocks, some belongings, modest retirement provisions. Yet sometimes we're scared of what the future holds. In Strasbourg today, an orange costs 50 cents, a sandwich $3, a hotel room $80. Will we make it in retirement? We got our four children through college—$200,000 later, we hope they will find success, happiness, jobs. Why this slight unease amid all this affluence? They say any middle-class person in America is just one paycheck or one medical incident away from poverty. In a money economy, we don't enjoy the face to face need and help of past generations. Most of my ancestors were poor. I doubt whether they had the financial anxiety I have in my faithless moments.

I've stolen a lot in my life. Change at the drug store where I once worked. And that peach. I would never have returned to Rome with the chalice one priest did who paid too little. I've stolen glory from the rightful recipient on numerous occasions. If John had amplified this command, he would probably have said, "Did you take anything undeserved?" If so, I frantically steal day by day. Life and health, pleasure and satisfying work, like teaching a class and writing this book.

I feel my privilege is costing some others misery. I don't think I could give up my salvation, as Paul intimated, that others might be saved. I've robbed my own kids, wife and parents of a Christian witness because I found it embarrassing. I didn't take up seminary work with its poverty until I had educated our children and somewhat secured our future.

So this command "Do not steal" hits home. Everything I am and have in life is stolen in grace, kidnapped in the redemption Jesus had to ante up. I hope I can let go some day of all that I've taken and let myself be taken.

IX. Lying: A Theology of Veracity

Error, in itself and by itself, whether a great error in great matters or a small error in small affairs, is always a bad thing. For who, except in error, denies that it is bad to approve the false as though it were the truth, or to disapprove the truth as though it were falsehood, or to hold what is certain as if it were uncertain, or what is uncertain as if it were certain?
Augustine, Enchiridion[152]

Two beliefs often support the rigid rejection of all lies: that God rules out all lies and that He will punish those who lie. These beliefs cannot be proved or disproved. Many, including many Christians, refuse to accept one or both. Other religions, while condemning lying, rarely do so without exceptions. Thus the most frequent religious act of Buddhists is to recite each day five precepts, the fourth of which is an undertaking to abstain from telling lies. But certain lies are commonly regarded as not being sins, and thus not going against the precept. Similarly, while Jewish texts regard lying as prohibited, certain lies, and especially those told to preserve the peace of the household, are regarded as exceptions. All these traditions, therefore, leave room for a rejection of the absolutist prohibition of all lies.
Sissela Bok[153]

'Again, you have heard that our forefathers were told, "Do not break your oath," and "Oaths sworn to the Lord must be kept." But what I tell you is this: You are not to swear at all—not by heaven, for it is God's throne, nor by the

---

[152] *Library of Christian Classics,* Vol. 7. Albert Outler, ed., Philadelphia: Westminster, 1955, p. 350.
[153] *Lying: Moral Choice in Public and Private Life.* New York: Vintage, 1979, pp. 47-8.

earth, for it is his footstool, nor by Jerusalem, for it is the city of the great King, nor by your own head, because you cannot turn one hair of it white or black. Plain "Yes" or "No" is all you need to say; anything beyond that comes from the evil one
(Matthew 5: 33- 37).

Jake: "You lied to me."
Elwood: "It wasn't lies - just bullshit."
Jake to Elwood who picks him up after release from Joliet prison in what seems a sad replacement for the grand cadillac.
The Blues Brothers, 1980

Incursus

"What is the ethical hell?" queries the professor. The students in class then unwind the classic ethical quandary, peculiarly Polish. The patient (Dekalog II) is dying but his impending death must be certified by the doctor otherwise the estranged wife will abort her baby, fathered by another. Is false witness, the lie, excusable even obligatory to save the baby? The class continues as an American visitor weaves in her own complicated story of being saved as a six year old Jewish girl, who the gestapo would have shipped off to the ovens of Aushwitz, but for the lie that she was a baptized Christian. The professor, then an imperiled young wife of a member of the Polish underground, had denied this requested protection by virtue of the false witness commandment (claiming baptism). Now she has come to see that protection and affirmation of persons and the love of children is a higher value than the principle of "not lying." She is Hillel, Shammai or Joshua ben Josef revived.

Now 40 years later the child once saved returns to the scene of the crime and the deliverance. The mind wanders to the last marathon film we viewed before Decalogue—Shoah. This epic about the Polish holocaust took 8 hours to unwind a grotesque story of false witness, prejudice, murder and vicious, silent complicity. The American's mind seeks to discern her own story of damnation and salvation. As she kneels at the foot of the bed that night as guest of the professor her conversation of the afternoon finds focus:

"You don't mention God in your books, or in your class."
"God is the One who is in all of us."
"Today we must be free to choose."

Situation ethicists have always excused the life-saving lie, the lie that saves the family in Kant's treatise, the priest who covers for Jean Val Jean who has stolen a loaf of bread and now the plate of the cloister. Now, as Augustine explores in the Enchiridion, the drama of the lie and the ethics of saving-life emerge in prominence, separating illusion from reality, deception from veracity, falsehood from truth.

...NO FALSE WITNESS

Introduction

The great sins, more uncommon, are tucked away in the middle of the Decalogue: killing, adultery, stealing. At the end we are confronted with the pervasive and ubiquitous sins, lying and envying. It is as if the Decalogue teases us along like the rich young man, "Yes, I've kept all these from my youth", then come C-9 and C-10, and everyone is nailed—no one escapes. And the troubling footnote—having kept or broken the last you have broken or kept..."all."

Veracity is a virtue that can be grounded in many ways. Enlightened self-interest is one. Kant and the philosophical tradition has discountenanced lying because it sets in motion (rationally affirms) a cycle of untruth that eventually recoils back to everything another ever says to you. Biblically, veracity is grounded in the truth of God, taken at God's Word.

The courts must assume veracity and they attempt to safe guard it with perjury statutes, testimony oaths, etc. Modern law, regrettably has built falsehood and gamesmanship so much into the adversarial process that the very foundations of truth in legal process have become suspect. No one, on any side expected truth to emerge in the OJ Simpson proceedings, for example. The search for loopholes; the playing off of what is said and left unsaid, and most seriously, the commendable right to defense even when one is known to be guilty, all severely challenge the veracity of legal activity.

The commonplace setting of C-9 is conveyed in a thirteenth century Jewish *Mazor*, a picture of two persons standing before a judge, accusation has been brought against one, and another behind him raises his hand. The phenomenon of the witness across history comes to mind. Sometimes a friend or enemy lies and betrays you (or doesn't stand up for you). Sometimes a witness is bribed. Sometimes you thought you had escaped clean, even though you were guilty (as happens often in medical malpractice cases, or in sexual harassment cases when no one will squeal or whistle blow), then, an unsuspected witness rises in the back of the room, raises his hand and tells the true story. Will anyone object to Bill marrying Jane? Nowadays, we usually drop this invitation for a disturbing witness. God knows what might come out and we're not sure in any case what difference any accusation would or should make. In other words, we no longer have ethical basis for bans or disallowing marriage.

As we will see as this chapter unfolds, the textual base of C-9 is quite narrow. It refers to court proceedings against a neighbor. The tradition, though, expands the ethics to matters of calumny, conspiracy, collusion and a wide range of compromises to a person's right to fair process. In our homes we try to give each person a fair hearing. But personal animosities and skewed perspectives most often leave us with the facts confused and everyone trusting no one to arbitrate.

Text

YOU SHALL NOT BRING FALSE WITNESS

Jeremiah 32: 12 shows that the original textual meaning of C-9 was the right to truthful witness when one is accused either in the market-place (commerce) or in the courts. Whether in formal juridical process or in commonplace human transactions, witnesses are obliged to veracity and the accused has the right to that truthfulness.

The connection with the paradise garden has been noted. As soon as the man eats the forbidden fruit, the process of false accusation begins, which has gone on in endless cycle ever since. Actually, in the passing-the-buck story there is truth in each witness. It was the woman, it was the snake. The meaning of the story, though, is that all parties knew the prohibition and all sought to transfer blame. So, underneath that primal experience of false word was false will and false heart.

Rabbinic exegetes take the commandment to mean the wrongs inflicted on our neighbor from slander, backbiting, defamation and misrepresentation. Perhaps no people have been falsely accused as often throughout history as the Jews. When Hitler's henchmen burn down the Reichstag building and blame it on Jewish communists, a long tradition of violation of C-9 is reenacted. The fact that at some points Christian history repudiates the Decalogue (even Emil Brunner) may show troubled Christian conscience in this matter. The claim by narrow exegetes that C-9 refers only to the Jew and his literal Jewish neighbor violates the deep spirit of Decalogue. Jesus' answer to the question "who is my neighbor" is fully rabbinic.

> ...A man went down from Jerusalem to Jericho...(Luke 10:29)

The ramifications and implications of C-9 can be amplified out of keeping with the commandment but the obvious cross reference to C-3 not to use God's name falsely or deceptively (Jeremiah 7: 9) witnesses to a more generic meaning.

The talonic law of "scheming witnesses" in Deuteronomy 19: 16-19, where witnesses differ in the court at the gate, is protected against by this commandment. Remember also the contrary witnesses in Solomon's court with the two mothers and the disputed child. *Ed seqer*, the lie, seems to be the earliest text. The cross references in the Hebrew Testament (Psalm 27: 12, Proverbs 6: 19, 12: 17, 14: 5, 19: 59, 25: 18) all point in this broader direction.

If the theme of "lying witness" is the correct textual meaning, we can now see the meaning of Job and Micah 6: 1-8 where Yahweh summons the people as a plaintiff himself, "Oh people what have I done to you? Answer me."

Because of the pervasiveness in human affairs of the false witness no person shall be put to death on the testimony of one witness (Numbers 35: 30).

Israelite society functioned as a system of citizen jurisdiction. As we see in Ruth 4 and Jeremiah 26, every citizen could be involved as a judge or witness. The crucial importance of veracity in all such processes for solidarity and social cohesion is evident. The biblical tradition of textual interpretation of C-9 includes:

- Proverbs 17: 4—The wicked person is known by his "false lips."

- Psalms 35: 11—The root of much violence is some initial false charge.

- Proverbs 21: 28—There is a natural law (perhaps even a divine retribution) that will recycle the initial lie back to the original perpetrator.

- Ezekiel 21: 23, Zecheriah 10: 2—The diviners, fortune-tellers (especially fortune cookies), the obsequious, full of shallow compliments, are suspect. The "say nice things" therapists also join the genre of false witnesses.

- Psalm 27: 12, 119: 104, 128—The plight of our lives is constantly being assaulted and insulted by false accusations. Words hurt us every bit as much as sticks and stones.

- Jeremiah 14: 14, 23: 32—The real danger of false prophets and preachers is that they dishonor God and disgrace us with their "smooth words" (Isaiah 30: 10), misguiding predictions, or false accusation.

- Jeremiah 51: 17—The false witness is a total abrogation of Decalogue. It entails false gods, false names, false worship.

We side with the liberal textual tradition that funds a broad range of application implicit in the ninth commandment. As we move now to a survey of law, the tradition appropriates its ethical meaning and we see further evidence of this broader intent. Augustine's *Enchiridion* is one of several systematic works which he obviously intends to interpret biblical ethics and the Decalogue. Here he deals with C-9 in a separate chapter on "lying." This manual, something to have "at hand" as one seeks to live out a life of faith, uses the Lord's Prayer and Creed as particular guides. The Decalogue is not far in the background, even though it often recedes to a more remote position in Augustine's exuberant and sometimes antinomian faith.

Augustine had written about "lying" twice before this Enchiridion. In *Ad Consentium contra mendacium* and *De Mendacio* he developed his serious concern about C-9. For Augustine, every lie is a sin no matter how efficacious it is thought to be. Perhaps the most notable witness of this self delusion in history might have been Pilate's " I find no fault in the man" (John 18: 38). While this passage may be wishful thinking on the Evangelists' part, the fact is that for reason of truth or expediency, Pilate did find fault and his witness or judgment based on the false witness was the death sentence to the Lord of life. Was this a lie? Was it false witness? Augustine struggles with the issue of the "helpful lie."

The subtlety of Augustine's thought on this matter is found in his closing illustration. Suppose a man rightly calls adultery bad and chastity good but calls (witnesses to) a particular man good in ignorance of the fact that he is an adulterer. When we are called to bring witness or testimony against another, in everyday conversation, as well as in court, our own knowledge, perception and intention is refracted, biased and full of malice and self-service. Witness against another, lying if you will, is therefore almost by definition, flawed. Either we are biased in favor of the subject and distort the truth into protective false witness, or we are inclined toward disfavor, and distort the truth toward condemnation. Again, case at point, the O.J. Simpson trial and the total absence of any objectivity in parties to the case: attorneys, jurors, judge, public. Given these human proclivities, lying is a sin and veracity the chastening virtue.[154]

Luther further elaborates this complicated meaning of C-9 in the *Larger Catechism*. The good now at stake is honor or reputation. We have affirmed, thus far, he claims, the goods of body, spouse and possessions. Now we turn to honor and respect. This public reputation hinges on our character and reputation in righteousness or on our own character flaws, misdeeds or soiled reputation by reason of fact or the misrepresentation of others. Jesus, we recall, was caricatured as an immoral man. He blasphemed by associating himself with God (John 5: 30ff). In this passage we have a circuitous dealing with C-9 exploring the meaning of self-recrimination or witness about or against oneself. Unfortunately Jesus couldn't plead the Fifth Amendment. Jesus also associated with sinners, enjoyed their company, dined with them. He thus compromised his reputation and honor, at least in the eyes of some. His cross is seen as ultimate depletion (Philippians 2) and dereliction (Isaiah 53). He is "numbered among the transgressors."

The fundamental meaning of C-9 to Luther is its *prima facie* meaning in Hebrew:

> Pertaining to the public courts of justice, where a poor, innocent man (the rich have advocates who get them off, guilty or not) is accused and oppressed by false witnesses in order to be punished in his body, property or honor.[155]

Aware of the Jesus experience of being misrepresented and falsely accused to death, Luther reflects on the false witness that will be brought whenever the Gospel is proclaimed. As history amply evidences, whenever the justice of the Gospel is announced detractors and the disturbed scramble to bring false

---

[154] Augustine, *Enchiridion, Library of Christian Classics* Vol. 7. London: SCM Press, 1995, p. 350.
[155] LC, p. 23.

accusation of adultery, blasphemy, etc, to the preacher and the true witness (i.e. martyr).

> Wherever there are godly preachers and Christians, they must bear the sentence of the world that they are called seditious, apostates...the word must suffer...[156]

As is his wonderful proclivity, Luther also extends the commandment to those daily breaches of trust:

> ...evil speaking, lying, slandering as swine roll themselves in dirt and root in it with the snouts.[157]

The obvious reference above to ethics of the press and media takes on vivid meaning when you think of the wild boars that still inhabit the German and French forests. Calvin adds to our unfolding story. In the 1559 edition of *The Institutes*, Calvin roots C-9 in the nature of God. Since God is truth, God does not tolerate the lie. Since people are the express glory of God, we are to exhibit divine truthfulness in our dealings with one another. In our life we are to do and say all that we can to honor the being and belongings of our neighbors. This is the positive imperative in the command. The good name and reputation of the neighbor is a value that we must affirm in all possible ways. Calvin brings a subtle Puritan application, not as rude and delightful as Luther, but one perceptive, nevertheless:

> ...This precept extends to forbidding us to affect a fawning politeness barbed with bitter taunts under the guise of joking.[158]

Like Luther, Calvin extends the meaning of the commandment into all segments of the life of all people. Personal and public dimensions of ethics are addressed. When in the city of Geneva, the consistory called a believer to answer for certain actions of defamation, or when in modern history a corporation is castigated for rumor spreading that harms another firm (insider trading), we see the legacy of Calvin's construal of C-9.

Bucer and Calvin are very similar on C-9 in the catechisms. Bucer brings a fascinating new dimension to the development of C-9 others in his discussing the reign of Christ (*De Regno Christi*), in the era of persecution of Protestants in France. This work was written in 1550 for the young English King, Edward VI, the son and successor of Henry VIII. At that time, at Cramner's invitation, he had become Regis Professor of Divinity at Cambridge.

For Bucer, the true and good life is only possible in the christocracy. The administration of the holy and righteous life by civil and political leaders is

---

[156] *Ibid.*

[157] *Ibid.*, p. 24.

[158] *Institutes*, p. 412.

strongly affirmed. The church, state and home are three instruments for the rightful expression of justice in society. The moral laws of the Old and New Testaments were drawn for *Regno Christi* from the Decalogue and the "Golden Rule." The first four commandments compel the civil authorities to honor the one true God as revealed in Scripture and honored in worship, to suppress idols (unbelievers and cults) and to establish Christian sacraments and worship in order to honor the divine name and enhance the family of God. Bucer concludes this section with a treatise on the implications of the Second table of the law for Godly government.

> Then in the third place there may follow laws to regulate the exchanges of goods and services of this life and voluntary and involuntary contracts. Here the highest rule is that everyone do to others as he would have them do to him (cf. Matt. 7: 12), and this out of a sincere love. In the formulation, emendation, and elucidation of laws of this kind, one must take the greatest care to exclude from the commerce of the citizens all greed (i.e., excessive cupidity in seeking for oneself things, honors, or pleasures) and also all fraud and deceit. If such creeps in, it should receive the strictest attention and be gotten rid of. The citizen must be made to realize that that person ought not be tolerated, neither in the Church of Christ nor in any Christian commonwealth, who is found to prefer private to public advantage or to seek his own interests to the disadvantage of others, and who is not disposed to cultivate among his neighbors mutual benevolence and beneficence, trust, honesty, and appreciation.

> For when man has the will and desire to deceive, defraud, and harm his neighbors, although he may have the name and shape of a man, he is in nature and desire a savage beast, to whom nothing is lacking but the occasion for overthrowing not only private citizens but also the commonwealth itself. He will readily seize every opportunity to do so for he is a captive of Satan and subject to his deceitful lust which is in every way so ruinous for mankind. The Holy Spirit has borne witness to this when he affirmed that "he who hates his brother" (and knowingly and willingly harms someone hates him) "is a murderer: (I John 3: 15). Therefore, in every condemnation of the godless, Scripture always takes special note of fraud, malice, and lying, and execrates them.

> And so in all laws it must first of all be required that all selflove and all greed be suppressed and that everyone embrace and help his neighbors and transact all things with them in the same good faith that everyone wishes others to have in entering into and making contracts with himself. These things, therefore, should be considered and regarded by the correctors of all laws which are promulgated for the observance of so-called commutative justice, by which men are made to acknowledge that they have been born not for themselves but for God, Church, country, and neighbor, and that they wickedly injure God and the commonwealth and deserve to be rejected from the human community if they should be discovered to have preferred in any matter their own good to the

good of the commonwealth and their neighbor. This is part of the law of nature, not only of the gospel, which indeed all profess in Your Majesty's realm.[159]

Bucer thus pleas for the continuum from personal faith, through life in the sacred community, including the Eucharist, and out into the public society. The common thread connecting all levels of ethical action is the moral law disclosed in Decalogue and the New Testament law of love including the Golden Rule.

Theology

As we move into theological reflection about C-9, we start with its inner meaning in our spiritual and ethical existence. For Philo in *De Decalogo*, the essential wrong in false witness is the breach of trust. Someone we had counted on to defend our right, betrays us. Our experience is replete with instances of those we love and trust double-crossing us. We live and work in families, communities, institutions and nations. At any level those to whom we have entrusted our well being can turn against us, misconstrue the facts of situations to make case against us, and sometimes when matters go to that extent, actually testify against us in some decisive arbitration or court of law.

We live with such moral dynamics of C-9 in many settings. There is the court of family affairs. The dog kicks over the garbage can. Big brother blames little sister. She is punished. False witness. The husband and wife go together to a marriage counselor. Testimony (my side of the story) is presented from both sides. Through the three-partnered conversation each begins to see the misperception and misrepresentation that they and the spouse has made. Reconciliation occurs as that false witness is regulated and chastened not only by truth but by underlying disposition for justice and love. If hatred persists, the stalemate hardens.

In the corporate world, management has conflict with labor. Each falsely accuses the other. Actually, as in most human relations (as Augustine and Calvin have shown), there is a modicum of truth on both sides. Through some process of arbitration, human relations, intervention or, at last resort, the courts, the stalemate is worked through. Exaggeration, lying or false witness of some type is involved in nearly all manner of human relations.

At the personal and communal level there is another level of interaction with this commandment. It comes under the title of "not squealing" or "whistle-blowing." I have mentioned the tendency of professionals in the guilds, medicine, law, ministry in particular, to "cover up" for one another. The practice seems to stem from a basic pattern learned in school or play groups. Here is the situation: In an all-boys class the bully beats up the wimp, who then comes back into class with a bloody nose. "Who did this?" asks the teacher. No one will talk. They remain silent, we may surmise, both out of fear of reprisal and out of some

---

[159] Bucer, M. *De Regno Christi, Library of Christian Classics* Vol. 14, London: SCM Press, 1960, p. 360, 361.

basic code of honor that holds that persons should work out their own squabbles, including the establishing of the inevitable pecking-orders. This should be done, says the code without resorting to authority. There is a subtle presumption in C-9 reflection in general that one should leave well-enough alone, not turn small matters into federal cases, only say yes and no, and if ever called on to testify, to limit one's witness to absolute essentials of truth.

I think that the fundamental moral truth implied in this anthropological observation is that sustaining the positive spirit of C- 9 is to maintain the integrity, honor and "good name" of one another. To turn one "in" or turn one "over" to authorities is thought to be a basic violation of our human covenants one with the other.

One implication of this for the church, synagogue or sacred community is involved when we ask about "covering over" sins or bringing one before the body in honest confrontation of some wrong in which one is involved. In the church, even until the last century, persons would be called before the session or official Board for various moral lapses, some serious enough to merit censure, or even excommunication. Such rabbinical, canon law or ecclesiastical proceeding always involved accusation, witnesses and judgment. The woman brought to Jesus, taken in the act of adultery, is a moving case of such adjudication. The case also cautions us against employing the process.

The conviction that the church could only safeguard one's sacred honor or that one's good name could only be "cleared" in and by the sacred community is a fascinating issue for discussion of some contemporary matters. Before we turn to this one other theological point.

Paul in his letter to Romans reflects on the cosmic drama of honor, false witness, defamation, dishonor, forgiving or clearing one's good name and restoration of honor. In theology, we call it the drama of redemption. In the opening chapters of this brief, he appears to have the Decalogue before him. Let us trace this theological theme through Paul's letter, using the theme of witness. Romans 2: 15. . their conscience also bears witness..."

Paul begins the epistle with a discussion of the lost condition of people in the natural and godless state of their existence. We do not lustfully witness against sin in each other (2: 3) because we know that we are guilty of the same charge. After all, didn't Jesus say to the woman caught in adultery (John 8),

> "Woman, where are your accusers?" and "He who is without sin cast the first stone."

We have all sinned with or without the law (2: 12ff.). When we obey the law either by nature (instinct), or by instruction (Decalogue adherence), we are righteous and the "law is written on our hearts" (2: 15). But conscience also bears witness against us in our neglect and defiance of God's law. Does conscience bear false-witness or true-witness? Paul is complicated at this point. On the one hand, conscience condemns us in unfortunate ways by unworthy accusation (2 Timothy 3: 3, Titus 2: 3). On the other hand conscience, as with the law, condemns us rightly, and casts us upon Christ for mercy.

> ...you have been made God's children...when we cry abba!
> Father it is the Spirit bearing witness with our spirit that we are
> the children of God. (Romans 8: 16)

The law perjures in the providence of God to convict us of sin (7: 7). We know because of the Godly efficacy of the law that we have "fallen short of the glory of God." We know that by God's law we deserve to die. In various metaphors Paul then rehearses the grace of Christ which covers our sin (4: 7) and will not impute (accuse) sin against us (4: 8). Jesus Christ died to render our sin impotent and save us from death to life (6: 6-19). Christ takes the accusation and witness onto himself and becomes in the cross, sin for us and in resurrection, forgiveness and life.

> Living he loved me
> dying he saved me
> buried he carried my sin far away
> rising he justified...

Now a new voice of witness, one authentic and affirmative, confirms that we are God's children and that nothing can sever us from this relation and this love (Chapter 8).

Romans 9: 1 (Hebrews 2: 4)...My conscience bears me witness in the Holy Spirit. Now my conscience, liberated in Christ's spirit testifies, not in false accusation, but in affirmation.

The whole scene has been a courtroom. We have been called before the Bar, in front of the judge. False witnesses have been offered against us (Satan and conscience) but also valid accusers (the law). At the very moment when we are brought low by the testified evidence and are without excuse, an awesome event occurs. The judge, the only one lawful, pure and righteous, the only one able to witness against us, comes around the table and stands with us and for us. Like a good father, he takes the charge for his son (the modern film *Les Misérables*). In Bonhoeffer's words, he becomes guilt for us and thereby exonerates and sets us free.

The cosmic and existential drama summarized here is the root of the enduring relevance of C-9. We must not falsely accuse one another because each human being has received the justice of witness and has been exonerated in Christ's mercy. We now witness against one another only to the absolute truth of a sin or crime and not out of hateful, revengeful will but out of redemptive hope. We know "there but for the grace of God, go I." We know that in Christ, the will of God is that none should perish.

In light of Akedic theology and Decalogic ethics which we have explored thus far through inflicted false witness like imputed injustice brings about incorporation into the way and will of God which is inclusion in the redemptive being of God. This living God of Israel of the law and prophets, of the messiah is one who has gone out sacrificially toward the misunderstanding and malevolence of the world.

Today

Lying and false witnessing are fragile moral principles in our age of relativity and expediency. Even the Kantian logic of pervasive cyclical manifestation, rendering a moral world absurd and impossible, is unconvincing. We deceive the self, always a pushover; survive untouched in indulgent congregations; and happily thrive in a society riddled with falsehood. The experience of alcoholism and other mental and behavioral syndromes shows the tendency of the human mind to self-deception. We constantly think of ourselves more highly than we ought or, on the other hand, in self-loathing, constantly bring false witness against ourselves. Both postures are theologically and ethically unworthy. Decalogue holds before us the challenge and possibility of living a holy and just existence. On our own, no! But in the grace of God, with the aid of God's spirit, with the encouragement, and, yes, the enjoining of the sacred and human community, we can be responsible. We are made to be, and ought to be trained to be persons of faith, justice and love. That is what it means to be fully human.

The church should seek to be less a community of condemnation and more a community of consolation and mutual admonition. Today we seem to operate either out of harsh law or cheap grace. The wreckage of both mistakes is all around us. The young people who have rejected fundamentalist systems often flee to freedom and wreck their lives. Similarly, those who have been perpetually indulged, like spoiled children, often go astray. The structure of Decalogue ethics—rooted in the presence of God in theophany, in relationship with God, sustained in covenant fellowships, eucharist, the sacramental people, and worked out in constant catechesis and ritualistic renewal—can best sustain the sacred community in our generation.

Finally, what can be done to rescue a society that has made falsehood, truth and false witness, success? We call evil, good and good, evil. We are pluralistic states today with more and more pluralism and relativity in ethics. Even if Pat Buchanan or Pat Robertson succeeds in politics and somehow restores some "voice of God," Word of the Lord, right to life and moral fiber to this society, nothing will change. Our best hope is to restore the cultural legacy of the Decalogue. This would mean full human rights always expressed in terms of responsibilities. All freedoms should be secured by concomitant duties. And beneath it all truth in conversation and transaction. We need to post the ten commandments, not mourn classrooms (though I fail to see them offense but in the tablets of human hearts and from there into the public record).

Excursus

Some nights I wake up trembling. I have dreamed that I killed someone way back somewhere (C-6) and was involved in a complicated cover-up (C-9). The cover-up was starting to unravel. I am running when I awake, startled. While the subconscious accuses me the conscious mind assures me that it never happened. But Freud and Jung counseled us to rehearse and examine our dreams. Is there a residual consciousness and conscientiousness in all of us that demonstrates guilt over lethal words and deeds? Others report to me the same nightmares (Revelation 6). Residual universal conscience may confirm Philo's eternal Decalogue.

Much of my life has been lived at the fuzzy edge of truth and lie. Like most, I am engaged in a constant litany of self justification to both God and man. Though adaptive to the self, it is a lie. I love a good buy. "What a deal!" I bought six suits at a downtown Chicago shop going out of business - 90% discount. Was it a steal or a lie? Something's wrong somewhere. Someone pays or loses out. What about the stock market? Gambling? Veracity would insist on honesty and justice in every transaction of life, but where would that leave romance, investment, business, and job interviewing? False witness is ubiquitous. We live by exaggeration, compensation, denial and flattery — all lies.

Confession precedes forgiveness of sins. Confession is disavowal of the lie. Jung reported little neurosis in those who regularly made catholic confession. Forgiveness then must be essential to righteousness. Not as evasion "...I love sinning – God loves forgiving - this is the best of all possible worlds" - but as repentant resolve to do it right the next time. There is a power in Luther's reading of Paul's assessment of the Quandary of life "The good that I would I do not and the wrong I hate - that's what I do." *Non posse non pecattum.* But it must be possible to change or be changed. At least then we can wake up *simul justus et pecattor* and go on living despite haunting dreams. We rendevoux with Akedah:

> ...Those who follow the lamb wherever he goes
> The redeemed of mankind...
> ...in their mouth no lie was found
> (Revelation 14: 4,5)

X. I LIKE IT: A THEOLOGY OF CRAVING

> You shall not covet your neighbor's house; your neighbor's wife, his slave, ox or ass—anything that is your neighbor's.
> Exodus 20: 17

If a man steals an ox or a sheep, and kills it or sells it, he shall pay five oxen for an ox, and four sheep for a sheep. He shall make restitution; if he has nothing, then he shall be sold for his theft. If the stolen beast is found alive in his possession, whether it is an ox or an ass or a sheep, he shall pay double. If a thief is found breaking in, and is struck so that he dies, there shall be no blood guilt for him.
(Exodus 22: 1-2a)

But the people of Israel broke faith in regard to the devoted things; for Achan the son of Carmi, son of Zabdi, son of Zerah, of the tribe of Judah, took some of the devoted things; and the anger of the Lord burned against the people of Israel.

Joshua sent men from Jericho to Ai, which is near Beth-a'ven, east of Bethel, and said to them, "Go up and spy out the land." And the men went up and spied out Ai. And they returned to Joshua, and said to him, "Let not all the people go up, but let about two or three thousand men go up and attack Ai; do not make the whole people toil up there, for they are but few." So about three thousand went up there from the people; and they fled before the men of Ai, and the men of Ai killed about thirtysix men of them, and chased them before the gate as far as Sheb'arim, and slew them at the descent. And the hearts of the people melted, and became as water.

Then Joshua rent his clothes, and fell to the earth upon his face before the ark of the Lord until the evening, he and the elders of Israel; and they put dust upon their heads. And Joshua said, "Alas, O Lord God, why hast thou brought this people over the Jordan at all, to give us into the hands of the Amorites, to destroy us? Would that we had been content to dwell beyond the Jordan! O Lord, what can I say, when Israel has turned their backs before their enemies! For the Canaanites and all the inhabitants of the land will hear of it, and will surround us, and cut off our name from the earth; and what wilt thou do for thy great name?"

The Lord said to Joshua, "Arise, why have you thus fallen upon your face? Israel has sinned; they have transgressed my covenant which I commanded them; they have taken some of the devoted things; they have stolen and lied, and put them among their own stuff. Therefore the people of Israel cannot stand before their enemies; they turn their backs before their enemies, because they have become a thing for destruction. I will be with you no more, unless you destroy the devoted things from among you. Up, sanctify the people, and say, 'Sanctify yourselves for tomorrow; for thus says the Lord, God of Israel, "There are devoted things in the midst of you, O Israel; you cannot stand before your enemies, until you take away the devoted things from among you." In the morning therefore you shall be brought near by your tribes; and the tribe which the Lord takes shall come near by families; and the family which the Lord takes shall come near by households; and the household which the Lord takes shall come near man by man. And he who is taken with the devoted things shall be burned with fire, and he and all that he has, because he has transgressed the covenant of the Lord, and because he has done a shameful thing in Israel.' "

276

So Joshua rose early in the morning, and brought Israel near tribe by tribe, and the tribe of Judah was taken; and he brought near the families of Judah, and the family of the Zer'ahites was taken; and he brought near the family of the Zer'ahites man by man, and Achan the son of Carmi, son of Zabdi, son of Zerah, of the tribe of Judah, was taken. Then Joshua said to Achan, "My son, give glory to the Lord God of Israel, and render praise to him; and tell me now what you have done; do not hide it from me." And Achan answered Joshua, "of a truth I have sinned against the Lord God of Israel, and this is what I did: when I saw among the spoil a beautiful mantle from Shinar, and two hundred shekels of silver, and a bar of gold weighing fifty shekels, then I coveted them, and took them; and behold, they are hidden in the earth inside my tent, with the silver underneath."

So Joshua sent messengers, and they ran to the tent; and behold, it was hidden in his tent with the silver underneath. And they took them out of the tent and brought them to Joshua and all the people of Israel; and they laid them down before the Lord. And Joshua and all of Israel with him took Achan the son of Zerah, and the silver and the mantle of and the bar of gold, and his sons and daughters, and his oxen and asses and sheep, and his tent, and all that he had; and they brought them up to the Valleyof the Anchor. And Joshua said, "Why did you bring trouble on us? The Lord brings trouble on you today." And all Israel stoned him with stones; they burned him with fire, and stoned them with stones. And they raised over him a great heap of stones that remains to this day; then the Lord turned from his burning anger. Therefore to this day the name of that place is called the valley of Anchor.
(Joshua 7)

Now Naboth the Jezreelite had a vineyard in Jezreel, beside the palace of Ahab king of Sama'ria. And after this Ahab said to Naboth, "Give me your vineyard, that I may have it for a vegetable garden, because if is near my house; and I will give you a better vineyard for it; or, if it seems good to you, I will give you its value in money." But Naboth said to Ahab, "The Lord forbid that I should give you the inheritance of my fathers." And Ahab went into his house vexed and sullen because of what Naboth the Jezreelite had said to him; for he had said, "I will not give you the inheritance of my fathers." And he lay down on his bed, and turned away his face, and would eat no food.

But Jez'ebel his wife came to him, and said to him, "Why is your spirit so vexed that you eat no food?" And he said to her, "Because I spoke to Naboth the Jezreelite, and said to him, 'Give me your vineyard for money; or else, if it please you, I will give you another vineyard for it'; and he answered, 'I will not give you my vineyard.' "And Jez'ebel his wife said to him, "Do you now govern Israel? Arise, and eat bread, and let your heart be cheerful; I will give you the vineyard of Naboth the Jezreelite."

So she wrote letters in Ahab's name and sealed them with his seal, and she sent the letters to the elders and the nobles who dwelt with Naboth in his city. And she wrote in the letters, "Proclaim a fast, and set Naboth on high among the people; and set two base fellows opposite him, and let them bring a charge against him, saying, 'You have cursed God and the king.' Then take him out, and stone him to death." And the men of his city, did as Jez'ebel had sent word to them. As it was written in the letters which she had sent to them, they proclaimed a fast, and set Naboth on high among the people. And the two base fellows came in and sat opposite him; and the base fellows brought a charge against Naboth, in the presence of the people, saying, "Naboth cursed God and the king." So they took him outside the city, and stoned him to death with stones. Then they sent to Jez'ebel, saying, "Naboth has been stoned; he is dead."

As soon as Jez'ebel heard that Naboth had been stoned and was dead, Jez'ebel said to Ahab, "Arise, take possession of the vineyard of Naboth the Jezreelite, which he refused to give you for money; for Naboth is not alive, but dead." And as soon as Ahab heard that Naboth was dead, Ahab arose to go down to the vineyard of Naboth the Jezreelite, to take possession of it.

Then the word of the Lord came to Elijah the Tishbite, saying, "Arise, go down to meet Ahab king of Israel, who is in Sama'ria; behold, he is in the vineyard of Naboth, where he has gone to take possession. And you shall say to him, 'Thus says the Lord, "Have you killed, and also taken possession?" ' And you shall say to him, 'Thus says the Lord: "In the place where dogs licked up the blood of Naboth shall dogs lick your own blood."

Ahab said to Eli'jah, "Have you found me, O my enemy?" He answered, "I have found you, because you have sold yourself to do what is evil in the sight of the Lord. Behold, I will bring evil upon you; I will utterly sweep you away, and will cut off from Ahab every male, bond or free, in Israel; and I will make your house like the house of Jerobo'am the son of Nebat, and like the house of Ba'asha the son of Ahi'jah, for the anger to which you have provoked me, and because you have made Israel to sin. And of Jez'ebel the Lord also said, 'The dogs shall eat Jez'ebel within the bounds of Jezreel.' Any one belonging to Ahab who dies in the city the dogs shall eat; and any one of his who dies in the open country the birds of the air shall eat."

(There was none who sold himself to do what was evil in the sight of the Lord like Ahab, whom Jez'ebel his wife incited. He did very abominably in going after idols, as the Amorites had done, whom the Lord cast out before the people of Israel.)

And when Ahab heard those words, he rent his clothes, and put sackcloth upon his flesh, and fasted and lay in sackcloth, and went about dejectedly. And the word of the Lord came to Eli'jah the Tishbite, saying, "Have you seen how Ahab has humbled himself before me? Because he has humb led himself before me, I will not bring the evil in his days; but in his son's days I will bring the evil upon his house."
1 Kings 21

In the spring of the year, the time when kings go forth to battle, David sent Jo'ab, and his servants with him, and all Israel; andthey ravaged the Ammonites, and besieged Rabbah. But David remained at Jerusalem.

It happened, late one afternoon, when David arose from his couch and was walking upon the roof of the king's house, that he saw from the roof a woman bathing; and the woman was very beautiful. And David sent and inquired about the woman. And one said, "Is not this Bathshe'ba, the daughter of Eli'am, the wife of Uri'ah the Hittite?" So David sent messengers, and took her; and she came to him, and he lay with her. (Now she was purifying herself from her uncleanness.) Then she returned to her house. And the woman conceived; and she sent and told David, "I am with child."

So David sent word to Jo'ab, "Send me Uri'ah the Hittite." And Jo'ab sent Uri'ah to David. When Uri'ah came to him, David asked how Jo'ab was doing, and how the people fared, and how the war prospered. Then David said to Uri'ah, "Go down to your house, and wash your feet." And Uri'ah went out of the king's house, and there followed him a present from the king. But Uri'ah slept at the door of the king's house with all the servants of his lord, and did not go down to his house. When they told David, "Uri'ah did not go down to his house," David said to Uri'ah, "Have you not come from a journey? Why did you not go down to your house?" Uri'ah said to David, "The ark and Israel and Judah dwell in booths; and my lord Jo'ab and the servants of my lord are camping in the open field; shall I then go to my house, to eat and to drink, and to lie with my wife? As you live, and as your soul lives, I will not do this thing." Then David said to Uri'ah, "Remain here today also, and tomorrow I will let you depart." So Uri'ah remained in Jerusalem that day, and the next. And David invited him, and he ate in his presence and drank, so that he made him drunk; and in the evening he went out to lie on his couch with the servants of his lord, but he did not go down to his house.

In the morning David wrote a letter to Jo'ab, and sent it by the hand of Uri'ah. In the letter he wrote, "Set Uri'ah in the forefront of the hardest fighting, and then draw back from him, that he may be struck down, and die." And as Jo'ab was besieging the city, he assigned Uri'ah to the place where he knew there were valiant men. And the men of the city came out and fought with Jo'ab; and some of the servants of David among the people fell. Uri'ah the Hittite was slain also. Then Jo'ab sent and told David all the news about the fighting; and he instructed the messenger, "When you have finished telling all the news about the fighting to the king, then, if the king's anger arises, and if he says to you, 'Why did you go so near the city to fight? Did you not know that they would shoot from the wall? Who killed Abim'elech the son of Jerub'besheth? Did not a woman cast an upper millstone upon him from the wall, so that he died at Thebez? Why did you go so near the wall?' then you shall say, 'Your servant Uri'ah the Hittite is dead also.' "

So the messenger went, and came and told David all that Jo'ab had sent him to tell. The messenger said to David, "The men gained an advantage over us, and came out against us in the firld; but we drove them back to the entrance of the gate. Then the archers shot at your servants from the wall; some of the king's servants are dead; and your servant Uri'ah the Hittite is dead also." David said to the messenger, "Thus shall you say to Jo'ab, 'Do not let this matter trouble you, for the sword devours now one and now another; strengthen your attack upon the city, and overthrow it.' And encourage him."

When the wife of Uri'ah heard that Uri'ah her husband was dead, she made lamentation for her husband. And when the mourning was over, David sent and

brought her to his house, and she became his wife, and she bore him a son. But the thing that David had done displeased the Lord.
2 Samuel 11

Woe to those who devise wickedness and work evil upon their beds! When the morning dawns, they perform it, because it is in the power of their hand. They covet fields, and seize them; and houses, and take them away; they oppress a man and his house, a man and his inheritance.
Micah 2: 2

One's desire for the object may grow stronger, to the point of devising a scheme to obtain it, and one will not stop begging and pressing the owner to sell it, or give in exchange for something better or more valuable. If a person has his way, he breaks not only this prohibition (of craving) but "You shall not covet" as well, since by his persistence and scheming he has acquired a thing with which the owner did not want to part.
Maimonides, *Sejer ha Misnot*,
Jerusalem, 1971

Qu'est-ce que la propriété? Propriété, c'est le vol. (Property is theft.)
Pierre J. Proudhon, 1840

Incursus

Kieslowski accepts the listing of Augustine, Luther and modern Catholic catechism dividing the biblical (C-10) into coveting the neighbors wife, servants and animals (C-9) and the neighbors goods (C10). In this case the fertility internist is brutally honest with his surgeon colleague.

"I want to know the truth."
"Yours is a classic case, all the lab data confirms."

Untreatable irreversible infertility. Now begins the saga with his already unfaithful wife. She tries to convince the increasingly jealous and paranoiac husband of her love for him.

"Love isn't panting in bed 5 minutes a week."

While the surgeon is treating a brilliant young singer, this theme will be further developed in (*duble vie de veronique*). Her wound is a cardiac anomaly that threatens her musical career. The ethical dilemma; threatening surgery or medial therapy that is safer.

"...my mother needs me to be famous (covet's fame) but my heart won't take it."

The intrique deepens as the doctor's suspicion mounts and his wife has to decide her loyalty. Finally the decisional crisis ends in the doctor's near death and his wife's return. After tragic near misses as they each run toward destruction, he finally gets a call through from his hospital bed, "hello" - "It's me." To covet or wander into adultery is to find discontent with oneself - to not be at peace with oneself. Contentment with one's life is the *gebot* within the *verbot* of covetousness. Kieslowski's strong thesis is that love bestows such peace and succors one amid the world's terrors and temptations.

Decalogue ends in a riotous act. It's a Mel Brooks comedy of human foibles. The crazy team from White - purgatory or *fraternite*, (if you take colors of the flag of France) arises again as two brothers must live with a priceless stamp collection left by their father (the neighbor "Root" in the professor tale in #8). In Mel Brooks *The Story of Man* stage 4 in Shakespeare's famous 7 stages of life is "liver transplant." The organ retrieval team arrives at the door to perform the hepatectomy. When the two boys discover the stamp collection is worth millions (even though father never had enough for clothes or to feed them and they lived in semi squalor) the brothers catch the thrill and thralldom of acquisitiveness.

"I forgot how good it feels..."
"nothing bothers me anymore."

But then they must protect the inheritance - locks, bars, dogstotal obsession. Finally, one brother is extorted to donate a kidney to pay for a special stamp (the Austrian Rose Mercury to finish a set). As he leaves the hospital still in pain from the nephrectomy, the brother breaks down and cries. The big black Great Dane guard dogs had been part of a scam and they had been robbed of everything. Biblical wisdom is again born out:

"do not build up for yourselves treasures on earth where moths and rust consume and thieves break in and steal."
(Matthew 6:19)

"Follow the simple example of the one who did not covet equality with God as something to be grasped."
(Phillipians 2: 5-7)

Introduction

Even before creation envy was found among ambitious angels who coveted the power of father and son. The Decalogue in its entirety is a portrayal of the rightful relationship that humans ought to have with the God who established association with the first human beings to confront cooperatively that primeval envy and make the world new and good. The paradise event is the narrative background of this and all commandments. Here in mythic drama framed by the snake and the mysterious walker in the garden in the cool of the day (Genesis 3: 8) is depicted primal craving and desire which is the essence of covetousness. The inordinate yet inescapable desire to eat of the tree of good and evil and the irresistible sequel desire for the fruit of the tree of life itself must be rescinded by divine banishment from Eden. Just as life can only proceed if accompanied by death, to live forever would mean that life would cease. Cosmic death can only be avoided by refusing the usurpation of life. Covetousness is the primal yearning for freedom and immortality which, in curious inversion, is bondage and death; ascent is fall—fall is ascent.

The drama of covetousness and life and death is continued in the next pericope of Cain and Abel. Cain envies Yahweh's arbitrary favoritism to Abel's sacrifice. Playing on the primeval tension of farmer and herdsman where in the cosmic carnival pork rinds are preferred to sprouts, humans are cautioned against resenting God's arbitrary action and choices. We are sternly warned against brooding in lethal anger, the indwelling sin which is the destructive concomitant of coveting (Genesis 4: 7).

Ungrateful desire for something else or envious plotting for that which belongs to another is a violation of the divine gifts of life. Productive land, fields and vines (Deuteronomy 8: 7-9), a comfortable house (6: 11, 8: 12), and a good wife (24: 5, 28: 11, Proverbs 38) constitute the abundant life. Faith and righteousness beget the blessings of life. Irascible friends, improvident land, harsh work, alienated family life are the antitheses of "good life" entailed by envy and covetousness as they negate gratitude.

Scholars believe that beyond this theological origin, the Decalogue was a legal code for the concrete wordily life of the people of Israel. The tenth law is about respect and violation of the neighbor's house and household. When the people of Israel escaped their slavery, they settled in the first available home, Kadesh (Deuteronomy 1: 26), where they plied their bitter learned trade now for their own edification, brick-making and bricklaying. The commandment in its strict sense is honoring respective houses and households.

The commandment in its strict and literal sense means to want and take something that does not belong to you but to your neighbor. The neighbor is not the generic fellow human being but the family that lives in the next tent or house. Neighbor in the old German language was called *Nächsten, nachbar*— the next one, the proximate person. Israel's law is that no one can be dispossessed.

The Hebrew word covet *hamad* means not only desiring something, but plotting steps to take it. In the great body of law throughout the world, which proceeds from Sinai, this subtlety is subsumed in the notions of motive and act. Jesus' rendition of *Mitzvoh* in the Sermon on the Mount is fully Judaic—thoughts and acts can be evil. The cardinal act of coveting is depicted in Joshua 7. The story is the destruction of Jericho—the oath of destruction and the spoils belonging to Yahweh's treasury. The assumption here is radical:

- All things that we think of as possessions are actually blessings
- Our response ought to be thanksgiving not pride in procurement ("my might and the power of my hand have gotten me this wealth." Deuteronomy 8).

- In all things we are therefore stewards, not owners.

Text
DO NOT COVET ANYTHING THAT IS YOUR NEIGHBOR'S

We have cited in entirety the locus classicus of C-10: Aachen's deception, Nathan's vineyard, David and Bathsheba. To predatory desire, the animals killing for food, is now added inordinate desire. We will have it. Yet, even after we have it, we drop it. Mark locates this craving desire in a concise rehearsal of the Decalogue:

> And he called the people to him again, and said to them, "Hear me, all of you, and understand: there is nothing outside a man which by going into him can defile him; but the things which come out of a man are what defile him." And when he had entered the house, and left the people, his disciples asked him about the parable. And he said to them, then are you also without understanding? Do you not see that whatever goes into a man from the outside cannot defile him, since it enters, not his heart but his stomach, and so passes on?" (Thus he declared all foods clean.) And he said, "What comes out of a man is what defiles a man. For from within, out of the heart of man, come evil thoughts, fornication, theft, murder, adultery, coveting, wickedness, deceit, licentiousness, envy, slander, pride, foolishness. All these evil things come from within, and they defile a man."
> Mark 7: 14-23

The heart that does not covet something of another's will not lie, rob, kill or otherwise harm him. The human yearning and desire called coveting is rooted in the primal condition of humans who know of the tree of life and death but are denied access to it. This primal craving for immortality is the spring of all penultimate covetousness. Lucy cries out her longing to Charlie Brown in "Peanuts," "I want more, and more, and more..."

Although Jesus locates sin in the desire and action (Matthew 5), the rabbis, often in the spirit of Micah 2: 2, conclude that desire is inevitable and that sin comes only when the object is taken. When President Carter confessed to "lust in his heart" without ever acting that desire out as adultery, we still consider him a good man. In some way the desire is constant, but repressible. The great monastic and pietistic traditions at this point extol the virtue of suppressing or sublimating one's desires.

The biblical pathway of C-10 is intriguing with some twists.

- Proverbs 21: 26—The persistent nature of the impulse
- Acts 20: 33—The test of Apostolic devotion "I coveted no man's silver or gold"

- I Corinthian 12: 31—Covet the higher gifts. The energy directed to unobtainable objects should be relocated in spirit life and those gifts.

Tradition

Luther said that this command was not directed to "the rogues of the world" but to the powerful and pious, those who think they have followed all preceding commandments. Building on Rabbinic teaching, Luther said that breaking the last one meant breaking them all. C-10 is therefore an affirmation protecting the vulnerable—the world is the possession of the poor, they shall inherit the earth. Until that final shakedown, forecast by Isaiah, the wealthy and powerful will take the world's inheritance to themselves and concentrate it with the few.

Successful coveting, accumulating and hoarding the goods of the world perpetually incites the covetous impulse in everyone else. The miracle, in rabbinic wisdom, occurs when one breaks the cycle. In keeping this one commandment one keeps all.

When Schindler finally departs from the Jewish friends he has saved from genocide and kept working in his factories, they melt down the gold of their teeth and smelt a ring with the words, "Having saved one—you saved the whole world." The righteous gentile who rightly performs the one command, performs all.

We only rip off one another when we have distanced and dehumanized them, when we have removed them from the orbit of our family or neighborhood. The haunting implication of C-10 is that the neighbor in Jesus' midrash in Luke 10: 25-37 is the merciful Samaritan. The family of God is one's own family yes and the neighborhood and tribe—yes, but it also embraces the other, the alien, the Samaritan. Calvin comments at the end of his exposition on the coveting command.

> 'Who is my neighbor?' 'The more closely human beings are bound together by the ties of kinship, of acquaintanceship, or of neighborhood, the more responsibilities for one another they share...But I say: we ought to embrace the whole human race without exception in a single feeling of love...whatever the character of the human being, we must love him or her because we love God.'[160]

Proverbs summarizes:

> The wicked covet, the righteous give, and do not hold back.

---

[160] Calvin's Commentaries.

Bucer gives a twist to this commandment in his catechism of 1537. When we love God sufficiently, he says, we know that we have everything in Christ, we therefore need nothing more (p.86).

All is in Christ…God's dear Son of Lord of all.

Commandments 8-10 in Islam

Seizure, piracy and *Landnahmen* (expropriation of territory) are implicit in the war of and against terrorism. Taliban wait at crossroads and seize parcels and belongings. They kidnap and kill Mr. Daniel Pearl, the reporter. Kidnapping is the central biblical meaning of the Eighth Command. The grand exploits of colonialism—first that of the Ottomans, then that of Europe and the West lie behind the war on terrorism. The sins of exploitation and expropriation are the sins of the final set of commandments in the Holy tableau. Stealing, deceiving and coveting are misdirected desire where persons and peoples fail to honor the property and possessions of one another. The craving of cheap oil to fuel the intemperate ambitions of the West has been a grave violation of the resources of others. The primal crime in the Gulf War is now recognized to be the American and the West's grasping envy of Gulf Oil and Kuwait's siphoning off of the oil field lying underneath Iraq and Kuwait.

The seizure of the country of Afghanistan by the Taliban was reprehensible as was the preceding ambition of the Soviet Union. The cumulative effect of little deceptions, envies, covetings and seizures has created a fabric of malice and danger. The gun-running, drug trafficking, money-laundering and credentials—falsifying on all sides of the conflict has created a milieu of inhumanity and destruction. The betrayal, assassination, undermining of respect, war-lording and other violence has created an atmosphere where war and terrorism thrives and forgiveness and peace shrivels. Only a new day of equanimity and mutual affirmation can restore shalom to a war torn, rubble-strewn land like Afghanistan. In my comments after 9/11 I argued for a peace-corps to rebuild homes, clothe the naked, feed the hungry, heal the sick, educate the searchers, supply the needy. In shocked patriotic America, that didn't preach.

Theology

The theology of C-10 recapitulates the theology of C-1: "no other gods." We are to desire none other than our rightful sovereign. We belong, claims all faith, from Horeb to Heidelberg, from Beersheba to Barmen, to the only God, our Savior. We who have been delivered in Exodus and Easter owe devotion and allegiance only to God. We are given to our neighbors in service not seduction. The ascetic and frugal posture is incumbent in belief so that we do not crave the things of others nor do we in ostentation tempt envy in others. As Paul says to the elders at Ephesus, I coveted no one's silver, gold or approval; rather, I sought to minister to the weak. When we lust after houses, cars, stereos, wives, or success or accomplishment in others, we attach our being to that yearning and distort ourselves. Attachments make us different persons, less than free. Jesus is fully in the Qumran and Prophetic tradition when he claims that in possessing we are ourselves possessed.

The world economic structure is bent on incessant craving and covetousness. Modern economic life is structured on ever-enlarging markets for goods. Achieving market share means either enlarging consumer desire for new things—covetousness—or taking from those who presently have it—stealing. The best modern economists have warned that this hegemonic impulse will not only destroy peoples but our natural world and happiness itself. We must resign ourselves to some more steady and equilibrium state between resources and demands. Greed, which is the incessant demand for something more from someone else, has made the world a wasteland. Economic inequity, disparity and injustice has filled the world with theft and murder.

The personal and public manifestations of the sin of covetousness fill the world with wreckage and unsatiated desire.

"What do you give the man who has everything?" When Marshall Field's announces its Christmas catalogue, it includes a few exotic items for the man who has everything: A gold-plated toothpick case, your personal camel. The biblical doctrine of sufficiency transmutes covetousness into contentment, striving into service. Such transformation is grace.

> My grace is sufficient for you...my power is perfected in weakness.
> (2 Corinthians 12: 9)

The incomplete self is never satiated. The eucharistic self is satisfied. Keeping up with the Joneses has brought down many a family of Smiths. When the eye of contentment constantly scans the horizon for what others have, there is always something more that is needed. The consumer is one with perpetually unfulfilled needs. The advertiser must create needs from natural wants. Through explicit and subliminal advertising, we are constantly exposed to fresh needs. With noses pressed against the windows of the candy stores of life, our dreams are haunted by how we can get what we want.

Excursus

Want and desire animates the entire template of violation. They also hold the impulses of creativity and faithfulness. To create this good we must betray desire not only to disregard others but to succeed. The channeling of desire within this matrix of decalogue is to take it away from indulgence and place it along the pathways of goodness and justice. The apostle Paul exhibited enormous energy for the kingdom only after the destructive power of Saul was reclaimed by the risen Messiah.

The Hippolyte Baptism Ritual

As the apostolic age is enacted and the spirited Gospel catches fire throughout the Roman Empire, the substance and structure of Decalogue and

Lord's Prayer come to intertwine in the catechetical work and the nascent creed as persons are brought into the kingdom of Christ. By the second century, we have evidence that the lengthy process of preparing inquirers for baptism involves an intense process of examination and fortification, especially against idolatry and immortality in the surrounding culture. This iconoclastic cleansing venture is accomplished by means of Decalogue meditation. The Holy Spirit applies apostolic preaching to set people right with God. Freed to righteousness in the exuberant spirit of Christ, we are set on the life course of recompense and thanksgiving which is the spirit of Torah. We also now sense an urgent mood of armament against persecution and for kingdom battle. Only as comforted (strengthened) was one ready to affirm faith in God: Father, Son and Spirit. A holy commission and crusade is taking hold that will seek to transform the world into Messiah's kingdom.

Hippolytus of Rome (d. 235 CE) wrote the treatise *The Apostolic Tradition* in which he describes the process of coming to faith in God in the earliest church. It is 100 years after his predecessor, Clement of Rome, and a long tradition of believer formation has already transpired. Those who decided to come toward faith were interviewed with their sponsor. The first question asked was whether they were capable hearing the word. The focus was not so much on motive as on life-style. Did one have a mistress? Were slaves trying to please their masters? Did they work in city hallor theatre management (certain disqualifications)? Chapters 15-21 of the *Apostolic Tradition* seem to focus the issue of competence to be auditors toward faith on the seekers' rejection of the whole apparatus of paganism, its idolatry, immorality, violence and impurity. The scrutiny and cleansing of this first movement of faith must have been an exercise grounded in the Decalogue and the commandment of Christ.

When persons were accepted as catechumens, they listened to "the word" for three years. They were then admitted to the first part of the eucharistic liturgy and to the daily morning service of readings, instruction and prayer. At the end of the three-year probation period, they were examined as to their "worthiness" for baptism:

> Have they honored the widows, visited the sick…done every good work
> (Apostolic Tradition, 20).

The "law of Christ" (Galatians 6:2) and "pure and undefiled religion" (James 1:27) now has assumed the features of alymossary ministry which is extracted from various versions of Decalogue justice (e.g., Leviticus 19; Matthew 25) wherein being "right with God" is to care for the widow and orphan, the poor and the sick. "What does the Lord require of you: do justice, love mercy, walk humbly… (Micah 6:8)."

Conclusion

We have traced the contours of an ethical theology or a theological ethic, guided as biblical religion always has been by the Decalogue. We have not been able to stay in bounds and have spilled over into our next study, a eucharistical theology, as we have seen the connection between catechesis and communion. In Jewish tradition we have learned that Decalogue is joined with Shema in covenant worship. In Christian tradition, especially in moments of demoralization of the people like sixteenth century Europe, Decalogue precedes Eucharist as preparation for communion. A closer look at Rabbinic and Roman Catholic catechesis and communion, even in non-crisis times, shows the close connection of ethics and Eucharist.

Law takes measure of our sin. It is therefore also related to prayer and creed to which we now turn. Sin as transgression of God's will and Word is implicated in matters of health and life and suffering and death, which will be the thematic focus of Part III. We have explored certain meanings of law and ethics. Our thesis has been the salutary and redeeming function of law within faith. This approach betrays my own reliance on the traditions of biblical theology, hermeneutics and Judaic studies in recent theological work. My teacher Geza Vermes in Oxford, his associate E. P. Sanders and my colleague Dominic Crossan in Chicago have pioneered recent Jesus studies that show the ethical and political element in his words, acts and ministry. I side with their project of showing the essential Hebraic dimensions of Christology. I also affirm the project, of several decades, which has sought to dehellenize and rejudaize our understanding of the Christian heritage.

In this work I have also affirmed the Bonhoeffer tradition in his Decalogue studies, where he celebrates the concrete focus of Christian ethics derived from Torah. The rabbinic tradition is rightly impatient with overly generalized or spiritualized ethics: "do justice", "love your neighb or." I have not delved into the more complicated question of how specified and elaborated Torah must become before it becomes knit-picking casuistry seeking to trap and condemn rather than liberate. Jesus obviously rejected the trivialization of the law into endless exceptions and cases. Where the spirit of God is present vivid, compelling and concrete law for life is present. The 613 commandments, including Kosher laws and ceremonial practices need to be revised in the light of modern experience. But the fabric of ethical responsibility, the tapestry of Decalogue colors that show evils to be shunned and goods to be sought, remains valid.

Historically, I have sought to express the ethical genius of that moment in the continental Reformation when Martin Bucer and John Calvin meet and collaborate in Strasbourg. Working on sabbatical (a good Decalogic practice) in this wonderful university-city, has afforded me the opportunity to consult Luther, Bucer and Calvin scholars and trace the footsteps of these forerunners in faith at this momentous period: 1538-1541. What I have hoped to show is that here is a fascinatingly creative period where theology and ethics enjoy a renaissance of personal, ecclesial and public vitality. We need to discover this foundational sociological genius of Protestant culture, rejoin it firmly to

Judaism, Roman Catholicism and the resurgent world faiths, and fashion an ethos for our contemporary world that can deal more adequately with public issues like war and peace, crime and punishment, pleasure and sexuality, work and leisure, environment and habitat, men, women and children.

The issues that confront our world with lethal threat—climate change, water and air pollution; conflicts like Bosnia, Rwanda, Israel and Ireland; the deterioration of cities; the fading life-prospects of the poor, especially women and children; the endangering of the black male in America; sexual freedom and diversification; abortion and euthanasia; corporate greed and dishonesty; economic competition and international development—all these compelling ethical issues cry out for some fabric of ethical commitment, some synthetic theistic/humanistic moral wisdom.

I have devoted this study to the theoretical and cultural ethos that can help us fathom and concretely address such issues. The issues themselves have been sparingly treated since these depend on local action, specialization studies, e.g. bioethics, business ethics, and governmental and trans-governmental action. I place much of my hope for ethical renewal in our challenging world in structures like the United Nations, international Human Rights agencies, the Ecumenical and World Congress of Religious movements and the like. The ground of my hope is the parishes and congregations. I also place high expectations on the leaders of international technology, internet, international business, science, technology and the professions to lead the way.

The Deuteronomist holds before us two ways, life and death, and with the Decalogue cries,

> "Choose life!"
> (Deuteronomy 30:1)

> Jesus says, "I come to bring life, and that in abundance."
> (John 10:10)

Part III. Worship: Liturgy, Pastoral and Health Care

When I changed my career from bioethics to theology, my fascination with Judaism caused me to find in fundamental Christian theology a missing metaphor satisfied by Akedah. In ethics an evasion causing a particularly Christian amorality was redirected in the Decalogue. My growing appreciation of Islam confirmed in my mind that Christianity had ignored an essential Semitic dimension of its heritage. As I turned to pastoral and shephardic themes, including my familiar fare—Biotheology and Bioethics—I became aware of how dependent Christians were on Jewish prayer—that cache of disciplines where we lift anguish, petition and hope before the answering powers of transcendence. From the theoretical objectives and ambitions of science and medicine to the technical programs of health care, even specific ministries of birthing, living, and dying, a Judaic vision and value scheme is felt. We now turn to the prayer of the Rabbi Jesus, which is the expression of Jewish faith and life, which through Christian voice and Muslim appreciation now surrounds the world.

> Eternal Spirit,
> Earthmaker, Pain-bearer, Life-giver,
> Source of all that is and that shall be,
> Father and Mother of us all,
> Loving God, in whom is heaven:
> The hallowing of your name echo through the universe!
> The way of your justice be followed by the peoples of the world!
> Your heavenly will be done by all created beings!
> Your commonwealth of peace and freedom
> sustain our hope and come on earth.
> With the bread we need for today, feed us.
> In the hurts we absorb from one another, forgive us.
> In times of temptation and test, strengthen us.
> From trials too great to endure, spare us.
> From the grip of all that is evil, free us.
> For your reign in the glory of the power that is love,
> now and forever. Amen.
> **Maori Lord's Prayer**
> From the *New Zealand Book of Common Prayer*

The last time I taught "The Lord's Prayer" one of my students offered her testimony to this version of the prayer.

> The richly evocative, inclusive Maori Lord's Prayer speaks to me clearly. It is a comprehensive theology about who God is, what God gives us, and what God calls us to. God is creator of all, Mother/Father who gives us life. God as Son bears all pain. God as eternal indwelling Spirit calls us to justice. We are to bring about God's commonwealth, make a heaven here on earth. God's power is love, not mere might that makes right. God is neither dictator nor arbitrary dispenser of wrath. For the Maori, and for me, there is "a cross in the heart of God."

292

Introduction

It is the drama of life and death in six movements. Written in the last months of his life after the unsettling death of his friend Beethoven, the young composer was thirty years old. These last months of Franz Schubert's life would produce the song cycles *Schwanengesang* and *Die Winterreise*, The Mass in E Flat Major, and this masterpiece, the C Major String Quintet. "It is the story of our life," said the young father of three who played the viola that night. "The turmoil, the dissonance, the conflict, then the peace and resolution. It's all there!" How like the Book of Romans, I thought, as the quintet performed at the home of my colleague, Pauline scholar, Bob Jewett. Bob's life labor has been to fathom again that salient epistle. The quintet was so like the other masterwork I found myself pondering—"The Lord's Prayer". The noble ascription, the undergirding *cantus firma* of two cellos, the plaintive plea, the gentle and violent surges of joy and sorrow, the solemn and victorious climax.

"The Lord's Prayer" begins by announcing the ground that alone can secure and safeguard our existence. "Our Father—who art in heaven—holy be your name..." Rightful worship always begins by positioning our sin within God's goodness, our corruption, within God's holiness, our temporal death within God's eternal life. Human existence, faithful to *Torah* and *imitatio Christou,* positions our weakness within God's strength. Our rightful ground of being established by the Lord's Prayer affirms that we are to be conduits of divine grace toward the need of the world. We bring the there here. "Thy Kingdom come—thy will be done—on earth, as in heaven...." The prayer continues with what may have originally been *petitio/obligatio* couplets as captured in the Maori version and parallel ancient Jewish texts.

Give us our bread	As we feed others
Forgive our sins	As we forgive others
Save us from temptation	As we refrain from tempting others
Deliver us from evil	As we not mislead others

The prayer finally comes full circle to the all-ingathering ascription of praise to the one who makes all living and dying possible:

For you are Kingdom, Power, Glory, for all Eternity.

Franz Schubert has strains for the most "subtle thoughts and feelings, the tones and color of existence," "the events and conditions of Life...," wrote Robert Schumann. Schubert died at 31, a young man like his Lord. His was a comprehensive Catholic faith. Like *The Vaterunser*, he knew all the moods and tones of existence. "No composer," wrote Arthur Schnabel, "was so close to God."

The first part of our comprehensive Systematic Theology explored a Leitmotiv for a re-Judaized Christian faith. It was about our need, God's action, and our response. The second part, an Ethical Theology, focused on life-style tempered by Torah and Decalogue—Jesus' moral charter. Now, we move, from ethos to pathos, from *Aufgabe* to *Gabe*, from tasks of life to thanksgiving in and for life. Then, religious salience of our life was shaped by faith amid temptation and the moral atmosphere of our life was captured in the Decalogue—the ten God words. Now the dramatic ambience of our life is captured in the Kuriologue— The Lord's Prayer—seven Jesus requests. This paradigm text of expectant plea embraces the pathos of human existence— its joy and delight—its agony and its end. These are matters of prayer and work, *ora et labora*, liturgy and Eucharist.

The particular take I propose on the Lord's Prayer is to scan the arch of human existence with its pathos and ethos. We will stop at four points on the arch where we find binding touchstones.

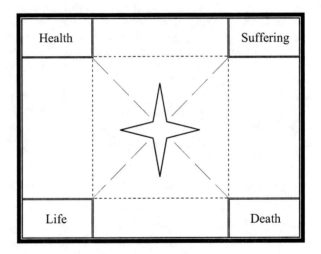

Health		Suffering
Life		Death

Building on the findings of our ethical theology, the panorama of divine requirement, I now offer a Eucharistic Theology, the panoply of human response to the law and grace of life. For Karl Barth the interpretation of the Lord's Prayer was the culmination of his uncompleted Systematic Theology. In that spirit, this elaboration of a theology of human existence is offered on the architecture of the Lord's Prayer. The question, "What we ought to be and do?" now becomes "How do we get there?" or "How ought we to pray?" This is *Leitourgia*—the offering of our common life. Speaking of the creed, code and prayer Luther would say: "We have learned what to believe and what to do. Now we need the strength to perform both: so we pray."

On close observation the Lord's Prayer is inextricably linked to Judaism through to the moral life—the Decalogue, and the Sermon on the Mount. Recall the sequence in Matthew 5—The Sermon on the Mount:

Be ye perfect...
When you fast or offer alms (works)...
When you pray...

The ethical is prelude to the eucharistical. This conjunction is perhaps most clear in the gospel of Thomas (6:1 and 14), that text so steeped in Jerusalem Jewish-Christian and Syriac flavor where law and Gospel blend:

His followers asked Him and said to him,
Do you want us to fast?
How should we pray?
Should we give to beggars?
Must we observe the (kosher) diet?

Jesus said to them:

If you fast you will bring sin on yourselves
If you pray, you will be condemned
If you give to charity, you will wound your souls.
When you go in to any region and people entertain you,
eat the food they offer and heal the sick among them.
What comes out doesn't defile. It's what goes in.
(My translation: Gospel of Thomas)

This enigmatic answer, echoed in the Synoptic Gospels (Matthew 9, Luke 10, and Mark 6), shows the radical character of the prayer and its link with life and death issues.

The Metzger Greek text of the New Testament in Matthew 5 and 6 shows this movement in its headings. After the wilderness temptations of Jesus to display power over life, bread and kingdom (the perennial moral temptations) we have:

The Beatitudes [What is the good (blessed)] life?	5:3-10
Salt and light	13-16
Teaching about law	17-20
Teaching about anger	21-26
Teaching about adultery	27-30
Teaching about divorce	31-32
Teaching about oaths	33-37
Teaching about retaliation	38-42
Love for enemies	43-48

Teaching about almsgiving	6:1-4
Teaching about prayer(includes Lord's Prayer)	5-14
Teaching about fasting	16-18

When *obligatio* and *petitio* are thus joined, eucharistical theology is **pastoral**; it speaks to the themes of solitude, suffering, dying, and courage in living. It is **commensal** having to do with survival, hunger, starvation, food, sustenance, and the Lord's meal. It is **existential** dealing with the anxieties, temptations, and comforts of life. A Eucharistical Theology is both **global** and **eternal**, linking the supplicant with all people throughout all time. Our Father...**forever**! As with the Decalogue, which is the child's utterance of devotion (How I will live?), the Lord's Prayer is the child's plea for help—a trustful song.

The Lord's Prayer is the perfect formulary about who we are, on this particular planet of life, given by the One who sets that world in process in expressed purpose. Its genius is extolled by Karl Barth:

> How shall we pray? It was not by chance that Jesus gave us a formulary in the Lord's Prayer to instruct men how to pray aright. God himself teaches us how we are to pray, for we have so many things to ask! And we think that what we desire is always so important! Besides, it is necessary for us to believe this. But in order that our act may become true prayer, we must accept the offer that God tenders us. We cannot pray by ourselves, and if we have deceptions in prayer, we must accept God's showing us the way of true prayer. He therefore starts us, with all our needs and problems, on a certain path by which we can bring everything to him; but we must take that path. This discipline is necessary for us. If it is absent, we must not be surprised that we cry out in a void, instead of finding ourselves engaged in a prayer that has already been heard.[161]

My son, a linguistics professor at Harvard, tells me that the Lord's Prayer, the prayer that spans the planet, is the universal tool of linguists, being the most ubiquitous text in the world. These few phrases are translated into more languages than any other extant text. As a written and oral document, it comprehends the divine nature and the human drama. Scholars and saints have read the prayer as social manifesto and spiritual compendium. Tolstoy called it the "Gospel in Brief."

In full concord with this early Christian tradition, especially the Paschal and Judaic tone and tenor of devotion, is the Islamic tradition of worship and prayers focused in the six pillars: *Salat* (worship and prayers); *Shahada* (oneness and mission of God); *Zakat* (philanthropy); *Saway* (Ramadan month of fasting, includes care for the poor-akedic sacrifice); *Hajj* (tax on income); pilgrimage to Mecca; *Jihad* (inner striving of thought and action). Theology is life and action, prayer is work.

---

[161] Karl Barth, *Prayer* (Westminster: Philadelphia, 1951), p. 25. *Jew, Christian and Muslim.*

Muslim Worship

In worship Muslims enter "the pavilion of light" which is their understanding of ritual rendezvous with God (Kenneth Cragg). In the vivid imagery of The Arabian Nights this transport dispels the realm of Satan into the light of angels where "...four ropes descend" with rescuing angels glorifying God—transposing the one in peril into forgiveness and the light of divine presence. Kenneth Cragg in his The Dome and the Rock (London: SPCK, 1964) call them the ropes of duty, protection, merit and communion. In splendid continuity with the commandments, prayer, provision and protection, the shield and salvation of pastoral care is bestowed on the faithful.

For Luther, who trembled at the spectre of Souleyman the Magnificent at the gates of Vienna, the Theology of Creation and redemption, sanctification and justification, saw all bound together in the prayer.[162] *Paternoster* is pivotal to Christian faith from the very onset. "It is Martin Luther that makes it the cornerstone of the theological construction." With these words Albrecht Peters begins an important new study of the "Lord's Prayer" in the context of Luther's Theology. Luther first undergirds his understanding of theology via *Vaterunser* with the premise that God is far away in heaven and we are way down here on earth. The distance *(widerspannung)* is enormous: *"Ach Vater Du bist im Himmel, Dein elend kind, auf Erden, in Elend weit von Dir"* (WA [*Weimarer Ausgabe*] 2:83, 30). Yet there is a child-to-father intimacy across the infinite Kierkegaardian chasm. This is not the message, "ET call home," across the vast universes of space, but the paradox of someone vastly different and distant, yet near as breath and dear as Mom. *"Du"* is a whispered closeness to one ever so near.

A second starting premise for Luther is that prayer must follow commandments and creed because we cannot perfectly keep the commands and we have only begun to believe. Prayer, in the Lord's mode, is the ratification of the will to follow and believe. Prayer fulfills the second (Luther) command to "not lightly dismiss or ignore the name of God but to call on that name." Prayer is the resourcing of our life - especially in trouble! In the large catechism (LC), Luther says that we should be incited and excited to pray, for God says:

"Call upon me in the day of trouble. I will deliver you"
(Psalm 50:15).

"Ask and it will be given you"
(Matthew 7:7).

The words of God, conveyed in that ever-near presence and command, convince and evince our response in godly behavior, belief and trust. Power is mediated in

---

[162] Albrecht Peters, *Kommentar zu Luthers Katechismen, Band 3, Das Vaterunser* (Gottingen: Vanderhoect & Ruprecht, 1992).

the same way that *memra* or that shimmering presence in The Ark (*Shekinah*) required response. You could try to box it up or run away from it (Psalm 139), but that love searches us out to the edge of the universe. God "pities our distress." In Luther and in the broader literature of "Theology of The Cross," the weakness, sadness, vulnerability and calamity (*Not und tragen*) of our lives is the occasion of God's grace. Not only are we more accessible to God in emergency and crisis, the crucified God is more accessible to us. Prayer is the conduit of that access. In *Vaterunser* we open our lives to the depths of God (*Theozentrische Tiefe*) and find in the depths of our own care (*Not*), the "*Not Gottes unter uns.*" The crucis of God undergirds our excruciation. God is compassioner (co-sufferer).

The structure of *vaterunser* is like the Decalogue, a section about God, then one about us. Luther calls the two sections the

"*Dein - Bitten*" — your name, your kingdom, your will...and the
"*Unser-bitten*" — our bread, our sins, lead us not, deliver us...

The deep theological cosmology inherent in the prayer is that God's kingdom of peace, order, health, justice and life arises over against the powers of chaos and evil (*chaosmächte, Satan, welt, fleisch*).

As Calvin would contend, after Luther, only *ecclesia*—only the church at work in the world (*ora et labora*) brings that cohering, sustaining cosmos to what otherwise would be overwhelming chaos. Prayer is thus closely related to politics (work), since that order also provisionally holds the world together.

Our invoking prayer invites this new reality. Jesus and the disciples brought a simple power to the houses and villages of Galilee and Judea: bread, healing, forgiveness, and peace. *Vaterunser* rehearses that primitive *Kerygma*. God's *Feste Burg* (strong fortress) staunchly defends our assaulted life from "*alt bösen Feindes*" (the old evil fiends ["ancient foe"]). The prayer is a simple kindergarten lesson for children, since only such can perceive the kingdom (Mark 10:13-16).

Our particular construal of the Lord's Prayer is taken from Luther and the reformers appropriation of it, especially in Luther's smaller and larger catechism. In the important Commentary on the Catechism, Albrecht Peters seizes on Luther's own rubrics to discuss the meaning of the Lord's Prayer. One of the central purposes Luther writes in the materials on the larger catechism is,

"...The Lord's prayer as Godly leading to fathom our misery (*not*)"
[LC 667:8].

The rich meanings of the German word "*Not*" are central to our exposition of the Lord's Prayer as Eucharistical Theology. "*Not*" means our crisis situation, our need, our misery (*le misere*), and our emergency. In Luther's sermon of October 12, 1516, his first recorded statement on the Lord's Prayer, he pleads

> *"Oratio Dominica, qua plenissime continent omnes tribulationes nostras et est cruce refortissima."*
> [WA 1.90.9]

Cyprian in the early church also prompted Luther to expound The Lord's Prayer in its succor to our abject weakness and anguish (*humiliationem et miseriam nostram*). Again *Vaterunser* was God's response to our *Elend und Dürftigkeit* (Fr. *dénoument, détresse, insuffiiance, indigence*). The forces and experiences of life that "bring us low," "cast us down," and crush our standing and dignity—sickness, shame, ostracism, neglect, disgrace—all are taken up in *Vaterunser* as they were taken up in Jesus' cross.163 [163]I will search out the Lord's Prayer as charter and succor in our life and death, health and suffering.

Within the Reformation heritage the particular construal of the prayer that I choose to guide this study is taken from my *Doktorvater*, Helmut Thielicke. Thielicke spoke from the Lord's Prayer to the terrified congregations of Stuttgart, during the air raids of 1940-42, first at the ancient Church of the Hospitallers until it was leveled, then at the small auditorium of St. Matthew's parish. In such times the prayer, like the enfolding Eucharist, became for the living and dying the litany of the meaning of life and health, suffering and death. These themes and those particular interpretations of Luther and Calvin will guide this study. For Thielicke, the Lord's Prayer draws together the heart of God and aching human hearts, served by the one who offered each to the other.

> ...(our father) was actually and beyond all conjecture with us in the dark forest and that when we cried "Father, Father" we were not merely victims of the illusions of our own yearnings.

> And this is the point in our train of thought at which we clearly see the tremendous importance that is to be attributed to the fact that it is *Jesus Christ himself who teaches us to pray the Lord's Prayer*. Remarkably enough, in this prayer he himself retires into the background. And time and again it has been concluded from this that Jesus himself had no intention whatsoever of being the "Son of God," but wished only to reveal the Father more clearly while he himself remained unrecognized in the background, like an unknown prophet, or at most was present in the way that medieval painters included their self-portraits somewhere in the background of their pictures.

> But now, suddenly we realize that it is fatefully significant that *he* is the one from whom we received this holy prayer of all Christendom. He is the invisible background of every one of its petitions. All of them are nothing less than geometrical loci that meet in him, even though he himself is never mentioned.

---

[163] Albrecht Peters, *Kommentar zu Luthers Katechismen* (Band 3: *Das Vaterunser*, Gottingen, Vanderhoeck & Ruprecht, 1992), p. 17.

For in him and in him alone did the miracle occur. In him and only in him was the one condition fulfilled of which we spoke: the miracle and the condition that the Father should have spoken to us first, that he actually has come to meet us in the dark forest. For this is the way the Bible views the appearance of Jesus. The prophetic vision sees him appearing against the dark background of night: darkness covers the earth and thick darkness the peoples. It is a world of pitilessness, of persecution, of loneliness, of anxiety, a world in which God is far away. Not because this is the way God made the world, but rather because a rift runs right through it and the weight of guilt hangs heavy upon it. Over all the world there reigns a night so dark that hope seems quite impossible. This is the prophets', the Bible's picture of the world.

And here, against that background, we are given the news, no, not only the "news," it is actually *demonstrated* to us in the fact of "Jesus," that this hope nevertheless is there, miraculously and incomprehensibly there—and that the heart of a Father is beating for us.

Everything that this Jesus says, and what is more, everything he does is the reflection, *the reverberation of that heart.* Every one of his sayings is a pastoral, brotherly address. And this is what he says to us:

"You, my human brothers, live in a world of wounds and sickness and war, and I hear you complaining and quarreling with your Father and my Father. I hear what you are saying to him: How, O Father, if you do exist, how can you allow these things to happen? How can you allow cancer and multiple sclerosis and these endless rows of graves? You yourself made the blossoms—why do you blight them? Why should we believe that you are our Father? That's what you're saying, isn't it, my brothers?

"But look, don't you see that everything that torments you and makes you complain grieves my Father and your Father? Your sorrows are his sorrows; otherwise would I be standing here among you? He has sent me into the midst of your sorrows.

"Every wound I lay my healing hand upon has ached a thousand times in me; every demon I cast out has leered at me; I died the death that I myself defeated; I let my own body be torn and buried in the earth. Who among you suffers and I do not suffer with you? Who among you dies and I do not die with you? I am your comrade and brother in every pain, whatever your lot may be. Do you understand that? Then understand this too: He who sees me sees the Father, and he who sees me suffering with you sees the Father suffering. God suffers pain for you and with you; do you understand this?"164[164]

Beyond the transient delight of life the story of all living things is strife and sickness until we succumb through suffering to the terror of death and beyond to the mystery of God's peace. Franz Schubert lived in intense poverty and was

---

[164] Helmut Thielicke, *Our Heavenly Father* (New York: Harper and Bros., 1960), p. 22, 23.

afflicted with venereal disease most of the creative years of his abruptly short life (31). He wrote to a friend:

> picture to yourself a man whose health can never be reestablished... one whose brilliant hopes have come to nothing, to whom proffered love and friendship are but anguish...Each night when I go to sleep I hope never again to awaken, and every morning reopens the wounds of yesterday.[165]

Like the living and dying of his contemporaries, Beethoven, Mozart, and Salieri, Schubert fathomed the depths of the divinehuman drama as enunciated in the Lord's Prayer.

When Martin Luther begins his project of moral and spiritual renewal in Germany in the early sixteenth century, he frequently draws on the "Lord's Prayer" as an instrument to remoralize discouraged people and inspire life amid life's distress. In 1520 he writes a Brief Explanation of the Ten Commandments, The Creed and the Lord's Prayer. The Longer Catechism follows the same order in 1529, and so on throughout his career. The assumption of Christian history is reclaimed. Here is the nexus of eucharistical and pastoral strength amid life's vicissitudes.

Prayer and Modern People

Just as individual human beings find themselves on precarious pilgrimage through the thrills, terrors, and temptations of life, so collective people find themselves in exodus experience as they ask for continuing sustenance and companionship. The Jesus community to whom the liberation of Easter has been added to Exodus is a people living in an ethical, eucharistical, and eschatological salience. They are people on the way, animated by the spirit of their departed, yet strangely present *rebbe*, committed to holy, exemplary life (which provokes demonic fury in an evil-bound world); a people ecstatically bonded to a future kingdom whose savior they already know.

The dirge is a plea against adversity, enemies and want. The history of Israel from original slavery in Egypt to penultimal anguish in Aushwitz is a pilgrimage of travail. Trying to be righteous and faithful, failing through disregard for God's law and disdain for God's will, plagued by disease, political antagonism, and the ultimate assault of genocide, this representative people of all humanity, this chosen people, struggles on. Just as in the crucifixion of Jesus, the world at enmity with God sought to obliterate goodness from the world, so the crucifixion of the Jews is the perennial temptation to test whether God's kingdom will in fact prevail on earth. The Lord's Prayer is perfectly in keeping with Jewish piety. Christian theology and theodicy must remain perfectly concordant with Judaic thought.

---

[165] Milton Cross, Encyclopedia of the Great Composers and Their Music (New York: Doubleday, 1953), p. 682.

Approach

In this part of our study I wish to explore a range of questions about the human condition and human prospect — questions of human identity, illness, suffering and death juxtaposed with questions of human life, health, hope and happiness. I will call this constellation of considerations a eucharistical theology. The theological approach which I have offered in previous work holds that within the divine milieu human suffering holds redemptive meaning. Indeed suffering is the secret meaning of life in Christ. The crucifixion of Jesus and the crucifixion of the Jews, as this transfigures (condemns and redeems) all genocide and homicide, indeed the universal plight of the oppressed, is not absurd, but is the inevitable consequence of Godly health, and good life. This grace of life antagonizes the world so as to provoke disease, evil and death. "The light has come into the world...," "but the world sought to put it out" (Matthew 26, John 16). Now the cataclysmic crises of suffering, death and transfiguration constitute the drama of redemption.

> "You meant it for evil, God meant it for good"
> (Genesis 50:20).

Jewish Prayer at the Time of Jesus

A telephone call to St. Peter at the receptionist's desk in Heaven. He intercoms back to God, "It's Jerry Falwell and he wants to know if you hear the prayers of Jews, gays and atheists?" The Lord responds: "Tell Falwell to stick to politics and leave religion to me." This was a cartoon at the time of Jerry Falwell's statement that God doesn't hear the prayers of Jews, gays and atheists.

Jesus was an observant Jew. He was part of the regular *Simhat Torah*, the celebration of the law. He knew intimately the heart of the father and how God delighted in the prayers of his people. God knew and sympathized with the anguish of his children. As a prayer from Jesus' contemporaries at Qumram reflected:

> On the day of my distress
> I will call to Yahweh, and my God will answer me.
> (4Q 381.24. 7-8)

Prayer in Jesus' time reflected the full glory of temple worship in Jerusalem:

> How lovely is your dwelling place, O Lord of Hosts.
> My soul longs, indeed yearns for the courts of the Lord;
> My heart and flesh shout for joy to the living God.
> (Psalm 84:2-3)

Johannes Brahms incorporates this peon of praise into his great treatise on life and death, *Ein Deutsches Requiem*.

The common elements and experiences of life, as these were offered continually in prayer, became the elements of the Lord's Prayer: Praise to Abba, plea that the world would recognize his holiness, appeal for God's rule on earth, request for daily sustenance and mercy, request for guidance from disorienting and destructive temptation and evil. High temple and low table traditions are blended in prayer:

> Blessed art thou, Lord our God, King of the universe, who sustainest the whole world with goodness, kindness and mercy. Thou givest food to all creatures, for thy mercy endures forever.[166]

Three texts by the early seventeenth century English poet, George Herbert, reflect the celestial grandeur and common ground of the "Lord's Prayer" as it arises in the context of contemporary Jewish literature:

> Let all the world in ev'ry corner sing My God and King.
> The Heav'ns are not too high, His praise may thither fly;
> The earth is not too low, His praises there may grow.
> Let all the world in ev'ry corner sing My God and King.
> Prayer the Church's banquet...
> Exalted manna, gladness of the best, Heaven in ordinary, man well drest,
> The Milky Way, the bird of Paradise...
> The land of spices; something understood.
> (Oxford Dictionary of Quotations, p. 248ff.)
> Come, my joy, my love, my Heart:
> Such a joy, as none can move:
> Such a love, as none can part:
> Such a Heart, as joys in love.
> (Oxford Book of Prayer, p. 7)

The Radical Christology of the Lord's Prayer

The prayer is firmly rooted in Jewish precedents, ancient and contemporaneous. It is also a profoundly original and unique document. This uniqueness also verifies the particular emphasis this study places on the prayer—health and life, suffering and death.

The "Our Father" as presented by Luke is related to Jesus' committal of his life to God in suffering and death:

> Father, into your hands I commend my spirit (23:46).

For Luke, Jesus' suffering and death are "necessary." The Christ must suffer (24:26, 46). The destiny of Jesus according to the evangelists is to embody and bear the sins of the world, to offer the sacrifice required by that sin in God's justice and in resurrection to pronounce vindication of humanity before God. All

---

[166] D. Birnbaum, *Daily Prayer Book* (New York: Hebrew Publishing Co., 1977), p. 759-760.

Jesus' words are colored and interpreted by this underlying destiny. The "Lord's Prayer" arises out of this "necessity"..."Christ must suffer" (Acts 3:18).

What cast does this evangelical orientation give to the prayer? From address to ascription and from petition to petition it alludes to Jesus' harmatologic, salvific and eschatologic destiny - to save humanity from death-bound sin and to renew the fallen cosmos. The prayer is thus about the endurance of shame and guilt, of suffering and death in a fallen cosmos, and the enfolding of this crisis by the good shepherd. This disgrace and the continuing pull of temptation and evil has been ultimately (though not yet penultimately) overwhelmed in Christ by the grace of life and health (salvation).

The Lord's Prayer expressed therefore the full ultimacy and immediacy of the human spirit. Persons invoked the prayer as assurance against the powers of heaven and the terrors of earth. The history of the prayer, from its earliest usage in cryptic and incantational magic during the first century Roman Empire to its late twentieth century use by starving refugees from the South Sudan, witnesses to its universality and particularity; its sublime solemnity and its mundane practicality. From earliest times the prayer's eucharistical usage spans the life cycle from christening to perishing, the broad horizon of life's work.

The Lord's Prayer: Recent Biblical Insights of the Jesus Movement

The "Lord's Prayer" itself (Matthew 6) stemming from oral-aural proto-experience is "the oldest part of Gospel tradition."167[167] A "cultic didache" (again the connection with the ethical), it is an instruction to followers (and teachers) cognate to the genre of "commandment" (cf. Matthew 5), "cultic law", "cultic practice" and the genre of "piety." We may assume therefore, that Matthew's version of the "Lord's Prayer" emerges from a well-established community of practicing believers (Jewish Christians) reaching out to other Jewish converts in the period before and during Paul's mission to the Greeks (C. 50 c.e).

In both the Hellenic and Hebraic precedent, righteousness (*dikaiosuné*) was seen as a composite posture involving piety, integrity, and purity; the total disposition of being to believe, behave, and belong. The simple gifts of the heart of simple people (the widow's mite) is the optimal sacrifice of righteousness, perfect mimesis of God (Matt. 5:48). The instruction in almsgiving and its prelude to the sacrifice of prayer is instruction on a wholistic good life under God.

Literary Structure

Invocation
Main Body (2 sets of 3 petitions)

---

[167] H. D. Betz, *Sermon on the Mount: Hermenia* (Minneapolis: Fortress Press, 1995), p. 330.

Benediction (perhaps a later addition)

The first set has the character of reminder (*hypomnesis*). God's promises are the grounds for the boldness and brashness of reminding God. As if God needed reminding! God's righteousness is invoked and these petitions affirm God's needs.

> Hallowed be thy name
> Thy kingdom come
> Thy will be done on earth as in heaven

In Peter Schaefer's play *Amadeus* he juxtaposes the pedantic Salieri to the frivolous Mozart, the latter's playfulness being the vehicle for God to make his way into the world. This caused Karl Barth to reflect,

> "...God needed Mozart to get himself into the world"[168]

The architecture of the Lord's Prayer provides a lattice for the construction of this offering in eight stages. This is an unfolding development of the preceding concept. The structure and substance is like the Decalogue. Between an address and ascription we have six petitions; three depicting the drama of ultimacy and three the drama of humanity. The generic and universal truths of the prayer are noted alongside each particular petition.

A. LIFE
  I. Our Father, who art in heaven - - -   Stabulum
  II. Hallowed be thy name - - -   Sanctus

B. HEALTH
  III. Thy Kingdom come   Salus
  IV. Thy will be done on earth as in heaven   Semblance

C. SUFFERING
  V. Give us this day our daily bread   Sustenance
  VI. Forgive us our sins as we forgive those
      who sin against us   Satisfaction

D. DEATH
  VII. Lead us not into temptation, but deliver
      us from evil   Suffering
  VIII. For thine is the Kingdom, the power
      And glory forever   Serenity

Perspective

I have suggested that a Systematic Theology dealing with code and creed must also have the dimension of "cry" or "call." Indeed this link of human

---

[168] Karl Barth, *Church Dogmatics III,* pp. 337ff.

response is necessary to complete the chain. The pathos of the human condition has to be recognized as one explores what one ought to do and believe. If Schliermacher's division of Systematic Theology (*Glaubenslehre*) into thoughts of man, world, and God is valid, then, this volume focuses on the human condition. The text of the "Lord's Prayer" along with that of its paradigmatic precursor—the "Twenty Third Psalm"—is the masterpiece of the human soul at journey in this world among the challenges of life, in the company of others, in the presence of the One. A comprehensive theology is presumed, for the prayer assumes human beings within a world, under God.

My particular take on this rich and salient text is the way in which it illumines the human condition. Luther's reading is that humans are commended to the posture of prayer in order to honor God, to change reality in accord with the divine will and to sanctify the self. My own emphasis will be on the pathos of the human condition in sustenance and support, in suffering and deliverance. Humans are the point of intersection between God and world. Each of the phrases speaks of divine providence in response to a human plea. In composite, the prayer is a panorama of provision proving that most awesome fact: we are not alone.

I also anchor this study in Martin Luther's use of the *vaterunser* in his Shorter Catechism. The raw simplicity and power of this small text that Luther prepared for pastors, schoolmasters, and housefathers, retains the incisive strength of the "Lord's Prayer" far beyond any theological treatment. I am also indebted to a new, moving commentary on the *Vaterunser* in Luther's Catechisms by Albrecht Peters.[169]

Peters draws five purposes of the "Our Father" from Luther's own catechetical texts. They resonate with the pathway of interpretation that we are offering in this book:

> The "Lord's Prayer" as God's guidance in acknowledging the crisis of our situation.
> The "Lord's Prayer" as God's given pattern for our prayer.
> The "Lord's Prayer" as God's command and promise grounding certainty that He hears us.
> The "Lord's Prayer" as defense and offense against the evil one.
> The "Lord's Prayer" as help in praying.

The existential, spiritual, even physical dimensions of life are paramount in the Shorter Catechism (SC). Luther also links what we are calling command, creed and cry (his order). This is the charter of life and death.

---

[169] Albrecht Peters, *Kommentar zu Luther's Katechismen*, Band III *"Das Vaterunser,"* (Gottingen: Vandenhoeck & Ruprecht, 1992).

A. Life

We awaken to life. Fresh on delivery as light strikes the baby's eyes. There is the gasp for air (*nephesh*/life). There is the cry of hunger. We are cast unwittingly into life, as Heidigger says. As Hans Jonas has shown, life is the primal phenomenon, it defines existence. The first awareness is (ought to be) that we are held, that we belong. There is a voice, a soft breast, other eyes, a smile, a lilting sound we will come to know as a voice—mom or dad. Receiving and trusting life and light we can enter the darkness and sleep.

> I will lay me down to rest
> for it is you Lord who makes me dwell in safety.
> (Psalm 4:8)

Life is a movement. It can be outgoing, neutral and waiting, or retiring. In the presence of enfolding care a life ventures out. The mouth opens, the arms wave. Being exudes praise.

> ...yet while I have being my God I will praise...

Life is receptivity. It responds to presence. It acknowledges other. We are beings—*Homo Religiosis*—by raw nature other searching, dependent, open. There is no such thing as "life" says a wise man, Ivan Illich. We cast around the words "right to life," "sanctity of life," etc. Yet there is no such thing as the substantive life, Illich claims. There are living beings. But life does not exist. It takes part from the source that imparts. There is God. God is life. God alone is (*ho on*). We take being from God.

> ...In him was life and that life was the light...
> ...I have come that you might have life...
> ...I set before you life and death...choose life.
> ...In him we live and move and have our being...

I. Stabulum: A Safe Place to Come Home to...Our Father

> ...*arena shebashamiyim*...

> OUR FATHER

>> Father eternal, ruler of creation, spirit of life who moved e're form was made...

>>> Once in royal David's city stood a lowly cattle shed,
>>> Where a mother laid her baby in a manger for his bed:
>>> Mary was that mother mild, Jesus Christ her little child.

>>> He came down to earth from heaven, who is God and Lord of all,

> And his shelter was a stable, And his cradle was a stall:
> With the poor, and mean, and lowly,
> lived on earth our Savior holy.
>> Cecil Frances Alexander, 1848
>> The Hymnbook (Presbyterian), 1955

> When Israel was young, I loved him;
> I called my son out of Egypt;
> But the more I called them,
> the further they went from me.

> Yet it was I who taught Ephraim to walk,
> I who had taken him in my arms.
> But they did not know that I was their redeemer.
> I drew them with human cords,
> with strings of love.
> I was to them like one who lifts a little child close against the chin.

> I bent down and gave him to eat.
> (Jeremiah 11:1 ff.)

Background

> *Tu fecisti nos ad te, Domine, et inquietum est cor nostrum, donec requiescat in te.*
> (Augustine, Confessions Bk 1:1)

The ultimate seed-bed of life is God. Within that AKEDIC assertion, the saga of human existence is projected against or defined by a perceived and received backdrop of divine stability, boldly designated as loving father. Not a purposeless void, but a kindly heart is affirmed as the *cantus firma* of the universe. I use the word stability in its old Latin meaning of a stable (in french, *etabile*) cowstall, a restful home. The Greek word *Ethos* and the Latin *habitus* mean a home, an atmosphere to shape living and behaving. The fatherhood of God may be the most revolutionary idea yet to have crossed the human mind. It sets the world at ease, at comfort, in stability. It grounds the human sense of contentment and of belonging. It gives persons a sense of tender protective care, of provision of needs, of authority and guidance against the threats of uncertainty and misdirection. Israel's God is introduced to the people by prophets, psalmists and patriarchs as the perfect embodiment of parental love— paternal power and maternal nurture.

While Jesus as God's son intensifies the notion of God as father and the world's people as children and siblings, the innovation comes with Judaism. While the prayers of Hebrew scripture do not begin with '*Abh* or *Abhinu* (...Our Father), Israel's covenanting Lord is clearly introduced in this fatherly mode. This is not a stern and mean father but the ideal of firm support and direction. With the eighth century prophet Hosea, the dominant picture of God becomes neither the capricious sky God nor a judgmental heavenly tyrant. God is depicted as a loving, guiding father. This image is reinforced by the later prophets, Jeremiah and Isaiah:

> Is Ephraim my dear son,
> a child in whom I delight?
> As often as I threaten him,
> I remember him:
> my most inward parts are moved for him.
> I must have mercy, I must have mercy upon him.
> (Jeremiah 31:20 NRSV)

> From this holy and glorious dwelling!
> Look down from heaven and behold
> Where is your zeal and your strength,
> the moving of your inmost parts and your mercy?
> Stand not aloof!
> For you are our father.
> Abraham ignores us
> and Israel does not acknowledge us.
> You, Yahweh, are our father,
> "Our redeemer" is your name from of old!
> (Isaiah 63:15 ff. NRSV)

A ninth-century Jewish prayer, "Our Father, Our King," exhibits the full-orbed divine and human tradition behind the Lord's prayer. It expounds the unfolding liturgy of health and life amid suffering and death.

> *"Our Father, Our King"*
> A Later Version (Ninth Century)
> Our Father, our King, we have sinned before You.
> Our Father, our King, we have no King but You.
> Our Father, our King, deal with us for the sake of Your Name.
> Our Father, our King, nullify evil decrees from us.
> Our Father, our King, renew for us good decrees.
> Our Father, our King, nullify from us the designs of those who hate us.
> Our Father, our King, confound the counsel of our enemies.
> Our Father, our King, send perfect healing to the sick of Your people.
> Our Father, our King, prevent the plague Your people.
> Our Father, our King, of pestilence, sword, famine and destruction rid the partners of Your covenant.
> Our Father, our King, remember that we are but dust.
> Our Father, our King, do it for Your sake, and not for ours.
> Our Father, our King, rend from us the evil judgment decreed against us.
> Our Father, our King, erase the records of our guilt.
> Our Father, our King, pardon and forgive our iniquities.
> Our Father, our King, blot out our transgressions, and make them pass away from our sight.
> Our Father, our King, let us return in perfect repentance before You.
> Our Father, our King, inscribe us in the book of life.
> Our Father, our King, inscribe us in the book of remembrance.

Our Father, our King, inscribe us in the book of merits.
Our Father, our King, inscribe us in the book of maintenance and sustenance.
Our Father, our King, let salvation sprout for us soon.
Our Father, our King, hear our voice, pity us, and have mercy upon us.
Our Father, our King, accept our prayer in mercy and in favour.
Our Father, our King, do it for the sake of Your great Name.
Our Father, our King, do it for the sake of Your abundant mercies; and have compassion upon us.
Our Father, our King, be gracious unto us and answer us, for we have no good works to show.
Deal charitably and kindly with us, and save us.[170]

The primary text resonating from Christian Scripture is Galatians 4. "God sent his son...that we might receive adoption as sons...And because you are sons. God has sent the Spirit of his son into our hearts crying, '*Abba*,' 'Father.'" (4:6,7)

The "Our Father," "*Pater Noster*," "*Vaterunser*," is a prayer in continuity with Jewish tradition. It sustains the profound theological revolution of that people who broke with all- remote "sky god" and fertile "earth god," precursors to worship *Yaweh*—the "I am" who addressed, claimed and led his people in love. The "*Abba*" father is also strikingly unique. In an exhaustive study of this usage, Joachim Jeremias concludes that "'*Abba*'...remained in Jesus' time a familiar word with which no one would have dared to address God. No Jew ever called God '*Abba*'...yet, the evangelists record that Jesus always called God '*Abba*', 'My Father.'"[171]

The radical charter and revolutionary insight of Hebrew faith, confuting all natural senses of self-sufficiency and abandonment, is the parenthood of God and the kinship of all creatures. Hebrew prayer in the traditional continuity and radical discontinuity of the "Lord's Prayer" exudes praise and expects protection. No other strength can anchor life and assuage anxiety. As John Calvin wrote:

> Surely, with good reason the Heavenly Father affirms that the only stronghold of safety is in calling upon his name. By so doing we invoke the presence both of his providence, through which he watches over us and guards our affairs. And of his power, through which he sustains us, weak as we are and well-nigh overcome, and of his goodness, through which he receives us, miserably burdened with sins, unto grace.[172]

The idea of a heavenly king and father is one of the central convictions of Israel *Avinu, Malkenu* (Our Father, Our King) was uttered by Rabbi Akibu c. 100 C.E. at the Ark of the Synagogue as a plea to end an extended draught. The

---

[170] J. J. Petuchowski and M. Brocke, *The Lord's Prayer and Jewish Liturgy* (New York: Seabury/Crossroad, 1978), pp. 39-40.

[171] Joachim Jeremias, *The Prayers of Jesus* (London: SCM Press, 1967), p. 111.

[172] John Calvin, *Institutes of the Christian Religion,* ed. J.T. McNeill (Philadelphia: Westminster Press, 1960), v. 2, p.851 (III. 20, 2).

juxtaposition of king and father expresses the Jewish cry for both a ruler and a caring parent. Israel's faith believed *Yaweh* to be one who attended to our woes and could do something about them.[173] The centrality of the prayer to a Heavenly Father in Jesus' ministry is striking. Many of the parables, for example, "The Prodigal Son" (Luke 15:11-32), so accent the paternal-filial quality of God's love for us that Thielicke was led to entitle his sermons on these parables, The Waiting Father. A father who knows, forgives, cares, guides and offers expectations is consistent with the Jewish awareness of God. Special nuances in Jews' relation with "Our Father" are instructive:

Ask what you will, in seclusion—"When you pray close the door."
(Matthew 6:6)

"Which father, when asked for bread, will give his son a stone?"
(Matthew 7:9)

The mark of Jesus' family—"Whoever does the will of my Father...is brother and sister."
(Matthew 12:50)

Our life is to reflect glory on the Father—"glorify your Father in Heaven."
(Matthew 5:16)

He feeds the creatures of the world—(the omniprovider giver of life to the world."Yet your heavenly Father feeds them."
(Matthew 6:26)

He sees and knows all—The omniscient presence over all. "Not a sparrow falls to the ground without your Father's knowledge."
(Matthew 6:32)

"That day" is known only to the Father—of "that day" no man knows.
(Mark 13:32)

His forgiveness is to be emulated—"Be ye merciful as your Father."
(Luke 6:36)

The Father's delight in the child's good—"It is the Father's good pleasure to give."
(Luke 12:32)

---

[173] B. Tenn. 25 a Quoted in G Vermes *The Religion of Jesus the Jew* (Philadelphia: Fortress, 1994), p. 153.

Sin is cosmic (natural) and paternal—"Father I have sinned against Heaven and you."
(Luke 15:21)

The good life honors the Father—"Who honors the Son, honors the Father."
(John 5:19 ff.)

The works of the father are pattern to us—"The works that I do...you will do greater..."
(John 10:25)

The one you go to in agonal suffering—"Father, Let this cup pass from me."
(Mark 14:36)

The one to whom you can cry over injustice and desolation—"Why have you forsaken me?"
(Mark 15:34)

In death he yields up his life—"Father into your hands I commit my spirit."
(Luke 23:46)

Tradition

From the earliest Christian theology, the Lord's Prayer has played a crucial role in shaping faith and piety. Its role in theology, liturgy, and pastoral devotion has been central. For Tertullian the "Our Father" clause recalled the rigor of "no other gods" from the Decalogue.

We are trained by the "Lord's Prayer" to see God and ourselves (especially Fathers) in a new way. Ontology begets ontogeny. God, known as the Father of our Lord Jesus Christ, shapes our being toward caring parentalism. Even in times like ours of "bad fathers," this clause is not invalidated by poor earthly fathers nor is it a Freudian projection on an uncaring universe. It annunciates how life is meant to be by virtue of who God is.

I will never forget the eleven-year-old Solevecic lad. He was dying from an incurable brain tumor in our Medical Center. His father and grandfather, distinguished rabbis, (Grandfather Aaron was the expert on the Jewish understanding of "brain death") refused to accept death, contending for further treatment even if only to prolong life (or dying) a short while. The mother, also the daughter of a rabbi, pleaded (successfully before the civil, though not rabbinic court), that he be allowed to die. In this poignant case, we all learned anew the meaning of fatherly (motherly) care, human and divine.

Cyprian and Origen accent the Pauline configuration of fathers, children and family as the characteristics of the human and divine life world. The doctrine of adoption assumes parental care not only by virtue of generative obligation (*Imago Dei*) but by outgoing care, transcending obligation and desert. God has chosen us as his own children across the chasm separating eternity from space and time. Besides belonging, this doctrine grounds the value of the human brotherhood/sisterhood.[174]

For Augustine one among many ramifications of the "Lord's Prayer" is its service as a guide (along with the creed) to the nterpretation of the theological virtues of faith, hope and love.

> Since, through sin, the human race stood grievously burdened by great misery and in deep need of mercy, a prophet, preaching in the time of God's grace, said "And it shall be that we who invoke the Lord's name will be saved (Joel 2:32).[175]

Augustine then adds the Pauline footnote, "How shall they call on one whom they have not heard or believed?" (Romans 10:14) A gracious encounter and visitation of God precedes the ability to pray. Luther sees the *vaterunser* as the invoked power by which we withstand the world, flesh and the devil, those powers that mitigate against trust in a loving father and lead us astray from our home. Luther's kindly reflections on God as father are all the more remarkable when we think of his brutal and coercive old father, Hans Luther, the Miner—Bureaucrat.

> "Our whole protection and defense lies in prayer alone"
> (LC, p.113).

For Luther, Bucer, Calvin and the reformers it was vitally important to place in the heart, mouth and memory the words of the Prayer, Decalogue and Creed as that powerful assertion of word against all the adversarial evil of the world. We must be able to draw automatically in life crises on this comfort.

> "One little word shall fell him..."
> (*festeburg*)

Calvin also expresses the honor and glory (C-1, C-3) bestowed on us to be called children of God with the privilege of praying in Jesus' name to God our Father. In a moving passage in The Institutes he writes:

> ...By the great sweetness of this name he frees us from all distrust, since no greater feeling of love can be found elsewhere than in Father.
> (Institutes LCC III, XX, 36)

---

[174] Cyprian, *On the Lord's Prayer* (Ch. 11). Origen, *On Prayer* (Ch. 22, 23), LCC.
[175] Augustine, *Enchiridion* (Ch. 2.7, LCC), p. 339.

Theology: A Parent in Life's Extremis

In fear and anguish we cry for a father. As Bosnia's children and families are separated and cleansed by the invading Serbs or as Jewish families were sacrificed at Buchenwald or as Palestinians watch their homes being crushed by Israeli bombs— humiliation often began with witnessed torture or murder of the father. In sickness we cling to mother who nursed us into life. When we die we call for mama.

> When Jesus approached his cross and death he cried, 'Abba, Father, all things are possible to you. Take this cup away from me: Yet not what I will, but what you will'
> (Mark 14:36)

The essence of stability is faith and trust. Jesus is gripped by terror as he feels the burden of dereliction, abandonment and the full disjunction of good and evil, God and world, created by humanity's collective sin. In mind, body and spirit Jesus vicariously endures the agony of physical pain, of dehydration and exsanguination, the waning of consciousness, the loss of the light, the disappearance of friends and all that is familiar in this dear world. "Abba, Father," he cries cosmic lament. "If it be possible"—"Yet not my will, but yours." Scare resolves into stasis—the father's home (John 14:2).

Christian theology holds that God allowed all of the world's suffering, and world's recalcitrance to God, to descend on Jesus and well up into his unjust execution. Jesus epitomizes Isaac, the sacrifice of the only begotten, beloved son (John 3:16). God, the Father, is willing to offer his son as was foreshadowed in Abraham's offering of Isaac to the sacrificial knife. While God does not remove the bitter cruelty of suffering death as Docetics and Gnostics assumed, He does not leave his son alone. The darkness and howling winds of Golgotha's mountain seem to envelop not only the son, but the eternal father. Golgotha answers the Holocaust historians' anguished question: "Why did the sky not darken?" (Arno Mayer).

Some recent feminist theologies reject the notion of God as a punishing father, a primitive sacrifice, who kills his own son and hangs him on a bloody cross. Such a vindictive infanticidal God, it is held, is not worthy of worship. In my view this view distorts the crucifixion. The God of the "sacred head now wounded" is in humanistic and theistic purview good and right, just what we need. Bernard of Clairvaux (c.1150) and Paul Gerhardt (c.1650) capture in the great hymn the blessed love of this good for those whose own heart breaks in the crucifixion agony of his "only son." It would be more natural and fatherly to play macho protector, spare the beloved son, and blast the assailant to smithereens with some cosmic Rambo assault gun. But God "so loved that he gave..." (John 3:16). He offered his son who willingly offered himself.

> My father loves me because I lay down my life

314

That I might take it up again. No man takes it from me
I have power to lay it down, and raise it up again.
(John 10:18)

There is an important theological connection in feminist theology—even in the Sophia, mother God assertions of recent controversy or in Mary Baker Eddy's spiritual science a century ago. The stabilizing being of God which anchors our life is best depicted by the best human words for a welcome home—mother *and* father.

A Child's Plea: Dada?

In a provocative study, the New Testament scholar, Joachim Jeremias, claims that the Aramaic word "*ABBA*" is the authentic voice of Jesus. In dissonance with the Hebraic tradition of respect and the Hellenic traditions of nobility and courage, Jesus speaks with innocent familiarity.

> It was something new, something unique and unheard of, that Jesus dared to take this step and to speak with God as a child with his father, simply, intimately, securely.[176]

One might even add presumptively, the child assumes and presumes on the presence and support of "daddy." That he is there for me is natural and self-evident. Heidigger's being cast into a loveless world without asking to be, now becomes a deserving to be "Daddy is pleased with me." *Abba* was childish babble, like a baby's first blathering cry. To this day Irish men in pubs still refer to "*da*," their father. *ABBA* was also a mature assertion of intimacy with the father in knowledge and vacation. In Jesus, *ABBA* connotes the basis of his *Selbstbewusstsein* (self-consciousness) and *sendungsbewusstsein* (mission awareness). In knowing the father, we know where we come from and where we are going—we are generative. Jesus came to call sinners, not the righteous, to repentance (Mark 2:17). Our destiny is to care all of the world into the enfolding arms of "*ABBA*."

A Fatherly or Fatherless Universe

The Bible and the Jesus story present a picture often foreign to we who live in the twentieth century. The experience of modern peoples' relationship with God does not come as naturally or easily as it may have in the past. Consider three texts: one reflecting the synthetic Christian view of reality (Dante), another on an early modern thinker (Bertrand Russell) and the third a very recent postmodern position (modern cosmology).

As in Beethoven's "*Die Ehre Gottes auf der Natur*" or Haydn's "The Heavens Declare the Glory of God," in Dante's Divine Comedy, we receive a lyric description of a cosmos of fatherly coherence and purpose.

---

[176] Joachim Jeremias, *The Central Message of the New Testament.* (New York: , 1965), p. 20.

The All-Mover's glory penetrates through the universe, and regloweth in one region more, and less in another.

In that heaven which most receiveth of his light, have I been; and have seen things which whoso descendeth from up there hath nor knowledge nor power to re-tell;

Because, as it draweth nigh to its desire, our intellect sinketh so deep, that memory cannot go back upon the track.

Nathless, whatever of the holy realm I had the power to treasure in my memory, shall now be matter of my song...

Much is granted there which is not granted here to our powers, in virtue of the place made as proper to the human race...

All things whatsoever observe a mutual order; and this the form that maketh the universe like unto God...

Gazing upon his son with the love which the one and the other eternally breathes forth, the primal and ineffable Worth,

Made whatsoever circleth through mind or space with so great order that whoso looketh on it may not be without some taste of him...

O, light supreme, who so far dost uplift thee o'er mortal thought, re-lend unto my mind a little of what thou then didst seem,

And give my tongue such power that it may leave only a single spark of thy glory unto the folk to come;

I hold that by the keenness of the living ray which I endured. I had been lost, had mine eyes turned aside from it.

And so I was the bolder, as I mind me, so long to sustain it as to unite my glance with the Worth infinite.

O grace abounding, wherein I presumed to fix my look on the eternal light so long that I consumed my sight thereon!

Within its depths I saw gathered, bound by love in one volume, the scattered leaves of all the universe;

Substance and accidents and their relations, as though together fused, after such fashion that what I tell of is one simple flame...

Thus all suspended did my mind gaze fixed, immoveable, intent, ever enkindled by its gazing.

Such at that light doth man become that to turn thence to any other sight could not by possibility be ever yielded.

For the good, which is the object of the will, is therein wholly gathered, and outside it that same thing is defective which therein is perfect...

O Light eternal, who only in thyself abidest, only thyself dost understand, and to thyself, self-understood, self-understanding, turnest love and smiling:

That circling which appeared in thee to be conceived as a reflected light, by mine eyes scanned some little,

In itself, of its own color, seemed to be painted with our effigy and there at my sight was all committed to it,

As the geometer who all sets himself to measure the circle and who findeth not, think as he may, the principle he lacketh;

Such was I at this new seen spectacle; I would perceive how the image consorteth with the circle, and how it settleth there; But not for this were my proper wings, save that my mind was smitten by a flash wherein its will came to it.

To the high fantasy here power failed; but already my desire and will were rolled —even as a wheel that moveth equally—by the Love that moves the sun and the other stars.[177]

Compare this with an excerpt from a representative contemporary philosopher of influence, which embodies a rather extreme statement of the doctrine of man widely current in modern times. After quoting the Mephistophelian account of creation as the performance of a quite heartless and capricious being, Bertrand Russell, by contrast, elucidates a cold, uncaring cosmos in which persons are orphaned.

Even more purposeless, more void of meaning, in the world which Science presents for our belief. Amid such a world, if anywhere, our ideals henceforward must find a home. That man is the product of causes which had no vision of the end they were achieving; that his origin, his growth, his hopes and fears, his loves and his beliefs, are but the outcome of accidental collocations of atoms; that no fire, no heroism, no intensity of thought and feeling, can preserve an individual life beyond the grave; that all the labours of the ages, all the devotion, all the inspiration, all the noonday brightness of human genius, are destined to extinction in the vast death of the solar system, and that the whole temple of Man's achievement must inevitably be buried beneath the debris of a universe in ruins—all these things, if not quite beyond dispute, are yet so nearly certain, that no philosophy which rejects them can hope to stand. Only within the scaffolding of these truths, only on the firm

---

[177] Selections from the *Paradiso*, Cantos I, X, and XXXIII, Temple Classics edition.

foundation of unyielding despair, can the soul's habitation henceforth be safely built....

Brief and powerless is Man's life; on him and all his race the show, sure doom falls pitiless and dark. Blind to good and evil, reckless of destruction, omnipotent matter rolls on its relentless way; for Man, condemned to-day to lose his dearest, to-morrow himself to pass through the gate of darkness, it remains only to cherish, ere yet the blow falls, the lofty thoughts that ennoble his little day; disdaining the cowardly terrors of the slave of fate, to worship at the shrine that his own hands have built; undismayed by the empire of chance, to preserve a mind free from the wanton tyranny that rules his outward life; proudly defiant of the irresistible forces that tolerate, for a moment, his knowledge and his condemnation, to sustain alone, a weary but unyielding Atlas, the world that his own ideals have fashioned despite the trampling march of unconscious power.[178]

Finally, recent cosmological reflection depicts an enigmatically coherent yet precariously tenuous universe:

In their audacious reach for understanding of the universe, cosmologists often draw back hands that are maddeningly empty. They know, for example, that there is more out there than meets the eye. But hard as they try, they are unable to grasp the nature of what lurks in the blackness enfolding the luminous stars and galaxies, that shadowy substance whose gravitational pull must be the organizing force for the evolution and overall structure of the universe. The abundance of this invisible mass, whatever it is, could dictate the fate of the universe. Unless there is more mass than scientists so far have been able to measure or infer, that fate would appear to be bleak indeed. Some of the cosmic mass, particle physicists suggest, could be in the form of fast-moving neutrinos, subatomic particles that pervade the universe. They are known byproducts of the "Big Bang," the theorized explosive event of cosmic creation, but no one yet is sure if neutrinos have any mass. Much more of the missing mass, physicists think, could be something more exotic and sluggish, which they call cold dark matter. For various theoretical reasons, such weakly interacting massive particles, dubbed WIMPS, could exist in great abundance. But they have never been detected.

This line of investigation could have profound philosophical implications. If most of the universe is discovered to be composed of exotic material never before seen and absolutely unlike the "ordinary" matter of stars, of earth and of all life, cosmologists point out, the effect on human thinking could be more startling and diminishing than the Copernican revolution, which almost five centuries ago revealed that Earth was not the center of the universe or even the solar system.[179]

---

[178] Bertrand Russell, *A Free Man's Worship (Mysticism and Logic),* (New York: 1918), p. 46ff.
[179] New York Times, November 29, 1994, Sec. B, p. 1.

Perhaps the astrophysicists are correct and a supernova will explode again within 30 light years of this blue-green planet frying the stratosphere, dissolving the ozone shield, allowing the scorching sun to radiate the sea plankton and with it most life in the world. The vast panorama of galaxies, the total infinite universe which we may wish to designate as the mind of God seems, in human terms, to be both violent and creative. The ozone fry and near total extermination of life on earth may occur every 200 million years. A calamitous meteor crash on earth may come every 45 thousand years. Yet life comes back—even though plankton is nearly decimated— cockroaches and great turtles survive along with life forms deep in the seas. The stars seem to be biogenic. DNA seems to be implicit in converging inorganic elements. H. Richard Niebuhr writes:

> Yet all of these social and personal reinterpretations of remembered pasts and anticipated futures do not radically change either our general pattern of understanding of action upon us or our general mode of fitting response so long as our sense of the ultimate context remains unrevised. Deep in our minds is the myth, the interpretive pattern of the metahistory, within which all our histories and biographies are enacted. It has variant forms. It appears as the story of recurring cycles, of golden, silver, bronze, and iron ages, or of the round of personal rebirth and death. It appears as the story of the infinite progress of a particular species, this human kind, moving outward into space with its conquests, forward in time with victories over nature, but leaving behind in its past forgotten, dead generations. And that is the great overarching myth. It is the almost unconquerable picture in the mind, of everlasting winter lying on the frozen wastes of existence before all its time and after all its time, or, otherwise, of all-destroying fire raging before and after the brief interval of its life upon our planet or in our galaxy. It is the image of myself as coming to that future when there is no more future. It is that understanding of the society, into whose actions I fit my actions, as bound with all the tragic empires of history toward eschaton, beyond which there is no healing of diseases, no resurrection. It has scores of forms, no doubt, this mythology of death. But all its forms lead to the same interpretations in the present; to the same way of evaluating the beings with whom we are compresent by dividing them into the good and evil. And all the forms lead to the ethos of defense, to the ethics of survival. The great religions in general, and Christianity in particular, make their not least significant attack on this universal human ethos by challenging our ultimate historical myth. They do present new laws; they do present to us new ideals. But beyond all this they make their impact on us by calling into question our whole conception of what is fitting-that is, of what really fits inby questioning our picture of the context into which we now fit our actions. Doubtless they develop certain accommodations in their popular forms to the mythology of death-as in those Christian teachings about heaven and hell that lead to a new Manichaeanism and to a new form of survival ethics. Doubtless they must also clothe in symbols and in legends the conviction that we are surrounded in history by life and not by death, by the power of being and not by ultimate destructiveness. These, like all human words and pictures, will be subject to misinterpretation, as when our existence in responsibility is all concentrated in the vision of a last judgement where the rule of law is thought to prevail. But despite all aberrations and deviations, the central work of revising our

> mythology of death into a history of life goes on and with it the redefining for us of what is a fitting response in a lifetime and a history surrounded by eternal life, as well as by the universal society of being.[180]

Despite the formidable challenge to faith of the changed scientific, even apocalyptic world view, the essential confrontation is ethical, not cosmological. The theodicy question, why evil, if God cares, is raised acutely in this first clause. Martin Buber characterized the mid-twentieth century as a time of the *Eclipse of God.*

> Eclipse of the light of heaven, eclipse of God—such, indeed, is the character of the historic hour through which the world is passing. But it is not a process which can be adequately accounted for by instancing the changes that have taken place in man's spirit. An eclipse of the sun is something that occurs between the sun and our eyes, not in the eye itself.[181]

What Buber speaks of is not the death of God that Nietzsche or Vahanian described, but the willful hiddenness of God. Perhaps God is revolted by human presumption and sin. Perhaps the powers of darkness have conspired to blot out the sun. Perhaps our vision has become obscured and opaque. Whatever the source of the eclipse, it is certain that the conspiracy of theological amnesia, ethical abnegation, terrorism, even simple secularism defined as "getting along perfectly well without God." Our self-sufficient affluence has made us orphans in a fatherless world. We are prodigal children. The psychic and political crises of modern life can be attributed to the anxiety that results from this loss.

The theodicy issue can be approached one of two ways: either God is pitiless and impotent against evil or God is a caring father, involved with us in our plight and in our efforts to ameliorate evil. We remember the words of Archibald McCliesh on Job:

> I heard upon this dry dung heap
> that man cry out who cannot sleep:
> "If God is God, He is not good,
> If God is good, He is not God;
> Take the even take the odd (J.B.).

God is present in the trenches of both armies at Verdun. God is present, inspiring Jenner in the discovery and development of penicillin. He is with one receiving the "old man's friend" of bacterial pneumonia.

---

[180] H. Richard Niebuhr, *The Responsible Self* (, 1961), p. 106, 107.
[181] Martin Buber, *Eclipse of God* (New York: Scribners, 1952), p. 34.

Other Crises in "Our Father"

Other difficulties arise with the fatherly clause of the "Lord's Prayer." Well-known are the atheist and feminist critiques. Friedrich Nietzsche articulates the composite critique of nineteenth-century figures such as Marx, Freud, and Feuerbach. In Beyond Good and Evil, he writes:

> Why Atheism nowadays? 'The father' in God is thoroughly refuted; equally so' the judge,' 'the rewarder.' Also his 'free will.' He does not hear—and even if he did, he would not know how to help. The worst is that he seems incapable of communicating himself clearly. This is what I have made out to be the cause of the decline of European theism.[182]

The son of the Lutheran pastor in Röcken is objecting to the presentations of a deity, ostensibly provident and redemptive, but in reality one who is impotent to prevent evil and who, in actuality, emasculates the human spirit by creating such projection and abject dependence. The paternal God presents problems for both deity and humanity. As in family relationality, the delicate balance between authority and autonomy, suffocating guidance and love-liberating maturity, can easily be breached. The good father is one who cares enough to set free and not smother. An equipoise between overweening concern and obsequious apathy must be struck. God's fatherly love is stabilizing, strengthening, and liberating.

We must not distort it and render it indulgent, crippling, masculating. The feminist critique is equally telling and clarifying. In her book, Beyond God the Father, Mary Daly expresses an impish and sparkling earth love over against a stern, paternal, authority in heaven:

> Our Father who art in heaven, stay there
> And we will stay on earth
> Which is at times so lovely With its mysteries of New York
> With its mysteries of Paris which absolutely outweigh the mystery of the Trinity.[183]

Dorothee Söelle formulates similar offense:

> My difficulties about God as father, begetter, ruler and the manager of history grew as I began to understand more clearly what it means to be born a woman and therefore 'incomplete,' and so to have to live in a patriarchal society. How could I want power to be the dominant characteristic of my life? And how could I worship a God who was only a Male? Male power, for me, is something to do with roaring, shooting and giving orders. I do not think that this patriarchal culture has done me any more damage than other women. It only

---

[182] Beyond Good and Evil., Oscar Levy, The Complete Works of Friedrich Nietzsche (New York: Vintage, 1914, v.12), p. 72.

[183] Quoted in J.J. Petuchowski and M. Brocke, eds., *The Lord's Prayer and Jewish Liturgy* (London: Burns Oates, 1974), p. 184.

became constantly more obvious to me that any identification with the aggressor, the ruler, the violator, is the worst thing that can happen to a woman.[184]

The God of biblical faith is not a male. Gender language is metaphoric not ontic. It was a distortion of the fourth century when Lactantius adopted the Christian God to a Constantinian ideology of *Dominus Pater ac Deus*, God, Father Almighty. This imported ideology distorted and colored western theology for centuries.

The feminist critique is well-founded, reminding us that God is like a good father or mother. Human metaphors fail. The divine mystery transcends gender, materially, historically, all that we know. The biblical use of parental metaphor uses both mother and father and thus transcends restriction.

Is he not your father who created you...
In the desert and howling wilderness work he sustained you
He shielded you, cared for you as the apple of his eye
Like an eagle she stirred up the nest and hovered over her young
Taking them up and bearing them aloft on its pinions.
(Deut. 32:1-11)

Elizabeth Johnson, in her important book, She Who Is: The Mystery of God in Feminist Theological Discourse, comments on the biblical "*Abba*":

"Abba connotes an intimacy of relation between Jesus and God, along with a sense of God's compassion over suffering, willing good in the midst of evil."[185]

Excursus: Bad Dads and Gingrich's Orphanages

It is called the welfare crisis. Mothers with dependent children languish in chronic generational cycles and repetitive dependence. The dads father the kids, then skip out, oblivious to their responsibilities. They couldn't help, economically speaking, even if they stayed home. There is no home, only inadequate shelter. There are no jobs. They could be there in love and presence, but that takes great ego security, a trait so rare in all of us. So the paternal benediction of a people is shattered from bottom to top; the biological dad, the familial circle, the neighborhood, the paternal function of city, state, and nation. Poor moms and kids are left to fend for themselves. Ten percent of Americans are on public assistance. Thirty percent of American children are born into poverty. A sizeable portion of these are settling into chronic economic and educational deprivation where the only avenue for creativity, if it arises at all, is the avenue of drugs and crime.

---

[184] D. Solle, "Paternalistic Religion as Experienced by Women," (Concilium 143 (1981), p. 72.

[185] Elizabeth Johnson, She Who Is: The Mystery of God in Feminist Theological Discourse (New York: Crossroad, 1992), p. 81.

The U.S. Census Bureau has disclosed that as of 1993, 30% of American families are headed by one parent, mostly single women (80%). In any given month, 45% of the single-parent families headed by women require some form of major public assistance such as food stamps, Medicaid, rent assistance, or aid to families with dependent children. Sixty-three percent of the nation's black families were headed by single parents, 90% women. In the cities of America, in other words, the majority of family units find themselves in a bitter struggle for economic, educational, employment, nutritional, medical, and motivational survival.[186]

What is the answer? Resurgent conservative politicians suggest a reemphasis on alymossary orphanages like Father Flanagan's Boy's Town. Liberals recall Oliver Twist. Good orphanages in the tradition of Boy's Town continue to make outstanding contributions. If massive private philanthropy could ensue from funds freed up in the clamor to reduce taxes, this might be a partial solution. Perhaps the impending budget surplus can be allocated here. It would be a splendid investment. Somehow one doubts that this synergy or effort will take place. Public welfare is a sham, everyone admits. We offer far too little, much too late. If we could develop a Scandinavian-like care system for families, especially mothers and children, that could work although we have a large and chronic underclass. We would have to increase our taxes probably by five percent. Disclaiming human paternity, personally and socially, continues to devastate our world. Faith-based human services might serve good purpose, but these should not be accompanied by diminished public action and funding.

How can we re-establish paternal provision in our increasingly fatherless world? Certainly we have to strengthen the earning power and equality, even superiority of women in the workplace. In our present sociologic situation where poverty concentrates in women and children, perhaps even in the universal and inherent situation where women naturally assume the total burden of childbearing and the greater burden of childrearing, women ought to receive greater economic remuneration than men. Bringing up children offers a society survival and a future. It must be honored and funded. Nationally, the most reasonable answer would seem to be a radically revised tax structure where the rapid concentration of wealth in a smaller and smaller portion of the community is exploited in order to strengthen the growing portion of needy and indigent.

Yet another critique precipitated by the "father" clause is that of psychological projection and dependence. In The Future of an Illusion and Moses and Monotheism, Sigmund Freud called to our attention the array of God-father images at play in the human psyche both engendering infantilizing dependence and of the soul's hard work of maturation and integrity which in ironic fashion elicit those same virtues. The wide community of theorists and therapists who have commented on the fatherhood of God have shown both the debilitating

---

[186] *The Chicago Tribune*, January 10, 1995, Sec. 1, p. 3.

legacy of the belief and its stabilizing and edifying effect. Disabusing persons of paternal idolatry makes possible the firm foundations of true parental comfort (Isaiah 44:20, 40:1-2). The theme of eternal stability is threatened as we look at temporal instability.

Paternal Vulnerability

"The world today," says Everett Fox, author of the new *Five Books of Moses*, "is not a hospitable place." We experience disease and doubt, war and deprivation. Human experience is full of fragility and vulnerability. The undergirding strength of personal insight and courage and of the sustenance we draw from one another amid life's vicissitudes are anticipations of that more basic stability found in God. Vulnerability in this ultimate unfolding is the precondition of ultimate belonging and safety. "Sadness," says the little girl in the film Ulee's Gold, "makes me feel still inside."

Population crisis also destabilizes the world placing precarious pressure on the world's resources and carrying capacity. An even broader and more profound insecurity of life on earth is reflected in the apocalyptic tenor of much scripture. ("I will shake the heavens and the earth," Haggai 2:6, Joel 3:16, Hebrews 12:26.) Ultimate foundational securing is established only in "our heavenly father."

Today, the heavens have become the domain of human beings. Astronauts float along the Hubbel telescope repairing a damaged satellite device, tracking down and catching a two-millimeter screw floating in weightless space, readjusting the optics on the great mirror. The heavens have become a home for humans. Yuri Gagarin, an early Russian cosmonaut, scanned the heavens and found no God. John Glenn, his American counterpart, did not expect to find his God out there in space. Cosmos can be seen not as an apocalyptic cataclysm, but a vast receptivity, an awesome coherence and mystery. We can now approach and comprehend how stars live and die. What we have known all along is true, the heavens have a friendly face. Even the vast death of the cosmos, the slow entropy of disorder to faith becomes a facet of intricate design. In some way, human finitude is part of infinite mystery and meaning.

The theological truth implicit in the first words of the Lord's Prayer, "Our Father, who art in Heaven," is the firm foundation of our being in the cherishing regard God has for us. Luther and Calvin, in turn, gave powerful expression to this foundation.

> This is our foundation. The gospel commands us not to look at our own good deeds or perfection but at the God of promise himself, at the Mediator Christ himself. This is how our theology achieves its assurance. We are torn away from ourselves and put outside ourselves, so as not to rely on our own powers,

conscience, experience, person, or works, but on that which is outside us, namely on the promise and truth of God which can never deceive us.[187]

We find the same stress in Calvin's persuasive comment on the doxology of the Lord's Prayer:

> This is the firm and tranquil repose of our faith. For if our prayers were to be commended to God by our worth, who would dare even mutter in his presence? Now, however miserable we may be, though unworthiest of all, however devoid of all commendation, we will never lack a reason to pray, never be short of assurance, since his Kingdom, power and glory can never be snatched away from our Father.[188]

Douglas John Hall writes,

> "[It is]...not so much the terror of death as the terror of life itself [which] impels most of us to seek some sphere of peace, security and permanence beyond the fluxes."[189]

A concluding footnote: Heaven, home and father come together as we approach death. "In my father's house are many mansions...I go to prepare a place for you" (John 14:2). Death "the last enemy" becomes the "desire to depart and be with Christ" (Philippians 1:23). The terrors of life resolve to still waters and green pastures. Even in the valley of the shadow of death we fear no evil. God is with us (Psalm 23). Our kindly father knows what we need before we ask. At this moment we recognize our call to the father as God's call to us. The pipes are calling from glen to glen and down the mountainside. He'll be there in sunshine and in sorrow. At the end of his long and full life, Karl Barth would often say, "To fold one's hands in prayer is the beginning of an uprising against the disorder of the world."[190]

Perhaps no reproach of life is as devastating as the death of a child. Fatherly protection has abdicated or failed. Innocence and potential has been violated. Providence and coherence have been shattered. Yet even amidst this grievous tragedy, underneath are the everlasting arms. Gustav Mahler gathered this crisis, enigma, this universal *Pieta*, in a peon of praise. The moving song cycle is called *Kindertotenlieder*.

In this weather, in this awful storm (Braus),

---

[187] M. Luther, "In epistolam S. Pauli and Galatas Commentarius, "in *D. Martin Luther's Werke: Kritische Gesamtausgabe* (Weimar: Hermann Bohlaus Nachfolger, 1911), vol. 40, pt. 1., p. 585.
[188] Calvin, *Institutes,* vol. 2, pp. 915-916 (III..20.47).
[189] Douglass John Hall, "The Theology and Ethics of the Lord's Prayer," in D. Migliori, *The Lord's Prayer* (Grand Rapids, MI.: Eerdmans, 1993), p. 127.
[190] Karl Barth quoted in Jan Milic Lochman, *The Lord's Prayer*, Grand Rapids: Eerdmans, 1990.

> I would never have let the children go out.
> I was afraid they would die tomorrow,
> but there is nothing to do about that now...
> In this weather, in this storm (Graus),
> in this gentle shower (Saus)
> They are resting.
> Resting as if they were at home with mother.
> rightened no more by storms,
> Watched over by God's hand,
> They are resting as if they were at home with mother.

The divine ground is the source of human life. Genesis, chapter 9, the Noahic covenant of life with life, is the restitution after the fall into existence symbolized by global deluge, back to the Edenic covenant with the primal family. With Noah and his family the innocence and sub-humanity of the race is resolved. The fruit of the tree of life is now given to humanity. Humans are now free to live and to die.

II. Sanctus: Hallowed Be Thy Name

Introduction

...Yiskadal v'yiskadash sh'may rabbo...

We have begun our exploration of a philosophy of life, what we see as a cache of ideas derivative from the historical conjunction of Judaism and Christianity, with the conviction that life itself is derivative—a divine epiphenomenon and not a phenomenon inherently explicable in naturalistic terms. Other interpretations of the phenomenon of life (see Hans Jonas) include philosophical vitalism, biologism and evolutionary theory and a wide range of views today which focus normativity on various neutral concepts of life as person, mind, brain, consciousness, thought and information. While these concepts possess the great value of embracing the data of emerging sciences like molecular genetics and neuropharmacology, they fail because of their specialization and fragmentation to comprehend a broad environment which includes elements of peace, home, rest, future and dissonance. Our view of life, per se, involves the composure of grounding and now, as we will see, the quality of integrity. Wholeness, holiness, sanctity is a correlate of life in the Abrahamic/Akedic/Christic perspective which we continue to elucidate. We proceed now to explain that context of integrity or meaning about life. We will consider elements which enhance coherence and wholeness and elements which bring corruption and disintegration. If cohabitation and synergy enhance vitalism, we have life. If contamination and disorientation inhabit being it leads to disintegration and death. We will use case studies such as sex, food, AIDS and death to illustrate these diverging directions of being.

The textual framework for this next level of discussion is the second phrase of the Lord's prayer—Hallowed be Thy name. Two greek words and their Aramaic/Hebraic precursors come into play. *Hagias the ta* (Holy...be the name) and *theoprepapteia* convey the conviction that life's setting (where it is at home and can thrive) is inthe divine-moral salience where life fits in, is worthy, is capable of entertaining not expelling the divine.

We have anchored our eschatological theology in the divine domesticity; the establishment of *Domus*, of a heavenly home, a haven of the body for our "barks so small and frail," adrift on life's tumultuous sea. The fitting response to such provident presence is dependence. In awe and wonder we ascribe holiness to God which in turn prompts desire and necessity for purity in ourselves. The Holy produces in persons a dynamic interplay of outer confrontation and inner condemnation and correction. The dynamic of life in God's presence is recognition, repentance, and restitution. The power of this logic is reflected in all great calls to ministry such as that of Isaiah:

> In the year that King Uzziah died, I saw the Lord sitting upon a throne, high and lifted up...and (the Seraphim) cried...Holy, Holy, Holy is the Lord of hosts, The whole earth is full of his glory...Then I said woe is me! for I am undone; because I am a man of unclean lips and dwell in the midst of a people of unclean lips: for my eyes have seen the King, the Lord of hosts. Then the Lord said " Who can I send—who will go for us?" I answered "Here I am—send me."
> (Isaiah 6:1-8).

Two ways, *didache*...ways of life or death; health or sickness .

Endearing presence calls forth loving devotion. Worthiness invites worship. Christina Rossetti wrote in a gentle Christmas ballad:

> In the bleak midwinter, frosty wind made moan,
> Earth stood hard as iron, water like a stone;
> Snow had fallen, snow on snow,
> In the bleak midwinter, long ago.
> What can I give him, poor as I am?
> If I were a shepherd, I would bring a lamb;
> If I were a wiseman, I would do my part;
> Yet what I can I give him, give my heart.
> The Oxford Book of Carols

Searching descriptions of eucharistical life, life entailing calling and sending, from Deuteronomy to *Didache* to *Devotio Moderna*, involve two ways. Purity or corruption, health or disease, life or death. All texts cry with the Deuteronomic Moses: "Choose life."

The precondition and salience of *stabulum*, of being at home, is sanctity or sanity, wholesomeness, wholeness. We will call the quality: sanctus. Holiness or

327

health is an intrapsychic, interpersonal, cosmic and divine-human phenomenon. To be at home with oneself, with others in the world and with God requires wellness in each of those relational dimensions. One can be at unease or well in thought, will, speech, and act as dimensions of being and in realms such as relationality and sexuality, disease and dying.

> Create in me a clean heart O God
> And renew a right spirit within me...
> Purge me with hyssop, and I shall be clean
> Wash me and I shall be whiter than snow (Psalm 51).

Though David cried out that his fundamental wrong was against God ("against thee and thee only have I sinned...") the immediate right relation that had been violated was with Uriah (murder C-6) and with Bathsheba (adultery C-7). Sin is systemic. Restitution is comprehensive. Happy (Blessed, Holy) are you Israel!" wrote Rabbi Akiba, "Who is it before whom you become clean? And who is it that makes you clean? Your father which is in heaven!" (Yoma, viii 9). Full forgiveness can only come from the heart of the father, from the arbiter of justice.

Purity has many synonyms in scripture: holiness, light, glory, grandeur, greatness, worthiness, worthship. The radiation of God into our being stimulates a range of ideals and negativities: light and darkness, glory and sullenness, publicity and secrecy, honesty and deception, crystal and soiled, perfect and imperfect, beautiful and ugly, good and evil. Each of these antinomies is the subject of authentic divine identification and dangerous human misdesignation.

Purity is a matter of justification, of worthiness (entrance) and of justice (ethics) "Pure and undefiled religion is this" wrote the Apostle James, "To care for the widows and homeless and to keep oneself uncontaminated by the world" (1:27).

We continue our depiction of the human condition, *sub specie aeternitatis*, by studying sanctity in God and in humans. Purity in persons is a response to holiness in God. The great burden of the sacramental and sacrificial traditions of religion, its Eucharistical heritage, finds that God and humans can only get together if there is similarity and compatibility. This is the cause and result of Akedah in the history of nature and of God. There must be affinity if not parity of the quality which is called holiness or sanctity. The holy God, holy name, holy mountain, holy place, can only be approached if one is clean, conscientious, and contrite. Such spirit or disposition is the precondition of holiness.

> Who shall ascend his Holy hill?
> He who has clean hands and a pure heart
> (Psalm 24).

Holiness or sanctity in one sense is an ethical matter confirmed by ritual. Clean hands and pure heart, rightness in action and intention, deed and will, is certified by ritual confession and cleansing.

In this first sense holiness is morality. Isaiah announces: The holy God shows himself holy in righteousness (5:16). The message is sounded throughout Christian scripture:

> Be pure and blameless for the day of Christ...
> Be filled with the fruits of righteousness
> (Philippians 1:11; I Peter 3:13).

Righteousness, enacted as in Judaism, imputed as in Christendom, or portrayed as in Islam, is the portal into divine presence. As the Easter Emmaeus text reads:

> Open our eyes, O loving and compassionate Jesus
> That we may see and behold thee, walking beside us in our sorrow
> Thou hast made death glorious and triumphant
> for through its portals we enter into the presence of the living God.
> (John Hays)

Sanctification, the process of becoming holy, is one where our lives express more and more fully the divine image within us. We do not become God or like gods, we manifest more and more God's good will. Human flesh, blood and frailty is lifted toward sanctity.

> Breathe on me breath of God, fill me with life anew
> that I may love as thou dost love, and do as thou wouldst do
> (Robert Jackson, 1894)

Purity, perfection or deepening holiness, in John Wesley's insight, is sanctity and service. Sanctification is an ethical process. We are being saved from sin and wrong into good and right. Ethics in its theocentric meaning, is that we live out the divine life toward the world in love and justice, purity and simplicity, freedom and peace. All this we have described in previous parts as Akedic and decalogic existence. Jesus inaugurated his mission with Isaiah's messianic words:

> The Spirit of the Lord is upon me, because he has anointed me to preach
> good news to the poor.
> He has sent me to proclaim release to the captives and recovery of sight to
> the blind, to set at liberty those who are oppressed, to proclaim the
> acceptable year of the Lord
> (Luke 4:18, 19; Isaiah 61:1-2).

Cultic Purity

The ethos of taboo and purity is strong in primitive religion. It finds vivid expression in the cult of Israel, especially in priestly religion and the holiness tradition, referred to, for example, in the book of Leviticus. As with *mitzvah*, the witness of Jesus confirms and deepens this tradition. He purifies his soul in the prayer and fasting of the temptation dessert. Yet he invites the publican and sinner, the tax collector, prostitute and Samaritan into his company. He acts with some freedom and nuance toward kosher and sabbath rules. Purity, in Jesus' purview, is thereby deepened and extended into its deepest *Torah* meaning— adoration and act. Jesus reaches out to make the unclean whole and well.

The religious ritualization of purification and contamination corresponds with the empirical human experience of disease, death and decay. The human arts of sanitation, prophylaxis, asepsis, food preservation and preparation, health care, sexual ethics, and death customs are human endeavors related to sanctity. The inner desire for holiness prompts behavioral will which, in turn, prompts concrete actions.

Monasteries embodied this cathartic presence and ambience. In an intriguing book related to the theme of our first chapter, Home: a History of an Idea, Witold Rybczynski, describes the Cistercian Monastery:

> It has been said that a blind monk could enter any of the more than seven hundred Cistercian monasteries and not get lost. Each complex included a *lavatorium*, or bathhouse, fitted with wooden tubs and with facilities for heating the water; small basins with constantly running cold water for hand-washing before and after meals were outside the refectory. The *misericord*, where dying monks were ritually bathed, was situated beside the infirmary, while the *reredorter*, a wing containing latrines, was built next to the dormitory (the *dorter*). The wastewaters from these facilities were carried away in covered-over streams, in effect underground sewers.[191]

The biological and theological dimensions of the response of sanctity (sanity) to divine holiness is part of a broader human response to what is an appropriate or becoming offering to God. The nostrils of God delight in sweet sacrifice (e.g., incense), not the stench of abomination. Instead of what transpires in secret or in darkness that which comes before God is light—in the open and public; it is not deceitful or a lie—it is honest and true; it is not stained or contaminated but clean; not cheap, it is valuable; not imperfect, but whole and perfect; not ugly, but beautiful; not evil, but good. We are prompted to bring the best that we are and have to God.

A slightly divergent Christian theme enters here. We may not be rich or intelligent, regal or lovely. Jesus' association with his own *anawim*—the simple, poor and unpretentious, forever hallows the simple gift of a pure heart. Jesus also hallows the outcasts, cripples, sick, and dying. The loathsome, lepers, diseased, and unclean are embraced in his welcoming heart. As at Emmaus, they dine in his heart-purifying presence.

---

[191] Witold Rybcanski, *Home: A History of an Idea,* (New York: Penguin, 1987), p. 29.

To Make Holy

The verb *hagiazein* (translating Hebrew *kadosh*) is usually spoken of as "making holy" in a cultic sense, to prepare and cleanse for divine offering (cf. Matthew 23:17,19). Christians are "made holy" in baptism (I Corinthians 6:11), in the bestowal of spirit (Romans 15:16), and in "the blood of Christ" (Hebrews 13:12; Acts 20:32, 26:18). On Palm Sunday, the pilgrim crowd shouted "Blessed"— "Hallowed" be he who comes in the name of the Lord" (Psalm 118:26). Cleansing is a personal and political matter. The Holy warrior—the Messiah—the conqueror of evil—must be a pure oblation. The inverse of hallowing or honoring God's name is blaspheming, defaming, smearing the same name (presence). Holiness is achieved by purity, integrity and justice; degradation by idolatry, pollution and injustice.

> ...They sell the righteous for silver,
> and the poor for a pair of shoes.
> They grind the poor into the ground
> and push the weak aside.
> Incest abounds as
> they profane my holy name.
> (Amos 2:6-8).

God promises to purify the people, making them a fit companion to his task. He will give them a new heart and a new spirit by which he will "sanctify his great name" (Ezekiel 36:22). He will punish the heathen who oppresses his people (Exodus 32:12f., Isaiah 48:11).

> So Jesus Sirach prays:
> As in us you have been sanctified before the foreign nations,
> So in them be magnified before us (36:3).

> Purity in humans is re-actio to the actio of God's holiness.
> "You shall be holy, for I am holy"
> (Leviticus 11:45).

The first request, "HOLY be your name," draws together the rich meanings of blasphemy, baptism and blessedness. The request recalls the second command, "Do not take the Lord's name in vain." It recalls that we are baptized "in the name" of Father, Son, and Spirit. It recalls that those who do justice bless the name and those who "trample the poor" profane the name (Amos 2:6-8). Again we see the intertwining of commandment and prayer. As in *Succoth*, the feast of Pentecost, when the tongues of flame rested on the believers, tongues representing the commandments, when the world was baptized by the Holy Spirit and fire as with tongues, when the Mosaic elders became the seventy apostles, so the ascription of the prayer "...Our Father," and the first request, ask that holiness be activated now on earth as it already is in heaven.

331

In this spirit, Luther rightly interprets the (*Erste Bitte*) to mean that in *Lehre* and *Leben*, *Wort* and *Werk* we are to thank, praise, and bless God and not curse, swear, or ignore the name (WA 671.13). Calvin adds that God's holiness (glory) is disclosed to us in his presence (being) and his works, therefore our responsive holiness or righteousness should also be expressed in ourselves, our words and our lives.[192]

Building on this foundational understanding, let us now explore two arguments: The Jesus revolution redefines (1) purity and (2) community, radically recasting for both theology and polity the rules of moral being and behavior and of human association—the meaning of sanctity. Eucharistics are the dynamics of holy association. This thesis will be developed by first reviewing traditional taboo, then biblical holiness doctrine in its revolutionary character, finally elucidating a new understanding of holiness with reference to practices of sexuality, disease interpretation and approach to dying.

Traditional Taboo

In the second part of his monumental work on superstitious behavior in primitive societies, James George Frazer reviews practices under the rubric "Taboo and the Perils of the Soul." A wide range of activities seek to safeguard "the life spirit" which is always in danger, it is believed, of leaking away, being lost or being contaminated. Restrictions and taboos are placed on representative leaders and common people. Kings or priests are intermediaries, they traffic between earth and heaven. The word priest, in Hebrew *cohen*, for example, combines roots meaning to kneel down and to lift up. The priest or king lifts the people up to God and draws God down to the people. For this concourse, purity is a necessity. Taboo customs pertaining to kings or priests are myriad. Their lives are circumscribed with taboos about eating, washing, walking, sleeping, and drinking. They must not be touched by a commoner, nor see or touch a dead body. To offer worthy intercession, the priest may not be castrated, hunch-backed, missing fingers or too ugly [Elvira Canons, 4th Century A.D.]. Sometimes for expiation of the sins of the people or his own transgression, the King must die. Abraham Lincoln is assassinated. Three French Priests die in Algeria. The king or priest must not be sullied by sex or scandal, lest he be sacrificed by the spurious purity of the sexually sinful and scandal ridden who feign self-righteousness. There is a connection between holiness and retributive violence. Sin provokes wrath, both divine and human. Therefore, Paul recalls Hebrew wisdom, "Vengeance is mine, I will repay, says the Lord" (Romans 12:19, Leviticus 19:18, Deuteronomy 32:35).

Jesus Christ is a new kind of mediator. He breaks the wall of hostility (Ephesians 2:14). As the book of Hebrews develops its holiness theology, we see that purity, as exemplified in Jesus, is more properly faithfulness, love of money is rejected (Chapter 13).

---

[192] *Institutes III 20, 40.*

The decalogic structure of the way of God is rehearsed. Faithfulness is filial piety. Christ made purification for sin, not in his angelic nature, but by virtue of the name he achieved in his obedient sonship.

> For to what angel did God ever say,
> thou art my Son, today I have begotten thee?
> Again, I will be to him a father, and he shall be to me a son?"
> (Hebrews 1:5).

Jesus pioneers a new purity and a new humanity. His purity is no longer superstitious sanitation or ritualistic perfection, but sure trust and expressed righteousness. Purity is goodness which is mercy and love. This holiness revolution forms the basis for a new community where publicans and sinners, the poor and outcasts, the diseased and deranged, prostitutes and the despicable, all are welcome. "They will have no need for a physician" (Luke 5:31). God, says Luther, saves the degraded in their dread and dereliction. Only the cast-down can be lifted up. Jesus comes to save sinners.

> ...where sin increased, grace abounded all the more...
> (Romans 5:20).

Holiness in one's individuality and in community now takes on a new character. Persons in Christ live in the awareness of being forgiven (The aorist tense in Greek suggests an enduring finality); of being welcomed and contributing to the family and history of God; of living the life of holiness out of thanksgiving. The ethical mood of holiness is one of commingled acceptance and expectancy. There is no longer a place for self-righteousness, works (earned) righteousness or condemnation of others. A rigorous self-expectation and mutual support now arises from an ethic of grace. The original and inherent spirit of Mizvoh and Torah is restored.

Biblical Holiness

Building on the perennial cathartic wisdom of scripture and tradition, Augustine writes:

> *Cum ergo dicimus: sanctificetur*
> *Nomen tuum, nos admonemus desiderare,*
> *Ut nomen eius quod semper sanctum est,*
> *Etiam apud homines santum habeatur,*
> *Hoc est non contemnatur.*

Divine holiness is enacted within the human. In both shorter and larger catechisms, Luther focused his reflection about this petition on the fact that God hallows his name within our words and deeds, our living and dying, our worship and work. The historic biblical rendition of sanctity is that God will exemplify his own holiness through ours.

I will sanctify myself in you (Isaiah 29:23). Our bodies are the temples wherein the sanctifying spirit of God abides. For this reason we glorify God in our bodies (I Corinthians 3:16, 17). The radical repository of *shekinah* in apostolic preaching places divine glory and grandeur (holiness) "not in temples made with hands" (Acts 7:48, 17:24), but in the life, breath and spirit of human beings. "A human life fulfilled," wrote Irenaeus of Lyon, "is the glory of God." Taboo contamination is now obliterated in the divine invitation and reception. God's name can only be hallowed if the world is hallowed. God's holiness abides in the father's heart, "the inmost depths in God's eternal breast" (Goethe) where he has secured human repose. With First Clement we therefore pray for "obedience to his most holy and glorious name, that we may tabernacle in confidence on the most sacred name of his majesty" (58:1).

The biblical *ordo salus* is holiness in order to goodness. Goodness is in order to wellness. A dominant theme in Hebrew tradition is that health is a blessing, the sequel of righteousness. God is a physician, a healer who wills the well-being of his people. God wills to make a home for his people, a promised land, a good place flowing with milk and honey (Exodus 3:8). The prophylactic import of the Mosaic code entails the protection of health and the prevention of illness as the benediction to pure lives well-lived. Cleanliness, sexual hygiene, care in the selection and preparation of foods, rest and sanitation all played into this salutary prescription.

The purity codes in the Torah are of two kinds: specific proscriptions and prescriptions for daily living habits seem to be an exquisite synthesis of ancient empirical wisdom about the behaviors which insure health; and the code of national life which includes rites of purification, worship and rules for cultic and priestly worthiness. The Hebrew people are called to peculiar separateness and exemplary life—called apart from the nations. Individuals within the nation are encouraged to lives of personal holiness. "Purity rules," writes William Countryman, "relate to the boundaries (between nations) and of the (boundaries of) human body, especially its orifices...whatever passes these boundaries has particular importance for purity law: foods, waste products, shed blood, menstrual blood, sexual emissions, sexual acts, birth, death."[193]

Synthesis and Case Studies

Brief examples can be drawn from the arenas of food, sex, disease and death and a case study of AIDS to illustrate this holiness tendency.

Food

In an important new study, Leon Kass writes of The Hungry Soul: Eating and the Perfecting of our Nature.[194] His essay captures the spiritual and ethical essence of the meaning of food and eating which is the foundational intent of the

---

[193] 193*Dirt, Greed and Sex* (Philadelphia: Fortress Press, 1988), p. 13.

[194] Leon Kass, *The Hungry Soul: Eating and the Perfecting of our Nature* (New York: The Free Press, 1994), p. 41.

purity tradition. Dining is a delight of life...who we are as persons, in community, within the divine milieu is expressed in the habitus of receiving the blessing of food. The near absolute taboos against eating bloody flesh and the lesser taboo of killing animals for our sustenance are symbolized in the use of cutlery as a distancing ritual from the act of killing. The ritual of eating with its traditional "blessing" or "grace" is an act of reverence or holiness. Ultimately, beyond the immediate and social ritual is the sanctification of food, says Kass, "as expressed in Jewish dietary laws."

In this act, as in all others, the threat of desanctifying that which is holy as it is done before "the Holy One" is ever present. Wolfing down a McDonald's "Big Mac" in front of the TV removes the art of partaking from the life of the world in its sacred and justice aspects. In eating, we give thanks and remember the hungry. We call to remembrance the contingency and need of our existence. We are drawn toward *askesis* (frugal conviviality) as we ponder starvation and sustenance. When we neglect this sacred dimension of thanksgiving and justice, we propel a society toward disregard. The Eucharistic meal verges Christ's death and our *momento mori* into Thanksgiving for here and now, near and far, there and then. Abraham's akedic offering is eventually transmutted into meal offerings.

An important new book by Robert Kaplan is entitled The Ends of the Earth. The social and economic injustice so rampant on the globe has led to two societies, not *Didache's* way of life and death, but one way of degradation, depression of life, desperation verging on resignation in one sector and an increasingly smug selfishness, indulgence and materialism in the other. AIDS is prevalent in the bands of disinheritance; poor West Africa, the American core cities, the impoverished rim of Asia, for example. Exuberant technological acquisitiveness and increasing disregard of the down-and-out is found in another luxuriant band; Western Europe, Israel, Japan, the dynamic commercial centers of Africa, Asia and India, and America's suburbs. The value indicative of poverty in American government statistics is calories of intake. Ethics is commensal, eucharistic.

"Our daily bread..."
More on this in the third request.

Sex

The responsive life of wholeness, of holiness, is as Mary Douglas has written

"a meditation on the oneness, purity and completeness of God."[195]

Human sexual intimacy and intercourse is mimesis of the divine wholeness, purity, completeness, and generativity. The character of the divine-human

---

[195] Mary Douglas, *Purity and Danger: An Analysis of Concepts of Pollution and Taboo* (London: Routledge and Kegan Paul, 1966), p. 57.

335

encounter controls and chastens interhuman relationships. God is faithful, singular, and undivided (complete) in devotion, wholly given to love and affirmation, loyal, unswerving and fruitful. Mimetic human sexuality therefore discontenances fornication and adultery, prostitution and incest, promiscuity and pederasty, divorce and abortion. Virtue holds these purities in check. In vice, dissolution occurs.

The words *Toebah* and *Shiqquts* in Hebrew Scriptures (translated abomination) refer to a range of pollution or impurities which soil or adulterate the divine-human and human-human companionship. They spoil a good thing. These spoilers include unclean food (Deut. 14:3, Leviticus 11), incest (Leviticus 17), idolatry, injustice and cheating (Leviticus 19), as well as sexual malpractice. The decalogue tablet observed wipes the sin slate clear. It fashions fidelity.

That which unifies and edifies the person, relationships and the community honors God, the giver of life in abundance. That which disunites and debases the person, the family or community is like idolatry, it obscures and threatens to obliterate the divine image. Holiness is Godliness, which is grace, getting through, making whole and well.

Disease

The classic biblical metaphor for disease is leprosy. As Susan Sontag has shown in her book Illness as Metaphor, it was syphilitics in the sixteenth century, tuberculars in the nineteenth, and persons with AIDS in the twentieth which symbolized "the unclean." Scripture's treatment is startling. This ancient scourge was not to be identified with today's leprosy (Hansen's disease) but with a range of skin diseases that literally ate away the flesh like a recent strain of staphylococcus infection and Eboli virus in Africa. This was cause for isolation and banishment as it blotched the otherwise complete and lovely being, and threatened the corporate well-being.

Priests must declare the leper unclean, ban contact between the afflicted one and the community, certify remission if healing occurs, purify the cleansed one and introduce reintegration into the community. The startling aspect of the story is that the completely, not partially, diseased person is also clean.

> If leprosy breaks out on the skin, so that leprosy covers all the skin of the diseased person from head to foot, so far as the priest can see, then the priest shall make an examination, and if the leprosy has covered all his body, he shall pronounce him clean of the disease; it has all turned white, and he is clean. (Leviticus 13:12-13 RSV)

Only one who has died to sin can be alive to life.

Beyond a purely technical diagnosis and prognosis which knows that a totally white and scar-tissued person with no open fleshy wounds is safe, and noninfectious, we have here an affirmation that disease pollutes but for a moment and restoration inevitably ensues. This is true to the point that we can say with an alumnus of our seminary, "Now that I have cancer, I am whole." Disease is an incompleteness over against the divine-human completeness. It is transient imperfection over against ultimate perfection. It is miasma, a temporary curse to be cleansed. As C.S. Lewis would say, "pain is a megaphone whereby God calls us home." Impurity, even in disease and death, is a call, a beckoning. It is a discrepancy, a declension away from what ought to be and will be.

Death

This foregoing analysis sets the stage to understand why death itself—the corpse, the remains, are part of the residue of impurity in our world. Certainly at one level decay is contaminating. The residual and omnipresent microbial bed finally has its day. In a deeper sense, death is offensive in its negation of life. But death is only a penultimate and passing disgrace. Through the cleansing of the great and cathartic river (Jordan's deep river) we come to the crystal shore of divine eternal life.

As I write these words, announcement comes from the Associated Press that Eduardo Mata, conductor of the Dallas Symphony, has crashed his small plane near Cuernavaca, Mexico. He and his companion, Marina, along with his daughter and another friend were killed. WFMT, our classical FM radio station, plays Bach's Suite #3 in D Major in meditative tribute. Bach, wrote Paul Hindemith, went to the edge of the established pure form of music and could not pass the curtain into perfection. Rituals of embalming, anointing and cleansing are cathartic in the dual sense of offering, cleaning, and preparing for this breakthrough into serene holiness which is the presence of God. All we can do now is kneel and serve.

> Now before the feast of the Passover, when Jesus knew that his hour had come to depart out of this world to the Father, having loved his own who were in the world, he loved them to the end. And during supper, when the devil had already put it into the heart of Judas Iscariot, Simon's son, to betray him, Jesus, knowing that the Father had given all things into his hands, and that he had come from God and was going to God, rose from supper, laid aside his garments, and girded himself with a towel. Then he poured water into a basin, and began to wash the disciples' feet, and to wipe them with the towel with which he was girded. He came to Simon Peter; and Peter said to him, "Lord, do you wash my feet?" Jesus answered him, "What I am doing you do not know now, but afterward you will understand." Peter said to him, "You shall never wash my feet." Jesus answered him, "If I do not wash you, you have no part in me." Simon Peter said to him, "Lord, not my feet only but also my hands and my head." Jesus said to him. "He who has bathed does not need to wash, except for his feet, but he is clean all over; and you are clean, but not every one of you." For he knew who was to betray him; that was why he said, "You are not all clean"
> (John 13:1-10 RSV).

Purity or holiness is the notion that defines the intervention, the interlude between God and people. God is Emmanuel—one who comes. We are *homo religiosis*, pilgrims toward heaven. Holiness is the order of the towel—the meeting ground.

Case Study: Aids

Two of the deepest mysteries and phobias of human existence, sex and death, lock hands in the AIDS pandemic. The subject is provocative, troubling yet unavoidable. It is now estimated that 40 million people worldwide are infected with HIV. By the end of this turbulent millennia—one which thought the suppression of plague to at long last be possible—100 million persons may be infected with this disease for which there is no cure. That we may be able to prolong the diseased condition short of death with protease inhibitors only compounds the problem. In our day we find an ambivalent national and global political mood. On the one hand it emphasizes personal responsibility and limited resources. On the other hand it emphasizes both freedom of expression and concern for justice and care for the sick and vulnerable. This ambivalence reflects the historic tension between purity and prophylactic values on the one hand and acceptance and provision of care on the other. A spate of moral imperatives in this age of the AIDS pandemic gather around the prophylactic pole and around the pole of free expression. Liberty and a sense of mercy and provision of help for people whom the vicissitudes of life have crushed, must be concomitant values.

Prophylactic Imperatives

First, a mixed imperative. Some claim that we ought to allow the free exchange of needles and the free availability of condoms in high schools. The moral idea here is prophylactic, i.e., we prevent a lethal contamination of human lives by sanitizing two vectors of transmission. These imperatives are somewhat dissonant with New Testament purity ethics which lays accent on holy care of the body as the temple of the Holy Spirit. On the other hand, such imperatives resonate with the Hebraic prophylactic ethic of protecting the society from harm by all political and public health measures.

Two recent prophylactic-type imperatives are now under debate in public policy. One asks whether pregnant mothers who are HIV positive should be coercively treated with AZT to diminish the incidence of transmission of the disease to the children they bear. The treatment works, with fifty percent fewer babies infected. A second issue is testing all newborns, say in New York City, to see if they are infected and to begin AZT treatment if they are found positive. As the practice of preventative medicine evolves the tension between a quick and temporary fix (technological fix) and fundamental change will become permanent. The fixes of automobiles (now apartments), antibiotics and contraceptives averting. The sequellae of detection, infection and conception have never removed the profound stigmata of sex. At the same time, we anguish whether health professionals should remain free in conscience to refuse or withdraw from the care of someone who is infected with the disease.

These representative imperatives variously express the prophylactic purification and disease preventive imperatives for individuals and society. In some way such imperatives cry out "clean up your act" and do what indeed can be done to prevent the transmission of disease.

However, there is a complementary imperative to this heavenly mandate which views the problem in its earthly dimension. This view is full of sympathy for the human condition. It recognizes our fall from grace and perfection. This accepting and accommodating mode embraces this world in its present plight, forgives sinners and proffers aid and support. In the AIDS pandemic such an apperception of kingdom emphasizes activities such as fair housing legislation seeking accommodation for persons with AIDS: the Housing for persons with AIDS Act. Help for the majoral victims of AIDS, poor persons in US cities and in Africa, and work for the extension of the Ryan White AIDS Care Act will move in resonance with this sympathy. That AIDS in the early third millennium afflicts mainly the poor and oppressed of the world (e.g. Africa) is a stigma of global injustice.

> Naaman, commander of the army of the king of Aram, was a great man and in high favor with his master, because by him the Lord had given victory to Aram. The man, though a mighty warrior, suffered from leprosy. Now the Arameans on one of their raids had taken a young girl captive from the land of Israel, and she served Naaman's wife. She said to her mistress, "If only my lord were with the prophet who is in Samaria! He would cure him of his leprosy." So Naaman went in and told his lord just what the girl from the land of Israel had said. And the king of Aram said, "Go then, and I will send along a letter to the king of Israel."

> He went, taking with him ten talents of silver, six thousand shekels of gold, and ten sets of garments. He brought the letter to the king of Israel, which read, "When this letter reaches you, know that I have sent to you my servant Naaman, that you may cure him of his leprosy." When the king of Israel read the letter, he tore his clothes and said, "Am I God, to give death or life, that this man sends word to me to cure a man of his leprosy? Just look and see how he is trying to pick a quarrel with me."

> But when Elisha the man of God heard that the king of Israel had torn his clothes, he sent a message to the king, "Why have you torn your clothes? Let him come to me, that he may learn that there is a prophet in Israel." So Naaman came with his horses and chariots, and halted at the entrance of Elisha's house. Elisha sent a messenger to him, saying, "Go, wash in the Jordan seven times, and your flesh shall be restored and you shall be clean." But Naaman became angry and went away, saying, "I thought that for me he would surely come out, and stand and call on the name of the Lord his God, and would wave his hand over the spot, and cure the leprosy! Are not Abana and Pharpar, the rivers of Damascus, better than all the waters of Israel? Could I not wash in them, and be

339

clean?" But his servants approached and said to him, "Father, if the prophet had commanded you to do something difficult, would you not have done it? How much more, when all he said to you was, 'Wash, and be clean'?" So he went down and immersed himself seven times in the Jordan, according to the word of the man of God; his flesh was restored like the flesh of a young boy, and he was clean.
(II Kings 5:1-14)

Comment: The God of Israel, the God of all nations, the God of all people is the God of the sick and vulnerable. The prophetic ministry of Elisha is the ministry of cleansing and healing. His witness is to the Syrian king through the king of Israel. The foreign is domesticated in the living, healing mercy of God. Like AIDS today, leprosy was the ancient stigma of uncleanness, of *Anfechtung* (Luther's attack) of vulnerability.

Excursus

"All Hallows" Day has just passed in Europe. France and Germany make much of this central day in Roman Catholic and Protestant faith. Tomorrow Americans (1996) will go to the polls to elect a new President. As I leave the Ecumenical Institute here in Strasburg I pass the United States Consulate where we have cast our absentee ballots. Some relief is evident there today since President Clinton has said that if he is elected he will keep the diplomatic corps in place and they need not submit their resignations.

Even in *abstentia* I have thought much this Fall about an issue that seemed to raise its head in campaign rhetoric. The question "values" of a "morality" and "character" which I take it, is contemporary lingo for what the tradition calls holiness or purity.

> "This [election] is about these words: 'Duty, honor, country.'"
> (former President George Bush)

> "If you want a President on the job, not on trial or in court, Bob Dole is your man."
> (Bob Dole)

> "Is there no sense of dignity, no honor? The person in this job should be at the center of ethical behavior."
> (Ross Perot)
> CBS Evening News Monday, Nov 4, 1996.

Two arguments have been forwarded in the campaign: In one scenario Dole is to be preferred to Clinton by reasons of positive vs. negative character.

Dole	Clinton
✓ Patriotic	✓ A draft-dodger
✓ Loyal to his wife	✓ A playboy
✓ True to his word	✓ Not trustworthy

In another scenario Clinton wins on the "Character," holiness issue:

Clinton	Dole
✓ Concerned for the poor	✓ Favors rich business interests
✓ Advocate of racial justice	✓ Favors status quo
✓ Advocates the rights of women	✓ Favors traditional "family (male dominant) values"

So...who wins? Answer: Clinton...then Bush...our ambilalence about moral purity.

Biblical holiness moves in both directions. Personal purity, sexual chastity, honesty, patriotism, and private virtue are features of holiness. At the same time, compassion, social justice, concern for the poor and commitment to peace are elements of holiness. So we pray "Hallowed be thy name," and the only winners are the spiritual Franciscans and Mother Theresa.

III. Salus: "Thy Kingdom Come...On Earth as in Heaven"

...ba 'shama yim re 'ma'al u' va' aretz mi'tachas...

A strange coincidence of events: Ted Kaczynski, a southside Chicago boy, Harvard student, Berkeley mathematician, is nabbed in his simple Montana cabin and accused of being the "Unabomber" whose first lethal missal was sent to a lab here at our university—Northwestern. An even more lethal missile meant for a Hezbollah rocket launcher inadvertently hit a UN refugee compound, killing scores in Lebanon. And the Luddite society holds its annual meeting. The common thread, in Marx's words, is a critique of heaven in name of earth—or a yearning to draw heaven down to earth. Human culture is a glorious obsession to fashion kingdom-come. Israel gave the world this transformative vision of Heaven to earth. It was called *Basilea tou theou*, the Kingdom of God. Jesus warned against coercing it in by force (Matthew 11:12).

The Luddites of nineteenth-century England smashed earth machines in the name of a heavenly bliss on earth. The Unabomber in his manifesto said that technology was destroying our humanity, which destruction he then proceeded to compound. Tim McVeigh envisioned a warrior kingdom of right and power which was confuted by bungling bureaucrats at Waco. Even if children were offered as "collateral damage" at Oklahoma City, this chaotic madness had to stop. Israeli, Iraqi, and American rockets launched in the service of peaceful security, heavenly shalom, have wrought hell on earth in recent times in the Middle East. Beware, wrote George Bernard Shaw, of the man (or nation) whose God is in the heavens; he likely is making hell on earth.

...on earth as in heaven...

We have pondered the home ground of our being in God, the Father, in heaven. We have pondered the quality of being necessary for access to our home—holiness. Now we can ponder the benefit of that homecoming and home being: wholeness (shalom) in that good household—the kingdom.

The Jewish (Aramaic) structure of the prayer and its rendition into Greek imply a parallelism of the first three petitions:

> Sanctified be...your name... *Onoma sou*
> Your kingdom come... *Basilea sou*
> Your will be done... *Thelema sou*
> on earth as in heaven... *Os en ourano*

Transmission to God beyond implies that we are travellers between two kingdoms. We appear as *Diognetus* pilgrims:

> They dwell in their own countries, but only as sojourners...
> Every foreign country is a fatherland to them,
> and every fatherland a foreign country.[196]

The second request (*zweite Bitte*: Luther) of the Lord's prayer "Thy kingdom come" takes us onto the richly varied terrain of the divine kingdom. Jaroslav Pelikan, whose book Jesus Through the Centuries develops the kingly picture of Jesus with two initial metaphors: *cosmokrator* and ruler of peoples, finds depicted a celestial and cosmic king. Secondly, there is a political king of nations. In The Historical Jesus, Dominic Crossan chooses another image exemplifying kingdom in the apostolic mission of healing and sharing bread with the poor and destitute. Let us consider these several pictures since they all agree that the good and mighty king (e.g., James of Scotland) dwells inconspicuously near, with, and for his suffering people.

Cosmic King

Taking its cue from the scriptural passages of lordship over the creation (e.g., Colossians 1:15-19), the early church envisioned and depicted Jesus as the King who is subduing all enemies and putting them under his feet (I Corinthians 15:25-26, Psalm 110:1, Isaiah 66:1, Mark 12:36, Acts 2:35, Hebrews 1:13). The *Cosmokrator* Jesus was shown on a fourth-century Roman sarcophagus with his foot resting on a personification of the cosmos. This conquering King will make death his last enemy. The king of the world and universe is a symbol that informs the doctrines of creation, providence, natural law and eschatology as kingdom embraces all given material and temporal reality out of the background of eternal and spiritual reality. As Calvin would say, creation is the "Theater of His glory." We therefore pray:

---

[196] Jaroslav Pelikan, *Jesus through the Centuries* (San Francisco: Harper, 1985).

Thy kingdom come on earth as in heaven...

Related to reign is reason. For the early church as it formulated its *Cosmokrator* doctrine (Basil of Caesarea c.350 C.E., for example), *Logos* was the binding ligature tying together divine and human consciousness and the world in its inner order and purpose. In Basil's phrase (reminiscent of Colossians), in Him "all things have their continuance and constitution."

Kyrios Christos is *Logos*

With words which recall the "Lord's Prayer," Jaroslav Pelikan concludes that this cosmic logos, who will restore all creation (*apokastatas ton panton*), "made sense out of the madness of the world and the power of evil."[197]

Political King

The world of first-century Palestinian Judaism also envisioned the Messiah (the Anointed One) to be a great King in the legacy of David. This is the political and military image. Luke records the angelic annunciation to Miriam, his mother:

> The Lord God will give to him the throne of his father David,
> and he will reign over the house of Jacob forever, and of his
> kingdom there will be no end
> (Luke 1:32-33).

The metaphor of the kingdom has been ambiguous from the beginning.

> Christ's kingdom is not of this world.
> (John 18:36)

> Seek first the kingdom of God and all else will be added unto you.
> (Luke 12:31)

> The kingdoms of the world have become The Kingdom of our Lord.
> (Revelations 1:15)

Judas and the Zealots, Constantine, even Augustine to some extent, identified the kingdom of God with material rule in this world. The Essenes then, the Mennonites now, and all the pacific mystics of the ages saw Kingdom as spiritual reign disjoined from political manifestation. A multitude of other Christian movements perceived the kingdom as having some blend of earthly and eternal dimension.

---

[197] Ibid., 69.

Christian martyrs in the early centuries would die rather than commit the blasphemy to own Caesar as Lord (*Kyrios Kaisar*). Tradition has it that Ignatius of Antioch on the verge of martyrdom told the Emperor Trajan to his face:

> I have Christ the King of Heaven...may I now enjoy his kingdom.

For Luther the Kingdom (which stands forever) is a mighty force against natural evil (*welt*) (*Tyrannai der Chaosmächte*) societal evil (*teufel*) Satan and subjective evil (*fleisch*) (*meine eigene wille*). Through the ages Christians have held various beliefs about Kingdom:

> The kingdom of God was to slowly displace the kingdom of this world (medieval Catholicism to nineteenth-century Protestant liberalism). The kingdom of God was to apocalyptically replace the increasingly decadent world.

> The kingdom of God would dialectically interplace God's will within ongoing secular history.[198]

Excursus: The Kingdom of God/Heaven in the Christian Testament

Tracing the understanding of the kingdom of God in the Hebrew testament is extremely complicated since every nation is called a kingdom and all kingdoms can have a divine commission (cf. Isaiah 44:28). The concept ranges from Saul's kingdom (I Chronicles 12:23) to the majestic reign of God over all creation (Psalm 103:18). The Christian testament notion of kingdom of God (*Basileou tou theou*) is multifaceted but falls into certain major meanings.

A. State of Being

- Blessed are the poor in spirit...Theirs is the kingdom of Heaven. (Matt 5:3)
- Suffer the little children...of such is the Kingdom of Heaven. (Matt 19:14)
- Prostitutes go in before you (priests and elders). (Matt 21:43)
- No one who puts hand to plow and turns back is fit for the Kingdom. (Luke 9:62)
- If I cast out demons, the Kingdom of God is come upon you. (Luke 11:20)
- The Kingdom of God is within you. (Luke 17:21)
- Unless born again cannot see Kingdom of God. (3:3)
- They went about preaching and teaching the Kingdom of God. (Acts 28:23)

---

[198] *"The Martyrdom of Ignatius,"* Pelikan, p. 48.

- The Kingdom is righteousness, joy and peace in the Holy Spirit. (Romans 14:17)
- He has translated us into the Kingdom of God. (Col 1:13)

B. Something Coming

Repent, the Kingdom of Heaven is at hand
Matthew 3:2

Jesus came preaching the Kingdom of God
Matthew 4:23

Thy Kingdom come
Matthew 6:10

Every scribe trained for the Kingdom of Heaven
Matthew 13:52

I'll drink it with you in the Kingdom
Matthew 26:29

You will not see death before the kingdom comes with power
Mark 9:1

The Lord...preserve me until the coming of His heavenly Kingdom
II Timothy 4:18

We are receiving a kingdom that cannot be shaken
Hebrews 2:28

The kingdoms of this world are become the Kingdom of God
Revelation 11:15

C. Society Here and there, Now and Then of Those Who Do the Will of God

(Whosoever) Breaks (does) least of commandments called least (greatest) in the Kingdom of Heaven
Matthew 5:19

Violent take it by force
Matthew 11:12

Hard for a rich man to enter the Kingdom of Heaven
Matthew 19:24

Inherit the Kingdom prepared for you
Matthew 25:34

Which commandment is first love God and neighbor "you arenot far from
the Kingdom"
Mark 12:34

It is your Father's good pleasure to give you the Kingdom
Luke 12:32

He shall eat bread in the Kingdom of God
Luke 14:15

You will eat and drink at my table in the Kingdom
Luke 22:29

Wrongdoers will not inherit the Kingdom of God
I Corinthians 6:9

D. Symbol for Something Beyond Words
Like one who sowed seed in the field
Matthew 13:24

What is Kingdom like? Mustard seed, leaven in bread
Luke 13:18

My Kingdom is not of this world
John 18:36

Kingdom of God is not talk but power
I Corinthians 4:20

Flesh and blood cannot inherit Kingdom
I Corinthians 15:50

Into the everlasting Kingdom of our Lord
2 Peter 1:11

All of these nuances and meanings of the Kingdom of God are embraced in the
Lord's Prayer. For our purposes let us first meditate on the cosmological and
communal (concern) for the poor before we refocus our inquiry toward concerns
of health and suffering.

Health in Judaic perspective is living out holiness. It is living out heavenly
other-worldness within the world. Health is a transaction of heaven on earth.
Dietrich Bonhoeffer accurately diagnosed the spiritual and ethical malaise of our
time when be observed that most persons were either excessively other-worldly

or excessively secular, making it impossible for them to both love God and the earth so fully that one could truly pray:

Thy kingdom come...on earth as in heaven.

Bonhoeffer's Kingdom Pilgrims

...are not..."wanderers who love the earth that carries them, Yet love it for here we meet that foreign land that we love above all things (a land that makes us wanderers here).... Only those who wander thus, who love earth and God in one, can believe in the Kingdom of God.[199]

The petition of the Lord's Prayer, under view in Bonhoeffer's intriguing diary, No Rusty Swords, contends that Don Quixote's rusty sword's cannot bring Heaven's Kingdom victory on earth. He challenges us to dissolve an excessive tendency toward either the spiritual or the material, one in neglect of the other.

Even in this day of a collapsed Communist world (that projected evil empire), as Bonhoeffer saw the two philosophies that still vie for human allegiance are humanistic materialism, an exaggerated secularism, critical of spirituality, and Abrahamic, biblical spirituality, critical of materialism. Only coalescence and cooperation between these two world-views can save our abandoned and endangered, yet visited and engraced planet. God's kingdom is in, though not of, this world.

To illumine the ideas behind this ethical crisis, and this vision of kingdom come, consider two texts. A century-and-a-half ago, Karl Marx wrote in his introduction to Critique of Hegel's Philosophy of Law:

Religious distress is at the same time the expression of real distress and a protest against real distress. Religion is the sigh of the oppressed creature, the heart of a heartless world, just as it is the spirit of a spiritless situation. It is the opium of the people. The abolition of religion as the illusory happiness of the people is required for their real happiness. The demand to give up the illusions about its condition is the demand to give up a condition which needs illusions. The criticism of religion is therefore in embryo the criticism of the vale of woe, the halo of which is religion.[200]

Marx seems to be drawing from Paul's letter to the Christians in Rome two millennia earlier:

For the creation waits with eager longing for the revealing of the sons of God; for the creation was subjected to futility, not of its own will but by the will of him who subjected it; in hope, because the creation itself will be set free from

---

[199] Dietrich Bonhoeffer, *"Dein Reich Komme" in Gesammelte Schriften* (Munchen: Kaiser Verlag, 1960), 3:270.2.
[200] A. Th. Van Leeuwen, *Critique of Heaven* (New York: Scribner's, 1964), p. 10.

> its bondage to decay and obtain the glorious liberty of the children of God. We
> know that the whole creation has been groaning in travail together until now;
> and not only the creation, but we ourselves, who have the first fruits of the
> Spirit, groan inwardly as we wait for adoption as sons, the redemption of our
> bodies (Romans 8:18).[201]

Illusion is the contradiction of redemption. Fantasy is otherworldly obsession.
Hope enacts liberation here and now, yet it disavows utopia. Can we find mutual
connection and convergence in these two charters of ethical obligation? "Beware
of the man, whose God is in the sky," wrote George Bernard Shaw. "He is likely
making hell on earth."

Advent is a bright season of good news, of unfailing oil lamps (*Hanukkah*)
occurs amid the bitter darkness of a people's struggle for survival. The world-
transforming story of a Madonna and child occurs against the dark backdrop of
Herod's "Slaughter of the Innocents." The brilliant drama today of birth and
new life is shadowed by the despair of poor mothers and children and the
concomitant teenage violence that springs from our neglect of their plight.

In this season we need the grace of refreshed faith and action. Piety and politics
are inextricably intertwined. "Pure and true religion is this," wrote the Apostle
James, "To tend the widows and homeless and to keep oneself uncorrupted from
the world" (James 1:27).

> *adveniat regnum tuum—Amen*

Today the kingdoms of the world are caught up in desperation and hope and the
metaphors of 'kingdom come' again seem powerful and vivid. I have just heard
a prayer from a Hungarian theologian at a meeting at the Council of Europe in
Strasbourg. He speaks of the dilemmas of living in a nation newly liberated from
the Soviet block, yearning to be assimilated into the new European Community,
struggling to discern its identity as it has been shaped by Eastern Orthodoxy,
Roman Catholicism and Protestantism, yet torn by all of theses political and
religious meanings of being a nation. On the one hand there is the upsurge of
affirmation of national, ethnic and religious identity. How does a people
faithfully become God's people? What is the theological meaning of "nation"?
True to the apocalyptic tenor of his culture and the neighboring Czech republic,
he speaks of the turmoil when

> nation shall rise against nation and kingdom against kingdom.
> (Matthew 24:7)

He speaks as if this applied to nations in crisis today. At the same time he extols
the universal messianic vision which animates the United Nations and the
European Community by recalling Isaiah:

---

[201] See Robert Jewett, "*Romans: A Commentary*" (Fortress/Hermeneia) [forthcoming].

Nations shall not lift up sword against nation neither shall they learn war anymore, They shall beat their swords into plowshares.
(Isaiah 2:4)

Here he identifies the new pluralism, toleration, human rights commitments and social justice enactments of a united Europe as the embodiment of the Kingdom of God. In the case of caught-between nations like his beloved Hungary, we find a rich mixture of ideals and actualities.

The more we probe the petition "thy kingdom come," the more that we discover that it is an admixture of earthly hope and heavenly blessing. The prayer for kingdom come is the prayer for salvation which is *shalom*. Our poor word, in English, is wholeness or health. The long history of words such as *salus, salve, save,* health, hale, heil, holy, and whole all display the rich constellation of meaning contained in this concept. The drama of health or *salus* is a drama of heaven and earth. We are saved from captivity within the conditions of existence; sin, sickness and death. We are saved from the earth, finitude and the cosmic destiny of matter which is decay, dissolution and entropy (disorganization and dissipation of energy). Salvation reposes human life in the eternal life of God: We are rescued from death to life. New life coalesces the cells of Spring.

Salvation from the destructive grip of the world is not escape from life in the world but entrance into divine life in the world. It is inauguration of kingdom. Freedom enhances the range of possibility and action. It is by nature a worldly phenomenon. Redemption is a process wherein created reality is restored to its intention and renewed toward its inherent possibility. By the very nature of transformation dynamics, redemption is also a worldly phenomenon.

In biblical tradition, God is a dynamic entity and the salvation story is going somewhere—"God was, is, and is to come" (Revelation 1:4, 8; 4:8). In biblical language, the kingdom is coming. The Greek text of this petition is *elthe* to "may it come"— Homer uses *eltheto* in the Iliad (23.770), "Hear me, O goddess, come graciously to help me." Scripture anticipates, indeed beckons, epiphany, the appearance or manifestation of God. While theophanies and epiphanies are erratic and unexpected, *Basileia tou theou*, the kingdom of God, is the progressive, normative mode of God's intruding will and way into the world. As John Bright has written in his masterful study of The Kingdom of God: From Abraham, who set out to seek "the city...whose builder and maker is God (Genesis 12:1ff, Hebrews 11:10) to Revelation's..."Holy city, New Jerusalem coming down out of heaven from God (Revelation 21:2)...to grasp what is meant by the Kingdom of God is to come very close to the heart of the Bible's gospel of salvation."[202]

---

[202] John Bright, *The Kingdom of God* (Nashville: Abingdon, 1953), p. 7.

Health as Kingdom

Let us now explore what Dominic Crossan considers to be the essence of "Kingdom come." The apostolic commission is to bring healing and food—fellowship among the poor and needy of the world. For we recall that "the well have no need of a physician" (Luke 5:31). We have noted in the preceding discussion of food that for the Hebrews sustenance is of the very essence of divine provision for the world.

That the kingdom is in but not of this world is a clue to the nature of health. Here we are wanderers, seekers, sojourners. Kingdom always appears on the horizon of space and time. Likewise, health is an elusive, hidden phenomenon, always transcending human achievement. Health is manifest at the conjunction of body and soul. Paradoxically, health can appear amid sickness, even death. Health defies our attempts to manufacture it. In the words of a wise observer, "health flourishes best when watched least." Health is ascetic distraction from world obsessions. Sickness is obsession, absorption in the sin of the world. It is the stone of impediment in God's salutary world. In the Kingdom, diseases and death are the last enemy that Messiah is proleptically preparing to put under his feet (I Corinthians 15). Health is a manifestation of the kingdom. The dominant mode of Jesus' annunciation of the kingdom is healing. When the Kingdom comes the sick are made well, the broken, whole. Death is transfigured into life.

The world is believed to be in the grip of sin, death, and the devil as Paul the Apostle would have it, or subject to debt, temptation, and the evil one as in the Lord's Prayer. We live beset by the powers, fatalities, and afflictions of this world. Release from this bondage is liberation, light, life and health.

> "If it is by the finger of God that I cast out demons, then the kingdom of God has come upon you."
> (Luke 11:20)

The kingdom comes to those who need help, who repent and cry out for salvation. It comes to the sick, the poor, the persecuted and oppressed. Drawing on Isaiah, the annunciation of Jesus' kingdom is to those who sit in the shadow of death (Matthew 4:16, Isaiah 8:23ff.).

This image corresponds with the Rabbinic picture of the messiah which finds him not sitting on an elaborate throne but on the road by the city gate among the lepers. The kingdom is a realm of life, eternal life—*zoes eionios* (Matthew 7:13ff., 19:29). This healing aspect of kingdom corresponds with the truth of Hebrew history where the law of life often refers to health practices and divine blessing is seen to reside in well-being. Let us review these two facets of biblical tradition.

The Kingdom of God—associated with Yaweh's reign in the Mosaic covenant and in the premonarchic life of the *Habiru*, then associated with the great

350

political kingdom of Saul, David and Solomon, then with prophetic righteousness and priestly rectitude in exile and diaspora—is, in great part, a matter of obedience, which is wealth and health. Disavowal of covenant is curse, disease, and misfortune. As previously noted, Yawism is a prophylactic way of life posited on singular allegiance and devotion to God. Life style, sexual and cultic purity, and social justice are all offered in return for blessing, prosperity, longevity, generativity and peace. While the righteousness/blessing, sin/sickness equation is complicated in this mysterious world where the righteous also suffer, and sinners apparently prosper, the working assumption prevails that God cares for and rewards those who seek and follow the Way. Kingdom is the state of shalom where a people abide in this faithfulness, justice and bliss.

In the reformed and messianic movement of Judaism inaugurated by John the Baptist, Jesus, and James, his brother, prophylactic rigor and legal righteousness is displaced by repentance, the inner restitution of holiness, a disposition of mercy and sacrificial care for the weak. The expectation of healing and miracle is realized as the finger of God casts out demonic power. It remains the same healing and dynamic spirit. Miracle and healing manifest kingdom in the Jesus movement. The signs of God's reign—of wellness and wealth—are no longer predominantly material phenomena but are now transposed into that elusive ecstatic, evangelic, and eschatologic quality of life peculiarly introduced by primitive Christianity.

The Kingdom of God II: Healing, Eating, Sickness and Destitution

John Dominic Crossan in his masterfully crafted cultural anthropological view of Jesus and the companions in ministry believes that evidence shows a Mediterranean Jewish peasant emboldened with a ministry that combined prophetic economic justice and healing/exorcism symbolically centered in a wandering itinerancy (homelessness) expressed in preaching, healing and eating with the poor and destitute. Healing and eating, thus claims Crossan, was the essence of the Kingdom of God.

Jesus invoked the metaphor, "Kingdom of God," he continues," not as an apocalyptic event in the immanent future, but as a mode of life in the immediate present."[203] The ministry of justice and compassion for the destitute and the sick here and now is the Kingdom of God. Exorcism and Healing confront the demons which hold life captive to injustice, destitution, and sickness. These powers of evil will also eventually kill the disciple in Christ. But death has no power over life in Christ.

Crossan argues that miracle (healing) and meal is at the heart of Jesus program. The "Lord's Prayer" follows "will be done" with "daily bread"—the perennial longing of the destitute. The Kingdom is a corporate plan (an embodiment) not a

---

[203] John Dominic Crossan, *The Historical Jesus* (San Francisco: Harper, 1991), p. 304.

personal salvation. In words obviously borrowed from Gerd Thessen and Bob Jewett, Crossan concludes:

> ...The intersection of magic and meal, miracle and table is pointed directly and deliberately at the intersection of patronage and clientage, honor and shame, the very heart of ancient mediterranean society.[204]

To continue, magic, or healing, is to the spiritual world, to spiritual subjugation, what banditry is to politics—it robs from the rich to give to the poor. Magic or healing is liberation.

The prosperous have no need of a physician (Matthew 9:12).

Elijah and Elisha were magicians, says Crossan, and so were Honi and Hnina, and Jesus of Nazareth.

Daniel Callahan in his provocative studies on healthcare has examined the premises of the World Health Organization and its moral charter concerning the "right" of health. These principles coincide with the Hebraic/Christic manifestations of kingdom.

> God wills health and the good commonwealth wills and provides for it.
> Sickness rises where there is injustice.
> Peace restores health to the world.

These insights might lead us back to healing and eating—because we consume, we are attracted to magic. Hans Dieter Betz of the University of Chicago has traced the history of miracle and magic from the second century to the fifth century CE. He concludes:

> Magic has survived from time immemorial throughout history through the coming and going of entire religions, the scientific and technological revolutions, and the triumph of modern medicine.[205]

Howard Clark Kee phrases it another way in a comprehensive study, Medicine, Miracle and Magic in the New Testament:

> Medicine is a method of diagnosis of human ailments and a prescription for them based on a combination of theory about and observation of the body, its functions and malfunctions. Miracle embodies the claim that healing can be accomplished through appeal to, and subsequent action by the gods, either directly or through a chosen intermediary agent. Magic is a technique through word or act, by which a desired end is achieved, whether that end lies in the solution to the seeker's problem or in damage to the enemy who has caused the problem (1986:3). In other words, "if the technique is effective of itself in

---

[204] Ibid., p. 304.
[205] Crossan, *Historical Jesus,* p. 315.

overcoming a hostile force, then the action is magical. If it is viewed as the intervention of the god or goddess, then it is miraculous. If it is a facilitating of the natural function of the body, then it is medical (1986:4).[206]

Paul Achtemeier has found a twin five-fold text of miracle magic healings in Mark 4-8.

Walking on Water[1/2] Mark 4:35-41	Walking on Water Mark 6:45-52
The Gerasene Demoniac [2/1] Mark 5:1-20	Blind Man Healed Mark 8:22-26
Two Women Cured [2/1] Mark 5:21-24a, 35-43	Distant Girl Cured Mark 7:24-30
Two Women Cured [2/1] Mark 5:24b-34	Deaf Mute Cured Mark 7:31-37[207]
Bread and Fish [1/6] Mark 6:33-44	Bread and Fish [1/6] Mark 8:1-10

Wolfgang Roth has shown how this template is drawn from Ezekiel (see The Hebrew Gospel). The Gesarene Demoniac (Mark 5:1-17) shows the dynamic quality of unity and plurality.

> Now he was casting out a demon that was dumb; when the demon had gone out, the dumb man spoke, and the people marveled. But some of them said, "he casts out demons by Beelsebub, the prince of demons."...But he, knowing their thoughts, said to them, "every kingdom divided against itself is laid waste, and a divided household falls. And if Satan also is divided against himself, how will his kingdom stand?" (Saying Gospel Q, 2Q: Luke 11:14-15, 17-18a; Matthew 9:32-34; 12:22-26).

The first important element is that, in both sources, the accusation is preserved in strikingly similar language and the accusatory term begins as Beelzebub and ends as Satan. The former word preserves, as Joseph Fitzmyer notes, "the name of an old Canaanite god, meaning 'Baal, the prince,' or Baal of the Exalted Abode" (1981-85:920). But that unique epithet is the voice, surely, of the little tradition, an attack that bespeaks a village environment, Beelsebub needed to be rephrased as Satan when the transmissional process began to move from that original location.

---

[206].Howard Clark Kee, *Medicine, Miracle and Magic in the New Testament*, p. 306.
[207] Paul Achetemeier, *Brokerless Kingdom,* in Kee, op.cit., p. 229ff.

A second important element is the conjunction that Jesus creates between kingdom, house, and Satan. Although those first two expressions could be taken as innocent and random examples of division begetting destruction, they could also be taken as underlining the politico-social dimensions of exorcism. Satan now rules, as Douglas Oakman has suggested, through kingdoms and houses, maybe, for example, the house of Herod or the kingdom of Rome (1988:115). The association is delicate, indirect, and implicit but probably neither accidental nor innocuous.

A final consideration: one wonders how Jesus' opponents left themselves open for such a devastating rejoinder. How could one even imagine casting out demons by demonic possession? One answer was seen already in Ian Lewis' work as establishments struck back somewhat separately at shamanistic curers of possession by accusing them of witchcraft, that is, of causing what they cured. Another answer may lie in George Peter Murdock's survey of illness in a statistically valid sample of the world's cultures. He distinguishes between disease, "suggesting primarily the communicable virus-borne or bacteria-borne phenomena," and illness,"embracing any impairment of health serious enough to arouse concern, whether it be due to communicable disease, psychosomatic disturbance, organic failure, aggressive assault, or alleged accident or supernatural interference" (6). He concedes "that supernatural causes of illness far outweigh natural causes in the belief systems of the world's people" (26) but never really wonders about that fact, it being enough apparently to say that "magic is illusory technique whereas science is the most admirable component of man's ideational environment" (53). Be that as it may, he notes that, among the supernatural causes of illness, "spiritaggression... the direct hostile, arbitrary, or punitive action of some malevolent or affronted supernatural being" (20) is a "quasiuniversal... rated as important (i.e., predominant or significant)...most markedly so in...the Circum-Mediterranean" (73-74). Yet there is another, separate, and different explanation, witchcraft, which "is practically universal in the Circum-Mediterranean region but surprisingly rare elsewhere in the world"(21) so that "there are fairly substantial grounds for regarding the Circum-Mediterranean as a culture area in which one of the most characteristic and deep-seated traits is the belief in the causation of illness by witchcraft."[208]

We therefore have a vital connection between kingdom, house, Satan and healing, Crossan argues.

> They came to the other side of the sea, to the country of the Gerasenes. And when he had come out of the boat, there met him out of the tombs a man with an unclean spirit, who lived among the tombs; and no one could bind him any more, even with a chain; for he had often been bound with fetters and chains, but the chains he wrenched apart, and the fetters he broke in pieces; and no one had the strength to subdue him. Night and day among the tombs and on the

---

[208] Kee, *Magic and Meal, p. 318, 319.*

mountains he was always crying out, and bruising himself with stones. And when he saw Jesus from afar, he ran and worshipped him; and crying out with a loud voice, he said, "What have you to do with me, Jesus, Son of the Most High God? I adjure you by God, do not torment me." For he had said to him, "Come out of the man, you unclean spirit!" And Jesus asked him, "What is your name?" He replied, "My name is Legion; for we are many."And he begged him eagerly not to send them out of the country. Now a great herd of swine was feeding there on the hillside; and they begged him, "Send us to the swine, let us enter them." So he gave them leave. And the unclean spirits came out, and entered the swine; and the herd, numbering about two thousand, rushed down the steep bank into the sea, and were drowned in the sea. The herdsmen fled and told it in the city and in the country. And people came to see what it was that had happened. And they came to Jesus, and saw the demoniac sitting there, clothed and in his right mind, the man who had had the legion; and they were afraid. And those who had seen it told what had happened to the demoniac and to the swine. And they began to beg Jesus to depart from their neighborhood (Mark 5:1-7).[209]

The Kingdom of Health Come Today

The December 1994 issue of Daedelus, the journal of the American Academy of Arts and Sciences, is entitled "Wealth and Health." The provocative set of essays are culled from the broad Western tradition. (Ideas on the good life and the material and spiritual, earthy and heavenly wisdom, concerning health). As the symposium title suggests, there is a close association between prosperity and health, poverty and illness. Throughout the world, the poor have higher mortality rates and higher incidence of all kinds of morbidity —heart disease, hypertension, tooth decay, cancer and mental illness. Yet, the causal association is more subtle. Prosperity does not ensure well-being. New modes of anguish plague the rich, especially diseases of the mind and spirit. Divorce, unhappiness, even specific mental and physical disorders of indulgence and luxuriant life styles take their toll. Kingdom blessing in one sense is reserved for children, the innocent and the poor (Matthew 5-7).

> "Blessed (happy, healthy) are the poor in spirit. Theirs is the kingdom of Heaven"
> (Matthew 5:2)

This would suggest that true health or wealth is found in some synthesis of the material, spiritual and ethical factors. A moving exposition of this purview on the Kingdom of God is offered by the health theology of Paul Tillich.

A Contemporary Conceptualization

Tillich has conceptualized the kingdom or domain of health as follows:[210]

---

[209] Magic and Meal p. 314.

[210] Paul Tillich, *Three Ways of Healing, in Belgum, Religion and Health*, p. 26.

Three Ways of Healing (Paul Tillich)			
Modes	Spiritual *(Religious)*	Psychic *(Magical)*	Bodily *(Natural)*
Courses of Disease	Existence *(Threat of non-being)*	Estrangement	Environment *(Imperfections born in finitude)*
Consequences	Anxiety	Guilt	Genetic *(Endemic disorder disease)*
Healing Practice	Sacrifice *(Prayer)*	Counseling *(Incantation)*	Drugs *(knife)*

Tillich's anthropology, which affirms a unity of body, mind and spirit, holds for a very tight integration of these three dimensions. In contrast to a natural philosophy as illustrated by the thought of Henri Bergson or of a transcendental theology as illustrated by the thought of Karl Barth, Tillich contends that the transcendent is imbedded in the imminent. "The kingdom is within you" (Luke 17:21).

> The spiritual is not a sphere outside the mind, as the unconditioned is not a reality outside the conditioned, nor the ultimate a stage above the preliminary. The spiritual is a qualification of the mind, the unconditioned a dimension of the conditioned, and the ultimate is the point of reference for everything preliminary."[211]

The kingdom of God is in part a quality or value of human existence. Divine and human realms intertwine in the dimension of spirit which is the vehicle of the Kingdom of God. Human health is a blessing of the divine spirit as the dimensions of existence are integrated. In this sense health is manifestation of the kingdom. Health in individual existence is as peace in social existence—both miracles or signs of the kingdom are shalom. Health is life. Life is God.

---

[211] Paul Tillich, "The Relation of Religion and Health," in D. Belgum, *Religion and Health. p. 28.*

The eucharistical gift of life is well-being ultimately grounded in God. Beyond and within suffering and death, the grace of life taps the source of eternity eliciting thanksgiving and praise—*Euxares*.

The version of the kingdom of God implicit in the "Lord's Prayer" according to most modern interpreters is that of the *ShenomESre*—the eighteen Benedictions of first-century (Second Temple) Israel—whose contours and themes are obviously reflected in the prayer. Here the "coming" and "reign" of the kingdom being to God alone. James Charlesworth, the Princeton expert on firstcentury Palestinian Judaism, says:

> The Lord's Prayer...is deeply Jewish as reflected abundantly in the Jewish literature contemporaneous with Jesus.[212]

The Hebrew Benediction (*Berakhah*) means to fall to one's knees, to be brought low in the exquisite coincidence of need and praise. The pervasive *Berakhah* or Benediction of Judaism is well known and resonates with the "Lord's Prayer."

> *Barukh attah adonai eloheinu m a lech ha olam ha mozi lehem min ha arez.*

> Blessed art thou Lord God of the Universe - who brings forth bread from the earth.

After the ascription *Barukh attah adonai Eloheinu melek ha-Olom* particular benedictions can be offered for

daily bread
for grace of feeding all on earth
for forgiveness
for contiguous blessings of life
for guidance through temptation
on the senses of the body
on provident harvest
on the candles and oil for light
on crises of life: divorce, stolen goods, harm to one's fellow, etc.

The prayers are always linked to the commandments as each applies to a C-3 invocation of the Divine name. The *Barakhah* were recited as one took hold of the *tefilin*, the sash of the commandments, or *Mitzvot*.

God's kingdom for which we invoke the name and dare to pray is therefore the Jewish reign of the Sovereign *Yaweh*.

Martin Buber, in a 1917 letter to Franz Weefal, captures its essence:

> ...what Jesus calls the kingdom—no matter how tinged with a sense of the world's end or miraculous transformation it may be—is no other-world

---

[212] James H. Charlesworth, *Jesus' Jewishness,* (New York: Crossroad , 1991), p. 196.

consolation, no vague heavenly bliss. Nor is it an ecclesiastical or cultic association, or church. It is the perfect life of man with man. (It is)True community, and as such God's immediate realm, God's *basilea*, God's earthly kingdom.[213]

IV. Semblance: "Thy Will be Done...on Earth as in Heaven"

"Be strong as a leopard, and swift as an eagle, and fleet as a hart, and courageous as a lion, to do the will of thy Father which is in heaven."[214]
Jehuda ben Tema

"Do his will as thy will, that he may do Thy will as his will. Annihilate thy will before his will, that he may annihilate the others before they will."[215]

If, as we have argued, the reality of God is the sure foundation of the origination, constitution, and destination of human beings in the human family; if the nature and purpose of God is holiness and the quality of human wholeness is harmony with that holiness; if an unfolding kingdom which is health is the divine will for creation, then semblance of human will with the divine will is the goal of human existence and we therefore pray

"Thy will be done on earth as it is in heaven."

God created man in his image. He created you and me to be like him, to be the mirror of his spirit, his love. The more you allow God to look upon you and in you, the more like him you become. God looks at you in Jesus Christ, and when you allow yourself to be seen by God in Jesus Christ, you become like him.[216]
Emil Brunner

"Turn your eyes upon Jesus, look full in his wonderful face; and the things of earth will grow strangely dim in the light of his glory and grace"...on earth as in Heaven. It is his will to perfect us; to cleanse us of all evil and to place his Holy Spirit in us. God's view, God's looking at us, is a creative looking. He wills that we at the appearance of Jesus Christ become like him.

That I may know him and the power of his resurrection, that I may share his sufferings and become like him in his death.
(Philippians 3:10)

If anyone wills His will he will know my authority is of God not my own. . .
(John 7:17)

---

[213] James H. Charlesworth, "A Prolegomenon to a New Study of the Jewish Background of the Hymns and Prayers in the New Testament," in G. Vermes, J. Neuser, ed., *Essays in Honor of Yigael Yadin*, Oxford: University Press, 1982), pp. 265-285.
[214] Jehuda ben Tema.
[215] "Gamaliel" (Quoted in Interpreter's Dictionary of the Bible, Vol. III, p. 156.)
[216] Emil Brunner, *I Believe in the Living God* (London: Butterworth Press, 1961), p. 20.

Health is resonant with the divine will, disease is dissonant with the divine will.

"I have come that they might have life and that life in abundance"
(John 10:10)

Life and health are God's gift, the divine presence on earth. To spill blood and life is blasphemy, to harm health, deadly sin. God's will is life, health, and peace.

Often the prayer is offered in Gethsemane agony, on the eve of death, "Not my will, but thine be done" (Luke 22:42). Both kingdom and will are qualified and directed by earth and heaven. The oldest form of the synagogue Kaddish prayer which the Lord's Prayer resembles begins:

"Exhaulted and hallowed is His great name in the world which He created according to His will."

It is likely that Jesus was familiar with this prayer from his childhood. It expressed the great faith and confidence of the biblical conception of world and divine will that by that very will the world was brought into being (Ephesians 1, Colossians 1); that humanity was chosen and blessed in holy destiny (Ephesians 1:4-5); humanity forgiven in its trespasses (vs. 7,8); and molded into perfection and joy in its being in God's world (Romans 12:2, 15:32). Humans are endowed and destined in creation to Imago dei, life, health, freedom and immortality.

The will of God is the plan of God for life on earth, for history and the history of nature, for all creation, and each constituent being; for all that has been, is now, and ever will be. God has a blueprint for creation and for each creature. The will of God, wrote Karl Barth, is:

To maintain his creature, to save it, and to fulfill his work by the manifestation of his Kingdom.[217]

Paul Lehmann offers the same comprehension of the will of God as

. . . what God is doing in the world to make and keep human life human.[218]

The staggering inference of this petition is that human receptivity encourages or thwarts the coming of God's kingdom and the realization of God's will. God's will pauses at human recalcitrance. It flourishes in human receptivity. A shred of truth is found in the old saw, "God has no hands but our own." In any case, we are "fellow workers with God" (I Corinthians 3:9). The petition expresses the audacious and awesome sense of human responsibility under God as found in

---

[217] Karl Barth, *Prayer* (Philadelphia: The Westminster Press, 1952) p. 52.
[218] Paul Lehman, *Ethics in a Christian Context* (New York: Harper and Row, 1963).

Judaism. God's will is exerted in cooperation with persons and nations. Even Augustine and Calvin, with their accents on divine initiative and independent divine intention, saw the importance of human participation since much content of the divine will concerns people.

The sorry fact is that despite our noble endowment we choose sin over salvation, disease over health, violence over help, idolatry over faith. The petition "Thy will be done," is therefore a plea against our wayward inclination. Even Jesus, embracing the full disorienting force of our human will prayed, "Not my will, but thine be done."

Plea and Promise

Barth suggests that the petition implies a plea that the time in which we are living not be devoid of divine purpose—that we not live in vain. We pray that God will find us worthy to deal with despite our unworthiness, and that God's sheer grace and love will compel and sustain his active will with us in our time. We pray that God not give up on us. The prayer pleas that God will not tire through incessant disappointment and anger at a recalcitrant people, but will continue and intensify his reign until "every knee shall bow and tongue confess..." (Isaiah 45:23, Romans 14:11, Philippians 2:10) and all kingdoms of the world" become the kingdoms of our Lord and of his Christ" (Revelation 11:15).

God chooses to work through human faithfulness and righteousness. A new quality of world, anticipated in the redemptive purposes of Yaweh with Israel is now perpetuated in the messianic kingdom of Jesus. This kingdom will ensue as God's people live it out and communicate it to others. An eclipse of God (Buber) blots out kingdom radiance when human evil magnifies darkness in creation and obscures the sun. Arno Mayer, the great historian of the Jewish holocaust in Europe, asks "Why did the heavens not darken?"[219]

The heavens were bright, "brighter than a thousand suns" as a *Bhagavad Gita* text applied to the Hiroshima genocide would claim, because the softening ozone shield of God's grace almost let the earth burn up in a supernova conflagration in those dark days. "Thy kingdom come" is a petition to God and an affirmation by humankind. "Keep bringing it," it sighs, and "if possible, let me aid, at least not obstruct, its coming."

This passage, "Thy will be done," might be Beethoven's Passionata or Pathetique. It is a trembling text in which one fears he will go deaf and not hear the earth sounds of the music of the spheres. It cries the fear that God may cease to speak and lead. It is a cry for continuation of the covenant of compassion and sympathy. It is a message of passion and suffering. It calls for semblance of human and divine wills. It is a plea for the great resemblance. It pleas that God

---

[219] London: Verso, 1990.

and we will keep it together. The petition anticipates two great scriptural truths from Philippians: *Kenosis* and *Genosonai*.

> Have this mind among yourselves
> Which you have in Christ Jesus,
> Who, though he was in the form of God,
> Did not count equality with God a thing to be grasped,

> But emptied himself, taking the form of a servant,
> Being born in the likeness of men.
> And being found in the human form.
> (Philippians 2:7, 8)

> He humbled himself and became obedient in death
> That I may know him,
> And the power of his resurrection
> And may share his sufferings

> Becoming like him in his death
> That if possible I may attain the resurrection
> From the dead.
> (Philippians 3:10, 11)

In *Kenotic* incarnation, God emptied divinity, identified with us in our humanity and became like us in our suffering and death. In Paul's *Genotic* identification, we seal that resemblance from our side, becoming one with him in his suffering and death.

The word translated "will" is somewhat rare in scripture. *thelēma* in Greek, *ra,son* in Hebrew, *re tua* in Aramaic, symbolize desire or longing, joy or delight. The modern coloring of the word "will," in the sense of Kant, Schopenhauer, or Freud, is foreign to these biblical roots. The couplet heaven and earth has the distinct biblical meaning of world or age (*olam*). Heaven, of course, connotes the abode of deity and thus the transcendent abode of human spirits.

Compassion, fellow suffering, is an important dimension of the theological quality of semblance which is the inner meaning of the petition "thy will be done on earth as in heaven." God's nature and will is one of self-giving, of out-going, which of necessity entails disappointment, discouragement, and suffering. Reciprocity is the key feature of the God-human fellowship. As James Ashbrook claims, between God and people, "attachment and aspiration are reciprocal." In freedom, God chooses fellowship with us, which entails suffering. In love we relate to one another in concern. This brings joy and pain. Compassion is the call of our being.[220]

---

[220] James Ashbrook, "Making Sense of God: How I Got to the Brain," *Zygon*, 31 Sept. 1996, p. 401ff.

Dimensions of Compassion

Suffering which we now must begin to explore even under the rubric of health is a complex phenomenon. It has objective and subjective dimensions. Pain is a substratum of suffering. Pain can be physical, emotional, mental, or spiritual. Persons can enjoy material affluence and wellbeing and be anguished in mind and spirit. A similar malignant tumor can devastate one person and scarcely affect another. It can be destructive or redemptive. Suffering can be prevented, caused, ameliorated, shared, or endured.

Prevention

The human enterprise of culture—agriculture, science, technology, business, government, medicine, education, the arts and religion are all, in one sense, attempts to maximize human pleasure and minimize pain—to prevent suffering—to fill up joy in life. Food procurement and production prevents the anguish of hunger and starvation. Sanitation assures clean water free of contamination. Science and derivative technology heats homes, provides travel, eases work, stimulates the mind, offers consumer goods. Vaccines and biologicals specifically prevent another range of maladies. In the near future, a broad spectrum of human pains and diseases will be preventable through the combined safeguarding vectors of environmental safeguard, personal hygiene and biological inoculation. The global eradication of leprosy and smallpox attest to this awesome prevention of the plagues of nature and the preclusion of attendant suffering. It is unconscionable that preventable river blindness, schistosomiasis, and intestinal diarrhea, diseases that damage brains and bodies of children, still decimate the world.

Causation

Suffering can be caused by intention or negligence. Therefore, we pray forgiveness for "what we have done and what we have left undone." In this rigorous ethical sense, all suffering that could be prevented, but is not, is caused. Killings and shootings create needless suffering. Accidents occur and are part of the inexplicable burden of suffering and evil. Some accidents are predictable and preventable. We calculate the statistical lives we can afford to lose or cannot afford to save when we build highways foregoing or keeping dangerous curves, for example. Do we cause suffering when we knowingly allow a severely genetically damaged child to be born? New diagnostic technology often makes such knowledge possible. Much suffering is caused by the mean spirit, hostility, anger, revenge and apathy.

As C.S. Lewis noted in *The Problem of Pain*:

> God can't be blamed.... When souls meet...they hurt one another....

> This accounts for four-fifths of the sufferings of men.... It is men, not God, who have produced rocks, whips, prisons, slavery, guns, bayonets and bombs; it is

by human avarice or stupidity, not by the churlishness of nature, that we have poverty and overwork.[221]

Jon Margolis' column ("Gynosupremacism engenders a political revolt") is a frightening exercise in demagogic reasoning. Margolis greatly exaggerates the cultural currency of a marginal group of New Age feminists who imagine that there once existed an ancient prepatriarchal society in which there was no war or violence and men and women lived peacefully with each other.[222]

Amelioration

To relieve suffering is one of the most noble of human gifts: surgery repairing the lesion, psychiatry relieving mental anguish, therapeutic medicine relieving pain, the friend helping you in distress or tiding you over with a loan. Much of the moral architecture of the world, reflected, for example, in the Noahic and Mosaic covenant, seeks to ameliorate anguish by prevention and intervention, assuaging the pain and suffering inflicted on humans and animals. The Noahic code proscribes cruelty to animals as well as murder and adultery. To these are added the Mosaic proscriptions of theft, lying and coveting. Amelioration of injury is the retributive and pastoral imperative in all high religion.

Sharing

With amazing efficacy, the greatest relief of suffering comes not when it is eradicated but when it is shared

> Bear ye one another's burdens and so fulfill the law of Christ
> (Galatians 6:2)

Law, suffering and identification converge in the act of care. The ministry of convivial life in general and the particular ministries of imparted care (e.g., surgery, medicine, counseling, education) are designed mainly to relieve the miseries—body, mind and soul—of our fellows. At a deeper level, cosmic and conscious suffering, reflect the discord of creation, the dissonance of earth and human history with the will of God. It is into the breach of this nonresemblance that Jesus comes to redeem and restore God's kingdom. "He has broken down the dividing wall of enmity...He is our peace" (Ephesians 2:11 ff).

Endured

In life's disease we "abound in the sufferings of Christ and in his consolation" (Corinthians 1:5). A fall has breached creation. Frailty and finitude have for a time qualified the creation. Suffering, as Paul writes in Romans, is living in the now world in memory and hope, reminiscent of its "then," cognizant of its "when." We know that our present sufferings are not worthy to

---

[221] C.S. Lewis, *The Problem of Pain,* (London: Centenary, 1940), p. 77.

[222] Rosemary Ruether, *Chicago Tribune*, Feb.15, 1997. For Margolis, see Jan 30 issue.

be compared with the glory that will be revealed in us, for "if we suffer with him, we will also be glorified with him" (Romans 8:17, 18).

This entire burden of suffering is therefore, ultimately, comprehended theologically. Suffering, in Arthur McGill's words, becomes the "test of theological method." Our existence within the purview of God is life destined ultimately toward divine glory. Crisis and suffering at present is in some mysterious way a premonition of things to come. At present, we can and do suffer and the world experiences a terrible residue of disease, pain, suffering and death. All this is (1) absurd—devoid of purpose; (2) evil—an amoral process of free cause/effect occurrences defined by malevolent purpose; or (3) redemptive—purposive and significant of redemption. The crucifixion of God's chosen, Israel and Israel's messiah, points in this latter direction.

We now reach a turning point in the Lord's Prayer. It is as striking as the turning point in the Ten Commandments with C-4 or C-5 on the Sabbath and parents. The first part has been toward heaven—we now fix our gaze on earth. Christianity, like its parent Judaism, is a profoundly worldly and historical faith.

As we explore the theme of suffering within human existence we are confronted with one of the deepest mysteries of the reality of time and space, history and nature and also one of the inscrutable aspects of faith to humans across the ages. Dostoevsky for example, poses the theodicy question as an intellectual impediment to belief, but he still believes. For him Christ, who is truth, supersedes truth, per se. "If I were forced to choose between Christ and the truth," he claimed, "I choose Christ." The mystery of divine entanglement in human affairs both as the cosmic deity of natural law and the saving God of the caring father of Jesus Christ bring an ambivalent message about suffering within the theocentric meaning of life. In physical terms and in light of laws of the universe pain, suffering and death are the concomitants of freedom, indeed are necessary in a cosmos of cause and effect as well as a developing cosmos. In terms of the personal loving God, the father to whom the Lord Jesus Christ prays, it seems as if God guides us into suffering and sustains us through it. Again it appears necessary, still an affront and enigma, yet the occasion for sustenance and grace. The tenor of the Lord's Prayer is about this paradox of suffering.

Early in Luther's career when he was held in kidnapped safety by Frederick on the Wartburg, Melanchthon asked him to help him discern "true prophecy" and authentic faith among the radical followers of Thomas Münzer and the Anabaptists. Luther's reply includes carefully reasoned criteria of discernment regarding ministry and infant baptism, for example. It also includes a remarkable passage on suffering - the true test of faith:

> In order to explore their [the prophets] individual spirit, too, you should inquire whether they have experienced spiritual distress and the divine birth, death and hell. If you should hear that all (their experiences) are pleasant, quiet, devout

(as they say), and spiritual, then don't approve of them, even if they should say that they were caught up to the third of heaven. The sign of the Son of Man is then missing, which is the only touchstone of Christians and a certain differentiator between the spirits. Do you want to know the place, time manner of (true) conversations with God? Listen: 'Like a lion has he broken all my bones'; I am cast out before your eyes'; 'my soul is filled with grief, and my life has approached hell.' The (Divine) Majesty (as they call it) does not speak in such a direct way to man that man could (actually) see it; but rather, 'Man shall not see me and live." (Our) nature cannot bear even a small glimmer of God's (direct) speaking...God is a consuming fire! The dreams and visions of the saints are horrifying.... Therefore examine them and do not even listen if they speak of the glorified Jesus, unless you have first heard of the crucified Jesus.[223]

V. Sustenance: Give us Day by Day the Bread We Need

...Hu nosain lechem l'chol basar...

In this petition, "Give us today our daily bread," the prayer shifts focus to concerns about human need, anguish, the human condition. Like the Decalogue, we move from God to man. The great themes of hunger, sin, temptation and deliverance from evil now throb in staccato petitions. The Bread benediction of *Barukh adonai* provides much of the substance of this first humanistic petition.

The Text

"Give us, this day, our daily bread."

Hunger drives people to desperation before the sullen acquiescence of starvation sets in. Jean Valjean steals a loaf of bread to save and sustain his famished family and is hounded for the rest of his life by Javert and relentless law.

The meaning of the text of this petition is the subject of wide discussion. The text is established and certain without significant variants. Whether the bread is "our daily bread" on "this day," "each day," or "tomorrow's bread today," does not seem to present major difficulties. But fascination hovers around the word *epiousios (Ton epiousion dos-Amin s-ameron* [Matthew 6:11]). Does this phrase, unique to the Gospels, refer to the bread miraculously distributed to the hungry (Matthew 15:36, or Acts 6:2) or to the breaking of bread in the Lord's Supper (Luke 24:13ff, Acts 2:42)? Three times it is said of Jesus, "He took bread, gave thanks, broke it, and gave it to them (Matthew 14:19, 15:36, 26:26). The closest parallel texts seem to be John 6:11, 21:13, where "give bread" has a purely theological sense (*diadidonai*). Here in John, Jesus offers the bread from Heaven, imbreaded in himself as the "bread of life" (John 6:31ff).

---

[223] G. Rupp, *Martin Luther,* (London: Edward Arnold, 1970), p. 75.

The Jewish hearers reflecting on Moses and manna in the wilderness plead, "Lord, give us this bread always" (John 6:34). The Hebrew bearings of the text are illuminating. A feature of God's goodness and justice is that he feeds the hungry:

> [God] keeps faith forever; Who executes justice for the oppressed; Who gives food to the hungry.
> (Psalm 146:6-7)

> . . . He satisfies the thirsty, and the hungry he fills with good things.
> (Psalm 107:9)

This fundamental appeal to the provident supply and fertility of the earth firmly links human justice with hunger and food. Food is both a divine gift and a human creation and possession. To make bread, persons must have flour and grain. In agricultural economics, which were already well established in the Ancient Near East, some citizens own the fields. Others scratch for the scraps along the edges. Thus, Hebrew jubilee, returning first fruits to the generous God and leaving the remains for the poor. Despite the spiritualizing of heavenly food and the eucharistic reality that the body is more than food, the fact remains that people require sustenance or they die. Mechanisms of employment, money, and distribution of food are required for communities which live "under Good (God)." The connection of work and bread is deep in the ethical consciousness of culture formed in the biblical ethos:

> If anyone will not work, let him not eat.
> (2 Thessalonians 3:10)

A complex cycle of offering and responsibility is envisioned within the human community where God gives life and bread to the world but this provision is only activated when each person offers his work and shares with the needy thus ensuring that provision for all.

Death by Bread Alone, writes Dorothee Söelle is the outlook and disposition towards other people where we see them..."not as a gift, lesson, or stimulus, but as threat, danger, competition. It is the death that comes to all who try to live by bread alone."[224] The temptation scripture recited by Jesus recalls Akedah, anticipates Golgotha and presages the universal and eternal eucharist.

In the divine purview, cooperation, not competition, is envisioned as the sustaining spirit of community. Sharing or *koinonia* is to characterize the community of faith and the community-at-large. In modern society, the competitive ethos has overwhelmed the cooperative, especially in the public sphere. The ascendancy of freedom, free-market capitalism and competition has intensified the work/responsibility side of the bread equation and diminished the

---

[224] Dorothee Soelle, *Death by Bread Alone,* (Philadelphia: Fortress Press, 1975), p. 4.

sharing side. Part of the competitive ethos is the conviction, grounded in the Genesis fall, that persons should earn their bread by the sweat of their brow, that handouts are debilitating, engendering idleness (2 Thess. 3:11), that one should look out for one's own and that the burden of "too many mouths to feed" should be solved by the Darwinian/Malthusian mechanism of starvation and "survival of the fittest." The biblical logic stands in radical contradiction to this view. Its imperative simply and strongly affirms—God gives you food—therefore, give your bread to the hungry. The manna received in humility, offered in generosity, will multiply.

Suffering and Sustenance

The human condition as reflected in this petition of the prayer is one of vulnerability poised at the precipice of deprivation, destitution, even starvation. The plea for daily bread is urgent and poignant. It is a recognition of thanksgiving and blessing for what we have received day by day. Our bread is a gift of God, new every morning.

Luther's *Morgensegen* offers this thankful plea:

> Die Nacht ist vergangen, ein neuer Tag hat begonnen. Laßt uns
> wachen und nüchtern sein und abtun, was uns träge macht, daß
>
> wir ihn preisen, unseren Gott, mit unserem Leben vom ersten
> Morgenlied an bis zur Ruhe der Nacht.[225]

Our life and prayer is an acknowledgment of our perpetual and acute need and dependence. It is awareness of impending crisis. As the saying goes today, most people are just one paycheck away from poverty. This power is the presentation of justice and the imperative to generosity as the appropriate response and antidote to the human condition of want.

Calvin's ethic of providence and provision which arises from an economical theology has the following basic points:

> God has made the world so that we need one another's help (the rich need the
> poor and the poor need the rich). bread for the day and the morrow is the
> symbolic currency of this exchange. "The bread" (Luther's Eucharist)
> symbolizes the divine backdrop and pattern for this reciprocal human sharing.
> The delight of light and Grace of God is fulfilled in this transaction.[226]

The vast majority of human beings whose lives have appeared on earth have died from starvation. For the millennia before the modern era, a major cause of death was a weakened constitution provoked by inadequate nutrition. This

---

[225] Martin Luther, *Morgensegen*, (German Worship Book), p. 841.

[226] Andre Bielier, *The Social Humanism of Calvin*, (Richmond: John Knox Press, 1964), p. 13ff.

compromise made one a setup for infectious or other diseases which were the immediate causal vectors of mortality. In the modern world, fifty thousand children die each day from starvation. Even today when hunger should be eliminated by the providence of the world's breadbaskets, the major vector of demise among the world's five billion people is undernourishment and secondary vulnerability to disease.

Epiousios

Jesus' prayer exquisitely blends the immediate and the imminent. The salient word *epiousios* seems to draw on two compounds: *epieina* and *epi-iena*, meaning respectively, to be and to come. The ultimate invitation—the bread of heaven—instills *insouciance* here and now...take no thought what you shall eat....We can abandon anxiety about food here and now because "we will sit at feast in the kingdom of God" (Luke 14:15). Though we know in Grace that we "do not live by bread alone," at the same time we boldly share, for we know "we are blessed who now go hungry, for hunger will be satisfied" (Luke 6:21).

Among the many themes of human existence invoked in the petition "our daily bread," let us explore toil and work, hunger and justice, anorexia and obesity.

Toil and Work

The way God puts bread on the table is through human work. Work is *cooperatio dei* —we plow and seed, God suns and waters. In harvest hymn we sing:

> We plow the fields and scatter the good seed on the land, but it is fed and watered by God's almighty hand; He sends the snow in winter, the warmth to swell the grain, the breezes and the sunshine, and soft refreshing rain. "All good things around us are sent from heaven above ,Then thank the Lord for all his love."
> Matthias Claudius, 1782

Work is thanksgiving, liturgy, eucharist. Work is our return gift for divine favor. Our charisma is offered to the world's labor movement—a gesture of justice— an offering of help or health. The wholeness or holiness of the earth is substantiated by our gift by God's grace.

Hunger and Justice

A living causal sequence is conveyed in this petition. God gives and sustains, we toil and work, the offering for sin and to grace. Justice and *shalom* is thereby animated on the earth. In this purview, work is dignified. The farmer and housewife, store clerk and teacher, garbage collector and nurse, each offer their gift to the building of the earth. Accumulating or hoarding is not in keeping with this ethos.

> "Share your food with the hungry," counsels Isaiah (58:7).

Feed the hungry, Clothe the naked...counsels the evangelist
(Matthew 25)

If your enemy is hungry, feed him...counsels the apostle
(Romans 12:20)

An adequate, even abundant provision is placed into the earth. Every resource is there for the need of all life.

You open your hand and fulfill the desire of every living thing
(Psalm 145:16)

John Calvin writes of the exquisite proportion and ration set into the world. On the food passage in Second Corinthians he comments:

God wills that there be equality among us. None should have too much and none too little.[227]
(cf. II Corinthians)

Commenting on Psalm 112. Paul writes of this giving and receiving.

The point is this: he who sows sparingly will also reap sparingly, and he who sows bountifully will also reap bountifully. Each one must do as he has made up his mind, not reluctantly or under compulsion, for God loves a cheerful giver. And God is able to provide you with every blessing in abundance, so that you may always have enough of everything and may provide in abundance for every good work. As it is written, "He scatters abroad, he gives to the poor, his righteousness endures for ever."

He who supplies seed to the sower and bread for food will supply and multiply your resources and increase the harvest of your righteousness. You will be enriched in every way for great generosity, which through us will produce thanksgiving to God; for the rendering of this service not only supplies the wants of the saints but also overflows in many thanksgivings to God.
(II Corinthians 9:6-12)

Violating this equation constitutes ingratitude and injustice. Manna hoarded and withheld from the community rotted and was spoiled overnight. St. Basil, whose fourth-century community sought to emulate and promulgate this benediction wrote:

The bread that is spoiling in your house belongs to the hungry. The shoes that are mildewing under your bed belong to those who have none. The clothes

---

[227] John Calvin, Commentary on Second Corinthians, Calvin's Commentaries. Eerdmans, 1958.

stored away in your trunk belong to those who are naked. The money that depreciates in your treasury belongs to the poor.[228]

This primitive and pristine communism is contradiction and offense to the Darwinian and capitalist spirit which in its selfish distortion says, "Grab all you can from this world and grind down those who can't make it."

Bread, Hunger, Politics and Poverty
The headline was stark:

> People are hungry because they are poor, not because the earth is running out of food.[229]

The news and commentary magazines again focused this week on the issue of bread for the world: Rwanda and Zaire as refugees have fled the Hutu-Tutsi strife and sought refuge and food in camps across the border. In the precarious "gang-governed" environs back home, millions were destitute. On return, their homes and substance were gone except for a few parcels carried on their heads. Also in the news was the world food summit in Rome. This conference again bogged down in dissension among the Malthusians who have argued for one hundred years that population growth must be checked lest it overwhelm the world's food resources and trigger the Darwinian mechanism of starvation. The technophiles on the other hand held forth in the green revolution and found politics at fault. All agreed that massive sharing of bread among the nations was urgently required. "Technophiles," on the other hand, held faith in the "green revolution" to support more and more "mouths to feed," all the while correctly doubting the "crash scenario" of projected births. Politics and the failure of world government was the problem, and new institutional arrangements and mechanisms were perfectly capable of ameliorating the crisis. All at the conference agreed that "sharing" of the world's bread was urgently required.

As might be expected the conservative and business oriented Economist found poverty to be the problem. If farmers could just function in free competitive markets and if the poor could be magically woven into the market economy, Adam Smith's invisible hand would wave its miracle wand.

> "What is needed," the editorial concluded, "...is not another break-through in farm technology, but a breakthrough in government policy. Western countries need to open their markets to the poor. Poor countries need to permit higher incomes on agriculture. This would raise rural incomes—even for the landless—and spur economic development more broadly."[230]

---

[228] St. Basil, *The Lord's Pryaer: The Prayer of Internal Liberation.* ed. Leonardo Bott, (Maryknoll, NY: Orbis, 1983), p. 84.
[229] *The Economist,* November 16, 1996, p. 18.
[230] *The Economist,* p. 18.

Meanwhile in this period of conservative governmental and economic policies this very approach has been taken and empirically refuted as the distance between rich and poor grows greater and the misery of the poor and hungry gets worse.

Give us today tomorrow's bread...

The prayer is corporeal and political. Our common life has to find a way to feed the people of the world. Optimally we need to ensure self-sufficiency.

Give a man a fish...Teach him to fish...

Our complex world of division of labor requires farmers who grow, bakers who bake, truckers who deliver (they now block the highway in France in yet another manifestation), shops who sell, etc.. Today it is harder to give away the loaf or to steal it (*Les Miserables*). We find ourselves at the mercy of one another and of the systems we have created.

The rich I know would like to help but chafe at higher taxes. The Rwanda/Zaire crisis or Sudan is typical. International humanitarian aid is profuse and ready to go—but where? The Zaire warlords want the food to give to their own people. The central government is inept with President Mubutu in Lausanne, France suffering from cancer. The rude crisis is Somalia (1994) was about food and starvation and we hightailed it out. In Rwanda, the minority (20%) Tutsi rule and want the supplies for themselves. Human avarice and exploitation block sharing, it seems, at every point. And this prayer continues...forgive our sins...

Anorexia and Obesity

It may seem ridiculous, even blasphemous that in such a world we would have "fats" and "skinnies." Yet an interesting correlate of the above discussion is the phenomenon of anorexia and obesity. The anorexic, typically a young woman, seems to be possessed of distorted consciousness, something like a hyper-fasting syndrome, where she sees herself as big and ugly, or as the kids would say, "gross", when in actuality she is thin as a rail. Psychological disorientation becomes physiological pathology as the person begins to emaciate and starve herself. The condition may be accompanied by cathartic and purgative rituals although this is more common in the related eating disorder, bulimia.

Obesity builds on the medieval vice of gluttony. Although this condition, like anorexia, often has genetic and deep behavioral roots, it tends to be a disease of unabated consumption, one cannot get enough. The delicate equipoise of partaking and giving is distorted in both conditions. These are personal and idiosyncratic disorders. They also reflect societal patterns of indulgence or frugality. In some cultures of the world, for example, India and China, anorexia is rarely found. The correlation of these eating disorders with economic and religious factors is striking.

The example from this analogous biological and emotional condition demonstrates that the interrogative and imperative dimensions of the "bread" petition are both voluntary and involuntary. Hunting and food gathering are at once ethological and ethical (etiquette) matters. Hunger drives persons to desperation. We think of Jean Val Jean in Victor Hugo's Les Miserables who stole a loaf of bread to feed his hungry family. If bread is the bread of God, ought it not be free and accessible like the sun, water and air? To withhold feeding in medical care seems morally intolerable to many.

Stones and Bread
(Sermon preached at the University of Chicago.)

Oscar Wilde has finally found his niche. After long controversy he lies in rest in the Poets Corner of Westminster Abbey, in London, next to W. H. Auden, as might seem fitting. I cannot wait to be there again. The delight might be like the night our family was crossing to France from Portsmouth and stopped in Winchester Cathedral. In the darkness and serene moonlight, I told Sara to look down at the marble plate on which she stood. The thankful pleasure of countless blessed hours flooded her eyes as she looked down on Jane Austen. In Wilde's play Lady Wandermere's Fan, Wilde reflects on a dissipated life with the words, "I couldn't help it - I can resist everything except temptation." The lectionary today tells of one who for us resisted even temptation, indeed triumphed through it.

TEMPTATION:
    The ubiquitous condition of our moral existence: personal, familial,
    national, and corporeal
    Shall we succumb to sexual enticements and entanglements devoid of love
    and liberty, full of danger, even death?
    Shall we yield to the perpetual threat of shame, guilt and self-reproach?
    Shall we trash our neighbors and colleagues to bolster our fragile egos?
    Shall we step on others as we climb the corporate ladder?
    Shall we compromise conscience for cash?
    Shall we fail to speak out against injustice, so as not to offend?
    Shall we stoop and help those who cry in pain, or pull the gingerly Jericho
    road sidestep which we have so well mastered?
    Shall we side with troubled nations, and advocate the plight of the
    oppressed, or plead the gutless virtue of
    noninterference, bomb them to silence, or undermine their economies?

TEMPTATION:
    The human condition- Luther called it *Anfechtung*, the duel to death,
    the relentless grip of a disorienting lure away from who we are and
    ought to be.

TEMPTATION:
   The sign of tragedy emblazoned on our brow
   Yet strangely and ironically, the impulse to our creativity
   Always the precondition of responsible freedom

We stand this morning:
   At the threshold of **Lent**
   At the eve of **Ramadan**
   Poised for the beginning of **Purim**

It is the universal season of food and fast. Of revelry, then remorse; of Mardi Gras and Ash Wednesday; of delight in vitality and awareness of mortality; of joy in conviviality; of the necessity of solitude. It is seed time and spring.

The lectionary today leads with **Deuteronomy**...
   The wandering Aramean has come home—the fruit baskets are offered— the nourishing land of milk and honey is celebrated with solemn thanksgiving and severe recommitment

Then **Psalm 91**, a cultic song of sustenance and support:
   The shelter of Her great and strong wings
   God is the shield of immunity against pestilence. When cast down,
   angels will bear us up.
   You may wonder about this "destruction that wastes us at
   noonday"
   This is probably the scorching, dehydrating sun and not lunch at
   the dorm.

Finally, the **Gospel** lection, Luke's diary of the temptations of Jesus at the inauguration of his ministry. At one level, this profound story is about our human plight, which is our glory. It is also about a striking hesitancy in divine omnipotence, a resounding NO WAY! To such an opportunity for wonderful suasion. There will be no miracle, no dazzling impression, no wizardry, no bread, no circus. This confrontation with evil, this resistance to temptation, must not yield; it must go all the way, all the way to the cross, over to death, down into hell, up to resurrection.

As often in Scripture, we deal with great recurrences, patterns, analogies: Eden and east of Jordan wilderness, Adam and Jesus, the tempter, in the garden and now on the prairie, forty days in the wilderness, Israel's forty years in Sinai, Abraham's ten trials. The fast of Moses and Elijah, and now Jesus.

   times to purify the soul
   times to prepare for the presence of God
   times to confront the power of evil
   times for the wandering Aramean to become the people of the

Way
times for the pioneer of our faith to become that way, the truth,
      the life
times for the Messiah, people and person, to become the
      vehicles, instruments, conduits for life and light, justice and
      peace, power and victory into the life world

The temptations are perennial and persistent
stones to bread
the world is yours - If you will only bow down.
throw yourself down—you are invincible, invulnerable—angels
      will catch you.

Every person, every nation confronts these temptations en route to becoming whole and free. Each of us cannot become well and certainly not assume a healing ministry until we have confronted our destiny in God.

We must go out into our desert
In our own season of temptation
By ourselves with no one to shield us
Driven by that uncanny yet irresistible spirit
with old *Diabolos* himself waiting there for us
seeking to split and splinter, break us down
the innocent bystander, interrogator a revisit from paradisic asking "has God really said?"

or simply distracting the scholar on the verge of insight and integrity—
remember Screwtape's auto suggestion in the library, "It's time for lunch"

The resistances are also perennial and reliant

symbolic answers against the diabolic
dictates of word against gnawing doubt
choices for life against death
we do not live by bread alone—but by Godly nourishment
worship and serve the only one worthy of that inclination
Do not tempt the Lord your God

In one of the moving passages of Russian literature, Dostoevsky reflects on the meaning of the temptations in the poem "The Grand Inquisitor" in Brothers Karamazov. Ivan and Alyosha are contending about human justice and godly goodness in the world, especially in face of the death of children.

"Listen", says Ivan, "I took the case of children only to make my case clearer. Of the other tears of humanity with which the earth is soaked from its crust to its center, I will say nothing.... We men ourselves are to blame. Given paradise we wanted freedom....

Now amid the flaming torches of victims of the inquisition, a silent visitor, one who had promised to come in glory, now walks the streets of Seville, burning with heretics. On his face "a gentle smile of infinite compassion." A funeral procession passes the cathedral. The parents cry out. He raises the maiden from her coffin. At that moment appears the unforgettable visage of the ancient Cardinal, almost ninety, with sunken yet brilliant eyes, robed in scarlet. The unwelcome intruder is led off to the dungeon. That breathless night with the air "fragrant with laurel and lemon," the old inquisitor pushes through the iron door of the pitch-dark prison.

"Is it Thou?"— (silence)

He interrogates the prisoner reenacting the temptations:

> ...Do you see these stones in this parched and barren wilderness? Turn them into bread and mankind will run after you like a flock of sheep, grateful and obedient, though forever trembling, lest you withdraw your hand and deny them bread. But you would not deprive man of freedom, and rejected the office...How did you forget that man prefers peace and even death to freedom of choice in the knowledge of good and evil.[231]

Our text is about freedom and responsibility in personal and public moral choice. Reflect with me for a moment on these dimensions of stones and bread. It is this temptation that most troubles individuals today. It vexes modern nations as they struggle to serve values of liberty and community in our global economy. This temptation is at issue, in the choice in Washington, between laissez faire and social justice. It is at stake in Chicago's treasury and schools, in America's urban and rural war zones. It's the matter of Mexico, Chechnya, Palestine, Rwanda, Sudan, Birundi, Bosnia. It is the crisis of bread and government, of sustenance and church. The issue is literally companionship— sharing bread together.

I've been moved by Leon Kass' new book, Hunger and the Soul. By Martha McClintock's work on psyche and eating. I'm concerned, as you are, with both Clinton's covenant and Gingrich's contract—both seem terribly stonehearted, not leavenous. The spirit of companionship is wanting. And our geographically proximate companions in Mexico, Latin America, Africa, Asia—as the big bread on the big board succumbs to the fickle laws of the global economy—as on the Mexican Day of the Dead, we offer a few morsels to the deceased but we are in panic!

Individuals and families, cities and states, nations, singular and united, are being severely tested, as was Jesus:

---

[231] F. Dostoevsky, *The Brothers Karamazov,* (New York: Random House, 1951), p. 299.

375

> Feed the hungry
> Clothe the naked
> Shelter the homeless
> Heal the sick
> Educate the latent

Though the cry is acute—debt depleted budgets fail—the yeast is spent and, though we know the moral requirement of fathers when asked for bread, we offer stones to the world's children.

> cut them off
> make them work, curtail chronic welfare
> build more prisons—Dostoevsky's dungeons of bread and
> water, what Dorothee Söelle calls the "death by bread
> alone"

> mute our last and most vital soul sustenance: the arts
> its all on the chopping block: welfare, student subsidy,
> WIC, school lunches, medicaid, social security

Have we become so rich that we are poor? The bread of idleness molds and rots like overdrawn manna and children's soft voices cry their last hunger sobs, 50,000 each week, in our wretched world, this good pantheon. Before we end all true religion offers a tough twist to this text.

> "We do not live by bread alone"
> "Take no thought for what you shall eat"

Higher than material values are needed to sustain the human spirit. We exist and subsist by every word from the mouth of God. "Those Who abide in His Spirit," writes Thomas a Kempis in *imitation Christou*

> "find in His teaching the hidden manna."[232]

Nourished by this bread we never hunger, drinking at this font we never thirst. In this ascetic spirit, life flourishes, in such frugality is found true wealth. Now, in acute desert temptation we crave not the illusory oasis but the one who opens her hand and satisfies the desire of every living thing (Psalm 145:16).

Our most insidious temptation today is *Feurbach's Man ißt was Er isst*: we are what we eat. We are what we have, what we earn, what we produce, we are the impression we make— "just kneel down and worship me."

---

[232] Thomas a Kempis, *imitatio christou,* Ch. 1.

Because of the persistence of human weakness and the perpetuity of temptation from this bread bondage - the old inquisitors' slavery to church or state, earth or heaven—Jesus took all the way out to that fateful hour of Satan's revisit in Judas' soul at the table that night he took it to the outer edges of hell—and wretched as we are in these bodies of death, always tracked with temptation as Luther called, *Anfechtung*, forsaking any easy fix, loved to the uttermost and saved us to a holy freedom. And a freedom communal and global, God-given bread is for the world, not hoard. Remember Salvador Dali's painting, "Last Super Table"—it arches the globe. It was Nikos Kazantzakis' Zorba the Greek, who roared:

> "What strange creature man is, you put in bread, wine and radishes and out come laughter, sighs and dreams."

Our task today is to sustain such nobility, to fast and pray, to resist temptation, to act freely in justice and love.

VI. Satisfaction: Forgive our Sins as We Forgive

...she 'tislach lanu al cal chatosaino...

Judah—I've got to believe, there is a moral structure, purpose, a higher being, forgiveness..."
Ben, the Rabbi in Woody Allen's film,
Crimes and Misdemeanors

Forgive, Lord, my little jokes on Thee. And I'll forgive your great big one on me.[233]
Robert Frost

In Rachmaninoff's cantata Spring, the desperate husband-lover broods in the discovered infidelity of his wife. His desperation mounts across the last, cold, dark weeks of the Russian winter. Finally he takes the knife and walks toward her room. Just as he raises his hand to kill her as the wind howls the last gust of winter and a warm and gentle waft of spring crosses his face and the words:

"love while we can still love" "forgive while we can still forgive"
Spring, Sergei Rachmaninoff

Jesus' gentle kiss of forgiveness on the parched lips of the old Inquisitor in Seville is reenacted in another of the most moving scenes in literature. Jane Eyre returns to care for the dying Aunt Reed who has so meanly mistreated her as a child. A letter from John Eyre, bequesting Jane Eyre his estate is read and this monumental scene of the forgiveness of the "pure in heart".

---

[233] Robert Frost, *The Poetry of Robert Frost*, (NY: Holt, Rinehart, Winston, 1967), p. 428.

"Madam, will you have the goodness to send me the address of my niece, Jane Eyre, and to tell me how she is: it is my intention to write shortly and desire her to come to me at Madeira. Providence has blessed my endeavors to secure a competency; and as I am unmarried and childless, I wish to adopt her during my life, and bequeath her at my death whatever I may have to leave. " I am Madam, etc., etc.,

"JOHN EYRE, Madeira"

It was dated three years back.

"Why did I never hear of this?" I asked.

"Because I disliked you too fixedly and thoroughly ever to lend a hand in lifting you to prosperity. I could not forget your conduct to me, Jane - the fury with which you once turned on me; the tone in which you declared you abhorred me the worst of anybody in the world; the unchildlike look and voice with which you affirmed that the very thought of me made you sick , and asserted that I had treated you with miserable cruelty. I could not forget my own sensations when you thus started up and poured out the venom of your mind: I felt fear, as if an animal that I had struck or pushed had looked up at me with human eyes and cursed me in a man's voice. - Bring me some water! Oh! make haste!"

"Dear Mrs. Reed," said I, as I offered her the draught she required, "think no more of all this, let it pass away from your mind. Forgive me for my passionate language: I was a child then; eight, nine years have passed since that day."

She heeded nothing of what I said; but when she had tasted the water and drawn breath, she went on thus:-"I tell you I could not forget it; and I took my revenge; for you to be adopted by your uncle, and placed in a state of ease and comfort, was what I could not endure. I wrote to him; I said I was sorry for his disappointment, but Jane Eyre was dead: she had died of typhus fever at Lowood. Now act as you please: write and contradict my assertion – expose my falsehood as soon as you like. You were born, I think, to be my torment: my last hour is racked by the recollection of a deed, which, but for you, I should never have been tempted to commit."

"If you could be persuaded to think no more of it, aunt and to regard me with kindness and forgiveness"

"You have a very bad disposition," said she,"and one to this day I feel it impossible to understand: how for nine years you could be patient and quiescent under any treatment, and in the tenth break out all fire and violence, I can never comprehend." "My disposition is not so bad as you think: I am passionate, but not vindictive. Many a time, as a little child, I should have been glad to love you if you would have let me; and I long earnestly to be reconciled to you now: kiss me, aunt."

I approached my cheek to her lips: she would not touch it. She said I oppressed her by leaning over the bed; and again demanded water. As I laid her down -

for I raised her and supported her on my arm while she drank - I covered her icecold and clammy hand with mine: the feeble fingers shrank from my touch - the glazing eyes shunned my gaze.

"Love me, then, or hate me, as you will," I said at last, "you have my full and free forgiveness: ask now for God's: and be at peace."[234]

Jewish prayer provides the structure and substance of the Lord's Prayer. A good part of that formal and material tradition is the matter of sin and satisfaction—the theme again of justice.

The prayer in general and this passage on sins, debts and transgressions in particular, is illumined by the justice narrative prayers in Hebrew scripture such as Genesis 18:22-23; Exodus 32:7- 14; Numbers 11:4-34; Numbers 14:11-25; Joshua 7:7-9 and I Kings 17:17-24.[235]

In Numbers 14, for example, the Hebrew people stand poised to enter the promised land yet the entry is delayed. They murmur and grumble as they tarry in the wilderness both against the fairness and justice of God and against the "good sense" of their leaders: Moses, Aaron, even Joshua and Caleb who sought to still resentment and instill hope (vs. 9). The people asked if they were liberated from Egypt (not that bad a scene, really) only to die out here in the desert. They doubt God's trustworthiness, "But you promised!" On God's part, the ingratitude for provision and lack of trust are just becoming too much.

They have seen my glory, my miracles, yet they continue to
taunt me and do not heed my voice....Those who anger me will
not see the land I promised their fathers (vs. 22, 23).

Hebrew prayer, including the Lord's instruction, implies certain aspects of the divine nature and the human condition. First, all human experiences are enfolded in the overarching awareness and understanding of God. Much that happens to us is terribly harmful and enigmatic, seemly devoid of purpose. Much grief we bring on ourselves through unknowing or "all-too-wrong" transgression. Akedah suggests that even perfect obedience may end in agony and loss. Akedah in Islam is celebrated in *Id al idah,* the feast of The Abrahamic Sacrifice. Here Muslim families around the world buy and sacrifice an animal, most often *mouton* (lamb). It is cooked and then taken to the poor and destitute. In many lands, like Senegal, families go door to door and ask forgiveness. This is the spirit of Akedah, and of Prayer and of The Sacrifice. All of the events of personal and social existence transpire within a divine milieu. God knows what is going on, sympathizes and transforms toward good everything offered by the

---

[234] Charlotte Bronte, *Jane Eyre,* (New York: Washington Sqaure 1953), p. 236-238.

[235] Samuel E. Balentine, "Prayer in the Wilderness Traditions: In Pursuit of Divine Justice*,"* *Hebrew Annual Review*, 9, (1985), p. 53- 74 and "Prayers for Justice in the Old Testament, Theodicy and Theology," *Catholic Biblical Quarterly,* 51(1989): 597-616.

loving heart in faith. That life itself is gift and every delight and even every crisis a dispensation of grace is the supposition and disposition of prayer. Prayer is the theistic assumption. To pray, wrote Abraham Heschel, is "to bring God back into the world...to expand his presence...His being immanent in the world depends on us."[236]

In prayer, in general, and this petition of the Lord's Prayer in particular, we offer thanks for all that we have received, however adverse. We ask even as Jesus did, to be spared temptation and evil. Our prayer is efficacious. God receives our cry and relents his justice. Our plight moves God to temper justice with mercy and his mercy in turn prompts us toward justice. We prevail on God to stay with the world on the condition that we'll abide with him. Injustice and evil will endure and overwhelm the world only if we fail to cry out against violence and oppression. As Walter Brueggemann has said, silence on justice issues in the sanctuary will muffle those issues outside the sanctuary.[237]

The complex text of Numbers 14 begins with a historicalexistential crisis of the Hebrew people. The awesome yet ambiguous event of Exodus is underway. Yes, it is spectacular deliverance and rescue. But it is also a leading toward some unknown and frightening future. "Maybe we should turn back." Later priestly writers with their concerns for worship and faith, justice and guilt, forgiveness and renewal, insert the inner collective memory of the people, now refined across many centuries, a litany of sin and satisfaction, judgment, justice and expiation. These theologians ponder God's purposes, God's justice in its terror yet underlying goodness, God's incessant availability to dialogue even persuasion, God's consummate mercy and commitment to go on with the redemptive story. The text, in sum, announces God's justice, exhibits the cause and actual course of the punishment, then is moved to mercy and continuation of the mission.

> To err is human
> to forgive, divine.

Primitive justice requires that wrong be requited. As we have shown this sense of justice in the human psyche is perennial and universal. Wrongs will be brought to light

> ...God will get you (one day) if you get away with it here...

On his death bed Karl Barth received a call from his friend and fellow pastor, Eduard Thurneysen. Barth's closing words:

---

[236] Abraham J. Heschel, *The Insecurity of Freedom,* (New York: Farrar Straus and Giroux, 1966), p. 258.
[237] Walter Brueggemann. "Theodicy in a Social Dimension," *Journal for the Study of the Old Testament,* 33:1995, pp. 3-25.

Er sitz in Regiment

But does He? Barth was probably quoting Paul Gerhardt's Hymn

Gott sitz im Regimente
und führet alles wohl

God's good is our good not our desert...God's nature imparts a most surprising and contradictory impulse into the human spirit -forgiveness. God so loved the world - that he gave...and forgave. Love breaks the cycle of endless retaliation and forgives.

Pope John Paul II visits the jail cell of Mehmet Ali Age a terrorist who sought to kill him with a knife. He kneels at his feet and forgives him. Cardinal Bernadin visits the troubled young man who had wrongly accused him of sexual misdeeds - and forgave him. On the cross Jesus cries:

Father forgive them, for they know not what they do.

The rhythm of health in body and soul in family and society, in church and world, is acknowledgement of wrong, receipt of grace, awareness of forgiveness, new life.

In the Lord's prayer, this great tradition is rehearsed in capsule form. Praise and petition, lament and supplication go hand-in-hand. We repent our sin toward God and others. That sin is a pattern of distrust, disobedience expressed in a plethora of attitudes of disdain and harmful actions toward others. The pithy petition picks up the whole saga of divine action and human reaction. Our liability before God is intertwined with our liability toward our fellow human beings. Repentance, restitution and renewal toward each effects the other. Forgiven both ways we can move on in newness of life. Forgiving our neighbor or confessing our fault to him, seeking reconciliation, we can then repair to God in worship and offer our gift at the altar (Matthew 5:24). Forgiven by God, we can find the guts and gall to seek and share forgiveness within our vicious circles of reprisal, reproach and alienation.

This petition is about our sin and the sin of others. Sin is something we are, something we choose to be and things we do. The essence of sin is unrighteousness: failing to live in and live out God's righteousness. God's righteousness is conveyed in *mitzvah*. The entirety of God's command is the rich panoply yet simple invitation of God's will. The requirement of righteousness is summarized in many ways:

Love God and the neighbor.
(Deuteronomy 13:3, Matthew 22:37)

Do justice, love mercy, walk humbly.
(Micah 6:8)

God's righteousness or God's will might be defined as God's project.

I, the Lord have called you in righteousness. I will hold your hand and keep
you and give you as a covenant for the world, a light for all peoples to bring
sight to the blind and release to prisoners who feared they would never see the
light of day.
(Isaiah 42:6, 7 my paraphrase.)

And he came to Nazareth, where he had been brought up; and he went to the
synagogue, as his custom was, on the Sabbath day. And he stood up to read;
and there was given to him the book of the prophet Isaiah. He opened the book
and found the place where it was written, "The Spirit of the Lord is upon me,
because he has anointed me to preach good news to the poor. He has sent me to
proclaim release to the captives and recovering of sight to the blind, to set at
liberty those who are oppressed, to proclaim the acceptable year of the Lord."
And he closed the book, and gave it back to the attendant, and sat down; and
the eyes of all in the synagogue were fixed on him. And he began to say to
them, "today this scripture has been fulfilled in your hearing."
(Luke 4:16-21)

The Text

While Luke uses the word *Hamartias* (sins), Matthew and *Didache* use the
more original *Opheilan* (debts). These words capture the Hebrew words *nasa,
salah* and *kapor* which pertain to cultic purity, and the aramaic (*hob*) which
connotes excusing a financial loan. God wipes out the stain of the unholy. God
always buys back the debt. The other Hebraic meaning of "sin" is missing the
mark, falling short, going astray. The theme here is not so much purity and
pollution but misdirection, disorientation. Materialism or secularism expressed
as disregard for the centrality of God's spiritual and ethical will (righteousness)
is, for the prophets, the ground of personal and communal sin. Again the
background theological question is theodicy or explanation of suffering. Why
did the sovereign historical God of this people, one who had chosen them and
led them out in Exodus and into the inhabitation of Palestine, why did Yaweh,
this great "I am" or "I will lead" now lead them into two-fold destruction of
Jewish state under Assyria and then Rome? Why did exile and diaspora displace
Zionic residence and peace as the new habitation of this people? Why have half
the Jews who ever lived been killed? Why did the saga of unending suffering,
pogrom and holocaust come to displace the blessed peace of *shalom*?

This history is marked by the drama of human faithfulness and of faithlessness.
But is the equation justified between sin and suffering and obedience and
blessing? Christianity personalizes the covenant and renders sin more a matter
of existential choice and behavior. The corporate dimension remains and the
declension of the church and commonwealth is identified as a cause of the

dyptheria epidemic in Cotton Mather's Puritan New England. But the association-dissociation phenomenon now tends to focus in individuals. This Lord's Prayer petition can be read either way. We ask for forgiveness for "our" sin or "my" personal sin as I stand a part of a community of prayer.

Calvin's reading of the petition focuses on *ophelon* (debts). Emphasizing the commercial and juridical meanings where we have incurred a debt, owe something, deserve penalty and have been purchased (redeemed) from the market place where lives and loyalties are bought and sold. Christ gave himself as ransom (Romans 3:24) for our indebted and indentured lives. Forgiveness is the context of the free gift of the grace of life for which Messiah's suffering and death has paid the wages of our sin. The Greek verb stands in the aorist, thus signifying finality and completeness, as well as endurance. The resurrection transfigures life now into patterns of justice, peace, and renewal all lived out in grace and forgiveness.

How did sin enter the world? Is it infectious, inherited, inevitable? Theological questions abound about what Reinhold Niebuhr called the most verifiable fact in the world. As I write today, a suicide bomber plants one explosive at a busy bus stop in Beit Lid, north of Tel Aviv, and carries another strapped to his body. Nineteen persons, mostly Israeli soldiers are killed, sixty-five injured. Islamic Jihad claims it sponsored the deed in revenge for preceding Israeli killings of Arabs. Tonight officials in Israel plan reprisal killings. Where did it start?

**Meditation: Arab and Jew in Palestine; Catholic and
Protestant in Ireland. Where is the Original Sin?
Primal Crime/Ultimal Peace**
    Sermon preached in the Irish Presbyterian Church, Groomsport, Northern Ireland, June 2, 1991.

Texts: Genesis 4:3-16, I John 1:5-9

Thank you for the privilege of speaking with you this morning from the pulpit distinguished this quarter-century by our dear friend, David Irwin. Our friendship goes back 30 years to when we were young theologians roaming the crooks and crannies and of course the gloaming and generally terrorizing together the haunts of Edinburgh. Fortunately for Edinburgh, and ourselves, we soon met our respective "bonnie lassies": and in the words of the old hymn— "our traveling days were done."

Neither of us would have thought in 1961 that the span of our ministries would be marked by such momentous events. For him the bitter saga of the Ireland Story, for me, the U.S. Civil Rights struggle and our American war history from Vietnam to Kuwait.

Throughout these turbulent years, with the help of people like yourselves, who became our companions on the journey of faith, we have tried what does not come easy for 50 year-old men—to pray—to listen—and to hear if there is any Word from the Lord.

This morning there is such a Word. That word Karl Barth said comes with the Bible in one hand and the newspaper in the other. The scriptures catch us up and call us to attention. Genesis speaks to us of the unending cycle of human violence that coils its way from our deeds today back to the primal crime we symbolize by Cain's execution of Abel. John turns that onion into a rose. In his letter he speaks of the upsurging spring of love and ultimal peace that takes off from our single gestures of justice or care and then spirals heavenward into the eternal light of God. Let us focus our worship this morning—our hearing and doing of the Word—on primal crime and ultimal peace. Think first of that root—that radix, radish—that downward swirling whirlpool of danger and destruction.

Dateline Baghdad

The Kurds seem to have struck a deal with the now compliant Saddam Hussein and the Baghdad government. For the first time in modern history, we seem to have a chance for an independent Kurdistan. Could it be at last a homecoming for those exiled people who have been no people? Coming from East and West, North and South—from Iraq and Turkey, Syria, Iran and Russia will they at last find a continuing city? Could it be the start of homecoming for those other disinherited and disturbed peoples who have yet to find a secure place to call their own? The Palestinians, the Armenians, the Jews, the Tibetans—has not God made of one blood of all nations and appointed the bounds of their habitation? Right now the best we can do, as you well know, in the midst of fragile and uneasy plantations around the world, is keep the peace and minimize the deaths. In this case, bring the Kurds down from the mountains into temporary safe havens.

Where will it end? Where did it begin?

- Iraq's attack on Kuwait
- America's support for the Shah
- Israel's occupation of the West Bank and Palestine
- The West's plantation of Israel into Palestine in 1948
- The Nazi Holocaust that made that plantation necessary
- The British failure early this century to go all the way into Mesopotamia and secure Kurdistan earlier this century
- The expulsion of the Jews from Western Europe into Poland and Russia a few centuries ago
- The medieval pogroms
- The failure of Babylonian Judaism

384

- The Roman destruction of the temple and of the nation of Israel
- On and on, back we go to Cain - the primal crime

Dateline Jerusalem

It is October 8, 1990. The pious old men in black clothes and hats sway back and forth at the wailing wall. This is the only remaining facade of Herod's temple. Above, on the temple mount, is the mosque built on the spot where Mohammed took his leap of faith into heaven—close at hand was Golgotha— where Jesus was crucified—restless and agitated Palestinian youths gathered that afternoon on the mount. A parade had been threatened by Jewish extremists. As the crowd grew angry, boys pelted the police below with stones. As police will, they opened fire, and as dust settled, 19 Palestinians were dead with more to follow.

Where will it end? Where did it begin?

Forgive us our sins as we forgive those who have sinned against us.

- Nordiya, Hebron—the Tel Aviv bus
- The massacre General Sharon ordered on the Palestinian refugee camp of Ramullah
- The 1967 war
- The Warsaw Ghetto
- The Crusaders exterminating Jews in the Middle Ages
- The Bar Kochba revolt in 150 C.E.
- Cyrus and the Babylonian captivity
- The Hebrew exodus from Egypt and their occupation of Canaan by means of Holy War
- On and on, back we go to Cain—the primal crime

Dateline Belfast

We Americans come home to Ireland. We don't visit or sightsee, we come home to the hills of County Down or the setting sun on Galway Bay. No land has so deeply shaped the American character as has this Emerald Isle. The Scots' Irish migrations of the 18th century and the Down-state migrations during the potato famine of the 19th have made us the people we are. As we drove up this week through the Republic and into Northern Ireland, we became aware again of this precious heritage. Then one passes through the guntowers and barricades, through the border villages where so many have been killed—on into West Belfast and Shankhill Wall. And during these days of promise when Peter Brooke tries to set the table at Storemont for unions and nationalists to reason together, we become aware again of the descent of the serpent and the flight of the dove—the downward coil of evil, the upward spiral of hope.

Where will it end? Where did it begin?

- Was it the Gibralter 3
- The Shankhill Butchers or the Birmingham Six
- The Darclay massacre or Bloody Sunday in Londonderry
- The partition of the solemn leagues
- The Battle of the Bogne in 1690
- The plantation of the Scots by King James or the massacre by the natives
- Those furtive British campaigns against Ireland by Richard II and other Kings
- The Scots incursions from Ireland against the Roman Britons
- The violent Indo-European migrations against the Atlantic in the Second Millennium B.C.E. from MacCool and the Giant Causeway to Scotland
- The two swimming brothers and the right hand
- Cain and Abel
- On and on—back we go to Cain—the primal crime Forgive us our sins as we forgive those who sin against us.

We could speak of India, of South Africa—on and on—the tale is everywhere the same, like Shakespeare's Richard II, we find ourselves so deep in blood that sin plucketh sin.[238] The tale would be sad indeed were not that primal and perpetual crime has been decisively countered by a primal and perpetual love. The descent into hell and ascent into glory of Jesus Christ.

St. Augustine showed us how we were all engulfed in that primal and perpetual crime. He called it "original", even "inherited" sin. What he meant was not genetic, but genesis—the empirical fact that when we look around and inside ourselves we see an intricate web—first spun in Eden's Garden—now reaching its sticky fibers out through our own thoughts and deeds and into the tragic history of our age.

Pause for a moment at that momentous century of world history, the 17th century. The revolution that would inspire all freedom revolutions from the American and French down to the Russian was taking place: the English Civil War. Charles I lost his head and the Westminster Assemblies produced documents of church and state which would change the world and constitute our

---

[238] *The Tragedy of King Richard* II Complete Works of Shakepeare, David Barrington, ed. New York: Harper, 1992, p. 725.

faith. These same standards would bring accusations against the fledgling American nation that it was a Presbyterian revolt. Shortly after Cromwell's campaign in Ireland, Thomas Hobbes wrote about the state and the state of nature. He used the biblical image of the whale—Leviathan—plunging into the depths of the sea.

> "I have spoken," he writes, "of the natural kingdom of God and his natural laws." "I add this short declaration on his natural punishments." "There is no action of man in this life, that is not the beginning of so long a chain of consequences, as no human providence is high enough to give man a prospect to the end. Intemperance is naturally punished with diseases, negligent government with rebellion—rebellion with slaughter."[239]

Hobbes is brutally honest about the "wages of sin." The Bible is even more candid about the consequences of our actions—the fall—and all of its terror—its neverending cyclone of retribution, what the Greeks called nemesis. The Bible also knows that we have been lifted from this bottomless quicksand pit. Christ descended into hell, met this downsurge of gravity head on—and like the lady clinging to the onion in Dostoevsky, led all captivity captive in himself. The Bible answers the volcano of evil with the descent and ascent of the dove. In this summer season of the Christian year we celebrate ascension and pentecost— Whitsunday with roses and peonies, clamydia and pansies. We acknowledge the victory of life over death, beauty over disgrace, color over darkness, growth over degradation—Christ ascended, *regius* over the world. Hobbes' natural sanctions and tragic necessity no longer hold the world in grim sway. The treadmill has been stopped. Grace has overwhelmed sin, law and determininism. Now grace holds before us the wonderful option of forgiveness as freedom. It opens up to a vindictive and vengeful world the possibility of reconciliation. Where first Adam fell down—final Adam has risen up. Primal crime has yielded to ultimal peace. We need only to take hold of it and turn bulb to bloom, onion to rose.

How do we see this different world? How do we recognize peace in a world which appears to be still at war? We need to look with different eyes, and act with different hopes. We need to believe and behave mystically and morally. Christians see the world mystically, that is, mysteriously, sacramentally, full of surprise and serendipity. We see inside the curtain. Retaliation sees things materially — forgiveness sees things mystically. Vengeance acts materially, reconciliation acts mystically and morally. The mystic sees the hidden meaning in ordinary experiences:

- It was just another bush burning in the desert—or was it?
- He was just another passover traveler on the road to Emmaeus—or was he?

---

[239] Hobbes, *Leviathan.*

- It was just someone else sick or hungry, naked or homeless—or was it?

When did we see you...?

Political events are also pregnant or portentous in this way. In his great historical novel, Les Miserables, Victor Hugo expresses the idea that historical events, though seemingly directed by chance and vicissitude, are actually reflections of a higher power, what the Bible calls "judgment". Reflecting on the Battle of Waterloo and the defeat of Napoleon, Hugo writes that the apparent and immediate cause was the failure of reinforcements to arrive because some peasant gave them a bum steer....Because on the afternoon of a certain day, a shepherd said to a Prussian in the forest, "go this way and not that." But the real cause was more profound. Hugo writes:

> End of the dictatorship. A whole European system crumbled away! Was it possible that Napoleon should have won the battle? We answer no—why? Because of Wellington? Because of Blucher? No, because of God...Napoleon had been denounced to the infinite and his fall has been decided on. He embarrassed God. Waterloo is not a battle; it is a change of front on part of the universe.[240]

To see what is really going on behind the scenes we must look with the eyes of faith, but act as if peace had already overwhelmed crime. Vision and virtue changes the world. In love Christ has overcome crime. He has broken down the dividing wall of hostility between us—be that wall in Jerusalem, Berlin, or on Shankhill Road. He has broken it down. It cost him. It will cost us!

Our president, Jimmy Carter, was a wall-breaker. He could put his arms on the shoulders of Presidents Sadat and Begin and say, "Let us pray." Needless to say, he was run out of office. Some had suggested him or the Dali Lama to chair the Stormont talks, "a good idea," I say.

God in Christ is present in this world. He stands beside us silently as he stood alongside the Grand Inquisitior. He suffers with us knowing our sorrow. He tries to bring common sense and humanity to our violent propensity. He wants to transform our retaliative passion into reconciling peace. Though we coil toward Cain, in Christ's spirit we spiral toward hope. In the mighty creed we boldly affirm Christ suffered, was crucified, died, and was buried. He descended into hell. He rose again and ascended into heaven from whence he comes to judge the world of the living and the dead....

We live and die under God's mercy which is his judgment and his judgment which is his mercy. Psalm 90 gathers this humiliation and exaltation into one

---

[240] V. Hugo, *Les Miserables*. Cossette, Bk 1, Ch. XVI, ix.

culminating vision on which we have focused our mediation. With its mighty words we close—

> Lord, thou hast been our dwelling-place in all generations. Before the mountains were brought forth, or ever thou hadst formed the earth and the world Even from everlasting to everlasting thou art God. Thou turnest man to destruction and sayest "return, ye children of men for a thousand years in thy sight are but as yesterday, when it is past and as a watch in the night...Thou hast set our iniquities before thee and our secret sins in the light of thy countinance For all our days are passed away in thy wrath; we spend our years as a tale that is told. So reach us to number our days that we may apply our hearts unto wisdom...all through the night—the dark and long and seemingly endless night—we are kept by The One. Amen.

One deep enigma confronted as we approach the question of sin or debt is that pondered by the Old and New Testaments and from works like Josephus' Antiquities of the Jews, Augustine's City of God, Samuel Usque's Consolation for the Tribulations of Israel, or Elie Wiesel's Night. Did the people of Israel or the body of Christ go wrong? Was sin the cause of the fall of the Jewish or Christian state? Each of these classic writings along with the scriptural texts find a deeper mystery at work in the vicissitudes and vindications of history.

The Biology and Psychology of Forgiveness
In accord with one Leitmotiv, the drama and trauma of human existence is fathomed in the "Lord's Prayer." Let us reflect briefly on the biology and psychology of forgiveness. A delicate balance between aggression and acquiescence makes for health. Riding roughshod over everything that gets in your way brings you down in the process. Lying down and letting others walk over you is equally flattening. This is the best of all possible worlds. I love sinning—God loves forgiving. How so?

This is a portrayal of cheap grace that weakens persons and ridicules God— reducing the Sovereign Lord of Abraham and Jesus to "Ludicrous Twaddle" (Kierkegaard). Strong love in body and mind requires strong forgiveness within a context of strong responsibility.

In the opening scene of Ingmar Berman's film about his parents, *Best Intentions*, Henrik Bergman confronts his grandfather. His grandmother is dying and asks for forgiveness for the years of abuse of the young boy and his mother. Henrik refuses Grandfather's offer to pay for his theological studies at Uppsala and rebukes the old lady's contrite plea:

> "I hate you...I never want to be like you."

The splendid film then weaves the life-fabric of this dialectic of demand and forgiveness. Our life, like Henrik's, is redeemed and damned by the way we transact wrong, and justice, forgiveness and restitution, in the relations and associations of life.

389

In the eucharistical theology of the Christian tradition baptism is "for the remission (forgiveness) of sins." This archaic and universal ritual recognizes that we must die and be buried to the relentless cycle of sin, guilt, and condemnation and be cleansed and raised to the life of renewal and freshness. We must be swallowed up in the abyss of sin and guilt. Only there, in complete dereliction and destitution, only as prodigal, can we be rescued by one who descended to the very pits of hell to effect our rescue and turnaround. Only thus can we find ourselves "being saved," being made whole.

Dietrich Bonhoeffer understood the dialectics and dynamics of grace and forgiveness. In his study of the "Lord's Prayer" within the mount sermon he wrote:

> Cheap grace means grace sold on the market like cheapjack's wares. The sacraments, the forgiveness of sin, and the consolations of religion are thrown away at cut prices. Grace is represented as the Church's inexhaustible treasury, from which she showers blessings with generous hands, without asking questions or fixing limits. Grace without price, grace without cost!

Bonhoeffer further expressed the same criticism:

> Cheap grace means grace as a doctrine, a principle, a system. It means forgiveness of sins proclaimed as a general truth, the love of God taught as the Christian "conception" of God. An intellectual assent to that idea is held to be of itself sufficient to secure remission of sins. The Church which holds the correct doctrine of Grace has, it is supposed, ipso facto a part in that grace. In such a church the world finds a cheap covering for its sins; no contrition is required, still less any real desire to be delivered from sin.[241]

Bonhoeffer is arguing for the concreteness of forgiveness. This grace, though spiritual and perhaps unique to human society among the species, is almost physical. It is specifically theologically related to creation, incarnation, and history, thanks to pneumatology and eschatology. Mercy is at root christological. Jesus is the personification of God's forgiveness.

Desmond Morris in his study of animal ethology and its application to people speaks of forgiveness as a "remotivating act." This is a gesture that animates one to try again or renew effort.[242]

The domestic dog, for example, can and must be shamed and punished, say, for dropping his load on the kitchen floor. But censure must be followed by love and reincorporation so that he can try again, and hopefully do better next time. Similarly, a child has to learn acceptable behavior sometimes with a stern word,

---

[241] Dietrich Bonhoeffer, *The Cost of Discipleship,* (New York: Macmillan, 1959) p. 35.
[242] Desmond Morris, *Manwatching: A Field Guide to Human Behavior,* (New York: Harry N. Abrams, 1977) p. 184-185.

but then must come the customary care and affirmation —a remotivation. In the physical and biological world there is something like a natural order of respect, live and let live.

Cooperation	♦	Everyone plays a part
Justice	♦	Censure a harmful action
	AND	
Mercy	♦	Let's try again.

When the natural environment enters crisis and the carrying capacity constricts or the food source diminishes, crowding disrupts space, incites anxiety, then aggression ensues and the natural equilibrium is disrupted. Then terror follows, exemplified by the paranoic schizophrenic who huddles in the corner afraid of the life-field of play. Forgiveness is a mode of psychic or soul healing which invites the estranged one into participation. This restitution rights the external and the internal relation. As Lew Smedes writes in his good study on the subject:

> "...My own guess is that God asks us to repent not as a condition he needs, but as a condition we need to bring his forgiveness full circle into our own experience."[243]

Shakespeare is the genius of the human necessity of forgiveness in body and soul, that life may go on. For the Bard it is the divine exemplification that exhibits the fundamental human necessity. We remember of course, Portia's magnificent speech in the Merchant of Venice,

> "...the quality of Mercy is not strained"

and in Richard II (1.1. 154-157):

> This we prescribe though no physician, deep malice makes too deep incision; forget, forgive, conclude, and be agreed; Our doctors say this is no month to bleed.

Sin, Grace, Responsibility and Renewal Reconsidered

In the conclusion of reflection on the petition "forgive our debts," I offer another interpretation. As we consider characteristics of Jewish prayer along with the features of Jewish theodicy and theology, it might be appropriate to recast the entire set of inter- and intrahuman petitions and so keep inner meaning of

Give us our daily bread
Forgive our debts

---

[243] Lewis Smedes, "Forgiving People Who Do Not Care," *Reformed Journal,* 33:13-18, 1983.

> Lead us not into temptation
> Deliver us from evil.

Building on what is explicit only in the forgiveness passage, perhaps these four petitions should be rendered:

- Give us our daily bread...as we share bread with others
- Forgive us our debts...as we forgive our debtors
- Lead us not into temptation...as we avoid tempting others
- And deliver us from evil...as we protect others from evil.

A different structure of sin and responsibility is conveyed in these revisions, one that would accord well with Jewish parallels and Aramaic (linguistic) potentials. God's law and will is the foundation for righteousness and the good life. Violating or failing to live and do that will is sin. Sin breaks the cycle of providence. If we fail to feed the hungry we too will miss the ultimal banquet. We may live, even thrive now, but finally we will be disinherited.

> "When did we see you hungry?" "Inasmuch as you refused it to the least
> of my brothers—you did it not to me"
> "...and these shall go away into everlasting punishment."
> (Matthew 25)

This interpretation of the structure of evil is somewhat at variance with a radical theology of grace as found in the Psalms, Paul's letter to Galatians, Luther's Lectures on Romans, and Barth's Dogmatics (ii, 1). This stream of thought rightfully claims that God's grace is constant and will continue regardless of human response or the lack of response.

But the more apocalyptic, Judaic, and reciprocal idea I propose is found in Matthew after Jesus recites the Lord's Prayer.

> For if you forgive men their trespasses, your heavenly father
> also will forgive you; but if you do not forgive men their
> trespasses,
> Neither will your Father forgive your trespasses.
> (Matthew 8:14-15)

This gift/task (*Gabe/aufgabe*) structure is also clearly articulated in the parable of the unforgiven servant (Matthew 18:21-35). I take this passage to show the more normative sense of God's action and human reaction as together constitutive of the gift of grace to the world.

God's justice requires satisfaction for the sin of the world. Christ's atonement satisfies that justice. As the Korean theology of *Ming Jung* states, the *Han* of people—the deep pathos and suffering born—the cross of pain—must be satisfied. Justice, which is grace, must prevail.

D. Death

We now turn to the culminating rhythm of our Eucharistical Theology. "The Lord's Prayer" certainly remembers David's Psalm:

> Though I walk through the valley of the Shadow of death I will fear no evil, for thou art with me (23)

It was at the funeral of Gianni Versace in Milan, Italy (July 22, 1997) that Elton John and Sting offered a mournful rendition of the Twenty-third Psalm, "The Lord is my Shepherd." At the outset, we announced our perspective on the prayer being concerned with the human drama of life and health, suffering and death. The divine disclosure to us in Scripture and Savior passes through the same process. Eucharist *itself* is a gathering of this divine story into a demonstrable form. In the Lord's Supper and baptism we lift our life and health, suffering and death up into the offering of God's descent and ascent, suffering, death, and resurrection joy in Christ's spirit. The "Lord's Prayer" is God's prayer within and for us for

> We do not know how to pray so the spirit intercedes for us...with sighs too deep for words.
> (Romans 8:26)

Death is the human reality which casts us up against the unknown and the transcendent. The premonition of death in ourselves, the witnessing of it in our loved ones, the grim reminder of it in war, starvation and accidents, the fact that animals die and are killed, the swift execution of accidents and illnesses, all render our minds and hearts eucharistically vulnerable. We seek to make sense of this enigma. Or better, if scripture, religious and philosophical traditions are correct, death seeks to make sense of us. The awareness of death makes us alive to self and reality and to the reality of God. Luther reports that he was "in terror and agony of sudden death" which led him both into denying compensation (the Monastery) and to true insight (WA VIII 573). Death premonition makes our lives eucharistical, cruciform, *Homo Religiosis*.

VII. Suffering: "Lead us not into Temptation...but Deliver us..."

Biblical theology finds the human condition beset by the limitations and temptations of the world, flesh and the devil. In modern language we are not free but are restricted by forces over which we have no control. Eden's garden stories identify our disobedience and free human usurpation of forbidden knowledge and power as the ground for the beginning of human sin, finitude, and cosmic evil. Yet the source of temptation is there before the fall, symbolized by the serpent. The Book of James, Luther's "straw epistle" (faith without works is dead), refuses to let us attribute temptation to God. This despite the fact that throughout Scripture God allows, leads into, or protects from, temptation:

> Let no one say when he is tempted, "I am tempted by God," for
> God cannot be tempted with evil, and he himself tempts no one.
> (James 1:13)

The primeval temptation of the Genesis garden is recapitulated at the inauguration of Jesus' ministry in (Matthew 4) with the desert temptation:

> ...Turn these stones to bread
> ...Throw yourself down
> ...Bow down and worship me

and in the midst, the ironic *GEGRAPTAI*

> "It is written—you shall not tempt the Lord your God."

Even so, the Bible has been called The Book of Temptations. After the paradise garden we have Abram and Jacob in Mesopotamia (4:7), and David and Job being "put to the test." In Psalm 119:8 we find the correlation of forsaking God's commandments and being forsaken into temptation. Jewish morning and evening prayer grounds this association:

> Set my portion in thy law and accustom me to the performance
> of religious duties...and lead me not into sin, or into iniquity, or
> into temptation or into contempt."[244]

In Corinthians (10:13ff) it is confided that "God is faithful, and will not let you be tempted beyond your strength" but will provide a pathway to relief and endurance.

In the book of Hebrews, to "be tempted" is the equivalent of suffering:

> for because he himself has suffered and been tempted, he is able to help those
> who are tempted." (2:18)

Suffering is therefore a state of being, characterized by pain, usually fired in the cauldron of judgment and condemnation, a state of anguish in body, mind, and spirit. The cosmos and order of life slips back toward chaos and dissolution. We are thrown back against the dark recesses of incoherence, absurdity, and pain. Death finally becomes a release from such agony.

Temptation, Evil and Death

Death is the ultimate temptation and evil. Abraham is drawn to the precipice of infanticide. Job cries, "though he slay me yet will I trust in him" (Job 13:15). In David's Psalm, "In the valley of life's darkest shadows, in the valley of death, we will fear no evil." For the apostle, "the wages of sin is death" (Romans 6:23).

---

[244] *Berak,*op.ci., p. 606.

Pascal's wager and Faust's temptation ultimately challenge life and death itself. Death is the ultimate enticement. In Freud's language, *Todestrieb*, the lure of placid stillness is a return to the womb and to the hollows of the pre-creation. In the shadowlands of Sheol and in the recesses of death, there is no life. We are no longer free, temptation ceases. Delivery from evil is rescue from the lion's mouth (II Timothy 4:17ff).

Temptation is the human condition. Paul here claims with another of his school that what we experience is "common to humanity" and Jesus, it is asserted, was "tempted at all points as we are, yet without sin" (Hebrews 4:15).

The petition "Lead us not into temptation, but deliver us from evil" has as its active verb, *eispherein*. The verb implies displacement or being moved from one place to another. Jesus is "led up by the spirit," *eispherein*, into the desert. We are often transferred from our home to some wilderness or strange place. The transfer is often from security to some terrifying and unknown place. Abraham walks his trusting son, *Yitsak*, into the mountains of Moriah (Genesis 22). The dislocation from life to death, from health to disease, from peace to war, from serenity to fear, is the crisis of temptation. The Lord's Prayer in this passage of crescendo of foreboding surely recalls the great psalm of *eispherein*.

> Though I walk through the valley of the shadow of death, I will fear no evil...
> (Psalm 23).

The ultimate terror of such temptation is pain and abandonment. Human experience in faith has proven that we can go through anything if "thou art with us" and if "thou preparest a table." Suffering through temptation becomes intolerable when it is meaningless and unaccompanied. Thousands of martyrs and heroes throughout the ages have laid down their lives unnoticed and unacknowledged. Only God knows their saving act. We can transact the paths of danger and fear if we know we are being "led in paths of righteousness for his name's sake." The ultimate meaning of temptation is judgment. All penultimate temptations prefigure an ultimate "great tribulation that will quake all creation." Through the cataclysmic trial, Christ will keep his own who endure:

> I will keep you from the hour of trial, which is coming to the whole world, to test those who dwell upon the earth"
> (Revelation 3:10).

The greatest incentive to faith is that this is God's world even in the presence of evil. Three senses of evil are comprehended in this petition. First, there is human evil. In C.S. Lewis' book, The Problem of Pain, he chides that we can't chalk up to God's carelessness our clubs and guns. Much evil in the world in caused by human thoughtlessness and malevolence. In Matthew 5:11 we read, "They will say all kinds of evil against you...." Much of the evil in the world is chosen, willed and inflicted.

As I write, a major commemoration is occurring at the fiftieth anniversary of the liberation of Auschwitz-Birkenau concentration camp and gas chambers. Poland acknowledges that even though tens of thousands of its citizens, including intellectuals and priests, were killed here by the Nazis, the vast burden of evil came to rest on Jewish men, women, and children. The Catholic Church acknowledges its silence and complicity with the evil of the holocaust. Elie Wiesel, who survived the camp, is the speaker at the event. He calls for love and understanding grounded in perpetual remembrance: "Not all to be killed were Jews, but all Jews were to be killed." The German government acknowledges its direct guilt. In America, it is a day when one political leader calls another, "Barney Fag," oblivious to the bitter fact that many gays went to the ovens along with the Jews succeeding the One who was "despised and rejected." It is a day where American complicity in Auschwitz, its denial of entry to that flood of "illegal immigrants," goes unacknowledged. Intimidated by the American Legion, we also fail to acknowledge in a Smithsonian fiftieth anniversary exhibition our genocide at Hiroshima and Nagasaki, Hamburg and Dresden. America remains triumphant and unrepentant. Our cooperation with evil remains sometimes acknowledged, most times ignored.

The evening news also carries the story of another kind of unassuming evil. A nineteen- year-old boy, of obviously rudimentary intelligence and learning, has been convicted by a judge of defacing a Jewish synagogue in Wisconsin with Nazi symbols and phrases like "we told you so." He is sentenced to a lengthy course of study with a survivor of the Auschwitz camp.

Evil is also found in a fabric of corporate or structural process. We all participate almost unconsciously in this ethos. A recent book by James North, *The Structures of Sin*, examines the inequality between the industrialized nations and the third world. The concentration of wealth in fewer and fewer hands is not willful evil, it just happens. Transcending the malevolence and maleficence of particular individuals, there seems to be a greater measure and mounting of evil at work in the world. *Tas Ponerias* (evil) seems to refer to a general mood and atmosphere, a kind of condition, salience, or state of affairs that permeates the world drawing all life toward injustice, harm and destruction.

Tou Ponerou (the evil one) is yet a third notion conveyed in the petition. This is evil personified, given a name. This is Beliar, Beelzebub, Satan, the Devil. This is *Diabolos*—the one who splits open and fractures wholeness and unity (*symbolos*). The Germans have the word *zerissenheit*, what Anne Morrow Lindbergh translated "torn-to-pieces-hood." *Diabolos* is one who lures us into temptation, accuses us "day and night before God," delivers us to death hoping to capture our eternal soul, casts doubt on the veracity of the way and will of God. The product of fierce apocalyptic imagination, the adventic dragon capitulates the archaic serpent as the metaphoric creature who personally wishes to lead us astray and separate us from God, our rightful home. Satan seeks to construct a separate cosmos of association based on the wayward tendencies in our nature.

Luther calls this the "*Doppelbitte*"

> Lead us not...
> But deliver us...

Calvin also unites it into one unified petition. Luther's powerful language clearly conveys that we must anchor ourselves in the strong sustenance and protection of God, the Savior, in the midst of these primal forces for which Luther uses primitive German words *korunga* and *bikorunga* which both convey the possessing ensnarement of the word "*anfechtung*."

The petition also has an urgent future and eschatic meaning. Like the "daily bread" clause it means now and then. We may be safe and secure for the moment, but night comes as does tomorrow. What will a day bring?

Jeremias draws in the parallel of an ancient Jewish Prayer:

> Keep my paths from the power of sin and do not bring me under the power of guilt or the power of temptation or the power of shame.[245]

These ominous forces which are able to undo us are always around. Only the strong safety of the Lord God can encircle us with safety. In Luther the prayer has further eschatological bearing, namely, my own end. Save us now—in the coming final temptation (Revelation 3) and in my own death—receive us into heaven (*sich nehmen in den himmel K.K.*). In the lovely song that concludes Claude-Michel Schöenberg's Les Miserables, at the end of battle and of a weary life, where one has tried his best, he sings for Marius, the young patriot on the barricades:

> ...BRING HIM HOME

In St Augustine's words, which in their platonic serenity and surprise do not allow for our all-too- dualistic construal of good and evil:

> ...we believe in faith that both the good and evil in all things in creation if fully understood (in faith) are God's good.[246]

The New Testament crafts a rich cosmology of evil including elements from apocalyptic Judaism, Mesopotamian mystery religion and Persian dualism. A counter kingdom of beings cohabit this world with us. In the moving passage of temptation, betrayal and persecution in Matthew 10, demonic powers are

---

[245] Joachin Jeremias, *Vaterunser,* (Stuttgart: Fuache Verlag, 1962), p.17.
[246] *Enchirdion* II 7, 8, 9 Library of Christian Classics.

envisaged as householders here in God's world where we thought we were safe. Here and now Satan holds sway. This petition of the prayer is thus a counter petition to the ascription: "Our father." The *stabulum*, home, ethos is disturbed and inhabited. We have been disowned or exiled into this world which still lies in the fading ownership of rebellious power. Alienation, sickness and death in our bodies are symptoms of this exile. The wiley tempter is outraged, however, since the house of this world has been visited by the one "in whom was life and that life was the light of all people" (John 1). Setting up his tent among ours (John 1:14), God's possession is re-established.

Yet this "evil one" remains entrenched in this world. He is the strong one who lives safely in his house "with his goods," exerting harm toward people and disturbing God's comfort (Matthew 12:29). Martin Luther, who as a medieval man with the dark, troubled psyche of that generation, was consumed with the imagery of demonic inhabitation, in part foisted by the church to foster allegiance, constructed a world of strong fortress (*feste burg*) of Christ's protective salvation against this invading kingdom.

> His rage we can endure
> for lo his doom is sure
> One little word shall fell him.

Luther lived in the same cosmos as primitive Christianity, where a principal ritual was exorcising of devils.

Now indeed, Satan, the evil one himself, is being dispossessed. He is being "cast out" by the erupting kingdom. There is no room or home for both. Satan cannot cast out Satan (Mark 3:23). Only God and manifest kingdom can eject this intruder, this squatter. Just as behind all evil we find Satan, beyond all good, we find God. The raison d'etre of Satan is temptation: *Proprium Satanas est tentare* (John Calvin, I Thessalonians 3:15). The essential nature of God is emancipation from evil, deliverance and wholeness.

> God sent the son into the world—not to condemn the world—but that the
> world through Him might be saved.
> (John 3:17)

In the crucible of temptation, the living force of the evil one is condemnation. The living force of God is forgiveness and wholeness.

The verbs in this petition are dynamic, personal and active. The text speaks of leading, tempting, delivering. One is acting. One is responding. This is not abstract theology, it is movement. Not being, it is going. An indissoluble bond or yoke is placed between suppliant and supplier, between the vulnerable and the vanguard.

Luther read the text as does Augustine:

We pray that our father in heaven will deliver us from all ill to body and soul, to goods and honour.

In Luther's great fortress hymn he follows the stirring conclusion of the Lord's Prayer.

Let goods and kindred go (*Gut, ehe, kind* and *weib*)
This mortal life also
The body they may kill
God's truth abideth still
His kingdom is forever.

Jesus taught the world that the world, however good and provident, cannot ultimately make us safe. Here we are vulnerable, weak and exposed to every danger. We can invent air bags to prevent auto crash injuries and inherit a rash of air-bag injuries. We can develop the new line of neuro-specific psychiatric drugs and inherit even more telling side effects. Our security systems of espionage and weapons turn against us. Iraq turns against Britain and America with lethal weapons and knowledge that these two nations provided. In the words of the writer of Hebrews:

...Here we have no abiding city (Hebrews 13:14)

We therefore trust through him in God, the builder and maker of that lasting city, that kingdom which has no end.

VIII. Serenity: For Thine is the Kingdom

The final doxology gathers all of the human drama—its sadness and needs, its loss and challenge, its hunger, hope and love—all into one song of praise and resolution—into God's ultimal peace. Circumstantial and chosen evil, random and calculated harm, the surge and delights of life and health, the terror of suffering and death., the gruesome reality of life and its residue of guilt and grief, the shimmering of hope on that distant yet so near horizon all are drawn here into a consummate love.

For thine is the kingdom, the power, and the glory forever, Amen.

The Didache, our most incisive glimpse of the ethics and liturgics of the very earliest apostolic church, ends the "Lord's Prayer" with the doxology "for thine is the power and glory forever." Obviously, the addition is not present in the first or third Gospel, but was added for worship purposes by the early Christian community, particularly the church in Syria. Jesus may have appended some doxology to the original model prayer since each petition of the contemporary eighteen benedictions ends with a doxology. These model prayers of the Great Synagogue tradition of the earliest centuries of the Christian era likely reach back to the time of Jesus and were familiar to him.

In his preface to the letter to the Galatians, Paul gathers a texture of colors together which show the purpose of the conclusion and completeness of the Lord's Prayer.

> Grace to you and peace from God the Father and our Lord Jesus Christ, who gave himself for our sins to deliver us from the present evil age, according to the will of our God and Father, to whom be the glory forever and ever. Amen. (Galatians 1:3-5)

As with Bach's masterful opus, the hymn *"Dei Gloria"* is offered in the face of the powers of this world. As Bach writes in the Cantata *"Christ Lag in Todesbanden,"* we offer our doxology in the jaws of death. The ramparts of the kingdom are safe and sure even in the presence of the full fury of the world, flesh, death and the devil.

> "For thine is the kingdom"

No intruding principality or power can separate...their occupation is temporary, fleeting and has been superseded as it was preceded for

> His kingdom is forever.
> (*das Reich muss uns doch bleiben*: Martin Luther, 1528)

The mystery of the kingdom is eucharistic. The good gift of victory over evil and of accomplished salvation is here already, finished and complete. But it does not yet appear to be in effect. Suffering and disease, violence and death, injustice and evil, still seem to have the upper hand. The eucharistic love feast has a similar bivalent meaning. Here and now we offer the simple gifts of bread and wine in memory of that terrifying night when Jesus was given over to his death. Like its paradigm Passover meal, we remember the bitter herbs and blood-smeared doorposts of Pharaoh's lethal assault. Bondage and oppression remain the human plight in this "not yet" time.

Eucharist is also communion of the saints, the heavenly banquet, the glorious victory of our God. It is a *fait accompli*. An admittedly weak illustration: the Gulf War. The conclusion was foregone. Joint Chiefs of Staff chair Colin Powell announced it to the world media before the air war with Iraq began.

Here is my report at that time:

> The war would be swift and horrible. General Colin Powell, chairman of the U.S. Joint Chiefs of Staff, and Secretary of State James Baker, would make that point clear that week to Iraq and the world. In blitzkrieg that would make the attacks on Dresden and Hamburg look like child's play, every advanced U.S. weapon would be used: F-117 stealth fighters would zoom through at low altitude raining laser-guided bombs on command bunkers and missile control sites; F-46 Wild Weasels in concert with F-16 and F-15 fighters would attack

anti-aircraft installations with HARM radar-seeking missiles; FB-111 and F-15E bombers would smash air defense installations, severing contact between the Iraqi central command and field commanders. EF-111 and other electronic craft would jam and disrupt all Iraqi communications; Cruise missiles launched from the Gulf, the Indian Ocean, and the Red Sea would home in on Iraq's concentrated installations on the Kuwaiti border and governmental and military centers in Baghdad. Hundreds of B- 52s would drop thousands of 900-kilogram bombs on Iraq's 500,000-strong army. Thousands of tons of ordnance would obliterate every important Iraqi center of military, industrial, and governmental activity. And when the first wave of attacks was completed, a second would begin, and then a third, and a fourth. And a fifth. After two weeks this would be followed by a multi-pronged ground and amphibious assault. And then what?

Modern electronic, computerized warfare can be fully programmed and simulated before it takes place and the outcome can be predicted, even announced. America could and did announce to Japan what was to transpire when the Enola Gay and other planes would atomic bomb Hiroshima and Nagasaki, Japan in 1945 and 'big bertha' Iraq in 1990. For most people most of the time, annunciation is not convincing—we require actualization. God's accomplished kingdom, the *fait accompli* victory, is annunciated in the suffering, death, resurrection, ascension and pentecost of Christ. Even though the evil one acts as if he's still viable, he's finished.

> Though the cause of evil prosper,
> Yet 'tis truth alone is strong;
> Though her portion be the scaffold,
> And upon the throne be wrong,
> Yet that scaffold sways the future,
> And behind the dim unknown,
> Standeth God within the shadow
> Keeping watch above his own.
> James Russell Lowell, 1845

The kingdom is achieved, though still hidden. In this day of Israel and Iran, Palestine and Iraq and Afganistan and Korea in what sense are the kingdoms of this world becoming the kingdom of our God and of his Christ (Revelation 11:15)? In this day of cancer and AIDS, in what sense is the kingdom of life and health come among us (Luke 11:20)? In this day of Bosnia and Armenia, in what sense is the kingdom of peace (Luke 2:14) available in our world of conflict? In this day of gaping poverty domestically and internationally, in what sense is the kingdom of the poor (Matthew 6:20) at hand?

The Kingdom is hand ever so like that coming kingdom

In the sparkling eyes of the child at the mystery of the Christmas tree.
In the unheralded good deed of taking a homeless person home for a meal and a
night's sleep.
In the Lord's supper we celebrate in church with unseen but ever present

companions not only everywhere but ever-before and ever-after.
In the morsels of bread or the drops of cool water placed on the lips of the dying.
In the heart-felt though autonomic

> *Bon Jour*
>> *Bon Soir*
>>> Good Bye—God be with you. (K.V.)

Conclusion

We have explored the intermediate call back of humans in eucharistical theology responding to God's call of duty in ethical theology and preceding our creedal witness in evangelical theology. Eucharistics is the indisputable link in the chain of grace. God's action and man's response is ligatured by the worship act of plea and praise. Our task now remains to formulate that witness of action and life that is evangelical theology. I have argued that an evangelical, eucharistical and ethical theology is Judaic and Akedic. We have seen how a common heritage is constituted by a compelling Leitmotiv (Akedah). We have surveyed the common ethical charter which grows out of that shaping theology of sacrifice. We now have examined the contours of prayer. It remains to struggle through the difficult issues of a common and divergent creed and cause.

Part IV. War: Creed, Crusade and Conversion

Part IV. War: Creed, Crusade and Conversion

Incursus: War

Vietnam: turning point in the wars of liberation. In 1965 my brother was discharged from the U.S. Army amid concern about his philosophical objections to the Vietnam War and for having a photo of Ho Chi Minh in his locker at Fort Hood, Texas. To me he was a hero and his service to our country was honorable. As a young Pastor in the Presbyterian Church my theological and ethical convictions had led me in similar directions to wage war against that war. In his spirit I would eventually write critiques of the wars on Iraq and against terrorism (Westview, 1992, WIPF/Stock, 2002).

The Vaux brothers had reversed a long family history of patriotism grounded in participation in War II and I, the Civil War and American Revolution, the religious wars of the Reformation and on and on back to Cain and Abel. Some UR-Vaux was there in all these creed-campaigns wielding, I assume, word and sword.

The crucial issue was not what my brother opposed but what he affirmed. He conscientiously objected to dehumanizing some people into the category of sub-human enemies because they were Asian. His costly protest was an affirmation of the dignity of all people. His objection to Lt. Calley and My Lai and other village napalm holocausts and his horror at flame-strafing and frying old men and kids was his love and respect for children and elders. He believed and lived in idealist, i.e. Marxism's, solidarity with the poor, with workers, with the oppressed. He found himself led against the patriotic crusade because of his humanistic creed. He was a soldier for liberty, truth and justice.

But, Vietnam was a turning point. Was it a war for liberty or liberation? Vietnam sought to free itself from French colonialism and American hegemony in Asia. America and its allies sought to rid the peninsula and particularly the south of communism. In conspiracy with Russia after War II, we had arbitrarily and wrongly divided the country.

The Vietnam War and its aftermath significantly transformed the martial and moral values of the American people. Standing in the long western heritage of rejecting tyranny, defying injustice, and advocating liberty and democracy, this American nation had struggled and suffered through a series of liberation wars: the revolution against England's occupation; the war against slavery and threatened separation and breach of sovereignty in the civil war; two great World Wars in Europe and Asia. Finally—as the last war against tyranny and the first hot burst of cold war—the resistance to the incursion of North Korea into South had to be challenged. Sprinkled in between were lesser conflicts like the wars against the Native Americans and the Mexican Wars. Despite the pacific propensity in the American soul, fervent patriotism and willingness to sacrifice arose strongly against the threats of godless tyrannies. God-derived freedom is the quintessential value of the American soul.

The salutary aftermath of that war has been the personal and public reflection it has stimulated. We have been forced to reevaluate the worthiness of conducting war—when—where—and why. Even more deeply, as my reflections in this study suggest, we have been asked to engage even more searching questions. What in the world do we deem worth living for, fighting for, dying for? What is our creed? What crusade are we prepared to undertake for our beliefs? This reflection that I now set before you might be called "a military history of the Apostle's Creed." Christian creed is rooted in *shemah* and Decalogue, the creed of second temple Judaism, Jesus' own faith and life.

Vietnam marked a turning point. The poignant drama surrounding the "Nam" wall on the Washington mall, where millions of persons have made their way to touch Braille-like the neglected names of their loved ones, reflect the national ambivalence of admiration and shame and the questionable patriot-coward resolve to never get involved—to never get "bogged down" again. Only 9-11 and the war on terrorism would change that reticence into bold assertion against perceived threat.

Incursus: Peace

Requiem aeternam dona eis. The haunting voice of the lyric soprano faded against the background of chorus and orchestra. It was Verdi's REQUIEM MASS performed by the Chicago Symphony Orchestra during the 100th anniversary of the composer's death. Like Brahm's *DEUTSCHES REQUIEM*, this is a sacred and secular masterpiece. A piece of akedic wisdom, the Ravinia audience of thousands was liberally sprinkled by Jewish and Muslim acquaintances. The many comments they shared and which I overheard convinced me of the validity of this work's thesis—that universal theological and ethical wisdom is formed as Judaism creatively gives shape to Christian reality through the symbol of Akedah. The historical crisis of Abrahamic faith continues with the rise of Islam. As we prepare to explore the Christian creed and crusade in light of its Judaic origins, Verdi's use of the ancient Roman creed in his REQUIEM points to the touchstone of this common history.

Verdi's atheistic propensities are swallowed up in faith and hope in the REQUIEM. The death of his young wife and two children added to the agony of the death of Giaichomo Rossini and Alessandro Manzoni, the premier composer and writer of his day and formed the crucible of human experience that drew Verdi to the brink of the akedic mystery of death into life. The bass-baritone is both narrator and trembling sinner as he offers:

Tearful will be that day of wrath (*dies Irae*)
When from the ashes arises
An accused man to be judged

On that day the chorus howls:

The generations will dissolve into ashes

> How great a trembling there will be
> When the judge comes
> And severely scatters everything

Reminiscent of the two soldiers duet of Abraham's offeratorio in Benjamin Britten's WAR REQUIEM, the soprano and mezzo plead:

> *Agnus Dei, qui tollis peccata mundi,*
> *Dona eis requiem sempiternam*

Rest and eternal peace is consummately proffered in the delivering grace of God who has come out to the history of the world, shared the travail of human freedom and anguish, and through sacrificing love has victoriously transfigured that plight into resurrection.

> ...you who are compassionate (*pius es*)
> save us on that day when heaven and earth tremble
> and you shall judge the world by fire.

War and peace, offense and defense of the God-way in this world is the subject of this part of our study. We will begin with the complicated notion of cause or mandate.

Introduction

> "Wrest that land from the wicked race and subject it to yourselves."
> Pope Urban's sermon at Clarmont, 1095 CE.

> "To protect the earth from the scum of the universe."
> Film, Men in Black, 1997

What noble purpose shall a people live and die for? What configuration of God (ultimate purpose), humanity, and the world shall triangulate human affairs? This Trinity stalks human belief. It compels confession and conviction animating assertion and defense. From the birth of Christianity in the bosom of first century Palestinian Judaism, we find a second temple Hebraic trinity shaping worldly existence under God: Decalogue, the eighteen benedictions, and the *Shema*. Jesus, we assume, was bar mitzvahed in this devotion. In the late first and early second century catechesis of the church he founded, this trinity now becomes the Decalogue, Lord's Prayer and Creed. Eventually, in the late second and third century, especially in the western church which had begun to dissociate from Judaism, the structure of faith becomes Father, Son and Spirit. The triumvirate or triadic theistic structure remains normative. In the Reformation, Luther assembles this ancient library in his shorter and longer catechisms: commandments, creed and prayer. Such a trilogy has always sought to summarize the essence of what we are to believe and how we are to live in the world. We ask of what is the faith we should fight for? "How ought we to contend for our convictions?"

The experiences which convinced me to look at the creed in this militant and activist way were two: As a young pastor in the church of Scotland I discovered, by visiting the village pubs on Saturday night before Sunday service, that the staunchest defenders of the faith and the Kirk were those who never darkened its door (this may explain the North Ireland crisis). After a few too many pints, these presumed defender-crusaders often came to blows over fine points of doctrine. Years later in my studies in Europe and the Middle East I discovered to my surprise that the Apostle's Creed was finally and firmly established in Western Christendom only under Charlemagne at the time of the rise and threat of Islam—strange coincidence! Creed is occasioned by and becomes the occasion for violence.

The Creed, as well as being a part of an ancient tri-unity, also sought to comprehend and defend that primal life-structure. The Christian creed in its biblical kernel [I Corinthians 12:3] or later formulation (Nicean, Chalcedonean, Apostle's) encapsulates the belief system and way of life that was the ancient structure of TANAKH, the Hebrew Bible—Hebrew Holy Scripture, that was known to Jesus and the Apostles. TANAKH included three parts: *Torah*—(Law)—*Nabiim*—(Prophets)—and *Kittim* (Wisdom writings). The fundamental rhythms and imperatives of the religious life are thus addressed as we are directed to faith (Decalogue), consolidated in faith (prayer) and sent to live out our faith in our lifeworld (creed).

This part of our study reflects my own evolving religious concept. Previous parts are based on the Decalogue and Lord's prayer. Now we begin to a study of the political field of faith and life (polity). I propose now to trace the societal defense of and assertion of the Gospel of Jesus Christ. I offer this all the while reclaiming our Judaic heritage. Put in more cultural terms, I am interested in what it is that we set out to advocate and defend as the way and truth of life. I will seek to track the history of that witness and confession of JESUS CHRIST. I am convinced that at most moments of creedal confession some gesture of social policy is at stake. When the Emperor Constantine convenes the Bishops at Nicea, we witness not only a watershed in spiritual belief, but an urgent political moment. As James Carroll vividly shows in The SWORD OF CONSTANTINE (2000) that history is marked by an antagonism to Judaism. Luther and Melanchton's Augsburg Confession (1530) and John Knox's Scots Confession of 1560 signal historical change as well as codification of extant belief.

I also seek to fathom the connection between war history and abrahamic religion. The military history of Christendom—Constantine through the crusades—down to the religious wars of the sixteenth and seventeenth centuries—even onto the modern strife among secularized states, say WW II—and the War on Iraq and on terrorism—is marked by tensions among the three Abrahamic faiths.

In Karen Armstrong's masterful book, THE BATTLE FOR GOD (Harper Collins, 2000), she traces two thresholds of this battle: 1492-1800 and the twentieth and early twenty-first century. In these two epochs the three Abrahamic faiths verge toward fundamentalism which portends, then activates militancy, provoking fervor in belief which seems inevitably to find bellicose expression.

Contemporary theological history seeks to remedy the errors of that past while confirming its strengths. History, as our calendar gives evidence, is the time process now bound and punctuated by the history of Jesus Christ—his annunciation through to his eschatic appearance that will mark the end of time. In the meanwhile, universal time is marked by His name and the history of His justice. Both good and evil are designated by reference to His name:

- Peter and Paul die in Rome and James, Jesus' brother in Jerusalem in 62 C.E.
- Nero dies in Rome in 68 C.E.
- Hitler dies in his Berlin bunker in 1945, Christian Era (C.E.)
- Schweitzer dies in Lambarene in 1965 C.E., the year of our Lord.

The moral history of the human race is a theological history. The great faiths and philosophies of East and West—religious and secular—all have their part. The non-historian must tread very lightly when he attempts an historical approach to a problem at hand. I seek, as a Systematic Theologian and a moral philosopher, to explore the history of the creed of faith in and the Way of life of Jesus Christ. This can only be done as the stem is anchored in the root of Judaism. I hope to thus uncover what this can mean to us today and how it functions in a contemporary personal and political history. I do not seek to rejuvenate Eusebius or Augustine in their triumphalist apologetic histories nor to emulate Joachim of Fiori in his apocalyptic ages of the Father, Son and Spirit. That scheme, it seems to me, is as misguided as Comte's division of history into ages of superstition, belief and science. I do not see inevitable organic patters of fertilization, fruition and finality in history as do Spengler, and Toynbee, for example. Nor do I hold to some progressive view of history as, for example, does Hegel. We are not moving to higher and higher modes of realization and ideals as history progresses. Reinhold Niebuhr seems closer to the mark when he says that history gets better and worse concurrently.

In some ways history moves toward greater freedom and salvation. In other ways it moves toward greater anomie and damnation. As victims of strife in Rwanda stream desperately across the Zaire border or ethnic Albanians forcibly forsake their homeland in Kosovo to a treacherous refugee winter in the mountains, or as lingering Taliban guerillas continue to kill in Western Asia ,we are aware that primitive tribal violence still stalks our "civilization." At millennium's close balkanization is as strong a phenomenon as is universalization. War in Palestine and Israel and the war with Iraq stalked the world like the apocalyptic horseman while the spectre of the twin towers or Tolkien's two Towers sear the conscience. Yet, religious culture is evolving towards greater tolerance and reciprocity in the ecumenical movement. But it also rushes toward greater tribalism and xenophobia in the resurgent fundamentalisms. We always live, as Charles Dickens wrote, in "the best of times...and the worst of times."

I wish therefore to sketch the ambiguity of Christian creedal history with an ethicist's penchant to celebrate its goodness and to condemn its injustice and violence. Each stage of the history of creedal crusade has a resplendently bright and an ominously dark side. If we are to move toward a peaceful world order and toward some finer proximation of the kingdom of God we must recognize the perpetual misconstrual of that authentic story. The challenge, indeed the survival necessity for us right now, is to get it right.

Faith, War and Piety: My Bias

My bias about the evangelical faith and authentic creed is as follows: Jesus has renewed for all humanity God's faith in the world and God's Way for the world. This belief and ethic grows fully from the roots of Israel as Israel is rooted in preceding and parallel religious truths and moralisms. It grows toward other world faiths, first through Hellenism, then out to the rest of the world. I see Christianity as a focusing of the spiritual and ethical wisdom present in primitive consciousness (Romans 1) in high faiths represented by prophets like Confucius, Buddha, and Zoroaster. This faith will show a fecundity—yielding philosophies and life patterns like Islamic humanism, and secular Marxism. It then proceeds toward a human future, safeguarding humanity and the earth as sacred trust. In biblical faith we call this Godly Will and Way for the world: God's WORD. For Luther, Jesus Christ as the Way, Truth, and Life, known through scripture and confession, is the Word of God. God's Word is dynamic. It is *cooperatio dei*; it seeks human reception and cooperation.

Evangelical faith is the publication or sharing of that WORD (evangel: news or message) with others. I see the messianic creed subsumed in Israel's mandate of Decalogue, *shemah* and light to the Gentiles. The process of forming evangelical faith occurs in sacred community. In the language of the Protestant Reformation in Europe—one vital moment in this historic process—we are saved (healed and made right with God) by God's grace through faith (also God's gift) for good works (the right [just] life).

This evangelical apostolate (going forth), an act of laity and civility, occurs throughout history, always generating two polar extremes and a middle—normative way. The polar extremes are exaggerations of the secular and sacred, the worldly and otherworldly dimensions of the faith, both essential ingredients of a divine gift, not kept in eternity but given to and through the world. The worldly exaggeration is holy war or civil religion. It is good and godly put partial and dangerous. Holy war, crusade and Jihad are energies of speech and spirit or coercion and violence. The danger comes when it becomes the sole expression of the divine faith and life in our midst. The other pole, also good and Godly, is spiritualism. Apocalypticism and world-betrayal occurs when this necessary and vital pole of authentic faith becomes exaggerated and all-exhausting. Creed can be distorted in either direction or it can seek the middle-way where the integrity and tension of the relation between God and the world is maintained. The history of receiving and appropriating God's faith to humanity is committed to human agency. It is thus a process of creedal crusade. This can be wholly worldly as in holy and just war or wholly spiritual as in monasticism or mysticism. Rightful via media is evangelical faith. The evangel is the watchman on the city wall, the messenger of good news (Isaiah 40),the one faithful in pacific JIHAD. This normative notion of fighting faith is the bias I bring to the analysis found in this book.

My viewpoint is also persuaded by a feature of human psychology. Human Beings want to live and die for some great cause. "That I have not lived in vain"; "that my life counts for something"; "that everything is not futility"; "That I do not end my days in senility or eroding malignancy having accomplished nothing"; all these sentiments are strong though deeply repressed aspects of the human psyche. As subliminal force they become the seedbed for the personal phenomenon of the "true believer" and the cultural phenomenon of evangelical crusade.

The Conjunction: Creed and Crusade

The church militant, church triumphant. All people of all worldviews live out and die for their creed. In one way the creed and the crusade of any given people have a singular intent and content throughout history. All peoples believe that their codified convictions and their way of life is to be both defended and extended. Even in the religiously pluralistic states of Western society in theocratic Muslim states and in secular states without a common faith, we find a body of philosophical principles and commitments to values—values such as freedom, toleration and human rights and social justice—ideals which are deemed worthy of vigorous defense and propagation. While such secular nations tend not to fight for their beliefs unless they are pushed to the brink and they do not seek to impose their values on other peoples, those convictions and commitments are held with serious tenacity. In both overt and subtle ways people commend them to others. Cultures, seen rightly, are defensive, apologetic, even aggressive. "We've a story to tell to the nations, that will turn their hearts to the right, a story of truth and mercy, a story of peace and light..."

Today, American, Western and even global society struggles with this issue in two ways. First Christian individuals and communities ask if they are meant to constitute a tribe, a society, a movement, a nation, a global civilization. Or is our faith transhistorical, founding a spiritual fellowship and not having to do with nations? Is the faith supra-secular, not of this world?

410

Gerd Theissen has argued that the monotheistic revolutions, which began throughout the world in the "Axis-Times" (800-200 BCE) and took a revolutionary leap in exile and post-exile Judaism, is just now in modern times working out its justice and peace.[247] Do we belong to some universal society of faith and values, one that transcends nations? Oliver O'Donovan's study The Desire of Nations (Cambridge, 1996) explores this issue. States where there is a national religion as well as a secular charter, states such as England, Scotland, Germany, France, Greece, Turkey, Armenia, Israel, and Iran continually agonize with this issue.

On the other hand we may ask if the purpose of God with the world is to establish righteous communities and nations where true faith and good life find expression.

(God) has established of one blood all nations that they should seek him. . .
(Acts 17:26)

In either case, we know today that we must seek to identify and clarify our beliefs and values in order to inform the national life and to have something to offer other nations. If America, for example, seeks willingly or reluctantly to dominate world affairs, geopolitically and geoeconomically, it needs to declare its own matrix of values. Do we believe in God or in some other ultimacy (power or money)? Do we believe in freedom, human rights and democracy? If so, what sort of freedom, which rights, what sort of democracy? America can probably never again be a Protestant commonwealth—internally or externally. It may never again extend a mission—say, to Korea (as it did early in the 20th Century or as some propose to do,now in Iraq)—a mission of political-cultural and spiritual influence. Does America seek to ensure, even enforce, human rights in Bosnia, Rwanda, Kosova, Turkey, Israel, China? What rights? Do we advocate and work for formal rights; speech, press, assembly, etc. for substantial rights: housing, work, health, etc., or both? When we intervene in Somalia, Bosnia, or Rwanda for presumably humanitarian concerns, what worldview, what ethic guides our programs? With Grounding in what worldview and anthropology do we resolve our ambivalent participation in the United Nations? The declaration of a spiritual and ethical standpoint is evidently necessary. The value of freedom can only mean relativity and plurality—an ethos of "do your own thing," unless there is some undergirding faith.

In contrast to these early modern secular-pluralist societies, most nations or peoples throughout history and even more today have a dominant "common faith" and "way of life." Israel is a Jewish State; Iran, Islamic; Spain, Catholic; and Scotland, Presbyterian. Some national religions are by their very nature nonevangelical. The Judaism of Israel, the Islam of Chechnya and Bosnia, the

---

[247] Gerd Theissen, *Biblical Faith: An Evolutionary Approach*, Trans. J. Bowden; Philadelphia: Fortress Press. 1985. Part IV. War: Creed, Crusade and Conversion.

Orthodoxy of Armenia and Serbia, the Anglicanism of England, the Buddhism and Shinto of Japan are such nonproselytizing societies. There is no compulsion to propagate the faith, at least not by overt action. Other societies are more conversionist and aggressive. Russian society in 1998 was struggling with reauthorizing the Orthodox Church to societal supremacy, thereby delegitimizing other faiths. Among most peoples at most times creed exudes social energies ranging from affirmation and assertion, to taking the stand, to engaging controversy and mounting battle cry. This more traditional pattern of culture throughout history has led societies to craft domestic constitutions and foreign political policies on the basis of some indigenous creed. Indeed creed is conceived as the impulse to crusade. Doctrinal display is a powerful concomitant alongside divisions of warriors. Indeed the divine word, vision or edict is most often "a call to arms," the mandate of warriors. Without creed there is no will to fight for anything. As Americans learned in Vietnam and the Russians learned in Chechnya, why go against an enemy if God or righteousness is not on your side? Again, my thesis contends that there is a legitimate and illegitimate holy war for individuals, families, tribes and nations.

Word Inducing War

The root faith of Abrahamic/AKEDIC faith—Judaism—presents a particularly difficult theological polity. At one or another time a faith, a way of life, an ethnicity, a nation-state—, Israel's peculiar identity and destiny is complex. Obviously the political character of her three children: Rabbinic Judaism, Christianity, and Islam—will be variously presented across history.

The ground work is further complicated by the fact that the Holy Writ of Judaism—TANAKH—may itself be a national epic—an apologia for the state. Historical moments such as David and Solomon in Judah (10th Century BCE) and Omri and Ahab (9th Century BCE), Josiah of Judah (7th Century BCE) or Ezra and Nehemiah from the Babylonian exile (6th Century BCE) converge with seasons of scriptural redaction such as the Mosaic coalescence, Josaian reform, the Deuteronomic Episode, and the Exile to form the national consciousness of Judaism. Further developments in the Persian, Greek, Roman, Christian and modern eras also take on a flavor of political polemic.[248] This background shapes political concepts as well as concrete actions such as nation-formation, treaties and war.

Generally throughout history Word prompts war: Israel was delivered from Egypt and drawn toward Palestine by Yahweh's command. Actually, we now think that the so-called conquest was an internal, more irenic consolidation of Highland Israelites with Valley Canaanites. Yet assertive and assimilating ideas formed a forceful new faith.

---

[248] See Isreal Finkelstein and Neil Asher Silberman, *The Bible Unearthed: Archealogy's New Vision of Ancient Israel and the Origin of Its Sacred Texts*, New York: The Free Press, 2001.

In the albeit unimpressive parade of Palms, Jesus presents a sop to the Jewish zealots and their passion for a kingdom in the guise if King David's splendorous might. Yet even this ironic gesture has a hidden irenic and akedic (see S. Kierkegaard on the Triumphal Entry) intent. Similarly:

- As the Roman Empire is about to succumb to the Barbarians at the gates, Augustine exhorts church and state to "compel them (unbelievers) to come in."
- In Islamic religion and Arabic tongue, *Jihad* means conquest by means of sword or word.
- Preacher and warrior, Mullah and Mujahidin, exert the crusades and counter-crusades.

On the other hand, the biblical mandate to such synthesis of message and might is admittedly ambiguous, discouraging aggression.

Word Refuting War

So much so that in all Abrahamic faith and high (ethical) religion we find repudiation of the battle-axe and Inquisition.

- King David is prohibited from building the temple because of the violence and blood on his hands. (II Kings 14:3)
- Jesus tells Peter to sheath his sword. His kingdom is a gentle interior gift, not political. (Matthew 26: 52)
- The apostle Paul spells out a spiritualized warfare writing to the faith community in Corinth.
- Islam means peace.

> …Some suspect us of acting in worldly fashion. For
> though we live in the world we are not carrying
> on a worldly war, for the weapons of our warfare are not
> worldly but have divine power to destroy
> strongholds. We destroy arguments and every proud
> obstacle to the knowledge of God…
> (II Corinthians 10:2ff)

And to those in Ephesus he describes these weapons so lacking in "steel and blood"

> Finally, be strong in the Lord and in the strength of his might. Put on the whole armor of God, that you may be able to stand against the wiles of the devil. For we are not contending against flesh and blood, but against the principalities, against the powers, against the world rulers of this present darkness, against the spiritual hosts of wickedness in the heavenly places. Therefore take the whole armor of God, that you may be able to withstand in the evil day, and having done all, to stand. Stand therefore, having girded your loins with truth, and

having put on the breastplate of righteousness, and having shod your feet with the equipment of the gospel of peace; beside all these, taking the shield of faith, with which you can quench all the flaming darts of the evil one. And take the word of God. Pray at all times in the Spirit, with all prayer and supplication. To that end keep alert with all perseverance, making supplication for all the saints, and also for me, that utterance may be given me in opening my mouth boldly to proclaim the mystery of the gospel, for which I am an ambassador in chains; that I may declare it boldly, as I ought to speak.
(Ephesians 6:10-20)

A Middle Way

Despite these apolitical appeals of Paul it is important to realize that he himself is in chains. He is not just oppressed in spirit. His preaching confutes Roman civil religion. It displaces Caesar *Kurios* with *Kurios* Jesus. That Jesus is Lord is incompatible with Caesar worship. Strife ensues. Creed is inevitably political.

Even at the outset of this study we see that we are dealing with a contradiction. As Jaroslav Pelikan depicts in his masterful *Jesus through the Centuries*[249], "the prince of peace" is often depicted as a warrior as in the Ravenna mosaic of Jesus as a Roman Soldier or Hagia Sophia's Jesus the Teacher between the Emperor and Empress Constantine. In light of this biblical and especially christic paradox we might go so far as to say that the two fundamental propensities to distort the Christian evangel are to reduce it to pure creed (belief) or to sheer crusade (contest). But the kingdom of God is somehow related both to the King Christ, the new David, and to the Prince of Peace (Isaiah 9:6). If so, then the artist at Ravenna (Church Militant—6th Century Mosaic, the Archepiscopal Chapel. Ravenna) and the evangelist John may have it right. Jesus is the soldier for peace, armed with the Holy Text.

Ego sum via, veritas et vita.
(John 14:6)

The evangelical impulse would therefore be to live out a godly (christic) way in the world so that the world—seeing our good works—"will glorify our father who is in heaven" (Matthew 5:16). The church will always be a small, hidden, non-political presence in the world—dispersed among all nations. But this is a personal and sectarian mandate. What about peoples and nations? Some faiths are intense in their worldly manifestation. Global Orthodox, Roman Catholic and Protestant Christianities and Islam are faiths of profound historico-political expression.

The most vivid contemporary throwback to creedal crusade is the Islamic doctrine of edicts (*Fatwa*). In 1993 the blind Sheik Abdel-Aziz Ibn Baaz,

---

[249] Jaroslav Pelikan, *Jesus Through the Centuries*, New Haven: Yale University Press, 1985.

supreme religious authority of Saudi Arabia, issued the following ill-founded world edict:

> "The earth is flat. Whoever claims it is round is an atheist deserving of punishment."

In a similar gesture, Baptist preacher, Paul Norwalt, pastor of the Merrimack, New Hampshire Baptist Temple, urged the town school board to give equal time to creationism alongside evolutionism in the public schools' science curriculum.[250]

Other noted Islamic edicts include Sheikh Omar Abdul Rahman's *Fatwa* authorizing five Islamic militants to assassinate Egypt's President Anwar Sadat in October, 1981. Another issued in 1989 by Ayatollah Khomeini of Iran called for the death of author, Salmon Rushdie.[251] Fortunately in 1998 Allah changed his mind on Rushdie and he walks the streets of London again.

These action edicts (*Fatwa*) are vestiges, anachronisms, and caricatures of an age where creed was expected to be translated into crusade. Pope Urban's Sermon at Clermont in 1095 declared:

> "Let us then reenact the law of our ancestors known as the truce of God." "Start upon the road to the Holy Sepulchre to wrest that land from the wicked race and subject it to yourselves."[252]

That road would wind through violent Muslim slaughter, synagogue burning, even fratricide of Christians in Byzantium with the faithful as fodder. Today creed is most often conveyed by non-violent and non-coercive persuasion. While some would question whether Billy now Frank Graham's or Jerry Falwell rallies are really non-coercive in light of their subliminal coercion, even brainwashing, in general, even the evangelical religious right resorts to gentle suasion and personal evangelism rather than overt political action. If direct action is initiated, as it was broadly in the 1994, 1998 and 2002 American elections, it is to unseat "liberal," "pro-welfare" or "anti-handgun" incumbents and candidates. In the 1996 elections the "Christian right" movement seemed to recede into a more passive and "spiritual" mode. Some critics indeed felt that the Dole Campaign was a "liberal ploy" to thus disarm the crusade and they vowed to return in 2000 with renewed vigor, next time "wise as serpents." They did.

My interest in this study of creed and crusade, is to show that exertion and ediction, even expedition and engagement, are integral dimensions of any dynamic creed. That exertion or evangel-ization may be mental or military. In

---

[250] *New York Times*, Sunday, February 12, 1995, p. A.4.

[251] *New York Times*, Monday, February 13, 1995, p. A.7.

[252] Quoted in George Weigel's *Tranquillitas Ordinis*. Oxford: Oxford University Press, 1987, p. 89.

this study of the Apostles' Creed, its Hebraic precursors, its Hellenic counterparts and its sequellae in Christian and Islamic history, I wish to show that overt political and military witness expresses the popular creed and that the hammered out and communally confessed creed is the grounding rationale of the crusade. In addition to this rather easily documented descriptive hypothesis, I will also offer the following normative thesis about how we ought to express a "living faith in God" in sublimely spiritual and powerfully physical ways.

> Culture is the substance of religion.
> Religion finds expression in culture.
> Paul Tillich

As Jews, Christians and Muslims rightfully comprehend the revelatory heritage of each other they will understand the proper connection of scripture and social action.

The Rightful Connection of Creed and Crusade

1. Human battle ought to resonate with the struggle of "God's power, justice and love, advocating life against unnatural death, righteousness against personal and social distortions, and joy in struggle toward the glorious liberty of the children of God."[253]

2. As the people's credo becomes more reflective of the true and living God, and becomes more expressive of the human condition, word will displace war and self-evidence in spirit will obviate the evangelical mandate of proclamation.

   > ...the earth will be filled with the glory of God as the waters cover the sea...
   > (Isaiah 11:9)

   > no longer will they teach each other...know the Lord for they will all know me.
   > (Jeremiah 31:34)

3. Even though regressive patterns of thought and deed abound today, glimmerings of this ultimal transmutation of creed and crusade into culminating peace are found as some ungodly and inhumane beliefs and behaviors are being challenged at this bimillenial moment of history.

As I develop this thesis, I will explore this confrontation of faith with

---

[253] Brian Fraser, Thomas D. Parker, *War and God's Justice*, Eds. Toronto: United Church Publishing House, 1989, p. x.

- secularism and scientism as intellectual heresy;
- injustice and hoarding (concentration of wealth) as sociological heresy;
- licentiousness and anomie as behavioral heresy;
- war and genocide as political heresy.

We're in a war. There is an enemy, to be sure. I'll try to draw the battle-lines.

The crusade hymn "Onward Christian Soldiers, Marching as to War" has been extirpated from the hymnbooks by our belief-impoverished, "political correctness" age. I want to ask how we can sing it again - this time in the spirit of those reluctant leaders – Moses and Jesus, not those presumptive leaders - Joshua and Constantine.

As a plan of attack I will divide the creed into the traditional threefold thematic architecture of the Apostles' Creed: God, Christ and Spirit. The reader will recall from the opening paragraph that I see this construal as rooted in Jewish Monotheism and radically remonotheized in Islam. The methodology of the essay will be to survey the stipulates of the creed in light of their more basic underlying convictions all in the context of their socio-historical setting. The drama of political and military history, which is the implicit and explicit background of this study, spans these epochal events:

Israel's war for Yahweh's home in Palestine	13-10 Century B.C.
Syria and Assyria's war against Israel	8th Century B.C.
Babylonia's war against Judah	6th Century B.C.
Persia's war against Chaldea and Jerusalem	5th Century B.C.
Alexander's conquests	4th Century B.C.
Roman wars and the destruction of Judea	1st Century A.D.
The struggle of Christianity with Gnosticism	1st-2nd Centuries A.D.
Armenia: The first Christian empire	3rd Century A.D.
Constantine's militant Christianization of the Eastern Empire	4th Century A.D.
The Germanic tribes conquest of the decaying Western Empire	4th Century A.D.
The Carolingian consolidation of the Northern Empire conciliation with Rome	8th, 9th Century A.D.
Islam's Jihad against Christendom	8th, 9th Century A.D.
The Christian Crusades against Islam (and Judaism)	10th-13th Century A.D.
The religious wars in Europe	16th, 17th Century A.D.
The Conquistadores, Euro-explorers and Exploiters wars against the Amerindians	17th -19th Century A.D.

• The wars for freedom: English, French and American revolutions	18th Century A.D.
• Crimean War: Anglicans and Russian Orthodox	18th century A.D
• The World Wars I and II: Crusades on Europe against demonic nationalism and anti-Semitism	20th Century A.D.
• The wars of the West against Communism: Korea and Vietnam	20th Century A.D.
• The Cold War: Star Wars and the cooperative venture into space	20th Century A.D.
• The furtive wars against hunger and for peace and human rights: Somalia, Bosnia, Haiti, Sudan, Kosovo, etc	20th Century A.D.
• The Bimillenial wars of God: Hindu and Muslim (1947 ff.), Jew and Arab (1948ff) The future war "terrorism"	1990's – 2000+

A Final Proviso

Beyond this war history, the modes of crusade embodying creed are myriad: Sometimes it takes the form of evangelization—preaching and teaching. Sometimes it finds expression as military conquest. Sometimes it is political and economic suasion and coercion. Sometimes it is the silent yet insidious transformation of culture, music, science, technology, films—the commerce and intercourse of peoples. In my view the word must not be corrupted by being coopted to ulterior economic, military or political purposes. Only those dimensions of a social purpose germane with and interior to the word itself should find expression. We will explicate and illustrate this bias as the argument unfolds. As illustration here I would argue that MEAN STREETS , TAXI DRIVER and GANGS OF NEW YORK of Martin Scorcese are genuine religious films ("redemption is in the streets") while Demille's THE TEN COMMANDMENTS is more nationalistic propaganda. I concur with the spirit of the cartoon in THE NEW YORKER. St. Peter calls back to the Lord at heaven's switchboard: "It's Falwell. He wants to know if you hear the prayers of Jews, Muslims and gays." The Lord retorts, "Tell Jerry to stick to politics and leave the religion to me."

The Impulse Behind the Creed/Crusade

There can and must be no war without word. The root phenomenon that is the basis of creed and crusade is what the Apostle Paul calls "The Mystery" (Ephesians 3:9, Colossians 1:24-29). Building on what W. F. Albright calls "Mosaic Yawehism as a missionary religion," the apostolic community, true to its name, is "sent forth" in a "mission to the nations." The earliest extant literature of the Christian tradition: the primitive *KERYGMA*, James and the fragments of primal Jewish Christianity, Paul's Letters, the Synoptic Gospels and their predecessors (Q), Acts and the late New Testament writings, all attest to the agenda and dynamism of this movement. It is a process of formulating conviction and sharing good news with the world.

It is transformative—changing lives, families, societies, nations and the world. We may indeed go so far as to see the New Testament in its earliest formation as the charter, agenda and didactic substance of this inaugural mission. Just as the epistles were written, beginning in the fifth decade of the Common Era, for specific occasions (often moral controversies or belief uncertainties), so the Gospels were composed beginning in the sixth decade of the Common Era for theological and liturgical purposes related to the evangelical mission. Bo Reicke has written that in the Synoptic Gospels

> "There is a heavy concentration of context-parallel triple traditions upon or around the text units that deal with Christ's baptism and passion."[254]

Though we must bracket in this work the Christian sacraments of baptism and the Lord's Supper, these are crucial themes in Systematic Theology because they devolve on the cardinal life events of Jesus, the Christ (baptism and passion), events which ground the fundamental doctrines of incarnation and redemptive death. These truths in turn initiate creed and inspire mission. Baptism and Eucharist in their deepest meaning are enlistments to sacrifice. We die in Christ in order to go and die for Him that we might live with Him.

In the same way that Jesus received martyrial baptism by John in the Jordan and then proceeded resolutely toward his Jerusalem passion, death and resurrection, so the apostolic (evangelical) community is incorporated, catechized, impassioned and commissioned to resolutely carry the cross forward. This urgent witness and mission is to the farthest reaches of humankind. It seeks to christically restore the fallen cosmos (John 3:16). Jesus came, lived, died, and arose that we might be born, live for, and rise with him, carrying his cross forward through space/time as eternal life is entrusted to us.

So we confess in the creed:

SYMBOLUM APOSTOLORUM

Credo in Deum Patrem omnipotentem
creatorem coeli et terrae.

Et in Iesum Christum

Filium eius unicum, dominum nostrum
qui conceptus est de Spiritu Sancto natus ex Maria Virgine

---

[254] Bo Reicke, *The Roots of the Synoptic Gospels*, Philadelphia: Fortress Press, 1986, p. 65.

passus sub Pontio Pilato, crucifixus, mortuus et sepultus

descendit ad inferno spertia die resurrexit a mortuis

ascendit ad coelos sedet ad dexteram Dei Patris omnipotentis

inde venturus est iudicare vivos et mortuos.
Credo in Spiritum Sanctum
sanctam Ecclesiam catholicam
sanctorum communionem

remissionem peccatorum
carnis resurectionem,
et vitam eternam

I believe in God, the Father, the almighty,

creator of heaven and earth.

And in Jesus Christ,
his only Son, our Lord,
conceived by the Holy Spirit,
born of the Virgin Mary,
suffered under Pontus Pilate,
crucified, dead and buried,

descended into the realm of death,
on the third day risen from the dead,
ascended into heaven;
he is seated at the right hand of God, the almighty Father;
from there he will come
to judge the living and the dead.

I believe in the Holy Spirit,
the holy catholic church,
communion of saints,
forgiveness of sins,
resurrection of the dead
and eternal life.

The historical and cultural setting of the creed is the great Christological controversy of the fourth century, focused in the competing theologies of Athanasias and Arius. It also reflects the political tensions between Roman and Germanic regions. It is also an anthropological controversy. "Who is Jesus as Christ?" is also the question "What is man?" The "Symbol", I will argue, is a divine designation, full of human implication correlated with political exemplification. All of this fine-grained delineation is continuation of the creedal formation process of Israel.

Creed History: Chart #1

Devine Designation	Human Implication	Political Exemplication
I Believe in God, the Father, the Almighty	God vs. gods	Israel, Syria, Babylon, Egypt, Persia
Creator of Heaven and Earth	Evolutionism vs.Creationism	Alexander the Great
And in Jesus Christ, His only Son, Our Lord	Caesar Kurios vs. Christos Kurios	Rome, Armenia
Conceived by the Holy Spirit Born of the Virgin Mary	Arius vs.Athanasius Tribal power vs.Augustine's rational state	Constantine Germanic tribes
Suffered under Pontius Pilate, crucified, dead and buried, descended into Hell, and on the third day rose again from the dead Ascended into Heaven	Christ vs. Mohammed	Islam Charlemagne Christian Crusades Normans
He is sitting at the right hand of God. From there He will come to judge the living and the dead. I believe in the Holy Spirit.	Magisterium vs. Conscience	Reformation
The Holy Catholic Church	Church vs. Freedom	Religious wars in Europe
The Communion of Saints		Conquistadores Crusades in Europe against Nationalism
The Forgiveness of Sins	God vs. State Wars against Communism	
Resurrection of the Dead		Cold War, Star wars
And Eternal Life	Jew vs. Arab Hindu vs. Muslim	Wars of God
Amen	Greed vs. Justice	Peace Wars, Virtual Wars?

Chart #1 suggests how we will display the panorama of events (crusades) along the course of world history against the background of the creed of Western Christendom exemplified by the Apostle's Creed. I will use the creed as text but also as pretext to elucidate that other Western credo which underlies and overlays the strictly ecclesial confession, the cultural credo about God, Humans and the world which often more indirectly animates political, economic, and military history.

Creed in the History of Belief

First we need to acknowledge the spiritual and theological nature of creed. At face value the creed is about the faith and beliefs of individual persons, collectivities such as families (Acts 16:15, Lydia and her household); nations (e.g. Edessa and Armenia, C. 300 C.E.), even empires (Constantine or Charlemagne). Though the hidden agenda is often polemical and political and though all creeds arise within some particular conflict or challenge, the heart of a confession or creed is to articulate belief for persons and communities (communions).

Christianity sustains the formulation and formation process of Israel much like the scriptural canonical process, whereby normative belief and life-pattern (ethics) is articulated. Luther places the Apostle's Creed between the Decalogue and Lord's Prayer in his catechisms. With various explanations he outlines the rationale for this novel arrangement. The commandments instruct us how to live under God and, with his Pauline proviso, show us that we cannot, in and of ourselves, live up to it. We need therefore a faith in God through Christ and in community, to respond to the law and to compose the troubled soul to allow the prayerful approach and access to God, our father.[255] Luther also has a systematic schema in mind as this order resonates with the three persons of the Trinity and the corresponding three works of the Godhead; creation, redemption and sanctification. The Trinitarian complexification of the monotheistic unification is necessary as the ideality of eternity is translated into this-worldly reality.

The use of the "symbol" (Apostles' Creed) had consolidated and become normative in church history by the late second or early third century. Irenaeas, Hippolytus in his catechetical theology, the Cappadocian, Marcellos of Ankaea in his Apology, and the early Roman bishops (e.g. Julius I, c. 340) attest to the fact that the creed has become central to the evangelical and ethical life (evangelism, witness, catechesis, etc.) of the early church. In the sixth to eighth centuries the creed is used in the Constantinian and European church, culminating in the establishment of orthodoxy in the Holy Roman Empire under Charlemagne (800 C.E.). The final establishment of orthodoxy comes as militant Islam hammers at the gates of the Western Empire.

---

[255] Albrecht Peters, *Kommentar Zur Luther's Katechismen*, Band 2: *"Der Glaube"* Göttinger: Vandenhoeck & Ruprecht, 1991, p. 13ff.

Luther accents the existential dimension of the creed as articulated by Augustine in his distinction between:

- Belief about
- Belief on and
- Belief in (*credere in Deum*).

The participation implied in the Greek word (*pistis*) and Latin word (*credo*) is also emphasized by Luther. Belief was not just cognition or intellectual conceptualization, it was trust, inclination, commitment, action, conviction, personal and communal, it is movement. Reformers (Zwingli, Calvin, Bucer and the rest) all emphasized the instrumentality of the creed to giving one's life over to God in devotion, commitment and trust. This wholehearted dedication, not merely passive assent, was seen to be the meaning of the creed. Here we see further the ground of will, movement, action, life-giving and consuming cause that we will emphasize in this study.

Creed in World War History
    Not content to just believe, people always fight for what they believe. We first fight for the right to believe. We exert and test (experiment, experience) our faith. We feel called on to defend or extend our beliefs about God, people and the world; our creed is our security, our defense, our crusade. War is too important to be left to the military, businessmen and politicians. War for right demands pacifism toward all petty war. Without war there is no credo. Without credo there is no war. To say and do it is to know and believe. We walk the talk. We may fight for land which is world in the creed. We may seek freedom, which derives from our anthropological doctrine. When governments or military-industrial complexes alone make war, they usually sputter out for lack of popular support. As much as Prosecutors, Pundits and Partisans sought to bring down a wayward President Clinton, without popular will they failed. Even Stalin had to temporarily suspend state atheism and coddle to the Russian Orthodox Church to restore patriotic fervor. Karl Marx contended that capitalism required the incessant incitement to war to sustain the market mechanism. Yet economics alone cannot justify or popularize war. Fervor and self-sacrifice and the willingness of parents to offer their children in sacrifice depends on more than philosophical rectitude or the cause being just. Going to battle must be for truth and right. It must be for God. The Second World War was fought against Hitler's demonic aggression and his infectious pagan ideology, yes. More vividly it was fight for freedom and faith, it was divinely impelled.

Of course, in some sense, God abhors all war and transcends our militancy in judgment. On careful reading, say of Israel's Holy War, we find scripture teaching against itself. In Kierkagardian paradox many pericopes parody surface meanings. One rabbinic teaching tells Moses and Joshua to silence their victory gloating over the drowned Egyptians at the Sea of Reeds. "These too are my children," says the Lord. Moses cannot enter the promised land and David is not allowed to build the temple for lack of faith and overt violence. Abraham Lincoln's memorable second inaugural address challenges the perception and fervent belief that God was on either the Union or Confederate side contending that God's judgments and mercy, in fact, far transcended those somewhat pathetic designations.

This study explores the phenomenon of faith quiescent and faith militant. It explores the politics of holy war and expedient war. Much has been made of the terror-filled interrogation of Jesus by Pontius Pilate over the charge of Jesus' claim to be "King of the Jews." Again, in John's purview, we have a disclaimer of political authority.

> My Kingship is not of this world; If my kingship were of this world, my servants would fight, that I might not be handed over to the Jews. But my kingship is not from the world.
> (John 18:33ff)

In this non-combatant spirit, the pre-creedal Christian movement is profoundly pacific. Jesus disappoints Jewish Holy War expectancy. Creedal Christendom picks up on the regal messiah motif and tends toward militancy. Such a dialectic frames the creedal-crusade history of western society.

In keeping with our AKEDIC thesis we find that under persecution the Church is more defensive (in the sense of creative faith), less aggressive and more authentic. The Christian community under Communism was, in some ways, more vital than is the present day establishment church.

"The blood of the martyrs is the seed of the church." Emil Brunner speaks of his Zurich congregation (*Fraumunsterkirche*) in the dark days of *Nazizeit*. His words, based on the Apostles' Creed, recall Paul's serene admonition to "stand fast":

> ...In these days nothing is so important as this, that we stand fast in the faith. The storm has not yet reached us; we have received only a small wind from its periphery...We will have to do everything in those days to strengthen ourselves out of God's Word and in prayer for coming difficulties...As a soldier receives provisions before combat and checks whether he has everything that belongs to his equipment, so we also want to examine and obtain the equipment of our faith so that we have it when the need comes...The struggle is...a war of faith.[256]

In minority status the church tends toward silent witness, creative passivity and martyrdom. In majority and ascendancy, the church may turn to hegemony and

---

[256] Emil Brunner, *I Believe in the Living God.* Trans. John Holden. London: Lutterworth Press, 1961, p. 16.

aggression. In both modes of witness there is strength. In faith we fight. It may be the fight to keep the faith, to retain the freedom to confess and teach. It may be the struggle against heresy or apathy. It may be a fight for the freedom to practice and propagate the faith. Going further, strife may ensue in the evangelical compulsion. There is a story to tell to the nations. The nations who sit in darkness are offended by the light. They prefer to stay in the comfortable dark. Practices of superstition, idolatry and oppression are to be challenged in the liberating faith. Though now receiving a well-deserved disgrace, the campaigns of Western colonialism, in Africa, Asia and the Americas at best were waged to share the Gospel and its derivative view of life and Way of life. The missionary churches most often challenged colonial, politicism, militarism and capitalism. Regrettably, at times, colonialism often proceeded not in the spirit of gospel freedom, respect and love but in exploitation, repressing native sensibility and culture. Very often it failed to appreciate indigenous grace and beauty. The gospel and its Way of life was often replaced by the idolatries of Iberia, Ionia, Germania. In the Americas indigenous cultures were brutally suppressed. A twentieth century epiphenomenon of classical religious creed is our promulgation of a way of life: free enterprise, democracy, human rights, pleasure embued consumer culture, and worse. "Good news" or "divine justice," the substance of the Way of God, splays along a spectrum of operational human values.

Today it is hard to imagine a day when people would fight, suffer and die for their faith. Fanatic self-sacrifice by Hindus and Muslims in modern day India or Iraq seems incredible. And Bonhoeffer and Cramner, Jean d'Arc, Paul and Peter being hung, torched or crucified for their faith is implausible—fanatic insanity. Nicene bishops being beaten and killed for what seems an iota of difference is absurd.

Yet, in recent years there seems to be a revitalization of living faith. In my denomination, the United Presbyterian Church, there has been a revolt. We have resolved to take theology seriously. Laypersons are on the rampage, rejecting years of "pop theology" and ethical "faddism". Reacting to the "reimagining conference," a controversial assembly of church women claiming their authentic voice in the church; responding adversely to the crisis about ordaining practicing homosexual persons to ministry and decrying a general malaise sapping the evangelical fervor of the communion, we have resolved in General Assembly to reclaim and reassert our theological confession with boldness and energy. We have affirmed that salvation is in Christ, and none other. This composite theological work, based on the Reformation Tryptich of Decalogue, Creed, and Prayer is part of that catechetical renaissance. While this may not mean that you will see staid Presbyterians preaching on a soapbox near Walgreen's on State Street or evangelizing outside McDonald's in Evanston, some kind of rearmament and readiness for battle is taking place. It may mean only a tightening of the defenses. It may prompt forays into pagan territory. Both ecclesiastical conformation and evangelical conversation are evident vitalities in the global church at the end of this second Christian millennium. In my view these evangelical impulses need to be conjoined with ethical piety. The thriving church is evangelically ethical. To cast some light on where we find ourselves today in creed and crusade, let us trace the story of the human and societal significance of the Apostles' Creed. The following chart shows how it follows the classical matrix of form and meaning which we find in the Decalogue and Lord's Prayer. Note the similarity in theme and movement.

Chart #2

Decalogue	Prayer	Creed
No other gods	Our Father in Heaven Holy be your name	God Father Almighty
No idols (earth crafted deities) Revere the name	Your kingdom come and will be done on Earth...as in Heaven	Maker of Heaven and Earth and in
Sabbath	Daily Bread	Jesus Christ His only Son, our Lord Born...suffered Was crucified
Parents Murder Adultery	Debts-debtors Temptation	Dead, buried, and decended into Hell
Do not Steal	Deliver from evil	On the third day...risen ascended is sitted... Will come Holy Spirit
No false witnesses No coveting	For thine is the kingdom, power and glory forever	Holy catholic Church Communion of Saints Forgiveness of sins Resurrection of body Life everlasting

Derivative Chart: Beliefs and Values We Propound and Defend

The following suggestive chart is derived from the Decalogue as it exemplifies and is elaborated in the greater faith-ethics structure of what I will call the Kuriologue and Ecclesialogue (Lord's Prayer and Creed). It develops the following positive and negative principles which form an offensive and defensive stance for God's people in the world. These are the forces that the people of God should fight for and fight against throughout history.

426

Value	Disvalue	Public Commitments
+ Worship of true and living God	- Atheisms, Statism, materialism, etc.	+ Freedom of faith + Liberty grounded in participatory democracy
+ Kingdom, bread, name, life of God for world	- Worship of any other false Lords and suppliants	- religious persecution + bread of life provided for world - starvation, ignorance
+ Worship, leisure, work, rest	- Denial of worship, torture, unjust labor, unemployment	+ Respected community
+ Integrity of family tribe, sovereignty of nation	- Family dissoulution, ethnocide (genocide), violation of national sovereignty	+ Pro-family public policy + Upheld honor of widows and orphans
+ Sanctity of life	- Murder and harm to persons	- proscribe killing + Just-war doctrine, healthcare
+ Sexual and marital fidelity	- promiscuity and adultery	+ Generativity and peace

Let us now explicate this creed:

I. I Believe in God, the Father Almighty: Credo in deum patrem omnipotem God vs. the Gods: Prelude

Monotheism is a *Götterdämmerung,* an imposed, if not self-imposed withdrawal of the pantheon of gods. When Jesus responds to Peter's confession that the "gates of hell shall not prevail against it" he refers to the penetration of this rock-truth into the darkest recesses of godless hell. The insinuation of Yahweh into human consciousness and into the history of nations is an assassination and annihilation of all other gods. It stymies the human propensity to idolization. It is a war against all pagan pretensions to and representations of deity. The creed appropriately incites crusade and appropriately begins with the Holy War of Israel against Satemi and Egypt's sun gods, Baal, Moloch, and the gods of Syria, Assyria, and Babylon. The complicating reality of this radical and incendiary factor is that Yahwism emerges from that same perennial religious culture of the ancient near east, borrowing from the indigenous theologies (e.g. Egyptian monotheism, Sumerian and Babylonian moral charters, etc.). This is not watering down the rigor of Yahweh but that God is the God of the nations, not in eclectic syncretism, but in the fact that the God of Israel is the same God who has inspired all the belief and righteousness from the origin of human life in the world. As Buddhists know there is an atheistic necessity in faith—that surrender might ensue. "I believe in God the father, Almighty" is the equivalent of commandments 1-3 and the ascription of the Lord's Prayer. On the surface "God, the Father Almighty" is an affirmation of God's absolute exclusivity and claim upon us, His human family. Secondarily, it is claim about what makes us human. The protocreed is Israel's declaration and Decalogue.

I am the Lord your God, who brought you out of the land of Egypt,

out of the house of bondage.
You shall have no other gods before me.
You shall not make yourself graven images.
You shall not take my name in vain.
(Exodus 20)

Our Father in Heaven,
Hallowed be your name
(Matthew 6)

The creed begins with a human affirmation—personal and communal: "credo—I believe." This is in contrast to the biblical Decalogue and Kurilogue. The Ten Commandments are cast in collective imperative: "You shall have no other gods"..."Remember the Sabbath day". The Lord's Prayer is also framed in striking communal language: "Our Father"..."Give us this day"...Here it is "I believe," personal and profound. As Hans Küng has shown with the insight of Luther, it is not "believe in something" (*credere en aliqued*) or even 'believing something' (*credere alieui*), it is 'believing in someone' (*credere en aliquen*). In a memorable phrase Luther says that it is the faith and trust of the human heart which makes both God and idol. The inclination and resting place of this human capacity in God or idol often comes into play in the militancy of faith. In some way all war is grounded either on faith or on idolatry. This is a further reason for the contention of this essay that creed and crusade are inseparable. The creed in one sense is the theological expression of the ethical crusade of the human heart, collectively rendered. As Girard has shown in his study of VIOLENCE AND THE SACRED there is an expected violence of the human heart that cascades throughout history. There is also the healing eschatological kingdom of the Messiah. Damnation and redemption proceed concurrently through time. Rightful crusade is the ethical expression of collective belief. As the prophet Isaiah told King Ahab of Judah, "If you do not believe, surely you will not be established." (Isaiah 7:9) Yahweh is a God who requires trust, seeks to join us to his reign, then takes us on his campaign. When we set out on our own, or with others, we err.

God is moving somewhere. We are to faithfully come along as companions in the quest and struggle. The God Abraham meets, calls and leads. "I will be who I will be." The God of Exodus and Easter is one who beckons us to "come and follow."[257] The first element of the creed is radical monotheism. The first war is a campaign against polytheism and paganism. Idolatry and immorality are the twin preventers of divine-human fellowship. Missing the mark—vertically or horizontally—is sin. The numerous wars of God against unbelief are typified by the Holy War of the Yahwist tribes of Israel against the pagan threats within and without Palestine. While that war requires complete separation, holiness and *herem*—the holocaust and genocide of enemies—in a subtler sense Israel borrows from its precursor faiths and its monotheism (yahwism) builds on the spirituality and morality of its forerunners. The world of empires—Egypt, Syria, Persia and indigenous Palestinian cohabitants—Edom, Moab, Canaan—is in divine mystery a "fullness of time," a *(Kairos)*.

God has never left himself without a witness and as Paul claims in the letter to Romans:

> For what can be known about God is plain to them…Ever since the creation of the world his invisible nature, namely his eternal power and deity has been clearly perceived in the things that have been made.
> (Romans 1:19-20)

The movement I will trace in each chapter will proceed from creed to crusade. The reader will remember that the relationship between belief and action, worship and war, is very complex. Causally, initiative can begin at any point. Either pole can lead and precipitate the other. It is my choice to begin with creed, what we will call divine designation; proceed to conflict, what we will call Human Implication; and then move to crusade, what we will call Political Exemplification. We begin, therefore, with the first article of the Apostles' Creed.

First Article

Martin Luther
How the master of the house is to explain it as simply as possible to his household.

The First Article of Creation

I believe in God the Father Almighty, Maker of heaven and earth.

What does that mean?

> ANSWER: I believe that God has created me and all other creatures, and has given me, and preserves for me, body and soul, eyes, ears, and all my limbs, my reason and all my senses; and that daily he bestows on me clothes and

---

[257] Hans Küng, *Credo: The Apostles' Creed Explained for Today.* (New York: Doubleday), 1993, p. 11.

shoes, meat and drink, house and home, wife and child, fields and cattle, and all my goods, and supplies in abundance all needs and necessities of my body and life, and protects me from all perils, and guards and defends me from all evil. And this he does out of pure fatherly and divine goodness and mercy, without any merit or worthiness in me; for all which I am bound to thank him and praise him, and, moreover, to serve and obey him. This is a faithful saying.[258]

John Calvin
The Institutes of the Christian Religion
The Knowledge of God the Creator
CHAPTER I
The Knowledge of God and That of Ourselves Are
Connected. How They are Interrelated

Without Knowledge of self there is no knowledge of God.

Nearly all the wisdom we possess, that is to say, true and sound wisdom, consists of two parts: the knowledge of God and of ourselves. But, while joined by many bonds, which one precedes and brings forth the other is not easy to discern. In the first place, no one can look upon himself without immediately turning his thoughts to the contemplation of God, in whom he "lives and moves" [Acts 17:28]. For, quite clearly, the mighty gifts with which we are endowed are hardly from ourselves; indeed, our very being is nothing but subsistence in one God.[259]

Incursus: Halloween
A Strange Reversal! It is Halloween in France. In this strongly Catholic country one would expect a stronger *Le Jour Toute Saintes*. Across the Rhine in Deutschland *Alle Heiligen Tag* is more in evidence. But here they celebrate Halloween. The kids and big kids at heart wear costumes in Nancy and Bordeaux—the Lone Ranger and Bob Dole, Dracula and Bill Clinton (coming Tuesday is American election day). The omnipresent corruption of American culture has spoiled France: McDonalds, Pizza Hut and now Halloween. Protestants have always parodied the night and the day of All Hallows. No saints here, or better—all saints here. Luther's list commemorated this weekend in Wittenberg is something of a parody, as were the gesticulations of the indulgence-hawker Tetzel. He should have been left alone to run his silly course like the selfproclaimed lone Druid in costume I saw last night in a documentary on Stone Henge on the Salisbury Plain—the audacity to compare a fool like himself to those brilliant, mystic cosmologists.

Yet the Protestant principle is true, we are saved and hallowed by Christ, not by our nobility and good works, though surely the rapprochement today with Catholicism and Judaism casts those Puritan good works in a better light.

---

[258] Luther's Short Catechism, July 1529, in G.E. Rupp and Benjamin Drewery, *Martin Luther: Documents in Modern History*, London: Edward Arnold, 1970, pp. 141, 142.
[259] *Library of Christian Classics*, John Mc Neill, p. 35.

Running through my soul is the hymn that embraces creed on this point. I learned it in high school church camp or "Young Life" or "Intervarsity." My evangelical congregations at Second Presbyterian (African-American) and Church of Christ (Japanese-American) in Chicago taught me to reappreciate it even in my theological disdain for such fervor. It capsulates creed:

> One day when Heaven was filled with his glory
> One day when sin was as black as could be
> Jesus came forth to be born of a virgin
> Dwelt among men our example to be
> Living he loved me
> Dying he saved me
> Buried he carried my sins far away
> Rising He justified, freely, forever!
> One day He's coming
> O Glorious Day!

As leaves color and fall and a chill fills the air we know that soon it will be Advent and we imagine and anticipate one

> ...Born under the law...to redeem those under the law.
> (Galatians 4:4-5)

I Believe in God the Father Almighty...

Karl Barth links the words "credo" and "in Deum" in the Symbol. (Symbol is the old Latin word for the Roman Creed.) Though God's being and activity is manifested to all persons in all time through the natural world, this natural revelation usually leads to idolatry or *götterschöpfung*, the fabrication of gods. Humans are *homoreligiosis*, naturally religious. We sense the divine power in creation (*cognoscibile Dei*: Romans 1:19). We respond in awe and terror. But rather than staying on the search for the pure, holy and righteous one, we curtail the quest and fashion our pocket-gods, familial and tribal deities. In the process we violate all the stipulates of creed, prayer and commandments; focused belief, devotion and the life of love and justice. Sometimes throughout history, even before the special depictions of God in Israel's story, the Jesus movement and the decisive events of Exodus and Easter, individuals have worshipped the true God and lived the good life and it has been counted to them as righteousness. Most often pagan impulses, idolatry, sacrifice and immorality have ensued. Though this natural religiosity, more often perverts than prepares the way for God, it is to this natural revelation and piety that the introduction of the strong and good God is offered. The natural and unschooled search for the love of God is the ground of revealed faith. As Paul preached at the altar of the unknown God at Athens (Acts 17:23):

> What you worship as unknown, I now display to you

Paul continues (Acts 17:24-28):

431

"The God who made the world and everything in it, being Lord of heaven and earth, does not live in shrines made by man, nor is he served by human hands, as though he needed anything, since he himself gives to all men life and breath and everything. And he made from one every nation of men to live on all the face of the earth, having determined allotted periods and the boundaries of their habitation, that they should seek God, in the hope that they might feel after him and find him. Yet he is not far from each one of us, for 'in him we live and move and have our being'; as even some of your poets have said, 'For we are indeed his offspring.'

Being then God's offspring, we ought not to think that the Deity is like gold, or silver, or stone, a representation by the art and imagination of man. The times of ignorance God overlooked, but now he commands all men everywhere to repent, because he has fixed a day on which he will judge the world in righteousness by a man who he has appointed, and of this he has given assurance to all by raising him from the dead."

The import of this passage for theology and for our thesis in this book is that we are found by God even while we search for God. God is a searcher, communicator, savior and leader. God's way is surveillance. Searching for God as the 'essence of our being' or the 'culmination of our finest aspirations' is misguided. God is not identical with our projections. Indeed God is not an object of consciousness, one object among others. God is not out there. God transcends the capacities and powers of our consciousness and intelligence. God is not *summum bonum*. To understand God, according to Barth, is to stand under God, to receive God's power, love, holiness and justice.[260]

God, the father almighty, a phrase somewhat foreign to scripture, emerges out of Israel's prophetic history, against the background of strife against contending powers such as Syria, Assyria and Babylonia. The designation of God as the mighty father is therefore in one sense a military image. God not only is, he is doing something in the world. One way to speak of this activity is to say that God is establishing and extending his reign. The concept of God, as Gordon Kaufman and David Tracy have shown in their masterful studies, "is the principle of ultimacy, the power to which we attribute Lordship, rule, dominion. The first stipulate of the creed points to the *führerprinzip*; the ultimate ground for all that we are and all that we do."[261]

Underneath the apocalyptic notion was the monarchic spirit where the God of Israel exerts his kingly reign from the throne of judgment and mercy. (Psalm 89). Jesus Christ, the Son of the Father, ascends to co-reign over the world with the Father from the right hand of the throne. The archaic Godhead is resettled. The dispensations of justice and mercy that proceed from this bivalent throne

---

[260] See Karl Barth, *Credo*. New York: Scribners, 1936, p. 5ff.

[261] Kaufman, Gordon D. *God, Mystery and Diversity: Christian Theology in a Pluralistic World*, Minneapolis: Fortress Press, 1996. Tracey, David. *Blessed Rage for Order: The New Pluralism in Theology*, Chicago: University of Chicago Press, 1996.

constitute the disease, hunger, war and death-history as well as the health, wealth, peace and life-history of humankind (Revelation 6). Human wars are either righteous goods, or idolatrous evils or some admixture of the two. Victor Hugo envisioned in *Les Misrables* that these contentions contain the inscrutable and paradoxical mystery of God. Although the history of God is war, war may not be of God because God also is the one who "shatters the spear and makes wars to cease" (Psalm 46:9).

The idea that God is father and is mighty contains elements both coincident and contrary. The image "father" connotes both authority and compassion. Authority resonates with power. Compassion, however, connotes vulnerability and limitation. The idea of father both defines and limits power, at least in the dimension of omnipotence. An earthly father by nature enjoys a dominion, precedence and importance over his child, among other distinctive qualities. The child in some sense is always dependent, beholden and subject to filial piety imbedded in the very nature of protection. But fatherhood also implies risk, vulnerability, susceptibility to rebellion,

failed love and misunderstanding. A father is unfree, at least in the sense of being bound by love and obligation to his offspring. Fatherhood is also a personal quality implying finitude and limits of subjectivity. The father lives for his family in an exquisite, invincible vulnerability. Power is an abstract quality, fatherhood, personal—another incompatibility or at least contrariety.

In an important sense "God as father" is a Christian invention or at least a distinctive emphasis of Christianity. When the chatechumen asserted her belief in God the father almighty, the reference was specific. It was to the God and father of the Lord Jesus Christ. The God of the Christian creed is the father of Jesus. This loving parent is consonant with Yahweh of Israel and in some sense even compatible with the natural god-power of the universe; the Canaanites creator God EL, the Babylonian moon/god Sin, Egypt's sun-sustainer, and the Greek's Zeus. Yet now this background power of the world has taken on personal focus. It is like One we know and love.

In the Heidelberg Catechism we affirm "that the eternal Father of our Lord Jesus Christ...is for the sake of Jesus Christ His Son, my God and my Father..." (Q.26).

It is in this personal bearing that power transpires. The *Pasa patria* (Ephesians 3:15) the father of fathers by whom every family in the world is named is like the Islamic "mother of all battles." It is a decisive definition of both spiritual paternity and patriotism.

The primal theological battle in world history is one between the personal, paternal, potent and pastoral God of Israel and the capricious and cajoling fertility deities regnant in the superstition of primitive tribal and early civil culture. The radical particularity of the Israel-Israel covenant "you alone I have loved among the nations of earth" entails deicide to the rest (*götterdamerung*). To the believers in those gods YAWEH believers proffer genocide, conversion or toleration depending upon the pathology and political overlay of the faith movement. As background to the first article of the creed, let us initially consider Yahweh's holy war through Israel with the inhabitants of Canaan.

Holy War and Canaan

The conquest or consolidation (internal guerrilla revolt) whereby Israel settles in Canaan is a victory for this people of austere theology and justice ethics. It is also the victory of Yahweh, a paternal deity of power, over the maternal gods of nature and fertility. This historical movement further defines, for better and worse, the *pater potestas* theology of Abrahamic religion. That Israel historically is on the war path and moving toward occupation gives a certain aggressive color and tone to its religion and theology. As one woman rightly quipped, "men are those who rape and kill." The sexist distortions of our non-gender God infect the deityconsciousness of people with this distortion.

From its first experience in the Sinai, Israel experiences Yahweh as an awesome, fearful and powerful God, a person and force who requires pure and intense allegiance, one who has in mind and will surprising and trying events for his exclusive people AND His beloved world. The seed planted in the soul through Abraham's faith has begun to grow. Detractors quip, "How odd of God to choose the Jews." Jews themselves ask "Why us?" The blessing and bane of being chosen remains. As Wolfhart Pannenberg states… "the idea of the divine almighty power is specifically Israelite."[262]

When the power God of the conquest, monarchy and of the prophets is joined to resurrection power or the Christian dispensation (Romans 4:24), the symbol becomes authentic, compelling, and universal. When the potent father theology is shaped by the prevalent patriarchal society, it becomes relativized and problematic. As it mediates the truth and justice of divine reality it provides revolutionary insight for human history. As "Almighty father" projects a contingent socio-political phenomenon it's currency is qualified.

The Holy War of ancient Israel aimed to establish God's reign in the world. It involved rebellious release from oppression in Egypt (Exodus 15:21). It continued in the militant introduction of a divine plantation in Canaan (Exodus 15:13, 17-18). The total campaign of liberation and occupation serves the purpose of establishing the solitary preeminence and authority of this God, Yahweh, creating a residence and eventually a temple for his presence. Roland de Vaux claims that Israel did not fight for her faith but for her existence.[263] The first fight is against those who would eliminate the divine presence by

---

[262] *The Apostles' Creed*, Philadelphia: The Westminster Press, 1972, p. 30.
[263] *Ancient Israel: Its Life and Institutions*. 2nd ed. London: DLT, 1968, p. 258.

exterminating the believing people. The very existence of this people is a theological entity since it is faith, not ethnicity or geography that defines her existence and *raison d-être*.

In an important essay Paul Hanson seeks to penetrate the sordid and severe side of Israelite "Holy War" in the Canaan consolidation finding herem and the ban whereby the annihilation of all men and women and children, even animals is required. This triumphalist reading of the actual historical events by the tenth and ninth century monarchs and their scribes becomes the "Royal" history. Building on DeVaux's creative idea, Hanson argues that "the biblical themes of liberation from oppression and creation from chaos undergird another justification for "Holy War" i.e. the establishment of true "shalom" in the world.[264] In my view in this essay it is the coerced establishment and creative efficacy of a new "Way of Yahweh" in the world that justifies the exploits of biblical Israel. The disgrace of biblical genocide must be acknowledged as an aberration of the deeper prophetic ethics of creation and covenant.

The chronicle of events in Israel's occupying and infiltrating Holy War are:

- The crossing of Jordan
- The fall of Jericho
- The negotiated settlement at Gibron
- The defeat of Hazor and King Jabin
- The wars with the Canaanites
- The campaign against the intrusion of the Philistines
- The death of Saul c. 1005 B.C.E.
- End of David's reign c. 966 B.C.E.
- Death of Solomon c. 926 B.C.E.

The "Yahweh Wars" (VonRad) referring to Numbers 21:14 are seen as fulfilling the creedal and crusading promises made to the patriarchs:

I will bring you out of the afflictions of Egypt
to the land of the Canaanites, Hittites, and Jebusites,
a land flowing with milk and honey.
(Exodus 3:17, 18)

A covenant partnership is the theological structure or creed which animates the conquest. Though the image is not used, the meaning of the campaign is that of sons and family following the leading father (divine king) in order to secure his

---

[264] Paul Hanson, "War, Peace and Justice in Early Israel" *Biblical Review* 3:32-45, 1987.

domain and terrain. Israel's Holy War is to make a home for God in the world. The Abrahamic covenant begins with Melchizedek's blessing:

> Blessed be God Most High, who has delivered
> Your enemies into your hand.
> (Genesis 14:20)

In Exodus, Yahweh is a "man of war." (Exodus 15:3) The war begins in an act of emancipation. Yahweh war is an act of liberation, or rectifying injustice. War decisively challenges the threat of annihilation. Slavery was oppression and Yahweh's first campaign is action in the spirit of old Greek holy war (*hieros polemos*)—a punishment for a sacrilege. The Egyptian incarceration was unjust and unholy. Freedom and rightful worship had been violated. Pharaoh must be punished (plagues) and the Egyptians miraculously killed (crossing the sea). The first campaign therefore involves escape and rescue at sea. Yahweh's victory over Pharaoh constitutes the belief which will subsequently be defended and pursued in Canaan:

> Yahweh saved Israel that day from the Land of the Egyptians. Israel saw the Egyptians dead upon the seashore…The people feared Yahweh, and believed in Yahweh and his servant Moses.
> (Exodus 14:30, 31)

The mighty acts of God inspire belief, credo. Credo in turn articulates and promulgates "almighty God." The war of armies now yields to the war of words and the war of the worlds.

The Hebrew literary and religious tradition through history follows this course of tactical and tacit warfare. The prophets remonstrate not only on the internal (domestic) credulity (authenticating of faith and ethics) but on external (international) relations. In the early monarchy, relations with cognate tribes, Philistines, Amorites, Amalekites, etc., and eventually in the later Kingly history, especially in the age of divided kingdom, with Assyria and Persia, Israel's devotion and righteousness are put to the test. As the mettle is tried, cognate nations became friends or foes all under the subscription of YAWEH who simultaneously wages holy war with and against his chosen people. From this we can extrapolate that God is at war with the world for righteousness and against injustice, for truth against the phony all by reason of his great love for the world. God's redemption of the world is the purpose of His election of Israel and formation of the Messianic Church. Creedal history, the holy war of JIHAD, the war of the soul and conscience that precedes physical war, is more about belief and concordant living than about physical and historical strife. All of the aforementioned material is formed and refined by the Jewish community in exile. It is during this period that the historical theology of the Deuteronomist, the salvation-history of the prophets and the good/evil equations of the priests take shape. As we eventually see in the re-entry texts of Ezra/Nehemiah, a militancy, xenophobia and quasi-aggressive mentality has grown during the exile which gives a certain defensive and belligerent flavor to the Hebrew scriptures.

Creation

> Men like you build the H Bomb
> you'll kill 3 billion people
> So creative…but you can't create life…life in the bosom
> Sarah Connor in the film Terminator II

In Luther's catechism and creedal history, in general, the first article is about proper attention to, adoration toward and emulation of God almighty. Though the metaphor used is one of power, confrontation and intended conquest, the approach of Yahweh as warrior does not coerce us in humiliation, but rather honors our human freedom and seeks our spiritual surrender and subjection. The creed therefore inextricably links God the almighty with creation through the assenting soul of a human person. Luther offers the subtle yet seismic change from the medieval creed by saying I believe in (not on) the father almighty. *Imago dei* is the link between the yielding soul, the creation and the almighty. *Coram deo* conquers *ego e îmí* through *Imago dei*. God's mighty creative power shields us from the powers of destruction (*von der böse mächte*) [WA 11.49.30]. The creator is taken by Luther to be a via media between a high overlord and the good father of the parables.

> *Quando qui deum est omnipotens…pater est…*[265]

As creator, God daily draws us near, fashioning our growth in life and the body and in spiritual vitality (*Leib, Seele und Leben*). Just as in the microcosmos strife and growth, assault and integration, death and life, mark the vital process, so in the macrocosmos of nature and history the supernal process of contention, subjugation and redemption was enacted for creation's redemption. Indeed, in all our pastoral life world—day and night, sun and stars, house and home, land and livestock (*Haus und Hof, Land und Vieh*, WA 30.I.88.5)—the creator remains father-protector and safeguards and flourishes our existence. God's war in history is the conquest of our being amid the distortions and distractions of this world. Rightful creation—grounded evangelization (article I) asserts this possession. Holy or Just war is the affirmation of and allegiance to God's contention for this handiwork. Again, the redemptive battle is to redeem and renew the creation, not to despoil or destroy it.

Maker of Heaven and Earth: Creatorum coeli et terrae

"The Maker of Heaven and Earth." When we move from the existential to the historical plane, the defining war context again is Israel's conquest of Canaan. The rivals now are the spiritual God, ahweh, and the fertility god, Baal. The confrontation is epitomized on Mt. Carmel with the duel of the competing,

---

[265] Sermon on first article, 4/3/1523; WA 11.50.5.

consuming, slaughtering prophets (I Kings 18). In the background of this struggle is the warfare of the competing gods of the ancient Near East: The Babylonian moon-god Sin; the Canaanite's creator god, EL; the Philistine's nature god, Dagon; Egypt's god, Satemi; and Zeus of the Greeks.

The contention of Yahweh and Baal with their respective kings and prophets is the war over "pure spiritual worship" and worship of nature and fertility. God seeks the worship of humanity "in spirit and in truth" (John 4:24). This contest also anticipates the coming intellectual tension between science and superstition, the religious tension between orgiastic theosis and ascetic protection of the divine-human distance and the ethical tension between hedonism and duty philosophy (deontology).

The warfare annunciated in this classic text is not only between true and pretender deities, between Yahweh and pagan prophesy, it also presages the war of science and religion. In conjunction with this clause of the first article of the creed we will examine that ancient struggle of evolutionism and creationism. The first and second century struggle behind this clause in the creed is the battle with Gnosticism. The threat of Gnosticism to God's truth in the world includes creation and artifact, as well as realism and knowledge that touches on the nature of God and the good. Undertaken mainly in the realm of ideas, debates, letters and dueling tracts, there was little physical violence in what was a mighty spiritual confrontation. *Jihad* is often a battle of mind and will.

An exposition of the creedal clause "maker of Heaven and Earth," requires that we first review the two derivative struggles which supply the historical background and theological meaning to the affirmation; the contention with Baal and Gnosis. The basic texts of Hebrew scripture involve the call of Abraham, the possessing of the land and the contention of the prophets of YAWEH and Baal on Mt. Carmel.

Genesis

Now the LORD said to Abram, "Go from your country and your kindred and your father's house to the land that I will show you. I will make of you a great nation, and I will bless you, and make your name great, so that you will be a blessing. I will bless those who bless you, and the one who curses you I will curse; and in you all the families of the earth shall be blessed.

So Abram went, as the LORD had told him; and Lot went with him. Abram was seventy-five years old when he departed from Haran. Abram took his wife Sarai and his brother's son Lot, and all the possessions that they had gathered, and the persons whom they had acquired in Haran; and they set forth to go to the land of Canaan. When they had come to the land of Canaan, Abram passed through the land to the place at Schechem, to the oak of Moreh. At that time the Canaanites were in the land. Then the LORD appeared to Abram, and said, "To your offspring I will give this land." So he built there an altar to the LORD, who had appeared to him. (Genesis 12:1-7)

Deuteronomy

When the LORD your God Brings you into the land that you are about to enter and occupy, and he clears away many nations before you—the Hittites, the Girgashites, the Amorites, the Canaanites, the Perizzites, the Hivites, and the Jebusites, seven nations mightier and more numerous than you—and when the LORD your God gives them over to you and you defeat them, then you must utterly destroy them. Make no covenant with them and show them no mercy. Do not intermarry with them, giving your daughters to their sons or taking their daughters for your sons, for that would turn away your children from following me, to serve other gods then the anger of the LORD would be kindled against you, and he would destroy you quickly. But this is how you must deal with them, break down their altars, smash their pillars, hew down their sacred poles, and burn their idols with fire. For you are a people holy to the LORD your God; the LORD your God has chosen you out of all the peoples on earth to be his people, his treasured possession. It was not because you were more numerous than any other people that the LORD set his heart on you and chose you—for you were the fewest of all peoples. It was because the LORD loved you and kept the oath that he swore to your ancestors, the LORD has brought you out with a mighty hand, and redeemed you from the house of slavery, from the hand of Pharaoh king of Egypt. Know therefore that the LORD your God is God, the faithful God who maintains covenant loyalty with those who love him and keep his commandments, to a thousand generations, and who repays in their own person those who reject him. Therefore, observe diligently the commandment—the statues, and the ordinances—that I am commanding you today.
(Deuteronomy 7:1-11 NRSV)

Exodus

I am going to send an angel in front of you, to guard you on the way and to bring you to the place that I have prepared. Be attentive to him and listen to his voice; do not rebel against him, for he will not pardon your transgression; for my name is in him.

But if you listen attentively to his voice and do all that I say, then I will be an enemy to your enemies and a foe to your foes.

When my angel goes in front of you, and brings you to the Amorites, the Hittites, the Perizzites, the Canaanites, the Hivites, and the Jubusites, and I blot them out, you shall not bow down to their gods, or worship them, or follow their practices, but you shall utterly demolish them and break their pillars in pieces. You shall worship the LORD your God, and I will bless your bread and your water; and I will take sickness away from among you. No one shall miscarry or be barren in your land; I will fulfill the number of your days. I will send my terror in front of you, and will throw into confusion all the people against whom you shall come, and I will make all your enemies turn their backs to you. And I will send the pestilence in front of you, which shall drive out the Hivites, the Canaanites, and the Hittites from before you.
(Exodus 23:20-28 NRSV)

These biblical texts immediately point us to the necessity of linking creed to crusade in biblical history and to the serious problems involved when we do that very thing. Abraham is promised a land now occupied by some other people. The Bible is candid in acknowledging that a *landnahme* ("land-nabbing") will be involved. Ignoring the historical fact that tribes were still migrating in this phase of Bronze-Age—early Iron Age history—Scripture acknowledges, without shame, it seems, that this will be done violently with genocidal cleansing. This is not only strategically necessary to consolidate authority, it is the divine will to exert the two-fold purpose of removing abominable presence and practice from YAHWEH's cognizance and of providing an atmosphere for pure faith and ethics.

On a recent stay in Jerusalem I met Rabbi Jeremy Milgram, a saintly figure like his parents. He chairs the Rabbi's for Peace Fellowship in Jerusalem and is one of the few rabbis deeply involved in the Palestinian and Christian-Arab cause. These suffering communities and not his own Jewish congregation are his primary fellowship. Out of these commitments he wondered with us about the authenticity, and if authentic, of the wisdom of the conquest (or infiltration) of Canaan. In his faith YAWEH is the kindly and just God of all peoples, then and now, including the Canaanites, whose obliteration is ordered. Does creed require crusade? Does crusade require iconoclastic cleansing? Does YAWEH desire uncontaminated faith? Might the God who is a multifaceted jewel prefer eclectic faith and pluralistic traditions? These profound questions surface when we read the biblical texts about Canaan and Baal. The contest of the respective debating and dueling prophets is also illuminating:

> So Ahab sent to all the Israelites, and assembled the prophets at Mount Carmel. Elijah then came near to all the people, and said, "How long will you go limping with two different opinions? If the LORD is God, follow him; but if Baal, then follow him." The people did not answer him a word. Then Elijah said to the people, "I, even I only, am left a prophet of the LORD; but Baal's prophets number four hundred fifty. Let two bulls be given to us; let them choose one bull for themselves, cut it in pieces, and lay it on the wood, but put no fire to it; I will prepare the other bull and lay it on the wood, but put no fire to it. Then you call on the name of your god and I will call on the name of the Lord; the god who answers by fire is indeed God." All the people answered, "Well spoken!" Then Elijah said to the prophets of Baal, "choose for yourselves one bull and prepare it first, for you are many; then call on the name of your god, but put no fire to it." So they took the bull that was given them, prepared it, and called on the name of Baal from morning until noon, crying, "O Baal, answer us!" But there was no voice, and no answer. They limped about the altar that they had made. At noon Elijah mocked them, saying "cry aloud! Surely he is a god; either he is meditating, or he was wandered away, or he is on a journey, or perhaps he is asleep and must be awakened." They then cried aloud and, as was their custom, they cut themselves with swords and lances until the blood gushed out over them. As midday passed, they raved on until the time of the offering of the oblation, but there was no voice, no answer, and no response.
>
> Then Elijah said to all the people, "come closer to me"; and all the people came closer to him. First he repaired the altar of the Lord that had been thrown down;

Elijah took twelve stones, according to the number of the tribes of the of the sons of Jacob, to whom the word of the LORD came saying, "Israel shall be your name"; with the stones he built an altar in the name of the LORD. Then he made a trench around the altar, large enough to contain two measures of seed. Next he put the wood in order, cut the bull in pieces, and laid it on the wood. He said, "fill four jars with water and pour it on the burnt offering and on the wood." Then he said, "Do it a second time"; and they did it a second time. Again he said, "Do it a third time"; and they did it a third time, so that the water ran all around the altar, and filled the trench also with water.

At the time of the offering of the oblation, the prophet Elijah came near and said, "O LORD, God of Abraham, Isaac, and Israel, let it be known this day that you are God in Israel, that I am your servant, and that I have done all these things at your bidding. Answer me, O LORD, answer me, so that this people may know that you, O LORD, are God, and that you have turned their hearts back." Then the fire of the LORD fell and consumed the burnt offering, the wood the stones, and the dust, and even licked up the water that was in the trench. When all the people saw it, they fell on their faces and said, "The LORD indeed is God; the LORD indeed is God." Elijah said to them, "seize the prophets of Baal; do not let one of them escape." They then seized them; and Elijah brought them down to the Wadi Kishon, and killed them there.
(I Kings 18:20-40)

The false gods, who are no gods, detract God's people from the one God, the true God, who alone gives life and salvation. As Calvin would contend in Strasburg, then Geneva, in the mid-sixteenth century, there is no eclectic god, no syncretistic diety in-between or neutral option. A people must choose whom they will serve. Each nation lives either by faith in God or by faith in some impotent and therefore destructive pretender. Neutrality or eclectic toleration is destructive evil. If we will accept this thesis, even with its grave cost of requiring allegiance and not tolerance, we have entered into the biblical world of creedal crusade. Baal must go, as must Ashtarte and *Caesar Kurios*.

Gnosis

In the decades and centuries of the appearance of the Evangel an even more attractive and therefore insidious adversary emerges to the one good and great God of Israel and the bible, at least to the puritanical consciousness of the consolidating creedal-crusading church. That adversary, Gnosticism, is like a malignancy, woven into the very cells and tissues of the faith itself. Indeed, whenever Pythagorean, Platonic, dualistic, Persian or new-Platonic thought infiltrates the nascent Christian organism we are dealing with something like Gnosticism. The terrible perhaps (*schrechliche vielleicht*) is that even biblical faith must be formulated in terms of human philosophy. Yet, that fruit of human reason is always inadequate to formulate God and the good.

Monumental studies of Gnosticism exist thanks to Hans Jonas and Elaine Pagels. If the Hebraic pole of Christian conviction tends toward the materialist and worldly—i.e. towards Baal, the pole of the Gnostic heresy tends toward the spiritualist. Obedience is the moral concomitant of orthodoxy—freedom in

441

gnosticism. Inclination towards Gnosticism is grounds for its rejection from the canon of Scripture (e.g. Gospel of Thomas), even though Scripture itself is profuse with Gnostic-like perspectives (John, Hebrews, etc.). The issue riddles through the early church's depiction of Jesus as the God-man. It lies underneath all of the Christology controversies. It animates the intellectual-theological wars of post-Constantine history and erupts into especial fury against the Barbarian invaders of Europe starting with the baptism of Clovis in 496 C.E. which we have just celebrated in France with the Pope's visit to Reims cathedral. Clovis' descendent, Charlemagne (c. 800) extends the Frankish dominion against the threat of Eastern tribalism, including Islam, as he makes the Apostles Creed ecclesial and political orthodoxy.

Gnosticism is found in Judaism and Hellenism as well as in Egyptian and Persian thought. It was seen as a popular and political threat because it claimed secret and particular access to God and because it threatened not only monotheism but derivative monocultures. Gnosticism in its quasi-mystical quality mitigates against the divine-king and the theocratic state. Its "anti-cosmic" dualism (Hans Jonas) threatens most modes of consolidation of sacred and secular spheres. Its astrological speculations were offensive to Hebrew creation (*ex nihilo*) theology. Its libertinism challenged Decalogue rigor. Its dualism undermined the sacral state.

Yet Gnosticism has left an enduring legacy. It was in many ways a winsome and generous philosophy. It has amplified the good/evil tension of Judaism, though often repudiating the goodness of creation and of the human body, doctrines so central to that faith. It has accented the mystical essence of religion so that faith can never be seen only as a physical-worldly phenomenon. It takes some of the fight out of the faith by projecting aggression and the conceptualization and dreams of cosmic warfare (the sacrificial system, etc) onto the eschatological plane.

False deity and false ideology are the enemies confronted in the creed/crusade of the first article. The warfare against Baal's prophets and the Canaanite protectorate in eighth-century Israel, against Caesar in first century Palestine, or against Hitler, then Stalin, in twentieth century Europe, is the war against a false god. The struggle of the indigenous Vietnamese against the French, then American, hegemony; of the Sandanistas in Nicaragua against vaunted and oppressing power, is the same struggle. That the church was found on both the sides of the oppressor and the oppressed shows the finegrained discernment of acuity of the first three commandments that is required in divine *Jihad*.

False ideology is also the necessary cause of thought war, lively debate, propaganda, even on occasion, resistance and battle. The contention of Vaclav Havel or Father Tókês against communism and the resistance of Bonhoeffer to Nazism as a false idol, diabolic ideology and anti-Semitic injustice were the twentieth century counterparts of the early church's contention with Gnosticism and Marcionism in the first centuries of the Christian era. God comes to humanity not only in person (presence) but in Logos and thought. Great humility is required in exerting iconoclasm. Our own god may be a less worthy idol than the one we attack. All human thought, especially, all ideology, is suspect. The American Imperium is suspect. The office of the exposition of faith and the office of the Inquisition ought to function with a perpetually troubled conscience.

What is the contemporary military meaning of the first article of the creed? Communism is dead, having collapsed of its own weight and inner contradictions. History has discovered that justice was impossible without God. Western Europe, North America, Japan, South Africa and Israel still seek to fashion secular-humanist states in the spirit of the now-liberated and unopposed capitalism. But this false god, mammon, will also fall. Indeed, it already languishes as global economic market centers (North America, Europe, East Asia, China) strive for affluent preeminence all to the neglect of the struggling, oppressed and exploited sectors of the world (Latin and South America, Africa, India). Worshipping the almighty dollar or Euro will only hasten the decline of the West within the divine economy. Today as Western investors sap the vitalities of the Asian, Middle-European and South American markets into their own accounts so that those very people find their economies in paradoxical flourish and near-collapse, we see the bitter fruits of such misplaced worship. The Asian, Argentinian and Russian crisis may be the most telling symptom of ethical economics of the early 21st century.

Spiritually speaking, religious vitality has already passed to Africa, Latin America (including holiness and evangelical enclaves in the luxuriant West), and Asia. Religion in the old crucible of faith in Greece, Asia Minor, Byzantium (Russia), Europe and North America is already in latency if not moribund. The creator God is turning the world upside down. Power almighty is not what we think it is. The world remains under the sovereign authority of the God of Israel and of Jesus Christ. The faith of Islam as it speaks to the poor of Arabia, Asia and Africa, and the exiled affluence seekers of the Arab peoples in the first world may be the *Avant gard*, the *Jihad* of the first article. Gospel exuberance, Catholic and Pentecostal faith, traces the same path around the world as that marked by desperate poverty. "The well" have no need of a physician.

Today, the lonely orthodox metropolitan-sitting in Istanbul, completely without a constituency, rejects the proposal of neo- Islamicized Turkey that Haj Sophia, Constantine's majestic central cathedral of Christendom, now a museum, become a theatre and mosque for the celebration of Muslim services. The die of ultimate irony is cast. The human forms and shapes of official religion have displaced pure belief in

God the father almighty...maker of heaven and earth.

The fight of faith in the world of privilege has moved to the prophetic underground and to the loyal remnant. Some will not bend the knee to Baal and Mammon. There Spirit is alive. I find it in the Taize community in France. Some resist the standard line, the packaged ideology, the prescribed program. In quiet ways they pray to God, do His justice, love His friends, heal and tend the earth and the powers-that-be fire across the bows of their boats or assassinate them on warm sub-tropical nights.

Seven phases of war in the world have to do with this initial phase of the creed.

- Israel's war for Yahweh's home in Palestine
- Syria and Assyria's war against Israel
- Babylonia's war against Judah
- Persia's war against Chaldea, liberating the Jews
- Alexander's conquests and Empire
- The Roman Empire and its war against Judea
- The struggle of Christianity against gnosticism and paganism

What are the continuing theological-political repercussions of those wars?

Israel/Palestine
The war for occupation of Palestine continues today. It is a strange religious phenomenon. On the one hand Zionism is the product of nineteenth century enlightenment (post-religious) European Judaism. Martin Buber's lectures on Zion in 1947 call for a magnanimous cosmopolitan state where Jews, Christians and Muslims live together in concord. In this spirit the establishment of the State of Israel was also the search for an out and guilt-offering from the theogenic genocide by European Christendom after the induction of Islam into world history. On the other hand, the State of Israel seeks today to exert its religious particularity in strident confrontation with Arabic Islam and Palestinian Christianity. Today (July 2001) a settler claims that God gave Israel this land. The spirit is sullied. In 1996 the seizing and securing of the land as a cleansed home for YAWEH has all the features of the first conquest. In the early summer of 1997 orthodox men (*Habarim*) stoned and pelted with feces conservative Jews (men and women) who dared pray at the Wailing Wall. The law of return and conversion threatens to fracture the fragile state. Under threat cleansing and purification becomes time—tuned resort as a nation turns away from Yahweh and in upon itself. Where is the Jerusalem where nations will stream up to Zion and swords will be recast into plowshares? Israel must make a bold, though dangerous, risk for justice and peace.

Syria/Israel
Though Damascus, Antioch and Edessa are intriguing cites in the civil history of theology, today they are not the cities of the Apostle Paul and the

philosopher Bardaisan, but of the son of the ancient ruler, President Hassan, an antagonist of Israel. Contending for a place in the new world order, where influence might be exerted over places like Lebanon, Jordan, Palestine, even Iran and Iraq, Syria struggles today with Israel over issues of regional power, survival and political ascendancy in this rapidly changing and volatile region of the world.

As Egyptian world domination ended toward the end of the new kingdom and the time of the Hebrew Exodus (c. 1200 BCE) the Assyrian power arose with powerful kings such as Tiglath Pileser (c. 730 BCE). Today, Syria's tanks have gone out against Israel as did old Assyria's war chariots. The stables and chariots of Israel were then no longer formidable as they were in Solomon's Megiddo and then the then divided kingdom melted before the awesome foe. Today, with America supplying $1000 per year, per person, in military aid to Israel, and with Europe and American supplying jet aircraft, missiles and nuclear capacity, any war in the Middle East is no contest. Israel is as plenipotent in the region as America is in the world. The search for co-existence and peace is the only alternative to suicidal folly. One fails to see any reason why Israel or Palestine or Egypt or Syria should make peace, but for the justice and mercy of Abrahamic/AKEDIC theology and ethics. Unless Israel, Syria and Palestinian militants end the present belligerence there may be a powerful Israel and a less powerful Syria, both lacking any moral credibility on which to establish a "Blessed Kingdom."

As every history museum in the world attests, Syria lived by a theophany and theogony that was almighty and fearsome but one which ultimately went the way of *götterdamering* invoked by the presence of Judaism, Christianity and Islam. These Semitic and Abrahamic creeds with their Noachic and Mosaic ethical aspects now guide Syrian society. The Noachic ethos is perhaps strongest in a society that seeks to be secular as well as a home to Islam and to orthodox Christianity. Here the norm of monotheism (no idolatry or blasphemy), fidelity (no adultery), and non-violence (killing) to people, animals, and nature, pertain. (cf. Genesis 9). In secular terms it seems to prescribe a state of justice and morality all within the embrace of its extraordinary hospitality. Syria will be swept, only reluctantly, onto the stage of international conflict if her existence is threatened, her sustenance (oil or global markets) is compromised, or if resurgent proselytic Islam comes to prevail as in Iran, Algeria, Afghanistan, and Turkey. Syria now seeks to live by the creed extrapolated from the Christian creed in the European Enlightenment by Hobbes and Locke, Rousseau and Voltaire, Hegel and Kant—a human rights based, liberty-focused, pluralistic and tolerant state. An economic vitality and political sovereignty are the principal "almighty fathers" of this global creed.

Other Historic Wars Coincident with the Creed (First Article)

We are exploring the thesis that the creed of Abrahamic faith, especially as embodied in Judaism covenant, the Christian Apostles' Creed and Islamic Jihad gives rise to a pattern of transforming history where idolatry is challenged, injustice is resisted, amelioration of evil is effected and a new realm of righteousness is sought. This redemptive process is shaped by numerous encounters through history.

We could speak of the Babylonian and Persian liberation of Israel from captivity. We could speak of the modern ideological and military strife between Iran and Iraq, Iran and Israel, Iran and the West. The prospects for global peace must remain in doubt as these apocalyptic nations come to possess weapons of mass destruction: nuclear, chemical, and biological. We could see how the exacerbation of global terrorism under the influence of the militant fundamentalist theology of the Ayatollah Khomeini or Osamo bin Laden is a conflict between the aforementioned secular-liberal sequel to a monotheistic-puritan creed in European and especially American Christendom and the newly intensified Islam of the post- Shah era. Since 1997 Iran apparently has elected a more tolerant and progressive Mullah to govern the State. The two nations met with competitive respect at the World Cup in France. We are too close to this contemporary history of creed and crusade to see clearly its outlines except to say that faith and ethics are again central. As we begin to dedemonize Islam in the post-modern period terrorists still in the movie Air Force One must be Kazakistan Muslims. As we come to respect Islamic and Arabic people not only in their indigenous nations but as sizable minorities in the modern Western democracies, we will begin to recast the Judaic-christic creed, particularly in the first article toward a more ecumenical formulation with this sister Abrahamic-Saraic faith.

Greece and Rome

The heritage of Greece and Rome is also still with us and these remarkable constitutive empires of antiquity still exert formidable influence in the creedal-crusades of the contemporary world. Even though Italy, Greece and Spain are poor stepsister nation-economies, even in the emerging European commonwealth, their heritage in thought, belief, culture and politics has been monumental. The philosophical and juridical ethos of today's world culture is still steeped in the worldview of the Hellenistic *oikumene* of the successor Roman and Holy Roman civilization. These two cultures also gave their indelible stamp to Christian belief and ecclesial and social structures which endure into the present time. Secular philosophy still begins with Plato and Aristotle and our legal systems still involve mutations of Athenian, Roman, and Justinian jurisprudence.

What about creed and crusade? Though Greek boats try to plant the flag on a rock Island or charge the UN border zone in Cyprus; and although they seek power in the European community and the Holy See is a governmental body in the European parliament, the Greco-Roman influence on the contemporary creed, even in those nations to say nothing of the emerging global society, is largely subliminal and nominal. But these cultures have given the world understandings of truth, good and beauty which have become universal. Pythagoras' structure of music is the formal architecture of Beethoven and Mozart, which is the national music of Japan and Israel. The Word has gone out and will not return void...(Isaiah 45:23).

Summary
What has been the technical history, i.e. the historic yield, of the first article? Whitehead would find in its impulse the logic and momentum of science. A disenchanted nature joined to the idea of Jehovah as a "righteous energy" imbuing reality with the dimension of purposive time is probably the gift of Jewish, Christic and Muslim theological iconoclasm to world history. Monotheism displaced polytheism in the great Christian and Muslim empires of this era. The military and economic ascendancy of western civilization in the recent four centuries of this millennium can also be traced to a political messianism implicit in the first article and in the Hebraic theology it conveys. Scientific technology, war and colonial history are all aggressive and annihilating and therefore ethically ambiguous. In the language of Durban they are blessings and "crimes against humanity." More benign are the convictions of freedom, responsibility, human rights, the imperatives of justice and the general cultural Geist which arise from the value of "*Soli Deo Gloriam.*" A caché of ideas, convictions and values roughly coincident with the Decalogue (see Part II) now pertains in world history as a constellation of truth worth living, fighting and dying for. This is the creative yield of the First Article.

But the credo goes on—"the law came through Moses, grace and truth through Jesus Christ." A subtle and gentle impulse is joined to the God sense of the first article that will invest culture with a different sentiment.

"And yet a spirit still and bright with something of Angelic light."
W. Wordsworth

Excursus: Creation, Creed and War
Today, in our nuclear age, war will afflict and destroy not only the human creature but the creation itself. As Robert Jungk (*Brighter than a Thousand Suns*) has pointed out, an ultimate act of punishment and vengeance or security and pre-emptive prevention (the two justifications of war) by superpowers possessing nuclear weapons (or other weapons of mass destruction) would be suicidal and ecocidal. It is no mistake that genocide accompanies modern war. This is the case not only in the reversion to primitive violence as in Rwanda and Bosnia where simple weapons— knives and machetes, rifles and mines are aimed at another kind of people—but in the targeted mass civilian deaths inflicted by the allied bombing of German and Japanese cities at the dawn of the nuclear age. In our modern world genocide is inevitably liked to war. War is suicide.

All out (total war) and even limited war today must therefore be seen as an assault on the creation. It is linked in belief and intention to a creedal inversion where in our destructive will we deny the creator and the creation itself. To provoke or prosecute a war or even to wait or hope for a final conflagration today is miscreed and anticreed, misdeed and anti-deed. The first article of the creed therefore requires a war of the mind and soul against war. To be faithful to the almighty father and creator in this age we must find peace credible (believable and possible) and contingent, i.e., we have the power to cause it or prevent it. The building of stringent international controls; the United Nations and its agencies, regional governments and associations of nations like the European, Asian and African communities, interlocking international economic arrangements, all have the power to actualize this creed. But underneath must be the creedal bedrock...on this rock...(Matthew 16:18).

My teacher, Carl Friedrich Von Weizsäcker, the physicistphilosopher, taught a course on peace at Hamburg in the 1960's. In one session he recalled the incident of going to the theologian Karl Barth and asking him if he could ethically and theologically continue his research on the nuclear secrets. Barth replied: "If you believe, what Christians have always believed, that we live in the twilight of history and that God will consummate the world—you can continue." Barth's masterful and monumental exposition of the first article of the creed should have led him to an undergirding theology of peace in the creation even beneath the necessity to war against Hitler. Yes creation and its consummation are ultimately in God's hands alone, but in frightful and wonderful freedom he has placed penultimate authority in ours. We are now gods in the earth.

II. Second Article
Luther

> And in Jesus Christ, his only Son, our Lord, who was conceived by the Holy Ghost, born of the Virgin Mary; suffered under Pontius Pilate; was crucified, dead and buried, he descended into hell; the third day he rose again from the dead; he ascended into heaven and sitteth at the right hand of the Father Almighty; form thence he shall come to judge the quick and the dead.

> *What does that mean?*

> ANSWER: I believe that Jesus Christ, very God, born of the Father in eternity, and also very man, born of the Virgin Mary is my Lord, who has redeemed me, a lost and damned man, and has won and delivered me from all sins, from death, and from the power of the devil, not with gold and silver, but with his holy and precious blood and with his innocent passion and death, so that I might be his own, and might live under him in his kingdom, and serve him in everlasting righteousness, innocence, and a blessing, just as he rose from the dead, and lives and reigns in all eternity. This is a faithful saying.[266]

---

[266] G.E. Rupp & Benjamin Drewery, *Martin Luther: Documents in Modern History,* London: Edward Arnold, 1970, p. 141-2.

Calvin:

>...since we have fallen from life into death, the whole knowledge of God the Creator that we have discussed would be useless unless faith also followed, setting forth for us God our Father in Christ. The natural order was that the frame of the universe should be the school in which we were to learn piety, and from it pass over to eternal life and perfect felicity. But after man's rebellion, our eyes—wherever they turn—encounter God's curse. This curse, while it seizes and envelops innocent creatures through our fault, must overwhelm our souls with despair. For even if God wills to manifest his father favor to us in many ways, yet we cannot by contemplating the universe infer that he is Father. Rather, conscience presses us within and shows in our sin just cause for his disowning us and not regarding or recognizing us as his sons. Dullness and ingratitude follow, for our minds, as they have been blinded, do not perceive what is true. And as all our senses have become perverted, we wickedly defraud God of his glory. We must, for this reason, come to Paul's statement: "Since in the wisdom of God the world did not know God through wisdom, it pleased God through the folly of preaching to save those who believe" [I Cor. 1:21]. This magnificent theater of heaven and earth, crammed with innumerable miracles, Paul calls the "wisdom of God." Contemplating it, we ought in wisdom to have known God. But because we have profited so little by it, he calls us to the faith of Christ, which, because it appears foolish, the unbelievers despise.

>Therefore, although the preaching of the cross does not agree with our human inclination, if we desire to return to God our Author and Maker, from whom we have been estranged, in order that he may again begin to be our Father, we ought nevertheless to embrace it humbly. Surely, after the fall of the first man no knowledge of God apart from the Mediator has had power unto salvation [cf. Rom. 1:16; I Cor. 1:24]. For Christ not only speaks of his own age, but comprehends all ages when he says: "This is eternal life, to know the father to be the one true God, and Jesus Christ whom he has sent" [John 17:3].[267]

The theme is thoroughly Judaic and AKEDIC. The emphasis is the *Shemah* and Decalogue in the sanctification, glorification and unification of the Name. With a gun to her head the young girl at Columbine High School was asked if she believed in God, when she confessed that she did, he pulled the trigger.

II. And in Jesus Christ God's Only Son: Et in Jesum Christum filium eius unicum, Dominum Nostrum

The second article is the stipulation of anthropological theology and theological anthropology. It expresses the truth about human life under God, in the world. In scripture and early creed the affirmation that God the almighty father is maker of heaven and earth is a resounding call to the Hellenic and pagan society that Yahweh, the God of Israel, is God alone. The Jesus article is the clarion call to Hebraic society and through the Jews to the whole world that Jesus is Messiah, that Yahweh and Jesus are One.

---

[267] J.T. McNeil, LCC. p. 201.

The Jesus drama is *militial*-a war saga. It concerns vanquishment and victory. These military images capture the meaning of the Christ event. Calvary and Easter, like Exile and Exodus, convey defeat and conquest. These are the Leitmotivs of the history of God.

The second article is the heart of the creed. In theology this is the drama of reconciliation and redemption. What has been created, then lost, is now bought back with the costly cross. Article one and three hinge on the Christ claim. The God and father, the God of Israel, is Jesus' God and father. The world's God now and forever is the God Jesus taught the world, regardless of the presence or place of the second article in any particular creed. The Spirit is Christ's gift and legacy to the creation and history. The oldest precursors of the Apostle's Creed therefore place the Christ clause in the primary position. Second Corinthians 13:13, for example, offers the classic benediction:

- The grace of the Lord Jesus Christ
- The love of God the father
- The communion of the Holy Spirit

The essence of the Jesus affirmation is that he is Christ, MESSIAH. This complex notion has rich meanings but central always is the meaning of anointed one, the deliverer and emancipator from oppression. The word messiah or Christ is a military or political designation. In scripture the anointed one can be the Isaiaic servant or Cyrus the Persian and King Josiah may be the first messianic personage in the history of Israel.[268] The fragments of the UR creed, gospel (*evangellion*) and message (*kerygma*) in the New Testament relate the life, death and resurrection of Jesus as his messianic vocation.

> For I passed on to you in the first place what I had myself received
> That Christ died for our sins according to the Scriptures,
> and that He was buried,
> and that He was raised on the third day according to the Scriptures,
> And that He appeared to Cephas,
> Then to the Twelve,
> then to more than five hundred brothers at once...
> then He appeared to James,
> then to all the apostles...
> (I Corinthians 15:3ff)
>
> Concerning His Son,
> Who was born of David's seed by natural descent,
> Who was declared Son of God with power by the Spirit of holiness
> When He was raised from the dead,
> Jesus Christ our Lord,

---

[268] Ref. Sweeney, M.A. King, *Josiah of Judeah*. (Oxford: Oxford University Press, 2001).

Through Whom we have received grace,
Romans 1:3ff

Christ Jesus Who died, or rather
Has been raised from the dead,
who is on the right hand of God,
who also makes intercession for us,
Romans 8:34

Remember Jesus Christ,
raised from the dead,
of the seed of David (according to my gospel).
II Timothy 2:8

For Christ also suffered for sins,
The just for the unjust, to bring us to God,
Slain indeed in the flesh but quickened in the Spirit,
In which He went and preached to the spirits in prison
...through the rising again of Jesus Christ,
who is on the right hand of God,
having descended to heaven,
angels, authorities and powers having been subjected to Him.
I Peter 3:18ff

Who was revealed in the flesh,
Was justified in the Spirit,
Appeared to angels,
Was preached among the Gentiles,
Was believed on throughout the world,
Was taken up in glory.
I Timothy 3:16

We, however, have one God the Father,
From Whom are all things, and we to Him,
And one Lord Jesus Christ,
Through Whom are all things, and we through Him.
I Corinthians 8:6

For there is one God,
Likewise one mediator between God and men,
The man Jesus Christ,
Who gave Himself as a ransom for all...
I Timothy 2:5ff.

I charge you in the sight of
God Who gives life to all things,
And Christ Jesus Who witnessed the fine confession
In the time of Pontius Pilate,
That you keep your commission spotless,
Without reproach, until
The manifestation of our Lord Jesus Christ. (I Timothy 6:13ff)

> Because of us…who believe
> On Him Who has raised
> Jesus our Lord from the dead,
> Who was delivered up for our transgressions
> And was raised for our justification.
> (Romans 4:24)

In primitive Christianity, this kernel of the creed forms and flourishes as needs arise for chatechesis and missionary expansion. Warfare in the nascent Christian community is waged against backsliding into pagan idolatry and immorality on the part of the vulnerable new believers. The creed is also a code or checklist of orthodox belief as missionaries encounter the competing Greco- Roman theologies and philosophies such as seeking the unknown God of Athens (Acts 17:23) or the Gnostic and Roman ideologies. Formulations of orthodoxy and orthopraxy abound especially when the heat is turned up on aggressive sects by the normally magnanimous and tolerant Roman Empire. Jude speaks of the defense against the assault of false teachers: "Contend for the faith which was once for all delivered to the saints." (verse 3) Paul counsels believers to exert noble life styles against a society rife with deleterious habits… "behave in a manner worthy of the God who calls you." (I Thess. 2:12).

The newfound relationship born in the human encounter with God in Christ is founded in hearing and receiving the Gospel. Successive stages of understanding and declaring this relationship can be called

- faith, then
- creed, then
- christianity, then
- christian culture.

Eventually the Cheshire cat is gone and only the smile remains—and it is a threatening grin! In the words of Aarend Van Leeuwen:

> Christianity is an historical phenomenon: that is, it accompanies the passage of the Gospel through human history and like all history, it lies under the judgment—and the patience—of God[269]

While Gospel and faith rarely and creed seldom become adversarial, Christianity and Christian culture—the sociopolitical derivatives of the primal piety—are often engaged in defensive and offensive action. Creed is the first stage of abstracting the faith relation away from the pacific and eschatological, toward

---

[269] Aarend Van Leeuwen, *Christianity in World History*. New York, Macmillan, 1964, p. 20.

militancy. Perhaps the worst and final declension away from vital faith is the warring secular society like modern Germany, Russia, England, France or America that thinks, because of its residual Christian culture, that its crusades against Europe, Vietnam, the Falklands, Chechnya, or Iraq are holy wars.

The model of Holy warfare in Israel—exodus, emancipation, entrance, establishment, is now the paradigm for the vocation of Jesus as Christ.

- He came out from eternity and encamped among us (John 1:14)
- He came to his own even though they didn't receive him (John 1:11)
- By making us children he re-established God's family on earth (John 1:12)
- He was interrogated by religious authority and incarcerated by civil authority because his mission transformed and threatened both realms
- In the cross he transected the deep river of humanity's sin and death
- He was rescued from the cruel entrapment of death
- In His descent into hell he strove against and conquered sin, death and the devil
- In his ascent from hell he leads captivity captive in himself (envisaged as a Roman Conqueror (Ephesians 4:8, Revelation 13:10).

The Christological kerygma is the redemptive story conceived as release and renewal of life. The humiliation and exaltation (Philippians 2:6-11) of the Son of God, son of man, son of David, is the drama of filial obedience which effects the salvation of humanity and creation. Because Jesus is *Christus Victor* he is the author of peace, the one worthy of worship and praise. The adoration and divine attribution of Jesus in the early church, as Larry Hortado has shown, attribution so foreign, even offensive to Judaism, is that given to a divine conqueror. Recent Christology, in Scotland, for example, shows this imputation of Lordship derives from Hebrew monotheism. By the early fourth century Jesus is a Roman Soldier. Constantine is Messiah and Savior. In popular imagination the two images converge. The Christian story as shown in James Carroll's The Sword of Constantine now becomes more anti-Judaic and spiritually and morally suspect.

Thine be the glory, risen, conquering son;
Endless is the victory, thou o'er death has won.
Edmund Budry, 1884
Music G.F. Handel from Judas Maccabeas, 1747.

Our Lord...*Dominum Nostrum*

God of our fathers, know of old,
Lord of our far-flung battle line,
Beneath whose awful Hand we hold
Dominion over palm and pine
Lord God of hosts; be with us yet,
Lest we forget—lest we forget.
(Rudyard Kipling, Recessional, 1897)

A militant and authoritative ascription indeed. But also a common designation. There are many Lords in today's world; Lord Linsey and Lord Ashbrook along with many other privileged scholars who come up to Oxford. There were many Lords in the New Testament world. The landowners and political overlords, among others, held this title and received appropriate respect and obeisance.

The Jesus community, the apostles, including Paul, had the distinctive, powerful and Godly designation in mind when they designated Jesus as Christ—our Lord. This was *Kurios*, in the sense that the Hebrew word Yahweh was translated into the Greek. *Kurios* is Yahweh. This was the co-laborer in the creation. In Nicea Constantinopolitan language this is "very God of very God:"

'The one by whom all things were made'
In whom all things subsist
And 'before whom every knee shall bow.'
(Colossians 1:16, 17; Philippians 2:10.

Christianity was born of Judaism. The long history of active belief in Israel is the cradle of Christian faith. The strange intermingling of theology, ethnicity and nationality that is *Judentum* will also mark *Christentum*. The story of Israel is one of spirituality and ethics acted out against the background of political history. The European holocaust and the fact that, in the second millennium of the Christian era, one out of every two Jews born was killed, is part of that biblical history. This is true for Jews, Christians and for humanity itself. Far from being the *Endlösung* (final solution) of the Jewish question, it remains the central question of the meaning of history. In sublime irony from the present purview Islam may prove the ultimate vindication of Israel.

In the 1990's we lived through an exciting age of retrieval of the Jewish roots of Christian faith. We also moved beyond positivistic renditions of the meaning of history as we recovered, even amid the birth pangs of the State of Israel, broader conceptions of spirit and purpose. As we undertake our study of evangelical theology as a crusading creed we, too, begin with Israel.

The rule or reign of God is the heartland of the transformation that Jesus brings to the world. Though the concept takes on cosmic, eschatological and apocalyptic connotation in the early Christian centuries, the root concept of Kingdom is Davidic and Solomonic, that is a Mosaic covenantal rule in human history. God extends rule into the world through a chosen people who live among and for universal humanity. The Christian appropriation of David standing threatened though, in God, victorious over the Philistines is re-enacted in Hugh of St. Victor in the twelfth century, who envisions himself amid an army with Christ against the devil—an army of Jews and Christians. At other times Christians, especially paganized Christian nations, became the instruments of holy war against Israel. The crusades of the 11th to 14th centuries slaughtered most of the Jews in Europe and in the Eastern Mediterranean. The portrayal of *Christentum* and *Judentum* in the 13th century Strasbourg cathedral depicts this violence. Here *Judentum* is shriveled and deformed. *Christentum* is erect and upright. Islam, is the satanic horde.

One can offer with ironic twist the words of Augustine on the "slumping" form of Jesus:

> Who had no form or comeliness that we should desire him (Isaiah 53:12) ... in the form of a slave, he humbled himself. (Philippians 2:7)[270]

> The deformity of Christ forms you. If he had not willed to be deformed, you would not have recovered the form which you had lost. Therefore he was deformed when he hung on the cross. But his deformity is our comeliness. In this life, therefore, let us hold fast to the deformed Christ.[271]

This concerted messianic mission has often been disjoined in religious history. It was Norman Perrin following Harnack, Bultmann, Käsemann and the Tübingen School defining Jesus' character and mission in its dissimilarity with Judaism, that a decisive break occurs that lead one scholar to speak of "The Christian Blasphemy: A Non-Jewish Jesus."[272] For Perrin, the kingdom of God of Jesus was radically different from the Jewish kingdom. For Perrin, the kingdom was a "tensive symbol" conveying a range of experiential meanings which coalesced into a comprehensive myth of the transformation of the self. In contrast to this "salvific" and mythic Christian thought is the worldly and political biblical thought which sees God and Christ, Jews and Christians as decisive victors over the actual and worldly forces of chaos and inimical threats to human purposes in nature itself and over political tyrants unpliable to divine purpose. The symbols of creation and exodus signal decisive military victory over the inimical powers of nature and history. In the words of John Kraus, the great expositor of the Psalms:

> steps forth as a fighter for his people and for humankind.[273]

---

[270] Q p. 104.
[271] Augustine, *Sermons,* 44.6.6.
[272] James H. Charlesworth, ed. *Jews and Christians*, New York: Crossroad, 1990. p. 211ff.
[273] John Kraus, *Theologische Religionkritik,* Neurkirchen-Vluyn, 1982, pp. 132-133.

The God of the Bible, of Israel and Jesus, is an immanent historical presence. There is no hint as yet of an ontological or metaphysical being. This will be the preserve of Greek culture's elaboration of the meaning of Jesus' appearance on earth that would come with Paul and the gentile mission. God, in the Hebrew Bible, comes to us and acts for us in the concrete events of history. God, in the words of Job, is advocate and avenger, the pursuer of worldly justice. Yes, God is transcendent in power and holiness but even these biblically derived, though ontologically projected qualities, are in order to the achievement of historical purposes, with people, in the world. God is the liberator of the oppressed, the vindicator of the righteous, the judge and prosecutor of the vicious—a righteous warrior (in Christ). God is one who offers and claims faith, extends love and demands response. This is the essential meaning of the first article of the creed. The language is historical, tangible, and practical. It is the earthly language of creation, the cosmic language of heaven and earth.

Practically speaking, first century Judaism and therefore first century Christianity were steeped in a Jewish apocalyptic which fostered a militant and revolutionary mentality in two ways: in theological terms a cosmic warfare ensued between good and evil, God and the forces of wrong, even in the heavens. This supernatural conflict spilled over onto the earth and effected human affairs. Among these precipitated crises was the vivid and present historical conflict of Second Temple Israel with the occupying Roman Empire. Two senses of immanent and impending warfare against a cosmic background fired a militant mentality which found wide-ranging expression from fantastic schemata of the cosmic conflicts to concrete guerrilla raids on garrisons of Roman soldiers.

The Christian Gospel and URCREDO was formed within the historical crucible of Jewish Holy War against the occupying Roman Empire in Palestine. This cultural fact forever stamps the Christian movement as a conjunction of creed and crusade.

If, "only son" denotes the relation to the father, "Our Lord" denotes Jesus' relationship to the world. If God the father language is meant to anchor for the Gentiles the Hebraic tenor of the Gospel, the Christ article is word to the Jewish community, that Jesus is the fulfillment of Israel's hope, the cosmic liberator, Yahweh's cosmic culmination of the historic Exodus.

Christ possesses dominion over the creation and the creature. In Barth's understanding this entails:

> Lordship of the creator of our life...the
> owner of our new life as those who in Him
> have been saved from sin and death.[274]

---

[274] *Credo*, p. 55.

Christ has conscripted our being in several senses. He is our creator. We were created in, through, and for Him. God has redeemed (rescued, ransomed) us through Him and we are his possession by virtue of his saving death and resurrection. He creates in us a new/loyalty, a new *Espirit de Corps*. He is our new being. He initiates new life within us, and seals our belonging to Him. All human existence after Christ must be existence in Christ either to salvation or damnation. Human life is Christ. All humanity is embraced in Christ's redemption. We die in Christ. If we have not died with Christ, we do not live with him. In Christ's choice and our assent, we pass from death to life. All persons on earth until the end of time are in Christ either to redemption or perdition. We live *Anno Domine*.

> ...If one died for all, then all were dead:
> and that he died for all that they which live
> henceforth should not live unto themselves
> but unto him which died for them, and rose again.
> (I Corinthians 5:14, 15 [KJV])

Further texts elucidate the significance of Jesus as Lord:

> No one can call Jesus Lord, except through the Holy Spirit
> (I Corinthians 12:3)

> Why do you call me Lord, Lord and not do my will?
> (Luke 12:46)

To be able to authentically call Jesus Lord is to be captivated by the spirit of his will. The very act of credo is elicited and confirmed by spiritual and ethical reality. Creed, especially in this crucial second article, is something to be lived out. It is something worth living and dying for. It is truth to be tested and promulgated. It is conviction to do battle for. The historic battle that arises over this section of the creed is called the Christological controversy of the first three centuries of what would become the Christian era.

The drama remains profoundly worldly and historical. It is in occupied Palestine, within the Roman Empire, "the mistress of nations," that we receive the intrusion or exclusion of Jesus into the world.

> Born of a woman...born under the law
> to ransom those under the law.
> (Galatians 4:5)

It was "in the fullness of time," at the right moment—the break in cover on the day of evacuating Dunkirk—that the emissary—the lone warrior was sent. The birth and life, suffering and death of Jesus is the decisive battle against the evil that had come to grip the world. He is David come out alone, as representative human against the Philistines and the gargantuan Goliath of wrong in the world. For Augustine it is the decisive battle of history

> Christ died for our sins
> > once and for all,
> > > and, rising from the dead
> > > > dies no more.[275]

Saddam Hussein, it has been argued, in the absolutely absurd Western rhetoric which still kills the children of Iraq, through cruel embargo, was left alive after the Gulf War to rebuild and come back to demand another sacrifice. By contrast in images from Hebrew holy war and Greco-Roman war theory, this Christic victory is final. Against this Terminator I, II, III the stainless mercury adversary cannot suck up the drooping Daliesque christic globules of steel and reform again. This time Satan drops into the white molten tank of eternal dissolution.

Jesus' Gospel and Violence

Before moving into later Christian history we can summarize the military effect of Jesus' gospel. Recent scholars find an aggressive, even violent impulse in that gospel and in the Christian scriptures. This assertive spirit is at the heart of what I call the evangelical commitment. Beneath the dominant tone of magnanimity, exemplified in the irenic mood of the gospel words, the peace premise of the gospels and the pacific theology and ethics of Paul, Michael Desjardin finds this rigorous tendency in the New Testament; its fascination with end-of-the-world-violence, the reality of male domination and the grouping of humanity into the lost "damned" and saved "insiders."[276]

The most virulent if not violent energy released into world history with the gospel of Jesus Christ is the spread of gospel salvation. The primitive Christian community perceives in the resurrection appearances of Jesus, in the experiences of Christ alive in the Pentecost enthusiasm and in the mandate of the Great Commission, an urgent mission to preach the word, to call persons to repentance, and to transform society toward freedom for gospel witness and righteous living. While the evangelization of the world is a benign voluntaristic force, a gentile conversion force ensues which issues ultimately in national conversions such as Armenia (c.300), Constantine (c. 320), Augustine's Theology of compulsion ("compel them to come in"), and the reconquister reclamation of Spain from the Muslim moors.

Desjardin finds the source of gospel aggression in Judaism and in the extrajudaic parentage of Christianity. The assurance of "chosenness" implies misfortune in the unchosen. Ironically this parental father then becomes the castigated even in Gospel texts to "the Jews" or "the Pharisees." Although Judaism generally shuns proselytizing, the spirit that there is "no other salvation" (Acts 4:2) is grounded in Jewish faith. Surprisingly, in light of Jesus' radical passion and the rejection of zealotry, primitive Christianity becomes virulent. The impenetrability and

---

[275] *City of God,* 12.13.
[276] *Peace, Violence and the New Testament,* Sheffield: Sheffield Academic Press, 1987.

resistance of Judaism to the Gospel fueled a conversionist intensity that betrayed an underlying aggression. Desjardin laments:

> Christian missionaries at the end of the first century received as much respect from outsiders as the Jehovah's Witnesses do today when they knock on doors. Given this situation, it is not surprising to find a certain seriousness and desperation to the Christian preaching.[277]

When Christians preach to Jews and Muslims, there is not only amnesia toward Akedah but a frantic violence. Christians believed that they had been given and now possessed the truth. Not only the truth about God and salvation but the truth about human nature and destiny was now known. The proper way of life for persons and nations was now a perceived body of truth constituting

the legitimate cache of a witness to the world—the truthful vision of God—the rightful way of life—a residual trust which is our duty to take to and defend before the world. It also holds the seeds of an illegitimate burden, one which deeply violates those who don't have it.

Jesus gospel, or Abrahamic faith, for that matter, benign and winsome, becomes malign and offensive, when we feel that it is our exclusive possession and not the work of God for all peoples. Stripped of Judaic and Hellenic universality, creed quickly degenerates into crusade. That defensive and offensive posture becomes more virulent when faith is second-hand, doubt-ridden and nominal. A more wholesome faith, truly evangelical, prophetic and psalmic sings:

> ...God is working his purpose out as year proceeds to year
> God is working his purpose out and the time is drawing near
> nearer and nearer draws the time, the time that shall surely be
> when the earth shall be filled with the glory of God as the waters cover
> the sea.

> Hymn "God is Working His Purpose Out,"
> Arthur Campbell Ainger, based on Isaiah 11.

Luther and Calvin

While in the Pauline and Petrine ages, the conversionist spirit prevails. The reformers in a Pauline renaissance find in the second article an impressive victory over the adversary. For Calvin we havenot only been taken captive into sin and are held captive and hostage, we have been killed in the battle, have fallen into death and cannot even hope for, let alone, accomplish our own release. The very knowledge of God, the hope of Terry Waite and Ben Wier for rescue in Lebanon, is gone. The redeemer must come across the land mines and confront, even those that will kill him. But in this agapic death this divine warrior will kill death and in resurrected life he will revive us so that we know

---

[277] Desjardin, Ibid., p. 68.

again who and whose we are. We can take the helicopter rescue from the prison compound.

> ...He has won and delivered me
> that I might be His own
> and live under his Kingdom.[278]

The "tyrants and jailers"[279] have been ousted and Jesus has restored us to his realm.

The man Jesus of Nazareth has been developed by Luther into the Messiah, the only Son of God, our Lord, following the classical Christological formulation. Building on the Christology doctrine of Paul and the church fathers, especially Augustine, Luther articulates a credo "I believe in Christ" that compounds the images of Davidic king, Yahwist Lord, Hellenist soter (warrior savior), medieval knight rescuing the captive princess, and the saint-subduer (*Hagios Georgios*) of the dragons of the world, flesh and the devil. The theatre of this most real drama of life is the struggling soul of the believer.

For Luther, the world still lies in darkness (*finsternis*). Luther was not as serene in Christ's victory as was his *nachfolger*, Johann Sebastian Bach, who saw Christ no longer lying "*in todesbanden*" but "*ressurexit*" and alive in the world. For Luther the world is still full of devils. His cosmos, in this sense, is still medieval, even Christian Romanesque, when, as Shirley Jackson Case says:

> the sky hung low in the ancient world...and traffic was heavy on the highway between heaven and earth. Gods and spirits thickly populated the upper air, where they stood in readines to intervene at any moment in the affairs of mortals. And demonic powers, emerging from the lower world or residents in remote corners of the earth, were a constant menace to human welfare. All nature was alive—alive with supernatural forces.[280]

..."Though this world with devils filled should threaten to undo us" or Thomas Carlyle's better translation:

> ...and were this world all devils o'er,
> and watching to devour us...

or the raw original of "Ein feste Burg"

> *...und wenn die welt voll Teufel wär
> und wollt uns gar verschlingen...*

---

[278] "Tyrannen and Stockmeister," Luther, *Shorter Catechism*. GK 65.2.2.F.
[279] Ibid.
[280] Shirley Jackson Case, *The Origins of Christian Supernaturalism,* (Chicago: University Press), 1946, p. 1.

Luther wrote to Spalatin, 15 August 1521:

> Last Monday, I went hunting for a couple of days to see what that 'bitter-sweet' pleasure of heroes is like. We caught two hares and a few poor partridges—a worthy occupation for men with nothing to do! I theologized even among the snares and the dogs: the pleasure that this spectacle afforded was balanced by the mystery of the misery and pain it also inflicted. It was nothing else than an image of the devil hunting innocent little creatures with his ambushes and his hounds—those ungodly teachers the bishops and the theologians. I was only too conscious of this tragic image of simple and faithful souls. A still more dreadful image followed, when at my insistence we had saved alive a little rabbit. I had it rolled up into the sleeve of my cloak. I moved away some distance, and meanwhile the dogs found the poor creature, bit through the cloak, broke its right leg, choked it and killed it. Even such the fury of the Pope and of Satan, raging to destroy even the souls that have been saved, and heeding naught of my efforts. I have had a surfeit of this kind of hunting. I prefer the more agreeable kind in which bears, wolves, foxes—and all that breed of godless teachers—are pierced with spears and arrows.
>
> Yet it consoles me that here to hand is an allegory of salvation. Hares and innocent creatures are captured by men not by bears, wolves, hawks of prey and such like Bishops and theologians: to be swallowed up by the latter means hell, but by the former heaven!
>
> I'm writing all this with my tongue in my cheek—don't miss the point that you courtiers, so keen on the chase, will yourselves be wild beasts in paradise, and even Christ, the supreme hunter, will have his hands full to catch and save you! While you are playing around hunting, you are being made game of yourselves…
>
> WARTBURG, Latin in W.A. Br.W., II, 380 *et seq.*[281]

Luther dwells on the passage in Luke (22:53) where Jesus quells the violent protective impulses of his followers who drew the sword and wounded the ear of the high Priest's servant. He healed the ear and said:

> Have you come for me with swords and clubs as if I were a thief?
>
> I was with you every day in the temple…
> But this house belongs to you and to the power of darkness

Luther inherited a cosmology of perpetual warfare in the world. The unholy trinity of evil forces (world, flesh, devil) which dated back at least to St. Anthony of the Egyptian desert was now decisively contested by the blood of Christ, the sacrifice (Eucharist) and the exorcizing power of the triune Name in word and sacrament. Yet their terror and threat stood, encouraging souls to cling to the safety of Christ's citadel. Part of this ethos was to project demons onto

---

[281] p. 73, 74 Rupp.

various actual adversaries like Jews, Turks, peasants and the Pope. Even partners in faith; Calvinists, Zwinglians and the Anabaptists were not spared.

Today the stark terror-rescue theology of Luther lacks currency since, for most, the sense of accusation, damnation, fall and imprisonment to sin is missing, Yet, as we will see in our next section on the anthropology of the second article, the Augustinian view of the human condition is being revived after the failure of the progressive age of Enlightenment—which stressed the inherent goodness of humanity. On the eve of Pearl Harbor, just four months after the German invasion of Russia, the columnist Walter Lippman could write:

> The modern skeptical world has been taught for some 200 years a conception of human nature in which the reality of evil, so well known to the ages of faith, has been discounted. Almost all of us grew up in an environment of such easy optimism that we can scarcely know what is meant, though our ancestors knew it well, by the satanic will. We shall have to recover this forgotten but essential truth—along with so many others that we lost when, thinking we were enlightened and advanced, we were merely shallow and blind.[282]

In the *Institutes* and in the Geneva catechism Calvin takes a cue from Luther and organizes the explanation of the second article around Christ's three fold office of prophet, priest and king. In each of these offices rich biblical metaphors are unfolded in a grand design of discernment, mediation and lordship as Christ redeems his own. Yet a serene and victorious Christology was hard to come by. The nuances of Christological Theology show the subtleties of the definitions and meanings which evolved.

The Christological Controversy

Why such a fuss? Why go to war, why lose your life for such a trifle? As the Roman officer must have said to the aged Polycarp before his martyr death, "Come on now, what harm can there be in just saying that Caesar is Lord?" How did *Kurios Iaesus*, that name, ecome a life or death credo? Surprising that those who know the name YAHWEH and the third command should be surprised. At Nicea, surely it's only an iota of difference, or is it? Why have your Achilles tendon severed and one eye gouged out? For two little words? Let us trace the outlines of the battlements of this war, a war much more one of conviction and idea than of sword and shield, but one far more decisive and determinative of the course of history than the outcome of any battlefield.

Born of the Virgin Mary: Natus ex Maria virgine

The hint is now made clear. God has become a person. The first movement of the second article in some sense is an extension of the God the father theology. Jesus...God's son...our Lord. Now the radical meaning—historical, worldly, human—becomes clear: conceived by the Holy Spirit, born of the

---

[282] Ronald Steel, *Walter Lippmann and the American Century,* Boston: Little, Brown, 1980, p. 390-391.

Virgin Mary. There is still a mood of spirit and transcendence, of course. The descent of the divine into human flesh is the longest conceivable journey. But the message is one of humanity. The misplaced *theotokos* (mother of God) controversy and the perennial dispute about the virgin birth both reflect the intellectual offense of the God-man notion and the charge, that borders on heresy, to say it isn't so.

My teacher at Princeton Seminary, John Hick, was eventually censured by the New Brunswick Presbytery, for denying the "virgin birth." Hick's problem, as an astute theologian, was to believe too firmly in the incarnation. Incarnation confounds our incessant spirituality, our contempt for earth in the name of heaven. The point of the evolving of Jesus tradition in the apostolic community, the tradition that eventually found creedal formulation in the second article, was the seminality, natality, the humanity of Jesus. Again incarnation and creation are strange doctrines only to those who forget that they are Jews. See the formidable *The Human God* (Walter Wink, 2002).

The concepts of incarnation in the general (especially Eastern Orthodox and Protestant) Christian tradition and the doctrines of Mary

- Virgin birth
- Immaculate conception (free form original sin)
- Assumption

are being explored in creative ways in the twentieth century. In an age of muted iconoclasm various films have depicted the life of Jesus in profoundly secular terms. *Jesus of Montreal* and *The Gospel According to Matthew* are examples. The affinity of Jesus with the oppressed has been drawn by this media as well as in the novels and poetry of writers from W.B. Yates, and Lawrence Ferlingetti to Nikos Kazantzakis. Mary and Jesus are actors in a present drama of hope and revolution where:

> ...the mighty will be brought low and the lowly will be lifted up.
> (Luke 1:46-55; I Samuel 2:1-10)

A wave of historians are also renewing an inquiry into the historical and Jewish Jesus. E.P. Sanders, Geza Vermes, Dominic Crossan and James Charlesworth, among others, have drawn colorful portraits of the human, historical Jesus. Another circle of wonderful writers, including Philip Yancy and Tom Wright have jumped on the "Jesus" wagon and sketched more traditional and evangelical portraits.

What has this Jesus renaissance to do with the motif of this study—creed and crusade? The message is mixed and we will review it closely in the upcoming section of the cross of Christ—*Passus sub pontio pilato, crucifixus est.* Suffice it to say now, that both humanistic and theistic treatments of Jesus stress both evangelical fervor and gentle pacifism.

Regarding Mary, there has been an intriguing deflation among Roman Catholics and inflation among Protestants as we seek an ecumenical convergence. Today as Lutherans and Catholics, for example, have approved a major joint document on "Justification by faith" under the auspices of our *Institute Oikumenique* in Strasbourg, France, both sides accent a central place for Mary in Christian devotion and esteem. She is chief among the members of the church, the only Christian thus far totally glorified, etc. As prepartions are being made for a significant rapprochement between Lutherans and Catholics, on the order of Rome's reunification with Eastern orthodoxy, this intensification of both the human and God-chosen qualities of Miriam, Jesus' mother are intriguing. The creed records this respectful pause—"born of the virgin (Jungfrau: Luther) Maria."

If "son" and "Lord" at the second article's head in addressed to the Hebrew, "conceived" and "born" is addressed to the Hellene. Here, word is uttered against the mythical and mystical gnostic, the spiritualist, the asensualist. In later christological phrasing, this "very God of very God" is now "bone of our bone, flesh of our flesh." Simultaneous and synthetic Godhood and manhood is the message. Karl Barth summarizes:

> True God: *conceptus de spiritus sancto*
> True man: *natus ex Maria Virgine*
> (*Credo*, p. 64, 65)

In the words of Barth's student and successor at Basel, Jan Milic Lochman,

> The ancient church now conducted its battle against monophysitism on two fronts—the enemy above and the enemy below.[283]

The question which now forces itself is why did God become human? Why did word become flesh? Something must have happened in the body of humanity which kept it from God's companionship. Some warfare, alienation, oppression and captivity must have set in the being of humanity (*Menschensein*: Barth). This ontological alienation, this disloyalty and digression from our true self, this rebellion, this flight and fight, necessitated the reenaction of Exodus or in Christian terms, Easter. The universal consummation of God's liberation of Israel and the concomitant covenant of life were sustained. Human disregard for and negation of this Adamic, Noahic and Mosaic covenant of life with life brought death to humanity and danger to the world. Jesus reenacts exodus and exile—God's holy war for and against Israel. For the sake of humanity and the world, Jesus becomes the enemy of God. In Easter, Jesus absorbs and thereby conquers the wrath of God—the cumulative burden of human malevolence.

---

[283] *The Faith We Confess*. Philadelphia: Fortress, 1984, p. 105.

This plight of humanity and the world is the presupposition of this clause in the creed. The full exposition of the second article then follows, with the retelling of the Jesus story of the apostolic preaching. He was born—crucified—suffered—died—was buried—rose again—ascended. In this death-defeating death and life-giving revival, Jesus ameliorated the human condition—healed the irreparable wound—made the creature one again with the creator. A war would now ensue throughout world history and the history of nature (Weizsacker) to extend the Gospel liberation and Gospel ethic to all of humanity and all of creation forevermore, in order that redemption might be complete (*TIKKUN OLAM*).

An Enduring Theology of Peace and Punishment

"He is our peace—who has broken down the dividing wall of hostility"
(Ephesians 2:14ff)

The community of the crucified and risen one in history is commissioned to perpetuate an ethical and political theology in the life of the world. The two sides of this societal theology are peace and punishment. The grounding and sustenance of good and the censure and containment of evil are the two faces of the coinage of Christ's realm. Traditionally the Churches' vocation has been conceived of as purveying the peace of God meaning the substance of reconciliation and healing (Shalom) into the life of the world. The state is to bear the sword, that instrumentality also undergirded by the spiritual—ethical conviction and commission of the people. The theology of punishment manifests itself in society in policies ranging from war-making and war-prevention to the legal system, criminal justice, incarceration, and capital punishment.

The broader social and political spirit of pursuing good and resisting harm manifests itself in economic, educational, employment and ecological policies, as these provide the salience and substance of preventing harms and maximizing the options for life-fulfillment among the citizens. This dual imperative is the root impulse of religious social ethics. In broadest construal establishing such peace and effecting such judgment is the enactment of the reign of God in the world.

The work of truth, justice and peace may involve force and coercion. Federal troops must be sent to Little Rock, Arkansas to insure the safety of black students achieving the court's order of school desegregation. Iraq's incursion into Kuwait must be challenged. But the opacities, hesitancies, ambivalences and political colorations of justice are pronounced and grievous. All human justice is imperfect. The Israeli government confiscates Arab lands in East Jerusalem with impunity. Mr. Karadic, an indicted war criminal, moves freely in Bosnia. Mr. Milosevic ridicules the jurisdiction of The Hague war crimes court. Justice is always severely refracted, even misdirected. Therefore the necessity endures of always intertwining punishment, peace, mercy and justice. That divine justice is mercy and mercy is justice grounds this morning's decisions in

South Chicago to grant ministers one million dollars to create correctional, penitential and reformational programs for youths convicted of crimes in lieu of dumping them in the states' overcrowded prison facilities.

Strife and warfare now and throughout history is a process of "filling up the sufferings of Christ" (I Peter 1,4). The travail of righteousness continues throughout history as Christ and the Holy Spirit confront the "principalities and powers of evil" (Romans 8:38, Ephesians 6:12). The inner theological meaning of political and military history is therefore the extension of justice. Forever throughout history there will be holy war (often not consonant with what we call Holy War) and the holy waging of peace. One example from modern war history is the American Civil War—though Abraham Lincoln was correct in his Second Inaugural Address, saying that God's judgments in the war were inscrutable, still war was the enaction of God's justice.

> One eighth of the whole population were colored slaves, not distributed generally over the Union, but localized in the Southern part of it. These slaves constituted a peculiar and powerful interest. All knew that this interest was, somehow, the cause of the war. To strengthen, perpetuate, and extend this interest was the object for which the insurgents would rend the Union, even by war; while the government claimed no right to do more than to restrict the territorial enlargement of it. Neither party expected for the war, the magnitude, or the duration, which it has already attained. Neither anticipated that the *cause* of the conflict might cease with, or even before, the conflict itself should cease. Each looked for an easier triumph, and a result less fundamental and astounding. Both read the same Bible, and pray to the same God; and each invokes His aid against the other. It may seem strange that any men should dare to ask a just God's assistance in wringing the bread from the sweat of other men's faces; but let us judge not that we be not judged. The prayers of both could not be answered; that of neither has been answered fully. The Almighty has His own purposes. "Woe unto the world because of offenses! For it must needs be that offences come; but woe to that man by whom the offence cometh!" If we shall suppose that American Slavery is one of those offenses which, in the providence of God, must needs come, but which, having continued through His appointed time, He now wills to remove, and that He gives both North and South, this terrible war, as the woe due to those by whom the offence came, shall we discern therein any departure from those divine attributes which the believers in a Living God always ascribe to him? Fondly we do hope—fervently do we pray—that this mighty scourge of war may speedily pass away. Yet, if God wills that it continue, until all the wealth piled by the bond-man's two hundred and fifty years of unrequited toil shall be sunk, and until every drop of blood drawn with the lash shall be paid by another drawn with the sword, as was said three thousand years ago, so still it must be said "the judgments of the Lord, are true and righteous altogether."

> With malice toward none; with charity for all; with firmness in the right, as God gives us to see the right, let us strive on to finish the work we are in;to bind up the nation's wounds; to care of him for shall have borne the battle, and for his widow, and his orphan—to do all which may achieve and cherish a just, and a lasting peace, among ourselves, and with all nations.

466

Lincoln's magnanimity and humility show us again that the second article is as much about human nature as it is about the divine. The doctrine (God became man) discloses both true God and true man. The great christological controversies across the ages are as much about human power and prerogative as they are about God's nature and work. Instances of human arrogation and abrogation of power, constant themes in military and creedal history, are therefore bound into the anthropological christology. The appearance of the kenotic Christ, where one omnipotent appears as a servant (Philippians 2) leads to a more modest appraisal of human power.

An excellent example of a war episode which illumines this exaltation motif is found in American history, in the span of two decades from the end of WWII to the war in Vietnam. Tracing the trajectory of the tension between Truman and McArthur, The Kennan report through to the Ridgeway doctrine illustrate the oscillating sense of valuing power and humility as ethical norms.

At the conclusion of WWII George F. Kennan - *Charge de Affaires* in Moscow - who would become architect of Truman's doctrines of international power and war ethics and the powerful geopolitical doctrine of "containment," noted in the American character a "legalistic—moralistic approach to international problems and a "rhetoric" and "habitual patterns of eschatology".[284] In his view this militant, triumphalist spirit would better yield to a more prudent, pragmatic view which sought not the extermination and eradication of enemies (the evil empire) but the balance and coexistence of powers in the world.

President Harry Truman, it will be remembered, exhibited the same political realism accenting "defense only" and nonprovocation which came into conflict with that more imperialistic "finish-the-job" creed of General Douglas McArthur. At the end of WWII McArthur would preside over the unconditional surrender of Japan. In Korea he would seek to extend American conquest deeply into the heart of communism. We should not only penetrate into the North of Korea, but into the land of China. He lived out the same patriotic ethic expressed by General Ridgeway's statement to the Eighth Army at the dawn of the Korean War on January 21, 1951:

> What are we fighting for? The real issues are whether the power of Western Civilization, as God has permitted it to flower in our own beloved land, shall defy and defeat communism…the issue is… whether communism or individual freedom shall prevail.[285]

The confrontation of capitalism and communism, freedom and socialism is ultimately the tension between two readings of the incarnation, Christic

---

[284] James A. Thomas, *Holy War.* New Rochelle, NY: Arlington House, 1973, p. 41.
[285] Matthew B. Ridgeway, *The Korean War,* New York, 1967, p. 264-265.

individuality or Chistic commonality. The confrontation continues into our own time as the Pope visits one of the last communist nations on earth—Cuba.

Here are my notes from that event:

January 22, 1998—Jose Martin International Airport, Cuba

- Fidel Castro condemns the Conqistadores' colonialism in Cuba and the suppression of scientific knowledge. He calls for an end of the present economic genocide (American Embargo) and for equality and the equal distribution of wealth "which we have achieved in Cuba." These values should be made universal.

- Pope John Paul XXII then speaks: "may this land by strengthened in freedom, reciprocal confidence, freedom for the justice and peace which belongs to all especially the poor, the sick, and the underprivileged...may Cuba open itself to all its possibilities (human rights including freedom of religion) and may the world open itself (end embargo) to Cuba.

- Both agree that justice requires the end of the accelerating imperialistic domination of the rich north over the poor south.

Throughout recent political history we find this oscillation between concepts of lordly and servile humanity—the legacy of the second article.

The Pope also began with bold and provocative proclamations. 500 years ago (Christopher Columbus) the cross of Christ was planted on this land celebrated as "the most beautiful on earth." What of the Christ of the *Conquistadores*? Are those 500 years years of grace or disgrace? Castro speaks of the disgrace—colonialism and suppression of science. Pope John Paul XXII celebrates the Gospel of grace, liberation and justice. Brutal inhuman arrogance and socialistic harm or Christic humanization—the verdict is still out.

The War of Body vs. Spirit: Christ and Sex
The clauses in the creed "conceived...and born" connote another battle that has marked Christendom; the battle of sex and the sexes. In 309 C.E., Bishops and Presbyters traveled the Roman roads to a basilica in Grenada (Alvira) in southern Spain. Here they formulated eighty-one canons, the first in the history of Christianity. Their burden is human sexuality. A decade after Armenia became the first Christian kingdom, two decades before Constantine consecrated the vast Roman Empire we have this glimpse of the true holy war going on in church and culture. (see S. Laechli, *Power and Sexuality*) For two and one half centuries profound strife ensued over the most profound question about human existence—who is God and who is the human being? Is the human person—in body and sexuality, in life and death, a natural spirit, self-sufficient, and ultimately mortal? Or is the person a divine soul, contingent and destined to

468

eternal life? The thought-war on these matters is intense throughout Christian history. What is normative and aberrant sexuality? Can priests marry? Can women be priests? Must they be celibate? What about gays and lesbians? At the turn of the millennium scandal shakes the Roman Catholic Church as these matters coalesce. The issue of sexuality lingers beneath all theological views however passionate or dispassionate the expression. They were lively in the formations of the creed and in all of its succession. They remain provocative and political today. If there is today something of a war of women against religion and the church it is historically wellgrounded and understandable.

Suffered under Pontius Pilate: Passus sub Pontio Pilato

Warfare is suffering. The agony is born by the innocents. Women and children, the old and weak, die and starve. Human power in the world is also given to prevent suffering and to punish its perpetrators. The full humanity of Jesus is exemplified in his suffering and is accented in this clause of the second article. The suffering of humanity is gathered into the cross of Christ and transformed to a new level of meaning. Redemptive suffering is the war of the lamb.

A series of texts from the Epistles unfolds this theological meaning:

> I consider that the sufferings of this present time are not worth comparing with the glory about to be revealed to us, for the creation waits with eager longing for the revealing of the children of God; for the creation was subjected to futility, not of its own will but by the will of the one who subjected it, in hope that the creation itself will be set free from its bondage to decay and will obtain the freedom of the glory of the children of God. We know that the whole creation has been groaning in labor pains until now; and not only the creation, but we ourselves, who have the first fruits of the Spirit, groan inwardly while we wait for adoption, the redemption of our bodies. For in hope we were saved. Now hope that is seen is not hope. For who hopes for what he has seen? But if we hope for what we do not see, we wait for it with patience.
> (Romans 8:18-25)

> For just as the sufferings of Christ are abundant for us, so also our consolation is abundant through Christ. If we are being afflicted, it is for your consolation; if we are being consoled it is for your consolation, which you show when you patiently endure the same sufferings that we are also suffering our hope for you is unshaken; for we know that as you share in our sufferings, so also you share in our consolation.
> (2 Corinthians 1:5-7)

> Yet whatever gains I had, these I have come to regard as loss because of Christ. More than that, I regard everything as loss because of the surpassing value of knowing Christ Jesus my Lord. For his sake I have suffered the loss of all things, and I regard them as rubbish, in order that I may gain Christ and be found in him, not having a righteousness of my own that comes from God based on faith. I want to know Christ and the power of his resurrection and the

sharing of his sufferings by becoming like him in his death, if somehow I may attain the resurrection form the dead.
(Philippians 3:10)

It was fitting that God, for whom and through whom all things exist, in bringing many children to glory, should make the pioneer of their salvation perfect through sufferings.
(Hebrews 2:10)

Slaves, accept the authority of your masters with all deference, not only those who are kind and gentle but also those who are harsh. For it is a credit to you if, being aware of God, you endure pain while suffering unjustly. If you endure when you are beaten for doing wrong, what credit is that? But if you endure when you do right and suffer for it, you have God's approval. For to this you have been called, because Christ also suffered for you, leaving you an example, so that you should follow in his steps

"He committed no sin, and no deceit was found in his mouth."

When he was abused, he did not return abuse; when he suffered, he did not threaten; but he entrusted himself to the one who judges justly. He himself bore our sins in his body on the cross, so that, free form sins, we might live for righteousness; by his wounds you have been healed. For you were going astray like sheep, but now you have returned to the shepherd and guardian of your souls. (I Peter 2:18-25)

Christic Suffering

The saga of personal human suffering in life and death points beyond to transcending theological meaning. The transcending axis of suffering then devolves back on the world.

Human history and the history of the world is a process of filling up the suffering of Christ. The conquest of evil in the creation is the meaning of the drama of redemption. Gregory of Nazianzus put it starkly: "What has not been assumed has not been redeemed." (Epistle c1) Only in full humanity, where Jesus has completely assumed our humanity, can salvation be affected.

In Dorothy Sayers' play, *The Man Born to be King*, she tells the story of that fateful night of the hearing before Pilate and of a dream experienced by Pilate's wife. She intervened with her husband to spare Jesus' life because of a dream in which she heard an unending chorus of all humanity reciting in all languages, the words of the creed..."Suffered under Pontius Pilate..." By man, Pilate, in this case, sin and suffering comes into the world. By this new man Jesus as Christ sin and suffering is absorbed into a redemptive strife and conquest by Godself. The contest or temptation abroad in the world is paradigmatically signaled by the suffering—death-resurrection experience of Abraham/Isaac's Akedah.

The insistence on naming Pontius Pilate—a vivid historical tag—retained in all major early creeds—signifies that Christ's suffering was a concrete political act. Here the human evil of the world squares off against divine peace and justice in the realm of public affaires. Pilate decrees the death of Jesus from his public office. Heretofore and hereafter human oppression and suffering must be seen as assault on the crucified One. It is amplification of the agony of the crucified God. The church militant, Christ's living body in history, like the martyr church, now at home the church triumphant, therefore wages wars against such evil. Most often the battle is passive and non-resistant, as the Lord's contention before Pilate. Since Christ suffered lifelong and his sufferings endurethroughout history, we remember his constant love in the face of constant adversity.

Question 37 of Heidelberg Catechism reads:

> What do you understand by this little word 'suffered'? and its answer: That all of the time of his life here on this earth but especially at the end thereof, he bore in body and soul the wrath of God against the sin of the whole human race so that by his suffering...he might redeem our body and soul.[286]

John Donne captures the same meaning in his Christmas sermon of 1626:

> The whole life of Christ was a continual passion; Others die Martyrs, but Christ was born a Martyr.[287]

Cosmic Suffering

Suffering is Christic and cosmic. Suffering is both sickness and oppression. It can manifest in the personal or corporate body. Suffering always involves a disequilibrium, imbalance, asymmetry of power. Jesus had the power to overwhelm the devil and impress the world in the wilderness temptations. He accepted the limitation. True conquest, moral in tone, must be transformative not magical.

> If Jesus had wanted for any mean thing—a star in the sky or a
> bird on the wing—or all of God's angels in heaven for to sing—
> He surely could have it for He was the King.
>
> I wonder as I wander...
> ("I Wonder as I Wander," an old Appalachian spiritual)

With Caiaphas and Pilate He again places himself at the mercy of prevailing power, "You would have no power over me were it not given you from above."

---

[286] Arthur Cochran, *Reformed Confessions of the Sixteenth Century.* Philadelphia: Westminster Press, 1966, p. 311.
[287] John Donne, *The Sermons of John Donne,* V.7. Berkeley: University of California Press, 1953, p. 279.

As Colin Ferguson, the crazed killer on the Long Island railroad faces his victims, one man who had been shot shouts as he is constrained by police, "I've suffered for 15 months. If I had five minutes with you, I'd show you what suffering is."

The law restrains unleashed and asymmetric power. A gun in the hand gives a scrawny, insecure punk power over the basketball giant, Ben Wilson, as he guns him down on a Chicago street.

If America or the free world could have intervened preventively in Bosnia, Rwanda, or Zaire or Kosovo, some of the immensity of human suffering might have been eliminated.

The absurd position of protecting Iraqi Kurds against Iraq and exposing them to Turkish aggression shows the terrible consequence of impotence in the powerful.

...our hands are tied the asymmetry of power

Suffering? What has it to do with the good and evil of war?

The prevention, amelioration and alleviation of suffering and perhaps punishment for perpetrators of suffering is the justification for war. The imposition and amplification of suffering is the evil of war.

Jesus suffered for the sin of the world. His overt and ignominious suffering expressed the temporal patience of God—a passionate, patient (suffering) for His creature throughout time and space. God allows his only begotten son to be given over (*Paradokein*) to the satanic power of the world which is the temporal and spatial amalgam of human sin.

Suffering and the First Christic War for Right: The Saga of Persecution

I. Early Church

I. Executions in Jerusalem Church: Stephen, James, the Apostle, James, the Just.

II. Roman Persecutions c. 60 A.D.

III. Charge of Atheism, Domitian (81-96)

IV. Trajan (98-117), Igantius, Polycarp—those who confess that they are Christians and refuse to sacrifice are to be executed.

V. Justin Martyr and Pothinus. In February 156 (the year has been the object of some controversy) Marcus Aurelius regarded the Christian

472

contempt of death as obstinate and theatrical. In 177 there was a violent anti-Christian outbreak at Lyon, in France.

- Perpetua and Felicity (203 or 202), Carthage.

- Alexander Severus (222-235), an edict was directed against the leaders of the church, ordering them to be put to death.

- Decian Persecution. Fabian was put to death at Rome on January 20, 250.

- Origen was arrested (probably at Caesarea), Gallus (251-253), renewed the persecution whin a plague ravished the empire. Valerian (257)

- Gallienus became sole ruler (260-268). He immediately put an end to the persecution, restoring to the Christians their places of worship

- Diocletian. Sol Invictus.

- Diocletian (284-305). In 303, four edicts were aimed at the extirpation of Christianity in the empire. The first was issued on Feb. 23, 303 and published the following day. It ordered the destruction of churches, the burning of sacred books, the cessation of religious gatherings, and the removal of civil rights and honors from those in high positions. The second edict enjoined the imprisonment of clerics; the third provided for their release if they would sacrifice and their execution for refusal to do so. The fourth edict required all Christians to offer sacrifice. These edicts were carried out with great severity throughout the empire, except in Gaul and Britain, which were governed by Constantius I. In the Province of Palestine alone there were 84 known martyrs, and in the Thebaid in Egypt there were mass executions of up to 1000 Christians at a time. Many of the most famous Roman martyrs are to be dated from this period.

- In February 313, Constantine I and Licinius—declared universal toleration generally known as the Convention or Edict (agreement) of Milan. In 324 war broke out between co-emperors. Licinius was defeated and executed, and the persecution was thus brought to a close.

- Julian the Apostate (361-363) initiated a pagan revival.

- Sapor II (310-380), urged on by Persian priests, began a severe anti-Christian persecution. Thousands perished in general massacres, including Simeon, Bishop of Seleucia (Sozemen, Hist. Eccl. 2.9-14). After a period of respite, the persecution was renewed by Bahram V (420-438). In 422 he made a treaty with Theodosius II guaranteeing liberty of conscience to the Christians, but he continued to put individual Christians to death. There were further persecutions under

Yazdgard II (438-457), Chodoes I (531-579) and Chosores II (590-628).

- Ulfilas (c. 311-383).

- Athanaric, a pagan Visigoth, began a persecution of the Christians that lasted for several years. Visigoths frequently plundered churches and murdered bishops and priests during their invasions of Italy, Gaul, and Spain in the 5th and 6th centuries.

- Vandals were the most hostile to the Catholics.

War against the Eradication of the Presence

In sum a central thesis of this book is that religious communities in general, but especially Judaism and Christianity in particular, have at times erroneously assumed that God's presence will be obliterated from the earth if their faith fails to survive. They therefore go on the warpath as preemptive strike. There is a certain truth to this felt nihilistic complex and while there is an urgency to the Jewish tasks of Torah transmission and Christian catechesis, the survival of the faith or more profoundly, the Shekinah—the very presence of the divine on earth—is not at our charge or discharge. Various Biblical promises assure God's enduring presence despite our efforts:

The Lord's Word will stand forever .
(Isaiah 40:08)

Upon this Rock (Peter's confession) I will build my church and
the gates of hell will not prevail against it.
(Matthew 16-18)

Yet war is witness (martyrdom) as the name is invoked and persecution ensues. The greatest agony of history that this thesis invokes has been the conviction in Palestinian Judaism of Jesus' era that the Christian movement must be obliterated (despite the noble counsel of Gamaliel… " if this plan is of God you will not be able to stop it…" (Acts 5:39). The mutual excommunication eventually transmutes the historic anti-Judaism in Christianity into virulent, genocidal anti-Semitism in 20th Century Christian Europe.

Just as Roland de Vaux contended that "Holy War" in Canaan was a survival struggle of the Isreali tribes, so the martyrial strife of early Christianity sought to survive the exterminating will of contemporaneous Judaism and Roman persecution.

2. Medieval Period

Saxons, Normans, and Slavs struck particular destruction on the Church. The letters to the Thessalonians, the Peter letters and Hebrews, all portray a profound warfare occurring in the world as persons choose allegiance—to Christ or to the state powers which find their credo a threat. Augustine also places the saga of persecution at a central point of his own analysis of the meaning of creed and crusade.

When we review the anthropological signification and military ramification of this part of the second article we will see the broad parameters of meaning which flow from the simple clause...*passus sub Pontio Pilato.*

Crucified, Buried, Descended: Crucifixus, mortuus et Sepultus

Incursus

I sit here in my office in Strasbourg, in Alsace, France, just on the French side of the Rhine and the land of Germany. Though a Calvinist myself, I am educated a Lutheran with Helmut Thielicke at Hamburg. Strasbourg in a city that bridges Luther's theology of the cross and Calvin's theology of glory all against the background of French Catholicism's eucharistical/national theology. But where do I stand? For Luther the theology of the cross was as close to the essence of his witness as was the authority of the Word of God or the doctrine of justification by grace through faith alone. *Crucifixus...* The heart of the Gospel is that Jesus' death by the grotesque mode of crucifixion (eventually banned by Constantine) was not a sad and absurd end to the Jesus story but its central meaning. The crucifixion was also at the heart of the thesis we are unfolding, namely that the strife of sin and salvation, death and life, defeat and victory— the AKEDIC logic - mark church militant as it moves toward church triumphant.

The Apostles' Creed rushes from "born of the virgin Mary" to "suffers and was crucified under Pontius Pilate." It's as if there is nothing in-between. The Apostle Paul is the author of the *theologia crucis*. In Paul there is precious little about Jesus' life, his miracles and teachings, even the culminating events of his life. The cross and the saving significance of Christ's death and resurrection totally consume "The Apostle."

> Far be it from me, he writes
> to glory except...in the cross of Christ.
> (Galatians 6:14)

and a majestic hymn faithfully echoes the words:

> ...forbid it not that I should boast save in the death of Christ, my God.[288]

Crucifixion is a doctrine that involves myself, Jesus Christ, the church, God and the world. Paul continues:

> ...by the cross of our Lord Jesus Christ the world has been crucified to me and I to the world.

---

[288] "When I Survey the Wondrous Cross." Isaac Watts, 1707.

The two clauses in the creed on suffering and crucifixion are linked in Christian perception. Not only did Jesus suffer in the hours-long harassment, the seizure, the ridicule, the imprisonment, the interrogation, the flogging, the torture and the VIA DOLOROSA, he suffered as foreshadowed in Isaiah 53, as the innocent, silent akedic lamb of God whose suffering was compounded because it was vicarious.

He was wounded for our transgressions

He was bruised for our iniquities.

The evangelists (Matthew 8:17, Acts 8:26-39) prompted, I must believe, by Jesus' self-consciousness and the uncompromising vocation he was living out, drew on the Isaianic image of the suffering messianic servant and Abraham's sacrifice of Isaac to comprehend the Christ-event. Like Grünewald's grotesque, but magnificent *Issenhiemer Triptrych* in the *Musea D'Unterdenlinder* in Colmar, France, Christ is pictured as a pierced and pocked (leper?) bruised and beaten, an ignominious criminal. So grotesque was the scene that

...we could not bear to look at him. (Isaiah 53:2, 3)

Martin Hengel has shown with brutal candor the horror of the cross:

> Crucifixion as a penalty was remarkably widespread in antiquity. It appears in various forms among numerous peoples of the ancient world even among the Greeks...It was and remained a political and military punishment. While among the Persians and Carthaginians it was imposed primarily on high officials (remember Polycrates) and commanders, as on rebels. Among the Romans it was inflicted above all on lower classes, i.e. slaves, violent criminals and the unruly elements in rebellious provinces, not least in Judaea. The chief reason for its use was its allegedly supreme efficacy as a deterrent, it was, of course, carried out publically...It was usually associated with other forms of torture, including at least flogging...By the public display of a naked victim at a prominent place—at a crossroads, in the theatre on high ground, at the place of his crime—crucifixion also represented his uttermost humiliation, which had a numinous dimension to it...[289]

Dominic Crossan in his *Jesus: A Revolutionary Biography* entitles one chapter: The "Dogs Beneath the Cross and a Corpse for the Wild Beasts."

> What exactly made crucifixion so terrible? The three supreme Roman penalties were the cross, fire and the beasts. What make them supreme was not just their inhuman cruelty or their public dishonor but the fact that there might be nothing left to bury at the end. That bodily destruction was involved in being cast into the fire or thrown to the beasts is obvious enough. But what we often

---

[289] *Crucifixion in the Ancient world and theFolly of the Message of the Cross*, Philadelphia: Fortress Press, 1977.

forget about crucifixion is that the carrion crow and scavenger dog respectively croak above and growl below the dead or dying body...[290]

In the cross all of the searing power of the world is leveled against all the sinless innocence of Christ, the sinful variance of humanity and the searching goodness of God. Though we are told the sky darkened and the earth quaked and the temple veil was ripped asunder, the power of evil had its day and the eerie silence and defeat of Salvador Dali's crucifixion hangs over Golgotha. Yet joined to the energy of Easter the cross assumes a power that will be called "the power of God," John of Damascus would say

> ...because of the might of God, that is, his victory over death, has been revealed through it.
> (The Orthodox Faith 4.11)

From this ignominious humiliation—victory? How absurd! Yet in the cosmic battle geography of the Christian tradition—starting with the New Testament—all of the anti-God, anti-human forces on earth have been decisively gathered, defeated and dismantled at Calvary. In his classic study, *Christus Victor*, Gustaf Aulén contends that the cross signaled

- God's invasion of enemy territory
- the miraculous duel (*mirabile duellum*) of the representative warriors Jesus and Satan (remember David and Goliath) and the
- defeat of the captor and release from oppression of captive humanity.[291]

The military metaphor will forever mark Christian history especially with its necessity of identifying the enemy(ies) and its implied triumphalism. Both tendencies will often prove to trouble the church and society. The wrong enemies will be designated and innocent bystanders will be caught in the crossfire. But it is the juxtaposition of cross and victory that is most amazing. The image becomes one of the royal king, the omnipotent Lord reducing himself to weakness and conquerability in order to allow himself to be killed. But in the cruel death is hidden victory for it is received vicariously for all of humanity (and creation) so that evil's destructive power is satiated as the centrifugal weight of human crime is reversed and God's justice is satisfied (Anselm).

Aulén traces the theological (creedal) history of the *Christus Victor* rendition of Christ's work.

---

[290] Dominic Crossan, *Jesus: A Revolutionary Biography,* San Francisco: Harper 1993, p. 126, 127.
[291] Christus Victor: *An Historical Study of the Three Main Types of Idea of Atonement,* New York: MacMillan, 1969, p. 4-7.

The "dramatic" view of the atonement is one where the theme is conflict and victory ...*Christus Victor* fights and triumphs over the evil powers of the world.

Paul sees Christ liberating humanity from the bondage and tyranny of the law and the sin and death that the law exemplifies. Death is ..."the last enemy to be destroyed." (1 Corinthians 15:26).

These "hostile forces": include "principalities, powers, thrones, dominions (Galatians 1:4, Colossians 2:15) Christ triumphed over these on the cross.

When Christ shall have put "all enemies under his feet" (Hebrews 10:13, I Corinthians 15:25) he will deliver the kingdom to the father (I Corinthians 15:24ff)

In this fourth century addendum to the old Roman Creed "descent into hell" is inserted to retain a critical dimension of Jesus' humanity and divinity. In suffering, execution, death, burial and descent into hell, he experiences the full power of separation from God. Hell is the absence of God's presence—the loss of fellowship and salvation. In death we lose the conviviality of God who is life. In hell we lose the heavenly companion. In descent into hell Jesus endures this human fate brought about by sin. He sees it through. The meaning of descent into hell for Luther is Jesus' agony of conscience. Yet God would not allow his Holy One to see corruption. (Psalm 16:10, Acts 2:27).

- In the gospels and epistles Christ confronts the captor of the world and ransoms his own (Mark 10:45; Ephesians 1:7; II Timothy 2:6; Hebrews 9:12; Revelation 1:5)

- The world that lieth in the evil one (1John 5:19) is thrown down and cast out (John 12:31)

- Jesus contended with the unclean spirits (Mark 3:22ff)

- Though all of this adversarial terrain is on the existential plane it is played against the actual physical background of sickness and death and the occupying Roman Empire. The biblical message is therefore one of spiritual victory but also of coming physical and historical victory.

- Irenaeus (the peace man of Lyon) offers the classic exposition of this view when he asks "*Ut quid enim descendebat?*" (Why did Christ come down from heaven?) and answers in very natural and physical terms that he came to make us divine and immortal.

- "He came down to destroy sin, overcome death and give life" (*Adversus Heresies* III.18.7)

- He bound the strong adversary, spoiled his goods and released his captive humanity. "He who had taken man captive was himself captured and his captive (humanity) was released from the bondage (condemnation and incarceration) (*Adversus Heresies* III.23.1)

- "The Word was made flesh in order to destroy death, bring humans to life, for we were led and bound in sin…and under the dominion of death" [*Epideixis, 37*]

- Jesus' victory is not by violence but by gentle persuasion (*secundun suadlam*) (*Adversus Heresies* V.1.1)

The christological drama complete, survival insured with Constantinian establishment, the churches contention then moved into the realm of ecclesiology, political formation and intellectual and artistic creativity. The years of waning Roman power and the ascending of Christian empire were marked by an intellectual degradation. As classical learning waned the spiritual and cultural vitalities of the superseding civilization would come slowly. Initially pagan intellectual culture was ambivalently received. Latin tradition is iconoclastic:

"What has Athens to do with Jerusalem? (Tertullian)

But the Greek tradition and Augustine would build on Plato, Aristotle and the Stoics.The spirit of the age-informing literature, music, dance, philosophy, grammar, rhetoric, politics and art- was slow to form toward Christian insight and value. This is JIHAD (assertion of mind and spirit). As this body of thought and culture, of law, political form and value takes shape it is preservation, not survival, which becomes the agenda of Christian society in history. The genius of Latin language and concepts is sustained. The "barbarian" tribes bring their own particular gifts—Celts, Franks, Germans, Lombards. They bring their own court poets, liturgists, jurists, and rhetoricians and slowly a new theological culture is born. This new heritage; grafted into classical wisdom and custom now becomes tradition to be preserved, vitalized and extended. During these salient centuries—erroneously caricatured as "Dark Ages"—a cache of ideas, e.g. truth; values e.g. freedom and convictions e.g. human rights of the sick and children, becomes codified. In both the Greek East and Roman West, Judeo-Christian civilization is now a way of life to be safeguarded.

Luther, claims Aulén, reasserts the power-warfare concepts of the atonement which he feels is "classic" and biblically orthodox. Protestantism, in its self-conception, becomes a liberation from oppression, rescue from a repressive system, deliverance from what Luther called "The Babylonian captivity of the Church." In the trilogy of treatises

- Appeal to the German nobility
- Freedom of the Christian man and
- The Babylonian captivity of the church

all written in 1520, the young Luther sets out a secular agenda of emancipation based on the still nascent theology of the cross and of *Christus Victor*.

Iranaeus' profound thought raises one important characteristic of Jesus' victory over evil. He does not conquer by violence but by love. The cross is finally a symbol of submission to God's good will and of the love of humanity. The guiding symbol of all Christian faith and life is Judaic and akedic.

> God so loved the world that He gave...(John 3:16)

The cross signals for all warfare and all history that love, forgiveness and peace have displaced hate, vengeance and war.

> He committed no sin – no guile was found on his lips when he was reviled – he did not revile in return when he suffered – he did not threaten, he trusted him who judges justly.
> (I Peter 2:21-23)

> He made peace through the blood of his cross.
> (Ephesians 2:15)

Love is a vital and aggressive power. It is stronger than hate. It is not *laissez faire*, non-concern. Like Holy War it seeks to persuade and win over. It seeks to liberate and repossess. As Girard has shown, love and violence are kindred impulses in the human spirit—individual and collective. The crucifixion of Chirst appears to be an act of impotence but in love it has become the most awesome force in Human history.

In the mercy of God Jesus was spared the grotesque postmortem described by Hengel and Crossan. Joseph of Aramatheia lay his dead body in the tomb. Was it the serene garden tomb just north of the Damascus gate in old Jerusalem? No matter! Even if the vultures and dogs had their day—no matter!

> God would not allow His holy one to see corruption.
> (Isaiah 38:17; Psalm 16:10; Acts 2:27-31)

The image of Jesus invading hell and leading captive humanity out as a Roman victory procession captures the apostolic fervor regarding the redemptive meaning of the crucifixion, death, burial and descent.

As son of man, Jesus endures humanity's full distance and depth of deprivation from God. As son of God, he rescues to the uttermost and leads captivity captive in his redemptively crucified body. (Psalm 58:18, Ephesians 4:8)

Jesus died an outcast. He died the ignominious death of the cross. He was a criminal, an offender to church and state. It was a disgraceful and deterrent death. It sought to humiliate the offender and discourage potential offenders. Yet its ignominity has become the glory of the ages.

Resurrection: Tertia die resurrexit a mortuos

> The strife is o'er the
> battle done
> The victory o'er death
> is won
> The song of triumph
> has begun
> Hallelujah
> Latin text. (Cologne) to Palestrina (1591)

I. Bible

The peace and victory of Easter morning makes the world new. This new dawn brings a silent end forever to spiritual strife and to the penchant for human violence. A new world, a new age, a new being has been inaugurated. The risen Jesus now says to his disciples "Go into all the world and preach the Gospel to every creature." (Mark 16:15f., Matt. 28:18-20, Luke 24:48-49). A new authority and assertion has been let loose in the world—the concourse of the Gospel. For John resurrection now means peace:

> The same evening, the doors shut for fear of the Jews
> Jesus came, stood among them and said
> Peace be with you—Showing them his hands
> and side the disciples were glad...
> Jesus said again, Peace be with you
> As the father has sent me, so I send you.
> (John 20:19-21)

The victorious aspect of the resurrection is found in its link back to the crucifixion and its link forward to the ascension. The crucifixion and death defeats the cumulative power of sin—through all ages throughout time and space—which is the power of evil. In ascension Jesus sits exalted at the right hand of God (Acts 2:33- 35)—reigning over creation in sustaining, now redeeming power. From here Spirit—convicting, convincing, conquering, spirit—is exuded into the world (Acts 2:34, 5:32, Eph. 4:9).

In the letter to Ephesus, Paul anchors the new *Christus Invictus*—the victorius, now invincible Christ—in his descent and ascent which accomplishes the warfare against sin and evil, the bestowal of charismata and the establishment of faith.

> ...Grace was given to each of us according to the measure of Christ's gift. Therefore, it is said, when he ascended on high he led a host of captives and he gave gifts to men. In saying "He ascended" what does it mean but that he had also descended into the lower parts of the earth? He who descended is he who also ascended far above all the heavens, that he might fill all things. His gifts were given...

- for the equipment of the saints
- for the work of ministry
- for the building up the body of Christ

> Until we all attain to the unity of the faith
> in knowledge of the Son of God
> to mature manhood
> to the measure of the stature of the fullness of Christ
> that we may no longer be blown here and
> there by every wind of doctrine
> (Ephesians 4:8ff)

The procession of Christ the victor now releases the gifts (or spoils, Luke 12:22,23, Hebrews 7:4) of this vanquishment of evil for the remaking of the peace, unity and salvation of the world now liberated from powers which held it in demonic grip. Paul is here drawing on Psalm 68, a song of the Holy War tradition. Let God arise, let his enemies be scattered...(Psalm 68:1)

II. Theology

The cry of death and defeat has now erupted into jubilation. The crucified one is now the risen one. The cross-grounded power of God (I Corinthians 1:18) is now verified throughout the creation through the resurrection (1 Cor. 15). The flashback of the Gospels across Jesus' life and ministry is a resurrection retrospective. The healings and miracles, the temptations and transfiguration, seen with the perfect vision of hindsight, already manifest Jesus' resurrection power over disease and death, time and space. The humiliation of the servant and the exaltation of the savior intertwine, each office coloring the other with theological significance. Now to be Christ's martyr [(witness) Acts 1:8] is to be a witness to the resurrection (Acts 1:22). Jesus is conqueror. He now sends the captives he has released, into the world, triumphant yet not triumphalist, servile warriors for his kingdom of peace.

The historical ground of this faith is the empty grave and the post-Easter appearances. The body has risen, not only the soul, the phantom. This is the central tenant of Christian faith. The resurrected body of Jesus Christ authorized and assured the general resurrection of the dead. The appearances; Emmaeus, the upperroom, on the seashore, all corroborate that physical fact of God's resurrection of Jesus' body. Now the ultimal transformation, one anticipated penultimately in the transfiguration, is actuated as Jesus' flesh becomes the incorruptible body. Our deaths are now incorporated into his transcorporeal body. The universal fate of death leading to dissolution is now reversed:

> As in Adam, all die, even so in Christ shall all be made alive…
> What is sown corruptible, is raised incorruptible.
> (I Corinthians 15)

III. War and History

The subject gets messy as we turn to concrete history. Jesus' resurrection, an event on the plane of transcendent history, in the realm of eternity, still occurs in time and space. Otherwise it is a fraud. But all concrete manifestations are parodies of reality. They appear like the illusions of Don Quixote de la Mancha or even worse as Slobadon Milosevich who now stands at the dock at The Hague war crimes tribunal. Just a few years ago he compared himself to a medieval knight defending the Orthodox Serbian homeland from Muslim, even Catholic enemies.

The resurrection of Christ completes what the covenant with Israel had begun—the establishment of God's command realm and commonwealth on earth. As Michael Walzer has shown in his masterful studies of the Puritans, the conviction arises from the Christian scriptures in their appropriation of the Hebrew Bible, that God's chosen people on earth have been perpetuated in a unique way in the Jesus community. The primitive church, Augustine, and the medieval church, further elucidate and embody this conviction that Gods' history with the world (*Heilsgeschite*) is now to be organized around this epicenter of the apostolic gathering—the new Israel. Israel is not superceded. Her founding role is honored and her salvation is expressed through the Christ dispensation within the dispensation of space/time. The God of Israel is the God of the nations. The formation of Christ's resurrected body among the nations of the world now constitutes a new battle for truth and a way of life.

That the resurrection of Jesus Christ has for two millennia transformed countless millions of lives toward faith, love and justice is beyond dispute. What dynamic has come into history through this epochal event? In 800 C.E. Pope Leo III crowned the king of the Franks Emperor of the Roman Empire. It was Charlemagne and his court which would standardize the Apostles' Creed as the orthodoxy of Western Christendom. This doctrine of the Son and the Father (*filoque*) would soon wreak havoc in the fragile universal church. This summer (2001) in the Ukraine, Pope John Paul II would try to mend that fracture. Then also in *Frankreich* the next two centuries would begin the crusades to exemplify that creed and reclaim its holy land and places from Islam. Centuries of strife preceded this consolidation and crusade. The focal battle had been between the Germanic Arian and the Italian Roman Catholic. What was the nature and import of that strife? The suffering, crucifixion and death, burial, descent and ascent of Jesus was the definitive explication of the nature of God. It was also the decisive explication of the nature of the human being. This is what is at stake in the resurrection. It defines therefore eternity and space/time as dimensions of reality. Historically the phenomenon of Christendom perpetuates the humanity and divinity, the *Zeitgeist* of the resurrection.

In his classic text on the Holy Roman Empire, James Bryce strikes the significance of Charlemagne's coronation:

> The coronation of Charles is not only the central event of the Middle Ages, it is also one of those very few events of which, taking them singly, it may be said that if they had not happened, the history of the world would have been different. In one sense indeed it has scarcely a parallel. The assassins of Julius Caesar thought that they had saved Rome from monarchy, but monarchy became inevitable in the next generation. The conversion of Constantine changed the face of the world, but Christianity was spreading fast, and its ultimate triumph was only a question of time. Had Columbus never spread his sails, the secret of the western sea would yet have been pierced by some later voyage; had Charles V broken his safe-conduct to Luther, the voice silenced at Wittenberg would have been taken up by echoes elsewhere. But if the Roman Empire had not been restored in the West in the person of Charles, it would never have been restored at all, and the inexhaustible train of consequences for good and for evil that followed could not have been.[292]

Before we sketch the military outgrowth of the Christ event we must announce its culmination which is the *denouement* of any other philosophy of history.

> He ascended into heaven…and is seated at the
> Right Hand of God the Father Almighty
>
> *Ascendit ad Coelos, Sedet ad Dexterem Dei*
> *Patris Omnipotentis*

The seal is set, the impact felt. History everafter is different by virtue of the ascension and session of Christ. There it is again…*Patris omnipotentis*. It recalls the opening of the creed—Credo in *Deum, Patrem Omnipotentem*.

The creed rests on Judaism—on the God of Israel, the God of Abraham, Isaac and Jacob. In the first announcement of the First Article we affirm God the God over all gods—the maker of Heaven and earth. Now in the final benediction of the Second Article we affirm the God of history—one who oversees, sustains, guides and judges the processes of nature and history. And at his side—the warrior—victor—the sympathizer—victim—the God-man who now supervenes, bringing life to and through the world that he gave his life to save. The words are awkward—the metaphors troubling—the imagery difficult—but the point is clear and true. The embodied principle and purpose of history now presides in

---

[292] James Bryce, *The Holy Roman Empire*. Philadelphia: Henry T. Coates and Company, 1886, p. 59.

session over its procession. Now One oversees history—judges its course—justifies its failings, bringing all reality toward its liberty, justice and peace—its inherent purpose. This One, who has come, will come again in consummate and culminating judgment.

What does the ascendancy of Jesus Christ mean for the history of the world? Several accomplishments deserve mention:

- The power of evil and death in the world is decisively overcome
- God in Christ is established as Lord of history
- Human affairs abide under the justice and mercy of God in Christ
- God is the Lord of nations and their affairs fall under His righteous will.

(Colossians 2)

Powers are disarmed and marshaled as captives shorn of weapons, parade down streets before the Roman conquerors. The biblical foundations of the ascension ground these truths:

...Who is to condemn?
...Is it Christ Jesus, who died, yes, who was raised
from the dead, who is at the right hand of God, who
indeed interceded for us?
...Who shall separate us from the Love of Christ?
...tribulation
...distress
...persecution
...famine
...nakedness
...peril
...sword?
(Romans 8:34ff)

The ascended Christ is the guardian of his believers against the destructive warhorses of this world. The binding love of Christ is more powerful and enduring than all of those violent human pretensions. The ascension teaches that beyond the vicissitudes of time and space, nature and history, shalom prevails. Here tribulation, persecution, devil and sword have no power. Where the vitalities of the eternal spirit are let loose in the world these destructive forces are disarmed.

...What is the immeasurable greatness of his power in us who believe, according to the working of his great might which he accomplished in Christ when he raised him from the dead and made him sit at his right hand in the heavenly places, far above all rule and authority and above every name that is

> named not only in this age but also in that which is to come; and he has put all
> things under his feet...
> (Ephesians 1:19ff)

A new superordination is placed over the world and a new subordination of all power and authority is placed in the world. As Karl Barth has said: "Jesus Christ became history in order to make history."[293] A new structure and momentum is given to the first and second dimension of universal reality.

> "When Christ had offered for all time a single
> sacrifice for sins, he sat down at the right
> hand of God, then to wait until his enemies
> should be made a stool for his feet."
> (Hebrew 1:3, 8:1, 10:12, 12:2)

The book of Hebrews interprets the ascension and session in terms of sacrifice, expiation and priestly representation. The fascinating bearing of 10:12, 13 implies that a heavenly conquest continues, a holy war ensues, a mopping-up operation goes on which will only be finished when He has "made his enemies his foot-stool."

Theology
Barth explicates the doctrine of ascension in terms of absolute authority over all alien powers:

> God's power over life and death...now has a fuller content: it is God's power to
> kill and make alive, to punish and reprieve to make the human cosmos grown
> old, that is, pass away, and when it has passed away, to awaken it to new life.[294]

He Will Come Again to Judge the Living and the Dead: Inde venturus est iudicare vivos et mortuos
A work had begun in the life and ministry of Jesus—the call to discipleship—the death, resurrection, and ascension—a work that one day must be completed. This culmination, this full circle completion of the drama of humiliation and exaultation, the ultimal transfiguration of his beloved world and humanity—will be finished only when he comes back. Much of the social strife, warfare, violence, science, peacemaking of world history is the patient or impatient waiting for this return.

The Michigan militia, through Terry Nichols, somehow implicated with the bombing of the Oklahoma City federal building on April 19, 1995, [(the anniversary of the Massachusetts militia uprising in (1775) and the destruction of the Waco Branch Davidian complex (1993)] was a group impatient at the delay of divine justice, frustrated at the presence of threat and the insecurity of American life, offended by the heavy hand of government in destroying the

---

[293] *Credo*, p. 109.
[294] Ibid., p. 110.

Branch Davidian fortress. They wanted to take parousia—the Jesus comeback—the restoration of godly order—into their own hands. The leader, a Baptist minister and gun shop owner articulated this fulminant fury on the eve of the Oklahoma City bombing: "They were a church" (Branch Davidian) "that the government destroyed." Recalling the deep resentment that Jews and early Christians felt toward the oppression and final suppression of their communities by the violent Roman Empire, such expectant communities have always coerced kingdom come out of their rabid frustration and impatience.

In so doing, they misunderstand Christ's session and intercession. Christ ever reigns over and returns to the living and the dead in justice and righteousness. But his remonstrance, for now is not historical and political, it is spiritual and ethical. Christ's warfare until the consummate end, is a reign of freedom, justice and peace.

We are therefore cautioned not to demand knowledge of the time and place (Acts 1) nor are we allowed to force the kingdom.

In Session

The resurrection, ascension, session and second coming are in one sense linked events. They all speak of the cosmic function of the risen Jesus.

The Russian armies returning from Chechnya were charged with war crimes. 220 civilians were killed in Chemaske—bombs, grenades, automatic rifles—on poor peasants. The soldiers didn't want to go—or do this—Yeltzin grieves over another vodka—Clinton worries. Russian human rights leaders prepare the case against themselves—the terrible mystery of evil. "He comes to judge the living and the dead." Why the atrocities against civilians? In Bosnia, documents have come to light, showing that the Serb leader Milosevich ordered genocide in the Muslim camps. He now is imprisoned as a war criminal, charged with ethnic cleansing, arbitrary killing and persecution. Robert McNamara's war memoirs of Vietnam were recently released. The architect of the Vietnam War now condemns his own construction. War crime. "He will come to judge the living and the dead." Last night again on the Fourth of July (2001) we decry the 58,000 Americans killed in Vietnam. Grief enough…But we fail to mention the 3 million Vietnamese and the 2.5 million Cambodians who died, in part because of our prosecution of that war. What happens morally when a people commit war crimes? As we know from the teaching of the prophet Hosea, when a nation violates the righteousness of God they call down natural sanctions such as domestic economic crisis, societal hardness of heart and long range cultural demise. Is this happening in America? … "He will come again to judge the living and the dead."

Princeton's Max Stackhouse has argued in *Creeds, Society and Human Rights* that convictions about human rights, immediately derived from

- modern experience—UN Charter of Human Rights, Nuremberg conventions, etc.
- early modern experience—John Locke and the American Constitution and Bill of Rights and
- fundamentally from biblical faith

have woven themselves into our contemporary creed. If this is the case, which I somewhat doubt (except in the fundamental sense), since enlightenment values and values from this century's historical experience seem to be only tenuously anchored in the second article of the creed, its justice endures:

"He will come to judge the living and the dead."

What do I mean?

- If General Ratko Mladic and president-psychiatrist Radovan Karazic are to be apprehended in Republika Serbska (Serbia-Bosnia) and charged with war crimes before the tribunal now convened in The Hague and if
- known leaders of Tutsi genocidal slaughter of Hutu are to be brought before that international tribunal
- If colonialism, slavery and Israel's occupation of Palestinian towns are condemned at Durban
- If Sharon and Arafat are ultimately called to account.

If human rights justice is to be done

- recompense for violations: e.g., war crimes
- provision of entitlements: e.g., the right to one's home

then it will only come as this phrase of the Apostles' Creed (which may have its origin in Serbia) is seen to demand that such human justice be done as imperative of Christ's righteousness and therefore human legal obligation.

The Anthropology of the Second Article

Paul Tillich, in the second volume (Christology) of his Systematic Theology gathers his thought around "Existence and the Christ." Humanity and divinity, the coincidence, the conflict, the paradox and the partnership of these two natures or qualities was the issue at Nicea (325) and Chalcedon (451). "Who was Jesus Christ?" was of course also the question. "Who is the human being?" In asking the Christ and Jesus question, the creedal formulations ask about the nature and range of human freedom and initiative. They inquire about the autonomy of human culture and society. They ask of the power of the church and state. In the crucial meetings of church leaders which hammer out the great christological creeds of the church, a belief structure is being formulated that will set the course of the historical and cultural agenda of Christendom. A cultural synthesis is now being born on the basis of a theology about Jesus that will now determine:

- the reaction to Islam
- the furtive crusades
- the European renaissance
- the Protestant reformation and
- the colonization of the world's of Asia, Africa and America

The war is underway.

The second article articulates the new view of the person and of humanity that Jesus brings to the world. In sum, it is the anthropology of human value: personal uniqueness and social solidarity. Jacob Burkhardt summarizes the contribution as the "theistic humanism of medievalism" which phases into the humanism of the renaissance. All this is a heritage of the Christ spirit:

> In the Middle Ages both sides of human consciousness—that which was turned within as that which was turned without—lay dreaming or half awake beneath a common veil. The veil was woven of faith, illusion, and childish prepossession, through which the world and history were seen clad in strange hues...[But in the Italian Renaissance] the *subjective* side...asserted itself...: man became a spiritual individual, and recognized himself as such. Observe the expressions *uomo singolare* and *uomo unico* for the higher and highest stages of individual development.[295]

The War History of the Second Article
Such a christological humanism provokes a war history which coincides with the age of christological formulation. It includes events such as:

- The Jewish persecutions of the first century represented by the stoning of Stephen (c.32 C.E.) and James, Jesus brother (c. 62 C.E.)

- The Roman persecutions under Nero and other emperors.

- The Roman-Jewish wars culminating in the destruction of Jerusalem (70) and Massada (73 C.E.)

- The Jewish revolts in Cyrenaeca, Egypt and Cyprus 117 C.E.

---

[295] Jacob Burkhardt, *The Civilization of the Renaissance in Italy,* New York: Harper, 1958, v. 1, p. 143.

- Persecutions under the second century emperors, e.g., Marcus Aurelius

- The Apologists: Justin Martyr, Tertullian, etc. c. 120-122 C.E.

- Persecutions of the Mesopotamian and Persian Christians by the Zoroastrian Sassanids.

- State Christianity in Edessa and Armenia c. 300 C.E.

- The conversion of Constantine 312 C.E.

- The conversion of the northern barbarians.

- The baptism of Clovis, 496 C.E.

- Justinian defeats Visigoths, Ostrogoths

- Charles Martel defeats Muslims at Poitiers 732 C.E.

- The coronation of Charlemagne s Holy Roman Emperor 800 C.E.

- Consolidation of Germanic and Italic people and faiths.

- Crusades

I.	1096-1099 French crusade created later kingdom of Jerusalem
II.	1147-1149 Led by Bernard of Clairvaux—France andGermany—failed to recapture Jerusalem.
III.	1188-1192 France,Germany, England - failed. Richard I made peace with Saladin.
IV.	1202-1204 West captured Constantinople - weakened Eastern bulwark against Islam.
V.	1212 Children's Crusade
VI.	1217-1221 mainly in Egypt - cross surrendered
VII.	1228-1229 Frederick II reclaimed Holy Land for 20 years
VIII.	1248-1254 Innocent IV. St. Louis of France
IX.	1270 St. Louis and Charles of Anjou

As with Herod's infanticidal order reported by Matthew (ch.2) Stephen's execution was at the hands of an all too fragile Judaic puppet regime centered in Jerusalem in the late third or fourth decade of what is now designated the Christian (common) era. The accusation leveled against the deacon of the Jerusalem congregation was that he said Jesus of Nazareth would destroy this place and change the customs of Moses..." [Acts 6:14, 7:48-50]. The persecution of Christians represented by Stephen's stoning which would spread throughout Judea and perhaps Samaria and even Syria was at the hands of the embattled pharisaic inquisition which was threatened by the urban rebellion of the Jewish zealots and by the similarly threatened Roman officials.

Paul's preaching and the mission to the Gentiles also provoked religious and political reaction wherever he went, especially in Ephesus, Phillipi, Berea and Thessalonica. The culminating persecution and execution of apostles and first generation Christians in Rome under Nero in the early sixties also represents early warfare for-and against the faith and its way of life.

The history of this persecution of the church, by Roman officials, sometimes instigated by Jews, began and became virulent under Nero. James, the just, the first Bishop of the church and leader of Jewish Christians, was killed at this time. Tactitus, reporting on Nero's persecutions, says that they were great in number and were popular although public sentiment eventually turned against Nero. Christians were accused of a "hatred for the human race" which we surmise was an extrapolate of their surpassing love of God in Christ and their contempt for the glory of this world. The apostle Peter we presume met his death, perhaps, though not likely, with Paul, during Nero's persecutions. Across the sea, James is dropped from the tower, beaten and stoned to death.

Under the second century emperors, persecution was prevalent especially in Asia Minor as we know from John' Apocalypse (Revelation). Pliny's letter to Trajen and the reply of Hadrian (c. 110 C.E.) tells of this crisis. Polycarp, approaching 90, was the last person of the generation who had been taught by the apostles and had talked with those who knew Jesus. He was executed in his hometown of Smyrna for refusing to disown his Lord at a Pagan festival.

Diocletian from the Balkans (now Bulgaria) exerted especially stringent persecutions on the Christians, beginning in 305. Eusebius tells of a Christian town in Asia Minor that was surrounded by Roman soldiers and burned to the ground with all of its inhabitants (Book VII ch. 11). By this time a profound power struggle had begun that would only end with Constantine's consolidation of power, a decade late. What was the nature of this theological—political struggle?

We know that the edict of Milan (313) extended toleration to the Christians. The year before he had battled against Maximentius and employed the Christian emblem XP on his standards which he had seen in a vision with the words: "Conquer by this sign." A long development of religious awareness and presumed political implication had gone before this moment. When the Emperor convenes the Ecumenical Council of Bishops in Nicea in 325 this long development comes to consummation.

What seems to have turned the tide? In sum the persecutions did not work—why? several conjectures can be offered:

- The philosophy which had disdained the new religion now found it to be rich in philosophical insights as it matured through the albeit strident anti-rationalism of Tertullian toward the sublime insights of Augustine (some 75 years after Constantine' council at Nicea).

- The moral vision of the Christians prevailed as the pagan practice to which they objected lost their attraction: polytheism, idolatry, amusements, etc. The nobility of the Christian ethic became attractive.

- Christians become more engaged in public life and citizenship.

- The persecutions had strengthened the church "The blood of the martyrs is the seed of the church"

- The creed of the church evolved from one mainly "otherworldly" to one that now implied secular responsibility. Leadership and government now became the aim of evangelization and the kingdom of Christ as it had been in locales like Edessa and greater Armenia now sought identity with the vaster empire. The Apostles' Creed, and its successor's (Nicea, Chalcedon, etc.) though literally wholly spiritual and eschatological, were interpreted in profoundly secular and worldly ways.

- Rodney Stark in his book The Rise of Christianity contends that Christians prevailed in the Roman empire for three sociological reasons:

  1) a satisfying explanation of suffering (thecross),
  2) a vivid belief in life after death (resurrection) and
  3) an abiding care (nursing) for the sick.

This is no surprise since the creed itself is anchored in world history:

- born
- suffered
- crucified
- risen
- coming

The creed had intensified in the life of the church and was related profoundly to baptism and Eucharist, the rituals of invitation and incorporation. This primary belonging and sense of kingdom of a growing number (often a majority) of citizens of the empire demanded some recognition within the structures of the society. Within the church, punishments for apostasy both here below and in heaven above, were intensified. There was a pagan and barbarian world out there and soon, in the matter of a few centuries, a new and alien faith would arise (Islam). The troops had to be steeled for conquest, consolidation and be made ready to resist and do battle. It is the threat of Islam that finally provokes the Apostles' Creed in the empire of Charlemagne.

Excursus: The Break with Judaism

By the time of Constantine, monumental historical and sociological changes had occurred in the bosom of Christianity. Far Eastern communities of Christians—in Persia, Bythinia, Egypt and Syria fell under severe persecution. These enclaves of Christian faith had remained closer to Judaism. The Christians of Edessa and Antioch, for example, were still deeply under the cultural and linguistic sway of Syriac and Aramean and had not been as deeply inculcated by Hellenic and Roman thought forms and ways of life as was the case in the Western Empire. In Western Asia, Asia Minor, Greece, Italy and Europe alienation sets in between Christians and Jews. As Jews had originally persecuted Christians in the first two centuries after Christ, agitating Roman officials for their arrest and execution, Christians now began to persecute the Jews. As Goldhagen has shown in his provocative book, the seeds of anti-Semitism prompting liquidations of all Jews resides very deep in the Germanic ethos. What he does not say is that all Europe, with only few exceptions, cooperated in the Holocaust. Of six million Jews killed 700,000 were German. The vast majority were Poles (3.5 million), Ukrainians (1.5 million) and others whose nations conspired against their own peoples. France, England and America were also in full complicity in mind and spirit as well as exerting specific exclusionary policies. Religious imperialism took victims among whom, most grievously, were the Jews. Christians now sought the conversion or the elimination of their ancestral brothers and sisters in faith.

Decisive creedal campaigns will now be undertaken as the barbarian tribes invade Europe. Attila and the Huns destroy cities in the wake of their advance. The Franks establish a stronghold that will become a kingdom in the North. In many places the church disappeared. The decimation was especially pronounced in the cities. Some of the tribes were Christian including tribes converted to Arian Faith. Warfare and strife was found among the Angles, Saxons, Celts, Franks, Vandals, Goths and Visigoths. The life of the indigenous peoples was a drama of conversion, conquest and consolidation. By the end of the fifth century in France most cities are Bishop seats and the monastic missionaries originating in Ireland are on the move christianizing the emerging social order.

The Goths were Arians and set up an Arian kingdom in Southern Gaul. the Bergundians moved south of the Rhine and consolidated with the indigenous Catholics. By this time the Roman armies were constituted largely by barbarian mercenaries and these became "Christian" soldiers. When Burgundians defeated the Huns they attributed it to their baptism and being staunch defenders of the Athanasian faith. This commitment was consolidated in an event celebrated by Pope John Paul II at Reims Cathedral (491 C.E.); the submission of Clovis, the Frankish king to baptism. His wife was a Roman Christian and his two children had been baptized. Was it a political gesture or a genuine conversion? God only knows. What is known is that the army quickly followed suit and a Roman Catholic culture was established in the center of Europe. Creedal conversion of the Franks was largely responsible for the Christianization of Europe following the reseeding of that region of the world by barbarian tribes. As the Teutonic invaders prepared their assault this consolidation was to prove determinative of the course of history.

At the end of the era of christological controversy and consolidation a literal war was going on for faith and control of culture. In the east it was against Zoroastrian Persian culture. In the north and west it was against pagan polytheism. In the far west we confront Celtic humanism, sometimes disguised as Pelagianism. On all borders of what will become The Holy Roman Empire, a drama is unfolding of conversion and conquest, creed and crusade.

The Coming Crisis of Creed and Crusade

Kenneth Scott Latourette makes the bold claim in the second volume of his monumental *History of the Expansion of Christianity* that Christianity was forced to surrender (in the millennium 500-1500 C.E.) about as much territory and as many adherents as it had gained in Northern Europe, Africa, Southeast Europe, Asia Minor, Syria, Palestine and Arabia."

The gentile mission seemed to have sputtered to a halt. Christianity was encapsulated as a power in the Western Empire. It was a vital presence, but scarcely a power in the East. Meanwhile the wall between Christians and Jews had hardened, Islam became a vibrant force and contender, and the ancient faiths and Buddism sealed the far East.

After the instrusion and conversion of:

- The Goths in Italy
- The Visigoths in Spain
- The Vandals in North Africa
- The Burgundians and Franks inWestern Europe
- The Angles and Saxons in Britain
- The Celts in Britain and Gaul

the Teutonic Lombards would conquer northern Italy for two centuries and the Avars and the Bulgars from western Asia would populate central Europe. Inspired by nascent Islam, the Arabs would invade Sicily, Mesopotamia and Persia. In the eighth century Viking raids began in Ireland, Britain, France, Spain and Russia. By the eleventh century the now Christianized Viking kingdoms were found in England, Sicily and Southern Italy. At this time we see the inauguration of the crusades of the 11th -13th centuries and the symbiotic missionary/ merchant/ military ventures of the 12th -14th centuries. These money and soul seeking adventures moved from Europe's shores, reaching even China.

Creed by this time had become a conglomerate of inculturated intellectual ideas, cultural elements and the code of life. Elements of learning, morality, and business intertwined with religious identity. This package of an organic society, finely honed in antagonism to Islam, especially the Turks, was exported in each boat to leave Venice or Genoa. At the same time Arabic and Islamic culture informed and enriched the West with the recovery of classical science and philosophy being its crowning achievement. In the 13th century, Genghis Khan and the Mongols moved and conquered China, Russia and when they became Muslims they even threatened Western Europe. At the end of this millennium, the Ottoman Turks would establish a mighty Kingdom in the Eastern and Western Mediterranean world and into the fringes of Europe. This widespread and volatile movement of peoples would be the environment within which creed and crusade would be inscribed and enacted.

Beginning in the sixth century we see a recovery of the first century pattern of "professional missionaries." The monasteries and monastic orders not only served to organize village life, including agriculture and commerce, say in Ireland or France, but as with Paul and his company, they also commissioned evangelists to carry the Word and Way to other cultures. The faith had brought a certain cosmos and coherence to the violent, marauding and rather chaotic existence that the tribes had introduced into Europe. While these rough peoples admired and adopted the culture of the church they imbued it with an ambition, aggression and conversionist energy. Christianity would now influence civil rulers with its evangelical zeal even as those rulers became sponsors to the propagation of the faith. The slow and sure, although somewhat coercive and violent crusade of creed and Christian culture achieved:

- The conversion of the Franks in the 6th century
- The conversion of the Angles, Saxons and Celts, 6th and 7th
- The conversion of the Rhine Valley in the 8th
- The conversion of the Slavs of central Europe and the Balkans in the 9th
- The conversion of the Scandinavians in the 11th
- The conversion of Poland and Sweden in the 12th
- The conversion of the peoples of the Baltic in the 13th
- The conversion of Russia and Lithuania in the 14th

How did the creed follow and shape the concourse of conversion? The millennium centered in the great Thomistic medieval synthesis is bracketed by two salient periods: The Augustinian period and the age of the reformers. Both parties sought to rationalize coercors and belligerence as well as irenic social action in terms of the Gospel. Though their reflections on "just war" pertain in particular to warmaking, these teachings can be applied to the broader justice of what we are calling the creedal crusade.

Augustine and Just War

The first prominent theological and political figure to draw together the threads of war and political development with faith and creed was St. Augustine. In *The City of God*, Augustine develops a theology of nature and history that will set the structure of orthodoxy and orthopraxy for a millennium. He lives in the waning triumphalism of the Constantinian Empire. The Vandals are poised to sack Rome. A cache of normative convictions about truth and right, beauty and civility, state and person, God and the world have developed within Christian culture to the point where Augustine can articulate a comprehensive theology of nature and history and a Christian philosophy. In 1500 years his magnificent vision has seldom been approached and never surpassed. Yet the civilization he extols was threatened. Not only the political coherence but the theological inheritance was at stake. In response to this impending crisis Augustine gathers the notions of statehood and extended dominion from Imperial Rome and the evangelistic imperative of the Apostolic and Pauline Kerygma and nascent Christendom into the creedal crusade that will become the charter of the Holy Roman Empire, of medieval Europe and of the subsequent history of western civilization.

Within this corpus of systematic active belief we find Augustine's doctrine of Just War. This pragmatic ideology will become the basis of war ethics in Western society. Augustine's legacy reaches forward to Thomas Aquinas, Vittoria, Suarez, Churchill, Eisenhower, George Bush and Michael Walzer. It reaches back to Cicero and to Hellenic and Hebraic holy war. More broadly Augustine's "just war theory" is a doctrine of rightful and obligatory conversion of the world. It is the contention of this section that Augustine's vision is still valid for it asks:

- What can and must we believe as followers of Christ?
- How may and must that truth and good be defended and extended in world history?

His ethics of war and peace evolve across several stages in his career:

A. In his early career in his philosophical dialogues he is struggling with the phenomenon of Manicheanism. The key issue with the followers of Mani was the nature of evil in the world. For Augustine, there was no evil antagonistic to God. In platonic spirit evil was the absence of or divergence from God and the good. Humans, in their reason, society and law ought to fashion a world where sin is punished and good is extolled and enforced.

The morality of killing is discussed in these early dialogues as a necessity sometimes for the public hangman.[296] The publicly viewed and publicly

---

[296] *DeOrdine* II.8.25.

accountable executioner who performs this act of human law reflecting eternal law, does justice not in a hidden or vengeful way but on behalf of the people.

War is the national counterpart of the public hangman. Punishment, even capital or militial punishment, is the proper suppression of evil in the preservation of the good. Propagation of the Gospel, and defense of the faith is similarly executed in the life of the church.

B. Augustine's thought then evolves toward a Christ-focused pacifism. Can one kill in self defense? He asks this in a letter to his young friend Evodius. Augustine now counsels us to turn the other cheek through "sermon on-the-mount" non-aggression. Now, only soldiers, the appointed public prosecutors against offense, may kill. Taking the life of those who have committed capital offense in murder or war is the response of justice in the defense and preservation of life.

C. Augustine's thought evolves further in Ch. 22 of Against Faustus the Manichee. Again rejecting the Manichean attack on the Old Testament, Augustine defends Moses who waged war on God's command. Like Abraham he would bring death even to his own son, to obey God's command. Augustine goes on in a Neoplatonic vein: "The real evils of war (since people are going to die sooner or later) are the love of violence, vengeful cruelty, fierce and implacable enmity, wild resistance, lust for power and such like."

The Manicheans said that the Hebrew patriarchs and their God were condemned by the pacific Gospel of Christ. Arguing from an ancient Persian dualism which held the polarity and incompatibility of light and darkness, Faustus contended that any militancy is a gross and crude confusion of the material with the spiritual.

Augustine disagrees and develops the following argument to justify war, though only when it is waged as a divine imperative within God's authority.

- If God can command war it can't be all wrong
- Jesus tells soldiers to be content with their lot (Luke 3:14) and to render to Caesar that which is Caesar's (Matt. 22:21)
- The natural order seeks the peace of mankind. If war is necessary to rebuke, crush or humble human pride, this must be a godly or righteous war.
- God's people will not be harmed (even if they are killed) for no power (even the sword—Romans 13:1ff) will come against God's beloved unless it is given from above.
- When Jesus said "turn the other cheek" he was describing an inner spiritual disposition not a stance of self non-defense or war policy.

497

- Jesus also claimed that he brought not peace but a sword to earth. (Matthew 10:24) Besides, he tells his disciples to carry a sword or two. (Luke 22:35-38)

- The actions and activities of people in the world are manifestations of sin or grace (construals of freedom) and the reactions of nature and history (including war) are the divine responses of justice and mercy. These ultimate divine sanctions are mediated through penultimate human political acts of punishment and forgiveness. Crusade enacts the judgments conveyed in creed. Justice defends truth.

- Whatever is good in the world is there by divine blessing; whatever is evil is there by divine judgment. (22:78)

- The origins of evil and human wickedness are in the fall.

- In the Apostolic age nonviolence was appropriate. Now in this Theodosian age (when the world has become a "choir praising Christ") force is prophetically sanctioned. In Christ's behalf we are to "compel them to come in." Theodosius' Empire (390 C.E.) is Christ's kingdom on earth.

- The social order is a chaos of conflicting purposes, tensions, prides, aggressions. Political, juridical and military power keeps check on this "hell on earth." (note the similarity to Hobbes).

- The wise man will wage just wars all the while lamenting the necessity which lays this duty upon him.

In one sense Augustine's vision, shapes Christian history, baptizes and extends the *Pax Romana*—the suppression of ethnic rivalry and violence under a tolerant and eclectic Roman empire. In another sense that same history provides expression for a particularly virulent conjunction of creed and crusade, one that through coercion and persuasion brings a new way of belief and behavior into world history. The vision is ultimately eschatological where God alone (and not humanly conceived political or ecclesial action) ushers in the times and places of kingdom.

Armenia

The establishment of the first Christian kingdom in Armenia in 301 C.E. is an assertion of faith and of a cultural way of life, law and politics amid the still strong Persian empire and the rapidly transforming Roman Empire.

The Armenian tradition has been surprisingly democratic from its very early history. In this manner it resembles Jewish culture in witnessing to an ebullient freedom, enterprising energy and participatory politic. The history of Armenia will typify the movement of the Christian creedal crusade in the epic of western civilization. Ecclesial consolidation, conflict with Islam, modern nationalism, genocide and post cold war freedom and ethnic struggles mark her history. This

498

history of suffering, courage, endurance and victory is a paradigm of the Gospel ethic in its historical manifestation. Attorney General John Ashcroft's placing of Armenians on the "terrorists" check list in 2002 was a colossal blunder.

Constantine

The Emperor Constantine's declaration that Christianity would be the official religion of the empire and his convention and guidance of the church council at Nicea was a watershed in the theological history of the human race and, if audacity can be excused, in the history of God. Nearly two millennia of history have been profoundly effected by the Christian world view. Even the radical break and reassertion of faith of the renaissance and reformation and the contemporary movements of nationalism and secularism have not impeded but only accelerated the momentum of this cultural change.

Augustine's ethics, in sum, justify creedal assertion (Matthew 28:19-20), ethical and spiritual conversion, even conflict and war when it honors good and countermands evil:

Goods to be protected	Evils to be resisted
• God's worship, name and holiness	• idolatry, blasphemy
• Human freedom, rights and worship	• Oppression and tyranny
• Divine truth, good and beauty	• Falsehood, evil and immorality.
• Human chastity, fidelity and integrity	• Degraded life

The conversion (often under compulsion, e.g., Armenia) and consolidation of the Christianized Roman Empire is a sometimes muted, sometimes overt war for minds, hearts peoples and lands. The crusades with their venomous anti-Semitism and destructive hatred of Muslims despoils the nobility of the purpose to safeguard Christian freedom, the life of the church and the historic heritage of the faith. The preceding and following conversions and confiscations of land were brought sometimes in the persuasive power of the Gospel, more often in dehumanizing coercion. The mass nationalpolitical conversions of nations like Armenia, Russia, Lithuania and Serbia raise questions of the spiritual authenticity and creedal integrity of the capitulation. It is only in the Protestant Reformation of the sixteenth century in Europe that the issues of corporate coercion and voluntaristic faith become clarified as helpfulsecularism is established.

Forerunning Luther's religio-political revolution are the significant faith/freedom revolutions of Wyclif, Hus, The Albigensians and the Waldensians, among others. Each of these individuals and groups attempt an intriguing rebellion and reformation seeking freedom from a tyrannical and oppressive church and/or state in the name of a claimed advocacy and protection of that state. They fought to the death for the truth and truce of God. Wyclif in the days of Sir John Oldcastle and the peasants rebellion (1381) sought to check papal power and enhance evangelical freedom by further empowering secular authority over against the church. Hus, Luther and Calvin made the same double–edged claim.

What is the ideology of conversion and conflict—what is the creedal crusade of the Protestant reformation? I draw here on Jaroslav Pelikan's chapter "The Prince of Peace" in *Jesus Through the Centuries*.

> There is a violent tenor to the effort to cleanse the Roman church and establish evangelical orthodoxy and orthopraxy. Not only do the Protestant bodies of the sixteenth century formulate creeds based on the Apostles' Creed, they stipulate rigors of sacrament (liturgy) and discipline (moral behavior) that will be held normative and enforced by censure, sanction, excommunication, even civil punishment. The papists and the Anabaptists along with Jews and Muslims were the targets of rigorous spiritual and physical strife as the new (restored old) faith was established.

John Comenius, the Bohemian Moravian of the early seventeen century would write of the Lord as

> the only real deliverer from all slavery of soul and body (John 8:32-36). For the way of peace they knew not at all, who about the kings of the earth, instead of a scepter, have gathered spears, swords, wheels, halters, crosses, flames, and headsmen, so making them rather to be feared than loved. Is this what was taught by the best of teachers? Does this proceed from, the teachings of Him who commended to His followers nought but love, and affection, and mutual help?[297]

Luther would reflect on Augustine's two kingdoms as he contemplated the justice of holy crusade. When the peasants' revolt threatened the integrity of evangelical faith in a political region he ruthlessly condoned

> "stab, slay, smite, whoever you can."[298]

Order and just government, he thought, must be coercively preserved, at all cost.

At the opposite extreme, he argued that if one is threatened with persecution even death for confessing faith in Christ, one must not resist or retaliate. In middle way he answers in the affirmative his question of whether soldiers can

---

[297] The Angel of Peace, New York: Pantheon. Jew, Christian and Muslim.
[298] "Against the Robbing and Murdering Hordes of Peasants," May 1525 in G. Rupp, *Martin Luther: Documents in Modern History*, London: Edward Arnold, p. 126.

and should serve the state, exerting the sword, proffering the justice and punishment of the state.

> Whether the Christian faith, by which we are accounted righteous before God, is compatible with being a soldier, going to war stabbing and killing, robbing and burning, as military law requires us to do to our enemies in wartime? Is this work sinful or unjust? Should it give us a bad conscience before God? Must a Christian only do good and love, and kill no one, nor do anyone any harm?[299]

"...my kingdom is not of this world." (John 18:36).

Military measures are not appropriate means to defend or extend the kingdom of Christ. The good ruler, who fights for the right to truly preach the Gospel and administer the sacraments is to be supported and his cause fought for. Suffering love, the way of the cross, was the mode of Christian witness. Zwingli was too militant, Munzer too revolutionary, and Calvin too political for brother Martin. Yet beneath this pacifist front is an advocacy for defending and extending the faith that is as bull-headed and belligerent as that of any of the reformers. You may not find Luther like Zwingli in the battlefield at Cappel or like Calvin negotiating the interest rates with bankers, but his presence and LEHRE is one of forceful material witness to the Gospel.

Luther sustained the Augustinian doctrine that the sword and the law of the state was to be used:

- To protect upright citizens
- To punish the wicked.

A certain creedal righteousness (e.g., decalogue) was the criteria employed to deem actions and teachings right or wrong. The purpose of wars is not exerted violence or even coerced belief, it is the achievement of justice and peace. The concourse of the Gospel for the reformers is a peaceful and non-coercive work of the church. Taking the cross against infidels (Turks or Jews) was not as Pope Urban II declared at Clermont on the eve of the First crusade, a "participation in the sufferings of Christ." It was a compounding of those sufferings. The brutality and senselessness of the religious wars of the reformation and counter-reformation, even though pursued for Christ and executed in his name, were what one writer has called "a betrayal of Christendom."

Luther's hunting down of Munzer and Munzer's bloodthirsty vision, Calvin's lethal decree on Servetus and the French Catholic genocide of the Huguenots were ugly blemishes on the worldly body of the church. Soderblom is correct in his judgment that "holy and just war was not just or holy."

---

[299] "Whether Soldiers Too Can Be Saved," LW 46:95.

In sum, the second article of the creed sets in motion a crusade first of thought, belief and way of life, second of political and military defense and extension.

Christ is, as the sixth century mosaic in the archiepiscopal chapel in Ravenna depicts, the way, truth, and life. There is a certain militancy, a fighting spirit in those gentle and pacific words of Jesus. The creed and its derivative crusades seek to:

- Bring the world to follow that way
- Disseminate that truth, and
- Offer that life to a dying world.

Law/Gospel: Concourse until Mohammed and Charlemagne

Mohammed claims to come on the stage of world history in the train of prophets-Moses and Jesus and in the spirit of law and Gospel. This new tribal faith with deep affinity to biblical religion – both Judaism and Christianity – arises in Arabia. Arabia's arising is marked by being shunned by Hebraic iconoclasm though seasoned by the Jewish diaspora, and leaped over by Christianity's (Paul's) tropism toward "the Occident"- Rome and the Western edges of Caesar's Empire. The eruption of Islam into both diaspora Judaism and Byzantium is a decisive moment in humanity's creed and crusade. The Apostles' creed, in fact, becomes normative in the holy Roman empire through the influence of Charlemagne and the Franks. Impulses to form creed and crusade are for the most part responses to the Islam that arises on the borders of Europe (Corpus Christianum).

The raw, eruptive power felt by Judaism is expressed to day (December 30, 1997) as Tatyana Suskin, a Russian-Jew is convicted in Jerusalem, for putting up posters in the Muslim sector of Hebron depicting Mohammed as a pig.[300] Going to the heart of kosher law, and purity statutes more generally, the provocation was held, in part, responsible for the bombing that killed nine German tourists in Egypt in September 1997.

In the sixth through eighth centuries, profound discussion occurred, much like the debates of the first Christian century of Jewish and gentile Christians, as to whether the law was binding on this new branch of Abrahamic (Yawistic) faith.

Today on New Years Eve 1997, President Clinton sends greetings on the eve of Ramadan to the Islamic community wishing all hope for "peace and spiritual renewal." What is the nature of the historical confrontation among Judaism, Christianity, and Islam, and among the respective assertions of Holy war crusade and Jihad?

---

[300] *Jerusalem Times*, December 30, 1997, p. 17.

The cultural achievement of the Hellenistic Roman Empire had by the fifth century (C.E.) yielded to the penetration of barbarian peoples; Germans and Franks, Vandals and Goths, who embraced the classical culture, adopted Christianity and exerted their united religion and political spirit on the Western empire. It was an aggressive, warring, defensive ethos. The Indo-European ancestry of these peoples, chronicled by Bruce Lincoln in *Myth, Cosmos and Society* now became manifest as they inculturated into the Roman empire.

In the middle of the fourth century Ulfila, a Goth convert, had taken the faith to the Germans, Vandals, and Burgundians. Surviving the assault of Attila (450c.e.), the carolingian kings, beginning with Clovis, combined, the Frankish and Germanic heritage into a vibrant notion of "*Christenheit*". The Apostles' creed, which had slowly evolved since the apostolic age, and had lain at the heart of the Constantinian consolidation, now became the political basis of the Merovingian, as it had in the Justinian empire. Here in Gaul, at the pagan, barbarian and heathen gates of the Mediterranean Christian empire, the Apostle's creed takes its final form and is superimposed back on Rome. Charlemagne reigns while Islamic tribes storm the Eastern ramparts.

It is at this curious yet crucial crux of history—the historical agony of Christianity and Judaism – that Islam appears. It's appearance and subsequent history is somehow related to the enigma of that Judeo-Christian saga. More deeply it has to do with a trinitarian theology of history—a history of father, son and spirit. The mystery of the age is the son manifest in that millennium of history which we call Christendom, yields to that exuberant and chaotic age of the Spirit—an age of Rennaissance, Reformation enlightenment, and secularism—an age marked by the impression of the Islamic and Ottoman Empire. The tulmult of that age now tends toward an ominous yet portentious age of power and fundamentalism—perhaps a new age of the Father—where Israel, Christ and Mohammed now contend for the filial piety and allegiance of earth's nations.

Many historians see the epoch of the invasion of Islam (from the seventh to twentieth centuries) into Western Christendom, African paganism, Asian orientalism as a reassertion of patriarchal familial, monotheistic and moralistic faith and ethics, the reconstitution of an ethos which Judaism and Christianity had abandoned to secularism. Henri Pirenno, in his classic Mohammed and Charlemagne (New York: Meridian, 1957) shows how the spiritual exhaustion of both Roman and Persian empires rendered each vulnerable to the movement which had subverted to paganism of ancient Arabia.

III. The Third Article

Luther

The Third Article: Sanctification

> I believe in the Holy Ghost, a holy Christian Church, the communion of saints, the forgiveness of sins, the resurrection of the body, and the life everlasting. Amen.

What does that mean?

> ANSWER: I believe that I cannot of my own understanding and strength believer in or come to Jesus Christ my Lord, but that the Holy Ghost has called me by the Gospel, and illuminated me with his gifts and sanctified and preserved me in the true faith, just as he calls, gathers together, illuminates, sanctifies and preserves in Jesus Christ all Christendom throughout the earth in one true faith; in which Christendom he daily bestows abundantly on me and all believers forgiveness of sins; and on the last day he will awaken me and all the dead, and will give to me and all that believe in Christ eternal life. This is a faithful saying...

Calvin

> First, the Holy Spirit is called the "spirit of adoption" because he is the witness to us of the free benevolence of God with which God the Father has embraced us in his beloved, onlybegotten Son to become a Father to us; and he encourages us to have trust in prayer. In fact, he supplies the very words so that we may fearlessly cry, "Abba, Father!" [Rom.8:25; Gal.4:6].

> For the same reason he is called "the guarantee and seal" of our inheritance [II Cor. 1:22;cf. Eph.1:14] because from heaven he so gives life to us, on pilgrimage in the world in the world and resembling dead men, as to assure us that our salvation is safe in God's unfailing care. He is called "life" because of righteousness [cf. Rom.8:10].

> By his secret watering the Spirit makes us fruitful to bring forth the buds of righteousness. Accordingly, he is frequently called "water," as in Isaiah: "Come, all ye who thirst, to the waters" [ch.55:1]. Also, "I shall pour out my Spirit upon him who thirsts, and rivers upon the dry land." [Isa.44:3.] To these verses Christ's statement, quoted above, corresponds: If anyone thirst, let him come to me" [John 7:37].

Although sometimes he is so called because of his power to cleanse and purify, as in Ezekiel, where the Lord promises "clean water" in which he will wash away the filth" of his people
[ch.36:25].

From the fact that he restores and nourishes unto vigor of life those on whom he has poured in the stream of his grace, he gets the names "oil" and "anointing"
[I John 2:20, 27].

On the other hand, persistently boiling away and burning up our vicious and inordinate desires, he enflames our hearts with the love of God and with zealous devotion. From this effect upon us he is also justly called "fire"
[Luke 3:16].

In short, he is described as the "spring" [John 4:14] whence all heavenly riches flow forth to us; or as the "hand of God" [Acts 11:21], by which he exercises his might. For by the inspiration of his power so breathes divine life into us that we are no longer actuated by ourselves, but are ruled by his action and prompting. Accordingly, whatever good things are in us are the fruits of his grace; and without him our gifts are darkness of mind and perversity of heart
[cf. Gal. 5:19-21]. (Institutes).

In spiritum sanctum

We now enter the season and structure of Spirit and Church.
We now consider the work of Spirit and Church in the world.

What was the Spirit of God that hovered over creation's waters and inspired kings and prophets? Why was the Holy Spirit released anew unto the world? What is the connection between Akedah, Decalogue, and Pentecost?

Why imbue nature and history with this new dynamic? Why was the Church established and energized by this same Spirit? Spirit, Church and Society are projects of God and Christ in the world. They are given to resist evil and achieve good and to restore God's will to the creation.

We live in the age of the Spirit, enfolded in the phenomenon of the Spirit. Yes, the Spirit of God has always been present in nature and history. The *Ruach Elohim* hovers over the primeval waters bringing cosmos form chaos. The Lord gave the Spirit to the seventy elders of Israel (Numbers 11:25). The age and atmosphere of the spirit, grounded in this Mosaic moment, is the Pentecost bequest of the ascended Christ to time and space. The tongues of fire now join decalogue Succoth with Christ's conjunction of Jewish water baptism and

John's apocalyptic fire baptism into a creed that will transform the world: Christ is Lord.

When the Nicene Creed expands the Apostles' and the old Roman Creed, the Spirit is spoken of as the Lord and giver of life. The third article of the creed charters the human enterprise as a divine spirited gift and project in the world. As Hegel claims in his vast *ouvre*, the realm of nature and human nature and the run of history is a phenomenon of Spirit (*Geist*). The vitalities and activities of the divine spirit are mediated in and through the personal and communal human spirit. In Luther's words', Christendom is sustained and intended in spirit through history.

The nature and destiny of the Holy Spirit is the renewal of life. If Christ's death is the death of death, His Spirit creation is the birth and nurturance of life.

As the world grows old, as entropy increases and the reign of violence and death prevails, the enlivening Spirit of God convicts, refreshes and renews the creation.

> We pray "take not your Holy Spirit from us…"

If God withdraws His Spirit, we collapse back to dust (Psalm 51:11). Spirit (resurrection) consumates akedic and Adamic dust. The Holy Spirit contemporizes and actualizes the reality of God in Christ.

> These things have I spoken to you,
> While I am still with you.
> But the counsellor, the Holy Spirit,
> Whom the Father will send in my name,
> He will teach you all things, and bring to
> Your remembrance all that I have said to you.
> Peace I leave with you. My peace I give to you;
> Not as the world gives, do I give to you.
> (John 14:25-27a)

The Communion of Saints: Communio sanctorum

The movements of God, the community of holy or set apart, recalls the covenant, remembers the Savior, reveres the martyrs and relies on the future of God. The phrase Communion of Saints, with its biblical foundation (Psalm 89:5, 2 Cor.6:14) finds its first creedal formulation in Serbia in the fourth century.[301]

"Communion of Saints" means the fellowship of Christians, past, present, and future. All the epistle ascriptions address this community: (Romans 1:7, I Cor. 1:1, Eph. 1:1, Phil. 1:1, Col.1:2). In the Augsburg Confession of 1530 it was the

---

[301] Wofhart Pannenberg, *The Apostles' Creed*. Philadelphia: Westminster Press, 1972, p. 148.

Congregatio Sanctorum, The Assembly of Saints. In Luther, it is the assembly of believers – *Congregatio Fidelium*. The communion of saints is the church in its various understandings and expressions. To be an Armenian or Copt is to be like a Jew, a member of an ethniclinguistic- ecclessial community. Genetic, geographic and *glaubenslehre* elements intertwine. Roman Catholics are part of an historic, hierarchical, global structure with a long and deep heritage. Europeans believe and belong more or less to the historic churches of the Reformation. Citizens of Hamburg are vaguely Lutheran, Strasburgers, nominally Calvinist. Evangelicals around the world, like Pentecostals, are bound together by faith or worship style.

Communio Sanctorum was the subject of the young Dietrich Bonhoeffer's "*Habilitationschrift*" – his professional treatise. In the spirit of Martin Luther, Bonhoeffer searched for the true spiritual church within the national community. Luther consciously and deliberately had changed the "Sancta Ecclesia" of the magisterial medieval church into the "*communio sanctorum*" of renewed holiness. Early Eastern faiths had used the same designation. The "German Christians" had become a corrupt, accommodating civil religion in the Nazi time. The "Confessing Church" resisted this idolatry and retained authenticity and faithfulness. As such it embodied the rightful *kirchenkampf* – the fight of faith. The Barmen Declaration was the charter of *communio sanctorum*.

Throughout church history "holy communities" and "purifying sects" often go on the offensive against dominant secularized bodies. Church sometimes fights State. The enthusiastic peasants rebel against the Lutheran princes. Often the "holiness separatists" are deeply pacifist. The persecuted church is often refined into purity by fire and sword. War is often waged by the secularized concomitant of the church with fervor and zeal appropriated from the "Holy fellowship." Stalin and Churchill, Saddam Hussein and President Bush invoke religious sentiment behind their schemes of political or economic warfare. Crusade can be disengaged from creed. The contention can be against unbeliever or infidel, rival or threat. The *ecclesia invisibiis* within *ecclesia visibilis* is the perennial enigma of the church voluntary and involuntary.

Forgiveness of Sins: Remissionem peccatorum
    What is the whole creed about? What is it for? What, for that matter is God's whole revelatory story and scripture for? Why is it given? What does it do? The answers clear and simple – the forgiveness of sins. All of the great sixteenth century creeds turn now to this rather abrupt focus of meaning. Why all this? What good is it? *Remissionem Pecatorum*. To turn Paul's provocative phrase and liberating logic – If we remain in our sins then Christ did not die and was not raised again, but now Christ is risen from the dead our sins and their deadly sting is gone! According to Barth we are dealing here with the core of the Gospel as received by the Apostolicum, embedded in creed by Christendom, refreshed and reasserted by the Reformation. Why is the phenomenon of forgiveness of sins so crucial? This continuum of meaning is best fathomed in

the mystery of ADEDAH. It entails sin, sacrifice, forgiveness, restitution. An errant world is restored to its good character and destiny. The destiny of the beloved son prevails.

Luther affirms the classic doctrine of the Holy Spirit as it appeared in the church fathers, Augustine and Aquinas. The Spirit akedically undertakes a threefold mission in the world: formation of the church, forgiveness of sins and resurrection or continuing vitalization of the world. Specifically the Spirit 1) appropriates to God's people the history of Jesus Christ – His words, His presence, His Gospel, His forgiving faith; 2) Secondly, the Spirit is creative; 3) Having animated creation and new creation we now can adore and obey God and gain a heart of love and justice for the neighbor.

In his *katechismusspredigten* of 21 September 1528 Luther attributes to the Holy Spirit the:

- Sanctification through the church
- Sanctification of our living through forgiveness and
- Sanctification of humanity and creation through resurrection and eternal life

The Third article, in other words, is suffused with the Spirit of God. In this train of Luther, Paul Tillich builds on the Third article the vast human creative project:

> Science, literature, the arts, history itself. The inspiration of culture as well as the vitalities of the church are God's Spirit –gift to the world.

If Tillich rightly senses the meaning of biblical pneumatology, as is likely, then conviction of truth, censure of error, pursuit of beauty, passion for human rights, the resistance to tyranny, the panoramic Jihad or Crusade of Faith is now at work in the world as the spirit of life over death is manifest. All of this is a work of the divine movement which she inaugurates linking the commandments (the meaning of the Pentecost) with the concourse of the Spirit forward into history.

Peter and Paul, like Stephen, are not afraid to die because they cannot die. With all believers, they have been translated to a new plane of existence where the Spirit imparts eternal life. And while we live here and now we live in and for the kingdom project which the Spirit is fashioning in human culture and history. The creed/crusade is therefore a manifestation of Spirit.

The essential teaching of the most culturally determinative strand of the theological tradition – that which can be traced as a thread through vastly more vibrant and colorful fabric – beginning in the priestly Genesis and weaving through the sacrality of the prophets – the depiction of Jesus the offering of God in the evangelists – Paul's exposition of the atonement – then elaborated in Augustine and Anselm – is the forgiveness of sins, appropriated in faith, saving persons and the world. Without grace the world remains embedded in death without God. Within grace, our sins are forgiven and the world is released to new life. Grace in Hebrew is an onamonopoetic word mimicing the cry of a mother camel searching in the desert for her lost son (Paul Scherer). The searching yearning of child for parent in Stanley Kubrick's last film AI is the meaning of the Spirit in history.

Continuing in the vein of Karl Barth's analysis of the creed, we could have placed at this point some other pivotal assertion. The heart of the matter could have been a new law for life, a true knowledge of or mediate communion with God. But legalism, gnosticism and mysticism, all profound meanings of the new life received in Christ, are turned aside by the receipt of redeeming mercy. This selection is all the more remarkable since the embracing Hebraic, Hellenic and Roman culture accented those achievable qualities as *summmum bonum*.

What is so grave about human sin and so great about divine forgiveness? The question goes to the core of the anthropological and theological question. What, if anything, has gone wrong in humanity? Of what concern is this to God? The biblical witness shows that people have taken a turn away from God and responsible living in the world and that this diversion in freedom has distorted our humanity and has damaged God's healing growth design for the world. God cannot be God, humans human, the world its true self, without forgiveness. Sin is the fall from wholeness and fullness, the discrepancy of is with ought. It is the acute and chronic disease of creation . It robs persons and the world of health and life. Unforgiven sin, as we know from Christ's dereliction cry and descent into hell entails eternal death and separation from God. The hymn lifts this dread disgrace toward proffered grace.

> Pardon for sin and a peace that endureth…
> Great is thy faithfulness

Forgiveness is the liberation of life from the bondage of distortion, decay and death. The forgiveness of sins, the justification and renewal of the sinner, the release of the creation in hope amid apparent futility (Romans 8:20-22) is the work of the living Spirit of Christ, the power the evangelists and early church designated as *hagios pneumatos, spiritum sanctum*. In forgiveness, life in the flesh, bodily life, material life, has become life in faith. Persons and our sympathetic environment, the world, have become new.

Origin and Biblical Setting

The phrase "forgiveness of sins" grounded in sacrifice and atonement, is associated particularly with the ritual of baptism. This is the akedic parting of the waters in Exodus deliverence. In parental or personal affirmation in infant or believer baptism we transpose our existence from one realm to another – from the realm of sin and death, to grace and life. In forgiveness we bury in death the body of death, drown without god and rise to the ocean's surface in recussitation, renewal of life. No longer does the terror of life or death hold sway. One has been released to another plane of existence. When Dietrich Bonhoeffer was being led to the gallows at Flossenberg, the guard noticing his serenity asked – "Are you not afraid, Herr Bonhoeffer?" "Afraid?," he answered, recalling an old comfort of Luther, "I have been baptized." As the text evolves from the Old Roman Creed toward the Nicene formulation, we "confess one baptism for the remission of sins." As Peter preaches his first sermon he appeals to everyone "...repent and be baptized in the name of Jesus Christ for he forgiveness of your sins." (Acts 2:38)

The biblical notion of forgiveness of sins seems to be about covering up, passing over, passing through or sending away (all akedic images) the residue of misdeeds and the concomitant guilt of the sinner and the rightful revenging anger of the offended. Just as the primal crime is lie and cover up so the antidote to sin is a therapeutic wipeout – a cleansing. Forgiveness cleans away the offense from all parties: God, the sinner and the sinned against. In Psalm 32 God's constant gifts become perceived blessing only in the experience and attitude of forgiveness.

> ...Blessed is he whose transgression is forgiven whose sin is covered (vs.1)

Apart from forgiveness we misconstrue reality. We take provision for granted. We take hardship with brutal bitterness. Grace upholds us amid the battering storm.

> ...In the floods of great waters he will say "you are my hiding place (vs.6,7)
> ...Though you pass through the waters, and through the fire...(Isaiah 43)

Since God is holy, sin offends. Jesus comes to rescue sinners.

Theology
Baptism for the forgiveness of sins is the primal experiential phenomenon behind the elaboration of theological doctrines such as justification and sanctification, penitence and regeneration.

Resurrection of the Body: Resurrectionem carnis
Luther's teaching on the resurrection of the body is anchored in the crucifixion/descent and resurrection/ascent of Jesus whereby Christ has now and will then rescue those ensnared by the devil in death...

> *Errettung aus der Satandisden Gewalten Zuruck*
> (rescued back from Satan's prison) (WA26.509.16)

> There is to be a general resurrection..."*Toten auferwacken*"
> And a deliverance of Christ's own..."*Glaubigen in Christo*"
> (WA512.8. (kk.).

The resurrection of the dead and life eternal have profound meaning for our thesis both in:

- The meaning of the beliefs for the doctrine of justice and
- The literal expectation of a return of the dead and/or the dead in Christ in the final battle.

The meaning of resurrection for a doctrine of justice moves in two directions. On the one hand, it fosters a doctrine of retributive justice, that is, it is the role of governments (the sword of the kingdom) to prosecute wars, punish wayward individuals and nations and restore the justice and peace of God. To use modern examples: when Hitler oversteps his bounds and invades Poland or when Saddam Hussein violates the sovereign integrity of Kuwait, it is the right, indeed duty, of "God fearing" nations, that is those whose public life is animated by the strictures of divine and human justice, and who have been entrusted with excelling power, to prosecute that injustice and restore equilibrium (shalom).

Perhaps the deepest primitive instinct in human justice is that which believes that divine judgment lies behind and beyond this life and that in the consummating reality and human affairs(that can be after one dies or in some cosmic and collective final judgment) scores will be settled.

- The little boy is beaten up at lunch time by the school bullies. He wisely doesn't retaliate believing that those ruffians "will get theirs…someday."
- The oppressed people of African slaves in America believe Dr. King when in his Nobel Prize speech he extols those who have…" suffered for righteousness sake."[302]

'When the years have rolled past and when the blazing light of truth is focused on the marvelous age in which we live, men and women will know and children will be taught that we have a finer land, a better people, a more noble civilization, because these humble children of God were willing to "suffer for righteousness' sake."[303]

The moral doctrine of justice, last-judgment and the ultimate righteousness of reality is a strong impulse in military and political action. For Abraham Lincoln in the second Inaugural Address the uncertainty of human judgment and certainty of divine judgment are sustained.

…both (North and South) read the same Bible, prayed to the
same God and each invoked His aid against the other
…Yet the judgments of God are true ad righteous altogether".

---

[302] David J. Garrow, *Bearing the Cross*, New York Vintage, 1986, p. 364.
[303] Ibid., p. 365

> Apocalyptic views of biblical justice sing
> "...I want to be in that number when the saints go marching in."

Lurking beneath many theologies of creedal – crusade is the anticipation of some ultimate victory of the saints and vanquishing of evil...This militant theology is ultimately drawn from the creed...

> ...The resurrection of the body and the life everlasting.

The Anthropology of the Third Article

Among active theologians in the modern world, Jurgen Moltmann comes closest to my project in reintegrating all dimensions of the creed – Father, Son and Spirit – and recapturing the ancient church and reformation emphasis of structuring theology around decalogue, prayer, and creed.

His rejudaizing project is most recently expressed in his 1991 publication *Der Geist des lebens*[304] he signals this purpose.

> In the degree to which Christianity cut itself off from its Hebrew roots and acquired Hellenistic and Roman form, it lost its eschatological hope and surrendered its apocalyptic alternative to this world of violence and death. It merged into late antiquity's gnostic religion of redemption. From Justin onwards, most of the Fathers revered Plato as a "Christian before Christ" and extolled his spiritual world. God's eternity now took the place of God's future, heaven replaced the coming kingdom, the spirit that redeemed the soul from the body supplanted the Spirit as "the well of life," the immortality of the soul displaced the resurrection of the body, and the yearning for another world became a substitute for changing this one.[305]

Moltmann is not content to sustain the Greek, Platonic and idealistic-Germanic tradition of theology as is, for example, Paul Tillich. In this tradition, the influence of Kant and Hegel is felt even in the doctrine of the Sprit. In Moltmann's Spirit of Life he offers a thorough-going Judaic (ethical and eschatological) understanding of the Spirit of God. As his friend and American interpreter, Douglas Meeks has written, Moltmann has moved to an eschatology of "immanence and presence" as he contemplates, like Abraham Joshua Heschel, "the cosmic *Shekinah* of God."[306]

Even though, in Moltmann's theology the trinity is offered as a structure for analysis it is a rejudaized and re-eschatlogized sense of the trinity, accenting the suffering of the Christ, historic Israel and the creation itself. In the theology that I have offered the biography of God is one of contending engagement with creation and humanity. Given in love, life entails suffering. Christ and Israel

---

[304] *The Spirit of Life*, Minneapolis: Fortress Press, 1992.
[305] Spirit, 89.
[306] M. Douglas Meeks, "Jurgen Moltmanns"s Systematic Contributions to Theology," *Religious Studies Review*, vol. 22, no.2, April 1996, p. 95.

collaborated in redemptive messianic suffering and the Holy Spirit of Life is manifest in the crises of health and suffering, life and death.

Metaphysically enriching the historical theology and ethics of biblical faith in the manner of Philo of Alexandria and contemporary Jewish philosophy, Moltmann offers two premises to interpret "what God is doing in the world" (Lehmann):

- God's being (suffering love) is affected by the world...as the world is embraced by God.
- God is present in the world giving life amid the omnipresence of destruction and death.

This divine ontology prompts an anthropology of freedom and responsibility where human beings are offered opportunity for wideranging liberty over creation (ecology), in society, in human relations and in self-fulfillment. But this freedom is refracted and dynamic (it is "on the way" – an Exodus freedom). It is incomplete, growing and always fraught with ambiguity. This crucial eshcatological dimension leads Moltmann to propose a

Theology of imagination (as) the Kingdom of God (comes to) the world and the world comes to the Kingdom of God.[307]

Critically and prophetically Kingdom of God theology interferes in public affairs- in the *res Publica* of a society.[308]

In this mood he concludes with an ecclesial or logical point...

...(we seek the) creative theological economics that is needed for the social and ecological reformation of the market society...

...I am seeking a critical ecclesiology which defines the position of the church of Christ in a globalized market economy.[309]

A theology and ethic rooted in the biblical tradition where God decisively intervened in the history of Israel and Jesus and reaching into the present world in which God is now involved in judging and redeeming, must begin with Barth's two sources of God's word: The bible and the daily newspaper. The world presents itself to the Word today as historic strife is transformed into global economy. The aggressive creedal energy that was expressed in the sixteenth century in the establishment of nation states is now expressed in this

---

[307] Meeks, p. 103.
[308] Ibid.
[309] Ibid., p. 105.

age of revolution and liberation as the dispossessed and oppressed throughout the world strive in a freedom revolution, becoming entrepreneurially free through our enterprising action with market economies. The dominant worldly phenomenon of the late twentieth century is this emerging global economy; the clustering of national powers into economic Conglomerates; the European community, North America, the Asian and African associations, for example. The battle for control and influence and for justice and equity in the world of the Twentieth Century – as the sphere of economics.

If wars and political hegemony have receded as vital world forces and the global economy has assumed overarching theological preeminence, what then is the spiritual and ethical challenge of this development.

The press toward a global economy falls under the justice and mercy of God as it offers new possibilities and hope for human life along with new human degradations. What of the justice of God? The manifestation of the divine Spirit of Christ, prophetically and pastorally conveyed into the world through the mystery of Christ's body in the church is realized and whenever and wherever redemptive life is breaking forth amid death redemption seeks the liberation of persons from oppression, seeks the enhancement of free creativity of persons and communities, seeks the redemption of love amid the ubiquity of hate. The grace of cooperation amid competition and the miracle of peace amid pervasive strife. Living well, prospering in the world, possessing shelter, food and the goods of life for all people is a dimension of spirit gifts to the world.

God seeks and our creed ought to affirm the salvation of persons; the strengthening of the healing and redemptive body in the world which is *communio sanctorum*, a mystery transcending all institutions. It affirms the amelioration of all inflicted pain and some inevitable pain (e.g., disease, natural calamity) as human afterthought of God's thoughts. It resists within space/time every diabolic distortion of that good life and creation that God gives and would give.

Specifically, what is the justice of God vis a vis the global economy? If divine justice is love and love is justice, if law is grace and grace is law, then the law of life (decalogue) ought to be written into the code of ethics of global business:

- Do not dishonor, kill, cheat, steal, lie and crave Rather
- Free, heal, pacify, love, forgive, and advocate

In the charters and agreements of the North American economic treaties (NAFTA) and of the European community, as well as those constellation of cultures shaped by biblical creed and Abrahamic faith, special responsibility for business ethics is called for. In Israel, South Africa, North America, and Africa, specific ethical guidelines should be affirmed and enforced including:

- Bottom line must never justify harm to persons or environment
- Justice and well-being for the poor ought to be the end result of economic activity
- Freedom and honesty ought to guide human relations in business
- Mutual enhancement of wealth and opportunity (the heart of the free market mechanism) rather than coercion, manipulation, cornering markets, deception and polarization of rich and poor ought to be the ethos undergirding the global economy.
- The OIKOS – the world house (economy, ecology, ecumenical) is God's house. We inhabitants are guests, not owners.

"People" said Martin Luther "live not for themselves but for others" "they live only for others and not for themselves." We have been enabled to labor, to acquire and preserve property in order to aid those who are in want. Thus may the stronger serve the weaker- as we bear one another's burdens. All other values – maximizing profits, survival of the fittest are not worthy of free and responsible human beings entrusted with the gifted goods of this world.

The War History of the Third Article
Modern history is replete with persons and armies going to war for and because of the faith:

- The peasants rise up in England in 1381 killing the Archbishop of Canterbury who unwisely "sics the Pope" on the crowd. In Germany in 1525 Luther calls on the princes to "crush" the peasants revolt. Confused and alarmed, the poor who always "hear the message gladly" retire back to their customary oppression until another season (18th and 19th centuries).
- The 30 year wars between Protestants and Catholics and the grievous 2 centuries (Huguenots, Henry IV, Louis XIV) was to eliminate Protestantism from France.
- The vigor with which Catholics (France and Spain) and Protestants (Scotland and Scandinavia) censure and cleanse the other parties remains a blight on Christ's faith and way among people. The only redeeming feature of these brutal conflicts was that they set the stage for more secular pluralistic-tolerant states that would have "no more" of confessional killing.

In Erasmus' *Enchiridion militis Christiani* (Handbook of the Christian Knight, 1503) he writes:

Make Christ the only goal of your life. Dedicate to Him all your enthusiasm, all your effort, your leisure as well as your business! And don't look upon Christ as the mere word, as empty expression, but rather as charity, simplicity, patience and purity...Jesus was the sole archetype of godliness...[310]

Dueling Standards

The restoration of a brilliant epic film INDEPENDENTA ROMANIEI (1912) by Grigore Brezeanu brings to life the long saga of creedal crusades and counter-crusades waged by the Ottoman Turkish empire (1299-1922) against the Byzantine East and the Roman/Protestant west. The wars were holy wars but not with the mystical fervor of the crusades. Although the fervor over Kosovo and Christian Serbia's defeat by Islamic powers still generates reminescent mystic power. In this film, a harsh reality of the bitter unholiness of war had already set in as had a secular, Clauswitzian doctrine of the brutal amoral necessity of war. The setting is the 1877 liberation of Romania as the warring Turkish power is beingsqueezed by the Russians and Czar Alexander II from the North and the Romanian King Carol first's forces from the south and west: The film depicts the awesome sacrifice and sacrament of war. As it begins the joy and dancing of simple sacral villages is interrupted by the call for mobilization. The calvary and infantry form as the distinguished elders (political and military) decide and plan the war of independence. The wives wail, even in their pride and patriotism as the children innocently continue their play. Mothers know, what is yet hidden from the children, that many of these men will not return, some will writhe in agony with battle wounds as they expire on the field, others will be carried home by ambulance there to die slowly at the hands of the surgeons or infections. Yet the victory thrill ensues and the parades. The children's pride finally comes home and the dancing goes on.

And the prayer for peace. The battle had been sacralized by the orthodox priests blessing the officers, troops and horses. Finally the standards, flags and banners are taken into the church and rituals, first conceived by Constantine and his standard cross, are reenacted (only when sacred ritual sets it right). Can units go to war, kill other men (even infidels), risk wound and death and endure the lonely nights torn from home and friends. The symbol: Father, Son and Spirit, is woven into the brilliant standards and crossed in faith through the holy salute.

Back in Ottoman strongholds the same rituals hallow the star and crescent—and the same rather-be-working and loving young men, the same families and children, then same fear and hope—and the same dancing fore and aft.

Elsewhere in Europe and the New World especially in:

- The 17th century English revolution
- The 18th century freedom revolution
  - ➤ America 1776
  - ➤ France 1789

---

[310] Enchiridon, 2.4 2.6 in John Patrick Dolan, *The Essential Erasmus*, New York: New American Library 1964, p. 58, 71.

> ➢ Germany 1848
- The 19th century Industrial Revolution
- The late 20th century technological (information) revolution

are fired by Gospel imperatives of personal liberty (Galatians 5), the infinite value of each person, and the truth of Mary's Magnificat that—the low will be exalted, and the mighty cast down. Even the poor can access the Internet.

Nineteenth-century Euro-American Expansion
The preeminent historian of church expansion, Kenneth Scott Lautorette, devotes three of his seven volumes to the nineteenth century, calling it "The Great Century." The great century of colonialism was the century of evangelism when Jesus' "great commission" was fully realized...

> All power is given unto me Go, and make disciples of all nations Baptizing them...And I am with you until the end of the age (Matthew 28:18ff)

In the Raj in India or the Dutch East Indian Company, in French, Dutch and British Africa, military and mission action often went together. As the modern world unfolds we realize that Adam Smith's project on free market enterprise is at root a visionary mission. In the concluding paragraph of The Theory of Moral Sentiments (1759) he promises (alluding to Wealth of Nations)

> ...in another discourse (I shall) endeavor to give an account of the general principles of law and government, and of the different revolutions they have undergone in the different ages and periods of society, not only in what is conscious justice but on what concerns policy revenue and arms, and whatever else is the object of law.[311]

The military and mercenary creed—often superceded the evangelistic creed to the lasting disgrace of the West. The fact that today the dynamic vital populational centers of Christianity are Korea, Africa, and South America is more a tribute to Christian forgiveness than to the commingled blood and bible exploits of the nineteenth century.

Mass conversions and baptisms following military defeat, absurd ritualsnot seen since medieval time, were again enacted. Zionism, dar al Islam, even Christendome became new ethnocentric entities in a world that had thought it had achieved secularism and pluralism. That the crusade was inevitably "Eurocentric" has come to haunt the West as indigenous churches in Africa and Asia now send their missionaries to "godless" Europe and America. Before the global calamity of the First World War, Hillaire Belloc coined the phrase "the faith is Europe and Europe is the faith."[312]

---

[311] EG West, *Adam Smith the Man and His Works*, Indianapolis: The Liberty Fund, 1976, p. 209.
[312] *Through the Centuries*, Pelican, p. 222.

That idolatrous faith was soon to be shattered and the faithfallacy exposed in Karl Barth's *Romerbrief* (1919). When Cyril and Methodius brought the Eastern creed and ritual to the Slavs in the ninth century they translated it into the beauty of the old church Slavonic. In the nineteenth century there was no such magnanimity and appreciation of indigenous culture. Now inculturation became new idolatry.

Perhaps the saving grace of the nineteenth century crusade into "all the world" has been the transmuting of the commission "in my name" from creedal orthodoxy to healing the sick and liberating the poor. Since the miracle—profused Gospels the kingdom and salvation has always had as one of its central meanings healing and health. Harnack notes:

> Into the world of craving for salvation the preaching of Christianity made its way. Long before it had achieved its final triumph by dint of an impressive philosophy of religion, its success was already assured by the fact that it promised and offered salvation—a feature in which it surpassed all other religions and cults. It did more than set up the actual Jesus against the imaginary Aesculapius of dreamland. *Deliberately and consciously it assumed the form of "the religion of salvation or healing," or "the medicine of soul and body," and at the same time it recognized that one of its chief duties was to care assiduously for the sick in body.*[313]

Since the tree of life depicted in Revelations 22:2 was "for the healing of the nations" it was significant that during the Crimean war and in the Geneva Convention of 1864 that "Just war" creed became concerned with "the wounded and sick armies on the field" and the innocent civilians injured in the collateral effects of war. The red cross, the inverted Swiss flag became the humanitarian symbol of crusade of mercy, a new accent of Christian initiative in the world.

Caring for the sick and poor of the world, a concomitant of early modern missions is personified in the nineteenth century English- Presbyterian physician David Livingstone and the twentieth century Alsacian genius Albert Schweitzer. As in first century Palestine the Word again goes out... "see how they love one another. By this they shall know that you are my disciples" (John 13:35). Rooney Stark and others have shown that the success of Christianity in the Roman Empire can be attributed mainly to its ameliorative and transformative power within the social order. Its genius was nursing, sustaining, caring in a world that had grown hopelessly self-obsessed and apathetic. Creedal crusade at its noblest and purist is exemplary love.

---

[313] A.W. Harnack, *The Mission and Expansion of Christianity*, London: Williams and Norgate, 1988, v.1, p. 108.

Recent War History

If our thesis thus far is correct and only creedal war is justified, unjustified war in the modern world would increase proportionately with the confusion in our creed. All war is now global in significance. All of the nearly 100 wars in the world in 1996 effect all persons everywhere. Now, in reality, in this age of global awareness, we can say with John Donne:

...no man is an island—each one's death diminishes me...

Consider in reverse order a sequence of representative modern conflicts:

- The conflict of Albanians and Serbs in Kosovo
- The refugee crisis in Zaire springing from the genocidal conflict (Tutsi/Hutu) in Rwanda and Brundi
- The crisis of Israel with Palestinian Arabs and Christians
- Russia/Chechnya
- The hunger crisis and tribal conflict in Somalia
- The genocidal conflict in Bosnia
- The Gulf War
- Panama, Grenada, The Falklands
- The cold-war and arms détente between Russia and the U.S.
- Vietnam
- Korea
- The Second and First World Wars

What have these crises to do with creed, crusade or church? In the humanitarian calamities of Somalia and Rwanda, the deeper crisis is spiritual and ethical. Competition and rivalry have displaced the common bond of humanity. These are crisis of the failure of the global economy and of world justice and order. The solidarity of the human race has been shattered. The world has accepted the false god of Darwin, "survival of the fittest." In creedal terms this is an assault on the spirit of life in the world—the Holy Spirit. It is an ecclesial crisis (Article 3), a crisis of the human fellowship in the world's Savior—the body of Christ (Article 2). It is a christological crisis—a deepening of the perpetual crucifixion of Jesus by an unjust and cruel world (Article 2). It is offense to God almighty, the maker and giver of the good heaven and earth (Article 1).

The extant creed has not been complemented by crusade. Word and deed have become disjoined. The eschatological features of the creed have overwhelmed the ethical and the whole substance has been damaged. The connection between commandments, Lord's prayer and creed has also been severed. The prayer for tomorrow's bread today and the commands not to steal, bear false witness or blaspheme have been undermined in the wars of the late twentieth century. War-weary and comfort-obsessed we have ceased to believe that there is anything worth living or dying for.

In our chart of "master interconnections" failure to feed the hungry (or to force hunger by unjust economic policies) is violation of the commandment against killing and stealing and of the creed's affirmation:

- That God created the heavens and Earth;
- That Christ suffered under Pontius Pilate; and,
- That He will come again to judge the living and dead (c.f. Dives and Lazarus, C. Dickens, A Christmas Carol.)

Today's crisis of Russia with Chechnya, Israel with Palestine, the U.S. with Iraq, Armenia with Azerbijean and other nations within the former Soviet Union is also global crisis. The world has a responsibility to integrate all nations into the body of world order and economy. Russia herself is of course responsible for violating the first article of the creed as clarified by the first three commandments. In accepting the inhuman idolatry of Lenin and Stalin it forfeited its chance to pursue the social justice of the young Marx. It thus plunged this ancient Christic people into the judgment of the living and the dead. The United States and the West also stands under this judgment for initiating (Manhattan Project) and accelerating the arms race which vitiated the Soviet economy and culture. The accelerating of military spending and the forcing of the entire world into the arms race in the 1980's will work havoc on the earth for a hundred years. In cruel irony, America, a blessed receptor of the contemporary Gospel, is the principal alms supplier to the world.

The creed which Russia had affirmed since 1100 C.E. in other words was violated in all three articles. God the almighty father was abandoned for atheism, the power of technology and war subjugation of peoples. Christ the Lord was forsaken as leader and people chose to serve materialism. The Holy Spirit of Life was denied as the nation undertook ethnic cleansing and godless existence. All this was in violation of the promise of the revolution of freedom, equity, justice and welfare for the peasantry and the destitute. It was also prompted by the mingled belligerence and insecurity of America and the West. The cold war legacy and the arms race was profoundly destructive of human value.

World War II was a just war, or in the words of Studs Terkel "the Good War". It was a creedal crusade with only a few side reservations:

1) The complicity of America and Europe in economically impoverishing Germany at Versailles following the First War.

520

2) The complicity of America, Europe and the rest of the world (except Scandinavia and Japan) in refusing immigration of European Jews.

3) The genocidal bombing of German and Japanese cities.

Beyond these grievous injustices the war was just. It fought against the following evils:

- Nazism as a godless, idolatrous ideology
- The victimization, killing and subjugation of other peoples
- The genocidal killing of European Jewry
- The seizing of the land of other peoples

It pursued the following goods:

- The protection of true worship
- Personal freedom (not tyranny)
- The democratic way of government
- Human rights, worship, assembly, press etc.
- The territorial integrity of nations and
- Personal integrity of persons, families and their properties.

When creed is amplified in a faith stance by the ethics of the Decalogue and the eucharistics of the Lord's prayer it contains a body of evils to be resisted and goods to be fought for. The Second World War was good and just, perhaps even holy in its repudiation and destruction of Hitler and the Third Reich. Christ's kingdom, not Caesar's I, II or III shall inherit the earth.

A New Mutation of Old Genes: Terrorist Holy War
In the middle of August, 1998, American missiles were launched at a so called "terrorist compound" in Afghanistan and a pharmaceutical factory in the Sudan. Newspapers heralded this as the beginning of a new mode and era of warfare. The New York Times called the raids and the precipitating conflict with terrorism, "the war of the future." On the heels of 9/11 now in 2003 the world is gripped with episodic terror, and nuclear threat, massive famine and economic collapse.

At first impression the "new" style of war looks very old. It feels all too much like Israel's ancient warfare against Mesopotamian paganism and early Hellenic Christianity's contention against Ebionite, Nestorian, Semitic versions of Christian faith. It recalls medieval and modern crusades against Islam and the Turkish Ottomans. It is old genes in newly cloned skins. The terrorist adversaries of President Harrison Ford in the film Air Force One are Khazakistan Muslims. In James Bond's latest, the enemy is a North Korean biologically mutated into a Nordic warrior (Die Another Day). The target of the August missiles is Osama bin Laden, a wealthy nomad, orchestrating, it is charged, in what many feel was a "wag the dog" like diversion from Clinton's sexual woes—a jihad against Satanic America.

National Security Advisor, Sandy Berger intones "This is an evil that is directed at the United States. It's going to persist." With religious, apocalyptic rhetoric The New York Times (Aug. 23, 1998) echoes:

> The enemy is a man, not a state
> Backed by acolytes, not armies.
> In this war high-tech weapons will
> Prove less effective than pick-ups packed with dynamite.

Have we come full cycle back to Israel's holy war on Canaan of the European crusades against the Islamic occupied Holy Land? Perhaps the enemy is no longer a foreign power but "the enemy within," a disenchanted patriot like Tim McVeigh or Ted Kaszinski. Perhaps even more Pogo has it right: "We have met the enemy and it is us!"

The new strife in the world involves power and money, opportunity and identity. It is the contention of creedal crusade—a matter of the deepest loyalties and devotions of a global humanity and of particular peoples. It is the engagement of faiths and ways of life. Somehow, in subtle mystery, it involves the judgmental strategies of God—ever redemptive.

Summary

We have traced the legacy of the Apostle's Creed. As the first text in western civilization of the principles and values "worth fighting for" it has enjoyed a noble and notorious history. As we noted in the introduction all peoples live by (crusade for) some creed. At times in Christian history specific fragments of the creed; "almighty father," "only son," "born of the virgin," "Holy catholic church," etc. have taken men to their deaths in battle, to prison or exile. At other periods of history they merge into secular equivalents: freedom, justice, equality, etc. The faith retracts into strict orthodoxy when confronted by adversaries and enlarges toward greater munificence in seasons of peace. All along history's course the ancient provincial functions of creed: catechesis of children, baptism of strangers to the faith and ongoing instruction to the faithful have been sustained alongside the public manifestation. Today the clear and continuing articulation of the "profession of faith" is in an offensive and defensive stance.

Today the creedal crusade stands at the center of an evangelical theology. What has the historic meeting of God with the world in Israel and Jesus meant for the world? What of sister faiths, and other creeds (or accents of the one creed) that arise in the providence of God? How do we know when alien systems of belief and practice damage and destroy humanity: Nazism, communism, materialism, commercialism, pleasure-obsession? The task of creed building and interpreting continues—as does the challenge to live it out

> In faith...
>> Justice
>>> ...peace
>>>> and love.

Excursus

It is November 18. Outside my window looking toward the cathedral it is snowing. *Blanche Neige*, as the French version of "Snow White" goes. A bit early for Strasbourg but we have to keep up with Chicago and Cleveland which had two feet last week. As I gaze up toward the cathedral there is a majestic old house with that ancient orange ceramic tile roof. Like so many *grand maison* in Strasbourg, the attic windows are gone. In previous centuries marksmen would go to these windows to defend home and city from some invader. Today I am fascinated not with the snipers but with the pigeons who make that attic their home and this window their portal.

All of the ridiculous antics of human strife are acted out in the ethological rituals of other animals and, it appears, of these dozen or so pigeons. At times they cooperate, share and seem to get along. At other times, like right now, posturing, strutting, intimidating, excluding, feather bristling and defensive pecking are the order of the day. A poor, weak, perhaps female has just flown in through the snow. She prances meekly in front of the small window while two arrogant, big breasted, Arnold Schwarzenegger types, block her entrance. There they strut like the *Gard Republican* that paraded on their horses with trumpets yesterday in *Place Kleber*. (I thought we had blown them away in Iraq.)

Ethnologists, like Edward Wilson who have studied animal behavior find (in the range of animal families) natural patterns of aggression and territoriality as well as natural patterns of cooperation and altruism. No animals except rats, they say, have risen to the fratricidal and suicidal violence of humans. To pattern, stylize and ritualize those aggressions and pompous power displays and enhance those salutary virtues (lit.) is the challenge of creed in our time. For here alone is found war which is word.

Conclusion

Conclusion

The journey now comes to a pause for rest. It will continue on into God's future as the faith peoples—The seed of Abraham, Hagar and Sarah—continue their Hegira. It will continue as other faith communities endure and appear in world history. It will continue as this perplexing world continues its search for truth and right, justice and peace. Inherent impulses toward disintegration and destruction will contend with forces inclined toward wholeness and goodness.

We have reviewed four dimensions of the three faiths of Abraham: Word, Way, Worship and War. We have examined the resonance and dissonance heard as the instruments of the three faiths—Judiasm, Christianity and Islam—play out in solo and interplay in concert in those four movements.

Though my thesis - that concord soothes the world while discord terrorizes - may be faddish in the aftermath of 9-11, I find myself anxiously and earnestly contending that mutual antagonism has set in deep distortions in each of Abraham's child-faiths. And that those distortions threaten, not only to spoil the witness of those communities, but to ruin God's good world.

This journey has occupied the last forty of my sixty-five years. That venture and adventure has been within the faith community and without in the realm of scientific and secular society. The akedic, decalogic, liturgic and pacific qualities of those two worlds—sacred and secular—continues to fascinate me as the clue to the deepest meaning of "what is going on" in the nature and history of reality as we are given to know and create that reality.

Appendix

The Gift of the Beloved Son
(Sermon delivered in First Presbyterian Church, Evanston,
Illinois, 1999)
Scripture: Genesis 22:1-4, John 3:10-17

Gene Siskel thought it the year's best. The film the Thin Red Line begins as a massive crocodile submerges silently in the algaed water. The primeval predator, a gnarled serpent representing the inertia and iniquity of the world, a Moby Dick, a massive embodiment of evil, a Leviathan, slides into the watery depths as a voice contemplates the two great issues of life: WHY IS THERE EVIL? WHAT IS GOOD?

- WHY IS THIS WAR AT THE HEART OF NATURE?
- HOW DID WE LOSE THE GOOD THAT WAS GIVEN US?
- HOW DID WE LET IT SLIP AWAY?

As we watched the film and heard these words my mind crossed to those murky baptismal waters of the Jordan River and those meditative words we have attended in this winter's lectionary, words which ponder those same great questions in terms of the one about the son:

It began at Christmastide:

The Word dwelt among us…as of the only beloved son of the
father
And from the Baptist…behold the Lamb of God who takes
away the sins of the world-and the baptismal dove and voice"
this is my beloved Son.
And the voice on transfiguration mountain…"This is my
beloved Son…"
And that strange inversion on temptation mount. " If you are the
son"…
And the reprise on Mt. Moriah, now Jesus Calvary "If you are
the Son…come down"
And now…God so loved the world that he gave his only
beloved son

Sounding further the primal issues of guilt and gift at the metaphysical foundation of the world, What went wrong and what now?…the film's scene shift back to beautiful dark-skinned children laying on the beach. With dexterity the camera scans the surging blue Pacific and the lush tropical forests of the island—Guadalcanal. It is the early 1940's. There's trouble in paradise—war in the garden— the music turns to the angelic Paradiso from Faure's REQUIEM:

In paradise…in the company of martyrs
In the holy city…Jerusalem, with the blessed of Abraham

Again my mind crosses back in the Mass to the ram of God…provided for Abraham in the tangled bramble …and Golgotha's cursed tree.

Agnus Dei, qui tollis peccata Mundi, dona eis requiem
(Lamb of God who takes away the sin of the world, give us rest)

The Questions push deeper.

Terrence Malick's film, like his earlier masterpieces: BADLANDS and DAYS OF HEAVEN, probes with ingenious technique and inspired text the mystery of human existence in a world that is more than it appears to be—a world that shimmers with intimations of transcendence—with dreadful terror and awesome wonder.

"A mythopetic capsule" writes one reviewer of the film, "searching for the reality behind reality."

Our Gospel lectionary text is such a capsule—a window into the ultimate mystery. God loved the world so, that he gave his only beloved Son. The Gospel in miniature it has been called. An intricately designed pearl cameo-A jewel whose myriad facets reflect and refract all creation's colors from sheer brilliance to deepest darkness—A symphony that resounds all the dissonance and harmony of the music of the spheres.

These words are often called the most beautiful in the world. They are coined in that small circle of bewildered and bedazzled witnesses to that gruesome execution and glorious reappearance of their itinerant rabbi from Nazareth. John and Peter, James the brother and Mary the mother. When they awoke on that perplexing first day they asked: What happened? What does it mean? What now? To fathom these mysteries and phrase their Gospel of redeeming love—of AGAPE—in the ensuing weeks they reached into the deepest symbol of the Hebrew lore: The Akedah—Abraham's binding and offering of Isaac.

The story of Abraham, is, in the words of one writer, central to the nervous system of Judaism and Christianity. Akedah with AGAPE are microminiatures of ultimate truth—Akedah fathoms what wrong in the world entails Abraham's offering of Isaac and God's gift of his only beloved son. It glimpses the delivering love that will rescue life from that death. Abraham's offeringof the beloved Son issac, says Oxford's Judaist, Geza Vermes, is the biblical annunciation of the love of God. AGAPE transforms that drama into the deepest meaning of the Cosmos. Together Akedah and AGAPE constitute what Harvard's Jon Levenson calls THE DEATH AND RESURRECTION OF THE BELOVED SON. Consider with me today that wondrous gift.

Akedah is a Hebrew word meaning binding, cutting, or dividing. It is used for tying Isaac to the bundle of sticks. It is also used for the parting of the seas as Israel escapes Egypt. It is about restriction and resurrection. This sense of the word religion—religare—ligatured to source and set free—is captured in David's psalm in our Ash Wednesday lectionary: "let the bones which you have broken rejoice."

At one level the story of Abraham and Isaac is about the crisis in the ancient world over human sacrifice. The primitive ritual, known in almost all cultures, sought to purchase life for a sinful world. Fertility of home and soil, protection from disease and death, but the purchase price is great. We think the Incas and the slaying of one to assure the corn harvest or of Agamemnon sacrificing his beloved daughter Iphegenia to assure victory in the Trojan War. But this universal practice created an acute crisis in Israel. By the time of the conquest and consolidation in the tenth century, this people, now shaped by the Mosaic covenant, found abomination in the baby belching Canaanite incinerator, just south of Jerusalem. Their selfgiving and life-commanding god, whom Abraham first met and followed, demanded both that we give over our very best, our first fruits, that which we dearly love, but also that we not kill. The texts of the morning now come into focus:

> Abraham, take your long-awaited, only begotten
> MONOGENOS-AGAPETOS (Septuagint)
> Your only beloved son.
> Abraham, do not lay a hand on the boy!
> God loved the world so, that he gave his AGAPETOS— his Only
> beloved son

Akedah, is a symbol which seeks to explain those great haunting questions of humanity and divinity. When we join Akedah with AGAPE we get close to the truth about life and the inextricable interdependence of the evangelical and the ethical: What can we believe and how ought we to live.

Akedah is a long and living tradition in Judaism, Christianity and Islam. From Abraham and John 3:16 it verges into the way that Jewish and Christian martyrs give meaning to their offering at the hands of Rome. It becomes the interpretive symbol for those across the ages who lay down their lives for God, for good or for their fellow human beings. Akedah texts seek to wrest meaning from the Holocaust and war in general. It grounds the general poetic and philosophical tradition of redemptive suffering. It captures the paradoxical truth of Socrates that it is better to suffer injustice than to inflict it thereby grounding the great heritage of non-violence and *Satyagraha*—love force.

In modern culture films like THIN RED LINE and BREAKING THE WAVES appropriate the theme of redemptive suffering from the great tradition of films about Jesus, Saint Francis and Jean d'arc. As we witnessed the Pope recently in Mexico we saw the symbol of Akedah/AGAPE applied to the plight of the poor, even those on death row. Remember Helen Prejan's portrayal of Matthew's redemption in DEAD MAN WALKING as the execution chair arches back against heaven like Dali's cosmic crucifixion. We think of the sacrifice of women and children, of the genocide of victimized peoples, of modern martyrs in India, Indonesia or Kosovo.

In recent work I have explored the symbol of Akedah as a way to reunite the tragically disjoined gifts of salvation and social justice, of lamb and law. Joining Akedah in Genesis 22 and AGAPE in John 3:16 provides a rich symbol for those who bear the cross in the world—through prophetic sacrifice, sickness, aging, witnessing to a hostile world— living the truth. We are called with Isaac and Jesus to lift high our cross and to find our only joy in that excruciating existence. For the joy that was set before him Jesus endured the cross... The cost of discipleship is to go out with Isaac with the logs of the fire and with Jesus with the crossbeam of that cursed tree.

AGAPE completed Akedah. AGAPE is the accomplishment of all that is anticipated in the Akedah. Mount Moriah is now Mount Calvary. If you visit Jerusalem today as our bell choir did over Christmas, these legendary mountains are just footsteps apart—Moriah at the Dome of the Rock and Calvary at the Church of the Holy Sepulchre. If you let your mind move by the wonder of legend here is the very rock altar where Abraham took Isaac and here the very hole in the rock where the cross was lifted high.

Here is the meeting point of heaven and earth. Here God came through to us while we languished in our plight. This lonely and unvisited planet had glimpsed its Maker in patriarch and prophet, now this wondrous and unspeakable gift, prepared from the foundation of the world an only begotten son, one fully human and divine, came through to us. While we were without hope and without God in the world he came through. While the world lay, like Isaac, like Jesus, crucified and buried, in Bach's words in *Todesbanden*, bound in death, while we were yet sinners, God set the beloved son into the world.

John uses the Greek word *cosmos* in 3:16. Cosmos is the fallen world. It is the belligerent, death-bound, lost and confused world. To this derelict and desperate World the searcher, the seeker, the savior, came through. This cosmos would not receive him but to those who did receive him he gave power to become AGAPETOI—children of God. It is this alienated and hostile world that God so loved Jesus offered himself against its fury and fire. He is Akedah AND AGAPE.

A moving painting of the First World War is entitled simply THROUGH. It shows a lone soldier, hanging like that ram on the barbed wire in the trenches of France. The smoke and gas waft through the air. In his clenched and dying fist are joined the severed ends of a broken telephone wire. In joining the connection he got "through". Let ET's glowing finger or that electric touch of Jehovah and

Adam on the Sistine ceiling—he got through. The mystery of Akedah—a ram caught in the bramble tree or the mystery of AGAPE—the lamb hanging on the tree, is that he got through, and reestablished contact, brought life from death. Like Matthew Shepherd, you remember the young man who was lashed to the farm fence in Wyoming or James Byrd dragged for three miles on a country road near Jasper, Texas or Australian missionary Graham Staines burned with his two son in his trailer in East India, Akedah/AGAPE asks eternally "when will you ever learn?" Wondrous love—unconditioned, full and free is manifest in the One Who lays down His life. One scorned and covered with scars, the immolated lamb of Revelation 4, reaching out to the bleeding, bruised and broken of this world and with whose wounds they become whole. " In the cross of Christ I glory—towering o'er the wrecks of time."

The cross, as a composite symbol of human need and divine action finds the human condition as one of acute peril. Our incapacity to receive God's nearness and righteousness causes us to experience Infinite distance from God and trembling anxiety. Soren Kierkegaard's FEAR AND TREMBLING and CONCEPT OF DREAD are the masterpieces depicting this plight.

Terry Malick, a philosopher-film maker is well acquainted with this tradition. In THIN RED LINE his meditative philosophy is evident when he deals throughout the film with human fear and trembling. As Guadalcanal's summit is assailed we often see American and Japanese soldiers quaking in uncontrollable dread and trembling: Shell-shock, bizarre laughter, shaking sobs, painsshudder, death shiver. When Luther read Abraham he said he felt *timor*, sheer terror. We remember the only fully human person who ever lived in the garden that night. As the moon shone over the Mount of Olives, illumining both yesteryears altar of Abraham and the morrow's place of the skull, he trembled sweat and blood, foreboding that cry of Isaac "Father, why have you forsaken me?" Now forever we must look up on that hill and ask: Were you there when they crucified my Lord? Sometimes it causes me to tremble.

To contemplate the costly coming to us of the Christ is to fall into convulsions of dread and wonder. It is to collapse into throbs of ecstasy and sobs of thankfulness. " What wondrous love is this, that caused the Lord of bliss to bear the heavy cross for my soul." We see in summary that our texts of AKEDAH and AGAPE show God's way in the world and our human condition. Our rightful and reasonable service is not to sacrifice ourselves or one another but to snatch life from the jaws of death and to live, as Dr. King said, after John, in beloved community. This is to present our bodies not as charred corpses but as living sacrifices. We need to strive as we do in this congregation for a strong synthesis and synergy of salvation and social justice boasting only in the cross of Christ our God" by whom the world is crucified to us and we are CRUCIFIED TO THE WORLD".

In the film, Staros the lawyer—officer in the name of life and love refuses to lead his troops into certain death even in he face of orders of his commander, the manic, Nick Nolte. As he departs he salutes his men in Greek, *Uioi Cardiamou*, you are my beloved sons, I live in you and you in me—the beloved community of John. In two subsequent scenes, in the river and in the field outside the camp a hero, Kierkegaard's word for Isaac and Jesus, draws the enemy to himself, offering his life to save his friends.

GREATER LOVE HAS NO MAN THAN THIS...

A moving Akedah text is Wilfred Owen's WW1 poem called THE OLD MAN AND THE YOUNG. It becomes the *Offeratorium* in Benjamin Britten's War Requiem. At the rededication of the bombed out Coventry Cathedral in 1962, two spared sons, Peter Pares and Dietrich Fischer-Diescau sing the haunting duet as a British and German soldier:

So Abraham rose and clave the wood and went,
And took the fire with him, and a knife.
And as they sojourned, both of them together,
Isaac, the first born spake and said, my father
Behold the preparations, fire and iron,
But where is the lamb for this burnt offering?
Then Abraham bound the youth with belts and straps,
And builded parapets and trenches there,
And stretched forth the knife to slay his son,
When lo, an angel called him out of heaven,
Saying, lay not thy hand upon the lad,
Neither do anything to him.
Behold a ram caught in a thicket by its horns
Offer the ram of pride instead of him
But the old man would not so, but slew his son
And half the seed of Europe, one by one.

The voice of God cries out eternally from heaven to stay our

propensity to slay
lay not a hand on the lad!
God love the world so much that he gave his beloved son
That whoever believes should not perish but have eternallife
God did not send the son to condemn-but to save

So Micah rightly concludes the matter:

Wherewith shall I then come before the Lord
And bow myself before the high God?
Shall I come before him with burnt offerings
Shall I give my first born, my MONOGENOS , for my transgressions
The fruit of my body for the sin of my soul?
He hath showed thee o Man what is good,

AND WHAT DOTH THE LORD REQUIRE OF THEE
BUT TO DO JUSTICE, LOVE MERCY
AND WALK HUMBLY WITH THY GOD.